Gender, Inequality, and Wages

IZA Prize in Labor Economics Series

Since 2002, the Institute for the Study of Labor (IZA) has awarded the annual IZA Prize in Labor Economics for outstanding contributions to policy-relevant labor market research and methodological progress in this sub-discipline of economic science. The IZA Prize is the only international science prize awarded exclusively to labor economists. This special focus acknowledges the global significance of high-quality basic research in labor economics and sound policy advice based on these research findings. As issues of employment and unemployment are among the most urgent challenges of our time, labor economists have an important task and responsibility. The IZA Prize in Labor Economics is today considered one of the most prestigious international awards in the field. It aims to stimulate further research on topics that have enormous implications for our future. All prize-winners contribute a volume to the IZA Prize in Labor Economics Series published by Oxford University Press, which has been established to provide an overview of the laureates' most significant findings.

The IZA Prize in Labor Economics has become an integral part of the institute's manifold activities to promote progress in labor market research. Based on nominations submitted by the IZA Research Fellows, a high-ranking IZA Prize Committee selects the prize-winner. In conjunction with the Award Ceremony the IZA Prize Conference brings together a number of renowned experts to discuss topical labor market issues.

It is not by coincidence that the IZA Prize in Labor Economics Series is published by Oxford University Press. This well-reputed publishing house has shown a great interest in the project from the very beginning as this exclusive series perfectly complements their range of publications. We gratefully acknowledge their excellent cooperation.

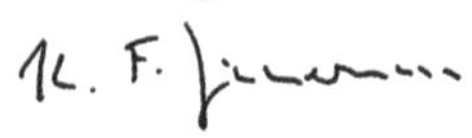

Klaus F. Zimmermann, IZA Director

Winners of the IZA Prize in Labor Economics

2011	George J. Borjas (Harvard University) Barry R. Chiswick (George Washington University)
2010	Francine D. Blau (Cornell University)
2009	Richard A. Easterlin (University of Southern California)
2008	Richard Layard (London School of Economics) Stephen J. Nickell (Nuffield College)
2007	Richard B. Freeman (Harvard University)
2006	David Card (University of California, Berkeley) Alan B. Krueger (Princeton University)
2005	Dale T. Mortensen (Northwestern University) Christopher A. Pissarides (London School of Economics)
2004	Edward P. Lazear (Stanford University)
2003	Orley C. Ashenfelter (Princeton University)
2002	Jacob Mincer (Columbia University)

Francine D. Blau
2010 IZA Prize Laureate

Gender, Inequality, and Wages

Francine D. Blau

Edited by
Anne C. Gielen
Klaus F. Zimmermann

OXFORD
UNIVERSITY PRESS

OXFORD
UNIVERSITY PRESS

Great Clarendon Street, Oxford, OX2 6DP,
United Kingdom

Oxford University Press is a department of the University of Oxford. It furthers the University's objective of excellence in research, scholarship, and education by publishing worldwide. Oxford is a registered trade mark of Oxford University Press in the UK and in certain other countries

First published 2012
First published in paperback 2016

Published in the United States of America by Oxford University Press
198 Madison Avenue, New York, NY 10016, United States of America

British Library Cataloguing in Publication Data
Data available

Library of Congress Cataloging in Publication Data
Data available

ISBN 978–0–19–966585–3 (Hbk.)
ISBN 978–0–19–877997–1 (Pbk.)

Award Statement of the IZA Prize Committee

The 2010 IZA Prize in Labor Economics is awarded to Francine D. Blau (Cornell University) for her seminal contributions to the economic analysis of labor market inequality. Professor Blau has written extensively on the role of women in the labor market and on gender differences in pay and many other aspects of economic life. Her work has profoundly shaped the view of scholars and policymakers on the causes and consequences of gender differences in economic outcomes, and on policies for advancing women's labor market position and well-being.

From the very beginning of her academic career, Francine Blau's work has concentrated on issues related to gender and inequality. In her first book, "Equal Pay in the Office" (published in 1977), she was one of the first scholars to study gender differences in labor market outcomes using detailed micro-level data on the occupational level. This approach allowed her to assess the relative importance of a wide range of potential causes for gender pay differentials, such as differences in qualifications between men and women, differences in the returns to skills, occupational segregation, and labor market discrimination. Her pioneering results were also published in the book "The Economics of Women, Men, and Work" (with Marianne Ferber), which has since become a standard textbook for scholars interested in gender issues in the labor market. In a later study with Lawrence Kahn, published in the *Journal of Economic Perspectives* in 2000, Francine Blau documented that the gender pay gap has narrowed since the 1970s. Their analysis shows that this change is attributable to a reduction in occupational segregation, whereby new cohorts of younger women have started to enter traditionally male dominated occupations, which tend to be better paid than jobs in predominantly female occupations. Despite this trend, her work has shown that there is little reason for euphoria: although the overall gender pay gap has decreased somewhat over time, the share of this gap that is unexplained by differences in qualifications and skills is increasing. This phenomenon may be due to labor market discrimination and the fact that women are still primarily responsible for childcare and housework duties, which in turn lowers women's labor market attachment and limits their employment opportunities. Policies aimed at facilitating the integration of work and family responsibilities are therefore essential to ensure more equal opportunities for men and women in the labor market.

In a series of papers with Lawrence Kahn, Francine Blau has further shown that gender inequality in pay is closely related to differences in labor market institutions. A comparative analysis for several OECD countries reveals that in about half of the countries studied, the gender pay gap is smaller than in the United States. According to Professor Blau, gender-specific factors, such as female qualification levels, labor market participation and occupational segregation by gender, could not explain why the U.S. does not perform better in an international comparison, since these factors are often more favorable than in other countries. Instead, her evaluation shows that country differences in gender pay gaps are intimately linked to the level of wage dispersion in a country (*American Economic Review*, 1992). In a later co-authored paper in the *Journal of Political Economy* (1996), Francine Blau investigates how the relationship between gender wage gaps and the degree of wage dispersion in a country can be explained by differences in labor market institutions. Compared to other countries, union coverage and the minimum wage are rather low in the U.S. Both centralized pay-setting institutions tend to reduce wage variation across firms and industries. The lack of such institutions in the U.S., where wages are more likely to be determined at a decentralized level, creates a much larger wage penalty for those with lower qualifications. Hence, the study shows that higher rewards to skills, rather than gender differences in skill levels as such, are among the main reasons for the relatively large gender pay gap in the U.S. compared to other industrialized countries with a more condensed wage distribution.

Apart from her ground-breaking work on gender and inequality, Francine Blau has also published influential studies on various other topics in labor economics, such as migration and racial discrimination. For instance, in her 1984 paper in the *Industrial and Labor Relations Review*, she challenged the prevailing view that immigrants constitute a burden on the U.S. welfare system by showing that, when controlling for all relevant characteristics, immigrant households are actually less likely to rely on social assistance than native households. Her sensitivity to fairness, which sparked her interest in gender inequality, also led to an important contribution in the area of racial discrimination, where she showed in a joint paper with Andrea Beller that black women performed better than black men in terms of annual earnings and estimated wages, but that both lagged behind compared to the earnings and wages of whites (*Review of Economics and Statistics*, 1992).

Francine Blau is a strong advocate of equity in the labor market. However, her work on gender differences in pay and labor market outcomes is not only inspired by a firm conviction in fairness. She also believes that social welfare can be maximized when all productive resources, including human labor resources, are fully utilized. In this respect, discrimination by gender implies a waste of otherwise equally skilled labor and hence lower economic efficiency. This strong belief in equity and efficiency is not only expressed in her published work, but also in her active role in various professional organizations and committees, such as the American Economic Association's Committee on the Status of Women in the Economics Profession (CSWEP). Searching for ways to reduce the under-representation of women in economics at the tenured level, she published an article in the *American Economic Review* (2010) in which she shows that mentoring programs for female assistant professors have positive effects on female academic productivity, and as such may help promote women's advance in the profession.

For almost four decades, Francine D. Blau has brought gender differences in the labor market to the attention of the public, both in her impressive body of research as well as through her professional activities in numerous institutions. The IZA Prize in Labor Economics 2010 honors this pioneering work, which has laid the foundation for more equality and equity in the labor market.

George A. Akerlof	University of California, Berkeley
Marco Caliendo	IZA
Richard Portes	London Business School; CEPR
Jan Svejnar	University of Michigan, Ann Arbor
Klaus F. Zimmermann	IZA; University of Bonn

For my husband, Lawrence Kahn,
and my children, Daniel Blau Kahn and Lisa Blau Kahn,
with love.

Acknowledgments

I am deeply indebted to a number of individuals who contributed to this volume. First and foremost, I thank my collaborators whose joint work appears here: Lawrence M. Kahn (Chapters 2, 3, 4, 5, 6, and 12), Andrea H. Beller (Chapters 2 and 9), Janet M. Currie, Rachel T. A. Croson, and Donna K. Ginther (Chapter 8), John W. Graham (Chapter 10), and Kerry Papps (Chapter 12). It has been a privilege to work with each of them. It was, of course, my receipt of the IZA Prize in Labor Economics that made this volume possible. For this and the great honor they bestowed on me, I thank IZA Director, Klaus F. Zimmermann, and the other IZA Prize Selection Committee members: George A. Akerlof, Marco Caliendo, Richard Portes, and Jan Svejnar. In preparing this volume I have benefited greatly from working closely with Anne C. Gielen and would like to warmly thank her and others at IZA, including Holger Hinte, for their help. I would also like to thank Peter Brummund for his excellent work in helping me to prepare the manuscript for Chapter 1 and Gary Cohen for his first-rate assistance in proofing the final manuscript.

Francine D. Blau

Contents

I

Equality and Fairness in the Labor Market

Anne C. Gielen and Klaus F. Zimmermann

Every year, the Institute for the Study of Labor awards the IZA Prize in Labor Economics to an individual who has made outstanding contributions to the field. Since its establishment in 2002, the Prize has been given to several distinguished labor economists; two of them later even received the Nobel Prize in Economics. The 2010 IZA Prize winner, Francine D. Blau, is now the first woman joining this group for her impressive and path breaking work on gender issues and other sources of inequality in the labor market.

One of the most important themes in Blau's work is the role of women in the labor market and gender differences in pay. In fact, she was among the first economists working on these topics. Even though the participation of women in the labor market was steeply rising in the 1970s, there were only very sparse empirical studies done in this area at that time, most of them coming from other disciplines than economics. Her earliest book, Equal Pay in the Office (1977) (see Chapter 1 of this book), was a pioneering study where she focused on the role of employment segregation by sex in influencing the gender pay gap within narrowly-defined occupational categories. In her second book (with Marianne Ferber and Anne Winkler), The Economics of Women, Men, and Work (first published in 1986 – now being in its 6th edition) she continued her ground breaking research by considering alternative explanations for the gender pay gap, as well as investigating time trends in gender differences. Over time, these early works of Francine Blau are not only considered to be classics in economics, but also in various other fields, such as sociology and social policy.

In her work on the trends in gender pay gaps over time (Blau and Beller 1988; Blau and Kahn 2000; 2006, see Chapter 2) Blau was the first to point at the fact that the gender pay gap has narrowed between the 1970s to the 1990s, mostly because of a decline in occupational segregation and the general increase in women's qualifications and skills. However, despite the overall decline, Blau stressed that women were still very much disadvantaged in the labor market. The fact that an increasing part of the gender pay gap could not be explained by differences in skills between men and women, suggested that women were still being discriminated against. Furthermore, the possibilities to build a career were limited as women were still primarily responsible for childcare and housework duties. To the extent that family responsibilities did play a role, this called for enhanced work-family policies to help address such responsibilities, the topic of her 1997 edited book with Ronald Ehrenberg on Gender and Family Issues in the Workplace.

Another innovative aspect in Blau's work has been her deviating from the traditional explanations for the gender pay gap, i.e. differences in human capital accumulation, occupational segregation and discrimination, and linking gender inequality to labor market institutions. Together with Lawrence Kahn, Blau has studied labor market institutions and how they vary across countries (see, for example, their 2002 book, At Home and Abroad: U.S. Labor Market Performance in International Perspective). Their results showed that the greater gender pay gaps in the U.S. as compared to other peer countries were not the result of differences in the most commonly known gender-specific determinants. Instead, their evaluation showed that a primary reason for the larger gender gap in the U.S. is the greater extent of wage dispersion in this country (see Part III of this book). The differences in wage dispersion are the result of weaker wage-setting institutions, lower union coverage, and minimum wages.

Nowadays, Blau's research on the unexplained gender pay gap still provides the foundation for many recent studies in this area. Many European researchers have followed Blau's approach in the European context to study gender pay differences in various European countries. Her work in the Industrial and Labor Relations Review with Andrea Beller (1988), which is one of the earliest papers looking at (trends in) gender differences in pay, has received over a hundred citations according to the Social Science Citation Index (SSCI) as well as 150 citations on Google Scholar. Other researchers have built upon

Blau's work and formulated alternative explanations for the (trends in the) gender pay gap (see Bertrand 2011 for an overview).

One recent popular explanation for gender differences in labor market outcomes are differences in psychological attributes and preferences between men and women. Since women are more risk averse than men (e.g., Croson and Gneezy 2009; Dohmen et al. 2011), they prefer to work in occupations with stable earnings. However, due to compensating wage differentials such jobs pay less on average. Additionally, women have different attitudes towards competition, which may cause them to stay away from competitive environments (e.g., Gneezy et al. 2003). Other experimental studies have shown that there are gender differences in social preferences (e.g., Croson and Gneezy 2009). All of these psychological factors may cause some occupations to be more attractive to women and others to be more attractive to men.

A second newly discussed explanation for gender differences is the existence of social norms, which dictate what men are expected to do and what is appropriate for women to do. Such social norms may cause differential occupational sorting between men and women (Akerlof and Kranton 2000). In this view, trends in gender labor market outcomes over time can be explained by changes in social norms, such as the introduction of the Pill (Goldin and Katz 2002) and the growing number of men who grew up with a working mother (Fernandez et al. 2004).

A third line of recent research focuses on biological influences – like brain structure or testosterone levels – causing gender inequality in the labor market (see Bertrand [2011] for a more detailed discussion).

Finally, some recent studies claim that the changes in gender differences in the labor market over time are the result of statistical artifacts, rather than being due to differential behavior between men and women. For example, in a recent IZA discussion paper, Lee and Lee (2011) suggest that the findings for the gender pay gap over time are also affected by the changing gender composition of survey respondents. They claim that about 11-34 percent of the earnings gap reduction from 1979 to 1989 is due to the fact that over time more and more female respondents participated in these surveys as the household representative reporting earnings information for themselves and their spouses. Furthermore, there are scientists who claim that the size of the gender pay gap is in fact biased by the gender of the researcher. Stanley and Jarrell (1998 and 2004) find that male researchers report larger gender wage gaps than female researchers. All in all, the pioneering work that Francine Blau has done in explaining gender differences in the labor market has set the stage for the much larger set of possible explanations that labor economists have at their disposal nowadays to explain differential labor market outcomes by gender.

Gender inequality in the labor market is nowadays a hot topic among policymakers. In the European Union, for example, the "Strategy for equality between women and men" (European Commission 2010) represents the Commission's work program on gender equality for the period 2010-2015. Furthermore, the EU's fundamental rights commissioner Viviane Reding strives to get more women in top positions across Europe, and has mentioned to impose gender quotas to achieve this goal. Recent academic studies suggest that quotas are effective. De Paola et al. (2010) find that Italian municipalities that adopted gender quotas on women's involvement in political activity have a higher women's representation in politics than other municipalities. Similar results have been found for other countries (see Pande and Ford (2011) for an overview).

However, gender equality in the labor market has not always been such a highly debated issue. In fact, when Blau started her pioneering work in the 1970s, gender issues were a risky territory, especially for female researchers. Traditional (labor) economics did not address women's economic behavior. For example, Adam Smith only scarcely mentioned women and gender issues, neither in his 1776 "The Wealth of Nations" nor in his 1759 "The Theory of Moral Sentiments" (Kuiper 2001). Similar, traditional labor supply theory was based on a male-headed family, where only the male's economic behavior was analyzed (Kuiper 2001). This leaves little opportunity for studying gender inequality and related gender issues. However, over the years, when also female labor market participation has increased substantially, this has changed a lot. One good example is Blau's 2000-paper with Lawrence Kahn in the Journal of Economic Perspectives which nowadays has over 700 citations on Google Scholar. However, it is not only the increase in female labor participation that has inspired the discussion of gender issues in the labor market, but also the change in the position of women in the labor market that is important in this respect. For example, the changes in labor market participation have changed the wages that women earned (see Chapter 6). Furthermore, the increased labor market participation of women has led young women to revise their expectations of future employment and, in turn, stimulated them to invest more in their education. A study by Goldin (2006) shows that in the 1970s and 1980s girls began to take more college preparation courses in high school, and consequently the female college attendance and graduation rates relative to males increased. This development has led to better educated women joining the labor force. A recent PISA survey (OECD 2010) adds to this that women also caught up in terms of school performance. Across the subjects (reading, mathematics and science), girls are now equally likely to be top performers as boys. The changing participation and qualification of women in the last decades will have a major impact on the labor supply of women in the near future.

However, despite the progress towards gender equality in many labor market dimensions (e.g., labor market participation, educational attainment), it is not quite clear that there is similar progress in other dimensions of gender equality. Chapter 7 discusses trends in well-being across men and women, and shows that the challenge of combining work and family still affects women differently than men. A recent study by Stevenson and Wolfers (2009) also shows that, despite decades of educational gains and a huge increase in their labor market opportunities, self-reported levels of life satisfaction for women have declined over time compared to those of men. Lalive and Stutzer (2010) explain this trend in a social norms framework, where they argue that women appear to be unhappy when they are expected to break away from traditional gender identity norms, even if they are successful in doing so. Since there is much more to learn about gender equality in other life domains, gender issues will continue to be an important topic of discussion, both in research and in policy.

The Institute for the Study of Labor has also witnessed the changing role of females in the labor market in her fellow network, where the female/male ratio of the IZA fellow network increased from 0.12 in 1998 to 0.26 in 2010. Furthermore, the enormous interest in gender equality issues these days is shown by the substantial number in IZA discussion papers dealing with gender inequality every year, which has more than tripled over the last 10 years.

The work of Blau on gender equality fits nicely with the mission and spirit of IZA. The institute has always strived for gender equality in the job application process and female researchers make up about 30 percent of the local IZA research team. Furthermore, since Winter

2010 IZA cooperates with the Federal Anti-Discrimination Agency in an experiment with anonymous applications initiated by the Agency to ensure equality and fairness for everyone in the job application process (Krause et al. 2010).

Blau's interest in gender and inequality issues is not only displayed in her research, but also in many other activities she has participated in to further the status of women in the economics profession. For example, Blau played a part in the establishment of the AEA Committee on the Status of Women in the Economics Profession (CSWEP), which was installed to monitor the status of women in the profession and formulate activities to improve their status, and served as a member of the first committee. Later on, she also served as a chair of the committee. Blau's immense contributions in furthering the status of women in the economics profession were recognized with the Carolyn Shaw Bell Award from CSWEP in 2001.

In her laudation during the IZA Prize Ceremony, Jane Waldfogel (Columbia University) named Francine Blau "an important role model and mentor for women in the economics profession." Not only is she an active mentor herself, she is also involved in promoting mentorship programs. Her recent AER article (Blau et al. [2010]; see Chapter 8) reports the results of an experimental study providing mentors for tenure-track women in economics. In addition to all these activities, Blau has also served as the president of the Society for Labor Economists and of the Labor and Employment Relations Association, and as a vice president of the American Economic Association.

Blau's work has profoundly shaped the view of scholars and policymakers on the causes and consequences of gender differences in economic outcomes, and on policies for advancing women's labor market position and well-being. Furthermore, her work on equality and equity has also inspired many labor economists' thinking on inequality with respect to race and with respect to origin. Blau's interest in fairness and equality, which made her work on gender inequality, also led to an important contribution in the area of racial discrimination, where she showed that blacks (and in particular female blacks) lagged behind in terms of earnings and wealth compared to whites (Chapters 9 and 10). Furthermore, in her influential 1984 paper (Blau 1984; Chapter 11 in this book) she challenged the prevailing belief that immigrants are a burden for the U.S. social assistance program by showing that immigrants are actually less likely to rely on social assistance than native Americans, once controlled for all relevant characteristics. Despite this, inequality with respect to origin may remain due to the important role of source country culture (Chapter 12) in economic behavior of immigrants.

This book consists of a collection of the most important contributions made by Francine Blau extended with a final section containing updated and new insights, and represents her incredible efforts to increase awareness and understanding for fairness and equality issues in the labor market.

II

The Gender Wage Gap: Determinants and Trends over Time for the United States

Introduction

When I first became interested in trying to better understand the gender pay gap, around 1970, attention to this issue among economists had been relatively sparse. Of course some crucial building blocks were in place, including the foundational work of Gary Becker (1993; 1st ed. 1964) and Jacob Mincer (1962b) on human capital theory and its application to wage determination and Becker's analysis of labor market discrimination (Becker 1971; 1st ed. 1957). And Jacob Mincer and Solomon Polachek's seminal elucidation of the role of human capital, particularly women's shorter and more discontinuous labor force attachment, in explaining the gender pay gap would appear in a few years (Mincer and Polachek 1974). But, there were relatively few empirical analyses focusing on possible inequities in labor market outcomes. Given this scarcity and a desire on my part to become familiar with a variety of approaches, I was motivated to read more broadly in other disciplines as well. One thing that particularly struck me – based on my readings in sociology (e.g., Gross 1968, Caplow 1954) – was that occupational segregation by sex appeared to be a central aspect of gender differences in the labor market, and one that had not been adequately explored by economists.

Moreover, as economists began to focus more on segregation, it was not clear to me that they viewed it correctly. For example, in one of the pioneering early analyses of the sources of the gender pay gap,

Sanborn (1964) interpreted Becker-type discrimination essentially as unequal pay for equal work and adjusted for gender differences in detailed occupational category in estimating the unexplained gender pay gap. McNulty (1967) and Buckley (1971) went even further and identified potentially discriminatory pay gaps between men and women in the same occupations only as those associated with gender pay differences within the same establishment. It seemed to me that including occupation (and industry) as controls in wage equations used in analyzing the gender gap was problematic in that gender differences in these variables might be due to the choices and preferences of workers but could also reflect discrimination by employers. Empirical work by economists did increasingly take this position - see Fuchs (1971) for an early example, and, later influential pieces by Oaxaca (1973b) and Blinder (1973). Of particular importance in the evolving view of occupational segregation was Barbara Bergmann's (1974) development of the "overcrowding model" which gave central importance to occupational segregation in explaining the gender pay gap. In Bergmann's model employer discrimination which excluded women from "male jobs" generated a gender pay gap as women crowded into "female jobs," depressing wages in the female jobs.

Nonetheless, I felt the source of occupational differences between the sexes would likely always be fraught with ambiguity regarding the relative role of supply- versus demand-side factors. This was one reason that in my dissertation, which became the basis of Equal Pay in the Office (1977) discussed in Chapter 1 below, I decided to focus on the role of employment segregation by sex in influencing the gender pay gap within narrowly-defined occupational categories. Not only did this have the advantage of abstracting from gender differences in occupational preferences but it also served to highlight an additional dimension of employment segregation that was getting considerably less attention at the time (and indeed still does) - sex segregation by establishment and industry. Moreover, the tabulations reported by McNulty (1967) and Buckley (1971) that showed that gender pay differentials within occupations and firms tended to be relatively small further encouraged me to believe that establishment segregation would be a useful dimension to consider, even though I disagreed with their interpretation that only within firm pay differentials should be considered as potentially discriminatory.

I developed a model that posited an internal wage structure that constrained the employer to pay the same base pay rate to all workers within an occupational category, as well as a wage hierarchy of firms for potentially equally productive labor that was consistent across occupational categories. I further assumed that employer tastes for discrimination against women à la Becker (1971; 1st ed. 1957) were widespread, but the ability to exercise them was constrained by the firm's position in the wage hierarchy. That is, the wages offered by the firm for each occupation were determined by a variety of institutional and market forces, and could not easily be altered to accommodate employer preferences for male versus female employees. At the time, my model was grounded in the internal labor market analysis of Doeringer and Piore (1971) and an older institutional literature. The new personnel economics would later greatly expand on within firm analyses (e.g., Lazear 1995) and an extensive later literature utilizing firm-worker matched data would provide considerable empirical support for the assumption of a wage hierarchy of firms, or "firm effects" (e.g., Abowd, Kramarz and Margolis 1999).

The model predicted that there would be considerable establishment segregation by sex within occupations. Moreover, women would be concentrated in firms which paid lower wages to both men and women, and conversely men would tend to be employed at the firms which paid higher wages to both sexes. The gender pay differential within occupations would be due primarily to pay differences among firms rather than pay differences within firms. These predictions were all strongly borne out by the data. The central finding – that pay differences between men and women within occupations were due (at least in a descriptive sense) to gender differences in employment across firms – was strongly corroborated in later work by Groshen (1991) using more recent data on narrowly-defined occupations. Bayard, Hellerstein, Neumark and Troske (2003), using matched employer-employee data (also of a more recent vintage), also confirmed the finding of a very substantial role for employment segregation, although, given their broader occupational categories, they found a more important role for within occupation, within firm gender pay differences than Groshen and I did.

One challenge raised in testing the model was determining whether or not within occupation employment segregation by firm existed. Given that a firm may hire just a small number of individuals within an occupation category, considerable sex segregation could exist just by chance. Thus, one would like to know whether, within the occupational category, each sex tends to work together within the same establishment to a significantly greater extent than would occur by chance. To examine this issue I developed an application of the binomial distribution to simulate the distribution of establishments by percent female in the occupational category that would occur under random hiring. The hypothesis of randomness was rejected in all cases. Subsequent applications of this basic approach by Carrington and Troske (1995, 1998) also produced evidence of employment segregation by sex at the plant level.

The next chapter in this part, Chapter 2, deals with trends in the gender pay gap in the United States. Before turning to the chapter, it is helpful to summarize these trends.

Figure II.I

U.S. Gender Earnings Ratios, Full-Time Workers (1955-2009)

Figure II.I presents data drawn from published government source on the U.S. gender earnings ratio (female divided by male earnings) of full-time workers. The focus on full-time workers is designed to adjust for gender differences in hours worked since women are more likely than men to work part-time. (Unfortunately, the government does not provide a similar long data series for hourly wages.) The figure presents two series available from published sources: annual earnings of workers who are employed year round, full-time (available since 1955); and weekly earnings of full-time workers (available since 1967). Both series tell the same story in terms of the trends. Until the late 1970s or early 1980s there was a remarkable constancy in the ratio, which hovered at around 60 percent. Then, over the 1980s, there was a period of strong, sustained increase in the ratio. However, during the 1990s and 2000s, the pace of convergence in both series slowed and both series behaved more erratically. Although cumulative gains were substantial – by 2009 the ratio was 77.0% based on annual earnings and 80.2% based on weekly earnings – a considerable gender pay gap remains.

Trends in the extent of occupational segregation are also relevant, since a wide literature shows that, controlling for measured characteristics of workers, predominantly female occupations pay less than predominantly male occupations.[1] The most commonly employed measure of segregation is that developed by Duncan and Duncan (1955), which indicates the proportion of women (or men) that would have to change occupations for the occupational distribution of men and women to be the same. Little change in the segregation index occurred prior to 1970 (Gross 1968; Blau and Hendricks 1979). However, a substantial decline in the index occurred in the 1970s (Beller 1985; Bianchi and Rytina 1986). The decrease in the segregation index persisted into the 1980s, at a somewhat diminished pace (Blau, Simpson and Anderson 1998). The pace of decrease fell still further in the 1990s and slowed to a virtual crawl in the 2000s (Blau, Brummund, and Liu forthcoming). Using the current (i.e., 2000) U.S. occupational classification system the index was 64.5% in 1970 and had fallen to 51.0% by 2009 (Blau, Brummund and Liu forthcoming). Thus, as with the earnings gap there has been a considerable decrease in occupational segregation, but the extent of occupational segregation by sex remains substantial.

The decline in the extent of occupational segregation over the 1970s provided a major motivation for my paper with Andrea Beller (1988) analyzing trends in the gender pay gap over the 1970s – discussed in the first section of Chapter 2. Although, as we have seen, the index of segregation had finally started to fall substantially during that decade, there had been no corresponding decline in the gender pay gap (at least based on published statistics). In undertaking our analysis we confronted two issues that are of considerable importance for investigations of this type. First, is the issue of selectivity bias that James Heckman (e.g., 1979; 1980) had brought to the attention of the profession. Wage comparisons between two groups and coefficients in wage regressions may be biased by self-selection into the wage sample. Arguably, one would like to compare the groups' wage offers rather than there actual observed wages. This is an important issue in the cross-section and is further magnified in importance when comparing different points in time if there have been substantial changes in participation rates, as there were for women over this period. In our study, Beller and I used a standard Heckman selectivity correction (see, e.g., Heckman 1979; 1980) to address this issue. Second, we needed a technique to identify the roles of specific factors that contributed to the trends, separating out the effect of gender differences in means and gender differences in coefficients (with the latter potentially representing the role of discrimination). We developed an application of the standard Oaxaca-Blinder decomposition to do this (Oaxaca 1973b; Blinder 1973).

Of course, as in all analyses of this type, it must be acknowledged that the unexplained gap is an imperfect indicator of discrimination, and our analysis is no exception to this (nor did we claim it to be). This was another attraction to us of focusing on the trends since the interest in one more study showing an unexplained pay gap between men and women was probably marginal. However, the meaty issue of what determined the trends had gotten less attention.

We found that the common focus on the median annual earnings of year-round, full-time workers available in the published statistics (shown in the figure above) was misleading in indicating that the gender ratio did not increase during the 1970s. Using the full sample of female workers (whether employed full- or part-time and full- or part-year) and a regression-based method to adjust for time inputs (hours and weeks worked), we found, on the contrary, that the earnings of both black and white women rose relative to men with similar time inputs over the decade. Moreover, focusing on wage offers (i.e., adjusting for selectivity bias), resulted in substantially higher estimates of the relative earnings gains of white, although not of black, women. We found that a variety of factors contributed to the narrowing of the earnings gap over this period. Of particular interest, we did find that the decline in occupational segregation contributed to a decrease in the gender pay gap as women increased their representation in male jobs and integrated jobs, but that this effect was offset by a decrease in the returns to such employment for women relative to men over the period.

The remainder of Chapter 2 focuses on my work with Lawrence Kahn on analyzing the trends in the gender pay gap over the 1980s and 1990s. Kahn and I first considered the 1980s trends and were confronted with something of a puzzle (Blau and Kahn 1997). As we saw in the figure, there was a considerable decrease in the gender pay gap in the 1980s. Yet the 1980s was a time of rising wage inequality in the U.S. driven by rising returns to skills (e.g., Juhn, Murphy, and Pierce 1993; and Katz and Murphy 1992). In the face of rising wage inequality, it could be argued that American women were essentially swimming upstream in a labor market growing increasingly unfavorable for workers with below average skills – while women's educational deficits were not large, women did lag considerably behind men in experience. Furthermore, they were concentrated in lower-paying industries and occupations that might be expected to be losing ground. In the face of rising rewards to labor market skills and higher-paying sectors, women would have to improve their relative skills, occupational and industrial distribution, and/or labor market treatment merely for the pay gap to remain constant; still larger gains would be necessary for it to be reduced. Progress in narrowing the black-white gap in earnings stalled during the 1980s in part due to rising returns to skills (Juhn, Murphy, and Pierce 1991), yet the gender pay gap was actually falling. How could we explain this?

In addressing this question, we applied a decomposition technique developed by Juhn, Murphy, and Pierce (1991). They called attention to the role of two broad sets of factors in influencing trends in wage differentials between groups. The first set is group-specific, or in this case gender-specific factors, like gender differences in qualifications and differences in the treatment of otherwise equally qualified male and female workers (i.e., labor market discrimination). Research on gender pay gaps had traditionally focused on such gender-specific factors. An important insight of Juhn, Murphy, and Pierce was to also focus on a second factor – the role of wage structure, or the array of prices the labor market sets for various skills and the rewards for employment in higher-paying sectors. Given gender differences in skills and in location in the labor market (i.e., occupation and industry), overall trends like rising inequality due to increasing returns to skills would be expected to impact men and women differently.

We found that women were indeed adversely affected by changes in returns to skills and sector over the decade but were able to swim against the current and narrow the gender gap by improving their relative qualifications, particularly their experience and occupational distribution. They also benefited from a substantial decline in the "unexplained" portion of the gender gap which could reflect improvements in unmeasured characteristics or reductions in discrimination. Some of our work also suggested that, given gender differences in occupational and industrial distributions, women benefited from a shift in the composition of demand favoring them relative to men overall, and particularly among low-skilled workers. This in turn implies that skill prices may not change at exactly the same pace across groups of workers that are imperfect substitutes.

As we saw in our examination of the figure above, progress in narrowing the gender pay gap appeared to falter in the 1990s. Kahn and I (2006) turned our attention to this development, extensively comparing the two decades (the 1980s and the 1990s) in order to gain insight into the factors behind the slowdown. This work is discussed in the second part of Chapter 2. We again utilized the Juhn, Murphy, and Pierce framework, paying closer attention to the residual (or unexplained gap) and factors that might influence it. An interesting feature of this paper was our experimentation with some alternate approaches to adjusting for selectivity bias, ranging from expanding the sample (from full-time to all workers), to locating wage observations from other years of our longitudinal data for individuals who currently did not have an observation on wages in the focal year, to implementing median regression in the spirit of Neal and Johnson's (1996) and Neal's (2004) analyses of black-white wage differentials.

Our decompositions showed that women improved their relative human capital to a comparable extent in the 1980s and the 1990s, with the narrowing of the gender experience gap playing a larger role in the 1980s and a reduction (indeed reversal) of the gender education gap playing a larger role in the 1990s. Occupational upgrading and de-unionization contributed to women's relative wage gains in both decades, however, the impact of these factors was greater in the 1980s. Thus, slowing convergence in sectoral location in the 1990s is part of the explanation for the slowdown in wage convergence, although just a small part. The results of our decompositions also indicated that changes in the price of skills and returns to location in favorable sectors of the economy could not explain why the gender pay gap fell faster in the 1980s than in the 1990s. These prices actually changed to women's detriment in the 1980s but had very little effect in the 1990s.

We found the major source of the difference between the two decades to be in the behavior of the residual or unexplained gap. Controlling for human capital, industry, occupation and unionism, and the prices of measured and unmeasured labor market skills, women made much larger gains in relative wages in the 1980s than in the 1990s. This larger decrease in the unexplained gap in the 1980s than in the 1990s was more than sufficient to fully account for the slowdown in wage convergence in the 1990s. We then considered the factors that may have contributed to these changes in the convergence of the unexplained gender pay gap, including changes in labor force selectivity, changes in the gender difference in unmeasured characteristics and in labor market discrimination, and changes in the favorableness of supply and demand shifts. We presented some evidence consistent with each of these factors, suggesting that each may have played a role in explaining the observed trends, with changes in selection, in particular, possibly accounting for as much of one quarter of the difference in trends in the gender gap between the two decades.[2]

1

Equal Pay in the Office

1.1. Introduction

The issue of pay differentials between male and female workers has been the focus of considerable theoretical interest and empirical research. The importance of some gender differences in qualifications, notably actual labor market experience (Mincer and Polachek 1974), has been identified. There have also been notable attempts to estimate the role of gender differences in extent of wage discrimination by sex in the labor market (Becker 1957). In empirical investigations of discrimination, the general practice has been to estimate the proportion of the male-female pay differential that is attributable to differences in those characteristics of male and female workers that are related to productivity. The residual, or unexplained portion of the differential, is then ascribed to possible discrimination.[1] The existence of large pay differentials between male and female workers that

This chapter is a revised and abridged version of Blau, F. D. (1977). Equal Pay in the Office, (Lexington, MA: Lexington Books, D.C. Heath 1977). © 1977 by Francine D. Blau. I am indebted to Peter Brummund for his assistance in readying the book files for editing and publication as a chapter. The original project benefited from the comments and suggestions of Peter Doeringer, Richard Freeman, Lawrence Kahn, Heidi Hartmann, Carol Jusenius, Richard Nelson, Andrew Kohen, Barbara Bergmann, Gilbert Nestel, Vahid Nowshirvani, Christopher Heady, Louis Silversin, Ann Freedman, Marianne Ferber, and Wallace Hendricks. I would like to thank the Bureau of Labor Statistics for granting me access to the unpublished data collected for the Area Wage Surveys, and Samuel Cohen and John Gracza for their role in making the data tape available. I am indebted to Christopher Heady, Donna Lustgarten, Sylvia Moore, and Kathryn Ross for their valuable research assistance on the original study. Portions of the material in this project were prepared under Grant No. 91-25-71-24 from the Manpower Administration, U.S. Department of Labor, under the authority of Title I of the Manpower Development and Training Act of 1962, as amended. Since researchers undertaking such projects are encouraged to express their own judgment freely, this study does not necessarily represent the official opinion or policy of the Department of Labor.

cannot be attributed to individual differences in productivity-related characteristics, and the large reduction in the size of the unexplained differential when detailed occupational classifications are taken into account have led a number of scholars to focus on the prevalence of sex segregation in the labor market.[2] The existence of sex segregation has generally been deduced from aggregate census data which indicate that a large number of detailed occupational categories tend to be either predominantly male or predominantly female, and that such segregated occupations involve relatively high proportions of the male and female labor forces (Gross 1968). A pay differential between men and women with similar productivity-related characteristics is commonly seen to result from this segregation, and the consequent "overcrowding" of the female sector (Bergmann 1974).

The purpose of this chapter is to shed further light on the causes and consequences of sex segregation in the labor market by going to the level of the establishment to examine the relationship of differences in the employment distribution of male and female workers among establishments to the male-female pay differential within selected white-collar occupations. In contrast to earlier studies, the establishment rather than the individual is taken as the unit of analysis. This approach makes it possible to examine data at the level of disaggregation at which many of the employment decisions which produce the observed patterns of employment segregation and pay differences are made. The use of establishment data permit us to observe the employment and pay practices of the firm across a variety of occupations, thus providing a fertile field within which to test a number of hypotheses concerning employer behavior.

This study also differs from previous empirical work at the time it was undertaken in the types of wage questions that are considered. The purpose is not to estimate what proportion of specific differentials between men and women workers may be attributed to discrimination. Rather, an effort is made to delineate the broad pattern of the relationship of within occupational differences in the distribution of men and women workers among establishments (i.e., employment segregation by sex) to male-female pay differentials, and to suggest reasonable hypotheses concerning the behavior which produces this pattern.

Given the high proportion of pay differences explained by occupational segregation, such differences between male and female workers in the same detailed occupational categories can account for only a small fraction of the aggregate pay differential between men and women in the labor market. Nonetheless, an understanding of the impact of distributional factors on male-female pay differences within occupational categories has considerable importance.

Different occupational categories may be thought of as requiring or emphasizing different training, skills, and abilities, although certainly some overlap exists in specific cases. Thus an explanation of the differences in the distribution of men and women among occupations would necessarily be exceedingly complex and would require some assessment of the impact of a large number of factors including early socialization and possibly even innate sex-linked characteristics, the role of educational institutions, historical forces, differing preferences of workers by sex, and the existence of various types of discrimination. Differences in the distribution of men and women among firms within occupational categories, since they occur among individuals of similar training, skills, and abilities, provide an opportunity to test some simpler hypotheses concerning the causes of segregation, which may then shed some light on the causes of segregation by occupation as well.

The interpretation of wage differences may also be less ambiguous within occupational categories where workers are relatively homogeneous. Examining pay data at the establishment level permits us to discern the pattern of the wage consequences of employment segregation within such homogeneous groups of workers.

An understanding of the scope and implications of sex segregation in employment requires some knowledge of its depth and dimensions. At the time this research was undertaken, little evidence existed regarding the extent of sex segregation by establishment within occupational categories. Further, it was not known whether establishments exhibit consistent patterns in the degree of utilization of women across occupational categories, or what characteristics of establishments are important in determining the sex composition of employment. This chapter is designed to extend our knowledge in these areas.

Although the extent of occupational segregation by sex remains substantial, considerable progress has been made since this research was undertaken in reducing it. This chapter is helpful in shedding light on the problems that remain after such integration is accomplished, since it is concerned with differences in the employment distribution and pay rates of men and women within occupational categories.

The results strongly suggest that employment segregation by sex is an important factor in explaining gender differences in pay within narrowly defined occupational categories. At the level of the occupational category, we find strong evidence that male and female workers in the same occupation are segregated by establishment. In most cases, women employed in firms that hire only women into the occupational category earn less on the average than those employed in firms that employ both sexes, while men in male-only firms tend to earn more than men in integrated establishments. Within the same firm, pay differentials by sex within occupations are shown to be small, on average, relative to market-wide occupational pay differences. Because of both the high level of segregation by establishment within occupations and the relatively small magnitude of pay differences by sex within firms, pay differences among firms are found to account for a high proportion of market-wide occupational pay differentials by sex.

At the level of the establishment, we demonstrate the existence of a wage hierarchy of establishments that is consistent across occupations and sex groups. We also show that establishment segregation does exist. After controlling for the occupation mix of the firm and thus the differential availability of women in each occupational category, we find that establishments exhibit consistent patterns with respect to the utilization of women across occupational categories. Further, the ranking of establishments with respect to the representation of women in the firm is inversely related to the ranking of establishments with respect to wage rates.

1.2. The Model

Analyses of employer discrimination generally proceed from an assumption of perfect competition in the labor market. We believe that the role of employer preferences can best be understood within a framework that takes explicit account of the institutional and market constraints under which employers operate. The institutional approach employed here is the internal labor market analysis (Doeringer and Piore 1971). This framework was derived primarily from the study of blue-collar labor markets. Thus the empirical verification of our model constitutes a test of the applicability of a model derived from these sources to office workers, as well as a test of the usefulness of such an approach for the analysis of employment segregation and sex differentials in wages.

The internal labor market analysis involves seeing the job structure of the firm as divided into two types of occupations. First are those job categories that are filled from sources external to the firm through the recruitment of new workers. Within clusters of related occupations, such entry jobs are generally restricted to lower-level positions. Second are those job categories that are filled from internal sources through advancement up well-defined promotion ladders. The process by which workers advance from entry-level positions to higher-level jobs is conceptualized as one in which they acquire, either formally or informally, added knowledge or skills that are to some significant extent firm specific.

The requirement of enterprise-specific skills for the performance of internally allocated jobs works to prevent the development of a competitive market (in the traditional sense) for these categories of occupations and widens the range of administrative influence within the firm. An internal labor market develops, that is, an administrative apparatus that allocates labor and determines wage rates within the firm. Thus the internal labor market structure may be seen as specifying a relatively rigid set of wage relationships and promotional possibilities, both of which are defined primarily in terms of job categories. The wage relationships among individuals and the promotional possibilities for any given individual are for the most part established as a consequence of workers' job assignments in the firm.

Two points of this analysis are particularly relevant to an understanding of sex discrimination in the labor market. The first point sheds light on the motive for such discrimination and the second on the form which such discrimination may be expected to take.

First, within the internal labor market, group or categorical treatment of individuals is the norm. Such group treatment will be more efficient (result in the discarding of less information) the greater the degree of intragroup homogeneity with respect to whatever characteristics are considered important. Thus statistical discrimination is likely to play an important role in rationing job opportunities in such a situation. If employers believe women are less stable workers than men, sex will be an obvious basis for differentiation among workers. Of course, employer distaste for hiring women or male employees' distaste for working with women (à la Becker 1957) could provide further incentives for differential treatment.

Second, within the internal labor market framework, segregation is the form discrimination may be expected to take and the mechanism by which pay differentials are produced because segregation is the primary way in which employers can differentiate between men and women, even with respect to wage rates. Under the constraints imposed by the administered system of the internal labor market, the latitude of the employer to differentiate among individuals (or between sex groups) is relatively broad with respect to hiring and job allocation. It is considerably narrower with respect to wage differentiation among individuals within the same job (unequal pay for equal work) and with respect to the alteration of wage relationships among occupational categories.

Thus employers may exclude women from certain entry-level positions and their associated promotion ladders or promote and upgrade women more slowly than men. Indeed the very structure of the jobs typically open to women is likely to reflect employer perceptions regarding the average characteristics of female workers. Predominantly female occupations may be characterized by fewer possibilities for promotion and more numerous ports of entry than comparable male jobs – the source of the common complaint that women's jobs are dead-end jobs. To the extent that exclusion occurs, it is likely to produce segregation both by occupation and, within occupations, by firm. In both cases, male-female pay differentials are likely to be associated with the restricted access of women to higher-paying opportunities. The primary concern in this chapter is with sex segregation by firm within occupational categories.

In our view, the role of employer preferences can best be understood within a model that takes explicit account of the institutional and market constraints under which employers operate. Two types of constraints are considered to be of particular importance.[3]

First are institutional considerations internal to the firm that place limits on the employer's ability to differentiate among individuals, and thus between men and women. Specifically, the employer is seen as being constrained to pay the same base pay rate to all workers within an occupational category. Wage differentiation among individuals within occupational categories is limited to seniority and merit considerations. In addition, the employer is believed to face a relatively rigid internal wage structure which specifies wage relationships among occupational categories.

Second are institutional and market considerations that determine the position of the establishment in the labor-market wage hierarchy. Given the interrelationships among occupational wage rates and the necessity of equal base occupational pay rates for both sexes, the relative wage position of the firm is postulated as being consistent across occupational categories and sex groups.

These factors are seen as operating on the demand side to yield a structure of occupational wage rates that may be offered by the firm, regardless of the sex of the worker employed. The wage relationships specified by the internal wage structure and the position of the firm in the wage hierarchy of establishments are shaped by a variety of factors and cannot easily be altered to accommodate employer preferences regarding the sex composition of specific occupational categories. Thus it is argued that while the preference for male over female labor is fairly widespread, the employer's ability to exercise this preference is constrained by the position of the establishment in the interfirm wage hierarchy. In each occupational category, male workers are primarily sought by and attracted to the higher-wage establishments, while female workers are likely to find employment in the lower-paying firms which, regardless of their preferences, are less able to compete for male labor.

The following testable hypotheses based on this model may be identified:

At the level of the occupational category:

- There will exist employment segregation within occupations.
- Within occupations, the average wage of women employed in women-only firms will be less than the average wage of women employed in integrated firms, while the average wage of men employed in male-only firms will be above the average wage of men employed in integrated firms.
- When both men and women are employed in the same firm, pay differentials by sex within occupations will be small relative to market-wide occupational pay differences.
- Market-wide occupational pay differentials by sex will be the result primarily of differences in pay rates among firms rather than of differences in pay rates within firms.

At the level of the establishment:

- Across occupations, there will exist segregation by establishment.
- Across occupations, there will exist an establishment wage hierarchy within the labor market.
- There will be an inverse relationship between the relative ranking of the establishment with respect to the representation of women and its ranking with respect to wages.
- Establishment characteristics that are positively related to wage rates will be negatively related to the representation of women in the establishments, and vice versa.
- To the extent that industry is an important factor in interfirm wage differences, we expect to find industry segregation.

The predictions of this model may be contrasted with two alternative cases which have been analyzed by Becker (1957). In the first case, discriminatory tastes are located in employers; in the second case, in employees.

In the Becker model, employers who have tastes for discrimination against female workers will hire women only if the wage difference between male and female labor is large enough to compensate for the disutility of employing women. One can postulate a structure of employer preferences that would result in some degree of employment segregation by occupation, establishment, and even by industry. However, two important differences between the two models emerge when we consider the relationship between employment and wage patterns. First, within occupational categories, there would be no significant pay differentials between the women employed in integrated firms and those employed in segregated firms, and the same would apply to male workers. It follows that the wage differential between men and women employed in the same firm would be roughly the same magnitude as the average market-wide sex differential within the occupation. These points follow from the traditional neoclassical view that a market wage rate is determined for both types of labor, and that no firm would pay wages above the market rate (nor could a firm pay less). Equally important, there would be no constraint within the firm that would prevent different pay rates for men and women in the same job (that is, wage flexibility is assumed). Second, even if we allow for some variation in rates of remuneration for male and female labor depending on the establishment in which they are employed, it would not be predicted that women would constitute a lower proportion of total employment in firms that pay higher wages to both men and women. That is, it is not expected that male and female pay rates will follow the same pattern by establishment of employment. On the contrary, we expect firms that hire a greater-than-expected proportion of male workers to be those firms that prefer men and will hire women only at a lower wage rate.

In the Becker model, the existence of employee discrimination may have significant effects on the employment of women even in the absence of employer discrimination. The major thrust of this factor would be towards segregation. Segregation results from the efforts of employers to avoid paying a premium to male workers to induce them to work with female labor. While a distaste on the part of male workers for working with women can produce segregation, it should not result in pay differences. However, complete segregation may not be possible. In particular, where the firm incurs substantial adjustment costs associated with hiring and firing workers, it is possible that it will not be profitable for the firm to entirely shift the sex composition of its work force in response to a wage differential between men and women (Arrow 1973: 22). Also working against the likelihood of complete segregation in the case of complementary labor is the fact that the existence of sex segregation by occupation may make it difficult to form single-sex work units. Where complete segregation is not possible, discriminatory tastes on the part of employees can lead to wage differences combined with tendencies toward segregation (Arrow 1973: 23). Under these circumstances, one might observe different rates of remuneration for male labor depending on whether it is employed with female labor. However, the wage implications of this model are quite different from those of our model. In the employee discrimination case it is expected that male workers will be paid a premium when they work with women and thus be more highly remunerated than when they work with men.

1.3. Data

The focus of this chapter is upon pay differentials and differences in the distribution of employment of male and female office workers in three large northeastern standard metropolitan statistical areas: Boston, New York, and Philadelphia. A wide variety of clerical, professional, and technical occupations are included in the sample. Occupations are narrowly defined and generally subdivided into skill classifications.

The data used in this study were collected by the Bureau of Labor Statistics for the Area Wage Surveys between April and November of 1970. The data provide information about standard weekly earnings and hours by sex and job category as well as by certain characteristics of the establishment including type of industry, size of firm, and union status of a majority of plant and office workers. Since B.L.S. field investigators classify workers by occupational category and skill grade, comparability across establishments is maximized. Working supervisors, apprentices, learners, beginners, trainees, and handicapped, part-time, temporary, and probationary workers are excluded from the sample by field investigators. The occupational-skill-class pay rates employed in this study are computed as standard weekly earnings divided by standard weekly hours and will be referred to as the wage. Overtime payments are not included in the estimate of earnings.

The occupation-skill classes included in this study of occupational wage rates and employment patterns are enumerated and described in Blau (1977), Appendix A. Throughout, we refer to each occupation-skill grade as an occupational category.

1.4. Occupational Wage Rates and Employment Patterns

In this section, we have selected a subsample of occupation-skill classes to test the hypotheses generated by our model with respect to wage rates and employment patterns when occupations are considered separately. Within this model, discrimination is manifested primarily through employer hiring practices that deny women access to the higher-wage establishments. These practices are seen to result, on the one hand, in sex segregation by establishment within occupational categories and, on the other hand, in pay differentials by sex within occupational categories that are primarily related to differences in wage rates among firms rather than to differences in wage rates within firms.

The features of this model may be contrasted to the operation of an unprejudiced system. In such a system, sex would not be a barrier to entry into the firm. Thus the sex composition of the establishment's occupational work force would be consistent with a selection process in which the sex of the worker hired was solely the result of random processes. Intrafirm pay differentials by sex within occupational categories would reflect differences in seniority and merit, while the advantage of employment in high-wage firms, and the burden of employment in low-wage firms, would be equally shared between men and women. Thus the sex differential in wages would be expected to be relatively small, and to be primarily the result of within firm pay differences.

At the most basic level, the impact of discrimination may be discerned by comparing the actual distribution of men and women among establishments and the wage outcomes of workers by sex with the situation that would obtain in an unprejudiced system. However, some caution must be exercised in this regard, particularly in interpreting the wage data presented in this chapter. While it would be tempting to attribute all of the sex differentials in wage rates associated with interfirm pay differences to the exclusionary behavior of high-wage firms, in the absence of direct data on the personal characteristics of individual workers such an approach cannot be justified. On the one hand, it is possible that the average quality of male labor is higher than the average quality of female labor and that such quality differences explain some portion of the sex differential. If this were the case, the impact of exclusion on pay differences would be overestimated. On the other hand, it is equally possible that, in the presence of sex discrimination in upgrading and promotion, as well as of other barriers to occupational mobility, female labor may be of higher average quality than male labor within specific occupational categories. In this case, the impact of exclusion on pay differences would be underestimated.

Moreover, it may be argued that, even in the presence of additional data, the impact on wage differences of discrimination through exclusion would be difficult to measure. Labor turnover, and thus the average level of seniority of workers within the establishment, is not a function solely of the personal characteristics of workers. The wage and promotion policies of the firm must also be considered. Further, even were direct measures of labor productivity obtainable, these would not take into account the effect of the wage and personnel practices of the firm on the diligence and effort of the establishment work force, nor differences across firms in the extent and effectiveness of on-the-job training programs or opportunities.

While we argue on the basis of theoretical considerations as well as empirical evidence that it is unlikely that interfirm pay differences are due solely to interfirm differences in the productivity-related characteristics of workers, in the absence of additional data it is not possible in specific cases to distinguish the gender pay differential within occupations resulting from individual characteristics from that resulting from other variables. Thus we trace the broad pattern of the relationship between differences in the distribution of men and women among firms and the male-female pay differential within occupational categories.

The occupation-skill classes included in this section are shown in Table 1.1. As noted above, we refer to each occupation-skill grade as an occupational category. Empirical results are reported for cities in which at least fifty firms contained observations on the occupational category, and in which at least seventy workers of each sex were employed in the sampled firms. Since occupational categories are considered separately, the designation of a firm as segregated or integrated is occupation specific, referring only to the sex composition of employment within the occupational category.

Table 1.1

Job Categories Included in the Study of Occupational Employment Patterns and Wage Rates

Office occupations
Accounting clerk
Class A
Class B
Order clerk
Payroll clerk
Office boy/girl
Tabulating machine operator
Class A
Class B
Professional and technical occupations
Systems analyst
Class B
Computer programer
Class A
Class B
Class C
Computer operator
Class B

1.4.1. *Sex Segregation by Establishment: Measurement and Magnitude*

The criterion for the existence of intraoccupational segregation (employment segregation within occupations) is whether, for given occupational categories, each sex tends to work together within the same establishment to a significantly greater extent than would occur by chance. Thus if one were to view the distribution of establishments according to the proportion that women comprise of each firm's occupational work force, this criterion would be met if there were a higher concentration of establishments in the tails of the distribution, employing relatively high or low proportions of women, than would be expected if the laws of chance were observed. The first requirement for applying this criterion is to specify the distribution of establishments that would obtain if the sex of the employee hired were the result of a random process.

1.4.1.1. A Model of Random Hiring

We here develop a model which enables us to specify the distribution of firms with respect to the sex composition of occupational employment under conditions of random hiring. We may then compare this theoretical distribution of establishments to the actual distribution to determine for each occupational category whether sex segregation by firm within occupations exists. For each occupation and city, let:

p = the proportion of the pool of individuals with the requisite occupational skills that is female.
$q = 1 - p$ = the proportion of the labor pool that is male.
x_i = the number of women employed in the occupation in firm i.
n_i = the total number of employees in the occupation in firm i.
$p_i = x_i/n_i \cdot 100$ = the percentage that women comprise of all workers in the occupation in firm i.

Then, x_i may be viewed as the outcome of n_i trials of an experiment where each trial consists of selecting an individual at random from the labor pool where the probability of obtaining a woman is p and the probability of obtaining a man is q. The binomial probability distribution may be employed to obtain the probability that x_i takes on any specified value (to be completely accurate we would have to postulate that the firms sample from the labor pool not only at random, but with replacement since it is only in this case that the outcomes of the n_i experiments can be independent):

(1.1) $$f_i(x=x_i)=\binom{n_i}{x_i}p^{x_i}q^{(n_i-x_i)}$$

To apply the model, establishments were grouped according to the number of employees in the occupational labor force. Each size category was composed of firms with the same value of n_i. The possible outcomes, x_i , were grouped into twelve categories according to the value of p_i. The twelve sex composition categories are: $p_i = 0$, $0 < p_i < 10$, $10 \leq p_i < 20$, $20 \leq p_i < 30$,... $90 \leq p_i < 100$, $p_i = 100$.

Let:

n_j = the number of firms in the jth size category.

p_{jk} = the probability that a firm selected at random from the jth size class has a value of p_i that falls in the kth sex composition category.

e_{jk} = the expected number of firms in the jth size class and the kth sex composition category.

E_k = the total expected number of firms in the kth sex composition category.

P_k = the probability of obtaining a firm in the kth sex composition category, given the size distribution of firms.

Then, p_{jk} may be computed from (1.1) as:

(1.2) $$p_{jk} = f(x_a \leq x \leq x_b) = \sum_{i=a}^{b} f_i(x = x_i)$$

Using the standard formula for expected value, e_{jk} may be computed as:

(1.3) $$e_{jk} = p_{jk} \cdot n_j$$

The e_{jk} represent the theoretical distribution of firms by the sex composition of establishment employment disaggregated by size category. To find the theoretical frequencies for the N firms in the sample, we may sum across size categories:

(1.4) $$E_k = \sum_j e_{jk}$$

And the theoretical probabilities for the sample may be defined as:

(1.5) $$P_k = E_k / N$$

Finally, the chi-square "goodness of fit" test may be employed to determine whether the theoretical probabilities are correct or the disparity between the observed and the expected frequencies is large enough to reject the hypothesis of randomness.

If we wish to examine the distribution of male and female workers among establishments that would prevail under the conditions of random hiring, the worker distributions may be derived directly from the theoretical establishment distributions.

Let:

n_{ij} = the number of employees in the occupational work force in firms included in the jth size class.

p_{jk} = the arithmetic mean of the pi included in the kth sex composition category divided by 100.

f_{jk} and m_{jk} = the expected number of women and men respectively employed in establishments which fall into the jth size class and kth sex composition category.

F_k and M_k = the total expected number of women and men respectively employed in firms included in the kth sex composition category.

Then we may approximate f_{jk} and m_{jk} in the following way:

$$f_{jk} = e_{jk} \cdot n_{jk} \cdot \overline{p}_{ik} \tag{1.6}$$

$$m_{jk} = (e_{jk} \cdots n_{ij}) - f_{jk} \tag{1.7}$$

And F_k and M_k may be obtained by summation:

$$F_k = \textstyle\sum_j f_{jk} \qquad M_k = \textstyle\sum_j m_{jk} \tag{1.8}$$

While the worker distributions yield no new information in terms of possible hypothesis testing, they may be employed to compute the index of segregation, which in this case is a summary measure of the degree of intraoccupational segregation (i.e., employment segregation by sex within occupations).

1.4.1.2. Conceptual Problems in the Application of the Model

Conceptually, the application of this model to establishment hiring poses certain problems of interdependence of outcomes. No difficulty would arise if firms sampled with replacement from the labor pool. However, since it is not reasonable to assume that firms do so, it may be helpful to consider whether problems of interdependence are serious enough to cast doubt on the ability of the theoretical distribution to serve as a fair and reasonable test for the existence of intraoccupational segregation.

The first area in which a question of interdependence arises is in the computation of p_{jk} in equation (1.2). It may be recalled that we viewed the number of women employed in the establishment, x_i, as the outcome of n_i trials of an experiment where each trial consists of selecting an individual at random from the labor pool. If firms were to sample from the labor pool with replacement, p, the probability of selecting a woman would be constant from trial to trial, and the outcome of each trial could be viewed as independent. However, when the firm samples without replacement from the labor pool, p is not constant, but rather changes slightly from trial to trial as either a man or a woman is selected. This type of interdependence could be modeled with the hypergeometric distribution. However, the larger the total universe (in this case the total labor pool) relative to the sample size (in this case the size of the firm), the smaller the divergence between the results obtained with the hypergeometric distribution and those obtained with the binomial distribution. It is doubtful that even the largest firms are sufficiently large relative to the labor pool to warrant the use of the hypergeometric distribution. Moreover, the utilization of the hypergeometric distribution poses its own problems, the most serious being the necessity of specifying and estimating the size of the total universe or labor pool.

A question of interdependence also arises in the computation of e_{jk} in Equation (1.3). Such a computation gives us the expected outcome of n_j replications of the experiment in which n_i workers are selected at random from the labor pool when the constant probability of obtaining a woman is p. Clearly such a computation requires independence of outcome of the $n.$ experiments. However, in the real world there would be some interdependence of outcomes among all firms, inside and outside the sample, and within and among size categories. The nature of this interdependence is difficult to specify. Certainly the labor pool, comprised of available individuals with the requisite occupational skills, includes some presently employed workers as well as those presently unemployed. Indeed some workers in the labor pool may be presently employed in other occupations as well as by other firms. Thus we do not have a simple form of interdependence whereby a worker employed by one firm is completely unavailable to other firms, and vice versa. While it is easy enough to imagine scenarios in which interdependence among establishments would be significant, most would involve a substantial departure from random behavior on the part of at least some of the firms or substantial differentials in interfirm mobility between male and female workers. Thus it was felt that considerations of interdependence among firms did not seriously challenge the applicability of the model.

An additional conceptual problem arises when the temporal dimension of the hiring process is considered. The representation of women in the occupational labor force of the establishment is the outcome of a selection procedure that takes place over a considerable, although unknown, period of time. It is possible that p has varied over time and that some of the interfirm differential in female employment reflects the time period in which the bulk of the establishment's occupational work force was recruited. In this sense, our estimate of p, the proportion that women presently comprise of total occupational employment, may be considered to reflect the average representation of women in the labor pool over time rather than the actual availability of women each time the firm hires an additional worker. However, it is doubtful that this factor could account for a uniform pattern of intraoccupational segregation in a wide variety of occupational categories.

In most cases, the actual distribution of establishments by sex composition of occupational employment is so heavily concentrated at both tails of the distribution that only radical changes in the proportion that women comprise of new entrants to the occupational labor force could produce this result (see Blau 1977, Appendix Table B-l). Moreover, in section 1.5 we present evidence of the existence of establishment and industry segregation (i.e., employment segregation of men and women by establishment and industry when occupations are considered jointly). Thus, for the temporal dimension of the hiring process to be the sole explanation for the observed patterns of sex segregation within occupations, it would be necessary for firms and industry groups to follow similar time patterns of recruitment across all occupational categories, and for all occupational categories to exhibit similar time patterns of changes in the level of p.

1.4.1.3. The Extent of Segregation within Occupations

To use the foregoing model to assess the magnitude of intraoccupational segregation, it is necessary to specify an estimate of p, the female proportion of the total labor supply pool in each occupation. We have here estimated p as the proportion women represent of all those actually employed in the occupation in each city. (P was estimated directly from our sample. Since the sample of establishments used by the Bureau of Labor Statistics in the Area Wage Surveys is a stratified and not a random sample, each observation was given its appropriate weight.) The size of the group of workers presently employed in an occupational category is a narrow definition of the pool of individuals with the requisite occupational skills. However, our definition of intraoccupational segregation takes as given the extent of segregation of men and women by occupation, that is, the proportion that women comprise of total employment in each occupational category. Thus this estimate of p is consistent with our definition.

The way in which the theoretical distribution of establishments is generated from the size classes is illustrated in Table 1.2 for class A accounting clerks in Boston. The expected distributions shown in the table were derived from the application of the model of random hiring. The actual distributions are of firms in the sample by sex composition category.

It may be noted that the total expected frequencies do not approximate a normal curve, but rather tend to cluster within a number of the sex composition categories. For a given value of p, the distribution of establishments among size classes is the most important factor in producing this clustering. Size of firm (which refers to the number of workers employed in the occupation category) affects the theoretical distribution in two ways. First, when n_i is small, p_i can take on only a limited number of values, due to indivisibilities. Thus, for example, when n_i equals 2, there are only three possible values for p_i: 0, 50, and 100. Second, as n_i or the number of trials is increased, the expected distribution of establishments would tend to cluster more tightly around p. However, for smaller values of n_i, the expected distribution is more diffuse. This is a simple application of the Law of Large Numbers. In most cases, there are a relatively large number of firms with small values of n_i, and thus these firms heavily influence the total distribution.

Table 1.2

Expected and Actual Distribution of Firms by Percent Female Employees and Size of Firm: Class A Accounting Clerks, Boston

Size of	Distribution	Percent Female												
Firm	(numbers)	0	1-9	10-19	20-29	30-39	40-49	50-59	60-69	70-79	80-89	90-99	100	Total
1	Expected	11.63	0.0	0.0	0.0	0.0	0.0	0.0	0.0	0.0	0.0	0.0	26.37	38
	Actual	12.00	0.0	0.0	0.0	0.0	0.0	0.0	0.0	0.0	0.0	0.0	26.00	38
2	Expected	2.53	0.0	0.0	0.0	0.0	0.0	11.47	0.0	0.0	0.0	0.0	13.00	27
	Actual	5.00	0.0	0.0	0.0	0.0	0.0	4.00	0.0	0.0	0.0	0.0	18.00	27
3	Expected	0.52	0.0	0.0	0.0	3.51	0.0	0.0	7.96	0.0	0.0	0.0	6.02	18
	Actual	2.00	0.0	0.0	0.0	4.00	0.0	0.0	2.00	0.0	0.0	0.0	10.00	18
4	Expected	0.12	0.0	0.0	1.11	0.0	0.0	3.79	0.0	5.73	0.0	0.0	3.25	14
	Actual	3.00	0.0	0.0	1.00	0.0	0.0	0.0	0.0	0.0	0.0	0.0	10.00	14
5	Expected	0.02	0.0	0.0	0.21	0.0	0.97	0.0	2.19	0.0	2.49	0.0	1.13	7
	Actual	0.0	0.0	0.0	0.0	0.0	0.0	0.0	0.0	0.0	4.00	0.0	3.00	7
6-9	Expected	0.01	0.0	0.12	0.28	0.87	0.80	4.29	4.62	4.82	5.41	0.0	1.79	23
	Actual	1.00	0.0	0.0	1.00	2.00	0.0	3.00	4.00	4.00	0.0	0.0	8.00	23
10-19	Expected	0.0	0.0	0.0	0.02	0.16	0.61	2.04	4.17	4.14	2.18	0.58	0.10	14
	Actual	0.0	0.0	0.0	1.00	3.00	0.0	2.00	3.00	0.0	0.0	0.0	5.00	14
20-39	Expected	0.0	0.0	0.0	0.0	0.01	0.12	0.90	3.45	3.21	1.20	0.10	0.0	9
	Actual	0.0	0.0	0.0	0.0	0.0	1.00	1.00	0.0	0.0	1.00	2.00	4.00	9
40+	Expected	0.0	0.0	0.0	0.0	0.0	0.01	0.26	1.78	1.75	0.20	0.0	0.0	4
	Actual	0.0	1.00	0.0	0.0	1.0	0.0	0.0	0.0	0.0	0.0	2.00	0.0	4
Total	Expected	14.82	0.0	0.12	1.63	4.54	2.50	22.74	24.17	19.65	11.47	0.68	51.66	154
	Actual	23.00	1.00	0.0	3.00	10.0	1.00	10.00	9.00	4.00	5.00	4.00	84.00	154

Source: Computed from unpublished Bureau of Labor Statistics data collected for the Area Wage Surveys between April and November 1970.
Note: Size of firm refers to the number of workers employed as Class A Accounting Clerks in each firm. If p_i is the percentage that women comprise of total occupational employment in firm i, then the 12 sex composition categories above are defined as: $p_i = 0, 0 < p_i < 10, 10$ $p_i < 20, 20 < p_i < 30, \ldots\ 90 < p_i < 100, p_i = 100$.

The total expected and actual distributions of establishments by occupation and city are shown in Blau (1977), Appendix B. Our findings are summarized in Table 1.3 which gives the chi-square values for two tests of the hypothesis of randomness in the distribution of firms by the sex composition of the establishment's occupational work force. The first test, X^2 (1), compares the actual to the expected frequencies of firms in three categories: firms employing only men, firms employing only women, and firms with mixed occupational work forces. The hypothesis of randomness is rejected in all cases. The second test, X^2 (2), compares the actual to the expected frequencies of firms in *k* sex composition categories, where the initial twelve categories were combined such that there was no category for which the expected frequency was less than 1. The hypothesis of randomness is again rejected in all cases.

Table 1.3

Chi-Square Values

Occupation	*P*	*N*	X^2 *(1)*	X^2 *(2)*	*k*
Accounting Clerk					
Class A					
Boston	0.694	154	43.51[a]	65.06[a]	9
New York	0.648	335	70.46[a]	118.53[a]	9
Philadelphia	0.731	171	28.03[a]	37.73[a]	7
Class B					
Boston	0.925	162	8.77[a]	13.44[b]	7
New York	0.759	322	66.01[a]	105.62[a]	7
Philadelphia	0.883	170	26.98[a]	36.89[a]	7
Order Clerk					
Boston	0.615	67	55.07[a]	61.59[a]	9
New York	0.833	106	46.52[a]	53.84[a]	7
Philadelphia	0.712	62	35.55[a]	41.05[a]	7
Payroll Clerk					
New York	0.855	223	23.6[a]	30.51[a]	7
Office boy/girl					
Boston	0.327	99	37.49[a]	49.43[a]	8
New York	0.248	279	113.51[a]	142.9[a]	8
Philadelphia	0.4	128	52.09[a]	66.09[a]	9

Table 1.3 (continued)

Occupation	*P*	*N*	X^2 *(1)*	X^2 *(2)*	*k*
Tabulating-machine operator					
Class A					
New York	0.38	52	51.79[a]	55.50[a]	8
Tabulating-machine operator					
Class B					
New York	0.271	66	27.38[a]	33.51[a]	8
Systems analyst					
Class B					
New York	0.149	93	13.55[a]	18.38[a]	7
Computer programmer					
Class A					
New York	0.208	122	12.72[a]	21.55[a]	8
Class B					
Boston	0.411	76	21.02[a]	32.69[a]	9
New York	0.261	138	13.97[a]	21.82[a]	8
Philadelphia	0.184	83	5.58[b]	11.82[b]	7
Class C					
New York	0.309	84	13.14[a]	18.82[a]	8
Computer Operator					
Class B					
New York	0.101	165	33.31[a]	34.18[a]	7
Philadelphia	0.103	110	24.96[a]	26.27[a]	7

Notes: To compute X^2 (1) the expected and actual frequencies were combined into three categories: $p_i = 0, 0 < p_i < 100, p_i = 100$. To compute X^2 (2) the expected and actual frequencies were combined into k categories such that there was no category for which the expected frequency was less than 1.

[a] Significant at the 0.5% level.

[b] Significant at the 5% level.

The impact of the establishment distributions on male and female employment is shown in Table 1.4, which gives the actual and expected values of the index of segregation. We employ the index of segregation developed by Duncan and Duncan (1955), which has frequently been used to measure gender segregation by occupation. In this case the index has been defined so as to measure employment segregation by sex within occupations or intraoccupational segregation. The index may take on any value between 0 and 100. In the present context, a value of 0 indicates that, within the occupational category, the distribution of women among the establishments in the sample closely approximates the distribution of male workers. Equivalently, this means that in each establishment the proportion of all those employed in the occupation who are women is roughly the same as the female share of total occupational employment. A value of 100 indi-

Table 1.4

Actual and Expected Indices of Segregation by City: Selected Occupations

		Index of Segregation		
Occupation	*City*	*Actual*	*Expected*	*Difference*
Office				
Accounting clerk				
Class A	Boston	72.62	28.92	43.70
	New York	59.54	27.77	31.77
	Philadelphia	72.58	32.32	40.26
Class B	Boston	59.53	43.91	15.62
	New York	58.69	28.06	30.63
	Philadelphia	82.22	34.60	47.62
Order clerk	Boston	85.47	35.85	49.62
	New York	84.21	35.25	48.95
	Philadelphia	90.05	28.68	61.37
Payroll clerk	New York	82.66	56.65	26.01
Office boy/girl	Boston	74.65	31.31	43.34
	New York	82.22	20.60	61.62
	Philadelphia	65.12	33.76	31.36
Tabulating-machine operator				
Class A	New York	84.65	26.45	58.19
Class B	New York	77.11	23.91	53.20
Professional and technical				
Systems analyst				
Class B	New York	40.83	27.30	13.52
Computer programmer				
Class A	New York	53.12	34.91	18.21
Class B	Boston	51.78	31.13	20.65
	New York	43.85	33.97	9.88
	Philadelphia	65.85	42.82	23.03
Class C	New York	40.60	31.52	9.08
Computer operator				
Class B	New York	82.08	47.48	34.60
	Philadelphia	85.79	54.00	31.79

Source: Computed from unpublished Bureau of Labor Statistics data collected for the Area Wage Surveys between April and November 1970.

Notes: Within each city, the index of segregation is computed in the following way: Let p_{hi} equal the percentage that women comprise of the labor force in occupation h within establishment i. Establishments are grouped into 12 sex composition categories depending on the value of p_{hi}. The categories are: $p_{hi} = 0, 0 < p_{hi} < 10, 10 \leq p_{hi} < 20, 20 \leq p_{hi} < 30, \ldots 90 \leq p_{hi} < 100, p_{hi} = 100$. Let f_{hk} equal the percentage of all female workers and m_{hk} equal the percentage of all male workers in occupation h who are employed in firms included in the kth sex composition category. The index of segregation for occupation h is then:

Table 1.4 (continued)

$$S_h = \frac{\sum_{k=1}^{12} | f_{hk} - m_{hk} |}{2}$$

The actual index of segregation utilizes the employment distributions of male and female workers from the sample. The expected index of segregation employs the theoretical distributions.

cates complete segregation, with women employed entirely in firms that hire only female workers into the occupation, and men working in establishments that employ only male workers in the occupation.

The actual index of segregation is computed on the basis of the employment distributions of male and female workers in the sample. The expected index of segregation utilizes the theoretical distributions derived from the application of the model of random hiring. While a fairly large degree of segregation would be expected even on the basis of random hiring (due to the large representation of firms with a small value of ni), the differences between the actual and expected values of the index (shown in the last column of Table 1.4) are generally of considerable magnitude. Thus a sizable proportion of women (or men) would have to be reallocated among firms for the actual distributions to approximate a situation of random hiring on the basis of sex.

It is interesting to note, however, that while the hypothesis of randomness has been rejected for all occupational categories, the values of the index of segregation indicate that in general the magnitude of segregation is smaller in the systems-analyst and computer-programmer categories. Inspection of the actual and expected distribution of firms by sex composition of establishment employment indicates a unique pattern among these classifications. While the actual number of male-only firms exceeds the expected number, the actual number of female-only firms is in every case less than the expected number, and the vast majority of women in each category are employed in integrated firms. This result may indicate a reluctance on the part of employers to entrust these highly responsible and skilled jobs to solely female work forces. However, it appears that, for a group of employers, mixed work forces may be just as acceptable as male work forces.

The apparent acceptability of mixed work forces in the systems-analyst and computer-programmer categories may be due, in part, to the rapid growth in demand for workers in these fields in the years preceding the study. The U.S. Census of the Population (1973, Table 2) records a twentyfold increase in the number of workers employed as systems analysts and computer programmers between 1960 and 1970. Since the computer jobs are relatively new, their wage standing in the firm is less influenced by historical and customary patterns. Thus it may be possible for most firms to set an occupational wage rate for these categories that is high enough to attract some male workers in the majority of cases. However, expanding demand, in combination with the necessity of recruiting workers with some training or skills in this area from sources external to the firm, may have induced employers to accept female workers more readily. (While some firms fill lower-level programmer jobs through the promotion of experienced clerical workers, outside sources of supply are important. Some training is generally required of new workers, although on-the-job training is also important in the skill acquisition process [U.S. Department of Labor 1970: 244-9].)

While employment expansion was no less rapid among computer operators, this occupational category differed from the other computer jobs in the greater tendency of firms to rely on recruitment of its members from internal sources. Often when employers installed electronic computers, they filled many of the operator positions by transferring presently employed workers from jobs as tabulating- and bookkeeping-machine operators, since such categories were no longer be needed after the computer was installed. In addition, both in the case of transferred workers and of those beginners hired from outside, the firm generally provided the training (U.S. Department of Labor 1970: 278-9). Thus, wage ranges in the computer operator category are expected to be more closely tied to rates of remuneration in clerical jobs than are the rates for programmers and systems analysts. The sex composition of the computer operator category within the firm is thus expected to more closely reflect the sex composition of the clerical occupations from which many operators were recruited.

1.4.2. The Relationship of Male and Female Wage Rates to the Distribution of Men and Women among Establishments

In assessing the importance of the pattern of sex segregation by establishment delineated in the preceding section, a crucial factor to be considered is the relationship between the differential distribution of male and female workers among establishments and the intraoccupational pay differential by sex (i.e, gender pay differences within occupations). In this section, we attempt to shed light on this question by examining the pattern of pay rates by establishment. First, the pattern of male and female wage rates by sector of employment is considered. Second, a method to estimate the contribution of pay differences within firms and pay differences among firms to the aggregate pay differential by sex is derived, and our findings are presented.

1.4.2.1. Male and Female Wage Rates by Sector

Since segregated establishments are viewed in our model as representing the extremes of the wage distribution, it is expected that the average wage of women in segregated firms will be below that of women employed in integrated firms, while the average wage of men employed in segregated firms will be above that of men employed in integrated firms. This also implies that the pay differential by sex will be larger in the segregated sector than in the integrated sector. These predictions of our model may be contrasted to the Becker models of employer and employee discrimination, as discussed above.

The Becker model of employer discrimination does not predict the existence of wage differentials by sector. Employers determine whether or not to hire women by comparing the market-wide sex differential to their coefficient of discrimination. The Becker case of employee preferences does not necessarily predict the existence of wage differences by sector. However, if such differences do in fact exist, the opposite pattern from that of our model is expected. That is, since men must be paid a premium to induce them to work with women, the average wage of men employed in segregated firms will be less than that of men employed in integrated firms. Further, since a profit-maximizing employer with no tastes for discrimination would hire men only if this imposed no cost disadvantage, the higher wages of men in integrated firms might have to be subsidized by female employees. If female labor is available to all firms at a lower wage than male labor, it is not necessarily true that women will earn less in integrated than in segregated firms. However, if a sectoral differential does exist, this is the direction that would be predicted. This reasoning further implies that the pay differential by sex will be larger in the integrated than in the segregated sector.

It may be helpful to summarize these alternative predictions more concisely.

Let:

W_{IF} = the average wage of women in integrated firms.
W_{SF} = the average wage of women in segregated firms.
W_{IM} = the average wage of men in integrated firms.
W_{SF} = the average wage of men in segregated firms.

Then, the three cases may be distinguished as follows:

1. Our model:
$W_{IF} - W_{SF}/W_{IF} > 0$
$W_{IM} - W_{SM}/W_{IM} < 0$
$W_{IM} - W_{IF}/W_{IM} < W_{SM} - W_{SF}/W_{SM}$

2. Unconstrained employer preferences:
$W_{IF} - W_{SF}/W_{IF} \approx 0$
$W_{IM} - W_{SM}/W_{IM} \approx 0$
$W_{IM} - W_{IF}/W_{IM} \approx W_{SM} - W_{SF}/W_{SM}$

3. Employee discrimination:
$W_{IF} - W_{SF}/W_{IF} \leq 0$
$W_{IM} - W_{SM}/W_{IM} \geq 0$
$W_{IM} - W_{IF}/W_{IM} \geq W_{SM} - W_{SF}/W_{SM}$

Before examining the empirical evidence with regard to these alternative hypotheses, it is important to consider how conclusive a test we are able to perform, given the limitations of the data. As noted earlier, it is our view that interfirm differences in pay rates generally exceed what would result from differences in the productivity-related characteristics of workers. It is not our contention that all interfirm wage differences unaccounted for by differences in the individual characteristics of workers actually represent cost differences per efficiency unit of labor, since establishment as well as individual characteristics influence labor productivity. Furthermore, costs of search and training must also be taken into account. While we hold this to be a reasonable view that is consistent with evidence from a variety of sources, it must be acknowledged that in the absence of additional data we cannot rule out the possibility that quality differences within the male work force or the female work force (or both) exist in sufficient magnitude to cause a reversal of some of the computed sectoral differentials. Thus our findings with regard to the merit of these alternative hypotheses must be considered as suggestive but not conclusive.

Mean wages by sector are shown in Table 1.5 for each occupational category and city. Let us first consider the clerical and computer-operator classifications, since our findings regarding the extent of segregation by firm are most uniform in these cases. In fifteen of the cases, the mean wage of women employed in integrated firms was above that of women employed in segregated firms, and in only three of these cases was the differential in favor of women employed in integrated firms less than 5 percent. In one case, that of messengers in New York, there was no difference. Among tabulating machine operators (class A) there was an 8 percent differential in favor of women employed in segregated firms; however, our estimate of W_{SF} was based on only twenty-four workers.

For male workers the results are somewhat uneven, but they do tend to support our model. The average wage rate of men employed in integrated firms was below that of men employed in segregated firms in twelve cases, although in six of these the differential in favor of men employed in segregated firms was less than 5 percent. Men employed in integrated firms had higher mean wages than men employed in segregated firms in five cases, although in only one of these was the differential greater than 5 percent.

Since there is only one case in which the pattern of differentials by sector goes against our hypothesis for both men and women, the one in which $W_{IF} - W_{SF}/W_{IF} > 0$ and $W_{IM} - W_{SM}/W_{IM} < 0$, the employee preference employee model does not appear to be confirmed. Similarly, the presence of differentials by sector is counter to the employer preference model.

A possible explanation for the few observed inconsistencies in the pattern of wage rates by sector is that, especially in the case of men, there is some overlap between the segregated and integrated sectors. That is, men are more highly represented in the higher-paying integrated establishments, while women are more highly represented in the lower-paying integrated establishments. This explanation will be confirmed if it is found in most cases, even within the integrated sector, that pay differences among firms explain a substantial proportion of the male-female pay differential.

The hypothesis that the male-female pay differential will be larger in the segregated than in the integrated sector is confirmed in the majority of cases. This finding follows directly from the fact that our

Table 1.5

Average Wages of Men and Women by Sector of Employment: Selected Occupations

Occupation			*Segregated Firms*			*Integrated Firms*		
			W	*N*	*s.d.*	*W*	*N*	*s.d.*
A Accounting Clerk								
	Boston							
		Men	$3.99	46	0.62	$3.63	299	0.4
		Women	3.16	375	0.49	3.38	393	0.45
	New York							
		Men	4.16	190	0.53	3.88	671	0.6
		Women	3.49	525	0.53	3.67	801	0.45
	Philadelphia							
		Men	3.83	126	0.5	3.78	133	0.51
		Women	2.97	414	0.47	3.43	339	0.57
B Accounting Clerk								
	Boston							
		Men	3.45	10	0.79	2.94	109	0.37
		Women	2.64	576	0.31	2.67	753	0.34
	New York							
		Men	3.38	98	0.41	3.23	505	0.46
		Women	2.86	894	0.42	3.06	1116	0.36
	Philadelphia							
		Men	3.59	20	0.83	3.54	356	0.43
		Women	2.46	871	0.31	2.72	474	0.57
Order Clerk								
	Boston							
		Men	3.75	51	0.66	3.91	58	0.65
		Women	2.56	159	0.32	3.12	42	0.59
	New York							
		Men	3.85	24	0.64	3.77	119	0.47
		Women	2.77	433	0.37	3.11	157	0.4
	Philadelphia							
		Men	3.46	40	0.49	3.64	74	0.64
		Women	2.38	305	0.44	2.8	32	0.65
Payroll Clerk								
	New York							
		Men	4.05	47	0.96	3.64	76	0.93
		Women	3.35	497	0.55	3.46	106	0.52
Office boy/girl								
	Boston							
		Men	2.39	202	0.24	2.37	144	0.18
		Women	2.24	65	0.23	2.27	188	0.15
	New York							
		Men	2.57	939	0.32	2.53	782	0.27
		Women	2.41	356	0.2	2.4	905	0.16
	Philadelphia							
		Men	2.31	224	0.33	2.6	158	0.64
		Women	2.1	66	0.19	2.36	219	0.55

Table 1.5 (continued)

	All Firms		Pay Differential between S and I Firms[a]	Pay Differential between Men and Women[b] (percentage)		
W	*N*	*s.d.*	*(Percentage)*	*S Firms*	*I Firms*	*All Firms*
$3.68	345	0.45	-10			
3.27	768	0.48	7	21	7	11
3.94	861	0.6	-7			
3.6	1326	0.49	5	16	5	9
3.8	259	0.51	-1			
3.18	753	0.56	13	22	9	16
2.98	119	0.44	-17			
2.66	1329	0.32	1	24	9	11
3.26	603	0.46	-4			
2.97	2010	0.4	7	15	5	9
3.54	376	0.46	-2			
2.55	1345	0.44	9	32	23	28
3.83	109	0.66	4			
2.68	201	0.45	18	32	20	30
3.78	143	0.5	-2			
2.86	590	0.41	11	28	17	24
3.58	114	0.59	5			
2.42	337	0.48	15	31	23	33
3.8	123	0.96	-11			
3.37	603	0.55	3	17	5	11
2.38	346	0.21	-1			
2.27	253	0.18	1	6	4	5
2.55	1721	0.3	-1			
2.4	1261	0.17	0	6	5	6
2.43	382	0.5	11			
2.3	285	0.51	11	9	9	5

Table 1.5 (continued)

Occupation	Segregated Firms			Integrated Firms		
	W	N	s.d.	W	N	s.d.
A Tabulating-machine operator						
New York						
Men	4.1	195	0.48	4.2	56	0.38
Women	4.07	24	0.66	3.79	133	0.29
B Tabulating-machine operator						
New York						
Men	3.51	241	0.39	3.28	195	0.36
Women	2.62	107	0.23	3.27	134	0.29
B Systems Analyst						
New York						
Men	7.01	220	0.97	6.9	492	0.75
Women	c	4	c	6.57	160	0.8
A Computer Programmer						
New York						
Men	6.96	198	0.94	6.52	345	0.54
Women	c	7	c	6.41	189	0.62
B Computer Programmer						
Boston						
Men	4.86	110	0.58	4.91	210	0.55
Women	3.47	13	0.35	4.95	109	0.71
New York						
Men	5.57	185	0.82	5.73	380	0.68
Women	4.96	18	0.84	5.68	201	0.61
Philadelphia						
Men	4.94	214	0.7	4.81	133	0.53
Women	c	7	c	4.83	87	0.53
C Computer Programmer						
New York						
Men	4.55	109	0.61	4.89	228	0.47
Women	3.99	12	0.41	4.91	165	0.45
B Computer Operator						
New York						
Men	3.94	677	0.61	4.12	271	0.5
Women	3.15	115	0.28	4.22	41	0.58
Philadelphia						
Men	3.66	412	0.46	3.38	102	0.43
Women	2.89	52	0.24	3.32	20	0.46

Source: Computed from unpublished Bureau of Labor Statistics data collected for the Area Wage Surveys between April and November 1970.

[a] Computed as $W_{IM} - W_{SM}/W_{IM}$ and $W_{IF} - W_{SF}/W_{IF}$ for men and women respectively.

[b] The pay differential for segregated, integrated, and all firms is computed as $W_{SM} - W_{SF}/W_{SM}$, $W_{IM} - W_{IF}/W_{IM}$, and $W_M - W_F/W_M$ respectively.

[c] Not reported because of small sample size.

Table 1.5 (continued)

All Firms			Pay Differential between S and I Firms[a]	Pay Differential between Men and Women[b] (percentage)		
W	*N*	*s.d.*	*(Percentage)*	*S Firms*	*I Firms*	*All Firms*
4.13	251	0.46	2			
3.83	157	0.38	-8	1	10	7
3.41	436	0.39	-7			
2.98	241	0.42	20	25	0	13
6.93	712	0.83	-2			
6.53	164	0.29	c	c	5	6
6.68	543	0.74	-7			
6.4	196	0.63	c	c	2	4
4.89	320	0.56	1			
4.79	122	0.82	30	29	-1	2
5.68	565	0.73	3			
5.62	219	0.66	13	11	1	1
4.89	347	0.64	-3			
4.79	94	0.56	c	c	-1	2
4.78	337	0.54	7			
4.85	177	0.51	19	12	0	-1
3.99	948	0.58	4			
3.43	156	0.61	25	20	-2	14
3.61	514	0.47	-8			
3.01	72	0.37	13	21	2	17

hypotheses concerning intersectoral differences in male-female wage rates were supported in most cases.

With respect to systems analysts and programmers, there are only three cases in which the absolute number of women employed in segregated firms is large enough to report, and even in these cases the number of observations is quite small. All three indicate that women receive higher wages in integrated firms. With respect to men, $W_{IM} - W_{IS}/W_{IM}$ is negative in three cases and positive in three cases, but the differential is small in absolute size in all six cases. This finding, in combination with the small size of the wage differential between men and women that is computed for all firms (in the case of class C computer programmers there is a small differential in favor of women) seems to indicate that the interfirm wage distribution is more compact in these categories. This result is consistent with our suggestion that employers are able to set the wage rates in these occupations at a level which is high enough in the majority of cases to attract some male workers.

A comparison of mean wages of male and female workers by sector of employment indicates for the most part that the distribution of men and women among firms is an important factor in pay differentials between male and female workers. However, this finding is only a first step in an examination of the relationship between the differential distribution of men and women among establishments and pay differentials by sex. While all of the wage differentials between men and women in the segregated sector may be associated with differences in wage rates among firms, the same relationship holds for some portion of the pay differential between men and women in the integrated sector. In the next section we examine the broader question of the contribution of pay differences within and among firms to the market-wide wage differential by sex.

1.4.2.2. The Contribution of Intrafirm and Interfirm Differences in Wage Rates to the Male-Female Pay Differential

Let us first consider the problem of estimating the contribution of pay differences within firms (intrafirm pay differences) and pay differences across firms (interfirm pay differences) to the overall sex pay differential for firms in the integrated sector. If there are such k firms, then for each occupational category and city, W_{IM}, the mean wage of male workers, and W_{IF}, the mean wage of female workers, may be computed as:

(1.9) $$W_{IM} = \sum_{i=1}^{k} p_{im} w_{im}$$

and

(1.10) $$W_{IF} = \sum_{i=1}^{k} p_{if} w_{if}$$

where
p_{im} = the proportion of all male workers in integrated firms employed in firm i.
p_{if} = the proportion of all female workers in integrated firms employed in firm i.
w_{im} = the mean wage of male workers employed in firm i.
w_{if} = the mean wage of female workers employed in firm i.

Two sources of variation between the male and female means may be identified. First is the difference between w_{im} and w_{if}, or the differential wage rate of men and women within each establishment. We label the absolute pay difference that is associated with pay differences within firms the intrafirm effect. Second is the difference between p_{im} and p_{if} or the differential distribution of men and women among firms. This differential may be considered to be associated with pay differences among firms. We label the absolute pay difference which arises from this source the interfirm effect.

The task of partitioning the total male-female differential in the integrated sector between these two sources of variation may be conceptualized in the following way:

(1.11) $$W_{IM} - W_{IF} = \sum_{i=1}^{k} p_{io}(w_{im} - w_{if}) + \sum_{i=1}^{k} w_{io}(p_{im} - p_{if})$$

where p_{io} and w_{io} represent the as yet unspecified weights.

The intrafirm effect would then be equal to:

(1.12) $$INTRA = \sum_{i=1}^{k} p_{io}(w_{im} - w_{if}) = \sum_{i=1}^{k} p_{io} w_{im} - \sum_{i=1}^{k} p_{io} w_{if}$$

As indicated in (1.12), the intrafirm effect may be viewed in two ways: first, as a weighted average of the wage differences by sex within each firm, and second, as the differential that would exist if men and women had an identical distribution among firms so that the only source of variation between the male and female means would be differential pay within firms. The interfirm effect would be represented by:

$$(1.13) \qquad INTRA = \sum_{i=1}^{k} w_{io}(p_{im} - p_{if}) = \sum_{i=1}^{k} p_{im}w_{io} - \sum_{i=1}^{k} p_{if}w_{io}$$

The interfirm effect may similarly be regarded in two ways: first, as a weighted average of the differential distributions of men and women among firms, and second, as the wage difference that would exist if within each establishment men and women received identical wage rates so that the only source of variation between the male and female means would be the differential distribution among firms.

It may readily be seen that this formulation raises the familiar index-number problems of arbitrariness and consistency, which we shall examine individually as they arise in this particular exercise.

The problem of arbitrariness may be stated quite simply. There are a wide variety of possible weights that might be employed, each of which would yield a different estimate of the relative magnitude of the intrafirm and interfirm effects. Moreover, there is little theoretical justification for preferring one set of weights over another. The two most obvious alternatives would be to utilize either p_{im} and w_{im} (the male distribution and the male wage) or p_{if} and w_{if} (the female distribution and the female wage) as the constant weights. A possible compromise would be to compute the intrafirm and interfirm effects in both ways. However, a serious problem of consistency would still remain.

The consistency problem arises because if both the intrafirm and interfirm effects are computed using a consistent set of weights, they will not necessarily sum to the total differential. To completely partition the total differential would require the utilization of an inconsistent weighting scheme. Thus it may easily be shown that:

$$(1.14) \qquad W_{IM} - W_{IF} = \sum_{i=1}^{k} p_{io}(w_{im} - w_{if}) = \sum_{i=1}^{k} w_{if}(p_{im} - p_{if})$$

or

(1.15) $$W_{IM} - W_{IF} = \sum_{i=1}^{k} p_{if}(w_{im} - w_{if}) = \sum_{i=1}^{k} w_{im}(p_{im} - p_{if})$$

However, the consistency problem may be solved if we employ a simple average of the male and female weights (this approach is recommended and further justified by Kitagawa 1955: 1168-93):

(1.16) $$p_{io} = \frac{p_{im} + p_{if}}{2}$$

(1.17) $$w_{io} = \frac{w_{im} + w_{if}}{2}$$

When (1.16) and (1.17) are employed as weights, the estimated intrafirm and interfirm effects will sum to the total differential. Further, it may be shown that when the two effects are computed in this way:

(1.18) $$INTRA = \frac{INTRA(M) + INTRA(F)}{2}$$

(1.19) $$INTRA = \frac{INTRA(M) + INTRA(F)}{2}$$

where (M) and (F) indicate that male and female weights have been used respectively.

Since there are no sound theoretical reasons for preferring any particular structure of weights, it was felt that this scheme was in some sense optimal since it provides for a solution of the consistency problem. Moreover, as can be seen in (1.18) and (1.19), these weights may be viewed as a compromise or summary measure since the results are equivalent to a simple average of the estimates derived from the utilization of male and female weights respectively.

In applying this method of analysis to the firms in our sample, one further problem must be considered. Many of the establishments employ entirely male or entirely female work forces within occupational categories. The total pay differential may be partitioned into two components by incorporating the results obtained for integrated firms using the appropriate weights.

If there are k firms which employ both men and women, m firms which employ only men, and n firms which employ only women, the intrafirm and interfirm effects may be computed as:

$$INTRA = \sum_{k=1}^{k} p_{io}(w_{im} - w_{if}) \tag{1.20}$$

and

$$\begin{aligned} INTER &= \sum_{i=1}^{k} p_{im}w_{io} + \sum_{i=k+1}^{m} p_{im}w_{im} - \sum_{i=1}^{k} p_{if}w_{io} - \sum_{i=k+1}^{n} p_{if}w_{if} \\ &= \sum_{i=k+1}^{m} p_{im}w_{im} - \sum_{i=k+1}^{n} p_{if}w_{if} - \sum_{i=1}^{k} w_{io}(p_{im} - p_{if}) \end{aligned} \tag{1.21}$$

where p_{im} and pif now represent the proportion of all male and female workers respectively employed in firm i, and p_{io} is computed as a simple average of p_{im} and p_{if}.

As can be seen in (1.20), the contribution of pay differences within firms to the total wage difference depends both on the size of such intrafirm wage differences and on the relative weight of the firm in total employment. The interfirm effect in (1.21) is computed by calculating male and female mean wages, substituting w_{io} for w_{im} and w_{if} in the case of integrated firms.

The results of the application of this estimation technique are shown in Table 1.6. The absolute wage differentials have been divided by the mean male wage to facilitate comparisons across cities and occupations. It may be recalled that our model predicts that intrafirm differences in wage rates between men and women will be relatively small compared to market-wide occupational wage differences. The intrafirm effect in integrated firms is a weighted average of mean wage differences between men and women within firms. Thus it is predicted that the magnitude of the intrafirm effect given in the first column of Table 1.6 will be small relative to the average pay differential between all male and female workers employed in the occupational category, given in column 6. Further, our model predicts that differences in wage rates among firms will account for a high proportion of the male-female differential in all firms, and for a substantial proportion of the differential between men and women employed in integrated firms. The proportion of the male-female wage differential in all firms that is accounted for by differences in wage rates among firms is shown in column 8, while interfirm wage differences as a percent of the male-female wage differential in integrated firms is given in column 7.

Table 1.6

The Contribution of Intrafirm and Interfirm Pay Differences to the Male-Female Pay Differential by City: Selected Occupations

	Male-Female Pay Difference (as a Percentage of the Male Wage)						*Interfirm Pay Difference (As a Percentage of the Total)*	
	Integrated Firms			*All Firms*				
Occupation	*Intrafirm*	*Interfirm*	*Total*	*Intrafirm*	*Interfirm*	*Total*	*Integrated Firms*	*All Firms*
A Accounting clerk								
Boston	2.1	4.6	6.7	1.5	9.4	10.9	69	86
New York	0.8	4.6	5.4	0.5	8.2	8.7	85	94
Philadelphia	3.9	5.4	9.3	1.8	14.6	16.4	58	89
B Accounting clerk								
Boston	3.8	5.3	9.1	2.8	8.1	10.9	58	74
New York	0.1	5.2	5.3	0.1	8.6	8.7	97	98
Philadelphia	7.0	16.2	23.2	4.6	23.4	28	70	83
Order clerk								
Boston	8.1	12.0	20.1	2.8	27.3	30.1	60	91
New York	2.5	14.9	17.4	1.7	22.6	24.3	85	93
Philadelphia	11.6	11.6	23.2	3.1	29.4	32.5	50	90
Payroll clerk								
New York	0.4	4.8	5.2	0.4	10.9	11.3	91	96
Office boy/girl								
Boston	2.7	1.3	4.0	1.6	3.3	4.9	31	67
New York	-2.2	7.4	5.2	-1.2	7.1	5.9	a	a
Philadelphia	1.9	7.2	9.1	1.4	3.9	5.3	79	74
A Tabulating-machine operator								
New York	-3.3	13.2	9.9	-2.6	9.8	7.2	a	a
B Tabulating-machine operator								
New York	-4.7	5.1	0.4	-2.5	15	12.5	a	a
B Systems analyst								
New York	3.5	1.3	4.8	2.9	2.9	5.8	26	50
A Computer programmer								
New York	0.1	1.7	1.8	0.0	4.3	4.3	92	99
B Computer programmer								
Boston	-0.6	-0.1	-0.7	-0.5	2.6	2.1	14*	a
New York	1.2	-0.2	1.0	0.9	0.1	1.0	b	10
Philadelphia	-0.4	-0.1	-0.5	-0.1	2.2	2.1	20*	a
C Computer programmer								
New York	—	—	0.0	0.1	-1.5	-1.4	—	a*
B Computer operator								
New York	0.4	-2.8	-2.4	0.0	14.1	14.1	a*	100
Philadelphia	1.2	0.7	1.9	0.3	16.3	16.6	37	98

Source: Computed from unpublished Bureau of Labor Statistics data collected for the Area Wage Surveys between April and November, 1970.

[a] The percentage of the total pay difference that is due to interfirm differences in pay rates is greater than 100.

[b] The percentage of the total pay difference that is due to interfirm differences in pay rates is less than zero.

* The female pay rate exceeds the male pay rate.

The employee discrimination model predicts exactly the opposite of these results if differentials by sector exist. That is, wage differentials should be largest when men and women are employed together in the same firm, and intrafirm differences in wage rates will account for a high proportion of the total pay differential.

The results presented in Table 1.6 support our hypotheses. In most cases the intrafirm effect in integrated firms is absolutely quite small. The average intrafirm pay differential is greater than 5 percent in only three cases: Class B accounting clerks in Philadelphia, and order clerks in Boston and Philadelphia. Moreover, in each of those three cases the magnitude of the intrafirm pay difference is small relative to the average male-female wage differential in both the integrated sector and all firms. There are five cases in which average intrafirm pay differences are in favor of women.

Differences in wage rates among firms, the interfirm effect, account for a substantial proportion of the male-female pay difference in integrated firms. In fifteen of the nineteen cases in which the male wage rate is greater than the female wage rate, interfirm differences in pay rates account for 50 percent or more of the total differential. In two of the three cases in which female mean wage exceeds the male mean, interfirm differences in pay rates account for 20 percent or less of the total differential, indicating that the wage advantage of women is primarily the result of the favorable intrafirm effect.

The importance of interfirm pay differences is even more strongly demonstrated when we consider all firms. Of the twenty-two cases in which the male mean wage exceeds the female mean, the proportion of the differential which is accounted for by interfirm differences in wage rates is over 80 percent in sixteen cases and at least 50 percent in twenty-one cases.

The model works fairly well even when the systems-analyst and computer-programmer categories are considered separately. The average magnitude of intrafirm differences in wage rates is less than 5 percent in all cases. Moreover, in four of the five cases in which the mean earnings of men in all firms exceed the mean earnings of women, interfirm wage differences account for 50 percent or more of the total differential. This suggests that the smaller average wage differences by sex among systems analysts and programmers reflect more compressed interfirm wage differences in these occupations, but a distributional pattern by sex within this narrower band that is similar to the other occupations in the sample.

Again, it is important to point out that, in the absence of direct information on the productivity-related characteristics of workers, it is not possible to argue that the interfirm effect is entirely due to the exclusion of women from the higher-wage establishments. However, the consistency of the observed relationships strongly suggests that the differential distribution of men and women among establishments is of great significance in explaining the sex differential within occupational categories.

1.5. Establishment Wage Rates and the Sex Composition of Employment

In the preceding section we have tested our model in terms of its implications for the employment distribution and wage rates of men and women when occupational categories are considered separately. It has been confirmed that, within occupational categories, male and female workers are differentially distributed among establishments to a degree in excess of what could be expected from the operation of random processes. Further, this differential distribution, which we have termed intraoccupational segregation, appears to be an important factor in the pay differential between male and female workers. In most cases, earnings differences between men and women in the same occupational category are primarily the result of differences in wage rates among firms rather than of differences in wage rates within firms. It may be recalled that within our model these differential employment patterns and wage outcomes for men and women were viewed as resulting from a predetermined wage hierarchy of firms. Within the context of this predetermined wage structure, employer hiring preferences were viewed as tending, in effect, to ration the higher-paying alternatives to male workers, while female workers would, for the most part, find employment in the lower-paying firms.

To verify the causal mechanism postulated in our model, it is necessary to consider occupations jointly to form a picture of establishment wage and employment patterns. Does there exist a hierarchy of firms with respect to wage rates? To answer this question in the affirmative, the relative wage standing of the firm with respect to one occupational category must be correlated with its ranking with respect to other categories. In addition, the wage standing of the firm must be estimated, holding the effect of the sex of the workers employed constant. That is, both male and female workers must receive higher wages than they would otherwise obtain when they are employed in the higher-paying establishments, while both sexes must earn less when employed by the lower-paying firms. Only if these two conditions are met can we confirm the existence of a wage hierarchy among establishments which may be viewed as a determinant of, rather than a response to, the sex of the job incumbents.

In the model, this wage hierarchy among firms is viewed as producing differential establishment patterns with respect to the employment of women, or what we have termed establishment segregation. For this to be the case, it is required that the standing of the firm with respect to the representation of women in one occupational category be positively correlated with its ranking with respect to other categories. Finally, our model implies that the ranking of the firms with respect to wage rates will be inversely related to the ranking of firms with respect to the representation of women.

We are also concerned with the establishment characteristics that generate the postulated wage hierarchy of firms that we have to this point considered to be predetermined. The impact on the wage standing of the firm of its size, industry, and union status is examined. The relationship of these factors to the representation of women in the establishment is also explored. The expectation is that establishment characteristics that are associated with higher wages will also be associated with a lower representation of women, and vice versa. Further, our view as to the importance of product market competition in enforcing homogeneity within industry groupings implies that industry would be an important variable in the determination of both the wage rates and the employment of women.

1.5.1. Establishment Wage Rates and Employment Patterns

Regression analysis with binary explanatory variables has been employed to examine the question of establishment differences in wage and employment patterns. This approach produces results equivalent to those of analysis of variance, but has the advantage that an equal number of observations in each cell is not required. Moreover, the use of regression analysis enables us to estimate coefficients for each firm that summarize its standing within the local labor market with respect to the wages paid to its employees and with respect to the representation of women. These coefficients will then be used as the dependent variables in the analysis of the determinants of wage and employment patterns. The following relation was estimated for each labor market to test for the existence of interfirm differences in wage rates across occupational categories and sex groups (since our estimate of wi is based on grouped data with unequal observations in each cell, observations have been weighted by the square root of employment to correct for the heteroskedasticity introduced by such grouping):

$$(1.22)\ w_i = \alpha + \gamma S_i + \beta_1 O_{i1} + \ldots + \beta_m O_{im} + \delta_1 F_{i1} + \ldots + \delta_n F_n + \varepsilon_i$$

where:

w_i = the mean wage of workers in the hth sex category, jth occupation group and kth firm.

S_i = 1 if the observation is on male workers and 0 otherwise.

O_{ij} = 1 if the observation is on the jth occupational category and 0 otherwise. There are $m + 1$ occupational categories and m occupation dummy variables.

F_{ik} = 1 if the observation is on the kth firm and 0 otherwise. There are $n + 1$ firms and n establishment dummy variables.

The coefficients on the establishment dummy variables in Equation (1.22) are estimates of the dollar-per-hour difference between the mean wage of workers employed in firm k and in an arbitrarily omitted firm, holding constant the estimated effect of occupation and sex of workers on wage rates. To obtain more efficient estimates of the establishment coefficients, the entire sample of occupations was included in this and the succeeding analysis of interfirm differences in the representation of women. The hypothesis that there are no significant differences among firms with regard to mean wages may be formulated in terms of Equation (1.22) as a test of the null hypothesis that $\delta_1, \delta_2 \ldots \delta_n$ are jointly equal to zero. The following F statistic is formed to test this hypothesis:

$$\frac{(SSR_Q - SSR_K)/(Q-K)}{SSE_Q/(N-Q)}$$

where:

$Q = m + n + 2$

$K = m + 2$

N = the total number of observations.

As stated earlier, this test produces equivalent results to analysis of variance (Kmenta 1971: 370, 415-18).

The rejection of the null hypothesis would imply the existence of a wage hierarchy among firms as we have defined it. That is, the wage standing of the firm would be consistent across occupational categories and for workers of both sexes. Were this not the case, the wage variation within firms would exceed the wage variation among firms, and the null hypothesis would be accepted. The rejection of the null hypothesis of no significant variation among firms does not, however, imply that none of the coefficients on the firm dummy variables are equal to zero, or equal to each other. Nor would such a finding be necessary to our argument.

Holding sex constant in the estimate of the firm coefficients is extremely important for our investigation of the relationship between the wage standing of the firm and the sex composition of establishment employment. Our expectation is that, after adjusting for the occupational mix of the establishment, men will comprise a higher proportion of the work force in firms which pay higher wages to both men and women, while women will be more highly represented in firms which pay lower wages to both sexes. It is in this sense that the wage standing of the firm may be viewed as determining the sex composition of its work force. However, were sex not held constant, the relationship between the establishment wage standing and the representation of women in the firm would become a virtual tautology. That is, since on average women receive lower wages, firms that employ a higher proportion of women would necessarily be "low-wage" firms.

The question of the representation of women in the establishment is approached in a similar fashion. The following equation is estimated for each city (observations have again been weighted by the square root of employment to correct for the heteroskedasticity introduced by the use of grouped data) so that:

$$(1.23) \qquad p_i = a + b_1O_{i1} + \ldots + b_mO_{im} + d_1F_{i1} + \ldots + d_nF_{in} + e_i$$

where:

p_i = the proportion of all workers employed in the kth firm and the jth occupational category who are female.

The coefficients of the firm dummy variables in Equation (1.23) are estimates of the percentage-point difference between the proportion of workers who are female in firm k and in an arbitrarily omitted firm, holding constant the estimated effect of occupational category on the representation of women in the firms. The occupational dummy variables are necessary because the availability of women to the firm differs by occupational category. The test for establishment segregation in Equation (1.23) may be formulated, as in Equation (1.22), as a test of the null hypothesis that $d_1, d_2 \ldots d_n$ are jointly equal to zero. The rejection of the null hypothesis of no significant difference among firms in the representation of women implies the existence of establishment segregation, that is, that not only are there significant differences among firms, but these differences are consistent across occupational categories.

Since there exist differences among occupational categories in the possible scope of interfirm variation in the representation of women, the estimated values of the coefficients d_k will differ depending on which occupations are included in the analysis. For example, more variation is feasible in an occupational category in which women comprise 50 percent of total employment than in the case of a classification in which women comprise 10 percent or 90 percent of all workers. The inclusion of the latter group of relatively sex-segregated occupations would tend to yield smaller estimated values of the dk. However, since some variation by firm is possible for every occupational category that we have included, it did not seem appropriate to discard this information by restricting the analysis to a relatively small group of highly integrated occupations. An additional consideration was the advisability of including the same sample of occupations in both the wage and proportion-female analyses. The inclusion of occupational categories with relatively high or low percentages of women tends to make it more difficult to obtain significant differences among firms with respect to the representation of women, thus strengthening our confidence in such a finding should it be obtained. (Establishments which contained observations only on relatively sex-segregated occupations were excluded from the sample.)

The estimated coefficients on the firm dummy variables in Equations (1.22) and (1.23) yield a ranking of firms with respect to wage rates and the representation of women for each labor market. Our findings are summarized in Tables 1.7 and 1.8. The F ratios for the significance of the group of establishment dummy variables are given in the last row of each table. All are significant at the 1 percent level. Thus we reject the null hypothesis of no difference among firms with respect to wage rates and the sex composition of employment.

Table 1.7

Distribution of Firms by Wage Standing of Establishment and City (Percentages)

Deviation from the Mean ($)		*Boston*		*New York*		*Philadelphia*	
		n	*percentage*[a]	*n*	*percentage*[a]	*n*	*percentage*[a]
Over 1.00		5	1.9	5	0.9	8	2.3
0.81-1.00		6	2.3	14	2.4	5	1.4
0.61-0.80		5	1.9	22	3.7	12	3.5
0.51-0.60		5	1.9	15	2.6	9	2.6
0.41-0.50	(+)	9	3.4	36	6.1	14	4.0
0.31-0.40		14	5.3	34	5.8	14	4.0
0.21-0.30		19	7.2	51	8.7	26	7.5
0.11-0.20		29	11.0	59	10.1	31	9.0
0.01-0.10		22	8.3	47	8.0	29	8.4
0		8	3.0	12	2.0	10	2.9
0.01-0.10		41	15.5	55	9.4	43	12.4
0.11-0.20		29	11.0	48	8.2	43	12.4
0.21-0.30		22	8.3	62	10.6	35	10.1
0.31-0.40	(-)	22	8.3	38	6.5	25	7.2
0.41-0.50		14	5.3	29	4.9	16	4.6
0.51-0.60		5	1.9	28	4.8	16	4.6
0.61-0.80		7	2.7	25	4.3	8	2.3
0.81-1.00		1	0.4	5	0.9	2	0.6
Over 1.00		1	0.4	2	0.3	0	0.0
Total		264	100.0	587	100.0	346	100.0
F ratio		9.27		6.76		10.46	

Source: Computed from unpublished Bureau of Labor Statistics data collected for the Area Wage Surveys between April and November 1970.
[a] Rows may not sum to column totals due to rounding.

Table 1.8

Distribution of Firms by Representation of Women in the Establishment and City (Percentages)

Deviation from the Mean (Percentage)		*Boston*		*New York*		*Philadelphia*	
		n	*percentage*[a]	*n*	*percentage*[a]	*n*	*percentage*[a]
Over 40		1	0.4	1	0.2	0	0.0
31-40		0	0.0	4	0.7	2	0.6
21-30		1	0.4	18	3.1	3	0.9
11-20	(+)	25	9.5	67	11.4	38	11.0
6-10		70	26.5	70	11.9	64	18.5
1-5		60	22.7	112	19.1	79	22.8
0		32	12.1	76	12.9	35	10.1
1-5		28	10.6	111	18.9	68	19.7
6-10		20	7.6	63	10.7	23	6.6
11-20		10	3.8	46	7.8	17	4.9
21-30	(-)	9	3.4	7	1.2	8	2.3
31-40		2	0.8	6	1.0	1	0.3
Over 40		6	2.3	6	1.0	8	2.3
Total		264	100.0	587	100.0	346	100.0
F ratio		2.00		2.28		3.78	

Source: Computed from unpublished Bureau of Labor Statistics data collected for the Area Wage Surveys between April and November 1970.
[a] Rows may not sum to column totals due to rounding.

The values of the coefficients have been expressed as deviations from the mean in each labor market to facilitate comparisons across cities. The establishment distributions are quite similar for the three cities. While there is a tendency for the distribution of establishments with respect to the value of both δ and d to cluster about the mean value for the local labor market, the range of variation is considerable. For example, in the case of the estimated values of the firm coefficients in the wage equation, we found that 22 percent of the firms in Boston, 31 percent in New York, and 26 percent in Philadelphia paid mean wages that were more than forty cents per hour above or below the average for the sample, after we controlled for the occupational mix of the establishment and the sex of the workers employed (this represents a pay differential of 14 percent in Boston, 12 percent in New York, and 15 percent in Philadelphia). Similar differences are exhibited with respect to the representation of women in the establishment. For 21 percent of the firms in Boston, 26 percent in New York, and 22 percent in Philadelphia, the proportion of women employed by the establishment deviated from the average for the labor market by over ten percentage points, after controlling for the occupational mix of the firm.

The values of the F ratios indicate that the probability is extremely small that the observed interfirm differences would be obtained by chance were the establishment means indeed the same. However, perhaps a stronger indication that this is not a random phenomenon is provided by the relationship between the ranking of establishments with respect to the value of δ and their ranking with respect to the value of d. Our model predicts an inverse relationship between the two variables and this is in fact what was obtained. The spearman rank correlation coefficient between the two variables is -0.35 for Boston, -0.27 for New York, and -0.26 for Philadelphia. All are significant at the .001 level. A nonparametric statistic was employed because it seemed to be the most suitable test of the model. An additional consideration was that the exact values of the firm coefficients, and dk, are subject to error, since they are stochastic variables. For this reason, somewhat more confidence may be placed in the rankings than in exact values. However, the computed values of the simple correlation coefficients were also highly statistically significant and negative in sign. (The values obtained were -0.34 for Boston, -0.21 for New York, and -0.24 for Philadelphia.)

In this section we have demonstrated the existence of a wage hierarchy among firms and of establishment segregation. We have also shown the expected inverse relationship between the ranking of the establishment with respect to the representation of women and its standing in the wage hierarchy. These results are counter to the predictions of the unconstrained employer preference model and the employee preference model. It may be recalled that in the case of employer preferences it is expected that the firms which hire a greater-than-expected proportion of men will be those firms that prefer men and will hire women only at a discount. In the case of employee preferences, men are expected to receive higher remuneration when they work with women. Thus in both cases male and female wage rates are not expected to follow the same pattern by establishment. Yet we have shown the establishment wage hierarchy to be consistent across sex groups. And moreover it is seen that men comprise a higher proportion of workers in those firms which pay higher wages to both sexes, while women are more highly represented in firms which pay lower wages to both sexes. As in our comparison of the predictions of these alternatives in section 1.4, we must bear in mind that in the absence of further information on worker quality our findings regarding these alternative explanations are suggestive but not conclusive.

1.5.2. The Determinants of Establishment Wage Rates and Employment Patterns

In this section we examine the relationship of establishment wage rates and employment patterns to a number of establishment characteristics. The model postulates that the establishment variables determine the standing of the firm in the wage hierarchy and thus the prices offered for labor in the various occupational categories. The differing availability of male labor to the high- and low-wage firms in conjunction with employer hiring preferences then determines the sex composition of employment. Although this model postulates that at the micro-level the causation runs from wage rates to sex composition of employment, we have chosen to consider both d, the standing of the firm with respect to the representation of women, and δ, the standing of the firm with respect to wage rates, as dependent variables that are determined by the same set of establishment variables (note that the number of observations is now equal to the number of firms, and thus the subscript i rather than k is associated with the establishment).

The logic of the model is illustrated by the following equations:

$$d_i = f(\delta_i, \phi_i) \tag{1.24}$$

$$\delta_i = f(E_{i1}, \ldots E_{in}) \tag{1.25}$$

$$\Rightarrow d_i = f(E_{i1}, \ldots E_{in}, \phi_i) \tag{1.26}$$

where:

ϕ_i = employer preferences regarding the employment of women in firm i.

$E_{i1}, \ldots, E_{in}$ = establishment characteristics that are related to wage rates.

A simultaneous equation system is postulated in Equations (1.24) and (1.25), where the variable ϕ is not observable, but will affect the relationship between d and δ. While it might be possible to estimate (1.24) and (1.25) directly, we chose to estimate the two equations (1.25) and (1.26) for three reasons.

First, the causal relationship between d and δ is not completely clear; that is, equations (1.24) and (1.25) may be oversimplified. The maintenance of a low-wage position requires that the firm be able to attract an adequate supply of labor, or else some adjustment will be necessary. Since the low-wage firm relies on female labor to a greater extent than does the high-wage firm, the availability of female labor to the firm may have an impact on wage rates. It was thus deemed advisable to relate both d and δ to a set of establishment variables that are truly exogenous. Second, both d and δ are stochastic variables subject to measurement error. A stochastic dependent variable does not pose serious statistical problems. However there are difficulties in utilizing a stochastic independent variable (Kmenta 1971, ch. 9) and thus the simpler approach of estimating the equations (1.25) and (1.26) seemed preferable. Third, it seemed possible that some of the establishment variables might be related to employer preferences, and thus have a direct effect on the proportion of women employed by the firm. While in general we would expect the coefficients of the establishment variables to be of opposite sign when δ and d are employed as dependent variables, it seemed worthwhile to test this expectation directly.

1.5.2.1. Empirical Results

To facilitate comparisons across cities, the coefficients of the firm dummy variables obtained through the estimation of equations (1.22) and (1.23) were transformed into indices. To obtain the wage index, the estimated mean wage of the establishment (after controlling for occupation mix and sex composition) was divided by the average for all establishments in the labor market. Similarly, to obtain the proportion-female index, the estimated average proportion that women comprise of establishment employment (after controlling for occupation mix) was divided by the average for all firms in the labor market. Thus, for each city, if $\overline{w}_o$ = the estimated average wage in the omitted firm obtained from equation (1.22), and $\overline{w}_i$ = the average wage in firm i, then $\overline{w}_i = \delta_i + \overline{w}_o$, and

$$WI_i = \frac{\overline{w}_i}{\sum_{i=0}^{n} w_i/n}$$

Similarly, if $\overline{p}_0$ = the estimated average proportion of women in the omitted firm obtained from Equation (1.23), and $\overline{p}_i$ = the average proportion of women in firm i, then $\overline{p}_i = d_i + \overline{w}_o$, and

$$FI_i = \frac{\overline{p}_i}{\sum_{i=0}^{n} p_i/n}$$

This standardization procedure involves only addition and division by a constant and therefore does not alter the rankings of firms, only the units in which the interfirm differences are measured.

The following regression equations were estimated to explain differences among establishments in wage rates and in the representation of women. (The dependent variables were obtained through the application of regression analysis, and, as noted earlier, are subject to measurement error. Estimates of the standard deviation of this error are available in the form of the estimated standard errors of the regression coefficients on the establishment dummy variables in Equations (1.22) and (1.23). Observations have been weighted by the inverse of the standard errors to correct for heteroskedasticity.):

$$WI_i = \alpha + \beta_1 I_{i1} + \ldots + \beta_n I_{in} + \gamma_1 U_{i1} + \gamma_2 U_{i2} + \eta_1 S_{i1} + \varepsilon_i \qquad (1.27)$$

$$(1.28) \qquad FI_i = a + b_1 I_{i1} + \ldots + b_n I_{in} + g_1 U_{i1} + g_2 U_{i2} + h_1 S_{i1} + e_i$$

where:

I_{i0} = 1 if the firm is in the wholesale trade-durable goods industry (SIC 50) and 0 otherwise. This is the reference dummy for the industry variables.

I_{ij} = 1 if the firm is in the jth industry group and 0 otherwise.

U_{io} = 1 if a majority of both plant and office workers in the firm are not unionized and 0 otherwise. This is the reference dummy for the union variables.

U_{i1} = 1 if a majority of both plant and office workers in the firm are unionized and 0 otherwise. (Three establishments in which a majority of office workers were unionized, but a majority of plant workers were not, were given a value of 1 for variable U_1.)

U_{i2} = 1 if a majority of plant workers in the firm are unionized, but a majority of office workers are not, and 0 otherwise.

S_{i0} = 1 if the firm employs between fifty and 999 workers and 0 otherwise. This is the reference dummy for the size of firm variable. (For the purposes of the Area Wage Survey, the Bureau of Labor Statistics includes in the sample only firms which employ fifty or more workers.)

S_{i1} = 1 if the firm employs 1,000 or more workers and 0 otherwise.

We refer to equation (1.27) as the wage regression, and to equation 1.28) as the proportion-female regression.

Before we discuss the regression results, some important qualifications are in order. First, the effect of industry on the wage standing of the firm and the representation of women in the establishment can best be tested when extremely fine industry classifications are employed. For our data, only two-digit SIC classifications are available. Further, it was necessary in some cases to form combinations of two-digit industries in order to obtain an adequate number of observations for each industry cell (see Appendix B-2 in Blau 1977). Thus our industry variable only approximates the product market distinctions that would provide the best test of the industry effect.

Second, while we are able to classify establishments by whether the majority of (plant or office) workers are unionized (covered by a collective bargaining contract), we have no further information on the characteristics of the union. Thus the union dummy variables provide only an imprecise indication of union power. Moreover, a common problem in the estimation of the impact of unions is that the effect of unionization on wage rates may be difficult to measure if nonunion firms pay union rates or higher ones to combat the threat of unionization (Lewis 1963). In addition, it is important to note that we are not able to assess the nonpecuniary benefits of unionization, which may be of considerable importance in workers' decisions to join unions (Ashenfelter and Johnson 1972: 491-2).

Third, we have no information regarding the locus of wage control in the establishments in our sample. It has often been noted that in the case of multiplant firms, wage decisions may be made at national headquarters, leaving the local management little discretion to adapt to local labor market conditions. Such local establishments may tend to be either high- or low-wage firms in the labor market. Thus we expect that the omission of this variable will detract from the explanatory power of the model.[4]

Finally it is important to note that the sample of establishments is not well distributed by industry, union status, and size of firm. We have indirectly alluded to this problem by reporting the necessity of combining two-digit industries. However, when the data are cross-classified by more than one dimension, it is clear that we must be cautious in our interpretation of the regression results. See Appendix B-2 (Blau 1977) for the distribution of sample establishments by industry, union status, and size. For example, in each city there are a large number of two-digit industry classifications, and even major industry groups (e.g., finance, insurance, and real estate), that have no observations on unionized firms. Similar problems exist with the size variable. This means at minimum that we cannot be sure that the estimated union and size effects would be of the same magnitude in such categories as in the rest of the sample. More probably it suggests that it is not possible to estimate statistically the pure effect of industry, union status, or size of firm on the dependent variables. This is especially true since we have in cases combined two-digit industries into larger groupings. Of course, what we face here is not simply a statistical problem, but a reflection of economic reality. Interindustry differences in the distribution of establishments by union status and size of firm are an important factor in the explanation of wage differences among industries (Fuchs 1968: 147-54). Moreover, there is considerable evidence of important interaction effects between industry characteristics and the impact of unions on wage rates (Segal 1964;

Weiss 1966). These problems are particularly serious in the case of Boston where considerable grouping of two-digit industries was necessary, and the absolute number both of unionized (plant and office) and of larger establishments (1,000 or more employees) was relatively small.

In light of these difficulties, the results presented in the section should be viewed primarily as a preliminary investigation of the importance of these types of factors in the determination of the ranking of the firm in the local labor market with respect to wage rates and the representation of women in white-collar occupations. It is our view that the results are promising enough to warrant further exploration of this approach.

The regression results for the three cities are presented in Tables 1.9 through 1.11 (the sample size in each city has been slightly reduced by the deletion of firms with missing SIC codes). Two sets of regression results are reported for each city. The first set shows our findings for the estimation of equations (1.27) and (1.28). The second set of regressions includes interaction effect(s) and must be regarded with particular caution due to the empty-cell and small-sample-size problem. Our findings with respect to the explanatory power of the regressions and the impact of the industry variables apply equally to both sets of regressions. We consider the differences between the two specifications in reference to the impact of union status and size of firm on the dependent variables.

All of the regression equations are statistically significant. The Boston proportion-female regressions are significant at the .05 level, while the remainder of the equations are significant at the .01 level, suggesting that the observed interfirm differences in wage rates and in the representation of women do, to some extent, follow discernible patterns with respect to economically meaningful establishment characteristics.

In each city we find that the proportion-female regressions explain a considerably smaller proportion of the total variance in the dependent variable and contain fewer significant explanatory variables than do the wage regressions. This finding is susceptible to a number of interpretations. It may indicate the range of employer latitude in determining the sex composition of employment, suggesting that hiring preferences are important. However, it is also possible that, as noted earlier, the inclusion of relatively sex-segregated occupations in the estimation of equation (1.23) tends to push the firm coefficients towards the mean, thus making it more difficult to obtain significant differences among firms or groups of firms.

Table 1.9

Wage and Proportion Female Regressions: Boston (Absolute *t*-values)

	Regressions- without Interaction Effect		*Regressions-with Interaction Effect*	
Independent Variables	*Wage I Coeff.*	*Fem I Coeff.*	*Wage I Coeff.*	*Fem I Coeff.*
Industry				
Manufacturing				
Food and kindred products	-0.0456	-0.0175	-0.0682	-0.0068
	(0.97)	(0.30)	(1.50)	(0.12)
Machinery, except electrical	-0.0035	0.0015	-0.0076	0.0035
	(0.09)	(0.03)	(0.21)	(0.07)
Electrical machinery	-0.0709	0.0766	-0.0871	0.0843
	(2.00)	(1.76)	(2.54)	(1.93)
Other nondurable goods	-0.0442	0.0887	-0.0795	0.1016
	(1.36)	(2.13)	(2.47)	(2.47)
Other durable goods	0.0102	0.0565	0.0042	0.0535
	(0.26)	(1.04)	(0.11)	(1.10)
Transportation and public utilities	-0.0114	0.0338	0.0536	0.0030
	(0.26)	(.6195)	(1.19)	(0.05)
Retail trade				
General merchandise	-0.1489	0.1482	-0.1206	0.1348
	(3.85)	(3.12)	(3.19)	(2.80)
Other retail	-0.0545	0.0562	-0.0579	0.0578
	(1.46)	(1.22)	(1.61)	(1.26)
Finance and insurance				
Finance	0.0533	0.0066	0.0501	0.0080
	(1.56)	(0.16)	(1.53)	(0.19)
Insurance	-0.0328	0.0384	-0.0359	0.0398
	(1.08)	(1.03)	(1.23)	(1.07)
Services				
Personal services	-0.0895	-0.0277	-0.0973	-0.0240
	(1.69)	(0.42)	(1.90)	(0.37)
Business and repair services	-0.0020	0.0113	-0.0065	0.0135
	(0.06)	(0.29)	(0.21)	(0.34)
Miscellaneous services	0.0957	0.0007	0.0896	0.0035
	(2.36)	(0.01)	(2.29)	(0.07)
Union status				
Union	0.1437	-0.1338	0.0307	-0.0802
	(4.13)	(3.12)	(0.72)	(1.49)
Plant only	0.0127	-0.0312	0.0159	-0.0328
	(0.61)	(1.23)	(0.80)	(1.29)
Size of firm				
Size 1 (1,000 and over)	0.0337	-0.0012	0.0265	0.0022
	(1.95)	(0.06)	(1.58)	(0.10)
Interaction term				
Manufacturing and union			0.2791	-0.1323
			(4.37)	(1.66)
Constant term	0.9979	0.9982	1,004	0.9953
	(46.38)	(37.65)	(48.34)	(37.59)
Statistics				
Corrected R^2	0.15	0.05	0.22	0.06
F ratio	3.81	1.79	4.99	1.86
Observations	248	248	248	248

Table 1.10

Wage and Proportion Female Regressions: New York (Absolute *t*-values)

	Regressions-without Interaction Effects		*Regressions-with Interaction Effects*	
Independent Variables	*Wage I Coeff.*	*Fem I Coeff.*	*Wage I Coeff.*	*Fem I Coeff.*
Industry				
Manufacturing				
Food and kindred products	-0.0309	0.0350	-0.0592	0.0706
	(1.29)	(1.08)	(2.37)	(2.09)
Apparel	-0.0997	0.0063	-0.1241	0.0382
	(2.27)	(0.11)	(2.83)	(0.64)
Printing and publishing	-0.0076	-0.0529	-0.0435	0.0041
	(0.35)	(1.74)	(1.87)	(0.13)
Chemicals	0.0061	0.0328	-0.0151	0.0580
	(0.26)	(1.02)	(0.61)	(1.74)
Machinery, except electrical	-0.0769	0.0128	-0.1109	0.0549
	(2.58)	(0.32)	(3.56)	(1.30)
Electrical machinery	-0.1239	0.0470	-0.1413	0.0685
	(5.28)	(1.48)	(5.94)	(2.12)
Instruments	-0.1198	0.0270	-0.1502	0.0645
	(4.16)	(0.69)	(5.02)	(1.59)
Miscellaneous mfg.	-0.1340	0.1093	-0.1476	0.1265
	(3.68)	(2.22)	(4.08)	(2.58)
Other nondurable goods	-0.0634	0.0523	-0.0813	0.0737
	(2.19)	(1.33)	(2.78)	(1.86)
Other durable goods	0.0141	-0.0194	-0.0011	-0.0011
	(0.65)	(0.66)	(0.05)	(0.04)
Transportation and public utilities				
Water transportation	0.0386	-0.1272	0.0510	-0.1424
	(1.20)	(2.92)	(1.59)	(3.27)
Air transportation	0.0097	0.0001	0.0214	-0.0144
	(0.40)	(0.00)	(0.87)	(0.44)
Communication	-0.0387	0.1035	-0.0181	0.0780
	(1.61)	(3.18)	(0.74)	(2.34)
Other transportation and public utilities	-0.0467	-0.0564	-0.0380	-0.0676
	(1.73)	(1.54)	(1.42)	(1.86)
Retail trade				
General merchandise	-0.1605	0.0872	-0.1435	0.0663
	(7.30)	(2.93)	(6.41)	(2.18)
Apparel and accessories	-0.0928	0.0266	-0.0835	0.0133
	(2.21)	(0.46)	(2.00)	(0.24)

Table 1.10 (continued)

Independent Variables	*Regressions- without Interaction Effects*		*Regressions- with Interaction Effects*	
	Wage I Coeff.	*Fem I Coeff.*	*Wage I Coeff.*	*Fem I Coeff.*
Other retail	-0.0617	0.1049	-0.0567	0.0993
	(1.83)	(2.30)	(1.70)	(2.19)
Finance, insurance and real estate				
Banking and credit	-0.0393	-0.0007	-0.0292	-0.0127
	(1.92)	(0.03)	(1.41)	(0.45)
Brokers and investment offices	-0.0553	-0.0794	-0.0490	-0.0865
	(2.65)	(2.81)	(2.36)	(3.07)
Insurance	-0.0532	0.0346	-0.0478	0.0284
	(2.52)	(1.21)	(2.26)	(0.99)
Real estate	0.0413	0.0716	0.0298	0.0854
	(0.63)	(0.80)	(0.46)	(0.97)
Services				
Personal services	-0.0822	0.0719	-0.0738	0.0610
	(2.72)	(1.76)	(2.47)	(1.50)
Business and repair services	-0.0536	-0.0164	-0.0542	-0.0199
	(2.69)	(0.61)	(2.55)	(0.74)
Other services	0.0230	-0.0450	0.0299	-0.0536
	(0.94)	(1.36)	(1.23)	(1.63)
Union status				
Union	0.0098	0.0088	-0.0093	0.0353
	(0.77)	(0.51)	(0.65)	(1.82)
Plant only	-0.0239	-0.0136	-0.0213	-0.0168
	(2.09)	(0.88)	(1.87)	(1.09)
Size of firm				
Size 1 (1,000 and over)	0.0016	0.0058	0.0169	0.0161
	(0.18)	(0.46)	(1.47)	(1.04)
Interaction terms				
Manufacturing and union			0.0715	-0.0997
			(2.67)	(2.74)
Manufacturing and size 1			0.0462	-0.0537
			(2.42)	(2.07)
Constant term	1.0583	0.9833	1.0625	0.9779
	(86.35)	(59.25)	(87.28)	(59.26)
Statistics				
Corrected R^2	0.18	0.09	0.20	0.11
F ratio	5.60	3.14	5.82	3.43
Observations	572	572	572	572

Table 1.11

Wage and Proportion Female Regressions: Philadelphia (Absolute *t*-values)

	Regressions- without Interaction Effects		*Regressions-with Interaction Effects*	
Independent Variables	*Wage I Coeff.*	*Fem I Coeff.*	*Wage I Coeff.*	*Fem I Coeff.*
Industry				
Manufacturing				
Food and kindred products	-0.0377	0.0448	-0.0718	0.0611
	(1.02)	(0.95)	(1.97)	(1.28)
Apparel	-0.1026	0.1329	-0.1236	0.1527
	(1.95)	(1.98)	(2.40)	(2.26)
Printing and publishing	-0.0534	0.0071	-0.1013	0.0268
	(1.29)	(0.13)	(2.43)	(0.49)
Chemicals	0.0782	0.0312	0.0367	0.0508
	(2.42)	(0.75)	(1.12)	(1.19)
Primary metals	-0.0245	-0.1369	-0.0701	-0.1107
	(0.64)	(2.80)	(1.81)	(2.19)
Fabricated metals	-0.0864	-0.0248	-0.1200	-0.0090
	(2.18)	(0.49)	(3.04)	(0.17)
Machinery, except	-0.1025	0.0005	-0.1443	0.0216
	(3.24)	(0.01)	(4.51)	(0.51)
Electrical machinery	-0.0867	0.0522	-0.1278	0.0792
	(2.59)	(1.32)	(4.01)	(1.90)
Other nondurable goods	-0.0208	0.0497	-0.0453	0.0629
	(0.57)	(1.06)	(1.26)	(1.33)
Other durable goods	-0.0074	0.0059	-0.0462	0.0278
	(0.26)	(0.16)	(1.60)	(0.73)
Transportation and	0.0238	0.0694	0.0342	0.0550
public utilities	(0.68)	(1.56)	(0.99)	(1.22)
Retail trade				
General merchandise	-0.1724	0.1662	-0.1011	0.1266
	(4.97)	(3.75)	(2.72)	(2.61)
Other retail	-0.0745	0.0182	-0.0287	0.0236
	(1.83)	(0.35)	(0.70)	(0.04)
Finance, insurance, and real estate				
Finance	-0.0674	0.0840	-0.0373	0.0724
	(2.15)	(2.09)	(1.19)	(1.77)
Insurance and real estate	-0.0444	0.0536	-0.0301	0.0482
	(1.57)	(1.48)	(1.08)	(1.33)
Services				
Personal services	-0.1372	0.0502	-0.1413	0.0483
	(2.82)	(0.81)	(2.99)	(0.78)

Table 1.11 (continued)

Independent Variables	*Regressions- without Interaction Effects*		*Regressions-with Interaction Effects*	
	Wage I Coeff.	*Fem I Coeff.*	*Wage I Coeff.*	*Fem I Coeff.*
Business and repair services	-0.0679	-0.0000	0.0734	0.0026
	(1.69)	(0.00)	(1.88)	(0.05)
Other services	-0.0442	-0.0419	0.0545	-0.0378
	(0.98)	(0.73)	(1.24)	(0.65)
Union status				
Union	0.0768	-0.0453	0.0129	0.0390
	(3.29)	(1.52)	(0.32)	(0.74)
Plant only	0.0108	0.0012	-0.0094	-0.0033
	(0.58)	(0.05)	(0.51)	(0.14)
Size of firm				
Size 1 (1,000 and over)	0.0402	0.0187	-0.0333	0.0097
	(2.70)	(0.98)	(1.47)	(0.33)
Interaction terms				
Manufacturing and union			0.0678	-0.1071
			(1.69)	(1.78)
Manufacturing and size 1			0.1205	-0.0434
			(4.10)	(1.13)
Constant term	1.0223	0.9856	1.0326	0.9815
	(47.40)	(35.83)	(48.99)	(35.62)
Statistics				
Corrected R^2	0.21	0.10	0.26	0.11
F ratio	5.26	2.78	6.00	2.79
Observations	336	336	336	336

The coefficients of the industry dummy variables in the regression equations indicate that there are significant differences among industry groups with respect to wage rates and the representation of women. Again, while this finding is weaker in the case of Boston, it is probably indicative of the aggregation problems. We have said that industry segregation occurs when workers in a sex group are employed together in the same industry to a greater extent than would be predicted by the laws of chance. The presence of significant coefficients for a number of the industry dummy variables suggests that such segregation does exist. In general, b_j, the regression coefficient for the jth industry category in the proportion-female regression is of the opposite sign from β_i, the regression coefficient for the jth industry category in the wage regression. This result confirms our expectation that women are more highly represented in industries which pay lower wages to both men and women. (However, our results do not indicate a one-to-one correspondence between the wage standing of the industry and the representation of women, either in terms of a comparison of the absolute magnitude of the coefficients or in terms of their levels of significance in the two equations. Again, it is not clear whether this represents the effect of employer preferences or estimation problems in the dependent variable in the proportion-female regressions.) While we have not explained the causes of the observed interindustry differentials, the existence of these differences suggests that product-market competition does enforce some degree of homogeneity in wage rates for office workers within industry groupings. This in turn suggests that wage differences do to some extent reflect differences in labor costs. In this regard, it appears likely that a finer industry classification would tend to produce sharper patterns.

The results for variable U_1 (plant and office workers unionized) were initially inconsistent across cities. For Boston a relatively large union effect was obtained in both the wage and proportion-female regressions. In Philadelphia the union effect was more moderate, but significant, while in New York there was no statistically significant relationship. To test for the possibility that sectoral differences underlay these inconsistencies, a manufacturing-union variable was created to measure the impact of unions in this sector. (The manufacturing-union variable equals 1 if the firm is both unionized and in the manufacturing sector, and 0 otherwise. It should be noted that this variable measures the union effect only for those manufacturing industries which had observations on union establishments.

The results that are reported in the second set of regressions indicate that there is evidence of a significant union effect on the dependent variables in the manufacturing sector of all three cities. Among these firms, unionization of a majority of plant and office workers produced a positive effect on the wage index, and a negative effect on the proportion-female index. The large impact of manufacturing-union status on the dependent variables in the Boston regressions is based on only five observations on unionized manufacturing firms and thus its magnitude is questionable. The impact of unionization in the manufacturing sector in New

York and Philadelphia is quite similar. Other things being equal, unionization increases the wage index by six percentage points in New York and eight percentage points in Philadelphia; similarly, it reduces the proportion-female index by six percentage points in New York, and seven percentage points in Philadelphia. These estimates are obtained by summing the coefficients on the union and manufacturing-union variables. After removing the effect of these unionized manufacturing firms, there is no evidence of a positive effect on unionization on wage rates for the rest of the sample.

In contrast to our findings for the impact of organization among both plant and office workers, with one exception we find no statistically significant relationships between the dependent variables and the presence of a union among a majority of plant workers. The exception, a small negative relationship between the wage index and blue-collar unionism in New York, may well be an artifact of the data. This finding regarding the lack of impact of blue-collar unions on white-collar wages is consistent with a number of other studies.[5] Superficially, these findings appear to contradict two empirical observations. First is the evidence that blue-collar unionism is positively related to the wage rates of manual workers (Weiss 1966; Raimon and Stoikov 1969). Second is the observation that many firms tend to grant white-collar workers pay increases comparable to those negotiated with blue-collar unions, possibly to avert attempts at unionization (Kassalow 1967: 360). However, there may in fact be no contradiction, since it may be that white-collar wages are lower relative to blue-collar wages in establishments where the former group is unorganized than in nonunion firms or in firms where both groups are organized. This relationship may then be preserved over time by granting both groups similar wage increases. This explanation has some intuitive appeal in that office workers are more likely to have information regarding union negotiated wage increases among manual workers in their own plant than about the relationship of white-collar to blue-collar earnings in other firms. Moreover, while their wages may be lower than those of organized white-collar workers, the latter group at present constitutes an extremely small proportion of the total (Kassalow 1967). An additional possibility suggested by Raimon and Stoikov (1969) is that the lack of impact of blue-collar unionism is due to the greater competitiveness of clerical labor markets.

For New York and Philadelphia our findings with regard to the impact of establishment size on the dependent variables are similar to those obtained for the (plant and office) union variable. (A small but significant positive relationship between establishment size and the wage index is obtained in the Boston first regression. However, the coefficient becomes marginally insignificant when the manufacturing union variable is included.[6]) In these cities the introduction of a variable reflecting the interaction of size and sector suggests that the consistent effect of large establishment size (over 1,000 employees) is mainly restricted to manufacturing (the manufacturing-size variable equals 1 if the firm is both large (over 1,000 employees) and in the manufacturing sector, and 0 otherwise). The magnitude of the manufacturing-size effect was similar in the two cities, contributing to an increase of six percentage points in the wage index in New York and nine percentage points in Philadelphia, and to a decrease of four percentage points in the proportion-female index in New York and three percentage points in Philadelphia (the last coefficient was not statistically significant).

1.6. Conclusions

This chapter is concerned with the relationship of differences in the distribution of men and women office workers among firms to the male-female pay differential within narrowly defined occupational categories. The study has been designed to place such distributional differences (employment segregation by sex) at the heart of the analysis. We have presented a model in which institutional and market factors are assumed to constrain the latitude of the employer to differentiate between male and female workers. The model is tested with a sample of clerical, professional, and technical occupations in three large northeastern labor markets: Boston, New York, and Philadelphia. It is our view that the model performs well and is deserving of further application with other data sets.

At the level of the occupational category it is found that men and women are differentially distributed among firms to a degree in excess of what could be expected from the operation of random processes, confirming the existence of sex segregation by firm within occupational categories. Further, this differential distribution is found to be an important factor in the sex differential in earnings. For the most part, earnings differentials by sex within occupations are primarily the result of differences in pay rates among firms rather than differences in pay rates within firms.

The causal mechanism postulated by the model is further verified by examining occupations jointly to form a picture of establishment wage and employment patterns. We demonstrate the existence of a wage hierarchy of firms within each labor market that is consistent across occupational categories and sex groups. In addition, after controlling for the occupational mix of the establishment (and thus the differing availability of women to the firm in each occupational category), we find that firms exhibit consistent patterns across occupational categories with respect to the representation of women. And, as expected, the wage standing of the firm is found to be inversely related to the representation of women in the establishment.

The relationship of establishment characteristics (industry, union status, and size of firm) to interfirm differences in wage rates and in the representation of women is also explored. Our findings suggest that structural variables are important for explaining the observed differences among firms in wage rates and the sex composition of establishment employment. In general it is found that variables that are positively related to establishment wage rates are negatively related to the representation of women in the establishment, and vice versa. In particular, industry is found to be an important explanatory factor in both cases, suggesting that the sexes are differentially distributed by industry and that such segregation is related to the wage standing of firms within the industry.

The view presented here is that demand-side factors play an important role in generating male-female pay differentials within occupational categories. Such differentials are seen as primarily the result of differences in the distribution of men and women among establishments stemming from the exclusionary practices of higher-wage firms. It is argued on the basis of theoretical considerations and empirical evidence that measured pay differentials among firms generally exceed differences that may reasonably be attributed to exogenously determined quality differences among workers (i.e., supply-side factors). Further, it is argued that worker quality is relatively homogeneous within the detailed occupational categories used in the analysis. However, in the absence of additional data on the personal characteristics of workers we do not attempt to measure and quantify the impact of discrimination on pay differentials in specific cases.

Rather, we are concerned with delineating the broad pattern of the relationship between pay differentials and distributional differences, observed across a variety of occupational categories. In addition, the results obtained when occupations are considered separately are linked to consistent establishment-wide patterns, again suggesting that demand-side factors are important. The results of this study suggest that demand-side factors produce pay differentials and employment segregation even when men and women have similar skills and abilities as evinced by their participation in the same narrowly defined occupational categories.

2

Trends in Earnings Differentials by Gender

*Based on papers with Andrea H. Beller and Lawrence M. Kahn**

2.1. 1970s *(based on a paper with Andrea H. Beller)*

How did women's earnings fare relative to men's earnings during the 1970s? One source of evidence on this question, the series of data on full-time, year-round workers derived from the Current Population Surveys (CPS), surprisingly indicates no change in women's relative economic position over that period: women's annual earnings were 59 percent of men's in both 1971 and 1981. The picture is complicated, however, by contradictory data from another series derived from the CPS, which shows that the ratio of weekly earnings of full-time

This chapter is a revised version of Blau, F. D., Beller, A. H. (1988). Trends in Earnings Differentials by Gender, 1971-1981, in: Industrial and Labor Relations Review, 41(4): 513-529 [Section 2.1] © 1988 Cornell University and a revised version of Blau, F. D., Kahn, L. M. (2006). The U.S. Gender Pay Gap in the 1990s: Slowing Convergence, in: Industrial and Labor Relations Review, 60(1): 45-66 [Section 2.2], © 2006 Cornell University.

For Section 2.1, the authors thank Lawrence Kahn, William Darity, Marianne Ferber, Claudia Goldin, Shelly Lundberg, Solomon Polachek, Sherwin Rosen, and James Smith for helpful comments on earlier drafts of this paper, and Adam Grossberg, Keith Chauvin, Kee-ok Kim Han, and Seung Chung for research assistance. For Section 2.2, the authors thank Nabanita Datta Gupta, Nicole Fortin, Caroline Hoxby, Ronald Oaxaca, and participants at the American Economic Association Meetings, Philadelphia, January 2005, the Society of Labor Economists Meetings, San Francisco, June 2005, and seminars at the Massachusetts Institute of Technology, Cornell University, the University of Washington, Seattle, Washington University, St. Louis, the London School of Economics, the Kennedy School of Government, the Wharton School, and IZA for helpful comments, and Fidan Kurtulus and Joan Moriarty for excellent research assistance. Portions of Section 2.2 were written while the authors were Visiting Fellows in the Economics Department of Princeton University, supported by the Industrial Relations Section. The authors are very grateful for this support.

female workers to that of full-time male workers rose from 61.7 to 64.6 percent between 1971 and 1981 (Blau and Ferber 1987; U.S. Department of Labor 1980).

Of the two series, that on annual earnings has attracted more attention and has puzzled observers. How could women's relative economic standing have stood still in a period that witnessed large increases in women's labor force participation (Blau and Ferber 1986), a decline in occupational segregation by gender (Beller 1985), and an impressive array of governmental anti-discrimination laws and regulations?

Previous research (O'Neill 1985; Smith and Ward 1984) suggests that there was a widening of the gender experience gap in the 1960s (as compared to the 1950s) and a modest reduction in the gap in the 1970s as women - particularly younger women - increased their average levels of experience.[1] These studies also find that, particularly in the 1960s, the educational attainment of women in the labor force declined relative to men, in part because the female labor force became less highly educated relative to the female population as a whole. These findings imply that - at least on the basis of these human capital factors - the lack of progress of women during the 1960s was perhaps understandable. The experience of the 1970s, however, seems worthy of closer scrutiny.

As for the 1980s, the two CPS series that yield conflicting pictures of women's fortunes in the 1970s are in agreement that the earnings gap has narrowed in the past few years, with annual earnings of year-round, full-time workers rising to 64.6 percent in 1986 and the female-male ratio of the weekly earnings of full-time workers rising to 69.2 percent. Indeed, in the second quarter of 1987 the female-male ratio of weekly earnings among full-time workers was 70.7 percent (U.S. Department of Labor 1987). Many of the considerations that help make these findings plausible are the same ones that make the finding of a stable female-male earnings differential in the 1970s perplexing.

This section examines the trends in gender differentials over the 1971-81 period and their determinants by means of a more detailed and disaggregated analysis than that contained in earlier work. We use data from the 1972 and 1982 Annual Demographic Files of the Current Population Surveys (CPS) for wage and salary workers aged 18-64.[2] Although these data sets unfortunately do not allow us to measure labor force experience, they do provide a rich source of information on the other determinants of wages. Indeed, of the available sources, only census data permit the examination of wage differentials over time for a large sample on a nationwide, comprehensive basis. By comparison, the major data set that contains information on actual labor force experience, the National Longitudinal Surveys, is available only for a much smaller sample and only for limited (and not always overlapping) age ranges of women and men.

At least two features of the analysis that follows set it apart from previous studies. First, we correct the estimated earnings functions for selectivity bias; and second, we estimate the extent to which changes in the degree of occupational segregation by gender contributed to changes in the earnings gap.

2.1.1. An Overview of Trends

The sample consists of individuals who worked at least one week during the previous year and whose wage and salary income was at least $100. Persons with any self-employment income were excluded, as were members of the military. Also, all individuals for whom data on income from wages and salaries were missing and therefore imputed by the Census are excluded.[3]

Trends in female-male earnings ratios for two different measures (geometric means and medians) and a variety of subgroups are presented in Table 2.1. We find a narrowing of gender differentials between 1971 and 1981, although the magnitude of the gains (in percentage terms) is somewhat larger when based on the geometric means than when based on the more commonly cited medians.[4] We use the geometric means in our analysis because the natural log of earnings is the dependent variable in the earnings regressions (see below).

It may also be seen that the magnitude of the gains varies among groups. Among all workers, larger gains are obtained for black women than for white women. Further, it is noteworthy that within each race group, full-time, year-round workers experienced the smallest gains. In the case of black women in this category, a small decrease in the ratio is actually found on the basis of the median. It is the trends for year-round, full-time workers that, as we have seen, have received the most public attention.[5]

One reason for focusing on year-round, full-time workers is to adjust for gender differences in time input (hours and weeks worked), because the CPS does not contain data on wages (hourly earnings). But it is quite possible that year-round, full-time female workers are not representative of the female labor force as a whole. We will therefore present an alternative technique for adjusting for time input, one that holds the characteristics of each race-gender group constant at their overall mean levels. The findings suggest that the focus on the subgroup of workers who are employed full-time and year-round has resulted in underestimates of the gains made by women during the 1970s.

Table 2.1

Trends in Female-Male Earnings Ratios, 1971-1981

	Based on Geometric Means[a]			Based on Medians[b]		
Group of Workers	1971 (%)	1981 (%)	% Change	1971 (%)	1981 (%)	% Change
Whites						
Annual Earnings						
All workers	39.5	45.4	14.9	43.2	47.1	9.0
Full-time, year-round	58.1	61.0	5.0	57.6	59.4	3.1
Weekly Earnings						
All workers	49.2	52.3	6.3	50.6	52.5	3.7
Full-time	56.2	61.3	9.1	55.8	59.2	6.1
Blacks						
Annual Earnings						
All workers	50.7	63.4	25.0	55.7	65.2	17.1
Full-time, year-round	73.1	75.4	3.1	73.5	73.1	-0.6
Weekly Earnings						
All workers	58.5	67.6	15.6	61.9	69.3	12.0
Full-time	70.0	74.0	5.7	69.2	72.1	4.1

[a] The geometric mean is the antilog of the mean of the natural log of earnings.
[b] The median is the level of earnings at which half the cases are higher and half lower.

2.1.2. *Strategy of the Analysis*

To gain a more accurate picture of trends in labor market treatment of women relative to men over this period, we consider trends in earnings ratios after adjustment for gender differences in selectivity bias, time input (hours and weeks worked), and other factors determining wages. Then, in order to identify specific influences that have worked to increase or reduce women's earnings relative to men's, we apply a standard technique (see, Blinder 1973, Oaxaca 1973a) to decompose the changes in earnings differentials over the period into (1) the component due to changes in the means of the variables (that is, due to the endowments of characteristics) and (2) the component due to changes in the coefficients of these variables (that is, due to the returns to characteristics).

One issue on which these findings have a bearing is the extent of discrimination against women over the period. The portion of the pay differential due to gender differences in returns to a given set of characteristics (that is, gender differences in coefficients, including the constant term) is conventionally used as an estimate of discrimination (Blinder 1973; Oaxaca 1973a). This basic approach has certain problems that can result in an overestimate or underestimate of the level of discrimination. On the one hand, available data sources do not allow for the measurement of all productivity-related characteristics. If, on average, men are more favorably endowed with the characteristics measured by these omitted variables, the extent of labor market discrimination will be overestimated. On the other hand, measured labor market discrimination is likely to be underestimated to the extent that factors representing the indirect effects of discrimination are controlled for. This study is in no way immune to those problems. Nevertheless, we believe that it is instructive to provide a consistent measure of discrimination across two different years using a single data source and methodology. As noted earlier, the CPS is the only data set providing information on a large sample of individuals of all ages over the decade.

The adjustment for selectivity bias is important and warrants fuller consideration. Gronau (1979), Reimers (1983), and others have suggested that, particularly when one is interested in potential differences in employer treatment of two groups, the focus should be on wage offers rather than observed wages. Since the latter are influenced by individuals' decisions about whether or not to participate in the wage and salary sector, analyses of observed wages may yield biased estimates of mean wage offers to individuals (with given measured characteristics), as well as of coefficients of earnings functions. The bias may be either positive or negative. If inclusion in the wage regression sample is selective of (favors) those with higher wage offers, the bias will be positive; that is, the mean of observed wages will be higher than the mean of wage offers. If inclusion in the sample is selective of (favors) those with lower values of time in alternative uses (such as non-market activities, self-employment, and the military), the bias will be negative; that is, the mean of observed wages will be lower than the mean of wage offers. If two groups differ in the direction or magnitude of this selectivity bias, estimates of differentials between those groups based on observed wages will be biased. The issue of sample selection bias assumes particular importance in this study because we are interested in comparing how women fared relative to men in the two years between which the labor force participation of each of the two groups changed. Intuitively, one might expect that shifts in labor force participation will be associated with changes in the degree of selectivity bias. In fact, such an expectation may or may not be borne out empirically; there is no necessary relationship between changes in labor force participation and selectivity bias.

To see why there is no necessary association between labor force participation rates and selectivity bias, consider the case at hand. The observed increase in women's labor force participation rate may be due to changes over time in the characteristics of the female population that influence participation (for example, educational attainment, proportion married, and the presence and ages of children), or changes in the behavior of women with given levels of these characteristics, or both. If changes in women's characteristics are responsible, there is obviously no change in the selectivity of the labor force relative to the population. If changes in the behavior of women are responsible, the female labor force may become less highly endowed relative to the population with some of the measured characteristics (for example, education) that influence wages. Since we control for these measured characteristics in our wage regression, however, no bias in the estimated coefficients need result. Such changes in labor force participation behavior are simply one of a number of factors that may cause a change in the measured qualifications of women in the labor force relative to those of men over the period.[6]

A technique suggested by Heckman (1980) is used to obtain consistent estimates of the coefficients and standard errors of the wage-offer function. The inverse of the Mills' ratio, X, from a probit equation predicting inclusion in the wage regression sample, is included as an explanatory variable in a wage regression estimated by weighted least squares. Specifically, the following wage equation is estimated separately for each race-gender group and year:

$$\ln w_i = B'X_i + b\lambda_i + v_i, \qquad (1)$$

where X is a vector of variables, B is a vector of coefficients, b is the covariance between the errors in the probit and wage equations (to be estimated), and v_i is an error term distributed $N(0, \sigma^2)$.[7]

For each group, then, $B'\overline{X}$ is an estimate of the wage offer for an individual with the average characteristics of those included in the wage regression, and $b\overline{\lambda}$ is an estimate of the selectivity bias in the average observed wage for the group (Reimers 1983). Since $\overline{\lambda}$ is inversely related to the probability of inclusion in the sample, it varies systematically with changes in participation rates over time. But since b is an estimate of the covariance between the unmeasured factors in the sample-inclusion and wage equations, it may again be seen that there is no necessary relationship between the sign or magnitude of b (or, by implication, $b\overline{\lambda}$) and changes in participation rates.[8]

2.1.3. Regression Model

Earnings regressions are estimated separately for race-gender groups in 1971 and 1981 as a function of individual human capital and other demographic characteristics and the 1970 gender composition of the individual's detailed (3- digit) occupational category. The human capital variables include education and a spline on education, potential labor market experience, weeks worked last year, and whether work was part-time. The demographic variables are measures of marital status, number of children, and age of children. The effect of the omission of actual labor market experience is minimized by the inclusion of these variables, which help to capture periods during which women are out of the labor force for childbearing and childrearing (Hill 1979). Further, as we have seen, the findings of O'Neill (1985) and Smith and Ward (1984) suggest that the omitted variable, actual experience, was if anything increasing for women during this period. We also control for veteran status (men only), government employment, and location. The variables are defined in Table 2.2.

Table 2.2

Variable Definitions

Variable Name	Definition
LNY	The natural log of annual earnings from wages and salaries
EDUC	Number of years of schooling completed
YRSLTB	For those with less than 8 years of schooling, the number of years less than 8; zero otherwise
YRSGTI2	For those with more than 12 years of schooling, the number of years greater than 12; zero otherwise
EXP	Potential experience, computed as AGE - EDUC - 6
EXPSQ	Square of EXP
LNWW	Natural log of weeks worked in previous year
PRTTIME	One if worked part-time (less than 35 hours per week) in the majority of weeks in the previous year; zero otherwise
MSP	One if married with spouse present; zero otherwise
NUMKIDS	Number of children
PRESLT6	One if one or more children under 6 years of age; zero otherwise
MALOCC	One if percent male in 1970 in the individual's 3-digit occupation was 70 or more; zero otherwise
INTOCC	One if percent male in 1970 in the individual's 3-digit occupation was 41 to 69 percent; zero otherwise
λ	Inverse of Mills' ratio predicted from a probit equation for inclusion in the wage sample

Unlike conventional specifications, our earnings functions include variables for the gender composition of the individual's detailed (3-digit) occupational category. Previous research suggests that, all else equal, predominantly male occupations and integrated occupations pay more than predominantly female occupations (Beller 1982b; Blau 1984, see Chapter 11). Under a human capital interpretation, such occupations are expected to pay more because individuals in them have made greater human capital investments (see, for example, Polachek 1979). According to the theory of occupational crowding, male occupations are expected to pay more because large numbers of women who are excluded from male jobs by discrimination are channeled into the labor market for jobs in which they face little or no discrimination, and the resultant increased supply of labor depresses wages in those female jobs (Bergmann 1974).

We do not propose in this section to test the relative merits of these alternative explanations, but rather to ascertain the importance of changes over time in occupational distributions and in the returns to being in a male or integrated job for earnings differentials. The human capital and crowding models imply that male occupations as a whole differ from female occupations as a whole rather than that the effect of occupational gender composition on earnings varies along a continuum corresponding to different proportions of men and women. Thus, we use a dummy variable specification for gender composition.[9] The gender composition of an occupation is defined on the basis of 1970 Census data; we thus identify a consistent set of male and integrated occupations for the two years (1971 and 1981), although a number of occupations shifted from male to integrated over the intervening period (Beller 1985).

Table 2.3 presents the earnings regression results and Table 2.4 presents the weighted means of the explanatory variables for each group. The findings for specific variables will be discussed in the course of our analyses of trends in the gender differential. But since the findings for the coefficients on λ (the variable used to correct for selectivity bias) are of particular interest, we summarize them here.

Among men, the coefficient on λ is negative for both years, although significantly so only for whites. This result suggests that, among those with the same measured characteristics, men with a higher value of time in activities other than wage- and salary-earning employment are the ones who tended not to participate in the labor force.[10] Thus, those who were omitted from the sample are estimated to have received higher wage offers than those included. The coeffiients on λ are found to decrease in absolute value over time for both

Table 2.3

Log Earnings Regression Results by Race and Gender, 1971 and 1981a (standard errors in parantheses)

	Without Selectivity Bias Correction				With Selectivity Bias Correction			
	1971		1981		1971		1981	
Variable	Female	Male	Female	Male	Female	Male	Female	Male
Whites								
EDUC	.067**	.065**	.054**	.082**	.067**	.069**	.061**	.082**
	(.004)	(.003)	(.004)	(.003)	(.004)	(.003)	(.005)	(.003)
YRSLT8	.043**	.016**	.019	.023**	.043**	.021**	.022*	.023**
	(.010)	(.006)	(.011)	(.007)	(.010)	(.006)	(.011)	(.007)
YRSGTI2	.024**	.020**	.022**	-.005	.024**	.026**	.018**	-.005
	(.006)	(.004)	(.005)	(.004)	(.006)	(.004)	(.006)	(.004)
EXP	.030**	.042**	.029**	.044**	.030**	.043**	.029**	.044**
	(.001)	(.001)	(.001)	(.001)	(.001)	(.001)	(.001)	(.001)
EXPSQ	$-.526 \times 10^{-3}$**	$-.693 \times 10^{-3}$**	549×10^{-3}**	$-.696 \times 10^{-3}$**	$-.526 \times 10^{-3}$**	$-.638 \times 10^{-3}$**	$-.612 \times 10^{-3}$**	$-.681 \times 10^{-3}$**
	$(.315 \times 10^{-4})$	$(.237 \times 10^{-4})$	298×10^{-4})	$(.247 \times 10^{-4})$	$(.334 \times 10^{-4})$	$(.250 \times 10^{-4})$	(.356 × 10-4)	$(.254 \times 10^{-4})$
LNWW	1.007**	.929**	1.123**	1.059**	1.007**	.924**	1.125**	1.056**
	(.007)	(.007)	(.007)	(.008)	(.007)	(.008)	(.007)	(.008)
PRTTIME	-.862**	-.857**	-.814**	-.849**	-.862**	-.855**	-.818**	-.846**
	(.011)	(.013)	(.009)	(.013)	(.011)	(.013)	(.009)	(.013)
MSP	.032**	.239**	.019*	.166**	.031*	.190**	.004	.159**
	(.010)	(.010)	(.009)	(.010)	(.012)	(.014)	(.010)	(.010)
NUMKIDS	-.050**	.014**	-.046**	.011**	-.051**	.020**	-.052**	.012**
	(.004)	(.003)	(.004)	(.003)	(.005)	(.003)	(.005)	(.003)
PRESLT6	.030*	.038**	.046**	.015	.030	.015	.021	.012
	(.014)	(.009)	(.012)	(.010)	(.018)	(.010)	(.014)	(.010)
MALOCC	.099**	.184**	.156**	.270**	.099**	.186**	.156**	.269**
	(.013)	(.012)	(.010)	(.012)	(.013)	(.012)	(.010)	(.012)
INTOCC	.065**	.099**	.092**	.161**	.065**	.101**	.092**	.161**
	(.013)	(.015)	(.011)	(.015)	(.013)	(.015)	(.011)	(.015)
λ	—	—	—	—	.002	-.413**	.146*	-.070*
					(.036)	(.073)	(.045)	(.029)
Constant	3.350**	3.702**	3.856**	3.696**	3.348**	3.896**	3.695**	3.735**
	(.055)	(.042)	(.058)	(.048)	(.061)	(.054)	(.076)	(.051)
Adjusted R^2	.719	.715	.716	.702	.719	.723	.714	.702
No. Observations	16,729	23,168	23,042	26,295	16,729	23,168	23,043	26,295

Table 2.3 (continued)

Variable	Without Selectivity Bias Correction				With Selectivity Bias Correction			
	1971		1981		1971		1981	
	Female	Male	Female	Male	Female	Male	Female	Male
Blacks								
EDUC	.066**	.044**	.077**	.062**	.070**	.045**	.091**	.062**
	(.010)	(.009)	(.012)	(.012)	(.012)	(.009)	(.021)	(.012)
YRSLT8	.063**	.033*	.059*	.043	.064**	.034*	.065*	.043
	(.019)	(.015)	(.027)	(.022)	(.019)	(.016)	(.028)	(.022)
YRSGTI2	.057**	.029*	.016	.015	.058**	.028	.010	.014
	(.016)	(.015)	(.015)	(.016)	(.016)	(.015)	(.017)	(.016)
EXP	.023**	.024**	.026**	.028**	.025**	.024**	.032**	.028**
	(.004)	(.003)	(.004)	(.004)	(.004)	(.004)	(.009)	(.005)
EXPSQ	$-.485 \times 10^{-3}$**	$-.400 \times 10^{-3}$**	$-.486 \times 10^{-3}$**	$-.442 \times 10^{-3}$**	$-.528 \times 10^{-3}$**	$-.387 \times 10^{-3}$**	$-.628 \times 10^{-3}$**	$-.438 \times 10^{-3}$**
	$(.784 \times 10^{-4})$	$(.706 \times 10^{-4})$	$(.817 \times 10^{-4})$	$(.822 \times 10^{-4})$	$(.977 \times 10^{-4})$	$(.851 \times 10^{-4})$	$(.197 \times 10^{-3})$	$(.114 \times 10^{-3})$
LNWW	.948**	.843**	1.115**	1.010**	.949**	.843**	1.115**	1.010**
	(.019)	(.022)	(.020)	(.025)	(.019)	(.022)	(.020)	(.025)
PRTTIME	-.891**	-.848**	-.721**	-.846**	-.891**	-.848**	-.722**	-.846**
	(.028)	(.041)	(.029)	(.044)	(.028)	(.041)	(.029)	(.044)
MSP	.035	.258**	.081 **	.198**	.036	.252**	.111*	.197**
	(.025)	(.029)	(.025)	(.034)	(.025)	(.037)	(.044)	(.042)
NUMKIDS	-.008	.009	-.028**	.006	-.011	.009	-.034**	.006
	(.008)	(.007)	(.010)	(.011)	(.009)	(.007)	(.013)	(.011)
PRESLT6	.094**	-.008	.041	.012	.088*	-.011	.039	.012
	(.034)	(.031)	(.033)	(.038)	(.035)	(.033)	(.033)	(.041)
MALOCC	.130**	.123**	.151 **	.154**	.132**	.123**	.150**	.154**
	(.037)	(.036)	(.031)	(.039)	(.037)	(.036)	(.031)	(.040)
INTOCC	.192**	.055	.161 **	.086	.192**	.054	.161**	.086
	(.033)	(.044)	(.032)	(.049)	(.033)	(.044)	(.032)	(.049)
λ	—	—	—	—	.080	-.039	.221	-.007
					(.112)	(.142)	(.275)	(.151)
Constant	3.493**	4.231**	3.491 **	4.105**	3.369**	4.253	3.092**	4.112**
	(.136)	(.131)	(.154)	(.162)	(.220)	(.155)	(.523)	(.220)
Adjusted R^2	.749	.675	.738	.695	.744	.674	.733	.694
No. Observations	2,326	2,304	2,492	2,159	2,326	2,304	2,492	2,159

[a] See Table 2 for variable definitions. Regressions include controls for region (North Central, South, and West), urban residence, veteran status (men only), and government employment.

* Significant at the 5 percent level; **significant at the 1 percent level (two-tailed tests).

Table 2.4

Weighted Means of Dependent and Independent Variables Included in Earnings Regressions by Race and Gender, 1971 and 1981[a]

	Whites				Blacks			
	1971		1981		1971		1981	
Variable	Female	Male	Female	Male	Female	Male	Female	Male
LNY	7.860	8.789	8.692	9.481	7.678	8.358	8.600	9.056
EDUC	12.048	11.941	12.728	12.732	10.936	10.172	11.976	11.585
YRSLT8	.098	.187	.061	.121	.316	.597	.120	.264
YRSGT12	.814	1.013	1.161	1.386	.509	.422	.803	.765
EXP	18.438	19.255	16.406	17.178	19.058	19.897	17.301	17.711
EXPSQ	544.190	564.430	436.429	463.360	546.957	585.115	460.420	483.907
LNWW	3.511	3.730	3.586	3.726	3.519	3.662	3.567	3.631
PRTTIME	.253	.076	.293	.089	.243	.090	.228	.112
MSP	.635	.744	.589	.650	.492	.608	.422	.517
NUMKIDS	1.012	1.270	.910	.954	1.412	1.348	1.248	.943
PRESLT6	.160	.249	.168	.202	.226	.237	.211	.186
MALOCC	.128	.802	.211	.806	.111	.759	.176	.742
INTOCC	.136	.118	.144	.110	.150	.135	.165	.143
λ	.764	.495	.687	.550	.695	.472	.760	.654

[a] See Table 2 for variable definitions. Observations are weighted by sampling weights provided in the CPS.

black and white men. This result accords with an intuitive expectation that as the group that did not participate in the wage and salary sector increased in size, it became less heavily comprised of those with high wage offers (high values of time spent in alternative activities). The coefficients on λ are smaller in absolute value and the trend over time is less pronounced for black men than for white men, perhaps because in the excluded group the categories "out of the labor force" and "unemployed" had greater relative importance (in comparison to self-employment) for blacks than for whites.

Among women, the coefficients on the selectivity variable are positive for blacks and whites in both years, although significantly so only for white women in 1981. A positive coefficient indicates that, among those with similar measured characteristics, women who are included in the sample had higher wage offers than the excluded group.[11] The degree of selectivity with respect to unmeasured characteristics was estimated to have increased over the period. This result conflicts with an intuitive expectation that as women's labor force participation increased the labor force should have become a less highly qualified group relative to the female population (in terms of its unmeasured characteristics). As discussed above, however, there is no necessary relationship between shifts in labor force participation and changes in the sign or magnitude of the coefficient on λ.[12]

2.1.4. Trends in Adjusted Female-Male Earnings Ratios

The trends in the unadjusted and adjusted differentials based on the estimated regression equations (with and without the selectivity bias correction) are shown in Table 2.5. For both whites and blacks, female-male earnings ratios of mean wage offers (earnings ratios adjusted for selectivity bias) are estimated to be lower in each year than earnings ratios based on observed wages, for example, 32.2% as compared to 39.6% among whites in 1971. The gender differential in earnings is widened by the selectivity adjustment because mean wage offers are above mean observed wages among men and below mean observed wages among women.

On the other hand, the impact on trends over time of the selectivity bias correction differs by race. For all race-gender groups, the group included in the wage regression sample became more selective relative to the excluded group over the period; that is, among individuals with the same measured characteristics, the mean wage offers of the included group rose relative to those of the excluded group. Among whites, the increase in the selectivity of the wage regression group was greater for men than women. Thus, adjusting for selectivity bias increased the gain in the relative earnings of women over the period from 14.6 to 22.7%. Among blacks, the increase in selectivity was greater for women than men. Thus, the earnings ratio based on observed wages increased 25.2%, whereas that based on wage offers was estimated to rise only 13.4%.

Table 2.5

Trends in Unadjusted and Adjusted Predicted Female-Male Earnings Ratios, 1971-1981

Type of Adjustment	Without Selectivity Bias Correction			With Selectivity Bias Correction		
	1971	1981	% Change	1971	1981	% Change
Whites						
Unadjusted[a]	39.6	45.4	14.6	39.6	45.4	14.6
Adjusted for:						
selectivity bias[b]				32.2	39.5	22.7
time input[c]	57.5	62.7	9.0	46.8	54.6	16.7
all variables[d]	62.7	69.7	11.2	50.3	60.4	20.1
Blacks						
Unadjusted[a]	50.7	63.5	25.2	50.7	63.5	25.2
Adjusted for:						
selectivity bias[b]				47.1	53.4	13.4
time input[c]	66.6	74.2	11.4	61.8	62.4	1.0
all variables[d]	69.0	79.2	14.8	64.0	66.6	4.1

[a] Computed by substituting the weighted means of the explanatory variables (including λ) for each group into the regression equation for that group.
[b] Computed as in (a), but by setting the term $b\bar{\lambda}$ equal to zero.
[c] Computed by adjusting for selectivity bias where indicated as in (b) and substituting the male weighted means for hours (PRTTIME) and weeks worked in the previous year (LNWW) into the female functions, with all the remaining variables given the female weighted means.
[d] Computed by adjusting for selectivity bias where indicated as in (b) and substituting the male means of all the explanatory variables into the female functions.

These estimates suggest that white women increased their relative earnings at a faster pace than black women. It is important to bear in mind, however, that although adjusting for selectivity bias has a considerable impact for blacks, the coefficients on X in the regressions for blacks were not statistically significant – a troublesome combination of findings. Thus, the results for blacks that include the selectivity bias correction must be interpreted with caution. Comparing the OLS results for blacks with the corrected results for whites results in nearly equal increases in the earnings ratio values for the two (22.7 percent for whites and 25.2 percent for blacks).

These findings suggest that the more rapid progress of black women over the period indicated by the unadjusted ratios is greatly reduced, and possibly even reversed, when selectivity bias is eliminated.

We next consider the impact of adjustment for time input, that is, for hours and weeks worked. The predicted means are adjusted for hours and weeks by substituting the male means of these variables into the female functions, while retaining the female means for the other explanatory variables. This technique enables us to examine the effect of adjustment for time input for a group of individuals with fixed characteristics: those who have the average characteristics of the sample in each race-gender group. As shown in Table 2.5, among whites the earnings ratio adjusted for time input is estimated to have increased by between 9.0 percent (OLS regressions) and 16.7 percent (regressions corrected for selectivity bias) over the period, considerably more than the 5.0 percent figure for the full-time, year-round group given in Table 2.1. Among blacks, OLS regressions indicate considerably larger gains (11.4 percent) than regressions corrected for selectivity bias (1.0 percent). The OLS result, in which we have more confidence, also substantially exceeds the 3.1 percent increase for year-round, full-time workers shown in Table 2.1.

Finally, findings for the fully adjusted ratios show that a woman earned more relative to a man with similar characteristics in 1981 than in 1971.[13] This result suggests that discrimination, as conventionally measured, declined over this period. Among whites, the adjusted earnings ratio increased by between 11.2 percent (OLS regressions) and 20.1 percent (selectivity bias-corrected regressions). The OLS results suggest that black women increased their earnings 14.8 percent relative to black men with similar characteristics. The gains are reduced to 4.1 percent when the results from the selectivity bias-corrected regressions are used.

Table 2.6 shows the trends in the adjusted earnings ratios by experience level, focusing on the selectivity bias-corrected results for whites and the OLS results for blacks. Changes in earnings ratios for the group with the indicated experience level in each year can be found by reading across the rows of data. Changes in the earnings ratio over time for a cohort with a given experience level in 1971 may be obtained by following the arrows. The table shows quite dramatic improvements in the relative earnings of younger white women. For white women, the extent of the gain declines steadily with experience, whereas for black women the gain is fairly uniform across experience groups. Also, all experience cohorts would have improved their earnings ratios as they aged if they had had the male means.[14] This result is cause for some hope that the younger cohorts will retain their relative earnings advantage as they age.

Table 2.6

Trends in Adjusted Predicted Female-Male Earnings Ratios by Experience Level, 1971-1981[a]

	Whites (With Selectivity Bias Correction)			Blacks (Without Selectivity Bias Correction)		
Experience Level	1971	1981	% Change[b]	1971	1981	% Change[b]
0	60.6	75.0	23.4	74.0	84.0	13.5
5	57.0	69.9	22.6	73.5	83.0	12.9
10	53.9	65.4	(7.9) 21.3	72.7	81.9	(10.7) 12.7
15	51.2	61.4	(7.7) 19.9	71.6	80.5	(9.5) 12.4
20	48.9	57.8	(7.2) 18.2	70.1	79.1	(8.8) 12.8
30	45.5	51.8	(5.9) 13.8	66.5	75.7	(8.0) 13.8
40	43.2	47.0	(3.3) 8.8	62.0	71.8	(8.0) 15.8

[a] For each year, the adjusted ratios are computed by substituting the overall male means of the explanatory variables into the female functions and evaluating at the indicated levels of experience.

[b] Percentage changes in the earnings ratios for cohorts are shown in parentheses.

2.1.5. *Decomposition of Trends in the Male-Female Differential*

In decomposing the change in the predicted male-female earnings differential, we again focus on the selectivity bias-corrected results for whites and the OLS results for blacks (Table 2.7). Overall, the predicted gender differential in the log of earnings declined by .1373 among whites and by .2255 among blacks between 1971 and 1981. These changes may be due to changes in the means or the coefficients of the variables (or both) for women relative to men. As shown in the table, we have categorized the variables into several groups representing education; (potential) experience, time in the labor market (over the year); demographic characteristics, gender composition of occupations, the constant term, and other variables. For whites, we also show the effect of changes in selectivity bias over time. Note that since we are analyzing changes in the male-female differential ($LNY_M - LNY_F$) over the period, a negative sign in Table 2.7 indicates that the factor worked to decrease the differential and a positive sign indicates that the factor worked to increase the differential.

To compute the mean effect for a group of variables (such as the education variables), we ask the following question: what would the 1971-81 change in the gender differential have been if the means of the variables in this group had changed to their 1981 levels (for both men and women), while all the coefficients and means of the remaining variables had remained at their 1971 levels?

Table 2.7

Decomposition of the Change in the Predicted Male-Female Differential in the Log of Earnings (LNY), 1971-1981. (1971 weights)

Groups of Variables[a]	Whites (With Selectivity Bias Correction) Means[b]	Coefficients[c]	Total[d]	Blacks (Without Selectivity Bias Correction) Means[b]	Coefficients[c]	Total[d]
Education	.0100	.2112	.2212	-.0121	.0887	.0766
Experience	-.0205	.0509	.0304	-.0136	.0011	-.0125
Time	-.0558	.0686	.0128	-.1039	-.0181	-.1220
Demographic Characteristics	-.0289	-.0137	-.0426	-.0239	-.0170	-.0409
Gender Composition of Occupation	-.0088	.0633	.0545	-.0130	.0303	.0173
Other Variables	.0071	.0400	.0471	-.0028	-.0249	-.0277
Constant term		-.5080	-.5080		-.1233	-.1233
Subtotal 1	-.0969	-.0877	-.1846	-.1693	-.0632	-.2325
λ	-.0224	.0593	.0369	—	—	—
Subtotal 2	-.1193	-.0284	-.1477			
Interaction[e]			.0104			.0070
Total			-.1373			-.2255

[a] The following explanatory variables are included in each group. Education: *EDUC*, *YRSLT8*, *YRSGT12*. Experience: *EXP*, *EXPSQ*. Time: *LNWW*, *PRTTIME*. Demographic Characteristics: *MSP*, *NUMKIDS*, *PRESLT6*. Gender Composition of Occupation: *MALOCC*, *INTOCC*. Other Variables: controls for region, urban residence, and government employment. See Table 2.2 for variable definitions.

[b] For variable x_i. computed as $b_{m71}\,(\overline{x}_{m81} - \overline{x}_{m71}) - b_{f71}\,(x_{f81} - x_{f71})$ where the i subscripts have been suppressed to simplify the expression and b_{jk} and $\overline{x}_{jk}$ are the regression coefficient and weighted mean of variable i for the jth gender group (m = males, f = females) and the kth year (k = 1971, 1981). Mean effects are summed over the variables indicated in footnote a.

[c] For variable x_i computed as $\overline{x}_{m71}\,(b_{m81} - b_{m71}) - \overline{x}_{f71}\,(b_{f81} - b_{f71})$. Coefficient effects are summed over the variables indicated in footnote a.

[d] Computed as the sum of the means and coefficient effects.

[e] The interaction term is equal to the difference between (1) the change in the differential predicted when the weighted means of the explanatory variables for each group (and year) are substituted into the regression equation for that group (and year) and (2) the sum of the mean and coefficient effects (i.e., Subtotal 1 for blacks and Subtotal 2 for whites).

Similarly, the total effect of changes in the means is obtained by computing the change in the gender differential that would have occurred if the means of all the variables had changed to their 1981 levels (for both genders), while all the coefficients had remained at their 1971 levels. In like manner, the coefficient effects are obtained by calculating the change in the gender differential that would have occurred if the coefficients had changed to their 1981 levels (for both men and women), while the means had remained at their 1971 levels. Since this procedure uses consistent 1971 weights to evaluate both the mean and coefficient effects, the sum of the two will not necessarily equal the change in the predicted gender differential (an example of the "index number problem"). The remainder of the change in the gender differential is assumed to be due to the interaction of changes in means and coefficient.

Previous research has shown that during the 1970s, the entry of women into the majority of male occupations increased (Beller 1985). We too find that the proportion of both black and white women employed in male and integrated jobs increased between 1971 and 1981 (Table 2.4). The increase was particularly substantial for male occupations. The proportion of white women in such jobs rose from 12.8 to 21.1 percent between 1971 and 1981, and the corresponding figures for black women were 11.1 and 17.6 percent. Further, we find an earnings premium for employment in male and integrated jobs (in comparison to female jobs) for all race-gender groups in all years (Table 2.3). The results in Table 2.7 indicate, however, that the *total* effect of occupational changes over the decade was to widen the gender differential in the log of annual earnings by .0545 among whites and .0173 among blacks. The increased entry of women into male (and integrated) occupations did narrow the differential slightly, but the change in the coefficients widened it. The return to being in a male or integrated occupation increased over the period among all race-gender groups (Table 2.3). For both races, however, it increased more for men than for women.[15] This gender difference was larger for whites than for blacks.

Why did the returns to being in a male occupation increase over the period? One possible explanation is an increase in crowding in the female sector. Such an increase would have widened the earnings differential between male and female occupations. The data do not allow a determination of whether supply expanded more rapidly than demand in female jobs, although we do know that employment in the female sector increased considerably over this period. Another possible explanation is the growth in the union-nonunion pay gap during the 1970s (Freeman and Medoff 1984). Since unions are more prevalent in male jobs than in female jobs, a growing union-nonunion differential could help to explain the widening premium for male jobs.

Given that the earnings of workers in male and integrated jobs rose relative to the earnings of workers in female occupations, there are several possible reasons for the greater increase in men's earnings than in women's. First, within the group of occupations identified as predominantly male in 1971, women would tend to be more highly represented in occupations that attracted a large influx of female workers over the 1970s. Their wages would thus be more greatly subject to any supply pressures than would the wages of workers in other male occupations. Second, the increase in the representation of women in male occupations over the 1970s is also likely to have increased the proportion of women in these occupations holding lower-paying, entry-level positions. Third, women's opportunities in the male sector may have been constrained by discrimination or other factors (Reskin and Roos 1987). Finally, since women's gains in the male sector were concentrated in professional and managerial rather than in blue-collar jobs (Beller 1985), women would have benefited less than men from any increase in the union wage premium during this period. Changes in both the coefficients and means of the demographic variables worked to lower the gender differential among both whites and blacks. The gender differential in the returns to marital status declined over the period for both races, reducing the male advantage. In addition, among whites, although the negative effect of children on women's earnings remained roughly constant, the positive effect of children on men's earnings decreased. These shifts in coefficients are consistent with some reduction in gender differences in specialization between the home and the market. Changes in the means of demographic variables that reduced the gender differential were decreases across all race-gender groups in the percentage married (with spouse present) and in the average number of children.

Relative returns to education shifted unfavorably for women over the decade, particularly among whites. An evaluation of the educational splines shows that, among whites, this pattern was due to adverse changes in the returns to years of high school. These returns were about the same for men and women in 1971, but increased by nearly two percentage points for men and fell by one-half a percentage point for women over the following ten years. (Returns to a college education fell for both genders, but were approximately the same for men and women in each year.) This unfavorable shift in the relative returns to education serves to widen the earnings gender differential more than any other single factor we have considered. Among blacks, the extent to which the returns to education for women exceeded those of men diminished over the decade. Returns to a college education fell for black women but not for black men; nevertheless, these returns were still higher in 1981 for black women than for any other group. Although returns to years of high school increased for both men and women, the increase was somewhat higher for men. Overall, the contribution of educational coefficients to widening the gender differential in earnings over the decade was considerably smaller for blacks than for whites.

Although we are measuring potential rather than actual experience, as noted above, controlling for the number of children has been shown to be a good proxy for work force interruptions. Moreover, gender differences in actual experience between 1971 and 1981 appear more likely to have decreased than to have grown. Thus, it is surprising that, among whites, the relative returns to (potential) experience fell for women, widening the differential. It should be borne in mind, however, that when younger women gain more rapidly relative to their male counterparts than do older women, it will appear in cross-sectional data as if the relative return to experience has declined for women. Estimates presented in Table 2.6 suggest that, among whites, young women have indeed been making more rapid gains than older women.

Among whites, the total effect of changes in means and coefficients of time spent in the labor force over the year was to increase the gender differential. On the one hand, changes in means lowered the differential. An increase in the proportion of women working part-time relative to men working part-time was counterbalanced by an increase in the female-male ratio of weeks worked. On the other hand, the effect of changes in coefficients was positive and somewhat larger than the negative effect of changes in means. Although the coefficient on the log of weeks worked (LNWW) shifted upward for both sexes, the increase was greater for men than for women. In contrast to the case among whites, changes in time inputs over the period lowered the gender differential substantially among blacks. This change was primarily due to a decrease in part-time work and an increase in weeks worked among women, with opposite changes occurring among men.

Of all the changes in variables over the decade, the change in the constant term contributed the most to narrowing the earnings differential between white women and white men. The gender difference in the constant term was virtually eliminated by 1981. Among blacks, the gender difference in the constant term remained large, despite a considerable reduction over the period. This shift in the constant term is difficult to interpret substantively. The constant term represents the expected wage of an individual with 0 values for all the variables included in the regression equation. Since it is not possible to assign primary responsibility for this shift to any specific variable (or variables), the shift must simply be interpreted as a decline in discrimination that cannot be associated with a relative increase in the returns to any particular characteristic.

Overall, changes in the means and coefficients contributed about equally to the decline in the gender differential among whites (subtotal 1 in Table 2.7). The results for the contribution of λ show that, as noted earlier, the gains for white women were to some extent masked by changes in selectivity bias over the period. Changes in means played a somewhat larger role among blacks, but even for this group, changes in coefficients explained 27 percent of the reduction in the gender differential. These findings in turn suggest that discrimination against women, as conventionally measured, declined between 1971 and 1981. As noted above, the same conclusion is supported by the fully adjusted female-male earnings ratios presented in Table 2.5.

2.1.6. Conclusion

The two major objectives in this section have been to clarify the trends in relative earnings by gender over the 1971 to 1981 period and to understand the reasons for those trends. The first major finding is that, overall, the increase in women's earnings relative to men's over that decade was greater than has been recognized. An analysis of wage offers results in substantially higher estimates of the earnings gains of white women relative to white men than does a more conventional analysis of observed wages (that is, an analysis uncorrected for selectivity bias) - specifically, an increase of 23 percent, as opposed to 15 percent, in the female-male earnings ratio. Among blacks, on the other hand, the effect of the selectivity bias correction is to lower the estimated increase in the earnings ratio from 25 to 13 percent. Since the coefficients on the selectivity variable were not significant for blacks, however, these results must be viewed with caution.

The common focus on the median annual earnings of year-round, full-time workers is partly accountable for the now-widespread view that the ratio of women's earnings to men's did not increase during the 1970s. Using a different method to adjust for time inputs (hours and weeks worked), we find, on the contrary, that the earnings of both black and white women rose relative to men with similar time inputs over the decade. Specifically, among blacks the earnings ratio rose by 11 percent (OLS regressions), and among whites it rose by between 9 percent (OLS regressions) and 17 percent (regressions corrected for selectivity bias).

Second, we examined the determinants of the observed changes. On the one hand, a variety of factors contributed to the narrowing of the earnings gap over this period. The findings suggest declining gender role specialization. For both blacks and whites, gender differences in the return to being married (with spouse present) decreased, and for whites, gender differences in the effect of children on earnings also narrowed. Another development benefiting women of both races, but particularly whites, was a large decrease in the gender differential in the constant term of the regression equations.

Not large enough to outweigh those influences, but still important, were some changes that adversely affected women's relative earnings. Perhaps surprisingly, the total effect of variables reflecting the gender composition of the individual's occupation was to widen the gender differential over the period. We found that although women increased their representation in male jobs and integrated jobs, the return to such employment decreased for women relative to men. This finding appears particularly important from a policy perspective. Another factor working to increase the differential, especially among whites, was a decline in the relative return to education for women.

Overall, we found that shifts in both the means and the coefficients of the explanatory variables played a role in reducing the gender earnings differential over the decade. These findings are consistent with a decrease in gender discrimination, as conventionally measured. There is evidence to suggest that the success of Equal Employment Opportunity laws may have contributed to this decline (Beller 1982a; 1982b). But changes in women's aspirations, as well as other unobservable factors, may also have played a role. We are inclined toward the view that both women's improved qualifications (see also O'Neill 1985; Smith and Ward 1984) and reduced discrimination against them contributed to a narrowing of the earnings gap during the 1970s. A similar process may well explain women's continued progress in the 1980s.

Our results also indicate that, among whites, relative gains were larger for young women than for older women. Published data suggest that this pattern has continued into the 1980s (Blau and Ferber 1987). If the younger women hold on to this advantage as they age - and our data suggest they may well do so - the relative earnings of white women will rise substantially in the future as more recent cohorts with relatively higher earnings replace earlier cohorts. The next section shows that the increase in relative earnings of women that were expected at the time this research on the 1970s were undertaken did indeed take place and explores the reasons for the female gains that occurred as well as their time pattern - i.e., faster increases in the 1980s than in the 1990s.

2.2. 1980s and 1990s *(based on a paper with Lawrence M. Kahn)*

After thirty years of relative constancy, the gender pay gap in the United States narrowed substantially in the 1980s. For example, published tabulations from the Census Bureau on the median annual earnings of year-round, full-time workers indicate that the female-to-male ratio rose from 59.7% to 68.7% between 1979 and 1989 - 9.0 percentage points. However, the rate of convergence slowed markedly in the following decade, with the ratio rising only to 72.2% by 1999 - 3.5 percentage points. As we saw in the previous section, the focus on year-round, full-time workers may have understated the 1970s gains; nonetheless these are dwarfed by the subsequent progress over the 1980s. In other work (see Blau and Kahn 1997), we have examined the 1980s gains in considerable detail.

In this section, we summarize those results and shed light on several possible sources of slowing convergence in the 1990s. In contrast to the the previous section, which was based on Current Population Survey (CPS) data, for the analysis of the 1980s and 1990s trends, we employ data from the Michigan Panel Study of Income Dynamics (PSID), the only nationally representative data base that contains information on workers' actual labor market experience. Labor market experience has been shown to be an extremely important factor in explaining the gender pay gap (Mincer and Polachek 1974) and its trends (for example, Blau and Kahn 1997; O'Neill and Polachek 1993). We focus on a number of hypotheses that might help to explain the slower progress of women in the 1990s.

First, relative improvements in women's measured characteristics or increases in their labor market commitment may have proceeded at a slower pace in the 1990s than in the 1980s. A slackening of relative gains in experience seems plausible, for example, given the reduction in the rate of increase of female labor force participation rates between the 1980s and 1990s (Blau, Ferber, and Winkler 2002, Chapter 4), although we note that it is not possible to directly infer trends in women's average experience levels from trends in their participation rates (see, for example, Goldin 1990). Another possibility is that discrimination narrowed at a slower pace in the 1990s. Views on this are mixed. On the one hand, the General Accounting Office (GAO) and members of Congress have raised concerns about glass ceilings in the late 1990s (GAO 2001; Offices of John D. Dingell and Carolyn B. Maloney 2002). On the other hand, O'Neill (2003) has argued that, at least within occupations, we have largely achieved pay parity between men and women, implying that the slowing in convergence was inevitable.[16] We will provide some suggestive evidence on glass ceilings.

Other explanations center around the possibility that demand- and supply-side shifts played out differently in the 1980s and 1990s, resulting in a larger decrease in the gender pay gap as well as a larger increase in wage inequality among men in the 1980s than in the 1990s. On the one hand, increases in the prices of labor market skills such as experience, for which women have a deficit, are expected to raise the gender pay gap or reduce the rate at which it falls (Blau and Kahn 1997). These skill price increases could in principle have proceeded more rapidly in the 1990s than the 1980s, helping to retard the rate of wage convergence. However, wage inequality in fact grew more rapidly in the 1980s than the 1990s (Autor, Katz, and Kearney 2005b), making such an explanation unlikely. On the other hand, Welch (2000), for example, pointed to a technology-based rise in the demand for intellectual skills relative to physical strength, which benefited women as a group relative to men and high-skilled compared to low-skilled men. In this view, the slowing increase in male inequality that occurred in the 1990s is consistent with a tapering off of these demand shifts and thus with slower relative progress of women.

Finally, labor force selection may cause changes in observed wage differentials between men and women. Data on wages are available only for a self-selected group of labor force participants. The possibility of selection bias (Heckman 1979) is of particular concern since women's labor force participation grew more rapidly in one period (the 1980s) than in the other (the 1990s).

After examining the overall patterns in the trends in the gender pay gap over the 1980s and 1990s, we use an accounting technique developed by Juhn, Murphy, and Pierce (1991) to decompose the reduction in the gender wage differential in each period into a portion due to changes in the measured characteristics of women compared to men; changes in the prices of measured characteristics; and changes in the unexplained gender pay gap. We then consider a number of possible explanations for the slowing convergence in the unexplained gap identified in the decomposition analysis as the major factor accounting for the difference in trends in the two periods. As explained above, we use PSID data for this analysis because it is the only nationally representative data for the United States that includes information on actual labor market experience for the full age range of the population.

2.2.1. *Trends in the Gender Pay Gap: Overall Patterns*

Table 2.8

Overview of Wage Inequality Trends, 1979, 1989, and 1998

				Changes (Average Annual Change X 10)	
	1979	1989	1998	1979-89	1989-98
Men					
Std. Dev. of Log Wage	0.506	0.569	0.601	0.063	0.036
90-50 Differential	0.516	0.630	0.761	0.114	0.145
50-10 Differential	0.654	0.787	0.700	0.133	-0.096
Sample Size	2816	2894	2336	—	—
Women					
Std. Dev.	0.484	0.543	0.566	0.060	0.026
90-50 Differential	0.603	0.646	0.675	0.043	0.031
50-10 Differential	0.534	0.719	0.696	0.186	-0.025
Sample Size	1922	2290	1804	—	—
Gender Log Wage Differential	0.459	0.295	0.227	-0.164	-0.075
Implied Female/Male Pay Ratio	0.632	0.745	0.797	0.113	0.058
Mean Female Percentile in the Male Wage Distribution[a]	24.31	35.16	38.93	10.85	4.19

Notes: Table contains full-time, nonfarm wage and salary workers aged 18-65 years from the Michigan Panel Study of Income Dynamics. Wages are computed as annual earnings divided by annual work hours. Years refer to the period during which income was earned. The Implied Female/Male Pay Ratio is (exp (ln w_f)/exp(ln w_m)), where ln w_f and ln w_m are, respectively, the average log female and log male wage.

[a] Computed by assigning each woman a percentile ranking in the indicated year's male wage distribution and calculating the female mean of these percentiles.

We now turn to the trends in the gender pay gap based on our PSID data for 1979, 1989, and 1998. These are shown in Table 2.8, which also contains information for these years on male and female wage inequality. Since our two time periods are of unequal length (ten and nine years), for comparability, we express changes over each period as the average annual change (uncompounded) multiplied by ten. Consistent with published data, we find that the pay gap fell substantially faster in the 1980s than in the 1990s: the gender differential in log wages fell 0.164 log points from 1979 to 1989 compared to a ten year rate of decline of .075 log points from 1989 to 1998. The implied female-male pay ratio rose from 63% in 1979 to 74% in 1989 and 80% in 1998. Wage inequality as measured by the standard deviation of log wages or the 90–50 and 50–10 gaps in log wages rose considerably in the 1980s both among men and among women; in the 1990s, 90–50 gaps continued to rise, while the 50–10 gap fell. The net effect on the standard deviation was a slowing increase in the 1990s compared to the 1980s. These inequality patterns among men and among women are consistent with Current Population Survey (CPS) data, as analyzed in an earlier version of this paper (Blau and Kahn 2004) and in Autor, Katz, and Kearney (2005b).

Figure 2.1, which displays the gender wage gap at the indicated percentiles of the male and female wage distributions, shows that the gender wage gap fell substantially throughout the wage distribution in the 1980s, with much smaller declines in the 1990s. The figure also indicates little wage convergence at the top of the distribution in the 1990s, a finding consistent with the concerns raised by the GAO report cited above. We will examine this issue below controlling for gender differences in measured characteristics by using quantile regression techniques.

Figure 2.1

Gender Gap, Log Hourly Earnings, by Percentile, Full-Time Workers, PSID

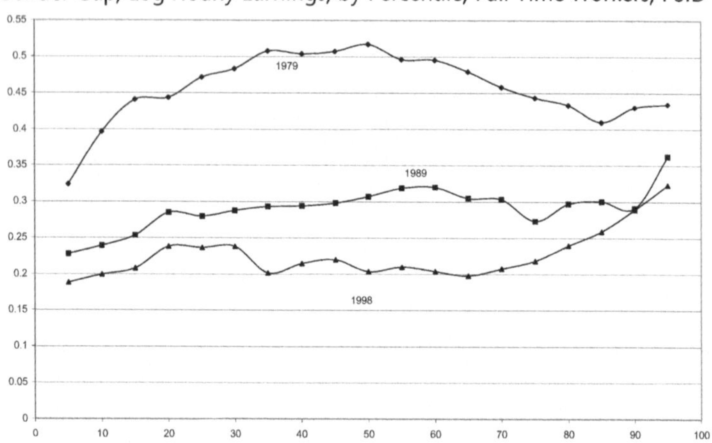

Rising skill prices may induce changes in the gender pay gap that are unrelated to women's relative qualifications or to the extent of discrimination against women. A simple measure that controls for such changes in wage structure is the mean female percentile in the male wage distribution. The female percentiles presented in Table 2.8 indicate that the behavior of this indicator was similar to the gender pay ratio: women moved up in the male pay distribution in both periods, but the pace of this upward progression was slower in the 1990s than in the 1980s. On average, women out-earned 24% of men in 1979, 35% in 1989, and 39% in 1998.

2.2.2. Decomposing the Changes in the Gender Wage Gap

2.2.2.1. Analytical Framework

In the previous section, focusing on the 1970s, the trends in the gender pay gap were analyzed with a decomposition derived from the classic Oaxaca-Blinder decomposition. Subsequently, Juhn, Murphy, and Pierce (1991) (hereafter, JMP) developed an alternative decomposition, which, as explained below, distinguishes between "gender-specific" factors and the overall impact of wage structure in influencing the trends in the gender pay gap. The analysis in this section utilizes this newer technique, which was previously implemented to analyze trends in the U.S. gender pay gap in the 1980s by Blau and Kahn (1997). Using the JMP decompostion, we identify, in an accounting sense, the contribution to changes over time in the gender pay gap of (i) changes in the measured characteristics of women compared to men; (ii) changes in the prices of measured characteristics; (iii) changes in the unexplained gap (corrected for the impact of changes in the prices of unmeasured characteristics); and (iv) changes in the prices of unmeasured characteristics.

The basic insight of the JMP framework is that, since prices change over time in ways that may advantage or disadvantage women, it is useful to identify the impact of gender specific factors like the relative qualifications of women and discrimination against them separately from the impact of wage structure (or price changes that are common to both sexes). Intuitively, if, as the human capital model suggests, women have less experience than men, on average, the higher the return to experience, all else equal, the higher will be the gender gap in pay. Similarly, if, due to discrimination or other factors, women tend to work in different occupations and industries from men, the higher the return to working in the male sector, the larger will be the gender pay gap. This reasoning suggests that rising wage inequality due to increasing returns to skill and sector would adversely affect women's relative pay. On the other hand, a rising relative demand for intellectual skills relative to physical strength (Welch 2000) or for white-collar relative to blue-collar workers (Berman, Bound, and Griliches 1994) due to technological advances may benefit women as a group relative to men but also increase male wage inequality (see also Blau and Kahn 1997).

Taking into account these alternative possibilities, rising wage inequality might be expected to have opposing negative and positive effects on women's relative wages, with the dominant effect being an empirical question. In terms of the JMP decomposition, the negative effects of adverse price changes are captured in the components that measure the impact of changes in measured and unmeasured prices on changes in the gender pay gap, while the impact of technological change and other factors that potentially positively affect the relative demand for female workers will be one of the possible factors included in the effect of changes in the unexplained portion of the gender pay gap.

Institutional changes are an additional factor that can affect the return to skill but may have gender-specific effects as well. For example, de-unionization likely raises wage inequality and the price of skills, since unions compress wages (DiNardo, Fortin, and Lemieux 1996). One might therefore expect that de-unionization would raise the gender pay gap by making wage floors less prevalent. But in the 1980s, the unionization rate fell more for men than for women, actually helping to explain the falling gender pay gap (Blau and Kahn 1997). We can directly assess the latter impact of de-unionization, since we can observe it directly. However, any more general effects of de-unionization through spill-over or threat effects on the nonunion sector will not be measured by our analysis.[17]

Using the JMP framework, we begin with a male wage equation,

$$Y_{it} = X_{it}B_t + \sigma_t\theta_{it} \tag{1}$$

where Y_{it} is the log of wages; X_{it} is a vector of explanatory variables; B_t is a vector of coefficients; θ_{it} is a standardized residual (that is, with mean zero and variance 1 for each year); and σ_t is the residual standard deviation of male wages (the level of male residual wage inequality) for that year.[18] The difference in the gender pay gap between two years 0 and 1 (1979–89 and 1989–98) can be decomposed into four components (for additional details, see Blau and Kahn 2004 and Juhn, Murphy, and Pierce 1991):

$$\text{Observed X's Effect} = (\Delta X_1 - \Delta X_0)B_1 \tag{2}$$

$$\text{Observed Prices Effect} = \Delta X_0(B_1 - B_0) \tag{3}$$

$$\text{Gap Effect} = (\Delta\theta_1 - \Delta\theta_0)\sigma_1 \tag{4}$$

$$\text{Unobserved Prices Effect} = \Delta\theta_0(\sigma_1 - \sigma_0) \tag{5}$$

where a Δ prefix signifies the average male-female difference for the variable immediately following.

The Observed X's Effect reflects the contribution of changing male-female differences in observed labor market qualifications (X). The Observed Prices Effect reflects the impact of changes in prices of observed labor market characteristics, as indexed by male prices. The Gap Effect measures the effect of changing differences in the relative positions of men and women in the male residual wage distribution, including the effect of an improvement in women's unmeasured characteristics or a reduction in the extent of discrimination against women. Finally, the Unobserved Prices Effect reflects the contribution to the change in the gender gap that would result if the percentile rankings of the female wage residuals had remained the same and only the extent of male residual wage inequality had changed. It measures changes in the female penalty to being below average in the distribution of male residuals. The sum of the gap and unobserved prices effects is equal to the change in the "unexplained" differential, which is commonly taken as an estimate of discrimination in a conventional decomposition but may also reflect unmeasured productivity differences between men and women. This decomposition has come under a variety of criticisms, particularly the decomposition of the residual (for discussion, see Blau and Kahn 2004). However, as shown below, our conclusions about the sources of the slowdown in the convergence of the gender pay gap in the 1990s are not affected by whether or not one decomposes the residual.

2.2.2.2. Data and Specifications

Three waves of the PSID are employed to compare the rate of convergence in the 1980s and the 1990s - 1980, 1990, and 1999[19] - allowing us to compute average hourly earnings for 1979, 1989, and 1998. The three survey years span the period of interest, and were also years of economic expansion, likely sharing similar overall macroeconomic conditions.[20] We initially restrict our analysis of wages to workers who were, as of the survey date, full-time, nonagricultural employees age 18–65; the self-employed were excluded. The analyses focus on full-time workers in the basic models in order to identify a group of men and women that is as homogeneous as possible with respect to labor market commitment. However, in some analyses below, we do include part-time workers in order to examine selection issues. To maximize sample size, we use both the PSID's random sample and its poverty over sample populations and, in all analyses, employ the sampling weights supplied in the PSID files. Patterns were similar when we restricted ourselves to the random sample. The wage measure is average real hourly earnings during the previous calendar year expressed in 1983 dollars using the Personal Consumption Expenditures deflator from the National Product Accounts. We exclude individuals earning less than \$1 or more than \$250 per hour in 1983 dollars. (Blau and Kahn (2004) contains details on the construction of the key experience variables.)

Two specifications are employed in implementing the decomposition. The "human capital" specification includes controls for race, education, and experience. The race variable is primarily a control. Sample sizes were insufficient to perform separate analyses for nonwhites, although results were very similar when we confined the sample to whites only. Education is measured by three variables: years of schooling, a dummy for college degree only, and a dummy for advanced degree. Experience includes full-time and part-time experience and their squares.[21]

The second "full" specification augments the human capital variables with a collective bargaining coverage indicator and a set of 19 occupation and 25 industry dummy variables that include some two-digit and some one-digit categories, depending on cell size. Controlling for sector in this way is potentially interesting, since existing research finds that much of the gender gap is associated with location of employment (Blau 1977; Groshen 1991; Bayard, Hellerstein, Neumark, and Troske 2003). Further, factors such as de-unionization and occupation and industry shifts clearly in part reflect changing demand for labor, and this specification allows us to examine the importance of these factors (in an accounting sense). We thus present some results controlling for these variables and, moreover, specify the categories in as much detail as we can in order to make the results as informative as possible. However, the sector variables are also potentially endogenous, as they themselves are likely to be affected by relative wages through both worker supply and employer demand decisions. Further, access to occupations, industries, and unionized workplaces may be affected by discrimination. We thus present results for both specifications but interpret the "full" specification cautiously.

As noted, to the extent that supply and demand shifts alter the extent of gender differences in occupation and industry, the direct effects of such shifts will, in an accounting sense, be captured in the portion of the change in the gender wage gap that is due to changes in gender differences in occupations and industries. However, to the extent, for example, that aggregate supply and demand shifts benefit women relative to men (as suggested by the discussion above), they should arguably raise the relative wages of women wherever they are employed. Such broader effects of supply and demand shifts will be included in the unexplained gap. We have not controlled for marital status or number of children, although they may be important factors influencing the pay gap. An alternative would have been to include them as productivity characteristics. Such an approach is problematic, however, because these variables may proxy higher skills for men but lower skills for women, even controlling for actual labor market experience (see, for example, Korenman and Neumark 1991; Waldfogel 1998). The approach we have followed clarifies the interpretation of the estimated impact of differences in labor market skills, and also allows marital and parental status to be endogenous.

2.2.2.3. Empirical Results

Tables 2.9a–b show the results of the JMP decomposition of changes in the gender pay gaps across our two periods: 1979–89 and 1989–98. We first consider the descriptive statistics presented in 2.9a and then the full decomposition results in 2.9b. Table 2.9a shows similar patterns of rising residual inequality for both men and women. The residual 90–10 gap increased more rapidly in the 1980s than in the 1990s, as did overall wage inequality (see Table 2.8). The similar trends in residual inequality for men and women give us some confidence in the validity of the JMP procedure's assumption of a common labor market for men and women. However, as noted above, supply and demand shifts that affect men and women differently will be captured in the unexplained portion of the differential and provide a possible explanation for changes in the unexplained gender pay gap over time.

In both specifications, the average female residual fell dramatically in absolute value in the 1980s but was virtually constant over the 1990s. Our results indicate that, controlling for the human capital variables, including actual labor market experience, the gender wage ratio increased from 70.8% to 81.8% between 1979 and 1989, and was roughly the same in 1998 at 81.2%. In the full specification, which adds controls for industry, occupation, and collective bargaining coverage, the ratio rose from 81.6% in 1979 to 91.0% in 1989 and remained at about 91% in 1998. The mean female percentile in the residual distribution, a measure that, in the context of the JMP framework, is independent of possible adverse shifts in the prices of unobservables, followed a similar pattern, rising sharply in the 1980s and only very slightly in the 1990s.

Table 2.9a

Decomposition of Changes in the Gender Pay Gap, 1979-89 and 1989-98 – Descriptive Statistics

	Human Capital	Full
Male Residual 90-10 Differential[a]		
1979	1.028	0.916
1989	1.124	1.028
1998	1.205	1.047
Female Residual 90-10 Differential[b]		
1979	0.939	0.845
1989	1.064	0.922
1998	1.152	0.979
Mean Female Residual from Male Wage Regression		
1979	-0.346	-0.204
1989	-0.200	-0.094
1998	-0.209	-0.094
Implied Gender Wage Ratio (Adjusted for Measured Xs)		
1979	0.708	0.816
1989	0.818	0.910
1998	0.812	0.911
Mean Female Residual Percentile		
1979	27.00	34.57
1989	36.71	43.15
1998	37.68	44.18

[a] Residuals from a male wage regression.
[b] Residuals from a female wage regression.
Notes: The human capital specification includes controls for race, education, and experience. The full specification includes, in addition, controls for occupation, industry, and collective bargaining coverage. See Blau and Kahn (2004), Table A2 for variable means and Table A3 for regression results.

Table 2.9b

Decomposition of Changes in the Gender Pay Gap, 1979-89 and 1989-98: Decomposition Results (Average Annual Changes X 10)

	1979-89		1989-98		(1989-98) - (1979-89)	
	Human Capital	Full	Human Capital	Full	Human Capital	Full
Change in Differential (D_1 - D_0)	-0.164	-0.164	-0.075	-0.075	0.089	0.089
Observed X's						
All X's	-0.049	-0.092	-0.056	-0.068	-0.007	0.025
(Standard errors)	(0.003)	(0.005)	(0.003)	(0.005)	(0.004)	(0.007)
Education variables	0.0002	-0.001	-0.035	-0.029	-0.036	-0.028
Experience variables	-0.053	-0.046	-0.019	-0.017	0.034	0.029
Occupation variables	—	-0.029	—	-0.019	—	0.010
Collective Bargaining	—	-0.022	—	-0.007	—	0.014
Industry variables	—	0.003	—	0.005	—	0.002
Observed Prices						
All B's	0.031	0.038	-0.028	-0.006	-0.059	-0.044
(Standard errors)	(0.009)	(0.023)	(0.032)	(0.024)	(0.034)	(0.033)
Education variables	0.004	0.004	0.003	0.002	-0.002	-0.002
Experience variables	0.025	0.022	-0.032	-0.027	-0.057	-0.048
Occupation variables	—	-0.018	—	0.054	—	0.072
Collective Bargaining	—	0.007	—	0.000	—	-0.008
Industry variables	—	0.022	—	-0.036	—	-0.058
Unexplained Differential	-0.146	-0.109	0.009	-0.001	0.155	0.108
Gap Effect	-0.18	-0.128	-0.006	-0.007	0.174	0.121
(Approximate standard errors)	(0.016)	(0.014)	(0.019)	(0.016)	(0.025)	(0.021)
Unobserved Prices	0.035	0.019	0.016	0.007	-0.019	-0.012
(Approximate standard errors)	(0.007)	(0.004)	(0.005)	(0.002)	(0.009)	(0.005)

Notes: The human capital specification includes controls for race, education and experience. The full specification includes, in addition, controls for occupation, industry, and collective bargaining coverage. See Blau and Kahn (2004), Table A2 for variable means and Table A3 for regression results. Standard errors of the All X's Effect and All B's Effect, and approximate standard errors of the Gap Effect and Unmeasured Price Effect computed using results from the Appendix to Datta Gupta, Oaxaca, and Smith (2006).

Table 2.9b shows the decompositions of the changes in the gender pay gap over the 1980s and the 1990s. Standard errors for the measured X and measured B effects, as well as approximate standard errors for the residual components, are based on the Appendix to Datta Gupta, Oaxaca, and Smith (2006). The 1980s decomposition results are very similar to those from our earlier work, which covered the 1979–88 period (Blau and Kahn 1997). Specifically, the human capital specification shows that women improved their relative experience levels in the 1980s, accounting for a 0.053 log point fall in the gender pay gap, or about 1/3 of the total decline. In addition, women moved up the male residual distribution, an effect contributing to a highly significant 0.180 log point decrease in the gender pay gap, or more than the actual decline. However, both measured prices and unmeasured prices underwent statistically significant changes to women's detriment, and together they served to increase the gender pay gap by 0.065 log points. The full specification for the 1980s yields a larger observed X effect and a gap effect that is smaller in absolute value, suggesting that more of the observed change in the gender pay gap can be explained with the addition of the occupation, industry, and union controls. In addition to the upgrading in female labor market experience, women's occupations improved, and de-unionization had a greater negative effect on men's than on women's wages, since men lost union jobs at a faster rate than women did. These changes in the All X's and Gap Effects between specifications for the 1980s were statistically significant. Measured and unmeasured price effects continued to raise the gender pay gap overall in the full specification, and were statistically significant or marginally significant overall, although occupational price effects were negative.[22]

Comparing the JMP decompositions for the 1980s and the 1990s can reveal some of the sources of the slowdown in the convergence of the gender pay gap. Using either the human capital or the full specification, we find that women upgraded their human capital as measured by education and experience to a similar degree in the two decades: for example, in the human capital specification, the difference in the All X's effect was only 0.007 log points, although it was marginally significant. In the 1980s, women's human capital upgrading consisted entirely of rising experience; moreover, consistent with speculations based on aggregate labor force participation rates, decreases in the gender gap in experience contributed considerably less to wage convergence in the 1990s than in the 1980s. The gender gap in years of full-time experience decreased by .7 years between 1989 and 1998, compared to 2.3 years between 1979 and 1989. However, rising relative educational attainment of women played a much larger role in the 1990s, and thus the sum of the effects of education and experience was similar in the 1980s and 1990s. Although men had an edge in the incidence of college degrees in earlier years, by 1998 the incidence of college degrees was slightly (1.2 percentage points) higher among women in our sample of full-time workers.

The full specification shows that, while occupational upgrading and de-unionization contributed to women's relative wage gains in both periods, these factors had larger effects in the 1980s than the 1990s, explaining roughly 0.024 log points of the 0.089 faster closing of the gender pay gap in the 1980s, or about 27 percent.[23] Occupational shifts were similar in a number of respects in both periods. Women increased their relative representation in managerial occupations and in professional jobs (both overall and excluding K–12 teaching) and reduced their relative representation in clerical and service jobs at about the same pace in the two decades. However, the gender difference in representation in craft and operator jobs declined more rapidly in the 1980s than the 1990s. This was because men moved out of (or lost) these jobs at a faster rate in the earlier decade. The results for collective bargaining coverage reflect a slowing pace of de-unionization for both men and women in the 1990s compared to the 1980s, with a smaller gender difference in the rate of de-unionization in the 1990s. The larger loss of relatively high-paying blue-collar and unionized employment for men in the 1980s than in the 1990s may be indicative of larger demand shifts favoring women in the 1980s. To the extent that such demand shifts occurred, they would plausibly have affected women's relative pay wherever men and women were employed. We explicitly examine evidence of such demand shifts below.

While more favorable shifts in occupations and collective bargaining coverage for women in the 1980s help to explain some of the faster convergence in that decade, trends in measured and unmeasured prices worked to widen the gender pay gap more in the 1980s than the 1990s. Specifically, trends in measured prices were estimated to slow convergence in the 1980s compared to the 1990s by .059 (human capital specification) to .044 (full specification) log points, although these differences were either only marginally significant or not significant; and trends in unmeasured prices worked to slow convergence in 1980s relative to the 1990s by 0.012 to 0.019 log points, statistically significant differences.

The results in Table 2.9b indicate that the primary factor accounting for the more rapid convergence in women's wages in the 1980s was the gap effect: unexplained gender differences in wages, corrected for unmeasured price changes using the JMP decomposition, narrowed more dramatically in both the human capital and full specifications in the 1980s than in the 1990s; and this highly statistically significant difference is more than sufficient to fully account for the slowdown in convergence in the 1990s. Women's more rapid movements up the male distribution in the 1980s produced gap effects narrowing the gender gap by 0.128 to 0.180 log points, in contrast to the much smaller reductions of 0.006 to 0.007 log points for the 1990s. This contrast means that, controlling for measured human capital and sector, women's relative labor market position improved much more in the 1980s than the 1990s. While it is reassuring to have a measure of changes in the unexplained gap that is corrected for the negative effects on women's wages (in some models) of widening residual male inequality, in fact our conclusions are similar if we restrict ourselves to changes in the conventionally defined unexplained differential also shown in Table 2.9b.[24]

2.2.3. *Factors Contributing to a Slowing Convergence in the Unexplained Gender Pay Gap in the 1990s*

The slower convergence in the unexplained gap in the 1990s than in the 1980s has at least three possible, non-mutually exclusive, substantive sources: first, gender differences in unmeasured characteristics may have narrowed at a faster pace in the 1980s than in the 1990s; second, reductions in labor market discrimination against women may have proceeded at a faster pace in the 1980s than in the 1990s; and finally, demand and supply conditions for women may have changed more favorably in the 1980s than the 1990s. An additional factor to be considered is the change in labor force selectivity among men and women in each period, which may have contributed to an apparent slowdown in wage convergence overall or in the unexplained gender pay gap (or both). Evidence on the impact of selectivity is considered before the assessment of the impact of the other factors since it is important to know whether the differential trends in the unexplained gap persist after adjusting for selection bias.

2.2.3.1. *Changes in Labor Force Selectivity*

Our approach to analyzing the impact of labor force selectivity on trends in the raw and unexplained gender wage gap is to get more information on the wages of those not included in our sample of full-time employed workers. An alternative would be to build sample selection models and then predict the wage offers of those without observed wages (Heckman 1979). However, since the identification conditions required for the successful implementation of such techniques are potentially severe, we take the more modest approach of looking harder for evidence on offers. We proceed in several stages, each of which allows us to include a successively larger portion of the adult population in our calculations.

First, we add all of those with observed hourly earnings in the current year to our base sample of full-time workers; that is, we include part-time workers. Second, for those with no earnings in a given year for which we measure wages, we use the longitudinal nature of the PSID to recover a real hourly earnings observation (using the Personal Consumption Expenditures deflator for the relevant year) from the most recent year for which one is available, with a maximum window of four years. Third, for those for whom we still have no observation on wages under these procedures, in the spirit of Neal and Johnson's (1996) and Neal's (2004) analyses of black-white wage differentials, we include some additional individuals by making assumptions about whether they place above or below the median of real wage offers. Specifically, we assume that individuals with at least a college degree and at least eight years of actual full-time labor market experience had above the median wage offer for their gender, and that those with less than a high school degree and less than eight years of actual full-time labor market experience had below-median wage offers for their gender. Note that this procedure takes into account that, particularly for women, it would not be appropriate to assume that all those outside the wage sample have below-median wage offers, since some women are outside the wage sample due to a high value of home time rather than a low wage offer. Further, our imputations take into account, in addition to education, actual labor market experience, a crucial variable influencing women's wages.[25] If these wage assumptions are valid, we can use median regression to estimate raw (that is, unadjusted) and human-capital-corrected gender differences in wage offers for the expanded group.[26] Koenker and Bassett (1978) showed that under some non-normal distributions, the sample median has a smaller asymptotic variance than the sample mean, suggesting that median regression may well estimate effects of explanatory variables with smaller errors than linear regression.

The fraction of the population included in our base sample of full-time workers is indeed very selective with respect to women, with only 41% of women in the population included in 1979, rising to 50% in 1989 and 53% in 1998.[27]

Moreover, since this group grew very quickly in the 1980s and more slowly in the 1990s, selection may have differentially affected the wage trends during these two periods. In contrast, the inclusion of men in the full-time sample is much greater and fluctuates less over time - including 80–83% of the population over the period. Thus, concerns about selection are centered primarily on women, and results for this group will drive our selection-correction adjustments. When we include all those with earnings in the prior year (that is, part-time workers), the share of all women with wage observations now ranges across years from 68% to 77%, while for men, the sample includes 92–94% of the population. Recovering past observed wages for those without current observations using a four-year window adds 10 to 13 percentage points to female coverage and 4 to 5 percentage points to male coverage. Finally, making our above- and below-median imputations for selected individuals without present or recovered past wage observations leads to very high rates of coverage of the population: fully 86–91% of women and 96–98% of men are now covered. Not only is the coverage within a given year much closer for men and women than under less inclusive definitions of the sample, but the increase in female coverage over time for the expanded sample – 4.3 percentage points (1979–89) and 0.4 percentage points (1989–98) – is much less than for the full-time employed sample – 8.7 percentage points (1979–89) and 2.8 percentage points (1989–98).

Table 2.10 shows median log wage gaps (panel A) and the changes in these gaps (panel B) for the four samples described above. Two estimates for each year are presented: the raw (unadjusted) gap, and the gap controlling for human capital. Panels A.I and B.I give our findings based on OLS regressions for full-time workers (repeated here for comparison). Panels A.II and B.II report our findings based on median (quantile .50) regressions estimated on the indicated samples. The raw gap is the difference between predicted median male and female log wages based on the estimated median regression coefficients from separate male and female regressions under the human capital specification and the actual male and female means of the explanatory variables.[28] The median gender log wage gap controlling for human capital is the difference in predicted median male and female log wages when both the male and female median regressions are evaluated at the female means.

As may be seen in panel A, median raw and human capital-corrected pay gaps for the sample of full-time employed workers are similar to those obtained using OLS regressions. Within each year, the size of the raw pay gap grows as we add individuals with less attachment to the labor force. Inspection of the predicted raw medians indicates that, on average, those included in the full-time employed sample are a positively selected group compared to those added to form our most inclusive sample (d). Since we add considerably more women than men and the added women had lower relative wages than the added men, the raw pay gap widens.[29]

Table 2.10 provides some indirect evidence on the potential impact of selection on the slowdown in convergence in the gender pay gap in the 1990s. Focusing on a comparison of the trends for the medians for the full-time employed sample and the most inclusive of the three expanded samples, we see that the raw gap closed more slowly in the 1980s for the expanded sample (0.153 log points) than for the full-time employed sample (0.174 log points). Similarly, convergence in the unexplained gap was also slower for the expanded sample (0.132 log points) than for full-time employed workers (0.158 log points).

The results imply that, due to sample selection, the 1980s gains in women's relative wage offers were overstated. At first glance it might be expected that using the observed wages of workers with full-time jobs should have caused us to understate the gains, since the female full-time work force was growing substantially over the 1980s, and median wage offers were lower among those without full-time jobs than among the full-time work force. The key to understanding why the gap in the selectivity-corrected offers closed more slowly than the gap in the observed wage offers in the 1980s lies in the changes in the degree of selectivity of the women included in the full-time sample (group a) as the female labor force grew. The results suggest that female labor force growth over this period was positively selected,[30] and this is indeed consistent with considerable evidence on female labor force participation trends. For example, Juhn and Murphy (1997) found that employment gains for married women over the 1970s and 1980s were largest for wives of middle- and high-wage men who themselves tended to be more skilled.[31] This pattern is in turn related to the rising returns to skills over this period, which drew high-skilled women into the labor force. These findings suggest that this positive selection characterized not only the observable characteristics of women in the labor force (as reflected in our results for the raw gap) but also their unobserved characteristics (as reflected in our results for the unexplained gap).

The selection adjustments had less impact for the 1990s, as might be expected based on the slower growth in the female labor force for that period. Convergence in the raw gap was somewhat faster in the expanded sample, where the gender gap fell by 0.100 log points, than in the full-time employed sample, where it decreased by 0.087 log points. This suggests that labor force growth over this period was negatively selected and may reflect the large entry of relatively low-

Table 2.10

Changes in Gender Pay Gaps at the Mean for Full-time Workers and at the Median Under Different Sample Inclusion Rules

	Raw Gap	Gap Controlling for Human Capital	Raw Gap	Gap Controlling for Human Capital	Raw Gap	Gap Controlling for Human Capital
A. Gender Pay Gaps	1979		1989		1998	
I. Mean (Full-time Employed Workers)	0.459	0.346	0.295	0.200	0.227	0.209
II. Median, Sample Inclusion Rule:						
a) Full Time Employed Workers	0.479	0.366	0.305	0.208	0.227	0.201
b) All with Hourly Earnings Observations	0.521	0.346	0.389	0.222	0.318	0.226
c) All with Hourly Earnings Observations in the Last Four Years	0.546	0.351	0.424	0.235	0.343	0.229
d) c) + those with (16+ yrs Educ and 8+ yrs Exp) or (<12 yrs Educ and < 8yrs Exp)	0.620	0.385	0.467	0.253	0.377	0.236
B. Chages in the Gender Pay Gaps	(Average Annual Changes X 10) 1979-1989		1989-1998		1989-98) - (1979-89)	
I. Mean (Full-time Employed Workers)	-0.164	-0.146	-0.075	0.009	0.089	0.155
II. Median, Sample Inclusion Rule:						
a) Full Time Employed Workers	-0.174	-0.158	-0.087	-0.008	0.087	0.150
b) All with Hourly Earnings Observations	-0.132	-0.124	-0.080	0.005	0.052	0.128
c) All with Hourly Earnings Observations in the Last Four Years	-0.121	-0.116	-0.090	-0.007	0.031	0.110
d) c) + those with (16+ yrs Educ and 8+ yrs Exp) or (<12 yrs Educ and < 8yrs Exp)	-0.153	-0.132	-0.100	-0.019	0.054	0.113

Source: PSID. Raw Gap is the difference in predicted mean or median log male and log female wage, which is $H_m X_m - H_f X_f$, where H_m and H_f are respectively vectors of male and female mean (Row I) or median (Rows IIa-d) human capital log wage regression coefficients and X_m and X_f are respectively male and female means for the vector of explanatory variables, which include a dummy for white, years of schooling, dummies for college degree and advanced degree, and part-time and full-time actual experience and their squares. The Gap Controlling For Human Capital is $(H_m - H_f)X_f$.

skilled, female single-family heads during this decade, about which there is a sizable literature related to changes in welfare laws (for example, Blank 2000; Meyer and Rosenbaum 2001). Reductions in the gender wage gap controlling for human capital were also slightly faster in the expanded sample (0.019 log points) than in the full-time sample (0.008 points).

Can sample selectivity help explain the slowdown in convergence between male and female wages in the 1990s? Table 2.10 suggests that it is indeed part of the explanation. Specifically, the last two columns of panel B compare changes in the raw and human capital-corrected gender pay gap in the 1990s and the 1980s. Looking at trends for the medians for our most restricted sample, the full-time employed, the raw pay gap converged 0.087 log points more slowly in the 1990s than in the 1980s, and the difference between the two decades in the human capital-corrected pay gap was even greater, closing 0.150 log points more slowly in the 1990s than in the 1980s. However, in our most inclusive sample (d), the raw gap closed 0.054 log points more slowly in the 1990s, and the human capital-corrected gap closed 0.113 log points more slowly. The comparison across the two samples implies that as much as 0.033 log points (that is, 0.087–0.054) of the 0.087 log point slower closing of the raw pay gap among the full-time employed in the 1990s was due to sample selection. Table 2.10 also shows a comparable effect of selection on the human capital-corrected gender pay gap: 0.037 log points of the 0.150 log point slower closing of the human capital-corrected gender pay gap in the 1990s was due to sample selection. This implies that sample selection can explain about 25% (0.037/0.150) of the slowdown in the narrowing of the unexplained pay gap (in the human capital specification) that we observe among the full-time employed. For the entire 1979–98 period, Table 2.10 implies that the human capital-corrected gap fell 0.165 log points when the analysis does not control for selection but 0.149 when it does. Thus, selection bias can explain about 10% of the closing of the ceteris paribus gender pay gap over the 1980s and 1990s taken together.[32] While our computations imply that selection appreciably affects the 1980s–1990s comparison, they do not alter our conclusion, based on OLS regressions for the full-time employed sample, that there was considerably less convergence in the unexplained gender pay gap in the 1990s than in the 1980s.[33]

2.2.3.2. *Changes in Gender Differences in Unmeasured Characteristics and Labor Market Discrimination*

This section considers two possible sources of the slower convergence in the unexplained gender wage gap in the 1990s that persists after our correction for sample selection – slower reductions during the 1990s (i) in the gender difference in unmeasured characteristics and (ii) in labor market discrimination. In the spirit of seeking as much homogeneity as possible between the female and male samples when addressing these issues, we return our focus to the full-time employed sample.

With respect to unmeasured characteristics, it is possible that increases in women's commitment to the labor market and their employers were greater in the 1980s than the 1990s, even controlling for measured human capital and sector. Changes in such unmeasured characteristics are, by definition, difficult to measure. However, Aguiar and Hurst's (2006) findings on changes in housework are consistent with the possibility that such shifts played a role. Specifically, based on time use diaries, the authors' data imply that the gender gap in housework hours among non-retired individuals age 21–65 declined by more in the 1980s than in the 1990s: between 1975 and 1985, this gap fell from a level of 18.3 hours per week to 12.6 hours; however, from 1985 to 1993, the gap only fell to 10.6 hours, with a further reduction to 8.6 hours by 2003. This pattern was also observed in analyses that controlled for the educational, age, and family composition of the sample, as well as the day of the week on which the data were collected. Specifically, in weekly housework regressions that pooled years separately by gender and controlled for these factors, the female year effect fell relative to the male year effect by 4.4 hours per week between 1975 and 1985, 1.7 hours between 1985 and 1993, and 2.6 hours between 1993 and 2003 (Aguiar and Hurst 2006: 45–6, 56).[34]

Additionally, retrospective data from the PSID for all full-time workers as well as married full-time workers show a pattern similar to that shown by the time diary data: declines in the housework gap were faster in the 1980s than in the 1990s (Blau and Kahn 2004). If housework reduces the effort one can put into a job (Becker 1985; Hersch and Stratton 1997), gender differences in potential effort on the job likely closed faster in the 1980s than in the 1990s. Of course, the observed changes in housework hours could have been in part a response to changing labor market opportunities. However, this does not invalidate the reasoning by which housework potentially exerts an independent effect on labor market success. More broadly, it seems likely to us that the differences in trends for gender differences in housework over the two decades are indicative of faster convergence over the 1980s in other unmeasured characteristics as well. The faster increase in female labor force participation in the 1980s, as well as the more rapid narrowing of the gender gap in experience in that decade, are also suggestive of a greater increase in women's commitment to the labor force in the earlier decade.[35]

It is also possible that discrimination decreased by more in the 1980s than in the 1990s. This might at first appear unlikely, given that civil rights legislation passed in 1991 made the legal environment more favorable toward anti-discrimination lawsuits in the 1990s than in the 1980s (Gould 1993). This contributed to a more rapid growth in job bias lawsuits over the 1990s, since representing defendants in such suits became more lucrative for private law firms operating on a contingency fee basis (Blau, Ferber, and Winkler 2002: 243). Nonetheless, if women's labor force commitment changed more in the 1980s, it is possible that employers' perceptions of women's labor force commitment also changed more in the 1980s. If so, one of the possible bases for statistical discrimination against women may have eroded faster in the 1980s than in the 1990s.

An additional scenario whereby discrimination could have narrowed more slowly in the 1990s is related to the glass ceiling hypothesis mentioned above. The so-called glass ceiling problem refers to the explicit or, more likely, subtle barriers that inhibit women's progress at the highest echelons. If there is indeed such a problem, it may have had a greater negative impact on women in the 1990s than in the 1980s, as women's 1980s gains placed more of them into the higher-level positions where glass-ceiling barriers might hinder their further upward progression. If women are indeed increasingly constrained by glass ceilings, then one might expect to find less wage convergence with men at the top of the distribution than at other points. We study this issue in Table 2.11.

As we saw in Figure 2.1, the gender pay gap closed more slowly in the 1990s at all points in the distribution, but the contrast was particularly large at the top of the distribution. Although this is consistent with greater glass ceiling problems, it could also have been due to different rates of change in women's relative qualifications in the two decades. The estimates in Table 2.11 are based on quantile regressions for the 50th and 90th percentiles and allow us to present estimates of the unexplained gender pay gap controlling for measured characteristics. (Of course, as in all analyses of this kind, the unexplained gender wage gap could also be due in whole or part to gender differences in unmeasured characteristics.) We focus on the results for the human capital specification because the implicit cell sizes within occupation-industry unionization cells in the PSID are rather small to support an analysis focusing on various points of the distribution.

Table 2.11 presents three sets of results. The first two apply the results of the male and female quantile regressions by evaluating them (I) at the actual female means and (II) for white college graduates with 15 years of full-time experience. That is, we take women with the indicated characteristics and compare the predicted wages from the male and female quantile regressions at the 50th and 90th percentiles given those characteristics.[36] The rationale for the simulations in (II) is that the popular understanding of the glass ceiling is that it potentially applies to relatively high-skilled/high-level workers. A different approach is used for the last set of results (III), where we construct counterfactual wage distributions for each year using a technique proposed by Machado and Mata (2005) and compute the gender gap at the 50th and 90th percentiles of these counterfactuals. Specifically, we first estimate 99 quantile regressions each year for men and women separately (that is, quantiles 1–99). These quantile regressions use the entire sample of full-time employed wage and salary workers. Next, we take a random sample of 100 women in each year and find 198 predicted wages for each woman applying each of the 99 estimated male and female quantile regressions. This results in two counterfactual "raw" wage distributions for the same sample of 100 women, one based on the male quantile regressions and one based on the female quantile regressions.[37]

Table 2.11

Unexplained Gender Pay Gaps Based on Quantile Regressions (Human Capital Specification)[a]

A. Unexplained Gender Pay Gap	1979	1989	1998
I. Evaluated at the Female Means			
50th Percentile	0.366	0.208	0.201
90th Percentile	0.377	0.209	0.269
II. Evaluated for White, College Graduates with 15 Years of Experience			
50th Percentile	0.243	0.164	0.169
90th Percentile	0.368	0.171	0.287
III. Evaluated Using Counterfactual Wage Distributions			
50th Percentile	0.393	0.198	0.197
90th Percentile	0.334	0.194	0.247
	Average Annual Change X 10		
B. Changes in the Unexplained Gender Pay Gap	1979-89 (1)	1989-98 (2)	Difference (2)-(1)
I. Evaluated at the Female Means			
50th Percentile	-0.158	-0.008	0.150
90th Percentile	-0.168	0.067	0.235
II. Evaluated for White, College Graduates with 15 Years of Experience			
50th Percentile	-0.079	0.005	0.084
90th Percentile	-0.197	0.116	0.313
III. Evaluated Using Counterfactual Wage Distributions			
50th Percentile	-0.195	0.0004	0.195
90th Percentile	-0.140	0.053	0.194

[a] The human capital specification includes controls for race, education, and experience.

Notes: In I and II, the unexplained gap is calculated as $(B_M - B_F)\ X_F$, where B_M and B_F are vectors of coefficients from male and female quantile regression equations and X_F is a vector of female characteristics, evaluated at the female means in I and for white, college graduates with 15 years of full-time experience in II. In III, counterfactual distributions are constructed from 99 male and 99 female quantile regressions estimated over the full male and female samples, with predicted wages based on a random sample of 100 women; see Machado and Mata (2005).

We then compare, for example, the 90th percentile of wages in the distribution based on the female and the male quantile regressions (that is, the female and male reward structures). A comparison of how individuals near the top (that is, 90th percentile) of these two distributions fare certainly incorporates an element of the glass ceiling idea. However, the characteristics of the individuals at the 90th percentile are not held constant in the comparison, as they are in approaches (I) and (II) - and as they traditionally are in studies of discrimination. That is, the male and female reward structures will likely result in different types of individuals ending up at the top, and comparison (III) asks how people at the top fare under the two reward structures (regardless of their characteristics). Looking at the calculations for the first approach (I), the results for the unexplained gender pay gap from median regressions are quite similar to those based on OLS regressions (see Tables 2.9a–b and Table 2.10). The unexplained gap fell substantially in the 1980s, with relatively little further convergence in the 1990s. At the 90th percentile, however, this pattern is even more pronounced, with the unexplained gap actually increasing in the 1990s. When the quantile regression results are evaluated for white college graduates with 15 years of experience, the disparity between the median and the 90th percentile is even more extreme, with women at the 90th found to be losing substantial ground relative to men at the 90th in the 1990s, ceteris paribus. Our findings for the third approach (III) differ in a key respect from (I) and (II). As in the earlier exercise, we find that both 50th and 90th percentile gaps fell much more quickly in the 1980s than the 1990s. But the results show that the magnitude of the slowdown in convergence was comparable at the 50th and 90th percentiles. This is not consistent with a worsening of the glass ceiling problem in the 1990s. Interestingly, though, the results for method (III) (unlike the results for I and II) suggest that women at the top were already showing a slower rate of progress than women at the median in the 1980s. And it is the continuation of this slower rate of progress of women at the 90th percentile into the 1990s that results in a comparable slowdown in convergence for the 50th and the 90th percentiles in the 1990s. Taking the evidence in Table 2.11 together, these methods of analyzing convergence at the top versus the middle of the distribution provide mixed evidence in favor of the notion that the glass ceiling problem worsened in the 1990s. We would again like to emphasize that even the results that are consistent with the glass ceiling story (I and II) may reflect, in whole or part, the impact of unmeasured characteristics rather than discrimination. For example, the high tech boom of the late 1990s may have especially benefited high-skill men (Echeverri-Carroll and Ayala 2006).

2.2.3.3 Shifts in Supply and Demand

In this section we consider the possibility those less favorable changes in supply of, and demand for, women during the 1990s than during the 1980s contributed to slower convergence in the unexplained gap during the 1990s. On the supply side, our longer paper (Blau and Kahn 2004) found evidence of a larger rightward shift in female relative labor supply in the 1980s than the 1990s. Thus, female labor supply shifts do not explain the wage convergence patterns. On the other hand, there is some evidence that demand shifts both between sectors and within sectors were more favorable to women in the 1980s than in the 1990s. First, looking at between-sector changes, we examine the degree to which changes in the industrial-occupational structure of employment favored women in the 1980s and the 1990s. To do this, we compute demand indexes similar to those specified by Katz and Murphy (1992). Following their procedure, we construct industry-occupation cells and view the "output" of particular occupation groups as an intermediate product. A relative demand index, $\ln(1+ \Delta DEMf)$, was computed for women relative to men for the two time periods 1980–90 and 1990–99,

$$\Delta DEM_f = \textstyle\sum_o c_{of}(\Delta E_o/E_f) \qquad (6)$$

where o refers to occupation-industry cell, c_{of} is the female share of the labor input in occupation-industry cell o over the pooled sample (1980, 1990, and 1999), ΔE_o is the difference between the 1990 and 1980 or 1999 and 1990 share of total labor input employed in cell o, and E_f is the 1980 or 1990 share of total labor input accounted for by women. The demand index thus measures the degree to which 1980–90 or 1990–99 shifts in occupation-industry structure favored women, using pooled 1980, 1990, and 1999 weights.

Estimates of such demand indexes are likely to be biased, so caution must be taken in interpreting the empirical results. When labor input is measured in hours or employment, the index will understate the shift in demand for women that would have occurred at constant relative wages, since women's wages rose more than men's over the sample period. This understatement will be more severe for the 1980s than for the 1990s, since women's relative wages were rising faster in the earlier decade. However, when labor input is measured in efficiency units (earnings), depending on the overall elasticity of demand for labor, the index could overstate or understate the shift in demand for women at constant relative wages. With inelastic labor demand, the index will overstate the shift toward women, while with elastic labor demand, the index will understate this shift; if the labor demand elasticity is –1, the index will accurately show the shift in labor demand at constant wages. In his review of many studies of labor demand, Hamermesh (1993) suggested that the elasticity of labor demand is less than zero but greater than –1, with a likely range of –0.15 to –0.75. This suggests that earnings-based measures of labor demand shift will overstate the shift toward women during this period and will do so by more in the 1980s than in the 1990s, in contrast to hours-based measures. Of course, the shift-share analysis does not measure within-sector changes in demand, and we will return to this issue below.

In computing the demand indexes, we use 1980, 1990, and 1999 March CPS data because the CPS sample sizes allow us to construct more detailed industry-occupation cells than the PSID. We include part-time and full-time nonagricultural workers, and both the self-employed and wage and salary workers. However, because of the difficulty in measuring self-employment income, earnings-based measures of labor income include only wage and salary earnings. As noted, the base shares of female labor input (cof) are computed using pooled 1980, 1990, and 1999 samples. In pooling these CPS files, we adjusted the CPS sampling weights so that each year received the same weight. We obtained similar results using either the 1980, 1990, or 1999 female shares as our base.

We defined sector as industry-occupation cells, with 43 mostly two-digit industries and five occupations: (a) professionals; (b) managers; (c) clerical and sales workers; (d) craft, operative, and laborer jobs; and (e) service occupations. For both hours and efficiency unit definitions of labor input, demand shifts were favorable toward women in the 1980s. The demand index, which is in log units of labor, was estimated to shift .056 units in the 1980s and only 0.015 units in the 1990s using the efficiency unit definition, with shifts of 0.033 in the 1980s and –0.0017 in the 1990s using hours. While these estimated demand shifts are consistent with the slowdown in wage convergence, our longer paper (Blau and Kahn 2004) showed that these demand shifts were too small to account for a major portion of the slowdown. In fact, they were smaller than changes in our estimated supply shifts. However, it is certainly possible that the shift-share analysis understates the true growth in demand, and particularly the extent of faster growth in the 1980s.

One possibility is that a substantial portion of the gender-biased increases in the demand for intellectual skills discussed by Welch (2000) manifested themselves within industry-occupation cells and are thus not captured by our shift-share analysis. One indicator of the increased demand for "brains" over "brawn" is the growth in the incidence of computer use at work. The observation that women are more likely than men to use computers at work suggests that women as a group may have benefited from shifts in demand associated with computerization.[38] Diffusion of computers likely also benefited women because computers restructure work in ways that de-emphasize physical strength (Weinberg 2000). Consistent with these arguments, Weinberg (2000) found for the 1984–93 period that, within industry-occupation cells, growth in overall computer usage in the cell increased women's share of hours worked among both computer users and nonusers. Computerization rose more rapidly in the 1980s than in the 1990s, and hence this may be a factor in explaining the slowdown in convergence in the 1990s. Friedberg (2003: 514) reported that computer use increased from 24.4% of workers in 1984 to 37.3% in 1989, for an annual rate of increase of 8.9%; in contrast, the annual increase between 1989 and 1997 was only 3.9%. Combining Weinberg's estimates of the impact of increased computer use on the female hours share with Friedberg's data on the growth in computer usage, we estimate that rising computer use increased women's share of hours by 0.077 log points over the 1980s compared to 0.030 log points over the 1990s under Weinberg's "high estimates," and 0.047 log points in the 1980s compared to 0.018 log points in the 1990s under his "low estimates."[39]

This suggests one plausible source of within-industry-occupation demand shifts favoring women to a greater extent in the 1980s than in the 1990s that is not captured by our shift-share analysis. While even if we added these estimates to those presented in the shift share analysis, we would still fall short of the demand shifts required by the simulation in Blau and Kahn (2004), this finding may be indicative of other factors positively affecting the demand for women within industry-occupation cells. A possible example of such within-sector changes in the demand for women is suggested by the work of Borghans, Weel, and Weinberg (2005), who found evidence that a growing influence of interpersonal interactions on wages (in part due to increased computer use) can help explain rapidly rising female relative wages in the 1980s as well as a slower rate of increase in the 1990s. Finally, as noted above, the effects of industry, occupation, and union coverage shown in Table 2.9b, taken together, are consistent with a slowdown in the growth of demand for women in the 1990s. Specifically, Table 2.9b shows that women's relative industry, occupation, and union status changes together contributed to a 0.048 log point closing in the gender wage gap in the 1980s, but to only a 0.021 log point closing in the 1990s, with both occupational shifts and de-unionization, in particular, contributing less to convergence in the 1990s. Of course, as noted, these effects only measure the direct impacts of shifting employment distributions on the gender gap. Demand shifts favoring women can have broader impacts, raising women's wages wherever they are employed and hence lowering the female residual. Interestingly, technical change has been widely cited as a factor in the shrinking of blue-collar employment (for example, Katz and Murphy 1992) and is likely also to be an important cause of de-unionization, as computers make it easier to substitute away from relatively unionized routine manual jobs (Autor, Levy, and Murnane 2003).

2.2.4. Conclusion

We have used PSID data to study the slowdown in the convergence of female and male wages in the 1990s compared to the 1980s. After decades of near constancy, between 1979 and 1989 the female/male hourly pay ratio rose by 17.8% – from 63.2% to 74.5%. However, convergence slowed in the 1990s, with the ratio rising to 79.7% in 1998, an increase of only 7.2% on a ten-year basis. We first decomposed the slowdown in convergence into a portion due to changes in women's relative human capital levels and other measured characteristics; a portion that was due to changes in measured labor market prices; a portion due to changes in women's position in the male wage distribution; and a portion due to changes in unmeasured labor market prices. Our decompositions showed that women improved their relative human capital to a comparable extent in the 1980s and the 1990s. In contrast, while occupational upgrading and de-unionization contributed to women's relative wage gains in both decades, the impact of these factors was greater in the 1980s. Thus, slowing convergence in sectoral location in the 1990s is part of the explanation for the slowdown in wage convergence. The results of our decompositions also indicate that changes in the price of skills and returns to location in favorable sectors of the economy cannot explain why the gender pay gap fell faster in the 1980s than in the 1990s. These prices changed to women's detriment in the 1980s and had very little effect in the 1990s.

Controlling for human capital, sector, and the prices of measured and unmeasured labor market skills, we found that women made much larger gains in relative wages in the 1980s than in the 1990s. This difference, which is "unexplained" by our regression analyses, was sufficient to more than fully account for the slowdown in wage convergence in the 1990s. We then considered the factors that may have contributed to these changes in the convergence of the unexplained gender pay gap, including changes in labor force selectivity, changes in the gender difference in unmeasured characteristics and in labor market discrimination, and changes in the favorableness of supply and demand shifts. We presented some evidence consistent with each of these factors, suggesting that each may have played a role in explaining the observed trends.

III

International Differences in the Gender Wage Gap and Wage Inequality: The Role of Wage Setting Institutions

Introduction

In this section, I discuss a series of papers with Lawrence Kahn that consider and attempt to explain international differences in the gender wage gap and wage inequality, including the link between the two. We began this line of research in the early 1990s when Richard Freeman and Lawrence Katz approached us to participate in an NBER project on "Difference and Changes in Wage Structures," which brought together a group of researchers focused on exploring and comparing developments in wage structure across a number of advanced industrialized nations, including the United States, Australia, Japan, Korea, and a number of European countries. They wanted Larry and me to consider the gender dimension, across the various countries. This was an exciting project that brought together an international group of scholars to discuss and debate the experience of these various countries at a time of rising wage inequality in the United States and many other advanced industrialized nations.[1]

What first struck us as we considered the data on the gender gap across the OECD countries was that the U.S. position represented something of a paradox. While a number of indicators suggested that the relative qualifications of American women were high compared to women in other countries and it was also the case that the United States had a longer and often stronger commitment to anti-discrimination laws than most industrialized nations, the United States at that time was among the countries with the largest gender gaps. This is illustrated in Figure III.I that shows female-male earnings ratios based on OECD data. The non-U.S. average includes the same nine OECD countries in each year,[2] but the results tend to be similar regardless of the specific set of countries (see Chapters 3 and 4 below, Blau and Kahn 2000b; Blau, Ferber and Winkler 2010: 372). While there are some countries with larger gender pay gaps than the United States (e.g., Japan which is included in the figure below and Switzerland which is not), the United States does have a smaller gender wage ratio (i.e., a larger gender gap) than most of the other advanced countries and lies below the non-U.S. average shown in the figure. As we saw in Part II, U.S. women succeeded in narrowing the gender pay gap in the post-1980 period. The figure indicates that, as a result, the United States did begin to catch up to the non-U.S. average, but it still lags behind the other countries where the pay gap has also been falling.

Figure III.I

Female-to-Male Ratios, Median Full-time Earnings

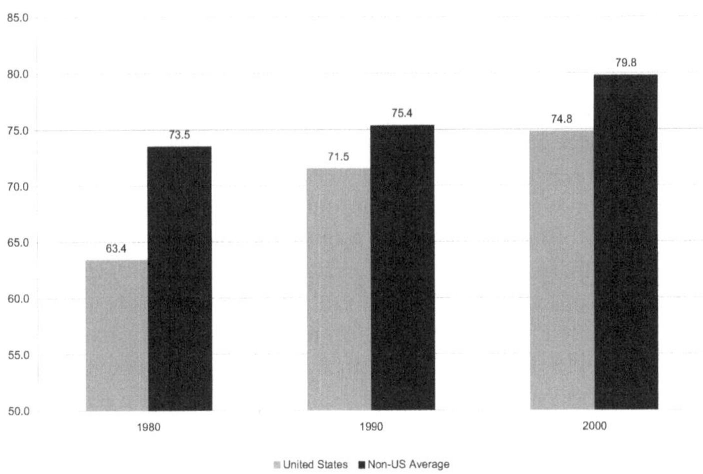

The emphasis on inequality in the project and the considerable interest and concern about that issue in the United States made us wonder if the substantially higher levels of wage inequality in the United States than elsewhere might help to explain our paradox. The reasoning that I outlined in my introduction to Part II, suggests the nature of such a link. It was our view that the larger role for unions and government in the other OECD countries compared to the decentralized wage-setting institutions in the United States lowered wage inequality in these countries relative to the United States – this argument is explicitly examined in Chapter 5 and I will discuss it in further detail below. We hypothesized that this wage compression also reduced the gender wage gap by lowering the rewards to skills and to employment in high-wage sectors. Since women in all these countries are less skilled on average (due to their lesser amount of labor market experience) and employed in less highly-rewarded sectors, they disproportionately benefit from such compression. Unions, in particular, tend to bring up the bottom of the wage distribution and, again, since women tend to be located at the bottom, they will disproportionately benefit and the gender wage gap will be reduced. Thus, centralized wage-setting institutions which tend to reduce the return to skills and compress interfirm and interindustry wage variation, and are often associated with conscious policies to raise the relative pay of low-wage workers (regardless of gender), may indirectly reduce the gender pay gap.

To test these ideas, one would like to differentiate between the role of gender-specific factors (i.e., labor market skills and discrimination) and wage structure in influencing international differences in the gender pay gap. Thus, the problem was similar to that outlined in the introduction to Part II where we examined trends over time in the gender wage gap, although in this case we were comparing across countries. As I explained there, the Juhn, Murphy, and Pierce (1991) decomposition is an excellent technique for identifying these factors; hence we used this approach in Chapter 3 below (see also, Blau and Kahn 1995). Interestingly, Juhn, Murphy, and Pierce developed their technique in order to analyze the trends in the black-white wage gap, where, as I noted in the introduction to Part II, progress had stalled in the late 1970s. Part of our insight was to realize its potential usefulness for understanding international difference in the gender pay gap. (In fact, we applied the Juhn, Murphy, and Pierce technique to analyzing international differences in the gender pay gap before we used it to examine trends.) The reasoning is quite similar in both cases. For example, suppose that in two countries, women have lower levels of labor market experience than men but that the gender difference in experience is the same in the two countries. If the return to experience is higher in one country, then that nation will have a larger gender pay gap. Or, as another example, suppose that the extent of occupational segregation by sex is the same in two countries but that the wage premium associated with employment in "male" jobs is higher in one country. Then, again, that country will have a higher pay gap.

One of the factors that increased our excitement about the project was that, in some respects, the international differences in wage setting institutions could be considered something of a natural experiment that could be used to establish the role of wage structure, a factor not generally considered in analyses of inter-group wage differentials, in affecting the magnitude of the gender pay gap. What was perhaps surprising even to us was the enormous importance of overall wage structure in explaining the lower ranking of U.S. women. Our results suggested that the U.S. gap would be similar to that in countries like Sweden and Australia (the countries in our sample with the smallest differentials) if the U.S. had their level of wage inequality. Our results strongly suggested that relying on a framework that considered only gender-specific factors would be inadequate to explain the relatively high gender pay gap in the United States.

This insight is further expanded in Chapter 4, where we ask whether wage structure has an important effect on the gender pay gap across a broad variety of countries, that is, whether wage structure explains a large component of international differences in the gender pay gap generally? Moreover, while the results of the Juhn, Murphy, and Pierce decomposition technique were consistent with a strong role for wage inequality and wage-setting institutions in affecting the gender gap, the methodology does not permit a direct test of this effect. Further, the technique requires some specific assumptions, notably that women will be affected by the same economic forces that influence the male wage distribution in a country. The decomposition of the wage residuals proposed by Juhn, Murphy, and Pierce had been particularly criticized (Suen 1997). In the study reported in Chapter 4, we were able to implement a more direct test of the impact of wage structure that provided considerable empirical support for our earlier findings and thus indirectly for the Juhn, Murphy, and Pierce decomposition technique itself.

To implement the analysis, we assembled microdata on 22 countries over the 1985–94 period to test the hypotheses that more egalitarian pay structures (as measured by the extent of male wage inequality) are associated with lower gender pay gaps. Our use of microdata on individual workers was crucial in that it permitted us to adjust for international differences in women's human capital in estimating the gender pay gap, and also to estimate the characteristics of the wage structure itself by enabling us to separate out labor force heterogeneity from the true effects of labor market prices. The regression-based approach that we used also enabled us to examine the impact of supply and demand conditions in the female labor market on a country's gender pay gap, a factor we had not previously considered.

The results provided support for the idea that egalitarian wage structures reduce the gender pay gap, where inequality was measured both in terms of the rewards to measured skills and the dispersion of the residuals from male wage equations estimated for each country. We also found that, controlling for wage structure, the gender differential is lower when women are in shorter supply relative to the favorableness of the country's demand structure for women (female "net supply"). As pointed out in Chapter 4, the latter finding is also consistent with positive selection of women into the labor force such that higher female participation rates are correlated with a larger gender gap.[3] The effect of pay structures on the gender pay gap was quantitatively very important: a large part of the difference in the gender differential between high-gap and low-gap countries is explained by the differences across these countries in overall wage structure, with another potentially important segment due to differences in female net supply.

In Chapter 5, we take a closer look at the sources of international differences in wage structure – measured in Chapters 3 and 4 by the extent of male inequality. Was the assumption underlying our work on international differences in the gender pay gap that wage setting institutions have an important influence on international differences in wage inequality correct? To address this issue, we again assembled a cross-country microdata set, in this case focusing on explaining international differences in male wage inequality. For wage-setting institutions to potentially play a role, a necessary condition would be that higher inequality in the United States be due at least in part to higher returns to skills, measured or unmeasured, where measured skills could include rewards to employment in favored sectors. Collecting evidence on this required us to net out the effect of differences across countries in the heterogeneity in the distribution of skills. To do this we employed a different, but related, Juhn, Murphy, and Pierce (1993) decomposition which provided a full distributional accounting scheme that permitted us to attribute U.S.-other country differences in inequality to differences in (i) the distribution of measured characteristics, (ii) wage functions, (iii) the distribution of wage residuals. We found that although greater heterogeneity in measured characteristics did explain some of the international differences, U.S. labor market prices - that is, higher rewards to measured and unmeasured characteristics - were indeed an important factor contributing to differences in inequality between the United States and other countries. This is consistent with a role for wage-setting institutions as outlined above, although differences in supply and demand factors across countries could also play a role.

We argued that if labor market institutions did indeed play a role, it would imply greater wage compression of the other countries compared to the United States at the bottom of the wage distribution than at the top - as unions and government policies are frequently directed at "bringing up the bottom."[4] And, this was indeed the pattern of inequality that we identified empirically. Interestingly, our results imply that union pay policies that bring up the bottom of the union wage distribution are common to all countries, including the United States, but that unions in other countries appeared to be more successful than U.S. unions both in reducing inequality in the union sector and in extending such policies to the nonunion sector. Finally, we presented some evidence that international differences in the supply of and demand for labor market skills did not provide a viable alternative explanation for the observed differences in inequality between the United States and other countries.

Our finding that both prices and worker heterogeneity played a role in explaining higher U.S. wage was based on analyses controlling for observed characteristics like age and education. However, labor market skills may differ even among observationally equivalent workers. In particular, it is believed that school systems in continental Europe produce a more uniform level of cognitive skills than the highly decentralized U.S. system. This view is supported by data from the International Adult Literacy Survey (IALS), which became available in the late 1990s. The IALS data show that, among those with little education, relative and absolute test performance is much lower in the United States than in the rest of the OECD (OECD 1998; Nickell and Layard 1999). This raises the possibility that unmeasured heterogeneity in cognitive skills might be sufficient to account for higher U.S. wage inequality, particularly its higher return to education (Nickell and Layard 1999). For this reason, in Blau and Kahn (2005b), we explicitly examined this issue using microdata from the IALS for nine countries. In addition to the traditional human capital measures of schooling and age, the IALS contains the results of comparable cognitive tests administered in a number of countries in the areas of arithmetic operations, prose literacy, and document-reading ability.

We found that while performance on cognitive tests plays a role in explaining greater U.S. wage inequality, higher labor market prices (i.e., higher returns to measured human capital and cognitive performance) and greater residual inequality still play important roles for both men and women. And, moreover, on average, prices were quantitatively considerably more important than differences in the distribution of test scores in explaining the relatively high levels of wage inequality in the United States. As in the case of our similar results in Chapter 5, this finding is consistent with a role either for international differences in wage-setting institutions or in labor market supply and demand, or both. We report some evidence in support of the institutional explanation: U.S.-other country differences in prices were significantly positively correlated with the country's collective bargaining coverage. Of course, this finding does not preclude a role for supply and demand as well. Moreover, as we point out (Blau and Kahn 2005b), the two may be related through feedback effects in that institutions may indirectly influence the supply of or demand for labor (see also Blau and Kahn 1999).

On the supply side, low wage premia for human capital investments due to institutional factors may deter individuals from making large human capital investments, thus yielding a smaller supply of high-skilled workers. Alternatively, to the extent that wage compression results in youth unemployment, the opportunity cost of investing in a college education may be reduced, encouraging attendance. On the demand side, Acemoglu (2003) suggests that union-induced wage compression can cause firms to increase their demand for less-skilled workers by making techniques that raise the productivity of less-skilled labor more profitable. Union policies may also directly affect supply or demand for labor. For example, Summers, Gruber, and Vergara (1993) argue that in heavily unionized, "corporatist" societies (i.e., where unions, management, and government play an important role in coordinating wage-setting at the national level), social spending - which could include spending on education - is likely to be higher. At the same time, institutions may themselves be endogenous and affected by characteristics of the population, such as homogeneity, which also influence the relative supplies of various skill groups.

If institutions are important and if employers are responding to de facto high wage floors, one indicator might be that various groups for whom the wage constraint is particularly binding may experience employment problems. Logical candidates would be the low-skilled, youth of both sexes, prime-aged women, and older individuals. In Chapter 5, we found some evidence consistent with this argument in that the low-skilled generally had a higher employment/population ratio relative to the higher-skilled in the United States than elsewhere. This result seems to be part of a broader pattern. Looking across a larger number of countries and for a longer time period, Kahn (2000) found that greater unionization lead to lower relative employment for less-skilled men. In work with Giuseppe Bertola (Bertola, Blau and Kahn 2007), Kahn and I probed this issue further, focusing on the effect of collective bargaining on the relative employment of youth, women, and older individuals. Using data from 17 OECD countries over the 1960–1996 period, we found that time-varying indicators of unionization decrease the employment–population ratio of young and older individuals relative to the prime-aged, and of prime-aged women relative to prime-aged men. We also found that unionization raises the unemployment rate of prime-aged women and, possibly, young men compared to prime-aged men. This is indirect evidence consistent with a role for institutions in determining international differences in skill prices through de facto wage floors. It also suggests that while wage-setting institutions may lower the gender pay gap through wage compression, it is at a price in terms of relative employment problems for women. As in other areas, there appears to be no free lunch here.

3

Wage Structure and Gender Earnings Differentials: An International Comparison

Based on a paper with Lawrence M. Kahn

Despite in many cases dramatic reductions in the male-female pay gap since the 1950s, gender differentials persist in all industrialized nations. However, the size of the gender gap varies considerably across countries. Published data suggest that, by the late 1980s, the Scandinavian countries, France, Australia, and New Zealand had female-male hourly pay ratios of 80-90%, while other countries in Western Europe and the United States had pay ratios of roughly 65-75%. The United States was amoung the countries with the larg-

---

This chapter is a revised version of Blau, F. D., Kahn, L. M. (1996b). Wage Structure and Wage Earnings Differentials: An International Comparison, in: Economica, 63 (250, suppl.): S29-S63. John Wiley & Sons Ltd.

The authors are most grateful to David Blanchflower for his efforts in making the International Social Survey Programme (ISSP) data available; to Andrea Ichino for providing the Bank of Italy data; and to Per-Anders Edin for supplying us with the Swedish Household Market and Nonmarket Activities Survey (HUS). We have benefited from the helpful comments on earlier stages of this project of Richard Freeman, Lawrence Katz, Claudia Goldin, Pamela Loprest and Ayal Kimhi, and of participants at the NBER/Ford Preconference and conference on 'Differences and Changes in Wage Structures' in London, September 1991, and Cambridge, Massachusetts, July 1992, the AEA Meetings in New Orleans, January 1992, the International Seminar on 'Economic Policy and Income Distribution' at Bar-Ilan University, May 1993, and to the University of Illinois, Harvard, University of Chicago, Cornell, Princeton, Massachusetts Institute of Technology, Brookings Institution, and University of Maryland Workshops. We also thank two anonymous referees for helpful comments and suggestions. This research was supported in part by a grant from the Ford Foundation to the NBER. Portions of this paper draw on our chapter on 'The Gender Earnings Gap: Some International Evidence' in Richard B. Freeman and Lawrence F. Katz, Differences and Changes in Wage Structures, Chicago. University of Chicago Press, National Bureau of Economic Research, 1995.

est differentials (OECD, ILO, USBLS). This chapter uses microdata to analyze international differences in the gender pay gap among a sample of ten industrialized nations. We focus particularly on explaining the surprisingly low ranking of the United States in comparison with other industrialized countries. An advantage of an international perspective is that countries vary considerably with respect to governmental policies, women's relative labor market qualifications, and wage-setting institutions. Such variability allows one to infer reasons for differences in the pay gap and, by implication, the impact of alternative government policies.

Empirical research on gender pay gaps has traditionally focused on the role of gender differences in qualifications and on differences in the treatment of otherwise equally qualified male and female workers (ie., labor market discrimination). Analyses of trends over time in the gender differential within countries as well as inter-country comparisons of gender earnings ratios have tended to emphasize these types of gender-specific factors. An innovative feature of the research reported in this chapter is to focus on the role of wage structure as an additional factor influencing the gender gap. To analyse the impact of wage structure, we adapt a framework developed by Juhn et al. (1991) to analyse trends over time in race differentials in the United States. Our findings suggest that labor market institutions that affect overall wage inequality have an extremely important effect on the gender earnings gap.

"Wage structure" describes the array of prices set for various labor market skills (measured and unmeasured) and rents received for employment in particular sectors of the economy. Research on gender-specific factors influencing the pay gap suggests that men and women tend to have different levels of labor market skills and to be employed in different sectors. This implies a potentially important role for wage structure in determining the pay gap. For example, suppose that in two countries women have lower levels of labor market experience than men but that the gender difference in experience is the same in the two countries: if the return to experience is higher in one country, then that nation will have a larger gender pay gap. Or, as another example, suppose that the extent of occupational segregation by sex is the same in two countries but that the wage premium associated with employment in male jobs is higher in one country: then, again, that country will have a higher pay gap.

Skill prices can be affected by relative supplies, by technology (e.g., high-tech industries place a premium on highly trained workers), by the composition of demand or, as emphasized in this chapter, by the wage-setting institutions of each country. Specifically, centralized wage-setting institutions, which tend to reduce interfirm and interindustry wage variation and are often associated with conscious policies to raise the relative pay of low-wage workers (regardless of gender), may indirectly reduce the gender pay gap.

The striking finding of this study is the enormous importance of overall wage structure in explaining the lower ranking of U.S. women. The higher level of wage inequality in the United States than elsewhere works to increase the U.S. gender differential relative to that in all the other countries in our sample. Our results suggest that the U.S. gap would be similar to that in countries like Sweden and Australia (the countries with the smallest gaps) if the United States had their levels of wage inequality. These results are consistent across our broadly based ten-country comparison, which employs microdata sets for each country and takes into account education, potential experience, major industry, occupation and unionism, and our supplemental detailed U.S.-Sweden comparison, in which we are able to take explicit account of actual labor force experience: a factor that has been found to be an important source of pay differences between men and women. While our focus is on explaining the relatively high pay gap in the United States compared with other industrialized countries, we do provide some evidence that wage inequality and decentralization in wage-setting are generally associated with higher gender gaps, particularly with regard to the component that may be attributed to wage structure.

This insight helps to resolve three puzzling sets of facts: (1) U.S. women compare favourably with women in other countries in terms of human capital and occupational distribution; (2) the United States has had a longer and often stronger commitment to equal pay and equal employment opportunity policies than have most of the other countries in our sample; but (3) the gender pay gap is larger in the United States than in most industrialized countries. An important part of the explanation of this pattern is that the U.S. labor market places a much larger penalty on those with lower levels of labor market skills (both measured and unmeasured). Put differently, our findings suggest that the gender gap in pay in the United States would be far less than it is if U.S. wage-setting processes more closely resembled those in the other countries, as long as U.S. women retained the same level of relative skills.[1]

3.1. An Overview of Data Sources and Gender Earnings Ratios

The microdata sets employed in this study were obtained from a variety of sources. We used the 1985-89 International Social Survey Programme (ISSP) for the following countries and time periods: Austria (1985-87 and 1989), West Germany (1985-88), Hungary (1986-88), Switzerland (1987), United Kingdom (1985-89), Norway (1989) and United States (1985-89). The 1985-89 ISSP files lack data on Sweden, and preliminary results suggested that the Australian data in the ISSP are inconsistent with other sources and that the Italian ISSP data contain very few observations on women. We therefore supplement the ISSP with the following three microdata sets in order to include these countries with very high gender earnings ratios: the Class Structure and Class Consciousness (CSCC) database, originally compiled by Erik Wright, for Sweden (1980) and, since it is also available, Norway (1982) (providing us with a second Norwegian data-set); the Income Distribution Survey (IDS) for Australia (1986); and a Bank of Italy (BI) survey for Italy (1987). These files constitute the data source for our broadly based ten-country comparisons. In addition, we perform a special comparison for 1984 between the United States and Sweden using two additional databases with information on actual labor market experience and a superior earnings measure: the Michigan Panel Study of Income Dynamics (PSID) and the Swedish Household Market and Non-market Activities Survey (HUS).[2] These results are presented in Section IV(d). In each case, the sample is restricted to individuals aged 18-65.

The specific earnings measures used in the data for each country are described in detail in the Appendix.[3] For all cases except the 1984 Sweden-U.S. comparison, the earnings figure is expressed on an annual or monthly basis. The computation of gender wage differentials from these data-sets is complicated by the omission from these files of information on annual weeks worked. Weekly hours worked is available, however, allowing for some adjustment of the earnings data for time input.[4] (The adjustment for time input is described below.) For the 1984 Sweden-U.S. comparison, we are able to compute average hourly earnings.

With the exception of the 1984 HUS (Sweden) and PSID (U.S.), the earnings variable is generally coded into categories.[5] A continuous earnings variable is constructed in the other cases by using the midpoint of the intervals. We arbitrarily coded the top (open-ended) category as 1.2 times its minimum value. However, the gender ratios were virtually identical when we experimented with alternative assumptions for the top category ranging from 1 to 1.5 times its minimum value. Finally, concern for adequate sample size led us to pool years of data for those countries in the ISSP surveyed more than once (see above).

International differences in gender gaps across the ten countries are summarized in Figure 3.1, which gives gender earnings ratios adjusted for hours. The figure indicates that Sweden, Australia, Austria, and Italy have the highest gender ratios. The United States ranks towards the bottom of the group, with six of the nine countries (Sweden, Norway, Australia, Austria, Italy, and Germany) having higher gender earnings ratios, and only three (the United Kingdom, Hungary, and Switzerland) having lower ratios.[6] The Italian ratio probably overstates the actual gender ratio in that country. Italy has an especially large proportion of workers who work in an informal sector in which government-mandated benefits are not paid. It is likely that informal-sector employment is underreported by the respondents in our survey-based data, possibly resulting in an understatement of the gender gap. None the less, it is likely that Italy is among the countries with smaller gender gaps.

Figure 3.1

Gender Earnings Ratios Adjusted for Hours Only (in percent)

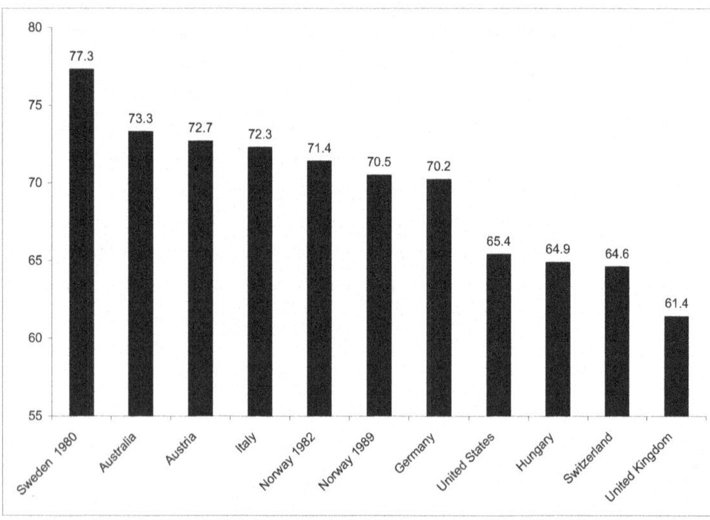

To illuminate the role of wage structure, we present the mean percentile rankings of women in the male wage distribution for each country in Figure 3.2.[7] Gender-specific factors, including differences in qualifications and the impact of labor market discrimination, are viewed as determining the percentile ranking of women in the male wage distribution, while the overall wage structure (as measured by the magnitude of male inequality) determines the wage penalty or reward associated with this position in the wage distribution. The basic premise is that males at the same percentile ranking as women may be viewed as comparable in the eyes of employers. Thus, the same set of factors will determine the relative rewards of women and of these comparable males, and differences between the rankings of countries in Figures 3.1 and 3.2 represent the role of wage structure.

Figure 3.2
Mean Female Percentile in Male Distribution

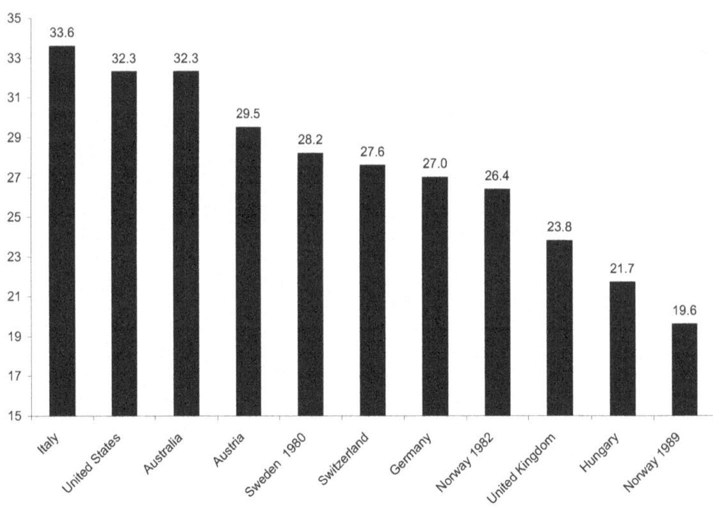

The most striking difference is for the United States. Whereas the United States ranks towards the bottom with respect to the female-male earnings ratios, it ranks second highest in terms of women's percentile ranking. Only Italy ranks higher and, as noted above, we have most likely overstated Italy's gender ratio. Thus, the relatively high gender pay gap in the United States does not appear to be due to a low ranking of women in the male wage distribution; rather, it is related to the higher level of wage inequality in the United States, which results in an especially large wage penalty for being below average in the distribution.

Also notable in comparing the two figures is the change in the rankings of the Scandinavian countries. Sweden falls from the highest ranked country in Figure 3.1 to the fifth-ranked in Figure 3.2, while the rankings for Norway, based on both of our microdata sets, also decline considerably. This suggests that the relatively more equal wage distribution in the Scandinavian countries is an important reason for the relatively high status of women there. So, for example, while the mean percentile ranking of women in the United States is 32.3, at the U.S. level of male wage inequality this corresponds to a wage that is 65.4% of the male mean. In contrast, Swedish women's percentile ranking of 28.2 corresponds to a wage that is 77.3% of the male mean and Norwegian women's ranking of 26.4 in 1982 corresponds to 71.4% of the male mean.

Figure 3.3(a)

Cumulative Distribution Function, Female Wages Relative to the Male Wage Distribution, USA, Germany, UK, Austria

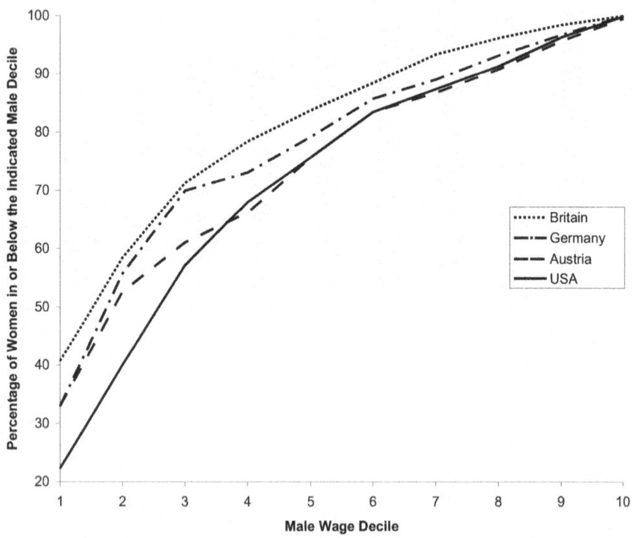

Figure 3.3(b)

Cumulative Distribution Function, Female Wages Relative to the Male Wage Distribution, USA, Switzerland, Hungary

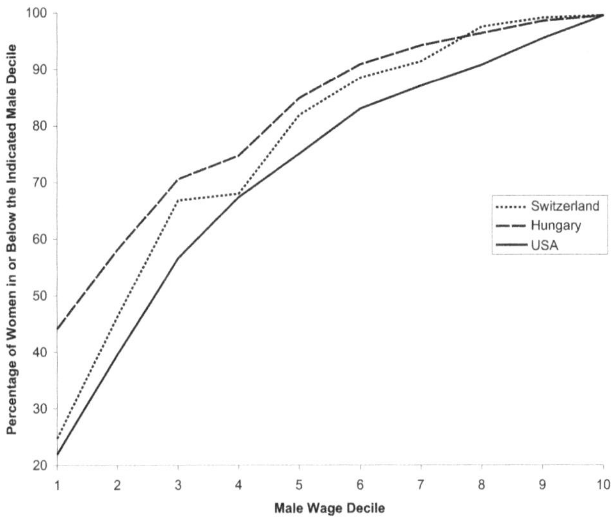

Figure 3.3(c)

Cumulative Distribution Function, Female Wages Relative to the Male Wage Distribution, USA, Sweden (1980), Norway (1980), Norway (1989)

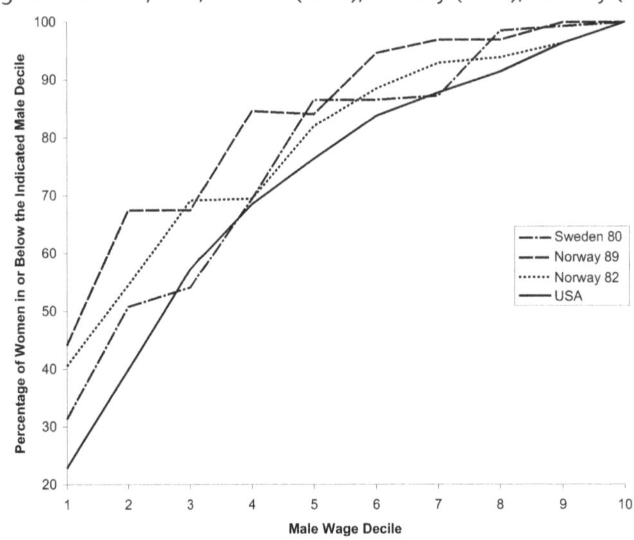

Figure 3.3(d)

Cumulative Distribution Function, Female Wages Relative to the Male Wage Distribution, USA, Italy, Australia

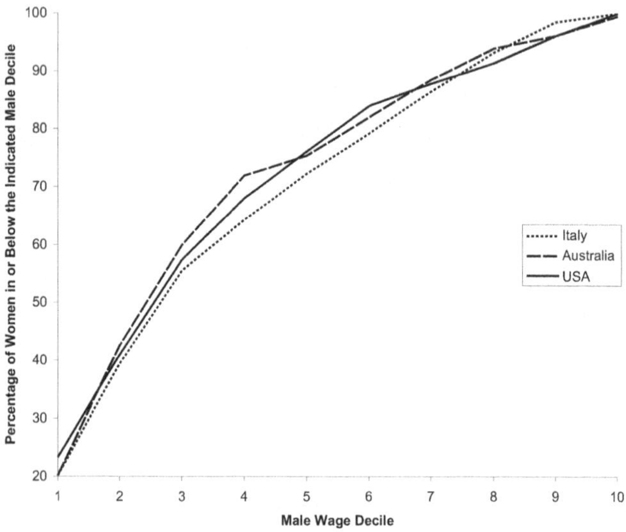

The female percentile comparisons of the United States and the other countries are shown in greater detail in Figure 3.3. Parts (a)-(d) give, for each country, the female cumulative distribution functions that result from placing women in male wage deciles on the basis of the male log wage cutoffs.[8] So, for example, in the United States approximately 22% of women fall in the first decile of the male distribution of log wages; almost 40% in or below the second male decile; etc. The comparison of the United States to the other countries has been made separately for two or three countries at a time to enhance clarity.

The results indicate that the conclusions based on a comparison of the mean female percentiles in the male distribution are fully supported by the more detailed comparison. Specifically, the U.S. female cumulative distribution function is quite similar to that of Italy and Australia, which have comparable levels of mean percentiles. The U.S. cumulative distribution lies below, or largely below, that of all the other countries. Particularly notable is the larger, often considerably larger, proportion of women in the lowest male wage decile in these other countries compared with the United States. This suggests an important role for labor market institutions which tend to "bring up the bottom" in reducing the gender pay gap in these countries relative to the United States. That is, although the percentage of women in other countries falling in the bottom male decile generally exceeds that in the United States, the gender pay gap tends to be smaller. This suggests that formal or de facto wage floors in these countries lessen the wage penalty for those in the bottom decile.

3.2. The Institutional Setting

In this section we review international differences in gender-specific policies and basic wage-setting institutions. Human capital is also a major determinant of gender pay gaps, and below, we present some international comparisons of indicators of women's relative levels of measured human capital. However, international differences in policies and institutions appear to be more dramatic than those in women's relative human capital levels, at least in our sample. Further, human capital can be affected by such policies and institutions as discussed below. We therefore begin with a comparison of the institutional setting.

Gender-specific policies include equal employment opportunity (EEO) and anti-discrimination laws, as well as laws and policies governing maternity and family leave.[9] The expected positive effect of the former on the earnings ratio is reasonably straightforward, although the impact will most likely depend on the effectiveness of the legislation as well as its provisions. In general, it is expected that, given considerable segregation of women by occupation and industry, equal pay laws mandating equal pay for equal work within the same occupation and firm will have a relatively small effect. Laws requiring equal opportunity, hiring preferences, and/or "comparable worth" (ie., equal pay for work of equal value to the firm, regardless of specific occupational category) have potentially larger impacts. In addition, since EEO laws involve occupational shifts, they may require considerable time to have an impact on pay. Thus, the comparable worth approach, which provides for immediate increases in relative pay in female-dominated occupations, may be expected to have the largest initial wage effect, possibly accompanied by a negative impact on female employment.

U.S. anti-discrimination policies compare relatively favourably on their face with those of the other countries in our sample. All of the OECD countries in the sample have passed some equal pay and equal opportunity legislation, but the U.S. commitment, particularly to equal employment opportunity, predates that in most of the other countries (see OECD 1988, Table 5.11: 167-8). The U.S. laws and regulations date to the 1960s and include the Equal Pay Act of 1963 (requiring equal pay for equal work), the Civil Rights Act of 1964 (requiring equal employment opportunity), and the Executive Order implemented in 1968 (which requires government contractors to take "affirmative action" to see that women and minorities are equitably treated). While Italy mandated equal pay through collective bargaining in the industrial sector in 1960 (predating the U.S. Equal Pay Act by three years), an Equal Employment Opportunity Act was not passed there until 1977. The earliest of the other countries, Australia and the United Kingdom, began to implement equal pay in 1969 and 1970. Equal opportunity measures were instituted in 1975 in Britain and 1978 in Norway. The remainder of the countries passed all relevant legislation in the 1980s. The one country with a clearly stronger intervention than the United States is Australia, the only one to have implemented a national policy of comparable worth through its labor courts (Gregory and Daly 1991; Killingsworth 1990).[10] Comparable worth pay policies remain rare in the U.S. private sector, although they have been adopted by a number of state governments (Blau and Ferber 1992).

The expected impact of family leave (disproportionately taken by women even when it is available to men) is unclear a priori. On the one hand, it is possible that such policies raise the relative earnings of women by encouraging the preservation of their ties to particular firms and hence by increasing the incentives of employers and women to invest in firm-specific training. On the other hand, the existence of such policies could increase the incidence and/or duration of temporary labor force withdrawals among women, raising the gender gap for the affected group. Further, the incremental costs associated with mandated leave policies may increase the incentive of employers to discriminate against women.

In contrast to anti-discrimination policy, as the only country in our sample that did not have government-mandated leave at the federal level during the period covered by our data (ILO 1988: Tables 2 and 3: 20-1),[11] the United States clearly lagged in the provision of family leave. However it did (and continues to) require that pregnancy be treated the same as any other medical disability. Thus, leave for the physical aspects of child-bearing must be covered under a firm's medical disability plan, if it has one. Further, voluntary provision of parental leave beyond this was not uncommon. For example, in the late 1980s, 40% of employees of large- and medium-size establishments were employed at firms that provided parental leave to women, the vast majority (92%) at firms offering unpaid leave (Hyland 1990). Plans allowed an average of 20 weeks off for unpaid leave. None the less, it remains the case that provision of maternity leave was less extensive as well as less generous in the United States than elsewhere. In contrast, it may be noted that provision for parental leave was articularly generous in Sweden, where nearly a year of paid parental leave is provided after 12 weeks of paid (at 90%) maternity leave.

With respect to wage structure, it seems likely that systems of centrally determined pay entail smaller gender wage differentials for a number of reasons. First, in the United States, a significant portion of the male-female pay gap is associated with interindustry or interfirm wage differentials that result from its relatively decentralized pay-setting institutions (Blau 1977; Johnson and Solon 1986; Sorensen 1990; Groshen 1991). Thus, centralized systems, which reduce the extent of wage variation across industries and firms are likely to lower the gender differential, all else equal. Second, since in all countries the female wage distribution lies below the male distribution, centralized systems that consciously raise minimum pay levels regardless of gender will also tend to lower male-female wage differentials. Finally, the impact of gender-specific policies to raise female wages may be greater under centralized systems, where such policies can be more speedily and effectively implemented.

U.S. pay-setting appears to be far less centralized than that in the other countries in this study.[12] U.S. unionization rates of 20.3% for male and 12.3% for female workers in our sample are considerably lower than elsewhere. Further, the collective bargaining process itself is very decentralized in the United States, with an emphasis on single-firm agreements, and the U.S. government exerts minimal intervention in wage-setting (Flanagan et al. 1989). In contrast, in most of the other countries in our sample, bargaining is conducted on an industry-wide or even an economy-wide level. Thus, there appears to be more scope for interfirm and interindustry wage differentials in the U.S. union sector. While a lower variance in the union sector of other countries could be achieved either by raising the bottom, restraining the top or both, centralized bargains often emphasize the setting of wage minima across diverse units. Events in the 1980s and 1990s have led to the decentralization of bargaining in virtually every industrialized country (Katz 1993; Edin and Holmlund 1995; Blau and Kahn 1996a, see Chapter 5). None the less, one's impression is that, with the possible exception of Britain, systems of collective bargaining remain more centralized in the other countries than in the United States.

Several factors also lead us to expect a wider dispersion of nonunion wages in the United States than elsewhere. These include the practice in many other countries of extending the terms of collective bargaining agreements to nonunion workers. To the extent that unions in all countries tend to compress wages at the bottom in the union sector, contract extension will not only reduce wage variation in the nonunion sector, but compress wages at the bottom as well. In addition, the higher degree of union organization outside the United States may produce more "voluntary" imitation of union pay structures by nonunion firms than in the United States (Kahn and Curme 1987). While the United States does have federal and state minimum wage legislation, the minimum is set at a relatively low level by international standards in contrast to the relatively high floors established via contract extension and other mechanisms in the other countries (EIRR 1992; Blau and Kahn 1996a, see Chapter 5).

3.3. Gender Differences in Worker Characteristics

Below we provide a formal decomposition of international differences in gender pay gaps into various components including gender differences in measured variables. Here we briefly examine the international differences in worker characteristics, including factors that may reveal qualitative differences in women's labor force commitment. Overall, we conclude that U.S. women compare favourably with those in other countries when we consider their labor market qualifications relative to those of men.

For most of our countries, indicators of measured human capital are limited to education and potential labor force experience. Gender differences in these variables are small for all the countries in our sample except Switzerland and Italy. In Switzerland the female labor force is less educated and younger than the male labor force, while in Italy women are more highly educated and younger than men.

While, unfortunately, in most cases we lack data on actual labor market experience, some indication of labor force commitment may be gained by an examination of the labor force participation (LFP) rates by gender-marital status groups for each country, shown in Table 3.1.

Table 3.1

Labor Force Participation Rates[a]

	Men			Women		
Country	Married	Not married	All	Married	Not married	All
Australia	0.8933	0.8688	0.8856	0.5624	0.6774	0.5956
Austria	0.7701	0.7956	0.7784	0.3883	0.5605	0.4444
Germany	0.8408	0.7047	0.7884	0.3742	0.5759	0.4477
Hungary	0.8552	0.8041	0.8423	0.6638	0.6320	0.6562
Italy (1980)	—	—	0.7880	—	—	0.4390
Norway (1982)	0.9067	0.7790	0.8778	0.5896	0.5960	0.5910
Sweden (1988)	—	—	0.9000	—	—	0.8500
Switzerland	0.9679	0.8477	0.9312	0.3949	0.8181	0.6045
UK	0.9211	0.8202	0.8930	0.5572	0.6686	0.5886
U.S.	0.9068	0.8564	0.8873	0.6200	0.7076	0.6614

[a] The labor force participation rate is defined in terms of labor force status in the survey week.

Sources: for Sweden: Lofstrom and Gustafsson (1991); for Italy: OECD, Labor Force Statistics (1990: 299); the remaining figures are calculated from the authors' microdata sets described in the text. In the case of countries from the ISSP, the 1985-88 ISSP files are employed.

As may be seen in the table, the labor force participation rate of U.S. women is higher than that in any of the other countries except Sweden. The absolute male-female differential in participation rates in the United States is comparable to that in Hungary and lower than that in any of the other countries apart from Sweden. While U.S. female labor force participation rates are higher than those of most of the other countries, this does not necessarily imply that the average employed American woman has more labor market experience. It is possible that in a country with a high female participation rate recent entrants comprise a high proportion of the labor force, and thus that women workers have less experience on average than in a country with a low female LFP rate. On the other hand, it may be that a country's high female LFP rate is due to a more continuous labor force attachment among women (Blau and Ferber 1992; O'Neill and Polachek 1993). Lacking complete international data on actual experience, we tentatively conclude that U.S. women are at least as oriented towards market work as women in most other countries. This conclusion is supported by data on actual experience, which are available to us for the United States and Sweden in 1984. These data indicate that the male-female gap in actual experience is only slightly higher in the United States (6 years) than in Sweden (5 years).

Table 3.2

Means For Part-Time Work (PART) by Marital Status, Employed Sample[a]

	Men			Women		
Country	All	Single	Married	All	Single	Married
Australia	0.0457	0.0674	0.0362	0.3740	0.2070	0.4641
Austria	0.0218	0.0233	0.0211	0.2821	0.1444	0.3855
Germany	0.0170	0.0280	0.0119	0.3455	0.1663	0.5076
Italy	0.0573	—	—	0.2613	—	—
Norway (1982)	0.0697	0.0679	0.0701	0.5251	0.2673	0.5875
Sweden (1980)	0.0525	0.0500	0.0534	0.4565	0.2766	0.5272
Switzerland	0.0232	0.0377	0.0177	0.2517	0.1386	0.5000
UK	0.0366	0.0464	0.0336	0.4485	0.2034	0.5506
U.S.	0.1145	0.1800	0.0771	0.2437	0.1915	0.2947

[a] PART is defined as employed for less than 35 hours per week. This variable is not available for Hungary. Marital status is not available for Italy.

Source: Microdata-sets described in the text; in the case of countries from the ISSP, the 1985-88 ISSP files are employed.

A similar conclusion is suggested by an examination of the incidence of part-time work shown in Table 3.2. A smaller percentage of employed women in the United States than in any other country works part-time (less than 35 hours per week). Further, since the incidence of part-time work among men is considerably higher in the United States than in other countries, the gender differential in part-time work is generally much smaller there than elsewhere. (While the incidence of part-time work is only slightly higher for Italian than for U.S. women, the Italian female labor force participation rate is much lower; see Table 3.1.) We particularly note the high incidence of part-time work among Scandinavian women. About 46% of Swedish and 53% of Norwegian employed women work part-time compared with only 24% of employed U.S. women.[13] The commitment of U.S. women to market work is further underscored by an examination of the incidence of part-time work by marital status, also shown in Table 3.2. In all countries, married women are more likely to work part-time than single women, and single men generally have a higher incidence of part-time work than married men. However, U.S. married women are far less likely to work part-time than those in any other country, while U.S. married men are slightly more likely to work part-time than those elsewhere.

Table 3.3

Gender Segregation Indexes by 1-Digit Occupation and Industry[a]

Country	Occupation	Industry
Australia	0.3807	0.3302
Austria	0.4020	0.3140
Germany	0.4216	0.3203
Hungary	0.4084	0.2467
Norway (1982)	0.4341	0.3893
Sweden (1980)	0.4614	0.4263
Switzerland	0.3222	0.2913
UK	0.4395	0.3488
U.S.	0.3568	0.3430

[a] The segregation index (1) represents the proportion of women (men) who would have to change jobs for the occupational (industrial) distribution of males and females to be the same. For each country, it is computed as follows (see Duncan and Duncan 1955):

$$I = \frac{1}{2} \Sigma_i \mid p_{im} - p_{if} \mid,$$

where p_{im} is the proportion of males in the labor force employed in occupation (industry) i and p_{if} is the proportion of females in the labor force employed in occupation (industry) i.

Source: Microdata-sets described in the text. In the case of countries from the ISSP, the 1985-88 ISSP files are employed.

Tables 3.1 and 3.2 are suggestive of a higher level of relative labor force commitment among U.S. women, particularly married women, than among those in most other countries.[14] Table 3.3 indicates a lower level of occupational segregation (at the one-digit level of aggregation) for U.S. women than for those in other countries (with the exception of Switzerland).[15] Industrial segregation, again measured at the one-digit level, is similar in the United States to that in other countries. The high levels of occupational and industrial segregation in Scandinavia are especially noteworthy and perhaps understandable in light of the high incidence of part-time work there. A country's level of occupational segregation is likely to reflect both women's relative training levels and labor force commitment, and the impact of employers and of governmental or union policies (Reskin et al. 1986; Blau and Ferber 1992). To the extent that it reflects training and commitment, we may again conclude that U.S. women's workforce credentials relative to men's equal or exceed those in other countries.

3.4. Analysis of International Differences in the Pay Gap: The Effects of Skills, Treatment of Women, and Overall Inequality

3.4.1. *A Method of Decomposing the International Differences in the Pay Gap*

Juhn et al. (1991) have devised a method for examining within-country trends in demographic differentials which we have adapted to decompose the international differences in gender pay gaps into a portion due to gender-specific factors and a portion due to differences in wage structure. Suppose that we have, for male worker i and country j, a male wage equation

$$Y_{ij} = X_{ij}B_j + \sigma_j\theta_{ij}, \tag{1}$$

where Y_{ij} is the log of wages; X_{ij} is a vector of explanatory variables; B_j is a vector of coefficients; θ_{ij} is a standarized residual (i.e., with mean 0 and variance 1 for each country); and σ_j is the country's residual standard deviation of wages (i.e., its level of residual wage inequality for males). Note that, following Juhn et al. (1991), our equation (1), which is used for expositional purposes, appears to impose symmetry on the distribution of residuals. As will become clear below however, in empirically implementing their decomposition neither they nor we in fact make this assumption.

Then the male-female log wage gap for country j is:

$$D_j \equiv Y_{mj} - Y_{fj} = \Delta X_jB_j + \sigma_j\Delta\theta_j, \tag{2}$$

where the m and f subscripts refer to male and female averages, respectively; and a Δ prefix signifies the average male-female difference for the variable immediately following. Equation (2) states that the country's pay gap can be decomposed into differences in measured qualifications ΔX_j and differences in the standardized residual $\Delta\theta_j$ (multiplied by the money value per unit difference in the standardized residual σ_j). Note that the final term of (2) corresponds to the "unexplained" differential in a standard decomposition of the gender differential when the contribution of the means is evaluated using the male function.

The gender pay gap difference between two countries j and k can then be decomposed, using (2):

$$D_j - D_k = (\Delta X_j - \Delta X_k)B_k + \Delta X_j(B_j - B_k) + (\Delta\theta_j - \Delta\theta_k)\sigma_k + \Delta\theta_j(\sigma_j - \sigma_k) \tag{3}$$

The first term in (3) reflects the contribution of inter-country differences in observed labor market qualifications (X) to the gender gap. For example, the pay gap in one country may be less than in another owing to women's higher relative levels of education. The second term reflects the impact of different measured prices across countries for observed labor market qualifications. For example, for a given (positive) male-female difference in schooling, a higher return to education will raise the male-female pay gap.

The third term measures the effect of international differences in the relative wage positions of men and women after controlling for measured characteristics (i.e., whether women rank higher or lower within the male residual wage distribution). That is, it gives the contribution to the international difference in the gender gap that would result if the two countries had the same levels of residual male wage inequality and differed only in their percentile rankings of the female wage residuals. In one country, for instance, the average woman's wage residual may be at the 35th percentile of the male distribution, while in another country, it may be at only the 25th percentile. This percentile ranking may reflect gender differences in unmeasured characteristics and/or the impact of labor market discrimination against women. In the empirical work that follows, we label this term the "gap" effect.

Finally, the fourth term of (3) reflects inter-country differences in residual inequality. It measures the contribution to the inter-country difference that would result if two countries had the same percentile rankings of the female wage residuals and differed only in the extent of male residual wage inequality. Suppose, as is likely, that, controlling for measured characteristics, the female mean log wage is less than the male mean in country j. Then, the larger is the inter-country difference in the overall residual inequality in wages ($\sigma_j - \sigma_k$). The larger difference there will be in the ultimate pay gaps in the two countries. That is, deficits in female unmeasured skills or discrimination lower women's position in the male distribution of wage residuals. The larger the penalty a country places on this lower position, the larger will be its pay gap. In the empirical work below, we label this the effect of "unobserved prices."

Under the assumption of normality, the third and fourth terms of (3) could be evaluated at the mean using the estimated value of σ for each country. Following Juhn et al. (1991), however, we estimate these terms empirically using the entire distribution of male and female residuals from the male wage equation for each country. For example, to compute $(\Delta\theta_j - \theta_k)\sigma_k$, we first give each woman in country j a percentile number based on the ranking of her wage residual (from the country j male wage regression) in country j's distribution of male wage residuals. We than impute each country j woman's wage residual given her percentile ranking in country j and the distribution of male wage residuals in country k. This imputed residual (multiplied by -1) is our estimate of $\Delta\theta_j\sigma_k$. (Recall that the mean male residual is always zero.) The actual mean female wage residual from the country k male distribution of residuals (multiplied by -1) constitutes our estimate of $\Delta\theta_k\sigma_k$. The difference between the mean of these imputed wage residuals for country j and the actual mean female wage residual for country k gives the estimate of $(\Delta\theta_j - \Delta\theta_k)\sigma_k$. The fourth term of (3), $\Delta\theta_j(\sigma_j - \sigma_k)$, is obtained analogously. Note that, by using the actual distribution of male residuals, this procedure does not impose any assumption of symmetry on the residual distribution.

According to (3), the full impact of gender-specific factors is reflected in the sum of the first and third terms, the effect of gender differences in qualifications and of gender differences in wage rankings at a given level of measured characteristics. Labor market structure is reflected in the sum of the second and fourth terms, the impact of inter-country differences in returns to measured and unmeasured characteristics. Within the framework of a traditional decomposition, the sum of the third and fourth terms represents the impact of inter-country differences in the "unexplained" differential which is commonly taken as an estimate of discrimination.

Note that equation (3) is an index number formulation, and that a change in any of the weights employed could alter the specific value obtained for each of the four components of the decomposition. For example, the formulation we employ is based on a male wage equation, rather than, say, a female equation differences in the coefficients from a male wage regression would be less affected by international differences in the extent of discrimination against women than would coefficients from a female or a pooled male-female equation. Since these coefficients constitute our estimate of each country's prices of observed characteristics, it is important that they be as uncontaminated as possible by the extent of discrimination against women in each country.[16] Similarly, in the empirical work below, each country j is compared with the United States (i.e., country k). This means that country j weights (i.e., ΔX_j and $\Delta\theta_j$) are used to evaluate the international differences in the components of wage structure - observed and unobserved prices (i.e., $(B_j - B_k)$ and $(\sigma_j - \sigma_k)$, while the U.S. weights (i.e., B_k and σ_k) are used to evaluate the contribution of international differences in gender-specific factors - observed Xs and women's rankings in the male residual wage distribution (i.e., $(\Delta X_j - \Delta X_k)$ and $(\Delta\theta_j - \Delta\theta_k)$). Reversing this, that is using country j weights to evaluate differences in gender-specific factors and U.S. weights to evaluate differences in wage structure, could alter the specific results somewhat. The use of one country (e.g., the United States) as a consistent frame of reference for all the pair-wise comparisons is desirable, since in that way the magnitude of U.S.-country j differences may be compared across countries in our sample. The selection of the United States as this reference country in the decomposition is logical, since this study is chiefly concerned with the sources of the relatively high genderwage gap in the United States.

The possibility of discrimination complicates the interpretation of the last term of (3). With labor market discrimination, this term in part reflects the interaction between country j's level of discrimination (which pushes women down the distribution of wages) and inter-country differences in the overall level of inequality, which determine how large the penalty is for that lower position in the distribution (Juhn et al. 1991). We will present some indirect evidence that, in the case of the countries compared here, this term at least in part reflects the impact of overall wage-setting. The observed price effect may also reflect discrimination if, for example, women are "crowded" by exclusion into certain sectors, lowering relative earnings there even for men (Bergmann 1974).

A final issue to note in interpreting our results is that they may be affected by selectivity bias (Heckman 1980). This is of particular concern in that, as may be seen in Table 3.1, countries vary considerably in their female labor force participation rates. While it is theoretically possible for labor force participants to be either a positively or negatively selected group in terms of their unmeasured characteristics (Blau and Beller 1988), a plausible possibility is that women are a more positively selected group in terms of their unmeasured characteristics in countries with relatively low female participation rates. A conventional approach to adjusting for selectivity bias in unmeasured characteristics is to employ a Heckman (1980) selectivity bias correction to obtain consistent estimates of the coefficients in the earnings equation. This approach, however, has come under increasing criticism for its lack of robustness: "seemingly small misspecifications may generate large biases in estimates [...]" (Manski 1989: 356). For this reason, we do not employ it here. Our use of the male earnings function to perform the decomposition helps to ameliorate this difficulty, since there is considerably less international variation in male than in female participation rates (Table 3.1). It is none the less true that the estimated gap effects may include the impact of gender differences in unmeasured characteristics as well as gender differences in discrimination - this is of course always the case in such decompositions. However, the international differences in female participation rates suggest that the magnitude of these two components may well vary across countries. This is not of undue concern for our study, however, since our major interest is in identifying the role of wage structure versus gender-specific factors, rather than identifying the importance of discrimination per se. Gender-specific factors include the impact of gender differences in both measured and unmeasured characteristics, as well as discrimination.

3.4.2. *Implementing the Decomposition*

We implement the decomposition using the Juhn et al. (1991) accounting method performed on equation (1). With the exception of the U.S.-Sweden 1984 comparison, each country's gross gender differential is expressed in terms of $YFULL$, log earnings corrected for hours. These estimates were obtained as follows. For each country, the following regression was run separately by sex:

$$(4) \qquad \ln EARN = b_0 + b_1 PART + b_2 HRPART + b_3 HRFULL + B'X + e,$$

where $\ln (EARN)$ is the natural log of earnings; $PART$ is a dummy variable for part-time employment defined as less than 35 hours per week;[17] $HRPART$ and $HRFULL$ are interactions of weekly work hours with part- and full-time status; X is a vector of explanatory variables described below; and e is an error term. The model allows for both a part-time shift term and different slopes for hours for part-time and full-time workers. A detailed adjustment for part-time employment is important in light of the prevalence of part-time work for women in many countries.

The $PART$, $HRPART$, and $HRFULL$ coefficients from (3) were used to adjust each person's earnings for work hours by assuming a 40-hour work week. That is, for each worker i, we have

$$YFULL_i = \ln EARN_i - b_1 PART_i - b_2 HRPART_i - b_3(HRFULL_i - 40) \quad (5)$$

where the coefficients, b_n, are obtained from estimating equation (4) for males and females separately.[18]

The explanatory variables in X include the traditional human capital variables of education, potential experience and its square, as well as union membership, and one-digit industry and occupation dummy variables.[19] (See the Appendix for variable definitions.) The structural variables (i.e., industry, occupation, and unionism) may reflect both worker skills and rents received by workers with these characteristics. Unfortunately, the data-sets available to us for the broad ten-country comparison lack information on actual labor market experience. Thus, this remains an important omitted variable in these analyses, although, to some degree, our controls for education, hours, industry, and occupation may pick up some of the effects of such omissions. Fortunately, data on actual experience are available for the 1984 Swedish-U.S. comparison presented in Section IV(d). As we shall see, those results are quite supportive of our findings based on potential experience for Sweden and the other countries.

We have not controlled for marital status in this analysis, although it may be an important factor influencing the pay gap. An alternative would have been to include martial status as a productivity characteristic. However, such an approach is problematic since this variable appears to measure higher skills for men (Korenman and Neumark 1991) but most likely lower skills for women, especially when data on actual labor market experience are lacking. The approach we have followed allows us to place a sharper interpretation in the decomposition on the impact of differences in labor market skills. Recognizing the potential importance of marital status, however, we also perform a decomposition of pay gaps among married and single workers based on our overall wage equation. Number of children was not explicitly available in most of our data-sets,[20] but similar considerations would have led us to exclude this variable as well. Number of children is likely to be an indicator of work discontinuity for women, but to measure greater workforce commitment for men. The availability of actual labor market experience for our 1984 Sweden-U.S. comparison presented below enables us to examine the sensitivity of our findings to this important omitted variable. As noted above, at least for this two-country comparison, our major findings are unchanged when we are able to include a measure of actual experience.

Before proceeding further, however, it is useful as a check on our basic approach to enquire whether a significant portion of the overall differences between the United States and other countries in these data-sets is due to differences in the marital status composition of the workforce. If this is the case, it would suggest a need to deal with marital status more explicitly in our estimating equation. To address this question, gross hours-corrected gender earnings ratios based on the mean of *YFULL* for married and single workers were calculated for each country and are shown in the first two columns of Table 3.4. As expected, in each country the gender gap is smaller for single than for married workers. (Marital status is of course in part a proxy for the presence of children.) Moreover, except for Hungary, for which we have no data on hours, the pay ratio is relatively high among single workers, ranging from 0.81 to 0.96.[21] Further, the rankings of the pay gaps for single workers are not always consistent with the overall rankings. In contrast, the pay gap is much larger for married workers and corresponds more consistently to the rankings for the overall labor force. None the less, since the ratios for married workers are always lower than those for single workers, a question may be raised as to whether the overall differences in ratios across countries are simply due to inter-country differences in family composition. This appears not to be the case, however. In the fourth column of Table 3.4, the earnings ratios for all workers are computed using the U.S. proportions of married and single workers. The implied ratios are similar to those for all workers shown in the third column of the table. In like manner, the mean percentile rankings computed using the U.S. proportions of female married and single workers are quite close to the actual mean female percentiles. These similarities indicate that cross-country differences in the family composition of the labor force do not account for the observed differences in relative pay gaps and percentile rankings.

Table 3.4

The Impact of Family Composition on Gender Earnings Ratios and Female Percentiles Corrected for Hours only[a]

	Gender ratio				Mean female wage percentile	
	Actual		All workers		All workers	
Country	Married workers	Single workers	Actual	U.S. family composition[b]	Actual	U.S. family composition[c]
Australia	0.6755	0.9044	0.7334	0.7386	32.3	31.6
Austria	0.6452	0.9111	0.7265	0.7343	29.5	29.6
Germany	0.5988	0.9641	0.7017	0.7171	27.0	27.0
Hungary	0.6084	0.7734	0.6488	0.6629	21.7	21.7
Norway (1982)	0.6756	0.8959	0.7139	0.7412	26.4	25.2
Norway (1989)	0.6722	0.8079	0.7054	0.7138	19.6	19.2
Sweden (1980)	0.7209	0.9435	0.7726	0.7866	28.2	28.6
Switzerland	0.6140	0.8710	0.6455	0.6873	27.6	28.3
UK	0.5585	0.8301	0.6142	0.6466	23.8	23.7
U.S.	0.5485	0.8681	0.6535	0.6535	32.3	32.3

[a] YFULL, earnings evaluated at full-time (40) hours (see equation (5)). The number of hours is not available for Hungary, but all workers are full-time.
[b] Computed using U.S. proportions of married and single workers.
[c] Computed using U.S. proportions of female married and single workers.

3.4.3. *Empirical Results: A Ten-Country Comparison*

The results of applying the decomposition for the whole labor force across our broad range of countries is summarized in Table 3.5. We see that the mean female residual percentile (i.e., the mean female percentile after controlling for measured characteristics)[22] ranges from 18.5 in Norway (1989) to 37.5 in Switzerland. It is noteworthy that U.S. women with a mean percentile ranking of 35.5 place with the top group (including Switzerland, Australia, Sweden 1980, and Italy). The column headed "Gap" shows the contribution of each country's female placement in the male residual wage distribution to its relative pay gap. The figure is positive for all countries except Australia, Italy, and Sweden,[23] indicating that these differences in rankings raise the differential relative to the United States, often substantially. (The unweighted average effect is 0.2333.) In contrast, the column headed "Unobserved prices" shows that the lower level of residual wage inequality in each of the other countries has a negative effect, often quite considerable, on its gap relative to that in the United States. (The unweighted average effect is -0.2560.)

Table 3.5

Analysis of Log Wages (YFULL), all workers

Country	D^a	Mean female residual	Mean female residual percentile[b]	Male residual std. dev.	Female residual std. rev.[c]	$D_i - D_{USA}$
Australia	0.3101	-0.2385	36.8	0.5998	0.6811	-0.1198
Austria	0.3195	-0.3019	28.1	0.3776	0.4315	-0.1059
Germany	0.3542	-0.3020	29.8	0.3780	0.4822	-0.0712
Hungary	0.4326	-0.4110	21.2	0.3898	0.3665	0.0129
Italy	0.3249	-0.2304	35.9	0.4731	0.4974	-0.1008
Norway (1982)	0.3370	-0.3070	29.5	0.4101	0.5120	-0.0884
Norway (1989)	0.3490	-0.3230	18.5	0.2724	0.3108	-0.0761
Sweden (1980)	0.2580	-0.1986	36.2	0.4231	0.4551	-0.1674
Switzerland	0.4377	-0.2232	37.5	0.4049	0.5236	0.0123
UK	0.4875	-0.4001	23.7	0.4068	0.4486	0.0621
U.S.	0.4254	-0.3079	35.5	0.6646	0.7699	—

Country	Observed *X*s	Observed prices	Gap	Unob-served prices	Sum gender-specific[d]	Sum wage structure[e]
Australia	0.0563	-0.0732	-0.0671	-0.0358	-0.0108	-0.1090
Austria	0.0575	-0.1573	0.2813	-0.2873	0.3388	-0.4446
Germany	0.0318	-0.0973	0.2421	-0.2480	0.2739	-0.3453
Hungary	-0.0567	-0.0287	0.6272	-0.5290	0.5705	-0.5577
Italy	0.0299	-0.0094	-0.0239	-0.0974	0.0060	-0.1068
Norway (1982)	0.00002	-0.0874	0.2112	-0.2121	0.2112	-0.2995
Norway (1989)	-0.0760	-0.0142	0.5829	-0.5688	0.5069	-0.5830
Sweden (1980)	-0.0309	-0.0270	-0.0122	-0.0971	-0.0431	-0.1241
Switzerland	0.1030	-0.0061	0.0683	-0.1530	0.1713	-0.1591
UK	0.0108	-0.0411	0.4232	-0.3310	0.4340	-0.3721
Average (unweighted)	0.0126	-0.0542	0.2333	-0.2560	0.2459	-0.3101

[a] The gender difference in YFULL, earnings evaluated at full-time (40) hours (see equation (5)).
[b] The mean female residual percentile in the male distribution of wage residuals.
[c] Calculated from female wage regressions.
[d] The sum of the observed Xs and gap effects.
[e] The sum of the observed and unobserved prices effects.

Notes: Regressions include controls for education, potential experience and its square, union status, and occupation, industry, and (where applicable) year dummy variables. The U.S. value used to calculate '$D_i - D_{USA}$' for Hungary, Australia, and Italy is based on hours corrections from U.S. regressions which conform to the specifications for each of those countries. However, the U.S. value in the 'D' column is based on the more detailed specification permitted by the ISSP and CSCC data files.

Table 3.5 also provides estimates of the impact of measured skills and their prices on inter-country differences in the pay gap. The "Observed *X*s" effect is, with three exceptions (i.e., Hungary, Norway 1989 and Sweden 1980), positive, indicating that U.S. women have relatively favourable levels of the measured variables. (The unweighted average effect is 0.0126.) The "Observed prices" effect is always negative, indicating that the male returns to the explanatory variables increase the pay gap in the United States relative to that in other countries. (The unweighted average effect is -0.0542.) However, these observed effects are much smaller in magnitude than the "Unobserved prices" and "Gap" effects.

The last two columns of the lower panel of Table 3.5 give the total effect of gender-specific factors and wage structure. As our discussion of the components suggest, U.S. women fare well with respect to gender-specific factors (as measured by the sum of the "Observed Xs" and the "Gap" effects). With a few exceptions, U.S. women tend to have relatively favorable levels of both productivity characteristics and gender-specific treatment in the labor market. The overall gender-specific effects are generally positive; the unweighted average is 0.2459. Negative effects are obtained only for Sweden (-0.0431) and Australia (-0.0108). One interpretation of the moderate gender-specific effects favouring Swedish and Australian women is that the types of gender-related interventions discussed above in Sweden (i.e., parental leave) and Australia (i.e., comparable worth) have had a particularly favorable impact. We may note two points in this regard. First, with respect to Sweden, our 1984 comparison, which contains data on actual labor market experience, does not find a negative gap effect for Sweden. This suggests that, in so far as Sweden's parental leave policy has produced positive effects for women, they are captured by the smaller gender difference in labor market experience there. Second, with respect to Australia, our Australian data-set does not include trade unionism and, thus, we are unable to control for this variable. Since men are more likely than women to be unionized, and since the return to unionism is particularly high in the United States (Blau and Kahn 1996a, see Chapter 5), it is possible that, were we able to control for unionism, the small gap effect favoring Australian women would be eliminated.

In contrast to the impact of gender-specific factors which favor U.S. women in all but two cases, the U.S. level of inequality (reflected in the sum of "Observed prices" and "Unobserved prices" effects) greatly raises its gender pay gap compared with each of the other countries in the sample; the unweighted average effect is -0.3101. This inequality effect is sufficient or more than sufficient to account for the higher pay gap in the United States than in four of the six countries with smaller gaps. In the remaining two cases, the wage structure effect accounts for 91% of the Australia-U.S. difference and for 74% of the Sweden-U.S. difference in the magnitude of the gender gap. As will be seen in greater detail below, however, using the more precise 1984 Sweden-U.S. comparison, wage structure is more than sufficient to account for the full difference in the gender gaps between these two countries.

An additional point of interest in Table 3.5 is that the residual standard deviation of the wage regressions is considerably higher for U.S. men and women than for men and women in other countries. (The female residual standard deviation is computed from a female wage regression.) Across all the countries in the sample, the correlation coefficient between the male and female residual standard deviations is 0.9427. The fact that the male and female residual standard deviations seem to move together in this manner adds credibility to our framework in which a country's overall level of inequality is assumed to affect both men and women. The standard deviation of gross hours corrected earnings (YFULL) is also higher in the United States than elsewhere (results not shown). Similarly, across all countries, the correlation of the male and female standard deviations is 0.9177.[24]

Summary results are presented separately for married workers (panel A) and single workers (panel B) in Table 3.6.[25] The first two columns provide descriptive statistics. In column (1) we show the actual male-female log wage gap for each group corresponding to the gender ratios shown in Table 3.4. Column (2) gives the male-female difference in the mean residuals from the overall male wage equation. Note that, since married and single men each comprise only a subgroup of all males, the mean male residual for each group is not zero: rather, the mean residual for married men tends to be positive and that for single men, negative. The male-female difference in mean residuals corresponds to the "unexplained" pay gap, where the gender differences in means are evaluated using the estimated coefficients from the overall male earnings regression.[26] As noted above, this is often used as a measure of the impact of discrimination.

Table 3.6

Analysis of Log Wages (YFULL), Married and Single Workers

	Descriptive statistics		$D_i - D_{USA}$			
			Male-female mean log wage		Male-female mean residual	
Country	Male-female mean log wage (1)	Male-female mean residual[a] (2)	Actual (3)	Adjusted for wage structure[b] (4)	Actual (5)	Adjusted for wage structure[c] (6)
A: Married						
Australia	0·3923	0·2968	-0·2082	-0·1405	-0·1378	-0·0914
Austria	0·4382	0·4000	-0·1624	0·2069	-0·0345	0·3504
Germany	0·5129	0·4558	-0·0877	0·2644	0·0212	0·4130
Hungary	0·4969	0·4534	-0·1037	0·4881	0·0188	0·6025
Norway (1982)	0·3921	0·3335	-0·2085	0·0649	-0·1010	0·1319
Norway (1989)	0·3972	0·3527	-0·2034	0·2642	-0·0818	0·5618
Sweden (1980)	0·3273	0·2283	-0·2733	-0·1062	-0·2063	-0·0895
Switzerland	0·4877	0·2860	-0·1128	0·0221	-0·1486	0·1131
UK	0·5825	0·4730	-0·0181	0·3775	0·0385	0·4396
U.S.	0·6006	0·4345	—	—	—	—
Unweighted non-US average	0·4475	0·3644	-0·1531	0·1602	-0·0702	0·2702
B: Single						
Australia	0·1005	0·1163	-0·0409	-0·0321	-0·0170	-0·0002
Austria	0·0931	0·1635	-0·0483	0·0662	0·0301	0·1873
Germany	0·0366	0·0923	-0·1048	-0·0778	-0·0410	0·0128
Hungary	0·2570	0·2766	0·1155	0·5449	0·1432	0·5058
Norway (1982)	0·1099	0·1975	-0·0315	0·0807	0·0641	0·1990
Norway (1989)	0·2133	0·2380	0·0719	0·3439	0·1046	0·4671
Sweden (1980)	0·0582	0·1189	-0·0832	-0·0453	-0·0145	0·0303
Switzerland	0·1382	0·1639	-0·0032	-0·0097	0·0306	0·1028
UK	0·1862	0·1952	0·0448	0·2036	0·0619	0·2071
U.S.	0·1414	0·1334	—	—	—	—
Unweighted non-US average	0·1325	0·1736	-0·0089	0·1194	0·0402	0·1902

[a] Male-female difference in mean residuals for the indicated marital status group from the overall male wage regression.

[b] Adjusted for wage structure based on the U.S. distribution of wages for all male workers.

[c] Adjusted for wage structure based on the U.S. male distribution of residuals from the overall male wage regression.

The U.S.-country i difference in the log wage gender gaps and the gender difference in mean wage residuals $(D_i - D_{USA})$ are shown in columns (3) and (5). Columns (4) and (6) give the estimates of the magnitude of each of these, i.e., the male-female log wage gap and the male-female difference in mean residuals, after adjusting for wage structure. To adjust for wage structure, we evaluate the country i gender difference at the U.S. level of wage inequality. In the case of the gender differences in mean residuals, this corresponds to the gap effect as defined in equation (3). The gender log wage differentials adjusted for wage structure are computed similarly, except we do not control for any variables. This approximates the total effect of gender-specific factors (i.e., the sum of the observed *X*s and gap effects) shown in Table 3.5, although it is computed somewhat differently. Note too that, in computing these effects for married and single workers, we use as our reference the overall male wage distribution.

Looking first at the results for married women, we see that our conclusions are quite similar to those for all workers. The U.S.-country *i* difference in gender log wage gaps shown in column (3) is always negative, indicating that the U.S. gap is larger, often considerably so; the unweighted average country *i*-U.S. difference is -0.1531 log points. After controlling for measured characteristics in the conventional fashion by looking at the differences in residuals shown in column (5), the U.S. gap remains larger in most cases (6 out of 9 possible comparisons); the unweighted average difference is -0.0702, and only three countries have somewhat larger gender gaps for married women than the United States: United Kingdom, Germany, and Hungary. When the gender difference in residuals is adjusted for wage structure, however, we find that the gender gap is generally larger in other countries, often considerably so; the unweighted average effect is 0.2702. Only two countries have smaller gaps: Sweden and Australia. Each of these countries also had negative gap effects for all workers in Table 3.5; however, the magnitude of the estimated effects is larger in absolute value for married workers than for all workers: -0.·0895 versus -0.0122 for Sweden and -0.0914 versus -0.0671 for Australia.

Findings for the actual log wage gap adjusted for wage structure (column 4) which represents the total gender-specific effect are similar. The unweighted average U.S.-country i difference is 0.1602, and only Sweden and Australia have smaller gaps than the United States. The estimated total gender-specific effects are again larger in absolute value for married workers than for all workers: -0.1062 versus -0.0431 for Sweden and -0.1405 versus -0.0108 for Australia. Thus, for married women we find that, as was the case in the full sample, with the exception of Australia and Sweden, higher U.S. inequality (i.e., wage structure) is sufficient or more than sufficient to explain the larger pay gap in the United States compared with the countries with smaller differentials. Wage structure explains 61% of the U.S.-Sweden difference and about one-third of the U.S.-Australia difference.

The results for single workers, shown in panel B of Table 3.6, also support the notion that wage structure is important. However, since, as noted in our discussion of Table 3.4, the initial U.S.-country *i* differences are smaller and the cross-country pattern of the differences is less consistently related to the pattern of international differences in overall gender ratios, the results are less informative. In general, the U.S. differential does exceed that in other countries, but three of the other countries - the United Kingdom, Hungary, and Norway 1989 - have larger gaps, as is indicated by a positive sign in column (3). Adjusting for measured characteristics through a comparison of gender differences in residuals leaves only three countries with smaller gender differentials than the United States: Germany, Sweden, and Australia column (5). After additionally adjusting for wage structure in column (6), all but one of the countries (i.e., Australia) has a larger differential than the United States and the Australia-U.S. difference is virtually zero. This contrasts with the fairly substantial negative gap effects obtained for married women in panel A of Table 3.6 for both Australia and Sweden. Finally, the gender log wage gaps adjusted for wage structure which are shown in column (4) suggest that the total gender-specific effect for single workers is generally positive (i.e., favours U.S. women), but is moderately negative in four cases: Sweden, Australia, Germany, and Switzerland. Both Sweden and Australia also had negative total gender-specific effects for married women in panel A, but these effects were considerably larger in absolute value for married than for single women: -0.1062 for married women versus -0.0453 for single women in Sweden (1980) and -0.1405 for married women versus -0.0321 for single women in Australia.

One interpretation of the more favourable gender-specific effects for married women than for single women for Sweden and Australia is that the types of gender-related intervention that we have identified as significant in these countries have had a disproportionate effect on married workers; that is, not surprisingly, parental leave (Sweden), but also comparable worth (Australia), may have especially large positive effects on the relative earnings of married women.

The striking finding of Tables 3.5 and 3.6 is the importance of wage structure in explaining the higher U.S. gender gap. However, as noted above, the observed and unobserved prices effects that represent the components of the wage structure effect could also reflect the impact of labor market discrimination. What are we thus to conclude about wage structure? From a number of indirect indicators, we conclude that it is important, even though it may not be possible precisely to estimate its effect.

First, our review of wage-setting institutions in each country strongly suggests that the U.S. system is considerably less centralized than in other countries, thus making a finding of the importance of wage structure plausible. Second, the United States has had a longer and often stronger commitment to Equal Pay and Employment Opportunity policies than most other countries in our sample.[27] Further, U.S. women compare favorably with women in other countries in terms of their qualifications and occupational distribution relative to men. Thus, it is credible that gender-specific factors do not explain the relatively high pay gap in the United States. Third, we found that the wage variation and residual wage variation of both men and women in the United States considerably exceeds that of the same gender group in other countries. Similarly, across all countries, female and male wage (and residual wage) variation were found to be highly correlated. This suggests that the same set of factors - measured and unmeasured prices and wage-setting institutions - affects the wages of both men and women in each country in a similar way. Finally, and perhaps most importantly, even though the estimated wage structure effect may include the impact of gender discrimination as it interacts with wage structure, our findings for the ten-country comparison none the less suggest an extremely important role for wage structure in affecting the overall gender ratio.

3.4.4. *Empirical Results: A Detailed Comparison of the United States and Sweden (1984)*

In this section we take advantage of the superior data available in the PSID for the United States and in the HUS for Sweden to verify the results obtained using our other data sources. Since these datasets contain information on weeks as well as hours worked, we are able to calculate a wage rate. The presence of information on actual labor market experience permits us to control for this important variable in our wage regressions and corresponding decompositions. Finally, since these data are available for the same year, 1984, we are able to compare the economic status of women in each of these two countries at the same point in time. The results obtained for this comparison strongly confirm the importance of wage structure in explaining the differences in the gender wage gaps in the two, countries and thus strengthen our confidence in the general findings of this study.

Table 3.7

Descriptive Statistics: Sweden and the United States, 1984[a]

	US	Sweden
Gender log wage differential	0·4019	0·1897
Gender wage ratio (%)	66·9	82·7
Mean female percentile	29·6	29·9
Male residual standard deviation	0·5110	0·2324
Female residual standard deviation[b]	0·4862	0·2283
Mean female residual	-0·1965	-0·0955
Adjusted wage ratio	82·2	90·9
Mean female residual percentile	36·6	37·4

[a] Based on HUS data for Sweden and PSID data for the United States.
[b] Calculated from female wage regressions.

Descriptive statistics for the 1984 comparison are shown in Table 3.7. The estimates of the gender ratio based on wages, of 66.9% for the United States and 82.7% for Sweden, are a bit higher for each country than the ratio adjusted for time inputs shown in Figure 3.1, but the differences are not large and, furthermore, the large U.S.-Sweden difference remains.[28] Swedish women also fare better after adjusting for all variables, including major industry and occupation: the adjusted wage ratio was 82.2% for the United States and 90.9% for Sweden. Despite these sizeable U.S.-Sweden differences in the adjusted and unadjusted gender ratios, the mean percentile rankings of women in the male wage distribution and residual wage distribution are virtually identical, suggesting an important role for wage structure in explaining the cross-country difference. Finally, looking at Figure 3.4, which gives a more detailed comparison of female percentile rankings in the two countries, we see that the female cumulative distribution functions (i.e., the percentage of women with earnings in or below the indicated male decile) are quite similar in the two countries. Indeed, a higher percentage of women in Sweden (29.1%) than in the United States (20.1%) fall in the lowest decile, as was also generally true in our ten-country comparison (Figure 3.3).

A detailed decomposition of the U.S.-Sweden difference is presented in Table 3.8. With respect to gender-specific factors, the overall impact of gender differences in the observed Xs in each country is negligible.

Figure 3.4

Cumulative Distribution Function, Female Wages Relative to the Male Wage Distribution, United States and Sweden, 1984

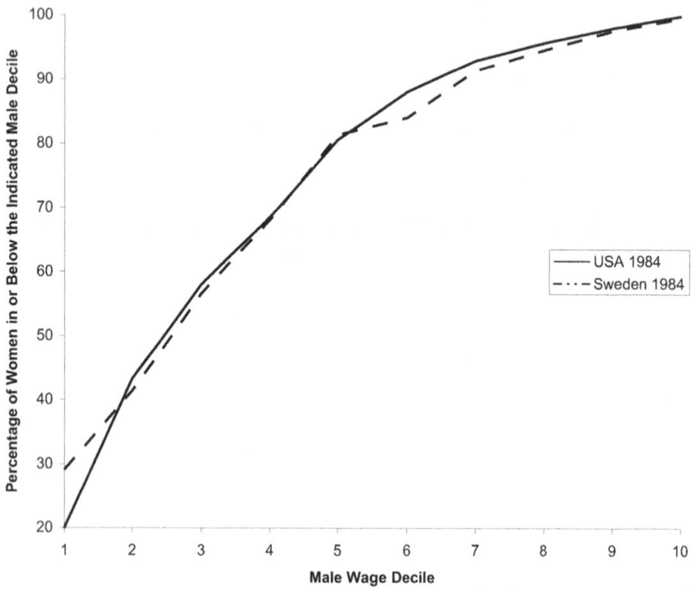

Table 3.8

Analysis of Differences in the Gender Pay Gap: Sweden and the United States, 1984[a]

Component	Contribution to the US-Sweden difference
Observed *X*s	-0·0054
Education variables	0·0226
Experience variables	-0·0313
Occupation variables	-0·0315
Industry variables	0·0348
Observed prices	-0·1058
Education variables	-0·0176
Experience variables	-0·0162
Occupation variables	-0·0031
Industry variables	-0·0689
Gap	0·0303
Unobserved prices	-0·1313
Sum gender-specific	0·0249
Sum wage structure	-0·2371
Total (D_{Sweden}-D_{USA})	-0·2122

[a] Based on HUS data for Sweden and PSID data for the United States.

This reflects a somewhat smaller gender difference in actual experience in Sweden (five years) than in the United States (six years) and a slightly more favorable relative occupational distribution of Swedish than of U.S. women. These factors are offset by differences favoring U.S. women relative to their male counterparts with respect to education and industrial distribution. In contrast to our results for the CSCC and ISSP data presented above, the gap effect somewhat favors U.S. women. This may indicate that, with better data on labor market experience, the impact of Sweden's more favorable maternity leave policy is captured by the smaller gender difference in measured experience. On net, the sum of gender-specific factors slightly favors U.S. women.

In contrast to the gender-specific factors, wage structure as indicated by the observed and unobserved prices effects strongly favors Swedish women. In terms of observed prices, the Swedish-U.S. difference in relative rewards to employment by industry is the most important factor, although less favorable (for women) prices of education and experience in the United States also play a role. Overall, the effect of wage structure, i.e., the higher level of wage inequality in the United States, is more than sufficient to account for the considerably larger gender gap in the United States.

The results for married and single women based on the overall male wage regression are shown in Table 3.9. As in the case of our ten-country comparison by marital status, we find that gender log wage gaps tend to be larger in both countries for married than for single women. This is also true of the gaps controlling for measured characteristics, as indicated by the male-female difference in the residuals. The Sweden-U.S. difference in gender gaps, both in log wages and in mean residuals, is also larger for married women. In comparing our results with those in Table 3.6, it is interesting to note that, using a measure of actual labor market experience, we no longer find either total or residual gender-specific effects favouring Swedish married women. Thus, wage structure is more than sufficient to explain both the U.S.-Sweden differences in overall gender gaps among married women, and gender gaps after controlling for measured characteristics. This again suggests that the favorable impact on women of Sweden's more generous parental leave policy is captured by the smaller difference between men and women in levels of experience in Sweden. For single women, the residual differential adjusted for wage structure is positive, indicating a favorable gap effect for U.S. women. While the log wage differential adjusted for wage structure is negative, wage structure is sufficient to explain 71% of the U.S.-Sweden difference in gender log ratios for single women. Since we have seen that the gap effect favors U.S. women, this must be due to differences in relative levels of observed *X*s favoring Swedish women.

Table 3.9

Analysis of Log Wages, Married and Single Workers: Sweden and the United States, 1984

	Married	Single
Descriptive statistics		
Male-female log wage		
Sweden	0·2068	0·0909
U.S.	0·4270	0·2689
Male-female residual		
Sweden	0·0976	0·0838
U.S.	0·2078	0·1586
Decomposition (D_{Sweden} - D_{USA})		
Male-female log wage		
Actual	-0·2203	-0·1780
Adjusted for wage structure	0·0436	-0·0518
Male-female residual		
Actual	-0·1103	-0·0748
Adjusted for wage structure	0·0229	0·0507

3.4.5. *Some General Evidence on the Effects of Institutions*

The evidence so far has suggested that the relatively higher level of wage inequality in the United States is an important factor working to increase the gender gap in the United States relative to other countries. We also speculated that the more decentralized wage-setting system in the United States is responsible, at least in part, for its higher wage dispersion. While our sample for the broad cross-country comparison is relatively small (10), it is still possible to obtain some indication of whether these relationships hold more generally, i.e., beyond the individual U.S.-other country comparisons that we have made up to this point. Specifically, we wish to know whether higher male wage inequality and decentralization of wage-setting institutions are generally associated with a larger gender gap, particularly a larger differential that may be attributed to wage structure. In the analyses below, we use as our measure of male inequality the U.S.-country *i* difference in the log wage difference between male workers at the 50th percentile of the male wage distribution and male workers at the 10th percentile of the distribution.[29]

Performing such a test also requires us to operationalize the concept of centralization in wage-setting. Several authors have produced rankings of countries with respect to the degree of centralization, including Blyth (1987), Bruno and Sachs (1985), Calmfors and Driffill (1988), Cameron (1984), and Schmitter (1981). These rankings take into account the degree of co-ordination within and between labor and management organizations, the level at which bargaining takes place, and the power of central bodies to conduct wage negotiations (Calmfors and Driffill 1988). We use as a measure of centralization the unweighted average of these rankings (which are shown individually in Calmfors and Driffill 1988: 18), correcting for differences across authors in the number of countries ranked. Based on this average ranking, Austria, with a ranking of 1.493 out of 17 countries, had the most centralized wage-setting system among the countries in our sample; while the United States, with a ranking of 15.191 out of 17, not surprisingly, had the least.[30] While Hungary as a Communist country in the 1980s was not included in the rankings, we assigned it the highest level of centralization since the government set wages there. This index which we term "decentralization," is then used as an inverse measure of centralization in regressions described below.

The dependent variables in our analyses are: (1) $D_i - D_{USA}$: the U.S.-country i difference in log wage gender differentials (defined in terms of $YFULL$, the log of hours-corrected earnings); (2) the sum of gender-specific factors (observed Xs plus gap effects); (3) the sum of wage structure effects (observed plus unobserved prices effects). Note that these dependent variables are measured relative to the United States. (We include the United States with a value of zero in each case.) These dependent variables are regressed on our indicator of the level of male inequality, the U.S.-country i difference in the 50-10 differential, and, in separate regressions, on the index of decentralization. The 50-10 differential is defined relative to the United States, as is decentralization, up to a constant.

Table 3.10 contains our results, both including and excluding Hungary. (The results are qualitatively similar whether or not Hungary is included.) Most striking are the findings for the wage structure effect. Both the magnitude of male inequality and the degree of decentralization of wage-setting is found to be positively associated with the wage structure effect; the coefficient is 2.6-2.8 times its standard error for the 50-10 differential and 2.7-3.4 times its standard error for decentralization. In contrast, male inequality and decentralization are negatively related to the gender-specific effect, although the coefficients are less precisely estimated; the coefficient is 1.6 times its standard error for the 50-10 differential and 1.1-1.7 its standard error for decentralization. One possibility here is that centralized wage-setting systems tend to narrow skill differentials and that this dispropor tionately negatively affects women's incentives to accumulate skills. Finally, we have some evidence that male inequality and decentralization are associated with a higher gender gap overall, with this coefficient smaller than its standard error for the 50-10 differential and 1.1-1.9 times its standard error for decentralization.

Table 3.10

The Effect of Male Wage Inequality and Male Wage-Setting Institutions on the Gender Pay Gap and its Components

	Dependent variables					
Explanatory variable	$D_i - D_{USA}$	Gender-specific effect	Wage structure effect	$D_i - D_{USA}$	Gender-specific effect	Wage structure effect
Decentralization	0·0054	-0·0197	0·0251	—	—	—
	(0·0048)	(0·0115)	(0·0075)			
Male 50-10 differential:	—	—	—	0·0905	0·4884	0·5789
Country *i* v. US				(0·1284)	(0·3055)	(0·2235)
Constant	-0·1021	0·369	-0·4711	-0·0143	0·0298	0·0155
	(0·0045)	(0·1092)	(0·0711)	(0·0688)	(0·1638)	(0·1198)
Hungary in?	yes	yes	yes	yes	yes	yes
R-squared	0·1419	0·2678	0·5835	0·0584	0·2421	0·456
n	10	10	10	10	10	10
	Dependent variables					
Explanatory variable	$D_i - D_{USA}$	Gender-specific effect	Wage structure effect	$D_i - D_{USA}$	Gender-specific effect	Wage structure effect
Decentralization	0·0088	-0·0125	0·0213	—	—	—
	(0·0046)	(0·0117)	(0·0080)			
Male 50-10 differential:	—	—	—	0·1085	-0·4161	0·5246
Country *i* v. US				(0·1289)	(0·2593)	(0·1867)
Constant	-0·1429	0·2809	-0·4237	-0·0143	0·0298	0·0155
	(0·0455)	(0·1170)	(0·0801)	(0·0685)	(0·1378)	(0·0992)
Hungary in?	no	no	no	no	no	no
R-squared	0·3454	0·1390	0·5001	0·092	0·2689	0·4631
n	9	9	9	9	9	9

The results of Table 3.10 suggest that male inequality and decentralization are positively associated with wage structure effects increasing the gender differential. One reason for this may be that centralized wage-setting has particularly strong effects in bringing up the bottom of the wage distribution (Blau and Kahn 1996a, see Chapter 5), which would disproportionately positively affect women. Admittedly, our sample of countries is extremely small - only ten. However, these results, in conjunction with the individual U.S.-other country comparisons, lend plausibility to the idea that wage-setting institutions are important.

3.5. Conclusions

In this chapter, we have used microdata to examine the gender pay gap in ten industrialized countries. Published data indicate that the gender gap is higher in the United States than in most industrialized countries, and it is higher than six of the countries in our sample. The striking finding is the importance of wage structure in explaining the larger U.S. gender gap. The higher level of wage inequality in the United States than elsewhere works to increase the gender differential in the United States relative to all the other countries in our sample. Our results suggest that the U.S. gap would be similar to that in countries like Sweden and Australia (the countries with the smallest gaps) if the United States had their level of wage inequality. This suggests that we need to focus both on the supply and demand for skills (i.e., some of the determinants of skill prices) and on wage-setting institutions to explain this important cause international differences in the gender pay gap. In a brief review of the institutional setting in each of these countries, we concluded that the wage-determination process in the United States is more decentralized than elsewhere, quite likely contributing to its higher level of wage inequality.

These findings have implications for analyses of trends in the gender gap across time as well as across countries. Much attention has been focused on women's growing relative levels of skills and labor force commitment as causes of changes in the pay gap. Our research suggests that, to understand changes in the gender pay gap fully, it is also important to examine the impact of changes in wage structure. As wage inequality has been rising in most industrialized countries (Freeman and Katz 1995), women may well have been swimming upstream in labor markets that are growing increasingly unfavorable to workers with below-average skills. In the face of rising rewards to labor market skills, women's relative skills and treatment have to improve merely for the pay gap to remain constant; still larger gains are necessary for it to be reduced.

Our work on trends in the gender gap in the United States (Blau and Kahn 1994b; Blau and Kahn 1997) suggests that rising inequality did indeed work to widen the gender gap over the 1970s and 1980s. Had there been no gender-specific improvements for women, the gender earnings ratio would have fallen from 60% in 1975 to 56% in 1987. Women were, however, able to swim against the current and narrow the gender gap by improving their relative qualifications, particularly their relative experience and occupational distribution. They also benefited from a substantial decline in the "unexplained" portion of the gender gap, which may reflect improvements in unmeasured characteristics or reductions in discrimination. An additional factor that may have contributed to this reduction in the unexplained gender differential was a shift in the composition of demand favoring women relative to men overall, and particularly among low-skilled workers. As a consequence of these offsetting gender-specific factors, the gender ratio had increased to 70% by 1987.

Appendix

Definitions of dependent variables

Australia	Annual earnings from all jobs
Austria	Net monthly income from employment
Germany and Switzerland	Net income per month after taxes and social insurance
Hungary	Monthly earnings
Italy	Annual labor income
Norway (1982)	Annual income from all jobs
Sweden (1980)	Income (from all sources) in previous year
Sweden (1984)	Average hourly earnings
U.S. (1985-89)	Previous year's earnings from occupation before taxes
U.S. (1984)	Average hourly earnings
UK	Total annual earnings before taxes

Definitions of explanatory variables

EDUC	= years of schooling completed
PEXP	= age-EDUC-6
PEXPSQ	= PEXP-squared
EXP	= actual experience (PSID and HUS only)
EXPSQ	= EXP-squared (PSID and HUS only)
MAR	= 1 if married spouse present and 0 otherwise
UNION	= dummy variable for union membership

Occupation dummy variables

PROF	= professional and technical workers (the omitted category)
MGR	= managers, except farm
CLER	= clerical workers
SALES	= sales workers
CRAFT	= craft workers
OPER	= operatives
LAB	= laborers, except farm
SERVWK	= service workers
FARMMGR	= farm managers
FARMLAB	= farm laborers

Industry dummy variables

AG	= agriculture, forestry, and fisheries
MINCON	= mining and construction
MANDUR	= durable goods manufacturing
MANNON	= nondurable goods manufacturing
TRANS	= transportation, communications and utilities
WTRADE	= the wholesale trade
RTRADE	= retail trade
FIRE	= finance, insurance, and real estate
SERVS	= services

GOVT	= government (the omitted category)

Industry dummy variables for Hungary

AG	(see above)
MINMAN	= mining and manufacturing
CONST	= construction
TRANS	(see above)
TRADE	= wholesale and retail trade
FISER V	= services, finance, insurance, and real estate
GOVT	(see above), the omitted category

Occupation dummy variables for Australia

MG	= managers and farm managers
CLER, CRAFT, and OPER	(see above)
LAB	= laborers and farm laborers
SALESW	=sales and service workers
PROF	(see above), the omitted category

Industry dummy variables for Australia

AG, TRANS, MINCON	(see above)
MANUF	= manufacturing
TRADE	= wholesale and retail trade
FISERV	(see above)
GOVT	(see above), the omitted category

Occupation dummy variables for Italy

BLUE	= blue-collar
WHITELO	= lower-level white-collar
WHITEHI	= higher-level white-collar, the omitted category

Industry dummy variables for Italy

AG, TRANS, TRADE	(see above)
IND	= mining, construction, and manufacturing
FIRE, GOVT	(see above)
SERVS	(see above), the omitted category

4

Understanding International Differences in the Gender Pay Gap

Based on a paper with Lawrence M. Kahn

4.1. Introduction

Virtually every industrialized country has passed laws mandating the equal treatment of women in the labor market. Yet the gender wage gap, while on the decline in many countries, is a persistent feature of virtually every nation's labor market. Moreover, the extent to which men outearn women varies substantially across countries. Among the 22 countries considered in this study, the gap in log earnings corrected for differences in weekly work hours between men and women averaged .307 log points over the 1985–94 period.[1] The standard de-

This chapter is a revised version of Blau, F. D., Kahn, L. M. (2003). Understanding International Differences in the Gender Pay Gap, in: Journal of Labor Economics, 21(1): 106–144. Chicago University Press.

Portions of this article were written while the authors were visiting scholars at the Russell Sage Foundation, to which we are grateful for research support. We are indebted to Danny Blanchflower for making the International Social Survey Programme (ISSP) data available and to Lisa Kahraman and Rachel Valente for excellent research assistance. We thank Rebecca Blank, Daniela Del Boca, Nicole Fortin, and participants at the following conferences and workshops for valuable suggestions and advice: Conference on Labor Market and Social Policies, International Centre for Economic Policy Research, Turin, Italy (April 1998); Society of Labor Economists annual meetings, San Francisco (May 1998); NBER Summer Institute Labor Studies Conference, Cambridge, MA (July 1998); American Economic Association/ Industrial Relations Research Association Meetings, New York (January 1999); seminars at Cornell University, the University of Uppsala, University of Aarhus, the University of Bergen, Queens College, Hunter College, the Federal Reserve Bank of New York, the City University of New York Graduate Center, New York University, and the Academia Sinica, Taipei. We are also indebted to Orley Ashenfelter and David Card, whose comments on our earlier work provided the motivation for this article.

viation (SD) of these gaps across countries was .145 log points, and the interquartile range (75-25 difference) in gender pay gaps across countries was .124 log points. In this chapter, we attempt to explain these international differences.

Economists have traditionally looked to gender-specific factors, such as female shortfalls in human capital or employer discrimination against women, to explain the size of the gender pay gap and its evolution over time. However, beginning with the work of Juhn, Murphy, and Pierce (1991), economists have recognized that overall wage structure, or the prices the labor market attaches to skills and the rents accruing to those in favored sectors, can have a major impact on the relative wages of different subgroups in the labor market. The logic behind this insight is straightforward. For example, since women have, on average, less labor market experience than men and tend to work in different occupations and industries, an increase in the return to experience or in sectoral differentials will raise the gender pay gap, all else equal. As we have pointed out in our earlier work (Blau and Kahn 1992; 1995; 1996b, see Chapter 3), the same reasoning applies across countries: countries with relatively high rewards to skill and relatively large sectoral differentials will tend to have larger gender pay gaps, all else equal. International comparisons provide a particularly fertile field in which to study the effects of wage structure on pay differentials between men and women because, due in part to substantial international differences in wage-setting institutions (Blau and Kahn 1996a, see Chapter 5), they provide greater variation in wage dispersion and labor market rewards than may generally be obtained by shifts in wage structure over time within a country. An important implication of this approach is that the factors that influence overall wage structure, such as supply of and demand for skills and wage-setting institutions, may well be extremely important determinants of international differences in the gender pay gap and, by implication, of trends in the gender pay gap within countries as well.

In previous work on international differences in the gender pay gap (Blau and Kahn 1992; 1995; 1996b, see Chapter 3), we used this insight to address a paradox: while the relative qualifications of American women are high as compared with those of women in other countries and the United States has had a longer and often stronger commitment to anti-discrimination laws than most economically advanced nations, the United States has traditionally been among the countries with the largest gender gaps. Due in part to its decentralized wage-setting institutions, the U.S. labor market places a much larger penalty on those with lower levels of labor market skills (both measured and unmeasured) or who are located in less favored sectors of the labor market. These are disproportionately women, whose relative wages are thus potentially reduced by labor market institutions in the United States. Based on pair-wise comparisons of the United States with nine other advanced countries, summarized in the previous chapter we presented evidence that the higher level of wage inequality in the United States is the primary reason for its relatively high gender pay gap.[2] In these comparisons, it was clear that relying on a framework that considered only gender-specific factors would have been inadequate to explain the relatively high gender pay gap in the United States.

In this chapter, we extend this analysis by asking whether wage structure has an important effect on the gender pay gap across a broad variety of countries. That is, while wage structure may be the most important reason for the relatively high gender pay gap in the United States, does this framework explain a large component of international differences in the gender pay gap generally? Moreover, our earlier research was based on two-country comparisons and a decomposition technique developed by Juhn et al. (1991).[3] The results suggested a strong role for wage inequality and wage-setting institutions in affecting the gender gap, but the methodology does not permit a direct test of this effect. The Juhn et al. technique requires some specific assumptions, notably that women will be affected by the same economic forces that influence the male wage distribution in a country. Thus, the estimated male prices of measured characteristics are assumed to affect men and women in the same way, and the residuals from a male wage regression are decomposed into a portion reflecting the prices of unmeasured skills and a portion reflecting the quantities of unmeasured skills, with the former affecting men and women similarly. This type of decomposition has been criticized by Suen (1997) in its decomposition of the wage residuals. In this chapter, we are able to implement a more direct test of these ideas that provides considerable empirical support for our earlier findings and thus indirectly for the Juhn et al. decomposition technique.

Some support for the notion that wage structure is important may be found in Rowthorn's (1992) observation, based on inspection of crosstabulations, that the gender pay gap (calculated from aggregate wage data) tended to be lower in countries with more centralized wage-setting institutions as measured by industrial relations researchers. In addition, in the previous chapter, we found a positive (though insignificant) correlation between a country's gender pay gap and the degree of decentralization of its wage setting across a small sample of 10 countries from the 1980s (Blau and Kahn 1996b, see Chapter 3).

In this chapter, we use microdata on 22 countries over the 1985–94 period to test whether more egalitarian pay structures (as measured by the extent of male wage inequality) are associated with lower gender pay gaps. In contrast to studies based on published data from sources such as the International Labor Organization (ILO) or the Organization for Economic Cooperation and Development (OECD), our microdata on individual workers allow us to adjust for international differences in women's human capital in estimating the gender pay gap, an important step in isolating the impact of wage structure. Data on individuals are also essential in estimating the characteristics of the wage structure itself if we are to separate out labor force heterogeneity from the true effects of labor market prices. A further contribution of the current study is that we are able to estimate the impact of supply and demand conditions in the female labor market on a country's gender pay gap.

The results provide support for the idea that egalitarian wage structures reduce the gender pay gap. We also find that, in some models, controlling for wage structure, the gender differential is lower when women are in shorter supply relative to the favorableness of the country's demand structure for women (female "net supply"). These results hold equally strongly even when we exclude the United States from the analysis, suggesting that the negative relationship between wage compression and the gender pay gap is not driven by the extreme case of the United States. Thus, to the extent that institutions are a major factor leading to more or less egalitarian wage structures (Blau and Kahn 1996a, see Chapter 5), we find strong evidence for the importance of institutions and some evidence for the effect of market forces in affecting the gender pay gap. Moreover, the effect of pay structures on the gender pay gap is quantitatively very important: a large part of the difference in the gender differential between high-gap and low-gap countries is explained by the differences across these countries in overall wage structure, with another potentially important segment due to differences in female net supply.

4.2. The Institutional Setting

In this section, we briefly summarize international differences in gender-specific policies and basic wage-setting institutions and their expected effects on the gender pay gap. Human capital is also a major determinant of gender pay gaps, and, in the work below, we control for international differences in women's measured human capital as compared with that of men. However, international variation in policies and institutions appears to be more dramatic than those in women's relative human capital levels, at least in our sample. Further, human capital can be affected by such policies and institutions, as we will discuss below. Differences across countries in institutions that affect the gender pay gap may be classified into those that are gender specific and those that affect the wage structure in general.

Gender-specific policies include equal employment opportunity (EEO) and anti-discrimination laws, as well as laws and policies governing parental leave and child care availability. The expected positive effect of EEO policies on the gender earnings ratio is reasonably straightforward, although the impact will most likely depend on the effectiveness of the legislation's enforcement as well as its provisions.

Virtually all OECD and European Community countries had passed equal pay and equal opportunity laws by the mid-1980s, although the United States implemented its anti-discrimination legislation before most other countries (Simona 1985; OECD 1988: 167–8). Of the Eastern European countries in our sample, only Russia and Hungary were listed by the ILO (1994) as having anti-discrimination laws as of 1994;[4] the other Eastern European nations in our sample - Bulgaria, the Czech Republic, Poland, and Slovenia - were not included in the ILO listing. However, Brainerd (2000) reports that, under socialism, in Eastern Europe and the Soviet Union, there were government guarantees of equal pay for equal work, and women's labor force participation was encouraged. One country with perhaps the strongest intervention against sex discrimination is Australia, the only one to have implemented a national policy of comparable worth through its labor courts (Killingsworth 1990; Gregory and Daly 1991).[5] Comparable worth pay policies remain rare in the U.S. private sector, although they have been adopted by a number of state and local governments (Blau, Ferber, and Winkler 2002).

The expected impact of family leave (disproportionately taken by women even when it is available to men) is unclear a priori. On the one hand, such policies may raise the relative earnings of women by encouraging the preservation of their ties to particular firms and hence increasing the incentives of employers and women workers to invest in firm-specific training. On the other hand, the existence of such policies could increase the incidence or duration of temporary labor force withdrawals among women, raising the gender gap for the affected group. Further, the incremental costs associated with mandated leave policies may increase employer incentives to discriminate against women in hiring or to discount their wages.

By international standards, the United States has a relatively weak entitlement to parental leave, consisting of an unpaid 13-week mandated period, which was only introduced in 1993. In contrast, other OECD countries implemented mandated leave earlier, and most have a much longer period of leave, usually paid (Ruhm 1998). While the theoretical effect of parental leave on the gender gap is ambiguous, research on its impact has tended to find a positive effect of short leave entitlements on women's relative wages, although some results suggest that extended leaves may have the opposite effect (Ruhm 1998; Waldfogel 1998). In some specifications, which we will describe below, we are able to control for the duration of parental leave entitlement, which in our data ranged from 0 to 156 weeks, although these data are not available for our full set of countries.

Child care is another important area of public policy that particularly affects women, but it is one that is difficult to summarize across a large set of countries. Although we were unable to secure data for an extended set of countries, some available evidence suggests that, as of the mid-1980s, the United States had a smaller share of young children in publicly funded child care than many other OECD countries but that it provided relatively generous tax relief for child-care expenses (Gornick, Meyers, and Ross 1997).

With respect to wage structure, there is a considerable body of evidence showing that wage-setting institutions affect a country's level of wage inequality. These institutions take the form of collective bargaining conventions, minimum wage laws, and governmentally mandated extensions of the terms of collective bargaining agreements to nonunion workers (Blau and Kahn 1999). In general, more heavily unionized economies in which collective bargaining takes place at highly centralized levels have been found to have the lowest overall wage dispersion (Freeman 1988; Rowthorn 1992; Blau and Kahn 1996a, see Chapter 5).

It seems likely that systems of centrally determined pay also entail smaller gender wage differentials for at least two reasons related to their impact on skill prices and sectoral differentials. First, in the United States, a significant portion of the male-female pay gap is associated with interindustry or interfirm wage differentials that result from its relatively decentralized pay setting institutions (e.g., Blau 1977; Sorensen 1990; Groshen 1991; Bayard et al. 1999). Thus, centralized systems, which reduce the extent of wage variation across industries and firms, are likely to lower the gender differential, all else equal. Second, since in all countries the female wage distribution lies below the male distribution, centralized systems that consciously raise minimum pay levels, regardless of gender, will also tend to lower male-female wage differentials.

There is considerable variation across countries, both in collective bargaining coverage and in the degree of centralization of wage setting in both the union and nonunion sectors. Among the OECD nations, the Scandinavian countries and Austria stand at one extreme with their high degree of collective bargaining coverage and union-negotiated wage agreements at the economy-wide or industry-wide level, while the United States stands at the other extreme with an especially low rate of collective bargaining coverage and pay setting that is often determined at the plant level even within the union sector. Moreover, in many of the OECD countries, but not in the United States, formal or informal mechanisms exist to extend union-negotiated pay rates to nonunion workers. In some specifications below, we look directly at the effect of collective bargaining coverage on the gender pay gap and find evidence of the expected negative effect.

Systems of pay compression may influence workers' incentives to invest in skill acquisition, although the direction of these effects is theoretically ambiguous. On the one hand, if the return to experience is reduced by wage compression, women will have less incentive to remain employed during periods of childbearing and child-rearing than in countries where there is a larger penalty for time out of the paid labor force. In our data, as well as in most microdata, we are unable to measure actual experience; thus, this type of labor supply response of women to pay compression will go largely undetected. This could bias us away from finding a positive effect of reduced male wage inequality and wage-compressing institutions on the relative pay of women, controlling for their measured, as opposed to actual, human capital levels. On the other hand, high wage floors may encourage women's labor force participation, raising their relative experience levels. Of course, these wage floors could still reduce women's employment if labor demand effects are important. In any case, wage-induced changes in female qualifications could produce a positive or a negative bias on our estimates of the impact of wage compression.

Another institution that directly affects the wage distribution is mandated minimum wage coverage. Studies of the impact of minimum wages in various countries on the wage distribution invariably find that such regulation compresses the bottom of the distribution (Machin and Manning 1994; Card and Krueger 1995; Katz, Loveman, and Blanchflower 1995; DiNardo, Fortin, and Lemieux 1996; Dolado et al. 1996). Further, Blau and Kahn (1997) concluded that falling real minimum wages over the 1980s retarded the narrowing of the pay gap between low-skill women and low-skill men. International differences in minimum wage levels, both those negotiated in collective bargaining and those imposed by government, are likely to be reflected in our measures of male wage inequality. Below, we also present some results designed to explicitly assess the impact of minimum wages on the gender pay gap.

An alternative perspective on these issues is provided in a recent paper by Fortin and Lemieux (1998). They suggest that relative gains for women can affect male wage inequality, in effect posing the opposite direction of causality to the one posited here.[6] As they point out, their approach is consistent with a pure job assignment model in which alterations in the relative position of women in the wage distribution do not affect the overall distribution of wages. This raises the possibility that a reduction in the gender gap could increase male inequality (as some women move up the wage distribution and some men move down); they present some evidence consistent with this for the United States over the 1980s. To the extent that female gains do come to some degree from male losses, this reverse causation will impose a negative bias on the measured effect of male inequality on the gender gap. This would make it more difficult for us to obtain the expected positive effect of male wage inequality on the gender gap that we postulate and would thus strengthen our confidence in such a finding. Given the possibility of reverse causation, in some specifications presented below, we attempt to avoid the simultaneity problem by taking a reduced-form approach in which institutional variables take the place of our measures of male inequality and female net supply.

4.3. Description of the Data

In this study, we use microdata from the 1985–94 annual files of the International Social Survey Programme (ISSP). The ISSP is a voluntary grouping of study teams in over 20 countries, with standardized questions asked of a random sample of adults. In addition to its annual theme questions concerning social attitudes, each year the ISSP administers a uniform set of questions on respondents' education, earnings, age, marital status, work hours, and gender. The sample design is a new random cross section in each available year for every country, with the exception of data for Australia in 1986–87, 1991, and 1994, and Hungary in 1990–94, which are panel follow-up samples. Our results were virtually identical when we excluded these country-year observations from the data.

The sample of countries with available wage data varies from year to year and is shown in Table 4.1.[7] Each country appears an average of 4.5 times during this period, yielding a total of 100 country-year observations. As may be seen in the table, the coverage of countries has grown from a relatively small number (four) in 1985 to 17 countries with usable data in 1994. A particularly interesting feature of the ISSP sample is the addition of several Eastern European countries, including the former East Germany, the Czech Republic, Hungary, Bulgaria, Russia, Slovenia, and Poland, mostly after 1990.

Table 4.1 also shows the earnings concept for each country. Unfortunately, there are some differences across countries in the exact definitions of the income variables in the ISSP data. While in over half of the cases the income data are measured before taxes, income is measured after taxes in the remainder. Although this difference is of some concern, it is reassuring that the empirical results reported below were not affected by the inclusion of a dummy variable indicating that net income was the income concept employed, nor was the coefficient for this dummy variable ever significant. In addition, because of the different possible tax treatment of single versus married women and the issue of before- versus after-tax earnings, besides our basic specification that includes all workers, we estimated some supplementary models confining ourselves to married workers only. Our results were very similar for the married subsample, providing some further indication that differing income definitions do not have a major impact on our results.

Table 4.1
Countries, Years, and Earnings Concepts in the ISSP Data

Country	Years of Data	Earnings Concept
Australia	1986–87, 1990–91, 1994	Annual gross wage and salary income
Austria	1985–87, 1989, 1991–92, 1994	Monthly net earnings
Britain	1985–94	Annual gross earnings
Bulgaria	1992–93	Monthly earnings
Canada	1992–94	Annual gross personal income
Czech Republic	1992, 1994	Monthly net income
East Germany	1990–93	Monthly net earnings
West Germany	1985–93	Monthly net earnings
Hungary	1988–94	Monthly gross earnings
Ireland	1988–90, 1993–94	Annual net earnings (1988–90); weekly net earnings (1993–94)
Israel	1993–94	Monthly earnings
Italy	1986, 1988, 1990, 1992–94	Monthly net income
Japan	1993–94	Annual gross earnings
Netherlands	1988–89	Annual net earnings
New Zealand	1991–94	Annual gross income
Norway	1989–94	Annual gross earnings
Poland	1991–94	Monthly net earnings, main job
Russia	1991–94	Monthly net earnings
Slovenia	1991–94	Monthly regular income
Sweden	1994	Monthly gross earnings
Switzerland	1987	Monthly net income
United States	1985–94	Annual gross earnings

As may also be seen in Table 4.1, with the exception of Ireland in 1993 and 1994, earnings are computed on either an annual or a monthly basis; thus, in general, we are not able to compute hourly or weekly earnings (the ISSP does not collect information on weeks worked). However, we do have information on hours worked per week, which, as described below, we used to estimate earnings adjusted for time input. Since the national surveys that make up the ISSP can change their focus from year to year, variables such as industry and union membership are not consistently available. However, occupational information is available for most country-year observations, and we used it in some supplementary analyses. Finally, it may be noted that not every country participates in every year, a factor that further contributes to the unbalanced nature of the country-year panel.

4.4. Estimation Strategy

Our analysis begins with log earnings equations estimated separately by gender for each country j and year t:

$$(1) \qquad \ln \text{EARN}_{ijt} = b_{0jt} + b_{1jt}\text{PART}_{ijt} + b_{2jt}\text{HRPART}_{ijt} + b_{3jt}\text{HRFULL}_{ijt} + X_{ijt}B_{jt} + e_{ijt},$$

where i indexes individuals; ln EARN is the natural log of earnings; PART is a dummy variable for part-time employment, defined as less than 35 hours per week;[8] HRPART and HRFULL are interactions of weekly work hours with part- and full-time status; X is a vector of explanatory variables, described below; and e is an error term. The model allows for both a part-time shift term and different slopes for hours for part-time and full-time workers. A detailed adjustment for part-time employment is important in light of the prevalence of part-time work for women in many countries. We use a linear specification for the hours variable and its interactions with the part-time and full-time dummies as part of a relatively unrestricted simple specification intended to capture the variation in labor input, given that we do not have information on weeks worked. Results were virtually identical when we used log hours instead of hours in equation (1).

The PART, HRPART, and HRFULL coefficients obtained from estimating equation (1) for males and females separately were used to compute for each individual ln EARN40, the log of earnings adjusted for work hours by assuming a 40-hour work week.[9] Thus, the gender difference in the mean of ln EARN40 in a given year and country is our best estimate of the gender gap in wage rates.[10] The explanatory variables in X include the traditional human capital variables of education, potential experience, and the square of potential experience, as well as a constant. Inclusion of marital status as a human capital characteristic is problematic in that it is likely to be positively associated with productivity for men but may be negatively so for women (e.g., Korenman and Neumark 1991). Because of this ambiguity, we do not control for marital status in the country-year microdata wage regressions used to estimate human capital-adjusted gender pay gaps; however, similar results were obtained when we did control for marital status and, as noted above, when we confined the sample to married individuals. In our main specification, both the self-employed and wage and salary workers are included in the regression sample, but results were similar when the sample was restricted to wage and salary workers only. The rationale for including the self-employed is that the size of this sector may be influenced by wage-setting institutions. For example, in economies where wage determination is heavily regulated, the self-employment sector may swell in an attempt to avoid such regulation.

In additional specifications for a subset of the country-year observations, we are able to estimate models that control for one-digit occupation.[11] We recognize that an individual's occupation is potentially endogenous since individuals may choose jobs on the basis of the opportunities available; further, a country's occupational structure may be affected by its wage structure. However, occupation is also likely to be an important indicator of human capital and may serve as a proxy for actual experience, which is not available in the ISSP. Thus, while we present results not controlling for occupation, we also estimate supplementary specifications with occupational controls. Our basic conclusions are robust with respect to this addition.

Having estimated (1) for each country and year (100 regressions for men and 100 for women), we then construct two different measures of the gender gap in hours-corrected earnings. We begin with the estimated raw gender log wage gap:

$$TOTALGAP_{jt} \equiv \ln \mathrm{EARN40}_{mjt} - \ln \mathrm{EARN40}_{fit}, \quad (2)$$

where $\ln \mathrm{EARN40}_{mjt}$ and $\ln \mathrm{EARN40}_{fjt}$ are, respectively, the average male and female levels of log full-time earnings for country j and time t. The raw gender gap represents the net effect of all of the forces that influence the gender gap in hours-corrected earnings, including gender differences in the explanatory variables.

While wage compression may, as argued above, affect women's and men's relative values of X, there may also be exogenous (e.g., cultural) reasons for men and women to have different relative levels of qualifications in different countries. For this reason, we primarily focus on results based on GAPUSCHARS, which estimates the predicted gender pay gap on the assumption that the men and women in each country-year microdata file have the same average levels of measured characteristics (i.e., X variables) as U.S. men and women for that year:

$$(3) \qquad \text{GAPUSCHARS}_{jt} = (40b_{3mjt} + X_{mut}B_{mjt}) - (40b_{3fjt} + X_{fut}B_{fjt}),$$

where u refers to the United States; X is a vector of U.S. means of the explanatory variables for the indicated group, b and B estimated in equation (1) separately for men and women in each country; and the subscripts f, m, and j are as defined above. Equation (3) provides a simulated gender pay gap that removes international differences in women's relative levels of measured characteristics. However, since gender differences in measured characteristics remain (i.e., at the U.S. levels), there is ample room for each country's wage structure to influence the magnitude of the gender pay gap through its effects on the returns to the measured X's. Finally, note that equation (3) simulates full-time earnings by valuing the country's own male and female full-time hours coefficients b_{3mjt} and b_{3fjt} at 40 hours.

Having described the construction of the basic dependent variables, we turn to the major explanatory variables: male wage compression and the favorableness of supply relative to demand for female labor. With respect to male wage compression, the simplest approach would be to use a measure of observed male wage inequality. However, observed male wage inequality is influenced by heterogeneity of productivity characteristics as well as by labor market prices, and it is prices that generate the compression of wages that are associated with collective bargaining institutions. To focus on prices, we construct two measures of male wage inequality that remove the effects of measured heterogeneity.[12] First, for each country and year, we take the U.S. sample of men for that year and compute yus, a predicted log wage for each U.S. male (ui) using the male price structure for country j and year t:

$$(4) \qquad (yus)_{ijt} = 40b_{3mjt} + X_{uit}B_{mjt}.$$

We then compute measures of inequality, including the SD and the 50-10 gap across the American male sample (the ui's) of these $(yus)_{ijt}$, which gives us a measure of the degree of male inequality that results from the prices of measured human capital in country j in year t. In this case, we include a control for marital status in X, since there is less ambiguity about the effect of this variable among men. The rationale behind examining the 50-10 gap is that it is a measure that may be especially relevant to those at the bottom of the distribution, such as women. Note that, while we use the mean of the $(yus)_{ijt}$ to compute the male part of the GAPUSCHARS in equation (3), we use the inequality in the distribution of the $(yus)_{ijt}$ as an indicator of the compression caused by human capital prices.

Second, an insight of Juhn et al.'s (1991) work is that wage residuals also potentially contain information about labor market prices, in this case, the prices of unmeasured characteristics. Accordingly, we also include as an explanatory variable the SD of (or the 50-10 gap in) the residuals from the male log wage equation estimated for country j in year t. Note that the regression residual includes not only the returns to unmeasured individual characteristics but also industry and firm wage effects, which we are not able to capture due to data limitations in the ISSP. There is evidence that industry wage effects vary significantly across countries (Barth and Zweimüller 1992; Edin and Zetterberg 1992; Kahn 1998), and firm wage effects are believed to do so as well (Teulings and Hartog 1998).[13] However, in addition to containing information about unmeasured prices, residual inequality is also affected by other factors including heterogeneity in unmeasured characteristics and measurement errors, while the inequality in predicted wages is a direct measure of labor market prices.

In addition to labor market prices and relative human capital levels, we also expect supply and demand conditions for women relative to men to influence the gender pay gap. If men and women are viewed as imperfect substitutes in the labor market, as assumed in supply and demand models of wage inequality (e.g., Bound and Johnson 1992; Katz and Murphy 1992; Juhn, Murphy, and Pierce 1993), then countries with higher demand for, or lower supplies of, women relative to men will have smaller gender pay gaps, other things equal. To measure these demand and supply factors, we construct demand and supply indexes for women relative to men in a manner similar to those employed in the wage inequality literature.

Turning first to demand, we wish to know, for each country-year observation, how favorable the composition of output by industry (and the consequent derived demand for labor) is for women. Following Katz and Murphy (1992), we constructed the demand index, FDEMAND, for women for each country j and year t relative to a base of 1989 in the United States:

(5a) $$\Delta D_{jt} = \sum_i c_{iu9}(E_{ijt} - E_{iu89})/E_{iu89},$$

(5b) $$\text{FDEMAND}_{jt} = \ln(1 + \Delta D_{jt}),$$

where i refers to one-digit industry cell, c_{iu89} is the fraction of all U.S. women workers who were employed in industry i in 1989, E_{ijt} is the share of total employment in industry i for country j in year t, and E_{iu89} is the share of total employment in industry i in the United States in 1989.[14] The demand index thus measures the degree to which the country j year t industry structure favors women relative to the United States in 1989, using U.S. weights.

Female supply indexes FSUPPLY are computed as follows

(6) $$\text{FSUPPLY}_{jt} = \ln F_{jt} - \ln F_{u89},$$

where F_{jt} is the share of country j's workers in year t who were women, and F_{u89} is the analogous fraction for the United States in 1989. Thus, the supply index shows the relative representation of women in country j's work force, using the 1989 U.S. share as the norm.

We may then compute net supply as:

(7) $$\text{FNETSUPPLY}_{jt} = \text{FSUPPLY}_{jt} - \text{FDEMAND}_{jt},$$

and (6) above. (Recall that all magnitudes are in log points and have been normalized relative to the United States in 1989.) As implied by Katz and Murphy's (1992) equilibrium model, differences across countries in the gender pay gap will be positively related to differences in female net supply, FNETSUPPLY_{jt}. Intuitively, the larger the supply of women relative to demand in country j, as compared with the United States, the worse women will fare in country j as compared with the United States.

While this net supply index represents our best measure of the relative abundance of women workers, we note that it is overstated (understated) for countries with relatively small (large) gender pay gaps. This is the case because, while we seek a measure of the position of the female relative supply curve in relation to the relative demand curve for female labor, our measures are based on employment outcomes. This means that countries with a low (high) gender pay gap will appear to have larger (smaller) female supply and smaller (larger) female demand indexes than otherwise because of the movements of workers and firms along their supply and demand schedules. Thus, the construction of the net supply index may lead to a bias away from finding that relative scarcity of women raises their relative wages. Another problem with this measure is that it does not reflect differences across countries or over time in the within-industry demand for women workers. Nonetheless, it is important to control for relative net supply, since this is potentially a key determinant of women's relative wages. Further, Topel (1994a) has argued that rising female labor supply has in fact contributed to rising male wage inequality. This is based on the idea that women compete in the labor market with low-skill men.[15] To the extent that this argument holds, our control for female net supply provides a sharper test of the effect of male prices on the gender pay gap. We interpret the impact of male prices as being their effect beyond any portion that may have been caused by female supply.

A final reason for including a measure of net supply concerns possible selection bias due to the fact that we observe earnings only for those with jobs. In addition to adjusting for the effect of relative scarcity on the gender gap, our control for net supply also accounts for the impact of the selectivity of the female and male labor forces on the gender pay differential. Note that we do not impose any functional form on this relationship, or even posit its sign.

Labor market prices and female net supply form the basic explanatory variables for our study of the determinants of the gender pay gap, as expressed in estimating equations of the following form:

$$(8) \quad \text{GENDERGAP}_{jt} = c_0 + c_1\text{INEQ(yus)}_{jt} + c_2\text{INEQRES}_{jt} + c_3 \text{FNETSUPPLY}_{jt} + \sum_s d_s YR_{st} + e_{jt},$$

where for each country j and year t, GENDERGAP is a measure of the gender log wage gap, INEQ(yus)_{jt} is male inequality in measured prices, INEQRES is male residual inequality, FNETSUPPLY is female net supply, YR_s, is a dummy variable for year s, with a range of 1986 to 1994 (1985 is the omitted year), and e is an error term.[16]

To test for the robustness of our findings with respect to wage compression and net supply, we add a number of controls for other policies, cultural differences, or other gender-specific factors that may influence the male-female pay gap. First, we control for whether a country was in the former Eastern bloc and test whether the impact of compression and net supply differ for these countries relative to the West. Second, using Ruhm and Teague (1997) and Nickell and Layard (1999), we construct, for a subset of our data, weeks of available parental leave and its square.[17] Parental leave information is available from these sources for 1981, 1991, and 1995. Since our data span the period 1985-94, we created an interpolated parental leave variable that incorporates some time variation. Third, again for a subset of observations for which data were available, we include a measure of the degree of occupational segregation by gender, using Anker's (1998) indexes, which were based on 75 occupational titles. Anker's indexes were collected at one time, typically 1990 (see the Data Appendix for further details). While this is not a time-varying measure, it includes a considerable amount of occupational detail, unlike published sources or the ISSP. Several of these variables may be affected by the male-female pay gap; yet each may also control for exogenous factors that influence the gender pay gap. Thus, one can make arguments for including or for excluding these additional variables. As we show below, our conclusions with respect to the effect of wage compression and net supply on the gender pay gap are robust with respect to the inclusion of these variables.[18]

In formulating our estimation strategy, we begin by noting that equation (8) combines two kinds of experiments: one is based upon between-country differences in levels of the dependent and explanatory variables, and the other is based upon within-country changes in these variables over time. Yet it is possible that these two sources of variation arise from different sources and hence have different consequences. Our review of the institutional literature on wage setting suggests that there are long-standing international differences in wage-setting mechanisms that lead to varying levels of wage compression and thus gender pay gaps. While institutions have changed in a number of countries over the 1980s and 1990s (Katz 1993; Boeri 2000), it is likely that, in most cases, the dominant factor driving changes in labor market prices within countries over time has been an increase in the demand for skilled workers due to such factors as skill-biased technological change and international trade (e.g., Freeman and Katz 1995). These technological changes included within-industry demand shifts that favored white-collar workers in general and thus, given traditional employment patterns, women relative to men (Katz and Murphy 1992; Berman, Bound, and Griliches 1994; Blau and Kahn 1997; Fortin and Lemieux 2000; Welch 2000).

If international differences in labor market prices are primarily driven by institutional differences while within country changes are caused mostly by technological factors, then time-series correlations of wage inequality and the gender pay gap within a country may in some sense not be comparable with cross-sectional associations between country averages of these variables. This creates an ambiguity in the empirically observed relationship between male inequality and the gender gap in the time series because our industry-based demand index will not be able to detect within-industry technological changes that have increased the demand for women. Thus, the same unobserved factor, technological change, may have tended to increase male inequality over time and reduced the gender gap in pay, possibly producing a spurious negative correlation between male prices and the gender pay gap in the time series. Moreover, while data limitations prevented us from formulating our demand indexes in terms of occupation-industry cells, it is unlikely that the problem could be surmounted even were the international data available at this level of disaggregation. Results of intertemporal studies within the United States are consistent with substantial increases in the demand for women workers within broad industry-occupation cells (Katz and Murphy 1992; Blau and Kahn 1997).

Another econometric issue relevant in estimating equation (8) is the possibility of reverse causation. For example, as discussed above, Fortin and Lemieux (1998) posit a negative reverse causality from the gender pay gap to the level of male wage inequality. Similarly, our earlier discussion suggests that the gender pay gap is likely to negatively affect our measure of female net supply through movements along demand and supply schedules. To the extent that such reverse causation exists, ordinary least squares (OLS) coefficients will be biased. To address the issue of reverse causality, in some analyses we replace the wage inequality and net supply variables with a variety of institutional variables, such as collective bargaining coverage, unemployment insurance (UI) system characteristics, minimum wage coverage, and the like. These models are, in effect, reduced forms.

Finally, due to our use of cross-section, time-series data, and the construction of our dependent and explanatory variables, there are a number of reasons to suspect that the classical assumptions regarding errors in least squares estimation are violated here. First, errors are likely to be heteroskedastic. This is the case both because there are multiple observations on the same country and error terms may thus be correlated across years within a country and because the dependent variable is based on regression coefficients with their own sampling variances. To address this issue, we use the Huber-White procedure and allow the error terms within a country to be correlated. Second, some of the explanatory variables are functions of regression coefficients and thus have sampling errors of their own. Murphy and Topel (1985) suggest a procedure for correcting standard errors (SEs) in such models. We used their procedure in several of our basic models with no change in the results. Finally, there may be country-level effects that are correlated with our explanatory variables. To address this concern, we add country dummies in some models, in effect performing a within-country analysis. While traditional panel data models consider both between- and within-unit analyses as providing different estimates of the same basic parameters, our discussion above suggests that, in this case, they may each be measuring the effects of different phenomena.

4.5. Results

The means of our main dependent and explanatory variables are shown in Table 4.2, which gives the unweighted averages across years for each country in our sample. The table shows a large range across countries in the raw gender pay gap, which averaged from .14 in Slovenia to .85 in Japan. Apart from these extremes, the countries with the largest gaps are Switzerland, the United States, Britain, and Russia, while the countries with relatively small gender gaps include the Eastern European countries of East Germany and Bulgaria, as well as Sweden, Italy, Ireland, and New Zealand.[19] Table 4.2 also shows GAPUSCHARS, the gender pay gap evaluated at U.S. values of male and female human capital characteristics (col. 2). This measure tends to be highly correlated with the raw gender gap.[20]

Table 4.2 also summarizes international differences in male labor market prices. As expected, the United States is at or near the top in each of the inequality measures. Further, while there is a positive correlation between the price effects of measured X's (SD yus or 50:10yus) and residual inequality (SD MALERES or 50:10MALERES),

Table 4.2

Means of Dependent and Explanatory Variables by Country (Unweighted Averages across Years for Each Country)

	TOTALGAP	GAPUSCHARS	SD yus	SD MALERES	50:10yus	50:10MALERES	FNETSUPPLY
Australia	.305	.267	.286	.536	.418	.547	-.054
Austria	.290	.199	.311	.404	.415	.439	.010
Britain	.366	.348	.442	.437	.515	.548	-.025
Bulgaria	.179	.233	.158	.498	.168	.639	.265
Canada	.282	.224	.297	.418	.472	.535	-.004
Czech Republic	.309	.293	.163	.399	.205	.412	.181
East Germany	.178	.121	.141	.323	.213	.356	.123
West Germany	.320	.222	.310	.363	.501	.416	-.062
Hungary	.291	.263	.224	.399	.269	.449	.147
Ireland	.220	.228	.347	.480	.499	.564	-.181
Israel	.314	.341	.222	.420	.266	.564	-.088
Italy	.228	.157	.220	.438	.323	.459	-.191
Japan	.852	.733	.386	.462	.539	.555	-.013
Netherlands	.274	.196	.272	.352	.447	.354	-.203
New Zealand	.188	.182	.222	.481	.34	.541	.018
Norway	.275	.263	.245	.357	.378	.409	.013
Poland	.292	.345	.313	.556	.347	.654	.239
Russia	.364	.357	.144	.702	.180	.727	.265
Slovenia	.144	.125	.228	.499	.259	.470	.199
Sweden	.216	.214	.216	.354	.305	.399	.048
Switzerland	.479	.262	.407	.461	.651	.624	-.110
United States	.395	.395	.408	.678	.579	.842	-.004

Note: TOTALGAP is the raw gender pay evaluated at 40 hours work; GAPUSCHARS is the predicted gender pay gap evaluated at U.S. values for male and female characteristics; SD yus and 50:10yus are, respectively, the standard deviation and the 50-10 gap of predicted log wages applying each country's male wage equation to U.S. men; SD MALERES and 50:10MALERES are, respectively the standard deviation and the 50-10 gap in each country's male log wage residuals calculated from its male wage equation; FNETSUPPLY is our measure of female net supply. See the text for further details.

a look at the rankings shows that they do appear to measure different things. For example, Australia has the tenth largest measured price variation (SD yus) out of the 22 countries but the fourth largest residual standard deviation, and Russia's comparison is particularly dramatic - it has the second smallest measured price variation but the largest residual standard deviation.[21] Finally the table shows net female supply relative to the United States in 1989. Ireland, Italy, and the Netherlands have much a smaller female net supply than the other countries, a pattern driven primarily by female labor supply rather than by the demand for women. On the other hand, the Eastern European countries have the highest net supply of women, again driven primarily by female labor supply.

Table 4.3

Basic Cross-Section, Time-Series Regression Results

	Dependent Variable = TOTALGAP				Dependent Variable = GAPUSCHARS			
	Coefficient	SE	Coefficient	SE	Coefficient	SE	Coefficient	SE
50:10yus	.3448	.1862			.3053	.1701		
50:10MALERES	.1097	.0818			.2573	.0949		
SD yus			.4138	.1928			.4850	.1512
SD MALERES			.1049	.0997			.2750	.0937
FNETSUPPLY	.2188	.1339	.1233	.1167	.2781	.1252	.2132	.1009
Year dummies	Yes		Yes		Yes		Yes	
Sample size	100		100		100		100	
R^2	.2641		.2284		.3310		.3268	

Note: The gender gap is computed from equations including education, potential experience, and the square of potential experience. Male prices and residuals are from equations that additionally include marital status. Standard errors are heteroskedasticity robust and are corrected for within-country error correlation. TOTALGAP is the raw gender pay evaluated at 40 hours work; GAPUSCHARS is the predicted gender pay gap evaluated at U.S. values for male and female characteristics; SD yus and 50:10yus are, respectively, the standard deviation and the 50-10 gap of predicted log wages applying each country's male wage equation to U.S. men; SD MALERES and 50:10MALERES are, respectively the standard deviation and the 50-10 gap in each country's male log wage residuals calculated from its male wage equation; FNETSUPPLY is our measure of female net supply. See the text for further details.

Table 4.3 shows regression results for the basic cross-section, time-series, estimation of equation (8). Across specifications with the two alternative dependent variables and two alternative measures of the labor market prices and residual inequality variables, the results consistently show that higher measured prices are associated with a higher gender pay gap.[22] The coefficients for the price variables are 1.79–1.85 times their SEs in the 50:10yus specification and statistically significant at better than the 5% level (on a two-tailed test) in the SD specification for both dependent variables. Residual inequality is also found to be positively related to the gender gap, and the estimated coefficients are always larger than their SEs; the coefficients on these variables are statistically significant at better than the 5% level (on a two-tailed test) in the GAPUSCHARS specification. Note that these findings for residual inequality strongly suggest that the male regression residual contains information regarding international differences in the prices of unmeasured skills, although it may also be influenced by international differences in the quantities of unmeasured skills as well as measurement error. Finally, in each specification, higher female net supply has the expected positive effect on the gender pay gap; its coefficient is always larger than its standard error and is statistically significant at better than the 5% level (on a two-tailed test) in the GAPUSCHARS specifications.[23]

The specifications in which male inequality is measured by the SD tend to perform somewhat better than those using the 50-10 specification. This is perhaps not surprising in that the SD takes into account inequality at all portions of the distribution and thus potentially conveys more information. The fact that the 50-10 specification performs nearly as well, despite its focus on only the bottom of the distribution, supports our expectation that it is this portion of the distribution that is particularly relevant for women.

Although the two measures of the gender gap are highly correlated, the most consistently statistically significant results in Table 4.3 are for the specification with GAPUSCHARS as the dependent variable. In this model, five of the six coefficients are significant at better than the 5% level, and the sixth is significant at the 8.7% level, all on two-tailed tests. It may be recalled that GAPUSCHARS is our preferred measure, since it nets out international differences in women's relative qualifications but reserves gender differences in measured characteristics (at the U.S. levels). Thus, in subsequent analyses, we focus on specifications that employ GAPUSCHARS as the dependent variable.

The effects implied by the estimated coefficients in Table 4.3 are important in magnitude as well as generally statistically significant. To see this, it is useful to simulate the impact on the gender pay gap of going from the twenty-fifth to the seventy-fifth percentile among country averages ranked according to the variability of male measured prices, male residual inequality, or female net supply. Using the GAPUSCHARS dependent variable and the standard deviation inequality specification, we find that such an increase in male measured price inequality would lead to a .055 log point increase in the gender log wage gap, which is 38% of the actual 75-25 difference in the country average GAPUSCHARS of .146 for our sample. A similar increase in male residual inequality is associated with an increase in the gender pay gap of .032 log points, or 22% of the actual 75-25 differential in GAPUSCHARS. Finally, a 75-25 increase in female net supply would lead to a .051 log point increase in the gender pay gap, or 35% of the 75-25 differential in the pay gap. These findings suggest a strong role for both labor market prices and female net supply in affecting the gender pay gap, with a quantitatively larger effect for measured prices and residuals together than for net supply.

Another indication of the quantitative importance of these variables is provided by the results presented in Table 4.4. The table shows, for selected Western countries, the percentage of the difference between the Western country average of GAPUSCHARS and the individual country's GAPUSCHARS that is accounted for by each explanatory variable.[24] Looking first at the findings for the United States, we see that the variables included in the regression are more than sufficient to account for the higher gender pay gap in the United States as compared with the other Western countries. This is primarily due to the impact of the wage inequality variables, although the higher net supply of women in the United States also plays a role. This conclusion strongly matches the results obtained in our previous work (Blau and Kahn 1992; 1995; 1996b, see Chapter 3), despite the very different methodology employed here. The fact that the actual difference between the United States and the other Western countries is less than would be expected based on the levels of the wage inequality and net supply variables implies that there are unmeasured factors favoring U.S. women as compared with women elsewhere. These may relate to women's unmeasured characteristics relative to men's or to laws, or policies benefiting women in the United States as compared with their counterparts abroad.

Table 4.4 also shows results for Sweden and Japan, two countries that are notable for their position at the extremes of the international distribution of gender gaps. The relatively low gender gap in Sweden is well explained by the male wage inequality and net supply variables. Specifically, the extremely low level of male wage inequality in Sweden would be more than sufficient to account for the lower gender pay gap there; however, its effect is offset somewhat by the relatively high net supply of women workers. Overall, the variables included in the regression are estimated to explain 63%–67% of the lower gender gap in Sweden than in other Western countries. That the regression variables can explain less than the full amount of the lower gender gap in Sweden suggests that, as in the case of the United States, there are unmeasured factors benefiting Swedish women relative to women elsewhere. Finally, the results for Japan indicate that the variables included in the regression analysis can explain only a relatively small proportion of the extremely large gender pay gap there: 11%–12%. This suggests that the large gender pay gap in Japan, to a considerable extent, reflects unmeasured factors that are highly unfavorable to women.

Table 4.4

Accounting for the Difference between Individual Country Gender Pay Gaps and the Average for the Western Nations: Selected Countries (Dependent Variable: GAPUSCHARS)

	SD	50-10 Gap
United States versus other Western countries:		
$(D_j - D_w) = .1209$:		
% of difference due to:		
Measured prices	44.0	36.7
Residual inequality	57.3	73.6
Net supply	9.9	13.0
Total	111.2	123.3
Sweden versus other Western countries:		
$(D_j - D_w) = .0734$:		
% of difference due to:		
Measured prices	63.6	61.4
Residual inequality	35.7	43.6
Net supply	-32.4	-42.3
Total	66.9	62.7
Japan versus other Western countries:		
$(D_j - D_w) = .4836$:		
% of difference due to:		
Measured prices	8.6	6.5
Residual inequality	1.2	2.0
Net supply	2.1	2.7
Total	11.9	11.2

Note: The variables D_j and D_w are, respectively, the average gender log wage gap (GAPUSCHARS) in country j and in Western countries.

We found the results in Table 4.3 to be robust to the inclusion of the additional controls discussed above – parental leave entitlement duration and its square, a control for Eastern European countries (EAST), and the degree of occupational segregation. Further, these additional controls did not have significant effects on the gender pay gap, and interactions between EAST and the male inequality and net supply variables also proved to be insignificant individually and as a group. Moreover, the results were similar when we estimated the gender pay gap controlling for one-digit occupation. Additional results also indicated that our findings are not due to the extreme case of the United States with its high level of wage inequality and relatively large gender pay gap.[25] Specifically, the results for GAPUSCHARS when the United States is omitted were virtually identical to those for the full sample in Table 4.3: male inequality and female net supply both continue to have large, usually statistically significant, positive effects on the gender pay gap. Moreover, the magnitudes of these effects are comparable with those reported above. Thus, while we found in earlier work (Blau and Kahn 1992; 1995; 1996b, see Chapter 3) that wage structure was important in explaining the differences between the gender pay gap in the United States and other countries, the results presented here strongly suggest that this conclusion holds more generally.

Table 4.A1 (in the Appendix) shows results in which we disaggregate the net supply variable into its component supply and demand indexes. The results indicate that the positive effects of net supply on the gender pay gap reported in Table 4.3 are driven by female supply. In particular, female supply has large positive, significant effects on the gender pay gap. In contrast, while the effects of female demand on the gender pay gap are always negative, as expected, they are smaller than their SEs in absolute value in each case. However, in each specification, we accept the hypothesis that the supply and demand coefficients are equal in magnitude and opposite in sign (and thus that the net supply variable is an appropriate specification). The poorer showing for the demand variable may reflect our inability to control for within-industry demand.

Other alternative specifications address a potential difficulty concerning the interpretation of our price variables. Specifically, because of omitted productivity characteristics, one country may have a seemingly higher return to education than another country, a difference that would be reflected in our measured price variability term. While we would like to interpret this variable as a measure of prices, it may instead reflect the variability of unmeasured skills that are correlated with education. For example, it has been pointed out that low-skill workers in the United States have lower relative levels of literacy than low-skill workers in other OECD countries (OECD 1998).

To take account of this possibility, we used data from the International Adult Literacy Survey 1994–96, as tabulated in OECD (1998), to form a rough control for average national levels of these unmeasured skill differences. In particular, for a subset of 11 of our 22 countries for which data were available, we computed the average difference in literacy test scores between those with upper secondary education only (i.e., middle levels) and those with less than upper-secondary levels of education (lower levels).[26] This is an estimate of average differences in unmeasured skills between workers with middle and low levels of education for each country. When we added this literacy variable to our basic models, the effects of prices and net supply were unaffected, and they were qualitatively similar to those for the full sample of 22 countries without the literacy variable included. Further, the literacy variable did not affect the gender pay gap. This alternative specification increases our confidence that our measured price variables really do reflect prices and that compressed returns to skills in general lead to a smaller gender pay gap.

We now present results that attempt to determine the degree to which our findings are due to differences across countries versus changes over time within countries. Table 4.5 presents our basic model with country dummies added. In this case, the variation in the dependent and explanatory variables is entirely due to within-country variation, while the results without country dummies (Table 4.3) combine the effects of within-country and between-country variation. In both the 50-10 and SD specifications, the estimated effect of male measured prices on the gender pay gap remains positive but is no longer significant. Male residual inequality is now estimated to have a negative effect on the gender pay gap, but the estimated coefficients are considerably smaller than their SEs. The effect of net supply remains positive but insignificant. Thus, the within-country estimates obtained by controlling for country dummies are considerably weaker and, in the case of male residual inequality, conflict with those not controlling for country dummies. This implies that the basic cross-section, time-series results are primarily due to differences between countries rather than to changes over time within countries.[27]

Table 4.5

Basic Cross-Section, Time-Series Regression Results with Country Effects (Dependent Variable = GAPUSCHARS)

	Coefficient	SE	Coefficient	SE
50:10yus	.1276	.1431		
50:10MALERES	-.0651	.1639		
SD yus			.1480	.2078
SD MALERES			-.0391	.1903
FNETSUPPLY	.3700	.6908	.3558	.7067
Year dummies	Yes		Yes	
Country dummies	Yes		Yes	
Sample size	100		100	
R^2	.7754		.7739	

Note: The gender gap is computed from equations including education, potential experience, and the square of potential experience. Male prices and residuals are from equations that additionally include marital status. Standard errors are heteroskedasticity robust and are corrected for within-country error correlation. GAPUSCHARS is the predicted gender pay gap evaluated at U.S. values for male and female characteristics; SD yus and 50:10yus are, respectively, the standard deviation and the 50-10 gap of predicted log wages applying each country's male wage equation to U.S. men; SD MALERES and 50:10MALERES are, respectively the standard deviation and the 50-10 gap in each country's male log wage residuals calculated from its male wage equation; FNETSUPPLY is our measure of female net supply. See the text for further details.

The divergence of the fixed effects results from the estimates without controlling for country effects likely reflects the different sources of variation in male inequality in each of the two cases, as discussed above. An additional factor working against obtaining equally strong results in the time series as in the cross-section is that most of the variation in the explanatory variables is between rather than within countries (Hamermesh 2000).[28] This is perhaps not surprising in that one of the attractions of international comparisons is the considerable variation in both the dependent and explanatory variables that such data provide, far exceeding what would be available for any individual country.

In light of the within-country results in Table 4.5, the cross-section, time-series results can be interpreted as primarily reflecting long-run differences across countries. One interpretation of the findings for male prices is that wage-setting institutions, such as collective bargaining contracts that call for high wage floors, lower male inequality and the gender pay gap as well. Further, where women are scarce in relation to the demand for labor in industries that traditionally employ them, the gender pay gap will be lower. This finding could reflect basic supply and demand in the labor market or selectivity of the female labor force.

But these interpretations can only be made subject to the usual caveat concerning cross-sectional differences across countries: there may be factors we cannot control for that influence male labor market prices and female net supply as well as the gender pay gap. The reduced form results presented in Tables 4.6, 4.7, and 4.8 shed additional light on this issue and also respond to the concern that wage inequality and possibly female net supply are potentially endogenous.

In Tables 4.6–4.8, we present a number of reduced-form specifications for the determination of the gender pay gap, omitting our measures of male wage inequality and instead including information on institutions that are expected to affect wage inequality in general or the gender gap specifically. These institutions include collective bargaining coverage, minimum wage laws, unemployment insurance systems, and job protection, as well as parental leave entitlements. The Data Appendix contains details on how these variables were constructed. As much as possible, we have constructed time-varying measures of these institutions to reflect the ongoing reforms of labor market institutions in the OECD (Boeri 2000). This analysis was based in most cases on the 14 countries for which we had this information.[29] There has been some relaxation of employment protection restrictions and some reduction in collective bargaining coverage in several countries over the 1980s and 1990s, and this is reflected in our institutional measures. However, as was the case with our wage-compression and net-supply measures, the cross-country variation in these institutions is much greater than their variation over time within countries. Specifically, between 89% and 99.96% of the total variation in collective bargaining coverage, unemployment insurance rules, parental leave entitlements, and job protection in our sample occurs between countries. Therefore, while there is time variation in these measures of labor market institutions, we are essentially looking at the effects of cross-sectional differences in them.

Table 4.6 shows results for including collective bargaining coverage alone (with year dummies) and with our original measures of wage compression and female net supply. With no covariates besides year dummies, collective bargaining coverage has a coefficient of -.0029 that is highly significant. This coefficient corresponds to a large impact of collective bargaining on the gender pay gap, implying that an increase in collective bargaining coverage from the twenty-fifth to the seventy-fifth percentile in our sample of 14 countries (i.e., going from 47% to 82% coverage) decreases the gender pay gap by .10 log points. This predicted fall is larger than the actual 75-25 differ-

Table 4.6

Results for Collective Bargaining Coverage and Wage Compression (Dependent Variable = GAPUSCHARS)

	Coefficient	SE	Coefficient	SE	Coefficient	SE	Coefficient	SE	Coefficient	SE
CBCOVERAGE	-.0029	.0007					-.0028	.0013	-.0024	.0012
50:10yus			.3638	.2184			.2780	.1753		
50:10MALERES			.1937	.1178			-.1323	.2085		
SD yus					.5344	.1786			.3519	.1722
SD MALERES					.2447	.1009			-.0878	.2318
FNETSUPPLY			.4274	.1748	.3803	.1673	.2283	.1200	.1883	.1336
Year dummies	Yes		Yes		Yes		Yes		Yes	
Sample size	71		71		71		71		71	
R^2	.4546		.3942		.4140		.5013		.5063	

Note: The gender gap is computed from equations including education, potential experience, and the square of potential experience. Male prices and residuals are from equations that additionally include marital status and are estimated across all workers. Standard errors are heteroskedasticity robust and are corrected for within-country error correlation. GAPUSCHARS is the predicted gender pay gap evaluated at U.S. values for male and female characteristics; CBCOVERAGE is the percentage of the country's workers covered by collective bargainin; SD yus and 50:10yus are, respectively, the standard deviation and the 50-10 gap of predicted log wages applying each country's male wage equation to U.S. men; SD MALERES and 50:10MALERES are, respectively the standard deviation and the 50-10 gap in each country's male log wage residuals calculated from its male wage equation; FNETSUPPLY is our measure of female net supply. See the text for further details.

ence in the gender pay gap among these countries of .07 log points. The second and third specifications in Table 4.6 reproduce the corresponding ones in Table 4.3 for the sample of countries for which information on collective bargaining is available. As may be seen in the table, we obtain results similar to those in Table 4.3 for this subsample: measured male price inequality, male residual wage inequality, and female net supply all have positive effects on the gender pay gap that are statistically significant or large relative to their SEs.

The final two specifications in Table 4.6 show that there is still a direct effect of collective bargaining even when wage compression and female net supply are included in the regression. In these instances, the collective bargaining coefficient is -.0024 to -.0028 and is two to 2.2 times its standard error in absolute value. A possible reason for this finding is that countries with very high levels of collective bargaining coverage have a greater coverage of female-dominated sectors of the labor market than countries with lower overall levels of collective bargaining. A further possibility is that the estimated direct effect of collective bargaining may be due in part to the fact that the extent of wage inequality is not perfectly captured by our inequality variables. Our estimate of the impact of measured prices is based on just a few variables reflecting education, potential experience, and marital status; and our measure of residual inequality reflects not only unmeasured prices but also differences across countries in the variation in unmeasured quantities and measurement error. Thus the extent of collective bargaining may continue to reflect the impact of wage compression, even when our inequality variables are included. When we control for collective bargaining, measured inequality in male prices and female net supply are still positively associated with the gender pay gap with effects that are from 1.6 to 2.0 (measured price inequality) or 1.4 to 1.9 (female net supply) times their SEs. However, in contrast to the results in Table 4.3, there is no longer a positive association between male residual wage inequality and the gender pay gap; this effect is negative and insignificant in Table 4.6.

Table 4.7 provides further evidence on the importance of institutions in affecting the gender pay gap by looking at both minimum wages and collective bargaining. The first column shows the impact of the minimum wage level (relative to the average wage) when only year dummies are included. The coefficient is significantly negative, suggesting a negative correlation between the "bite" of minimum wages and the gender pay gap.[30] However, when we control for collective bargaining coverage and minimum wages at the same time, the effect of minimum wages becomes much smaller and is now insignificant. The effect of collective bargaining, however, remains significantly negative and large in absolute value, even controlling for minimum wages. We further note that in several countries where there is a national wage floor, this is set in collective bargaining agreements covering most of the labor force (in our sample, this includes Austria, Norway, and Sweden) or in the application of collective bargaining agreements to nonunion workers (e.g., Germany, Italy, and Australia). In other countries, however, the government actually passes minimum wage legislation (e.g., Netherlands, the United Kingdom, Japan, New Zealand, Canada, the United States, and Ireland).[31] However, even where there is a statutory minimum, its level may be influenced by the strength of unions in influencing the political process. It may therefore be difficult to disentangle the impact of legislated minima from the effect of collective bargaining. Nonetheless, the results suggest that collective bargaining coverage has a stronger effect on the gender pay gap than minimum wage laws do. This conclusion makes sense if collective bargaining has larger wage effects at the bottom than statutory minimum wage laws.

Table 4.7

Results for Collective Bargaining Coverage and Minimum Wages (Dependent Variable = GAPUSCHARS)

Explanatory Variables	Coefficient	SE	Coefficient	SE
RELATIVEMINWAGE	-.6426	.1843	-.1674	.1912
CBCOVERAGE			-.0024	.0008
Year dummies	Yes		Yes	
Sample size	70		70	
R^2	.3927		.4634	

Note: The gender gap is computed from equations including education, potential experience, and the square of potential experience. Standard errors are heteroskedasticity robust and are corrected for within-country error correlation. GAPUSCHARS is the gender pay gap assuming U.S. male and female values for the X variables. RELATIVEMINWAGE is the country's minimum wage divided by its average wage, whether the minimum wage is set by law or in collective bargaining; CBCOVERAGE is the percentage of the country's workers covered by collective bargaining.

Table 4.8 shows results for collective bargaining, controlling for the effect of parental leave, unemployment insurance, and job protection policies and, in one specification, occupational segregation and female net supply as well. In all cases, collective bargaining continues to have a negative, significant effect on the gender pay gap that is large in absolute value. Evidence on the effects of the other policies was sensitive to the inclusion of the occupational segregation and female net supply variables. When these variables are not included (i.e., in the first and second specifications shown in the table), the labor market policies variables have insignificant effects both individually and as a group. However, controlling for net supply and segregation, these policy variables are significant at the 8% level as a group, although not individually.[32] Finally, the segregation index has the expected positive effect on the gender pay gap, although it is only 1.53 times its SE.

Table 4.8

Further Results for Collective Bargaining Coverage and Other Institutions (Dependent Variable: GAPUSCHARS)

	(1)		(2)		(3)	
	Coefficient	SE	Coefficient	SE	Coefficient	SE
CBCOVERAGE	-.0040	.0017	-.0041	.0023	-.0054	.0026
PARENTLEAVE	.0017	.0030	.0015	.0024	-.0006	.0032
(PARENTLEAVE)2/100	-.0004	.0016	-.0004	.0015	.0013	.0019
UIDURATION			.0017	.0167	.0011	.0279
Average UIREPRATE			-.0035	.0037	-.0059	.0040
Maximum UIREPRATE			.0014	.0022	.0011	.0026
PROTECTREGULAR			.0458	.0748	.0302	.0800
PROTECTTEMPORARY			.0137	.0241	.0344	.0303
SEGREGATION					1.2553	.8227
FNETSUPPLY					.1915	.4259
Year dummies	Yes		Yes		Yes	
Sample size	71		71		66	
R^2	.4872		.5202		.5779	

Note: The gender gap is computed from equations including education, potential experience, and the square of potential experience. Male prices and residuals are from equations that additionally include marital status and are estimated across all workers. Standard errors are heteroskedasticity robust and are corrected for within-country error correlation. GAPUSCHARS is the gender pay gap assuming U.S. male and female values for the X variables. CBCOVERAGE is the percentage of the country's workers covered by collective bargaining; PARENTLEAVE is weeks of mandated parental leave; UIDURATION is the maximum duration of unemployment insurance (UI) benefits; UIREPRATE is the UI replacement rate; PROTECTREGULAR and PROTECTTEMPORARY are, respectively, the OECD's index of mandated job protection for regular and temporary employees; SEGREGATION is the index of gender segregation by occupation; and FNETSUPPLY is our measure of female net supply.

These reduced form results for collective bargaining further strengthen our confidence in our basic findings for male wage inequality. Nonetheless, it is always possible that there are omitted variables that are correlated with collective bargaining coverage and the gender pay gap.[33] For example, there are other social programs that differ in generosity across countries that could potentially affect both male inequality and the gender gap. For instance, we do not have good data on the enforcement of equal employment opportunity laws, and variation in this factor may help explain differences in the gender pay gap. One possible indicator for such enforcement is the incidence of employment in very small firms, many of which are effectively exempt from labor market regulation (Carrington, McCue, and Pierce 2000). We examined this issue for the nine countries for which the OECD (1994) collected information during the 1990–92 period on the fraction of employment in firms with less than 20 workers.[34] While the sample size fell to 47 in this analysis, we still found a negative, significant effect of collective bargaining on the gender pay gap, while the effect of the incidence of employment in small firms was small and insignificant. Although the incidence of employment by firm size can clearly be affected by relative wages and by labor market institutions, the impact of collective bargaining was nonetheless robust with respect to this possible measure of the degree to which equal employment opportunity laws are enforced.

The results discussed above indicate that our findings for collective bargaining coverage are strong whether or not controls for other institutions are included. Further, according to Summers, Gruber, and Vergara (1993), it is centralizing wage-setting institutions that are primarily responsible for the growth of generous social programs in countries such as Sweden. If this is the case, then our models that exclude controls for other institutions can be viewed as reduced forms of such a process in which the prime mover is collective bargaining.

Another potential omitted variable would be social norms. For example, it is possible that a high degree of collective bargaining coverage, low male inequality, and a small gender gap all reflect an underlying social egalitarianism. While this is plausible, it seems unlikely to provide a full explanation for our findings. For one thing, there is considerable evidence that discontinuous changes in wage-setting institutions within countries do produce changes in wage inequality (Blau and Kahn 1999). For another thing, there are the examples of countries such as Austria and Italy that have highly centralized wage setting and relatively low male inequality and gender differentials and yet show little evidence of favorable treatment of women as a group otherwise.

A final consideration relates to a possible alternative interpretation of our finding of a negative association between wage compression and the gender pay gap, at least some of which appears to be due to the impact of collective bargaining coverage. We believe that these results indicate that bringing up the bottom of the pay distribution raises the relative wages of low-paid workers such as women. However, it is also possible that the negative relationship between pay compression and the gender pay gap reflects a positive impact of high wage floors on women's labor market skills, particularly their levels of actual labor market experience, although it may be recalled that the sign of this relationship is theoretically ambiguous. Some indication of the importance of this effect can be gained from panel data sets available for the United States, Sweden, and Germany which, unlike the ISSP, do have information on actual experience.

Germany and Sweden are both highly unionized societies with 80%–90% collective bargaining coverage, in contrast to the United States, with its 18% coverage rate in 1990. Table 4.2 shows that the male wage distribution is indeed much more compressed in these countries than in the United States. Using data sets we employed in earlier work (Blau and Kahn 1996b, see Chapter 3; Blau and Kahn 2000a), we find that the male-female gap in actual experience in 1984 was about 6 years in the United States and 5 years in Sweden and Germany. While these figures are consistent with the idea that high wage floors encourage female labor force commitment, in fact, female relative labor force participation rates among these three countries in the 1980s were highest in Sweden but higher in the United States than in West Germany.[35] Women in the United States are also much more likely to work full-time than women in these other countries (Blau and Kahn 1995). Thus, it is not clear that, taking all these indicators into account, women's labor force commitment was in fact higher in these other countries than in the United States. Moreover, the male-female experience gap in the United States declined steadily over the 1980s (Blau and Kahn 1997). Thus, by the end of the decade, it is quite possible that U.S. women had higher relative experience levels than women in several more highly unionized countries. It is, therefore, unlikely that a union effect on women's unmeasured labor market qualifications is responsible for our basic findings. Even if it were, however, one could still attribute an ultimate causal role to institutions of wage compression.

4.6. Conclusions

This article tested the hypotheses that overall wage compression and low female supply relative to demand reduce a country's gender pay gap. Using microdata for 22 countries over the 1985–94 period, we found that more compressed male wage structures and lower female net supply are both associated with a lower gender pay gap. Since it is likely that labor market institutions are responsible for an important portion of international differences in wage inequality, the inverse relationship between the gender pay gap and male wage inequality suggests that wage-setting mechanisms, such as encompassing collective bargaining agreements that provide for relatively high wage floors, raise the relative pay of women, who tend to be at the bottom of the wage distribution in all countries. Consistent with this view, we find that the extent of collective-bargaining coverage in each country is significantly negatively related to the gender gap. Overall, our results provide strong evidence that wage-setting institutions have important effects on the gender pay gap and some evidence of the impact of the market forces of supply and demand as well.

Appendix

Data Appendix

In this Appendix, we briefly describe the sources for the construction of the institutional variables used in Tables 4.6–4.8. See Table 4.A1 for a full summary of the variables.

Collective bargaining coverage was taken from OECD (1997), which had data for 1980, 1990, and 1994. We used linear interpolation to create a time series for this variable. For several countries, 1980 information was not available. In these cases, we used the 1990 figures. For Ireland, we assigned a value of 75 for collective bargaining coverage, in light of Layard, Nickell, and Jackman's (1991) classification of this country as having coverage in the "70% and above" range.

Parental leave was constructed from Ruhm and Teague (1997), who reported 1981 and 1991 values for parental leave, and Nickell and Layard (1999), who reported 1995 values for this variable. Again, we used linear interpolation to create a time series.

Regular and temporary employment protection were taken from OECD (1999), which reported indexes for protection for the late 1980s and the late 1990s. We used the late 1980s values for the years 1985–89 and the late 1990s values for the years 1990–94. Results were similar when we used a simple average of the late 1980s and the late 1990s for the 1990–94 period. The scales for these variables ranged from 0 to 4, with a higher value signifying more government restrictions on firms' use of labor.

Table 4.A1

Time-Series, Cross-Section Regression Results, Separate Female Supply, and Demand Effects (Dependent Variable: GAPUSCHARS)

	Coefficient	SE	Coefficient	SE
50:10yus	.2731	.2103		
50:10MALERES	.2560	.0932		
SD yus			.4276	.2084
SD MALERES			.2858	.0912
FSUPPLY	.3242	.1012	.2856	.1009
FDEMAND	-.1319	.3102	-.0195	.2503
F-test significance level for hypothesis: FSUPPLY effect = -1 × FDEMAND effect	.5344		.3623	
Year dummies	Yes		Yes	
Sample size	100		100	
R^2	.3372		.3388	

Notes: Gender gap is computed from equations including education, potential experience, and the square of potential experience. Male prices and residuals are from equations that additionally include marital status. Standard errors are heteroskedasticity robust and are corrected for within-country error correlation.Variable GAPUSCHARS is the gender pay gap assuming U.S. male and female values for the X variables. The variables SD yus and 50:10yus are, respectively, the standard deviation and the 50-10 gap of predicted log wages applying each country's male wage equation to U.S. men; SD MALERES and 50:10MALARES are, respectively the standard deviation and the 50-10 gap in each country's male log wage residuals calculated from its male wage equation.FDEMANDand FSUPPLYare female demand and supply indexes, respectively. See the text for further details.

Unemployment insurance (UI) benefit duration was taken from Nickell and Layard (1999) and is a one-time average for the period 1989–94. The average and maximum UI replacement rates were taken from Blanchard and Wolfers (2000). These authors compute 1985–89 and 1990–94 averages for these variables. We use the former for 1985–89 and the latter for 1990–94, thus creating a time-varying variable for UI replacement rates.

Minimum wages/average wages are a one-time average taken from Nickell and Layard (1999) and refer to the period 1991–94.

The Segregation Index comes from Anker (1998), Table 9.1. It is based on 75 nonagricultural two-digit occupations. Data refer to 1990 for Australia, Austria, Canada, Hungary, Japan, the Netherlands, Norway, and the United Kingdom; 1991 for Sweden and the United States; 1989 for West Germany; 1986 for New Zealand; 1980 for Switzerland; 1985 for Bulgaria; 1988 for Poland; and 1981 for Italy and Slovenia (former Yugoslavia).

5

International Differences in Male Wage Inequality: Institutions versus Market Forces

Based on a paper with Lawrence M. Kahn

5.1. Introduction

The level of wage inequality generated by a country's labor market is fundamentally important for those interested in understanding poverty, social stratification, and economic incentives facing workers. Labor earnings are by far the most important component of income for individuals who are employed; hence, in the absence of any compensatory government policies, low living standards in market economies will be associated with low labor incomes.[1] More generally, labor market inequality is a major determinant of disparities in living standards. The level of labor market inequality may also influence the solidarity that individuals feel with one another. Workers with similar earnings most likely feel more in com-

---

This chapter is a revised version of Blau, F. D., Kahn, L. M. (1996a). International Differences in Male Wage Inequality: Institutions versus Market Forces, in: The Journal of Political Economy, 104(4): 791-837: Chicago University Press. © 1996 by The University of Chicago. The authors are grateful to David Blanchflower, Per-Anders Edin, and Andrea Ichino for their help in acquiring data. Portions of this work were completed while they were visiting fellows at the Australian National University, Canberra. They have benefited from the helpful comments of participants at the University of Illinois, Cornell University, University of Oregon, and Columbia University Labor Economics Workshops, the 1994 NBER Summer Institute, and the 1995 meetings of the American Economic Association. They thank Robert Topel and an anonymous referee for helpful comments and suggestions.

mon with each other than those with vastly different economic rewards and status.

To the extent that labor market inequality reflects economic returns to skills, international differences in inequality imply differences in economic incentives. Countries with high rewards to skills have a wage structure that encourages skill acquisition by their workers. Moreover, centralized wage-setting mechanisms that reduce wage variation tend to limit firms' flexibility in responding to differences in market conditions across industries or geographical areas.[2] Also of concern is that relatively high wages for low-skill groups may reduce their relative employment.[3] On the other hand, a downside of high rewards to labor market skills is that they penalize demographic groups with below-average levels of skills, even in the absence of explicit discrimination against them. For example, the rising returns to skill in the United States in the 1980s have been found to reduce the relative wages of black workers (Juhn, Murphy, and Pierce 1991) and immigrants (LaLonde and Topel 1992) and to retard the economic progress of women (Blau and Kahn 1997). Similarly, Blau and Kahn (1992; 1995; 1996b, see Chapter 3) found that the higher rewards to skills in the United States compared to other industrialized countries were the most important reason for the relatively large gender pay gap in the United States.[4]

Considerable attention has been focused lately on the trend toward rising wage inequality that has been occurring in most of the industrialized countries.[5] Evidence that inequality increased in different countries with different institutional structures suggests that similar forces have been at work. For example, it has been suggested that technology and international trade have raised the relative demand for skilled workers among industrialized nations (Katz et al. 1995).

While changes in the demand for skilled labor appear to have led to a widening of the wage structures in many countries during the 1980s, considerable differences in the level of wage inequality remain. Of particular interest to us, the United States has a far greater dispersion of wages than other industrialized countries (Blanchflower and Freeman 1992; Blau and Kahn 1992; 1995; 1996b, see Chapter 3; OECD 1993). Previous international comparative work on wage inequality has focused on changes in wage dispersion. In this chapter, we are concerned with understanding the fundamental causes of the higher level of wage inequality in the United States compared to other industrialized countries in the 1980s. We concentrate on males in order to focus on a relatively homogeneous sample of workers for each country.[6]

Figure 5.1

Summary Measures of Male Log Wage Inequality

a)

b)

c)

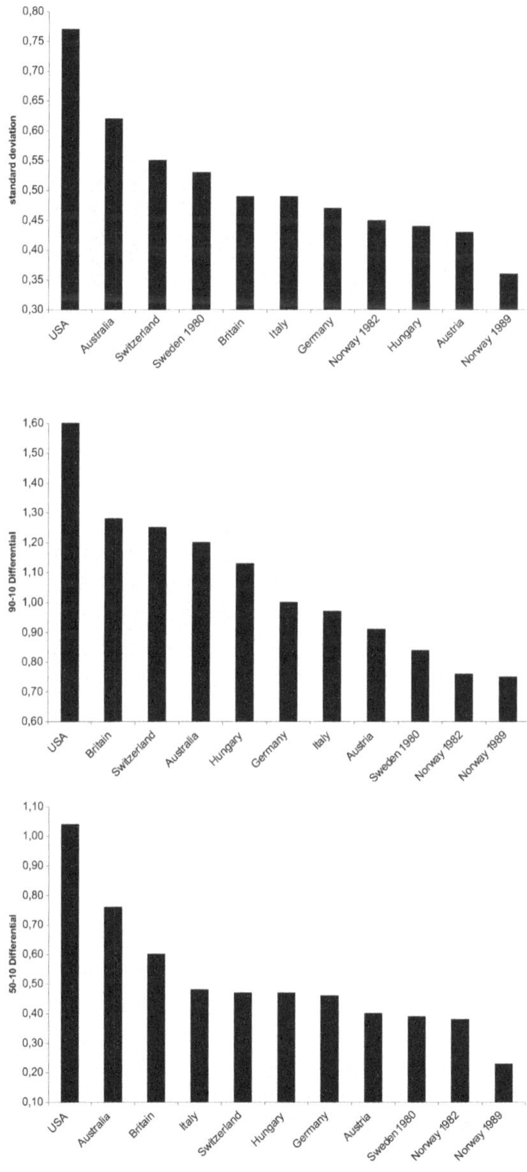

Figure 5.1 (continued)

d)

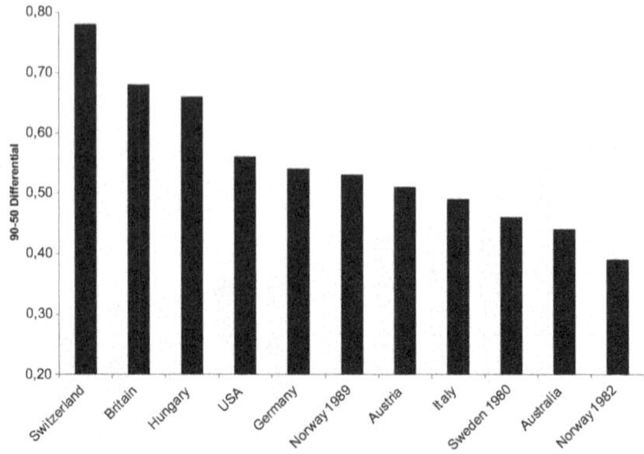

The basic pattern of international differences in wage inequality that we seek to explain is illustrated in Figure 5.1. (Details of the data sources and the method of calculating hours-corrected earnings are given below.) As expected on the basis of previous work, the United States has a considerably higher level of wage inequality than the other industrial countries in our sample. Panels a and b of Figure 5.1 indicate that both the standard deviation of log wages and the 90-10 percentile log wage differential are considerably greater in the United States than in the other countries. It is interesting, however, that this higher level of inequality reflects considerably more compression at the bottom of the distribution in the other countries relative to the United States but a much smaller difference in the degree of wage inequality at the top of the distribution. Thus, while the 50-10 percentile wage differential is much larger in the United States than elsewhere (panel c), the U.S. 90-50 differential is quite similar to that in several other countries in our sample (panel d).

Published data show a pattern similar to that of our microdata. Specifically, the OECD (1993) surveyed wage inequality in its member countries and found that the 50-10 gap was far larger in the United States than in other countries. While the 90-50 gap was also larger in the United States, the difference between the U.S. 90-50 gap and that of other countries was much smaller than the corresponding difference for the 50-10 gap.[7] This pattern of greater compression at the bottom is important from a policy perspective in that it implies that the labor market reward structure in other countries generates less poverty and relatively higher incomes for employed low-skill workers than in the United States.[8] Of course, as suggested above, there are potential costs of wage compression that would have to be compared to these benefits in deciding whether this is a desirable approach.

In the empirical work below, we focus on three possible explanations for these international differences in patterns of wage inequality. We first examine the role of differences across countries in the distribution of measured characteristics. We conclude that while measured characteristics help to explain some aspects of the international differences, U.S. labor market prices - that is, higher rewards to labor market skills and higher rents received for employment in favored sectors - are an important factor contributing to the observed differences in inequality between the United States and other countries.

Second, we assess the contribution of labor market institutions to explaining the differences in wage inequality. The United States has a largely nonunion labor market with very decentralized wage setting even in the union sector. The other countries have considerably higher rates of unionization, and most of them have much more centralized wage-setting processes than the U.S. union sector. Further, in several countries, the terms of collective bargaining agreements are routinely extended to cover nonunion workers, and their larger union sectors may also induce greater voluntary emulation of the union wage structure by the nonunion sector. Finally, in some of the countries, the government or the union movement has followed explicit policies to raise the relative pay of the lowest-paid workers.

Consideration of labor market institutions thus suggests less labor market inequality in these other countries than in the United States, and it may also imply greater compression at the bottom of the distribution than at the top. This is, of course, consistent with the pattern of inequality that we identify empirically. Moreover, we present information on the nature of union and nonunion patterns of inequality that reveals interesting features of the differences between the United States and other countries in the impact of labor market institutions. Specifically, our results imply that union pay policies that bring up the bottom of the union wage distribution are common to all countries, including the United States. However, unions in other countries appear to be more successful than U.S. unions both in reducing inequality in the union sector and in extending such policies to the nonunion sector.

Third, we examine international differences in the supply of and demand for labor market skills as an alternative explanation for the observed differences in inequality between the United States and other countries. We find that market forces, as best as we can measure them, do not appear to be a viable explanation for the international differences, further increasing our confidence that institutions are important. Finally, we present two additional pieces of empirical evidence suggesting that wage-setting institutions are an important determinant of international differences in wage distributions. First, examining the impact of centralization across the countries in our sample more generally, we find that the degree of wage centralization, as commonly measured by comparative industrial relations researchers, is negatively associated with wage dispersion, the 50-10 differential in the log of wages, and the pay gap between middle- and low-skill workers. Second, as would be expected on the basis of employer responses to de facto high wage floors, we generally find that the low-skilled have a higher employment/population ratio relative to the higher-skilled in the United States than elsewhere.

5.2. Determinants of Wage Inequality: Skills and Institutions

Wage inequality as measured by overall wage variation or by the wage gap between workers at different parts of the distribution (e.g., the tenth versus the fiftieth percentile) is affected by the distribution of skills, both measured and unmeasured, and the prices determined for those skills in the labor market. This price structure may include rents received by individuals employed in certain favored sectors. Prices, in turn, are influenced by both market and institutional forces.

Market forces determine skill prices through the interaction of the supply of and demand for skills. Suppose that workers of different skill levels (e.g., high school- or college-educated workers) are imperfect substitutes in production. Then differences in the relative supply of or demand for skills will produce differences in relative wages across countries.[9] The effects of demand can be felt both between and within industries. Final demand for output in one country may favor industries that (worldwide) disproportionately employ highly skilled workers. If such is the case, then the relative demand for skilled workers in this country will be higher than elsewhere; and, all else equal, we would expect skilled workers to do relatively well even in industries not directly affected by the high demand level. It is also possible that the relative demand for highly skilled labor is greater in each industry in one country than another, if different technologies are employed.

Institutional factors include the extent of collective bargaining coverage, the scope of collective bargaining where it occurs, union pay policies, and government policy toward the labor market. From each of these perspectives, we expect the United States to have a more unequal wage structure than other countries. The following decomposition of a country's overall level of wage inequality is useful in understanding the role of unions in producing differences in inequality across countries:

$$(1) \qquad v_i = \alpha_{ai}v_{ai} + (1-\alpha_{ai})v_{ni} + \alpha_{ai}(\omega_{ai}-\omega_i^*)^2 + (1-\alpha_{ai})(\omega_{ni}-\omega_i^*)^2,$$

where, for country i, v is the overall variance of log wages; α_a is the fraction of workers unionized; v_a and v_n are the variances of log union and nonunion wages; ω_a and ω_n are average log union and nonunion wages; and ω^* is the country's average log wage level.[10]

By the accounting scheme in equation (1), there are several routes through which the industrial relations system can affect overall wage inequality. First, unions typically raise their members' relative wages. This effect alone could increase or decrease overall wage dispersion, depending on where union workers would have been in the wage distribution in the absence of unionism. However, as suggested by the final two terms in equation (1), in an accounting sense, it is the union-nonunion wage gap (with other wage-influencing factors not controlled for) itself that is important in "explaining" the overall variance. All else equal, the larger this gap, however it is achieved, the larger the country's overall wage variance will be. And our data show that this gap is much higher for the United States than for other countries.[11]

Second, unions typically negotiate contracts that allow for less variation in pay than occurs in the nonunion sector (Freeman 1982; Blanchflower and Freeman 1992). Unions are much less prevalent in the United States than elsewhere; thus the lower union variance in pay would get a smaller weight in equation (1) in the United States. Hence, we would expect a higher overall variance in wages in the United States even if the variance of wages within the union and nonunion sectors were identical across countries. However, there are strong reasons for expecting both of these within-sector variances to be higher in the United States than elsewhere. These higher within-sector variances constitute a third route by which the U.S. industrial relations system raises wage inequality relative to other countries.

With respect to the union sector, collective bargaining in the United States is relatively decentralized, with an emphasis on single-firm agreements that, in most cases, are not firmwide (Hendricks and Kahn 1982). In contrast, as discussed below, in most of the other countries in our sample, bargaining is conducted on an industrywide or even an economywide level. Thus there appears to be more scope for interfirm and interindustry wage differentials in the United States than elsewhere, and a substantial portion of the wage inequality we observe in the United States is associated with such firm or industry wage effects (Blau 1977; Krueger and Summers 1988; Davis and Haltiwanger 1991; Groshen 1991).

While a lower variance in the union sector of other countries could be achieved either by raising the bottom, restraining the top, or both, centralized bargains often emphasize the setting of wage minima across diverse units. For example, in Austria, Germany, Italy, Sweden, and Switzerland (as well as in several European countries outside our sample), collective bargaining agreements, generally at the industry level, set minimum rates for the lowest pay group in a collective agreement ("Minimum Pay in 18 Countries," 1992). Such minima, to the extent that they are binding, will tend to bring up the floor among workers covered by the contract. In the limiting case, a contract that covered all workers in the economy might be expected to compress the bottom of the distribution, just as a high national minimum wage would. Thus we expect to find greater narrowing at the bottom than at the top in the union sector in most countries compared to the United States but regard this as to some extent an empirical question.

Several factors also lead us to expect more dispersion of nonunion wages in the United States than elsewhere. These factors include the practice in many other countries of extending the terms of collective bargaining agreements to nonunion workers. Such contract extensions blur the distinction between union and nonunion wage setting. To the extent that unions in all countries tend to compress wages at the bottom in the union sector, contract extension will not only reduce wage variation in the nonunion sector but compress wages at the bottom as well. In addition, the higher degree of union organization outside the United States should produce more "voluntary" imitation of union pay structures by nonunion firms than in the United

States.[12] Finally, the impact of these factors has been further strengthened by explicit union and government policies in some countries to bring up the bottom of the wage distribution.

5.3. Overview of International Differences in Labor Market Institutions

In this section, we provide a brief review of the institutional arrangements governing wage determination in the countries in our sample that suggests that wage setting is indeed more decentralized in both the union and nonunion sectors in the United States. In the union sector, Sweden and Norway exemplify a very high degree of centralization of wage setting in our sample of countries. There, the major union federation (LO) signs an agreement with the employer association (SAF in Sweden and NHO in Norway) covering a major portion of the labor force (Leion 1985; Thorsrud 1985; OECD 1989b). Austrian collective bargaining is also very centralized, with agreements in most cases covering an entire industry or group of industries throughout the country (Tomandl and Fuerboeck 1986). In Ger- many, contracts usually cover all employers in an industry in a state, providing a higher degree of centralization than in the United States but probably less than in Scandinavia or Austria (Kennedy 1980). And in Italy, master industrywide agreements negotiated at the national level between unions and employer associations have traditionally been the norm (Katz 1993).

Collective bargaining in Australia has also been characterized by considerable centralization, since the system relies heavily on government tribunals and compulsory arbitration in setting wages (Katz 1993). It has been estimated that about 90 percent of the Australian labor force has its pay set by these tribunals (Killingsworth 1990). Hungary was surveyed during the period of Communist party rule. While most workers were in unions, wages were controlled by the state, providing another example of centralized wage determination (Rezler 1973; U.S. Department of Labor 1992). For each of these countries, we would expect less dispersion of union wages than in the United States than in the countries discussed above, but likely more centralized than in the United States. While Britain, like the United States, had a mixture of single-firm and multiemployer agreements, in the 1970s, the latest period for which quantitative data are available, bargaining appeared to be more centralized in Britain. In the United

Kingdom for 1977-78, 25 percent of manufacturing contracts covered more than one firm (Deaton and Beaumont 1980), whereas for the United States the figure in 1975 was only 13 percent (Hendricks and Kahn 1982). Switzerland appears to have a mix of centralization and decentralization. On the one hand, many agreements exclude the subject of pay, leaving it to individual determination. On the other hand, there are no antitrust laws, and parties are encouraged to form associations, leaving open the possibility of de facto centralization (Wrong 1987). Further, it has been estimated that about half of the Swiss private-sector workforce is covered by industry collective bargaining agreements ("Minimum Pay in 18 Countries" 1992).

Events in the 1980s and 1990s have led to the decentralization of bargaining in virtually every industrialized country.[13] In Sweden and Norway, the influence of the central employer federation-LO agreement was reduced starting in the 1980s, though by the end of the decade, some recentralization had occurred in Norway. In Australia, tribunal decisions have allowed more interfirm variation in wage settlements. In Germany and Italy, bargaining has shifted in some cases from the industry to the plant level in the late 1980s. In Britain and the United States, multiemployer units continued to crumble in the 1980s and 1990s.

We have no way of knowing whether decentralization has proceeded faster outside the United States than inside. Nonetheless, ones impression is that, with the possible exception of Britain, systems of collective bargaining remain more centralized in the other countries than in the United States. The United States does not have the centralizing institutions that are still in place in these other countries. And deunionization proceeded much more rapidly in the United States than in other countries (including Britain), providing an extreme form of decentralization (Blanchflower and Freeman 1992; Katz 1993).

The structure of collective bargaining thus leads us to expect more dispersion of union wages in the United States than elsewhere. A review of labor market institutions in other countries leads us to expect more dispersion of nonunion wages in the United States as well. In Australia, wage tribunals set minimum pay rates across both the union and nonunion sectors, whereas in then - Communist Hungary, wages in both sectors were controlled by the state. In Germany, Austria, Italy, and Switzerland, the government routinely extends the terms of collective bargaining agreements to nonunion workers.[14] It has been estimated that as of 1992, legally binding industry or sectoral level agreements covered 90 percent of workers in Germany, 98 percent in Austria, "the vast majority" in Italy, and "nearly all" workplaces in Sweden ("Minimum Pay in 18 Countries" 1992). In Switzerland, in 1992, roughly 10 percent of all workers (or about 20 percent of nonunion workers) were nonunion employees whose wages had been set through contract extensions ("Minimum Pay in 18 Countries" 1992). These figures for 1992 suggest that whatever trends there have been toward decentralization in the 1980s and 1990s, wage setting remains considerably more centralized in Western Europe than in the United States.

Finally, in Sweden, Italy, Norway, and West Germany, explicit union and government policies have been followed that would be expected to lead to strong compression at the bottom of the distribution. From 1968 to 1974, the LO in Sweden made a conscious effort to raise the relative wages of lower-paid workers, leading to a sharp fall in inequality (Edin and Topel 1994). In Italy, the wage indexation system, the scala mobile, in place from 1975 to 1992, gave across-the- board lira increases in wages in response to inflation. The system was designed to reduce skilled-nonskilled pay differentials (Treu 1990; "Italy" 1992). By 1990, Italian employers claimed that accumulated indexation payments accounted for 40 percent of labor costs ("New Industrial Relations Talks Continue" 1990). While other aspects of the pay package to some degree counteracted the leveling effects of indexation, Erickson and Ichino (1995) found that the system still had some independent effect in reducing inequality. In Norway in 1980, a special fund for wage increases for the low-paid was established (U.S. Department of Labor 1984). Finally, in Germany, some unions have succeeded in getting above sectoral levels of wage increases for low-paid workers, in an attempt to raise the floor ("Minimum Pay Setting: Germany" 1992).

5.4. Results

5.4.1. Data Sources and the Definition of Hours-Corrected Earnings

We compiled microdata from several sources to examine international differences in male wage inequality. First, we used the International Social Survey Programme (ISSP) for the following countries and time periods: Austria (1985-87 and 1989), West Germany (1985-88), Hungary (1986-88), Switzerland (1987), Britain (1985- 89), the United States (1985-89), and Norway (1989). Second, we supplemented the

ISSP with several other microdata bases in order to expand our coverage of countries. Specifically, we used the Class Structure and Class Consciousness (CSCC) data base compiled by Erik Wright for Sweden (1980) and, since it is also available, Norway (1982) - providing us with a second Norwegian data set; the Income Distribution Survey (IDS) for Australia (1986); and a Bank of Italy survey for Italy (1987).[15] In all cases, the sample is restricted to wage and salary workers, aged 18-65. Third, we performed a special comparison for 1984 between the United States and Sweden using two additional databases with more detailed information on personal characteristics and earnings: the Michigan Panel Study of Income Dynamics (PSID) and the Swedish Household Market and Nonmarket Activities Survey (HUS).[16] In this portion of the analysis, the sample is further restricted to full-time workers and, in the case of the U.S. data, to whites. White males are used instead of all males in order to produce a relatively homogeneous U.S. sample to compare with the Swedish data. (The ISSP did not collect information on race.)

The specific earnings measures available in the data for each country are described in detail in Appendix Table 5.Al. For all cases except the 1984 Sweden-United States comparison, the earnings variable supplied by the data source is expressed on an annual or monthly basis. For example, the Appendix shows that in Britain, the United States, Australia, Italy, and Norway, the variable is annual earnings from all jobs; whereas in Austria, Germany, Switzerland, and Hungary, it is monthly earnings. For the 1980 data on Sweden, income is counted for the year and includes labor and nonlabor income, which is dominated by labor income (Rosenfeld and Kalleberg 1990). The computation of wage rates from such data is complicated by the omission of information on annual weeks worked. Data on weekly hours worked are available, however, allowing for some adjustment of earnings for time input (described below). But because of the lack of data on weeks worked for most of the countries, we cannot directly compute a wage rate, which would be the preferable measure of earnings. For the 1984 Sweden-United States comparison, however, we are able to compute hourly earnings.[17]

With the exception of the 1984 HUS (Sweden) and PSID (United States) data, the earnings variable in the raw data files generally arrived to us coded into categories. We used the midpoint of each interval as the actual earnings measure, except for the top interval, since it was open-ended. In the analyses presented below, we arbitrarily coded the top category as 1.2 times its minimum value. Our results were not sensitive to assumptions about top-coding.[18] Finally, concern about adequate sample size led us to pool years of data for those ISSP countries surveyed more than once (see above). However, since the multiple years of data on Sweden and Norway come from different sources, we do not pool them.

Because our basic data sources apart from the U.S. PSID and the Swedish HUS generally do not provide enough information to allow us to compute hourly earnings, we adjusted the raw earnings variable for time input, using the information available. Adjusting for time input is essential in studying the inequality of the price of labor across countries, since the distribution of working hours varies across countries. For example, Bjorklund and Freeman (1994) report that the variance of annual work hours is greater in the United States than in Sweden, and our microdata show that the U.S. variance in weekly work hours is greater than that in other countries, both among all workers and among full-time workers. To create the hours-corrected earnings measure, which was used to construct Figure 5.1 and in the analyses below, we implemented the following procedure.

For each worker i in country j, the following regression was estimated:

$$\ln \text{EARN}_{ij} = b_{j0} + b_{j1}\text{PART}_{ij} + b_{j2}\text{HPART}_{ij} + b_{j3}\text{HFULL}_{ij} + B_j'X_{ij} + \sum_t \tau_{it} YR_{ijt} + e_{ij}, \tag{2}$$

where ln EARN is the log of earnings; PART is a dummy variable for part-time work (less than 35 hours per week); HPART and HFULL are interactions of weekly work hours with part- and full-time status; X is a vector of explanatory variables including years of schooling, potential experience and its square, a dummy variable for those married, spouse present, a union membership dummy variable, and one-digit industry and occupation dummies; YR_t is a vector of dummies for the countries for which we pooled different years of data; and e is an error term. (For ease of notation, we have suppressed t subscripts for the dependent and explanatory variables besides YR_t and for the error term. See Appendix Table 5.A2 for variable definitions.)[19]

The PART, HPART, HFULL, and year dummy variable coefficients from (2) were used to adjust each person's earnings for work hours and year by assuming a 40-hour work week and the end year of the pooled years. That is, for each worker i and country j, we have

$$\text{(3)} \qquad \begin{aligned} \text{YFULL}_{ij} = {} & \ln \text{EARN}_{ij} - b_{j1}\text{PART}_{ij} - b_{j2}\text{HPART}_{ij} \\ & - b_{j3}(\text{HFULL}_{ij} - 40) - \sum_t \tau_{it}\text{YR}_{ijt}, \end{aligned}$$

where YFULL is the log of hours-corrected earnings, the b's and τ_t are coefficients estimated from equation (2), and the rest of the variables are defined above. We include part-time workers for sample size reasons and to have a representative sample. The share of part-time workers among male workers is small, ranging from 1 to 9 percent in the countries in our sample, and the distribution of hours-corrected earnings for full-time workers is similar to that for all workers in our sample.

In estimating the coefficients for the hours variables (the b's above) for the adjustment of earnings, we include all the explanatory variables in the basic wage determination model. We follow this procedure so that, as much as possible, the hours coefficients perform the function of adjusting for time input rather than picking up the effects of omitted variables. Of course, to some degree, even when one controls for human capital, marital status, industry, union status, and occupation, differences in hours may be associated with unmeasured productivity.[20] Nonetheless, for the purposes of computing an earnings measure with which to compare countries, we believe that it is important to adjust for hours input as fully as possible.[21] For the 1984 United States-Sweden comparison, we use the log of hourly earnings, based on the previous year's earnings divided by the previous year's work hours.[22]

Measures of inequality calculated on the basis of hours-corrected earnings were presented in Figure 5.1 and are also shown in panel A of Table 5.1. We again see that the United States has a considerably larger standard deviation of earnings and 90-10 gap than the other countries. However, whereas the U.S. 50-10 earnings differential is much larger than it is in the other countries (0.582 log points above the non-U.S. average), the 90-50 differential in the United States is smaller than in Britain, Switzerland, and Hungary and only slightly larger than in Germany, Austria, and Norway (1989). Overall, the U.S. 90-50 gap is only slightly larger (0.007 log points) than the unweighted average for the other countries. Similar results are obtained for a comparison of log hourly earnings between the United States and Sweden in 1984 (panel B). The U.S. 50-10 differential is much larger (0.518 log points) than it is in Sweden, whereas the 90-50 gap is only 0.158 log points higher. Further, these estimates of the U.S.-Swedish differences at the bottom and the top of the wage distribution are quite similar to those obtained for hours-corrected earnings using the ISSP data for the United States and the CSCC data for Sweden (panel A).[23]

Table 5.1

Summary Measures of Wage Inequality

	Standard Deviation	50-10 Percentile Differential	90-50 Percentile Differential	90-10 Percentile Differential
	A. Log Hours-Corrected Earnings			
Germany	.470	.456	.539	.995
Britain	.489	.594	.683	1.277
United States	.772	1.040	.552	1.592
Austria	.424	.391	.508	.899
Switzerland	.549	.464	.777	1.241
Sweden (1980)	.523	.382	.452	.834
Norway (1982)	.441	.372	.382	.754
Australia	.622	.755	.439	1.194
Hungary	.431	.462	.661	1.123
Italy	.488	.478	.486	.964
Norway (1989)	.360	.224	.525	.749
Non-U.S. average (unweighted)	.480	.458	.545	1.003
	B. Log Hourly Earnings			
Sweden (1984)	.343	.254	.388	.642
United States (1984)	.543	.772	.546	1.318

5.4.2. The Role of Prices and Measured Characteristics

A crucial question raised by the results shown in Table 5.1 is the degree to which the observed differences in wage dispersion between the United States and other countries are due to differences in measured characteristics versus differences in the prices of labor market skills (i.e., wage structure). To shed light on this issue, we employ a full distributional accounting scheme developed by Juhn et al. (1993) to study intertemporal changes in U.S. wage inequality. We begin with a wage equation for worker i in country j:

$$\text{YFULL}_{ij} = B_j' X_{ij} + c_j + e_{ij} \equiv B_j' X_{ij} + c_j + \sigma_j \theta_{ij}, \tag{4}$$

where YFULL is hours- (and year-) corrected log earnings as defined in equation (3), X is a vector of variables defined above, B is the vector of estimated coefficients from equation (2), and e is necessarily the same error term as in equation (2). Note that c_j (= $40b_{j3}$) derives from the computation of hours-corrected earnings in equation (3). Since it is constant across individuals in each country, it has no impact on our analysis of inter country differences in wage distributions, and thus, for simplicity, we suppress it from the equations below. (For the 1984 Sweden-United States comparison, the dependent variable is simply hourly earnings, and $c_j = 0$.)

In general, the analysis proceeds in one step in which we estimate the determinants of the raw earnings variable in equation (2) to obtain all the coefficients necessary for the hours adjustment of earnings and for the analysis of international differences in the distribution of hours-adjusted earnings (described below) at the same time. Thus, for the purposes of the decomposition, we treat the hours (and year dummy) variables as pure adjustment factors rather than as productivity characteristics or labor market structure indicators. While, as noted above, hours may be correlated with productivity, it is also a direct measure of labor supply. Our goal is to explain international differences in the distribution of the price of labor rather than of labor incomes. Since YFULL is adjusted for hours input, it does a better job of this than the unadjusted earnings variable (In EARN). However, as equations (2) and (4) show, the wage coefficients for the variables of substantive interest (B) and the residuals (e) are unchanged when we shift our focus from In EARN to YFULL.

To analyze the prices of skills as they influence international differences in the wage distribution, we begin by noting that, in the last term in equation (4), e is replaced by θ, a standardized residual with mean zero and variance one, multiplied by σ, the residual standard deviation of log hours-corrected earnings. Following Juhn et al. (1993), we may then create two hypothetical wage distributions for each country. First, for country j we construct the set of wages that would emerge if we applied the estimated U.S. wage function B_u, and residual standard deviation (σ_u) to each worker i in country j:

(5) $$Y(1)_{ij} = \mathbf{B}_u'\mathbf{X}_{ij} + \sigma_u\theta_{ij},$$

where $Y(1)_{ij}$ is computed for each worker in country j by valuing his measured characteristics at the U.S. coefficient vector B_u and his position in his own country's distribution of wage residuals (e.g., the thirty-fifth percentile) at the corresponding position in the U.S. residual distribution. The primary difference between the distribution of YFULL for the United States and of $Y(1)$ for country j is the substitution of country j's distribution of measured characteristics for those of the United States in the U.S. wage equation.[24] Construction of $Y(1)$ is important because it allows us to determine the extent to which international differences in the distribution of wages are due to differences in the distribution of measured characteristics.

The second hypothetical distribution for country j results from giving each person in country j his own country's estimated wage coefficients but the U.S. wage residual corresponding to his position in his own country's residual distribution:

$$\text{(6)} \qquad \mathrm{Y}(2)_{ij} = \mathbf{B}_j'\mathbf{X}_{ij} + \sigma_u\theta_{ij},$$

The difference between the distributions of $Y(2)_{ij}$ and $Y(1)_{ij}$ is entirely due to the difference between country j's wage function and that of the United States.

Finally, the impact of wage residuals on country j's wage distribution relative to that of the United States is the difference between the distribution of $YFULL_{ij}$ and $Y(2)_{ij}$. While we would like to interpret this as the effect of unmeasured prices (i.e., the difference between σ_u and σ_j), it also includes the effect of differences in the distribution of unmeasured productivity characteristics and measurement error. First, while the U.S. residual distribution may be more dispersed than that of other countries because of higher prices of unmeasured skills, it may also be the case that the U.S. labor force is more diverse in its unmeasured characteristics. Second, the need to deal with interval data and the different definitions of earnings may have introduced differential measurement errors across countries. Such differences in the distribution of unmeasured productivity and in measurement errors would be included in our estimate of the effect of wage residuals but do not reflect unmeasured prices. Our review of the literature on wage-setting institutions suggests that the United States does in fact have higher skill prices than other countries; but we cannot rule out the possibility that some portion of the cross-country differences in wage variation associated with the wage residuals reflects international differences in unmeasured quantities or measurement error as well as unmeasured prices.

To further support the notion that unmeasured prices are important, we supplement our other analyses with a comparison of 1984 data from the U.S. PSID and the Swedish HUS that are likely to be less contaminated by unmeasured heterogeneity than our other data sources. Specifically, as noted above, for the 1984 United States-Sweden comparison, we use a sample of white, full-time employed men from the United States and full-time employed men from Sweden. Thus racial heterogeneity in the United States will not directly affect this comparison. In addition, we are able to construct actual average hourly earnings in these samples, again reducing the scope for errors. Finally, we are able to control for actual, rather than potential, labor market experience. While potential labor market experience is a good proxy for actual experience for men, fewer errors will result if one has data on the real thing and if these data are themselves accurate.[25]

We perform the decomposition of differences in the wage distribution implied by equations (4)-(6) in two stages. Initially, we include only a vector of human capital characteristics (education, potential experience and its square, and marital status). Next, we augment the human capital variables with a vector of industry and occupation dummy variables and union status; that is, we estimate equation (2) above. A comparison of the results from the two specifications sheds light on the role of occupation, industry, and unionism in explaining the international differences.[26]

The results of performing this decomposition for the standard deviation of log wages are shown in Table 5.2. Panel A of the table shows the human capital specification results, and panel B shows the findings for the full specification. The actual U.S.-country j differences are shown in column 1. As may be seen in column 2 of the table, the distribution of measured characteristics explains relatively little (about 6 percent, on average) of the higher variation in wages in the United States than elsewhere under either specification. In contrast, prices appear to be important in explaining the differences in inequality between the United States and the other countries. In every instance, measured prices and residual effects serve to raise the U.S. standard deviation of wages compared to each country.

Table 5.2 indicates that prices of measured characteristics explain a larger share than the distribution of measured characteristics: 15-

20 percent on average, with the bulk of the difference between the United States and the other countries (74-79 percent) attributable to the larger residual variation of wages in the United States. Thus prices of labor market skills (both measured and unmeasured) appear to be the primary cause of the higher variation in wages in the United States, although we cannot rule out the possibility that the distribution of unmeasured characteristics and measurement error also play a role. The 1984 United States-Sweden comparison is instructive in this regard. Despite the more homogeneous U.S. sample and the better measure of wages and experience, the results are quite similar to those of the 1980 United States-Sweden comparison. Most notably, measured characteristics actually play a smaller part in explaining the U.S.-Swedish difference in the 1984 comparison.

Table 5.2

Decomposition of the U.S.-Country *j* Differences in the Standard Deviation of Log Wages

	U.S. Standard Deviation - Country *j* Standard Deviation	Measured Characteristics Effect	Wage Coefficients Effect	Wage Equation Residual Effect
	(1)	(2)	(3)	(4)
	A. Human Capital Specification			
Germany	.301	.008	.020	.274
Britain	.283	.044	.021	.218
Austria	.348	.006	.062	.279
Switzerland	.223	.001	.035	.187
Sweden (1980)	.248	.034	.017	.197
Norway (1982)	.331	.018	.047	.266
Australia	.150	.014	.036	.100
Hungary	.340	.038	.078	.224
Italy	.284	-.0004	.048	.236
Norway (1989)	.411	.023	.042	.347
Sweden (1984)	.200	-.001	.069	.132
Non-U.S. average (unweighted)	.284	.017	.043	.224
	B. Full Specification			
Germany	.301	.021	.032	.248
Britain	.283	.037	.037	.209
Austria	.348	.008	.075	.265
Switzerland	.223	-.004	.032	.195
Sweden (1980)	.248	.032	.018	.198
Norway (1982)	.331	.014	.071	.246
Australia	.150	.007	.051	.092
Hungary	.340	.025	.111	.205
Italy	.284	.020	.037	.227
Norway (1989)	.411	.008	.076	.327
Sweden (1984)	.200	.011	.080	.109
Non-U.S. average (unweighted)	.284	.016	.056	.211

We explicitly compare the magnitude and sources of the 50-10 and the 90-50 differentials in Table 5.3. The results for the human capital specification are again shown in panel A and the results for the full specification in panel B. Column 1 of both panels shows the actual U.S.-country *j* difference in the 50-10 and 90-50 log wage differentials. As we saw above, these differences are considerably greater for the 50-10 gap (0.576 log points, on average) than for the 90-50 gap (0.021 log points, on average).[27] Column 2 of Table 5.3 shows that these 50-10 versus 90-50 comparisons are substantially affected by the distribution of measured characteristics.

Table 5.3

Decomposition of the U.S.-Country *j* Differences in the 50-10 and 90-50 Differentials in Log Wages

	U.S. Differential - Country *j* Differential	Measured Characteristics Effect	Wage Coefficients Effect	Wage Equation Residual Effect
	(1)	(2)	(3)	(4)
	A. HUMAN CAPITAL SPECIFICATION			
	50-10 Log Wage Differential			
Germany	.584	.312	-.019	.291
Britain	.446	.083	.089	.274
Austria	.649	.299	-.005	.355
Switzerland	.576	.254	.053	.269
Sweden (1980)	.658	.385	.034	.239
Norway (1982)	.668	.331	-.013	.350
Australia	.285	.069	.068	.148
Hungary	.578	.158	.038	.382
Italy	.562	.246	.041	.275
Norway (1989)	.816	.338	-.037	.515
Sweden (1984)	.518	.225	.018	.275
Non-U.S. average (unweighted)	.576	.245	.024	.307
	90-50 Log Wage Differential			
Germany	.013	-.183	.095	.101
Britain	-.131	-.134	-.043	.046
Austria	.044	-.199	.121	.122
Switzerland	-.225	-.300	.046	.029
Sweden (1980)	.100	-.075	.078	.097
Norway (1982)	.170	-.132	.086	.216
Australia	.113	-.067	.054	.126
Hungary	-.109	-.190	.208	-.127
Italy	.066	-.151	.114	.103
Norway (1989)	.027	-.104	.065	.066
Sweden (1984)	.158	-.190	.152	.196
Non-U.S. average (unweighted)	.021	-.157	.089	.089

Table 5.3 (continued)

	U.S. Differential - Country *j* Differential	Measured Characteristics Effect	Wage Coefficients Effect	Wage Equation Residual Effect
	(1)	(2)	(3)	(4)
	B. FULL SPECIFICATION			
	50-10 Log Wage Differential			
Germany	.584	.301	.067	.216
Britain	.446	.010	.192	.244
Austria	.649	.208	.144	.297
Switzerland	.576	.218	.170	.188
Sweden (1980)	.658	.294	.205	.159
Norway (1982)	.668	.370	.057	.241
Australia	.285	.127	.046	.112
Hungary	.578	.145	.174	.259
Italy	.562	.233	.092	.237
Norway (1989)	.816	.212	.129	.475
Sweden (1984)	.518	.164	.104	.250
Non-U.S. average (unweighted)	.576	.207	.125	.243
	90-50 Log Wage Differential			
Germany	.013	-.177	.091	.099
Britain	-.131	-.149	-.056	.074
Austria	.044	-.151	.093	.102
Switzerland	-.225	-.231	-.049	.055
Sweden (1980)	.100	-.091	.080	.111
Norway (1982)	.170	-.191	.166	.195
Australia	.113	-.129	.098	.144
Hungary	-.109	-.206	.196	-.099
Italy	.066	-.108	.048	.126
Norway (1989)	.027	-.132	.056	.103
Sweden (1984)	.158	-.140	.132	.166
Non-U.S. average (unweighted)	.021	-.155	.078	.098

For each country j, the measured characteristics effect is the difference between $YFULL_u$ and $Y(1)_j$ at the indicated percentiles of the distribution. The positive effects for the 50-10 differentials for both specifications indicate that the U.S. distribution of measured characteristics widens the 50-10 gap compared to that in each country. These effects-0.245 log points for the human capital specification and 0.207 log points for the full specification, on average - are large indeed. A comparison of the results for the two specifications indicates that it is the U.S. distribution of human capital characteristics that is relevant in explaining the international differences, with the U.S. distribution of industry, occupation, and union status slightly lowering the 50-10 gap compared to other countries.[28] On average, measured characteristics are estimated to account for 35.9-43.4 percent of the higher U.S. 50-10 differential. In contrast, the distribution of measured characteristics lowers the 90-50 wage differential in the

United States compared to other countries. In each case, the effect is negative with an unweighted average effect of about -0.16 log points in both specifications. For both the 50-10 and 90-50 analyses, we find the impact of measured characteristics to be quite similar for the 1984 Sweden and 1980 Sweden comparisons, again suggesting that greater unmeasured heterogeneity of U.S. workers is not driving our results.

The findings for the measured characteristics effects imply that a considerable portion of the wider 50-10 gap relative to the 90-50 gap in the United States is accounted for by differences in the distribution of productive characteristics. With the same distribution of measured characteristics, the average difference between the U.S. 50-10 gap and that for the other countries would decline to 0.331-0.369 log points (from 0.576), whereas the figure for the 90-50 gap would increase to about 0.18 (from 0.021). Thus if we consider the part of the differential that is not accounted for by measured characteristics (i.e., the sum of the wage coefficients and wage residuals effects) as potentially due to wage structure, we find that the U.S. wage structure widens both the top and the bottom of the wage distribution relative to other countries. In particular, adding the wage coefficients and wage residuals effects, we find that in every case, U.S. prices lead to a widening of both the 50-10 and the 90-50 differentials compared to other countries.

In the decomposition shown in Tables 5.2 and 5.3, controlling for personal characteristics is especially important since it reveals the 90-50 widening effect of U.S. prices, an effect that is not apparent if one merely compares the raw 90-50 differential in the United States with that in other countries. Further, it reduces the likelihood that we are overstating the compression at the bottom (which would occur if one merely examined the raw 50-10 differentials). However, the U.S. wage structure continues to widen the bottom by more than the top. This is true on average and in 9 (full specification) or 10 (human capital specification) of 11 possible cases. Such an effect is consistent with government and trade union wage policies in other countries that have their biggest effect in bringing up the bottom of the distribution.

Columns 3 and 4 of Table 5.3 show the effects of wage coefficients and wage residuals separately. For the 50-10 gap, the U.S. human capital wage coefficients usually have a small widening effect compared to the other countries (accounting for 4.2 percent of the difference, on average), although the effect is negative in four cases. The coefficients effect is notably increased when the full specification is employed (accounting for 21.7 percent of the difference, on average), suggesting that it is the prices associated with the industry, occupation, and unionism variables that are particularly high in the United States. In both specifications, however, the wage residuals effect accounts for a substantial share (42.2-53.3 percent) of the U.S.-country j difference. In the case of the 90-50 gap, the coefficients and residual effects are generally positive and do not differ very much between the two specifications. This suggests that the impact of measured prices primarily reflects higher prices of the human capital variables in the United States. The coefficients and residual effects are roughly equal in size, on average.

5.4.3. The Effect of Institutions: Collective Bargaining and Contract Extension

Our discussion of trade unionism led us to expect greater U.S. wage dispersion than in other countries because of higher U.S. dispersion within the union and nonunion sectors, a greater U.S. union-nonunion wage differential, and a relatively smaller U.S. union sector. The relative size of the U.S.-other country difference in union versus nonunion wage dispersion is an empirical question. On the one hand, suppose that the wage spillover due to contract extension and voluntary imitation is virtually complete in the non-U.S. countries but that unions in these countries have only a slightly greater narrowing effect for their members than U.S. unions do. Then we would expect the nonunion differences in inequality between the United States and other countries to be larger because, outside the United States, workers not in unions would essentially be treated as union members. On the other hand, suppose that the spillover to nonunion workers in the non-U.S. countries is partial and that unions in these countries have a much greater narrowing effect for their members than U.S. unions do. Then U.S.-non-U.S. differences in union inequality could be greater than nonunion differences.

These issues are examined in detail in Blau and Kahn (1994a), and the results are summarized here. For the countries in our sample for which collective bargaining status was available,[29] we used equation (1) to decompose U.S.-other country differences in the log wage variance. We found that, on average, 86 percent of the larger U.S. variance was due to higher U.S. variances within the union and nonunion sectors.

Another substantial portion, about 12 percent, on average, was due to the smaller relative size of the low-variance (union) sector in the United States, whereas the higher U.S. union-nonunion wage differential accounted for only 2 percent of the larger U.S. log wage variance, on average. Thus we must look within the union and nonunion sectors to understand U.S.-other country differences in wage dispersion.

We found that the higher U.S. union and nonunion wage dispersion primarily reflected the larger 50-10 log wage gap within each sector in the United States than in the other countries, mirroring our findings for the aggregate wage distribution. The most striking finding pertained to the nonunion sector, where the U.S. 50-10 differential of 1.082 log points was much larger than the unweighted average of 0.516 for the other countries. The 50-10 gap was also larger for U.S. union workers, but the international difference was much less: 0.689 for the United States compared to an average of 0.404 elsewhere. In contrast, the 90-50 gap for U.S. nonunion workers was about the same as in the other countries, whereas the 90-50 gap for U.S. union workers was actually slightly smaller than that for non-U.S. workers.

This 50-10 pattern is suggestive of larger union spillover effects on nonunion wage structures in other countries than in the United States, although it could still be due to the impact of measured characteristics. In order to shed light on the impact of prices as opposed to the distribution of measured skills, we performed the Juhn et al. (1993) decomposition outlined in equations (4)-(6) separately for union and nonunion workers in each country using the full specification.[30] We find that the standard deviation of log wages continues to be substantially higher in the United States in both the union and nonunion sectors even after taking into account the distribution of measured characteristics. The same pattern obtains for the 50-10 differential: the U.S. gap remains larger than that of other countries in both sectors after adjustment for the distribution of characteristics, with the U.S.-country j difference being considerably greater, on average, for nonunion than for union workers (i.e., 0.423 versus 0.284 log points). In contrast, while the United States does tend to have a larger 90-50 gap than other countries after adjustment for the distribution of measured characteristics, the difference between the United States and the other countries is smaller than for the 50-10 gap and tends to be about the same size in the nonunion as in the union sector (i.e., 0.192 versus 0.166 log points, on average).

Finally, we used quantile regression analysis to compare the impact of unions on wages at different points of the conditional wage distribution (using the full specification). We found that, at each point of the distribution, the U.S. ceteris paribus union-nonunion wage differential was larger than that of other countries. The finding of a larger union premium in the United States also characterizes our ordinary least squares results and previous ordinary least squares analyses (Blanchflower and Freeman 1992) and is strongly suggestive of contract extension and other mechanisms by which union wages in other countries "spill over" into the nonunion sector, thus lowering their estimated ceteris paribus union-nonunion differentials relative to the United States.

Within virtually every country, the union wage effect was larger for the lower quantiles of the distribution. (This finding has previously been obtained in quantile regressions on U.S. data: see Chamberlain [1991].) This is consistent with union pay-leveling effects: being in a union matters more for one's wages the lower down one would have been in the nonunion wage distribution. However, the decline in union effects as we move up the conditional wage distribution is steeper in the United States than elsewhere. Thus it appears that union pay policies that bring up the bottom of the union wage distribution are common to all countries, including the United States. The difference between the United States and the other countries is that, in those countries, such policies are extended to the nonunion sector to a greater extent.

5.4.4. *An Alternative Explanation: Supply and Demand Effects*

The findings in Tables 5.2 and 5.3 indicate that prices of labor market skills play an important role in explaining international differences in inequality, since international differences in the distribution of measured characteristics do not fully account for the differences in wage inequality. While the results for union effects suggest that differences between countries in union pay-setting institutions are consistent with the observed patterns of wage inequality, we must also consider the possibility that supply and demand forces in the labor market are equally consistent.

To investigate the impact of supply and demand, we divide each country's labor force into three skill groups. We first pool the entire sample and estimate the following wage equation:

$$\text{(7)} \qquad \text{YFULL}_i = d_0 + d_1\text{ED}_i + d_2\text{EXP}_i + d_3\text{EXPSQ}_i + E'\text{N}_i + \epsilon_i,$$

where ED is education, EXP and EXPSQ are potential experience and its square, N is a vector of country dummies, and ϵ is an error term.[31] The estimated coefficients from equation (7) were used to compute SKILL, a predicted wage for each person i in each country j:

$$\text{(8)} \qquad \text{SKILL}_{ij} = d_0 + d_1\text{ED}_{ij} + d_2\text{EXP}_{ij} + d_3\text{EXPSQ}_{ij}.$$

This predicted wage is a measure of the person's skill based on a worldwide pooled regression including only productivity characteristics (and eliminating country shift terms).

We then divide each country's workforce into three skill groups based on the following percentiles of SKILL: 0-33, 33-67, and 67-100.[32] These percentiles are computed in two ways. First, we construct a set in which the percentiles refer to the country's own distribution of SKILL, so that the skill groups will be the same relative size across countries. This definition considers skill to be a relative concept, with, say, the thirty-third percentile of SKILL in one country considered comparable to the thirty-third percentile of SKILL in another country. One cannot analyze the effects of relative supply among these groups since, by construction, they are all proportionally the same size. Second, we construct a set of skill groups based on the U.S. cutoffs for SKILL. These percentiles consider skill to be an absolute concept: for example, those who place below the cutoff for the thirty-third percentile of the U.S. distribution of SKILL in one country are considered comparable to those who place below this level for the SKILL variable in another country. The relative sizes of the three groups can differ across countries under this latter definition. A similar analysis is performed separately for the 1984 U.S. PSID and Swedish HUS data samples.

Table 5.4 provides information on wage differentials by skill group. Panel A compares skill groups on the basis of own country cutoffs, and panel B uses U.S. skill group cutoffs. In both cases, the findings are similar to those obtained when we simply compared wage distributions. In particular, there is a larger pay gap between the middle- (33-67) and low- (0-33) skill groups in the United States than in each of the other countries. In contrast, the gap between high- and middle-skill groups tends to be fairly similar in the United States to that

Table 5.4
Wage Differentials by Skill Group

	33-67 vs. 0-33	67-100 vs. 33-67	67-100 vs. 0-33
	A. Own Country Skill Cutoffs		
Germany	.313	.269	.582
Britain	.238	.178	.416
United States (ISSP)	.530	.265	.795
Austria	.228	.223	.451
Switzerland	.396	.375	.772
Sweden (1980)	.357	.203	.560
Norway (1982)	.230	.265	.495
Australia	.414	.201	.615
Hungary	.195	.189	.385
Italy	.280	.306	.586
Norway (1989)	.180	.249	.430
Non-U.S. average (unweighted)	.283	.246	.529
Sweden (1984)	.133	.232	.365
United States (PSID, 1984)	.328	.300	.628
	B. U.S. Skill Group Cutoffs		
Germany	.320	.369	.689
Britain	.277	.343	.620
United States (ISSP)	.530	.265	.795
Austria	.215	.268	.483
Switzerland	.454	.343	.797
Sweden (1980)	.307	.361	.668
Norway (1982)	.274	.197	.471
Australia	.317	.269	.586
Hungary	.208	.243	.451
Italy	.293	.315	.608
Norway (1989)	.230	.285	.515
Non-U.S. average (unweighted)	.289	.299	.589
Sweden (1984)	.206	.178	.383
United States (PSID, 1984)	.328	.300	.628

in the other countries: the U.S. gap is about the same as the non-U.S. average when own country cutoffs are used and slightly smaller than the non-U.S. average when the U.S. cutoffs are employed. From the top to the bottom, the high (67-100) versus low (0-33) gap, with only one exception (Switzerland with the U.S. cut-offs), is larger in the United States than in each of the other countries. For the 1984 United States-Sweden comparison, the results are roughly similar when the relative cutoffs are used in that the U.S.-Swedish difference is considerably larger for the low-middle gap than for the middle-high gap. When the absolute cutoffs are used, however, the U.S.-Swedish difference between the middle-low gaps is now the same size as the difference between the middle-high gaps. Regardless of the cutoff used, however, the U.S. high-low gap exceeds the Swedish high-low gap.

To analyze the impact of supply and demand, we construct supply and demand indexes by skill group for each country relative to the United States in a manner similar to Katz and Murphy's (1992) analysis of changes over time in U.S. inequality. We focus on the results from panel B of Table 5.4 using the U.S. skill group cutoffs since they are more relevant for the supply indexes (and the net supply index we develop below). Thus the pattern we seek to explain is a relatively high pay gap between the middle- and low-skill groups in the United States combined with a high- versus middle-skill differential in the United States, which tends, with two exceptions (i.e., Sweden in 1984 and Norway in 1982), to be about the same as or smaller than those of other countries. Despite these countervailing differences, the pay gap between the top and bottom tends overwhelmingly to be higher in the United States.

Turning first to demand, we wish to know whether the composition of output by industry (and the consequent derived demand for labor) favors one skill group over another in the United States relative to other countries. Following Katz and Murphy (1992), we construct industry-occupation cells and view the "output" of particular occupation groups as an intermediate product. A demand index, $\ln(1 + \Delta D_k)$, was created for each skill group k for each country relative to the United States, where

$$\Delta D_k = \sum_o c_{ok} \left(\frac{\Delta E_o}{E_k} \right) \tag{9}$$

o refers to occupation-industry cell, c_{ok} is skill group k's share of employment in occupation-industry cell o in the United States, ΔE_o, is the difference between country j's and the U.S.' share of total labor input employed in cell o, and E_k is the U.S.' share of total labor input accounted for by skill group k. The demand index thus measures the degree to which the occupation-industry structure favors skill group k in country j relative to the United States, with U.S. weights.

Supply indexes ΔS_k are computed as follows:

$$\Delta S_k = \ln E_{kj} - \ln E_{ku}, \tag{10}$$

where E_{kj} and E_{ku} are, respectively, the share of country j's and the United States' total labor input consisting of skill group k, with the U.S. cutoffs for skill groups. Thus the supply indexes compare the relative representation of each skill group in country j's labor force, with the U.S. shares used as the norm.

We may then compute net supply as

$$\Delta NS_k = \Delta S_k - \ln(1+\Delta D_k), \tag{11}$$

where ΔS_k and ΔD_k are defined in equations (9) and (10) above. (Recall that all magnitudes are in log points and have been normalized relative to the United States.) As Katz and Murphy (1992) show using a simple equilibrium model, differences across countries in relative wages for each skill group will be negatively related to differences in net supply, ΔNS_k. Intuitively, the larger the supply of skill group k relative to demand in country j compared to that of the United States, the worse skill group k will fare in country j compared to the United States.

Tables 5.5 and 5.6 present the results for the demand and supply indexes, and Table 5.7 shows findings for net supply, which integrates the effects of supply and demand.[33] Because market forces include both supply and demand, we concentrate on the findings for net supply. Panel A gives the results when labor input is measured in hours, and panel B gives the results when earnings are used. Tables 5.5-5.7 clearly show that supply effects swamp the demand effects for low-skill workers: when both hours and earnings measures are used, net supply is positive for this group, on average, and within each country. While net supply is also positive, on average, for the middle-skill group, the average net supply figure for the low-skill group exceeds that for the middle-skill group for both the hours measure (0.331 versus 0.095) and the earnings measure (0.490 versus 0.146).[34] Thus the supply and demand analysis suggests that low-skill workers should in general fare worse relative to the middle in other countries than they do in the United States and cannot explain the smaller low-middle skill differentials that prevail in these countries.

In contrast to the pattern for the low-skill group, the net supply effects for the high-skill group are consistently negative. Further, they are, on average, quite large in absolute value (i.e., -0.785 with the hours measure and -0.710 with the earnings measure). While in two cases (Italy and Sweden in 1984) net supply is also negative for middle-skill workers (with both measures), in none of the four possible cases is the net supply figure for the high-skill group larger than the net supply figure for the middle-skill group. Thus supply and demand analysis would predict differentials in favor of high-skill workers in other countries relative to the United States. While this may be consistent with the findings from panel B of Table 5.4 that the U.S. differential is moderately (0.034) smaller than the non-U.S. average, when we consider the high (67-100) versus low (0-33) wage differential, the results are inconsistent with the predictions of supply and demand analysis in virtually every case.

Table 5.5

Demand Indexes by Skill Group Relative to the United States (Six Industries and Three Occupations)

	0-33	3-67	67-100
	A. Labor Input Measured in Hours		
Germany	-.007	.035	-.029
Britain	-.009	.026	-.018
Austria	.032	.036	-.068
Switzerland	-.127	-.054	.149
Sweden (1980)	.043	.047	-.092
Norway(1982)	.017	-.005	-.011
Australia	.068	.021	-.089
Hungary	.212	.076	-.346
Italy	.090	-.021	-.068
Norway (1989)	.027	.035	-.062
Sweden (1984)	.020	-.001	-.017
Non-U.S. average (unweighted)	.033	.018	-.059
	B. Labor Input Measured in Earnings		
Germany	.012	.039	-.036
Britain	-.008	.012	-.005
Austria	.078	.056	-.085
Switzerland	-.165	-.085	.125
Sweden (1980)	.100	.046	-.089
Norway (1982)	.066	.013	-.043
Australia	.109	.040	-.088
Hungary	.340	.103	-.317
Italy	.128	.016	-.079
Norway (1989)	.053	.024	-.045
Sweden (1984)	.062	.028	-.047
Non-U.S. average (unweighted)	.070	.026	-.065

Note: Units for demand indexes are log points.

Table 5.6

Supply Indexes by Skill Group Relative to the United States

	0-33	33-67	67-100
	A. Labor Input Measured in Hours		
Germany	.409	.211	-1.172
Britain	.039	.530	-1.291
Austria	.386	.095	-.746
Switzerland	.122	.208	-.423
Sweden (1980)	.440	.199	-1.267
Norway (1982)	.378	.021	-.578
Australia	.454	.110	-1.012
Hungary	.369	.104	-.719
Italy	.598	-.294	-.680
Norway (1989)	.313	.243	-.928
Sweden (1984)	.498	-.191	-.465
Non-U.S. average (unweighted)	.364	.112	-.844
	B. Labor Input Measured in Earnings		
Germany	.593	.289	-1.000
Britain	.233	.562	-1.173
Austria	.638	.133	-.746
Switzerland	.128	.257	-.335
Sweden (1980)	.672	.260	-1.119
Norway (1982)	.610	.070	-.597
Australia	.677	.186	-.938
Hungary	.607	.148	-.718
Italy	.786	-.232	-.519
Norway (1989)	.525	.297	-.879
Sweden (1984)	.702	-.069	-.497
Non-U.S. average (unweighted)	.561	.173	-.775

Note: Units for supply indexes are log points.

Table 5.7 indicates that high-skill workers are considerably scarcer relative to low-skill workers in other countries relative to the United States, yet Table 5.4 shows that, with one exception (Switzerland), they earn more relative to low-skill workers in the United States than elsewhere.

Thus differences in relative supplies and demands for skill in other countries compared to the United States are not broadly consistent with the observed pattern of relative wages by skill in other countries compared to the United States. In particular, they do not explain the most striking difference between the United States and the other countries, namely their greater wage compression at the bottom relative to the top or the middle. Having said that, we must note some important qualifications. First, since relative wages for low-skill workers are higher in other countries than in the United States and we use an employment-based measure of industry demand, we may have understated the demand for low-skill workers that would occur at constant wages relative to the United States. Similar reasoning implies that our supply estimates may have been overstated. Thus we may have overestimated net supply at constant relative prices. Second, our demand index does not include any differences across countries in within-industry-occupation demands for skill. It is unclear what effect this might have on our results.

Table 5.7

Net Supply Indexes by Skill Group Relative to the United States

	0-33	33-67	67-100
	A. Labor Input Measured in Hours		
Germany	.416	.176	-1.143
Britain	.049	.505	-1.274
Austria	.354	.059	-.678
Switzerland	.249	.262	-.572
Sweden (1980)	.396	.152	-1.175
Norway (1982)	.362	.026	-.568
Australia	.386	.089	-.923
Hungary	.157	.027	-.373
Italy	.508	-.273	-.612
Norway (1989)	.286	.208	-.866
Sweden (1984)	.478	-.190	-.448
Non-U.S. average (unweighted)	.331	.095	-.785
	B. Labor Input Measured in Earnings		
Germany	.581	.250	-.964
Britain	.241	.551	-1.168
Austria	.559	.077	-.661
Switzerland	.293	.342	-.460
Sweden (1980)	.572	.214	-1.031
Norway (1982)	.543	.057	-.554
Australia	.569	.147	-.851
Hungary	.267	.045	-.401
Italy	.658	-.248	-.440
Norway (1989)	.473	.273	-.834
Sweden (1984)	.640	-.097	-.450
Non-U.S. average (unweighted)	.490	.146	-.710

Notes: Units for net supply indexes are log points.

Third, we have implicitly assumed a separability in production between other factors and the three skill groups. However, other factors such as women's labor may not be equally substitutable for men's labor of different skill levels. Topel (1994b), for example, has suggested that women's labor is more substitutable on average for low-skill than for high- or medium-skill men. In our data, women's work hours account for a larger share of total hours worked in the United States (about 44 percent) than in the other countries (36 percent, on average). Topel's findings suggest that the relatively poor showing of low-skill men in the United States could be due to its high female labor supply. While this phenomenon may explain a portion of our results, we believe that it is not the whole story. In particular, as shown in the next subsection, female labor supply differences across countries are much less closely related to differences in male wage inequality than differences in wage-setting institutions are.

5.4.5. *The Effects of Institutions: Toward a General Test*

The evidence so far has suggested that the relatively decentralized wage-setting system in the United States is responsible for at least some of this country's higher wage dispersion and greater spread at the bottom of the distribution compared to the OECD countries in our sample. While our sample is relatively small (10), it is still possible to investigate whether this relationship between centralization and the wage distribution holds generally, that is, beyond the individual U.S.-other country comparisons we have made up to this point. Performing such a test requires one to operationalize the concept of centralization in wage setting. Several authors have produced rankings of countries with respect to their extent of centralization, including Blyth (1979), Schmitter (1981), Cameron (1984), Bruno and Sachs (1985), and Calmfors and Driffill (1988). These rankings take into account the degree of coordination within and between labor and management organizations, the level at which bargaining takes place, and the power of central bodies to conduct wage negotiations (Calmfors and Driffill 1988). We use as a measure of centralization the unweighted average of these rankings (which are shown individually in Calmfors and Driffill [1988: 18]), correcting for differences across authors in the number of countries ranked.

On the basis of this average ranking, Austria, with a ranking of 1.493 out of 17 countries, had the most centralized wage-setting system among the countries in our sample; the United States, with a ranking of 15.191 out of 17, not surprisingly, had the least.[35] While Hungary as a Communist country in the 1980s was not included in the rankings, we assigned it the highest level of centralization since the government set wages there. The results were qualitatively similar when Hungary was excluded.

We then used this (inverse) measure of centralization (DECENT) as an explanatory variable in two kinds of analyses. First, we ran regressions with the following dependent variables: (i) the country's standard deviation of YFULL (i.e., the log of hours-corrected earnings, as shown in Table 5.1); (ii) the 50-10 differential in YFULL (Table 5.1); (iii) the 90-50 differential in YFULL (Table 5.1); (iv) the standard deviation price effects, that is, the U.S.-country j difference net of personal characteristics, with the full specification (Table 5.2, panel B); (v) the 50-10 price effects; and (vi) the 90-50 price effects (Table 5.3, panel B).[36] In addition, in light of Topel's (1994b) findings on the impact of female labor supply on male wage inequality, we included the log of the share of total hours worked by women (LNFEM) as an explanatory variable in some specifications.[37]

The second kind of aggregate cross-country analysis involved estimating the determinants of the middle-low and high-middle skill group log wage differentials for absolute skill groups (i.e., using U.S. cutoffs for SKILL). Explanatory variables in this case included DECENT, the log of relative female labor supply measured in hours, and relative net supply. For example, in the analysis of the middle-low skill group wage differential, the net supply of the middle-skill relative to the low-skill group was included as a right-hand variable. Since the net supply measures are defined relative to the United States (Table 5.7), we define the wage differentials and female labor supply relative to the United States as well.[38]

Tables 5.8 and 5.9 contain our results. The major findings pertain to DECENT and are striking. First, decentralization of wage setting is found to be positively associated with the standard deviation of log wages (Table 5.8). This effect is 2.6-2.9 times its standard error and holds whether or not female labor supply is included and whether or not the effects of the distribution of male personal characteristics have been removed. Changing DECENT from, say, Sweden's level to Germany's (a change of 4.2) implies an increase in the standard deviation of log wages of about 0.06 log points, a moderate effect.

Table 5.8

Effects of Centralization of Wage Setting and Female Labor Supply on Male Wage Inequality (Sample Size 10)

	REGRESSION RESULTS FOR			
	DECENT	DECENT	LNFEM	LNFEM
DEPENDENT VARIABLE	(1)	(2)	(1)	(2)
Standard deviation of	.0133	.0148	.0392	.1747
YFULL	(.0051)	(.0054)	(.2307)	(.1780)
50-10 differential of	.0269	.0322	.3344	.6295
YFULL	(.0099)	(.0084)	(.4392)	(.2768)
90-50 differential of	.0044	.0040	-.0828	-.0457
YFULL	(.0072)	(.0080)	(.2437)	(.2663)
Standard deviation of	.0127	.0144	-.0679	.2001
YFULL, corrected for	(.0049)	(.0049)	(.2182)	(.1624)
personal characteristics				
50-10 differential, corrected	.0155	.0173	.0473	.2058
for personal characteristics	(.0072)	(.0077)	(.3003)	(.2547)
90-50 differential, corrected	.0095	.0108	.0648	.1642
for personal characteristics	(.0056)	(.0059)	(.2149)	(.1969)
Specification	DECENT	DECENT and	LNFEM	DECENT and
	only	LNFEM	only	LNFEM

Notes: DECENT. defined in the text. is an inverse measure of wage-setting centralization; LNFEM is the log of the share of total work hours accounted for by women. A constant term is included in all regressions.

Table 5.9

Effects of Centralization, Net Supply, and Female Labor Supply on Male Skill Group Wage Differentials (Sample Size 10)

	DEPENDENT VARIABLE			
EXPLANATORY	Middle vs. Low	High vs. Middle	Middle vs. Low	High vs. Middle
VARIABLE	DWMIDLOW	DWHIMID	DWMIDLOW	DWHIMID
Decentralization	.0113	.0024	.0122	.0025
	(.0057)	(.0027)	(.0048)	(.0031)
Net supply	.0540	-.0540	—	—
	(.0979)	(.0288)		
Female labor supply	-.0603	-.0807	—	—
	(.1882)	(.0942)		
Constant	-.3024	-.0447	-.3076	.0161
	(.0582)	(.0345)	(.0453)	(.0297)

Notes: Variables are relative to the United States, DWMIDLOW and DWHIMID are middle-low and high-middle skill group log wage gaps; net supply is the relative net supply of the relevant pair of skill groups; and female labor supply is LNFEM.

Second, as was the case in the U.S.-country *j* comparisons of Table 5.1, wage compression at the bottom of the distribution appears responsible for the association between centralization and the overall log wage variance. For example, in Table 5.8, decentralized wage setting has a positive association with the 50-10 log wage differential. The effect is robust with respect to controlling for the distribution of male personal characteristics and the inclusion of relative female labor supply. It is 2.2-3.8 times its standard error, and raising DECENT from Sweden's to Germany's level raises the 50-10 log wage gap by 0.11-0.14 log points. Similar findings for compression at the bottom of the distribution are obtained in Table 5.9, which examines wage differentials between skill groups: DECENT raises the middle-low wage differential.

In contrast to the strong positive association between decentralization and the widening of the wage distribution at the bottom, DECENT has very weak effects on the spread of wages at the top. In Tables 5.8 and 5.9, decentralization of pay setting has small positive effects on the 90-50 and high-middle-skill wage gaps, which are in every case but two smaller than their standard errors.

Unlike the findings for DECENT on the wage spread at the bottom of the distribution, the results for female labor supply are mixed and generally are not precisely estimated. The effects of net supply shown in Table 5.9 are also mixed. On the one hand, net supply has the "wrong" sign for the middle-low wage gap: it is positively associated with this gap. However, it is smaller than its standard error. On the other hand, net supply is negatively associated with the high-middle pay gap, as predicted and suggested by Tables 5.4 and 5.7, and is 1.9 times its standard error.

The results of Tables 5.8 and 5.9 suggest that wage centralization leads to less wage inequality generally and that it has a particularly strong effect in bringing up the bottom of the wage distribution. Admittedly, our sample of countries is extremely small - only 10 - and the causality between the wage distribution and wage-setting institutions, as well as our measures of female labor supply and net male labor supply, can run in both directions. However, these results in conjunction with the individual U.S.-other country comparisons lend plausibility to the idea that institutions are important.

5.4.6. *Implications: Employment Responses*

Our main finding that the centralized wage-setting institutions in other industrialized nations increase the relative wages of workers at the bottom of the distribution compared to the United States raises the possibility that these workers will experience greater relative employment problems as well. Not only is this in itself an important potential policy implication, it further suggests that wage-setting institutions can influence the distribution of productivity among employed workers, since the least-skilled are the most likely to lose their jobs (or not find jobs to begin with) when wage floors are instituted. Thus the distribution of measured and unmeasured productivity among employed workers may be influenced by wage floors, and our dichotomy between skills and institutions as explanations for inequality differences across countries may in fact be a false one. In this subsection, we examine these issues.

Some previous studies find evidence that wage floors have adverse employment effects for those at the bottom (see n. 3). We examine relative employment/population ratios by absolute skill group for the countries for which our data allow these ratios to be calculated.[39] The results are shown in Table 5.10. While not as strong as the wage compression results presented above, our findings do suggest higher relative employment/population ratios among low-skill workers in the United States than elsewhere.

Table 5.10

Employment/Population Ratios by Absolute Skill Group

A. Employment Population Ratios

	Low	Middle	High	Overall
Germany	.650	.860	.903	.756
Britain	.797	.812	.888	.815
United States	.792	.860	.904	.852
Austria	.694	.808	.809	.758
Australia	.793	.852	.898	.827
Norway (1982)	.777	.924	.926	.853
Norway (1989)	.740	.906	.987	.832

B. Differences Between Skill Groups in Log of Employment/ Population Ratio

	Middle-Low	High-Middle	High-Low
Germany	.279	.050	.329
Britain	.018	.089	.108
United States	.082	.049	.132
Austria	.152	.001	.153
Australia	.072	.053	.125
Norway (1982)	.173	.002	.175
Norway (1989)	.203	.085	.288

Panel A shows employment/population ratios for each skill group. In all cases, employment rates increase monotonically with skill within a country. Further, low-skill workers in the United States, Britain, and Australia have about the same employment rates, and they are moderately higher than the rates in the other countries. Panel B shows relative employment/population ratios by skill group (the differences across skill groups in the log of the employment/population ratio). For the key middle-low comparison, the U.S. difference is considerably smaller than that in Austria, Germany, and Norway, about the same as that in Australia, and larger than that in Britain. Thus Table 5.10 suggests that, in general, the low-skilled have fewer employment problems relative to other workers in the United States than in other countries.[40]

As we noted above, differences across countries in employment/population ratios can result in observed workers' being a more selected group in some countries than in others. Thus some of our observed *X*'s and residual effects might be due to the employment effects of wage floors. Panel A of Table 5.10 shows that the United States is at the top of the list (roughly tied with Norway in 1989) for the overall employment/population ratio. To get an idea of the possible selection effects this may imply, we made the simplifying assumption that the nonemployed are all less skilled than the employed (Juhn [1992] makes a similar assumption). Thus, in comparing, say, the U.S. wage distribution with that in Germany, we note that the U.S. employment/population ratio is .852, whereas Germany's is .756. To form a comparably selected U.S. labor force under our maintained assumption, we need to delete the bottom .113 of the U.S. sample.[41]

A similar procedure is followed for the other countries in Table 5.10. The results of this adjustment for selectivity do not affect our basic conclusion: the United States continues to have much less 50-10 compression than the other countries but about the same degree of 90-50 compression.[42]

While employment losses for unskilled workers are one possible response to high wage floors, public employment may be another, one that would prevent us from observing a decline in employment/population ratios. Both Bjorklund and Freeman (1994), and Edin and Topel (1994a) suggest that this argument has validity for analyzing Sweden's solidarity wage policy. To examine the hypothesis that the government acts as employer of last resort, we compared the share of government employment across skill groups in our microdata. In virtually all cases, the government demanded a relatively skilled workforce. Moreover, the differences in government employment across skill groups showed no particular pattern across countries.[43] Of course government policy can lead to employment changes in other industries. This and other issues related to the absorption of low-skill workers in the presence of wage compression merit further investigation.

5.5. Conclusions

In this chapter, we compare male wage inequality in the United States and nine other industrialized countries primarily in the middle to late 1980s. Consistent with previous work, the results indicate that overall wage inequality is much greater in the United States than elsewhere. However, when we disaggregate the measure of inequality to examine various parts of the wage distribution, we find that the distribution in other countries is much more compressed at the bottom than at the top relative to the United States. Thus, while the 50-10 differential is considerably larger in the United States than elsewhere, the U.S. 90-50 differential is only slightly larger.

We then evaluate several possible explanations for these patterns. First, differences in the distribution of measured characteristics across countries were found to be responsible for some but not all of the international differences in the wage distribution. If the United States had other countries' distribution of measured characteristics, its overall wage variation would remain much higher than that of other countries. Moreover, while the gap between the middle and bottom portions of the U.S. wage distribution would be reduced, the high-middle gap would be increased. Most important, the wage distribution in other countries would still be more compressed at the bottom than at the top relative to the United States. These results suggest that U.S. labor market prices contribute to our observed findings.

Second, we note that, unlike the United States, most of the other countries have very centralized systems of collective bargaining and many have provisions to extend the terms of union contracts to non-union workers. Voluntary emulation of the union wage structure by nonunion firms due to threat effects is also likely to be greater in these other countries given the larger size of their union sectors. Consistent with these observations, we find a larger variance of wages and less wage compression at the bottom within both the U.S. union and nonunion sectors compared to other countries. Indeed, the larger variance of overall wages in the United States is primarily due to the higher variance that prevails here within each of these sectors. Moreover, when one controls for the distribution of measured characteristics, both of these salient features of the U.S. distribution - a higher wage variance and a greater spread at the bottom – are more pronounced in the nonunion than in the union sector. This result suggests that contract extension and other mechanisms that extend union-determined wages to the nonunion sector in other countries have a larger effect on their wage structures relative to the United States than their more centralized wage-setting institutions within the union sector.

Third, we examine indexes of relative supplies and demands across countries to see whether market forces could provide an alternative explanation for the observed patterns, particularly for the high relative wages of low-skilled workers in other countries. Taking both supply and demand into account suggests that low-skill workers should fare worse relative to middle-skill workers in other countries than they do in the United States; thus this cannot explain the smaller low-middle skill differentials that prevail in these countries. Thus market forces, as best as we can measure them, do not appear to be consistent with the observed pattern of relative wages by skill in other countries compared to the United States.

Finally, we present two additional pieces of empirical evidence suggesting that wage-setting institutions are an important determinant of international differences in wage distributions. First, looking across countries, we find that wage centralization, as commonly measured by comparative industrial relations researchers, is negatively associated with wage dispersion, the 50-10 differential in the log of wages, and the pay gap between middle- and low-skill workers. Further, this compression at the bottom occurs even when we control for the distribution of personal characteristics, relative female labor supply, and relative male labor supply net of demand differences. Second, we examine possible employment responses to the pattern of greater wage compression at the bottom in other countries compared to the United States. As would be expected on the basis of employer responses to high wage floors, we generally find that the low-skilled have a higher employment/population ratio relative to the higher-skilled in the United States than in other countries.

To the extent that institutions are important in affecting wage inequality, we would expect adverse impacts on employment and productivity due to resource allocation effects. We have presented some evidence that this is the case. To some degree, labor market policies such as government employment or training programs and relocation subsidies can compensate for such effects, although we did not find evidence of disproportionate government employment among the low-skilled outside the United States. One interpretation of government labor market policy in many OECD countries is that wage-leveling policies are encouraged by the government on the one hand to achieve a desired level of wage inequality. The greater compression at the bottom, in particular, suggests that these other countries attempt to use the labor market to provide a "safety net" for low-wage workers to a greater extent than we do in the United States. On the other hand, their more activist government policies regarding employment, training, and relocation (see, e.g., Bjorklund and Freeman 1994; Edin and Topel 1994; Edin and Holmlund 1995) may be seen in part as corrective measures for the adverse employment and allocation effects of the wage distribution policies.

Appendix

Table 5.A1

Definitions of Dependent Variables

Australia	Annual earnings from all jobs
Austria	Net monthly income from employment
Britain	Total annual earnings before taxes
Germany and Switzerland	Net income per month after taxes and social insurance
Hungary	Monthly earnings
Italy	Annual labor income
Norway (1982)	Annual income from all jobs
Norway (1989)	Annual income from work
Sweden (1980)	Income (from all sources) in previous year
Sweden (1984)	Average hourly earnings
United States (1985-89)	Previous year's earnings from occupation before taxes
United States (1984)	Average hourly earnings

Table 5.A2

Definitions Of Explanatory Variables

EDUC	Years of schooling completed
PEXP	Age - EDUC - 6
PEXPSQ	PEXP squared
EXP	Actual experience (PSID and HUS only)
EXPSQ	EXP squared (PSID and HUS only)
MAR	One if married, spouse present; zero otherwise
UNION	Dummy variable for union membership
	Occupation Dummy Variables
PROF	Professional and technical workers (the omitted category)
MGR	Managers, except farm
CLER	Clerical workers
SALES	Sales workers
CRAFT	Craft workers
OPER	Operatives
LAB	Laborers, except farm
SERVWK	Service workers
FARMMGR	Farm managers
FARMLAB	Farm laborers
	Industry Dummy Variables
AG	Agriculture, forestry, and fisheries
MINCON	Mining and construction
MANDUR	Durable goods manufacturing
MANNON	Nondurable goods manufacturing
TRANS	Transportation, communications, and utilities
WTRADE	Wholesale trade
RTRADE	Retail trade
FIRE	Finance, insurance, and real estate
SERVS	Services
GOVT	Government (the omitted caregory)
	Industry Dummies for Hungary
AG	Agriculture, forestry, and fisheries
MINMAN	Mining and manufacturing
CONST	Construction
TRANS	Transportation, communications, and utilities
TRADE	Wholesale and retail trade
SERVS	Services, finance, insurance, and real estate
GOVT	Government (the omitted category)

Table 5.A2 (continued)

	Occupation Dummy Variables for Australia
MGR	Managers and farm managers
CLER	Clerical workers
CRAFT	Craft workers
OPER	Operatives
LAB	Laborers and farm laborers
SALESW	Sales and service workers
PROF	Professional and technical workers (the omitted category)
	Industry Dummy Variables for Australia
AG	Agriculture, forestry, and fisheries
TRANS	Transportation, communications, and utilities
MINCON	Mining and construction
MANUF	Manufacturing
TRADE	Wholesale and retail trade
FISERV	Finance, insurance, real estate, and services
GOVT	Government (the omitted category)
	Occupation Dummy Variables for Italy
BLUE	Blue-collar
WHITELOW	Lower-level white-collar
WHITEHI	Higher-level white-collar (the omitted category)
	Industry Dummy Variables for Italy
AG	Agriculture, forestry, and fisheries
TRANS	Transportation, communications, and utilities
TRADE	Wholesale and retail trade
IND	Mining, construction, and manufacturing
FIRE	Finance, insurance, and real estate
GOVT	Government
SERVS	Services, finance, insurance, and real estate (the omitted category)

IV

Other Dimensions of Gender Inequality and Policy Responses

Introduction

In this part, I consider additional dimensions of gender inequality, beyond the gender pay gap, and also the impact of a policy intervention aimed at reducing gender differences in outcomes for female economists. The first chapter in this part, Chapter 6, is based on a paper with Lawrence Kahn on female labor supply. The link between female labor supply and gender inequality is strong. At the most basic level, a major determinant of the gender wage gap is the gender difference in actual labor market experience – this is of course the cumulative result of labor supply decisions at various points in time. The relationship between trends in female labor force participation rates and the average experience level of the female labor force is not one-to-one, but the increase in female labor force participation that we have witnessed in recent decades has been associated with increased attachment of women to the labor force.[1] And, indeed, it is this increase in labor force attachment that has been the engine propelling the many gains in labor market outcomes that have occurred for women across most of the advanced industrialized nations in recent decades (e.g., Blau and Kahn 2008) – what Claudia Goldin has called a "quiet revolution" in gender roles (Goldin 2006).

But there are other reasons for those with an interest in gender equality to be interested in female labor force participation. Most obviously, with the increase in single female family heads and the growth of dual earner families where both partners are employed, the economic well-being of the family is increasingly dependent on the economic contribution of women within it. The relationship of increases in married women's labor force participation to overall inequality in family income is complex and under some debate, but there can be little doubt of its importance and relevance.[2] Finally, as I point out in Chapter 7, another factor suggesting the importance of women's labor force participation for gender equity is that family bargaining models suggest that, in married couple families, women's participation in the labor force and their level of earnings while employed are likely to positively affect their distribution within marriage (see, e.g., Lundberg and Pollak 1996).

Chapter 6 discusses joint work with Lawrence Kahn that is concerned with understanding the trends in female labor supply in the United States in the final decades of the last century. The initial motivation for this project was that, after years of strong, consistent increases in female labor force participation in the United States since World War II, the female participation rate began to plateau in the mid-1990s. Our focus in this Chapter is the 1980-2000 period, but the trend that first engaged our attention has continued since then - the female participation rate has continued to remain flat, even turning down slightly in recent years. We focus our analysis on married women whose behavior by and large drives the aggregate trends. The slowdown in female participation mirrored the slowing increase in the gender pay ratio discussed in Part II above, and made Kahn and I wonder if there was a connection - could slowing wage increases for women explain the flattening trend in participation rates? As we shall see, in fact this was not a major factor.

Explaining trends in married women's participation rates has always been somewhat up hill for economists. The important economic variables, own wages and husband wages (or income) perform as expected in the model but, for the most part, much of the increase in female participation remained unexplained by the traditional variables. Our findings were not exceptional in this regard: We found that most of the slowdown in the growth in labor supply over the 1990s was because the 1980s growth had been fueled by a large rightward shift in married women's labor supply function for annual hours in the 1980s, but that there was little shift in the function in the 1990s. That is, the unexplained source(s) of increase in married women's labor supply that had occurred in the 1980s did not continue into the 1990s.

What proved to be the major contribution of the paper was the dramatic decrease in the responsiveness of married women's labor supply to their own and husbands' wages that we found over the period: women's own wage elasticity fell by 50%–56%, while their cross wage elasticity fell by 38%–47% in absolute value.[3] In this respect women were becoming more like men, for whom both elasticities are generally estimated to be extremely small in absolute value. In addition to the shift in the labor supply curve noted above, women's decreasing own wage elasticities also contributed to the slowing growth in female labor force participation over this period.[4] Why has women's labor supply traditionally been considerably more sensitive to their own wages and to nonlabor income (or spouse's wages) than has men's and why have women's elasticities been getting more similar to men's? We argue that these developments are likely related to the traditional division of labor in the family and its diminished importance.

As Jacob Mincer (1962a) pointed out in important early work, women may be seen as substituting among market work, home production, and leisure, while men may be viewed as substituting only or primarily between market work and leisure. Although it is possible to substitute market goods for nonmarket time in leisure activities, these possibilities are relatively limited. In contrast, because purchased goods and services are in many cases useful substitutes for nonmarket time in producing the commodities the family wants, women have closer substitutes for time spent in market work than men do. Thus, changes in market wages are expected to have a larger substitution effect on women's labor supply, yielding a larger own wage elasticity for them than for men. One might also reason that, given traditional gender roles, women would generally be perceived as the secondary earner within the family and, thus, that their labor supply would be more responsive to changes in their husband's wage than vice versa. Based on this reasoning, one might argue that, to the extent that the traditional division of labor is breaking down and men and women are more equally sharing home and market responsibilities, we would expect women's labor supply elasticities to become more similar to men's over time, as our findings in Chapter 6 suggest occurred over the 1980s and 1990s.

We also saw our findings as fitting well with earlier developments traced by Claudia Goldin (1990), who provides an insightful analysis of changes in women's labor supply elasticities over the twentieth century. Goldin argues that, around 1900, when relatively few attractive labor market options were available to women and there was considerable stigma against wives working, married women's labor supply was largely determined by their husbands' labor market opportunities, rather than their own. Consistent with this, she reports that their own wage elasticity was small, while their nonlabor income (predominantly husband's income) elasticity was large in absolute value. According to Goldin, as women's education levels increased and white-collar employment opportunities became available to them, the stigma against married women working diminished. Again, the movements of the elasticities are consistent with her argument: women's own wage elasticity increased, while their responsiveness to changes in their husband's income decreased. Goldin further reasoned that, as divorce rates rose and women's jobs increasingly became careers as opposed to merely a means to earn income, not only should the effect of husbands' income continue to decline, but so should wives' own wage elasticity. That is, as women became more strongly attached to the labor force and more committed to their careers, they would be less likely to move in and out of the labor force or greatly change their hours worked in response to changes in their wages. Our findings of a decline in the magnitude of women's own and cross wage elasticities for the 1980-2000 period are consistent with this expectation.[5]

The impetus for the research discussed in Chapter 7 was an invitation from John Pencavel to write an article on gender for the Journal of Economic Literature, of which he was then editor. He particularly encouraged me to think broadly about women's economic status, beyond a narrow focus on the gender wage gap. I was enthusiastic about taking this on, and, as I thought about it, it seemed to me that the best approach would be to base the paper on original data analysis. This would allow me to summarize the trends in women's status across a number of indicators based on my own tabulations using the same data sources, breakdowns by subgroup, and time period. I focused on the United States over the 1970-95 period, and relied primarily on Current Population Survey data. While I did also briefly summarize the relevant literature, I felt a paper entirely based on the extant literature (as is generally the norm in the JEL) would, in this particular case, leave too many gaps and incomparabilities.

The notion that status is multidimensional is increasingly accepted in economics, with perhaps the most important influence pushing the field in this direction being Amartya Sen's "capability" approach for thinking about poverty, inequality, and human development (see, e.g., Sen 1999). Along that line, just as we now have indexes that take into account a number of different dimensions in measuring economic development, we also have such indexes for gender equity[6] This is a useful development, especially if information on components of the indexes is also made available. The indexes themselves are a bit problematic in that they require weights to be attached to the various components; clearly people may disagree about the appropriate weighting.

My findings for the period I examined were dramatic in showing increasing gender equality cross a broad range of indicators for virtually all age and education groups. However, parallel to the evidence of the declining labor market status of lower skilled men that was increasingly available at that time, I found that there had been a similar sharp decline in labor market outcomes for less educated women, especially high school dropouts, compared to other women. Moreover, less educated women struggled with an additional burden that less educated men did not have. Increasingly, they were single family heads and, during this period, the incidence of single headship among female high school dropouts increased sharply relative to more highly educated women. The concentration of the rise in female headship particularly on the less educated had not been widely noted at that time.

One question that this finding of a deteriorating position of high school dropouts raised, and a question that had received remarkably little attention in the literature at the time, was the possibility that such trends simply reflected shifts in the composition of the group rather than true changes in their opportunities or behavior. The share of the population with less than 12 years of education had fallen, and it had become increasingly comprised of immigrants whose economic status was declining, even relative to natives with similar levels of education (Borjas 1995). It is possible that as the high school dropout group dwindled in size it had become more negatively selected compared to more highly educated Americans. On the other hand, it could be argued that since the college educated group, which had fared especially well relative to high school dropouts, had markedly increased its share, it was becoming a less positively selected group. Thus, to the extent that compositional factors were important, their impact was an empirical question.

I used a fairly simple method for gaining insight into whether or not changes in the relative status of the less educated reflected true changes in outcomes and behavior versus solely compositional shifts

– one that had been previously used by Juhn, Murphy, and Pierce (1993) in their study of trends in male wage inequality. Specifically, I compared the magnitude of changes in each indicator for a cohort over time to changes experienced by successive cohorts of individuals of the same age. Because the former comparison could not have been affected by changes in the composition of the various education groups, similar findings for the "within cohort" and "across cohort" comparisons would suggest true changes in opportunities or behavior and not simply compositional effects. My findings strongly suggested that compositional shifts did not entirely account for the deteriorating economic position of less educated Americans.

Much of my research has looked at the extent and causes of gender and other types of inequality. My research in this area over the decades has left me with a profound respect for the complexity of the factors that contribute to these differences and the way that supply- and demand-side factors can interact to produce unequal outcomes. Consider the under-representation of women in high-paying traditionally male jobs and at the upper reaches of the hierarchies in business, unions, and government. Outright discrimination may play a role, but increasingly discrimination is subtle and even unconscious (e.g., Fiske 1998; Valian 1998; and Bertrand, Chugh, and Mullainathan 2005). And the barriers and difficulties facing women may transcend what we traditionally think of as discrimination. As Marianne Ferber, Anne Winkler, and I (2010, Chapter 7) discuss, they may include the absence of role models and mentors for younger women, as well as their limited access to predominantly male informal networks. Women may also need to deal with their own lack of self-confidence as they seek to enter nontraditional fields or make their way up job ladders where women have previously been absent. Further, the problem of combining work and family to achieve at the very highest levels has a special salience and import for women that it still lacks for most men. Thus, policies to facilitate the advancement of women likely need to go beyond traditional anti-discrimination policy (although such policies need to be included as well). Programs that are explicitly designed to better equip women to navigate the various obstacles and difficulties that they face in succeeding in highly competitive areas may be one fruitful line of approach.

The research discussed in Chapter 8, summarizing work with Janet Currie, Rachel Croson, and Donna Ginther, examines the consequences of just such an intervention that I had the opportunity to participate in developing; it was designed to improve the status of women in the economics profession in the United States. This was a mentoring program for junior women that was begun by the American Economic Association (AEA) Committee on the Status of Women in the Economics Profession (CSWEP) during my term as Chair of CSWEP. The CSWEP Mentoring Program (CeMENT) was supported by the National Science Foundation's (NSF) ADVANCE and Economics programs and the AEA. The aim of the program was to help female junior faculty prepare for the tenure hurdle. The need for such a program was based on the problem of the "leaky pipeline," the fall-off in the representation of women as one moves up the academic ranks, which had been documented in numerous CSWEP annual reports.

My own tie to CSWEP was a long one. While still a graduate student, I had been part of a group that worked to get the committee established and had served as a member of the first committee that was appointed. When I returned to the committee as its Chair, in 2003, I found there was considerable interest in implementing a mentoring initiative. CSWEP had an earlier one-shot mentoring effort in 1998 that was developed by the committee Chair at that time, Robin Bartlett. One of the CSWEP Board members, Rachel Croson, had herself participated in the program as a mentee and found it extremely beneficial.[7] In 2003, our goal was to launch a new mentoring program and, importantly, to institutionalize it first by securing adequate funding for a number of rounds of mentoring workshops and then, aided by what we hoped would be a positive evaluation of the program, gaining long-term support from the AEA. Rachel spearheaded our successful application to NSF to gain financial support for the program and also oversaw the first rounds of national workshops. When Rachel left the CSWEP Board, Donna Ginther joined the Board to take up this responsibility. Janet Currie, at the time a Board member, led the research/evaluation effort, and continued in this role after she left the Board.

The program is described in the chapter, but let me note that each mentoring workshop (offered to junior faculty every other year) lasted two days and was held in conjunction with the American Economic Association annual meetings.[8] The workshops brought together junior faculty mentees and senior faculty mentors from various institutions. This was important because, in a predominantly male field like economics, there are likely to be few (or even no) senior women at any particular institution and even junior women colleagues are likely to be relatively scarce. Further, the format of the workshops (which had been developed by Bartlett) brought junior women (mentees) together into small groups with similar research interests to work with a senior mentor (later two senior mentors). In addition to economizing on scarce senior women, anecdotal evidence based on discussions with former participants suggests that many mentees stayed in touch with other junior women whom they met through the program, and that these women became an important support network for them.

We advertized and solicited applications for the program – with the first workshop offered in 2004. Since the number of qualified applicants substantially exceeded the number we could offer the program to, we were able to use random assignment to evaluate the program. Our study compared the academic performance (i.e., papers, grants) of those who participated in the program by attending the workshop to controls who applied for the program but did not participate. To our knowledge, this randomized trial of a mentoring program was unique in academia.

One problem we encountered in evaluating the program was a low response rate on follow-up surveys designed to track the respondents' progress in subsequent years. Not surprisingly, this problem was particularly acute among the controls. Fortunately, however, we were able to collect and systematically code information from vitae of participants and controls; these vitae were generally available from public sources, particularly for individuals who remained in academia. We used this data in our evaluation. We were gratified to find that CeMENT increased top-tier publications, the total number of publications, and the total number of successful federal grants in treated women relative to controls. The effects were monotonic with respect to time from the intervention and robust to several specification checks designed to control for possible preexisting differences between treatments and controls. At the time of our evaluation, it was too early to say whether the intervention would have a significant effect on either the probability that women stayed in academia, or the probability that they received tenure.

6

Changes in the Labor Supply Behavior of Married Women: 1980–2000

Based on a paper with Lawrence M. Kahn

6.1. Introduction

One of the most dramatic developments in the United States since World War II has been the increasing labor force participation of women. Whereas in 1947 31.5% of women and 86.8% of men were in the labor force, by 2000, women's labor force participation rate had roughly doubled to 60%, while men's had fallen moderately to 74.8%.[1] What was a comparatively rare event in the late 1940s – women working outside the home – had become the mode by the 1990s. And, reflecting shifts in both men's and women's labor supply behavior, the gen-

This chapter is a revised version of Blau, F. D., Kahn, L. M. (2007). Changes in the Labor Supply of Married Women: 1980-2000, in: Journal of Labor Economics, 25(3): 393-438. © 2007 by The University of Chicago.
An earlier version of the original article was presented by Francine D. Blau as her presidential address at the 2006 Society of Labor Economists meetings in Cambridge, MA. The authors have benefited from comments of Henry Farber, Claudia Goldin, Reuben Gronau, Bradley Heim, Lawrence Katz, Solomon Polachek, Finis Welch, Anne Winkler, and participants at the NBER Public Economics meeting, the American Economic Association meetings, the Cornell University Labor Economics Workshop, the Princeton University Labor Economics Workshop, the University of Turin Economics Seminar, and the University of Washington Labor Economics Workshop, and are deeply grateful to Kerry Papps for excellent research assistance. Portions of the original article were written while the authors were Visiting Fellows in the Economics Department of Princeton University, supported by the Industrial Relations Section. We are very grateful for this support.

der gap in labor force participation rates fell from 55 to 15 percentage points, a 73% decline. Beginning in the late 1970s or early 1980s, women's relative wages also rose: the female/male ratio of annual earnings of full-time, full-year workers increased from 60.2% in 1980 to 73.3% in 2000. Moreover, during the post-1970 period, women's representation in high-paying professions and managerial jobs also greatly increased. Since 1990, however, women's increases in labor force participation and relative wages have slowed. For example, their labor force participation rose only from 57.5% to 60% between 1990 and 2000, a much slower rate of increase than in previous decades. Over the same period, the female-male ratio of annual earnings for full-time, full-year workers barely increased from 71.6% to 73.3%.

Since women's labor supply is positively affected by their own wages and negatively affected by men's wages, the concurrent slowdowns in both women's relative wage and employment increases in the 1990s suggest the possibility that the latter is a labor supply response. In this chapter, we shed light on the connection between wages and labor supply by using March Current Population Survey (CPS) data to investigate women's labor supply behavior over the 1980–2000 period. We focus on married couples in light of a long tradition in labor supply research that emphasizes the family context in which work and consumption decisions are made (Blundell and MaCurdy 1999). Moreover, changes in the labor supply behavior of married women have driven the changes in labor supply for women overall. Chiefly we focus on annual hours, including the nonemployed, but also investigate participation (i.e., positive work hours) and hours conditional on employment.

One goal of this chapter is to shed light on the reasons for these changes in labor supply. Why did married women's labor supply rise so much in the 1980s, and why did its increase slow in the 1990s? We study the impact of changing wage offers to women and men, as well as nonlabor income, and demographic factors (e.g., the number and age composition of children) as causes of the labor supply trends. These factors can be thought of as changes in the explanatory variables in women's labor supply function, and we find that they play some role in explaining the overall patterns. In addition, we study whether the function itself has changed over the 1980–2000 period, and it is the changes in the labor supply function that comprise the most dramatic of our findings.

We find that married women's real wages increased in both the 1980s and 1990s, and these caused comparable increases in labor supply in each decade, given women's positively sloped labor supply schedules. However, their labor supply function shifted sharply to the right in the 1980s, with little shift in the 1990s. In an accounting sense, this difference in supply shifts is the major reason for the more rapid growth of female labor supply in the 1980s than the 1990s. In addition, married men's real wages fell slightly in the 1980s but rose in the 1990s, a factor that contributed modestly to the slowdown in the growth of women's labor supply in the 1990s.

Most strikingly, we find that, over both decades, there was a steady and dramatic reduction in women's own wage labor supply elasticity, a significant new development. In addition, continuing a long-term trend, married women's labor supply also became substantially less responsive to their husbands' wages, particularly over the 1980s. Taking the 1980–2000 period as a whole, we estimate that married women's own wage elasticity was reduced by 50%–56%, while their cross wage elasticity fell by 38%–47% in absolute value. These reductions occurred at both the extensive and intensive margins; however, the decrease in own wage elasticities for annual hours occurred mostly through a reduction of responsiveness at the extensive margin. In contrast to the trends for wives, husbands' own wage elasticities were very small and did not show a strong pattern over time, and husbands showed little labor supply responsiveness with respect to their spouses' wages. Thus, married women's own and cross wage labor supply elasticities were becoming more like married men's. Such a development is likely to be due at least in part to the fact that, with rising participation rates, fewer and fewer married women are on the margin between participating and not participating in the labor force. Moreover, increasing divorce rates and increasing career orientation of married women are also expected to make their labor supply less sensitive to their own wages and to their husbands' wages (Goldin 1990).

We found that these patterns hold up in virtually all cases under a variety of alternative specifications and estimation methods. An innovative feature of one of these alternatives is to control for the selection into marriage, an important exercise since the incidence of marriage has been falling steadily. This raises the possibility that the sample of married women has become more "marriage-prone" over time relative to the whole population of women, and this compositional shift could influence measured labor supply elasticities among married women. However, our results hold up even when we account for this compositional factor.

The reduction in married women's labor supply elasticities implies that government policies such as income taxes that affect marginal wage rates have a much smaller distortionary effect on the quantity of labor supplied now than in the past. Conversely, our results imply that the potential for marginal tax rate cuts to increase labor supply is much smaller now than 30 years ago, since tax rates were much higher then and so was married women's labor supply responsiveness. In addition, the potential for increases in demand in the female labor market to raise the quantity of women's labor supply is also much smaller than previously; rather, any increases in demand for women will cause larger increases in women's relative wages than previously.

6.2. Recent Research on Female Labor Supply and Research Questions of the Study

As surveyed by Blundell and MaCurdy (1999), there have been numerous studies of female labor supply. We do not repeat such a survey here. Rather, we report on some recent studies of women's labor supply to provide both a sense of the econometric issues researchers have faced and the results that were obtained. As a baseline, Blundell and MaCurdy (1999) report that across 18–20 estimates of own wage labor supply elasticities in various recent studies, the median elasticity was 0.08 for men and 0.78 for married women.[2] For cross wage elasticities, Killingsworth (1983) reports a median spouse wage elasticity of 0.13 for married men's labor supply and -0.08 for married women's labor supply, although a recent study of the 1980s by Devereux (2004), analyzing labor supply conditional on having positive hours, reports a cross elasticity of roughly -0.4 to -0.5 for women and -.001 to -.06 for men.

These surveys suggest that women's labor supply is considerably more sensitive to their own wages than is men's. This difference is usually explained by the traditional division of labor in the family, in which women are seen as substituting among market work, home production, and leisure, while men are viewed as substituting only or primarily between market work and leisure (Mincer 1962a). Since women have closer substitutes for time spent in market work than men do, changes in market wages are expected to have larger substitution effects on women's labor supply. Further, since, given traditional gender roles, women are perceived as secondary earners within the family, their labor supply is likely to be more negatively affected by their spouse's wages (though issues of complementarity and substitutability of the home time of husband and wife also need to be considered). A corollary of this reasoning is that to the extent that the traditional division of labor is breaking down and men and women more equally share home and market responsibilities, we expect women's labor supply elasticities to approach men's over time.

A similar conclusion is reached by Goldin (1990). She reports that around 1900, when relatively few attractive labor market options were available to women and there was considerable stigma against wives working, married women's own wage elasticity was very small, but the cross elasticity with respect to their husbands' wages was negative and very large in absolute value. However, as women's education levels rose and their job opportunities became more varied, the stigma against married women working diminished. As a consequence, their own wage elasticity increased substantially while their responsiveness to other family income (primarily husband's income) decreased. Goldin further reasons that, as divorce rates have risen since 1960, and women's jobs have increasingly become careers as opposed to merely a means to earn income, not only should the effect of husbands' income continue to decline in magnitude, but the substitution effect of own wages on married women's labor supply should begin to fall as well. Studies reported in Goldin (1990), spanning data from 1900 through 1970 (Goldin 1990: 132–3), present clear evidence of a declining responsiveness to husband's income over this period. Some data reviewed by Goldin suggested declining own wage elasticities of married women after 1950. Indeed, based on one study (Mroz 1987), by 1975, women's labor supply responsiveness to wages and income looked like those for men. However, as we have seen, Blundell and MaCurdy's (1999) comprehensive review, with most of the data in the studies cited coming from the 1970s and early 1980s, continued to find a large gender difference in own wage elasticities, with men's elasticities near zero and women's at 0.8. Consistent with this, taking the 1968–70 to 1988–90 period as a whole, Juhn and Murphy (1997) find evidence not only of a continued reduction in the labor supply responsiveness of married women to their husbands' earnings, but of an increase in married women's responsiveness to their own wages. Nonetheless, Goldin's (1990) reasoning about women's careers and the anticipation of divorce does lead one to expect an eventual decline in own wage elasticities for married women as well as a continued decline in their responsiveness to husband's income. This expectation forms a central research focus of this chapter.[3]

Although married women's labor force participation increased dramatically over the 1960s and 1970s, it is not unreasonable that the expected decrease in own wage elasticities did not occur until the 1980s. Beginning in the 1960s, increases in the participation rates of married women were associated with a new pattern of entry of younger women, who previously tended to withdraw from the labor force during the childbearing and child-rearing years (Blau, Ferber, and Winkler 2006, 90–91). As this process continued and took hold more firmly, the resulting greater attachment of women to the labor force over the life cycle likely became more and more the norm, eventually generating the expected decline in married women's own wage elasticities. Lags may also have occurred in the response to rising divorce rates. The divorce rate increased substantially over the 1960s and 1970s but then leveled off and actually fell somewhat in the 1980s (Blau et al. 2006: 293-6). Nonetheless, it remained high, and it is reasonable that expectations of marital instability continued to be realigned to the (relatively) new higher levels.

Another strand of labor supply research takes as its central question the explanation of changes in the quantity of labor supplied by women, especially the rapid increases we have seen since the 1950s. Of course, supply responsiveness to wage opportunities will likely play an important role in such explanations. For example, Goldin (1990) takes existing estimates of women's labor supply elasticities and builds a simple supply and demand model of the female labor market to explain women's rising labor force participation over the 1890–1980 period. For the most recent time period analyzed, 1960–80, she concludes that the majority of the increase can be explained by responses to improving labor market opportunities, with a smaller portion explained by rightward shifts in women's labor supply functions.

More recent studies seek to explain the continued rise in women's labor supply in the 1980s and early 1990s. According to Juhn and Murphy (1997), a popular explanation for rising female participation in the 1970s and 1980s was that married women were forced to enter the labor market due to declining real wages and declining employment opportunities for their husbands. However, Juhn and Murphy cast doubt on this explanation by noting that the women with the fastest increases in labor supply during this period were married to men with high wages rather than to men with low wages, and high wage men experienced more rapid wage increases over this period than low wage men. If husbands' wages were playing a large role, then the labor supply of women married to low wage men should have increased the fastest. Juhn and Murphy (1997) conclude that changes in married women's own wage opportunities help explain the pattern of labor supply increases – women whose wages grew fastest also had the fastest increases in labor supply. However, as is the case in many labor supply analyses, they conclude that economic variables can account for only a small portion of the increase in the labor supply of married women. Similarly, in analyzing changes in women's labor supply over the 1975–94 period, Pencavel (1998) also concludes that rising own wage opportunities play a role. His estimates also leave a large portion of the increase in labor supply unexplained and thus due to shifts in labor supply functions.

For the 1990s taken separately, the question may again be raised about the relative importance of changes in own and husbands' wages in explaining the trends in married women's labor supply. Since husbands' real wage growth improved in the 1990s (see below), it is possible that this factor may explain some of the slowing of the increase in married women's labor supply during this decade. Estimates of the role of this factor will be provided in our empirical results below.

6.3. Econometric Issues in Estimating Labor Supply Models

Many analyses of labor supply use cross-sectional data on individuals to estimate functions such as the following static labor supply models:

$$H = a_0 + a_1 \ln W + a_2 I + B'X + u_a \text{ or} \tag{1a}$$

$$H = b_0 + b_1 \ln W + b_2 \ln W_s + b_3 A + C'X + u_b, \tag{1b}$$

where for each individual i (suppressing subscripts), H is hours worked, W is one's own hourly wage offer, I is family asset income plus spouse's earnings, X is a vector of control variables, W_s is one's spouse's hourly wage offer (assuming one is married), A is family asset income, and u_a and u_b are disturbance terms.

Model (1a) is a traditional static labor supply function in which coefficient a_2 indicates the income effect, while a_1 is the impact of an uncompensated wage increase. Model (1b) is more general than (1a) in that one's spouse's wage is allowed to have an effect on labor supply that is different from the impact of sources of income other than the labor income of either spouse (A). In this case, considerations of substitution or complementarity of husband's and wife's leisure can be taken into account (Ashenfelter and Heckman 1974). The model with husband's wages entered separately can also be interpreted in light of family bargaining models. In contrast to unitary family models in which it is assumed that all income is pooled, such models predict that individual labor supply and consumption behavior of husbands and wives is differentially influenced by their own sources of income (Lundberg and Pollak 1994; Manser and Brown 1980; McElroy and Horney 1981).[4]

Estimation of equations such as (1a) and (1b) presents an array of econometric difficulties that have been addressed by the literature on labor supply, and we use many of the techniques developed by this work. First, our sample focuses on married women, the most interesting group to study in a family context and the group whose behavior has driven the aggregate trends. During the period of our study, the share of women who were married with spouse present declined, raising the possibility that our results could be contaminated by changes in self-selection into the married group. As the marriage rate falls, married women may become more marriage-prone relative to the total population of women, on average. If unobserved marriage-proneness is correlated with the motivation to work in the market, then comparisons across years may reflect selection in addition to actual behavioral changes. Below, we implement some adjustments for this possibility.

Second, we do not observe wage offers for those without jobs. We impute wages for this group, as detailed in the data appendix, by assigning them the predicted wages for people with the same observed characteristics who had low (less than 20) weeks worked, a procedure similar in spirit to that used by Juhn (1992) and Juhn and Murphy (1997). The predictions come from wage regressions. As an alternative, we also implement a more traditional selectivity bias correction to assign wages to nonworkers, following Heckman (1979). In addition, unlike much work on female labor supply, in some models we explicitly account for taxes (including income and payroll taxes, as well as the earned income tax credit), using a design developed by Eissa and Hoynes (2004).

Third, the issue of measurement error in labor supply analysis is a potentially serious one, since in many data sources, including the CPS, the wage variable is computed by dividing annual earnings by annual work hours. Measurement error in work hours thus induces a negative bias on the wage. Fourth, a related problem concerns omitted variables. It is plausible that the omitted factors that influence a worker's wage offers such as motivation are also correlated with unmeasured willingness to work. Go-getters are likely to have high wages and long work hours, suggesting an alternative explanation besides upward-sloping labor supply for a positive sample correlation between wages and work hours.

Traditional solutions for the problems of measurement error and omitted variables involve finding instruments for wages, and as described more fully below, we perform instrumental variable (IV) analyses on equations ($1a$) and ($1b$). In addition, Angrist (1991), for example, shows that estimating labor supply models using grouped data is equivalent to IV on individual data with group averages serving as the instruments. Using group averages as the unit of analysis leads the measurement errors and the unmeasured factors mentioned above to cancel out as the number of observations within cells gets large. We are thus left with a wage-hours correlation that tends toward the true causal relationship. And unlike traditional IV approaches using individual data, the grouped data approach does not require the use of exclusion restrictions, many of which may be difficult to justify on theoretical grounds. However, as described below, the grouped data approach places more restrictions on the labor supply parameters than the traditional use of individual data does. In addition to Angrist (1991), several analysts have used grouped data to study labor supply, including Blundell, Duncan, and Meghir (1998), Pencavel (1998), and Devereux (2004), and we present some results using such methods here.

Fifth, equations ($1a$) and ($1b$) impose a linear functional form; that is, they treat the decision to increase one's work hours from, say, 0 to 100 similarly to an increase from 1,500 to 1,600. We thus test the robustness of our findings by separately examining participation (i.e., positive work hours) and conditional hours (i.e., work hours given participation). An additional functional form issue concerns the possible truncation of work hours for many workers at a conventional full-time, full-year level, possibly limiting the responsiveness of such workers to wage increases. We address this possibility by estimating median regressions, where the estimates are not sensitive to behavior at the tails of the distribution of work hours.

6.4. Data and Descriptive Patterns

As noted, we use March CPS data to analyze labor supply. To increase sample size and minimize the effect of the selection of end points, we use three sets of 3 years each: 1979–81 ("1980"), 1989–91 ("1990"), and 1999–2001 ("2000").[5] We restrict our regression analyses to married individuals ages 25–54 with a 25–54-year-old spouse present, in order to abstract from issues of school enrollment and retirement for both husbands and wives.[6] In all analyses we use CPS March Supplement sampling weights adjusted so that each year of data (e.g., 1979) receives the same total weight.

Our basic measure of labor supply is annual work hours: this is the product of usual hours worked per week and weeks worked per year. We include individuals with zero work hours as well but exclude anyone with allocated annual weeks worked or allocated hours worked per week. In supplementary analyses we also investigate participation (i.e., working positive hours) and hours conditional on working. As described in detail in the appendix, hourly wages are defined as annual earnings divided by annual work hours for wage and salary workers.[7] We consider hourly wage observations as invalid if they are less than \$2 or greater than \$200 per hour in 2000 dollars using the Personal Consumption Expenditures price index from the National Income and Product Market Accounts (see http://www.bea.gov). For nonworkers, the self-employed and those with invalid wage observations or allocated earnings, wages are imputed using a regression approach. A separate wage regression is run for each period (1979–81, 1989–91, or 1999–2001) for each of two gender by weeks worked (less than 20 or 20 and higher) cells. Nonworkers receive predicted wages based on the regression using the under-20-weeks-per-year sample. The other categories of workers whose wages are imputed (i.e., the self-employed and those with invalid wage observations or allocated earnings) are given imputations using the regression corresponding to the weeks they worked (i.e., less than 20 or 20 and higher). This imputation is similar in spirit to that proposed by Juhn (1992) and Juhn and Murphy (1997). Appendix Table 6.A1 compares own and spouse education and age, as well as number of children, across the samples of nonworkers and those working less than 20 weeks. It shows that the two samples are reasonably similar with respect to these variables, suggesting that those with short work weeks may be an appropriate base from which to estimate the wages of nonworkers. Nonwage income is defined as income from assets, including interest, dividend, and rental income.

Appendix Tables 6.A2 and 6.A3 provide some descriptive information on the CPS samples. Looking first at the labor supply trends in Table 6.A2, we see a clear pattern that manifests itself both for all women and for those married (spouse present) and for each measure of labor supply - unconditional work hours (i.e., average hours including those with zero hours), annual participation (i.e., whether they had any positive work hours in the past year), and average work hours conditional on working. We see dramatic increases over the 1980s, with noticeably smaller increases for the 1990s. Focusing on married women, we find that, over the 1980s, unconditional hours rose by 284 (29%); participation by 10 percentage points (15%); and conditional hours by 179 (12%). For the 1990s these increases were: 110 (9%) for unconditional hours, 1 percentage point (2%) for participation, and 114 (7%) for conditional hours. Married women's labor supply thus rose faster in the 1980s than in the 1990s both at the extensive and (to a lesser extent) intensive margins. For nonmarried women, this pattern is not observed for participation and is considerably more muted for unconditional hours, suggesting that married women are driving the aggregate trends. Hence, we focus in this study on the labor supply behavior of married women, where we see the more dramatic changes. It is also important to note that married women still comprise the majority of the prime-age female population and that the family context of labor supply is best tested on a sample of married women, where we can observe spouse-related variables.

Figure 6.1 indicates that this pattern of faster increases in labor supply in the 1980s than in the 1990s (illustrated for unconditional annual hours) is widespread among subgroups of married women. Disaggregating by education, we find a roughly similar pattern for each education group, albeit with more muted trends for the least educated (i.e., high school dropouts), who have considerably lower labor supply and labor supply increases in each period than the other groups. The same temporal pattern prevails among married mothers of children under 6 years old, as well as when we consider age groups separately.

Figure 6.1

Annual Hours Trends for Selected Groups of Married Women. Sample Includes those with Zero as Well as Positive Work Hours.

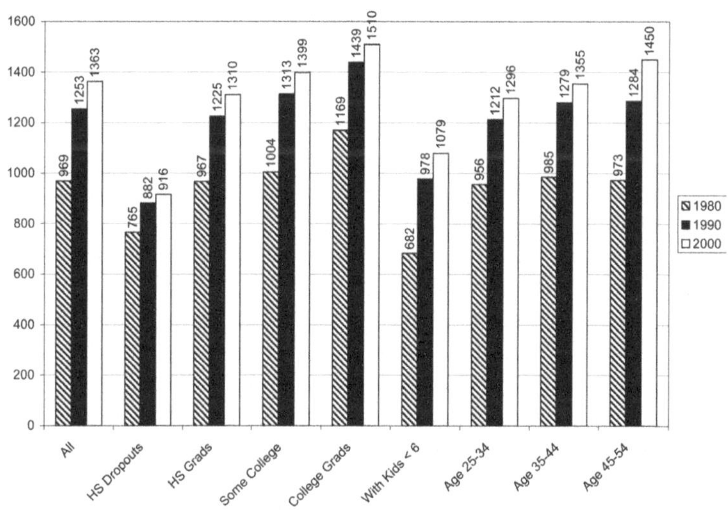

Table 6.A2 also indicates that men's labor supply was fairly stable across the three periods in all the dimensions shown, with relatively small changes in hours and participation for men in the aggregate, married men, and nonmarried men. The pattern for the 1980s is very similar to that found by Juhn (1992) for changes in men's annual participation rates (whether they worked at all) and fraction of weeks they worked: she found that in the aggregate, both of these outcomes for men were virtually constant between 1979–81 and 1985–87, the most recent period of her study.[8] Table 6.A2 also shows a decline in the incidence of marriage for women, from 73% in 1980 to 67% in 1990, with a smaller further decline to 64% by 2000. Not surprisingly, the incidence of marriage among men ages 25–54 also declined over the 1980–2000 period, with a pattern similar to women's.

Table 6.A3 shows descriptive data on some of our key explanatory variables, including women's own wages, spouse's wages, nonwage income, education, and number and ages of children. We present information on our imputed wages, for which everyone in the sample receives a value, as well as on actual wages for the subsample with valid observations (i.e., wage and salary workers with "legal" values for wages). Under either definition, married women's real wages rose substantially in the 1980s (about 12%), with an even more rapid increase in the 1990s (17%–20%). In contrast, married men's real wages fell slightly in the 1980s (by 1%–2%) and rose by 8%–9% in the 1990s. Taken together, these changes in real wages imply that the gender wage gap among married people closed faster in the 1980s than the 1990s, as also found by Blau and Kahn (2006) for the full male and female populations. The more rapid increase of married women's wages relative to married men's in the 1980s than the 1990s may have contributed to the higher growth rate in married women's labor supply in the 1980s.

Table 6.A3 also shows that the total number of own children present fell somewhat in the 1980s (from 1.55 to 1.34), with a very small further decline (1.34 to 1.31) in the 1990s. Most of the major changes in the number of children over the 2 decades were concentrated in those of school age (6–11 and 12–17) during the 1980s, with only small changes in the 1990s. Such a pattern, while consistent with a faster increase in labor supply in the 1980s, may not have a large impact if school age children tend to have modest effects on female labor supply (compared to younger children).

6.5. Empirical Procedures and Regression Results

6.5.1. Basic Regression Results

Our basic empirical procedure involves estimating equations (1a) and (1b) separately for married women and married men for each period: 1979–81, 1989–91, and 1999–2001. The dependent variable is annual work hours, and we treat this as a linear model, although results were very similar when we estimated a Tobit model in order to take into account the mass of observations at zero hours. In addition to the key wage and other income variables, we control in all models for own and spouse age and age squared; eight Census region dummies; a metropolitan area dummy; own and spouse dummies for black non-Hispanic, other race non-Hispanic, and Hispanic origin (with white non-Hispanic the omitted category); and year dummies (because we pool 3 years of data for each period).

Four specifications of (1a) and (1b) were estimated. We estimate specifications with (models 3 and 4) and without (models 1 and 2) controlling for own or spouse education.[9] There are several reasons one might wish to control for schooling. First, it may be an indicator of work orientation. In addition, it may be correlated with nonwage compensation, allowing us to place a sharper interpretation on the wage variable. And education may be an indicator of permanent income or wealth. If so, then Blundell and MaCurdy's (1999) discussion implies that the wage coefficient controlling for education may be an estimate of the intertemporal labor elasticity. However, with education excluded from the basic labor supply equation, the wage variable would refer to a change in wages that also raises lifetime wealth. Thus, we also estimate the models with education excluded. In addition to controlling for education in some models, we also estimate the models separately by education group, since responses to wages may differ across this dimension.

Each of these two broad specifications is estimated with (models 2 and 4) and without (models 1 and 3) a detailed set of controls for own children living in the household by age group (as shown in Table 6.A3). The decision of whether to control for the presence of children is based on the following considerations. On the one hand, suppose that fertility decisions depend primarily on preferences. Under such a scenario, it is likely that women with preferences for smaller families will have higher labor supply and will invest more in market-related human capital. This reasoning suggests that if we do not control for the number of children, we might observe a spurious positive correlation between wages and labor supply reflecting these preferences rather than a true labor supply effect. And since the impact of children is likely to vary according to the children's ages, we use a detailed child age specification. On the other hand, the decision to have children may be the result of an overall set of time allocation decisions including labor supply (Rosenzweig and Wolpin 1980; Angrist and Evans 1998). Specifically, higher wage offers may induce women to work more and to have fewer children, and controlling for the number of children may therefore lead us to understate the full effects of wages on labor supply. For this reason, we also estimate models with the children variables excluded, allowing wages to have their full effects.

We estimate these models using IV with own wage and spouse's wage each considered endogenous in the models where each spouse's wage is entered separately (i.e., eq. [1b]) and with own wage and other income each considered endogenous when spouse's earnings and other nonlabor income are added together (i.e., eq. [1a]). The excluded instruments include a series of dummy variables indicating the decile of actual or imputed wage (for both own and spouse wage). Using deciles corrects to some degree for measurement error in the wage (Baker and Benjamin 1997; Juhn and Murphy 1997; Blau et al. 2003). In addition, in all models, own and spouse education are included in the first stage log wage regressions. Thus, in the labor supply models without schooling controls, the education dummies comprise another set of excluded instruments.

Table 6.1 contains basic IV results for wives' unconditional hours of labor supply equations based on specification (1b): own and spouse wage rates are each entered separately. (Results with spouse's labor income aggregated into nonlabor income were very similar.) We present results for the four specifications mentioned earlier for each of the three periods; elasticities are shown at the bottom of the table.

We find a dramatic decrease in women's own wage elasticities. As indicated by our discussion of previous empirical findings, this is an important recent development. In addition, we find that the long-term trend toward declines in the magnitude of spouse's wage elasticities continued in this period, particularly in the 1980s. Taken together this pattern of reduced responsiveness of married women's labor supply to their own and their spouse's wages supports the pattern expected by Goldin (1990) as married women's employments shifted from "jobs" to "careers" and as married women responded to continued high divorce rates.

We now examine these results in more detail. Table 6.1 indicates that married women's labor supply is positively and significantly related to their own log wages in each specification and period. The coefficients on own log wages were roughly constant over the 1980s, ranging from 743 to 856 in 1980 to 732 to 805 in 1990, but they fell substantially over the 1990s to 487 to 563 in 2000.[10] Own wage elasticities evaluated at the mean of hours in each period fell steadily from .77 to .88 in 1980 to .58 to .64 in 1990 and .36 to .41 in 2000. It is notable that the 1980 figures are virtually the same as the modal estimates based on the surveys cited earlier. These studies themselves were largely based on data before the 1980s. The absolute declines in the elasticities were roughly similar over the 1980s (.18–.24) and the 1990s (.20–.25). In an accounting sense, the decreases were achieved

Table 6.1

Instrumental Variables Labor Supply Estimates for Wives (Dependent Variable Is Annual Hours, including Zeros)

	1979–81				1989–91				1999–2001			
	Model 1	Model 2	Model 3	Model 4	Model 1	Model 2	Model 3	Model 4	Model 1	Model 2	Model 3	Model 4
Own log wage	855.828**	779.630**	820.500**	743.209**	805.423**	753.600**	788.859**	731.527**	563.540**	547.054**	508.998**	487.197**
	(10.183)	(9.875)	(11.035)	(10.637)	(8.479)	(8.252)	(9.389)	(9.087)	(10.066)	(9.821)	(11.306)	(10.998)
Spouse log wage	-351.267**	-322.904**	-373.429**	-348.194**	-310.142**	-279.786**	-318.924**	-294.880**	-308.682**	-263.491**	-299.457**	-261.606**
	(10.117)	(9.679)	(10.866)	(10.400)	(8.974)	(8.620)	(9.714)	(9.330)	(10.463)	(10.161)	(11.466)	(11.128)
Nonwage income	-3.732**	-3.824**	-3.810**	-3.948**	-3.140**	-3.049**	-2.790**	-2.814**	-2.107**	-1.577**	-1.723**	-1.293**
	(.460)	(.439)	(.460)	(.439)	(.438)	(.420)	(.437)	(.419)	(.401)	(.388)	(.398)	(.386)
Number of children		-395.534**		-395.229**		-360.420**		-356.601**		-348.272**		-344.883**
age <1		(14.818)		(14.764)		(14.494)		(14.427)		(17.816)		(17.670)
Number of children		-534.435**		-532.195**		-449.911**		-449.690**		-425.845**		-423.952**
age 1		(14.096)		(14.045)		(13.775)		(13.707)		(16.938)		(16.805)
Number of children		-401.529**		-400.039**		-355.536**		-353.861**		-378.038**		-378.015**
age 2		(13.720)		(13.666)		(13.670)		(13.600)		(16.289)		(16.165)
Number of children		-315.800**		-314.862**		-295.215**		-293.669**		-286.517**		-282.766**
ages 3–5		(7.712)		(7.681)		(7.654)		(7.614)		(9.320)		(9.246)

Table 6.1 (continued)

	1979–81				1989–91				1999–2001			
	Model 1	Model 2	Model 3	Model 4	Model 1	Model 2	Model 3	Model 4	Model 1	Model 2	Model 3	Model 4
Number of children		-166.575**		-163.205**		-172.046**		-168.191**		-167.513**		-161.905**
ages 6–11		(4.660)		(4.648)		(4.974)		(4.951)		(5.783)		(5.741)
Number of children		-36.753**		-32.385**		-59.932**		-56.444**		-64.468**		-58.030**
ages 12–17		(4.444)		(4.438)		(5.427)		(5.406)		(6.076)		(6.032)
Own and spouse												
education	No	No	Yes	Yes	No	No	Yes	Yes	No	No	Yes	Yes
Observations	64,001	64,001	64,001	64,001	58,987	58,987	58,987	58,987	48,733	48,733	48,733	48,733
Elasticities (at mean, computed from the basic regressions):												
Own log wage	.883	.804	.846	.766	.643	.601	.630	.584	.413	.401	.373	.357
Spouse log wage	-.362	-.333	-.385	-.359	-.247	-.223	-.255	-.235	-.226	-.193	-.220	-.192
Nonwage income	-.004	-.004	-.004	-.004	-.003	-.002	-.002	-.002	-.002	-.001	-.001	-.001
Elasticities (at median hours and mean nonwage income, computed from median regressions):												
Own log wage	1.593	1.292	1.428	1.210	.643	.527	.612	.511	.342	.294	.297	.265
Spouse log wage	-.758	-.583	-.737	-.610	-.285	-.232	-.270	-.238	-.229	-.181	-.209	-.172
Nonwage income	-.009	-.010	-.009	-.010	-.008	-.006	-.006	-.006	-.007	-.004	-.006	-.003

Notes: A symptotic standard errors are in parentheses. All models include eight regional dummies; a metropolitan area dummy; age and age squared; spouse age and age squared; three race and Hispanic origin dummies; three race and Hispanic origin dummies for spouse; and two year dummies. All elasticities are significantly different from zero at the 1% level, two-tailed tests.

* Denotes significance at 5%, two-tailed tests.

** Denotes significance at 1%, two-tailed tests.

differently in the two periods. Although the hours coefficient was relatively stable over the 1980s, mean hours rose considerably. In contrast, over the 1990s, the hours coefficient fell sharply but the increase in mean hours was fairly small. The net effect was a comparable absolute decline in women's own wage labor supply elasticity in the two decades. One possible reason why the responsiveness of women's labor supply to their own wages declined is a statistically based one: it is possible that, as female labor supply increased, a growing share of women reached the point where it was virtually impossible for them to increase their work hours further, given that the distribution of work hours may effectively be truncated at the full-time, full-year level. We investigated this possibility by estimating women's labor supply functions using median regression, since hours at the median are not affected by truncation at the top: median work hours for women were 800 in 1980, 1,560 in 1990, and 1,785 in 2000, supporting this idea. As the bottom panel of Table 6.1 shows, labor supply elasticities and cross elasticities fell dramatically in magnitude at the median.[11] Further, the decline in female labor supply elasticities across the skill distribution reported below (including high school dropouts) also seems inconsistent with a simple hypothesis that our results are due to women moving to an inelastic portion of a constant labor supply function.

The own wage coefficient for women's labor supply is qualitatively similar across specifications in Table 6.1, although it does decline slightly when we control for schooling and again when we control for the number of children in the various age groups. The decline in the wage coefficient when we control for schooling is consistent with the idea that the education variables are positively correlated with unmeasured aspects of compensation or tastes for work, but not with the version of life-cycle model in which education is a proxy for the marginal utility of wealth. Since the hours coefficients on own education rise over time (results not shown), it is possible that the decline in the own wage coefficient between 1980 and 2000 is spurious. However, as discussed further below, the decline in women's own wage elasticity of labor supply occurs within education groups, suggesting that this finding does indeed reflect declining wage responsiveness of married women's labor supply.

The decline, though slight, in the own wage coefficients for women's labor supply when we control for children is an expected result in the two scenarios we described earlier: (i) the propensity to have children leads women to place a lower value on market time and on human capital investment, or (ii) higher wage offers lead women to shift some of their time allocation from home production (including having and raising children) to market work and human capital investment. Unfortunately, we cannot distinguish between these two scenarios, but the similarity of the results under models controlling and not controlling for children is reassuring. Also of interest, the coefficients on the children variables decline moderately in magnitude between 1980 and 1990 and again between 1990 and 2000. And relative to average labor supply, the effect of children falls even more dramatically. For example, not controlling for education, at the mean labor supply level, each child under 1 year of age lowers women's labor supply by 41% in 1980, 29% in 1990, and 26% in 2000.[12]

The second set of major results for women's labor supply shown in Table 6.1 concerns the impact of husband's wages. Consistent with earlier work based on the 1980s (Devereux 2004), we find significant negative effects of husbands' wages on wives' labor supply. These negative effects get smaller in absolute value over time, ranging from -323 to -373 in 1980; to -280 to -319 in 1990; and -262 to -309 in 2000. The elasticity (at the mean labor supply) with respect to husbands' wages falls in absolute value more dramatically than the raw hours effect, with particularly large decreases over the 1980s: from -0.33 to -0.39 in 1980, to -0.22 to -0.26 in 1990, to -0.19 to -0.23 in 2000. Finally, we note that, while the coefficients on nonwage income other than husbands' wages are significantly negative (as expected), they are very small in absolute value. For example, the negative elasticities in Table 6.1 are always below 0.01 in absolute value.

Turning now to a consideration of the labor supply results for husbands, the findings (available in our longer paper, Blau and Kahn [2005a]) can be quickly summarized. While men's labor supply is significantly positively affected by their own wages, the responsiveness is relatively small, as previous work has found. Specifically, the own wage elasticity at the mean work hours ranges from 0.01 to 0.07 in 1980, 0.09 to 0.14 in 1990, and 0.05 to 0.10 in 2000. The cross wage elasticity is even smaller than this range in absolute value and changes sign and significance level depending on the specification. And the impact of other income has the wrong sign (i.e., it is positive and significant) but implies an elasticity of less than 0.003 in every case.

Our results for married women's and men's labor supply suggest that Goldin's (1990) vision of falling married women's own wage and cross wage labor supply elasticities was coming to pass by 2000. We find that for married women, the own wage elasticity was cut roughly in half and the cross wage elasticity was reduced by about 40% in magnitude. Thus, women's labor supply responses did indeed much more closely resemble men's by 2000.[13]

6.5.2. *Pervasiveness of the Reduction in Female Labor Supply Elasticities*

Table 6.1 presents evidence of striking decreases in the labor supply responsiveness of married women. While these results may accurately reflect changes in average behavior, it is possible that the findings are driven by shifts in the composition of the female labor force that are not adequately controlled for in our basic analysis. For this reason, and because it is in any case of interest to know how far reaching these trends are, in this subsection we consider separate analyses of labor supply behavior by subgroup. We find that the decline in wage responsiveness was pervasive and dramatic across a variety of dimensions, including education, race, age, and marital status. It appears that women in general have either become more committed to the idea of working or anticipate spending a larger portion of their lives without spouses, with both phenomena implying reduced own wage labor supply elasticities. The similarity in the decline in elasticities across subgroups suggests that this commitment or expectation cuts across skill levels and even family type. For example, single women in 1980 may have anticipated being married for a longer portion of their lives than single women in 2000.

6.5.2.1. *Education Groups*

In addition to addressing shifts in the relative size of education groups, models disaggregated by education are of interest because compensation may be better measured within education groups, thus yielding a more precise estimate of the supply elasticity. This would be the case if education levels reflect unmeasured differences in wages because we have not been entirely successful in correcting for measurement error in wage rates or because education is positively correlated with total compensation, including the nonpecuniary benefits of various employments. The elasticities in Table 6.2 from estimating our basic labor supply model disaggregated by education group indicate that own and cross wage elasticities fall sharply in magnitude for all of the education groups. The decline for high school dropouts by 2000 is especially precipitous: own wage elasticities are not only extremely small in absolute value but also become negative (sometimes significantly so); elasticities remain negative but insignificant for spouse wages. Below, we explore the possibility that these findings are due to the failure to adjust for the impact of the EITC and taxes and find that this does not appear to be the case.[14]

6.5.2.2. Mothers of Young Children

Recent Bureau of Labor Statistics (BLS) reports have suggested that the labor market attachment of mothers with young children has declined and that this may mark a shift in women's labor supply behavior. For example, the Monthly Labor Review editor reports that labor force participation of women with infants fell each year except one between 1998 and 2003 (http://www.bls.gov/opub/ted/2004/apr/wk3/art04.htm). In contrast, Baker and Boushey (2004) report that during the recessionary period 2000–2002, employment-to-population ratios fell similarly for men and women with children and those without children, suggesting that there was nothing unique about the labor supply behavior of mothers during this period. In light of such data, we conducted additional analyses restricting the sample to married women with children under 6 years of age, in order to determine whether this group's labor supply behavior was changing over the long run in a manner different from other married women. We have already seen that the pattern of labor supply trends for this group mirrors those of the aggregate: a large rise in the 1980s followed by a much smaller rise in the 1990s, although at a somewhat lower level of labor supply (see Figure 6.1).

As may be seen in Table 6.2, we find very similar labor supply patterns for this group over the 1980–2000 period to those for married women overall. Specifically, the own wage elasticity for mothers of young children fell steadily between 1980 and 2000 (from .98–1.04 in 1980 to .49–.54 in 2000). And the cross wage elasticities for mothers of young children fell in absolute value from -0.56 (for all specifications) in 1980 to -0.32 to -0.35 in 1990, before rising slightly to -0.34 to -0.40 in 2000. The slight rise in magnitude of the cross elasticity for mothers of young children between 1990 and 2000 contrasts with the slight fall for married women as a whole. Nonetheless, for both samples, the cross elasticity was much smaller in magnitude in 2000

Table 6.2

Selected Instrumental Variables Results for Married Women by Subgroup

	1979–81				1989–91				1999–2001			
	Model 1	Model 2	Model 3	Model 4	Model 1	Model 2	Model 3	Model 4	Model 1	Model 2	Model 3	Model 4
Elasticities for education groups:												
Grade 11 or less:												
Own log wage	.850	.810	.868	.828	.746	.728	.747	.734	-.102^	-.121*	-.118*	-.127*
Spouse log wage	-.162	-.193	-.225	-.254	-.135	-.147	-.151	-.163	-.025^	-.009^	-.030^	-.020^
Nonwage income (divided by 1,000)	-.001^	-.002^	-.001^	-.001^	-.001^	-.001^	-.001^	-.001^	-.001^	-.001^	-.001^	-.001^
Grade 12:												
Own log wage	.899	.822	.901	.824	.688	.641	.691	.644	.384	.365	.412	.392
Spouse log wage	-.389	-.366	-.408	-.385	-.255	-.238	-.258	-.242	-.094	-.078	-.153	-.135
Nonwage income (divided by 1,000)	-.004	-.004	-.003	-.004	-.004	-.004	-.003	-.004	-.003^	-.003^	-.001^	-.001^
Some college:												
Own log wage	.688	.615	.693	.620	.612	.556	.613	.558	.452	.428	.472	.447
Spouse log wage	-.401	-.368	-.402	-.373	-.276	-.251	-.284	-.257	-.192	-.167	-.240	-.213
Nonwage income (divided by 1,000)	-.011	-.012	-.011	-.012	-.003^	-.003*	-.002^	-.002^	-.007	-.006	-.004	-.004
College graduates:												
Own log wage	.653	.548	.654	.548	.500	.449	.502	.452	.273	.261	.287	.273
Spouse log wage	-.441	-.381	-.438	-.380	-.275	-.244	-.282	-.251	-.248	-.224	-.266	-.240
Nonwage income (divided by 1,000)	-.010	-.011	-.009	-.010	-.010	-.011	-.009	-.010	-.007	-.005	-.005	-.003

Table 6.2 (continued)

	1979–81				1989–91				1999–2001			
	Model 1	Model 2	Model 3	Model 4	Model 1	Model 2	Model 3	Model 4	Model 1	Model 2	Model 3	Model 4
Elasticities for mothers with children under 6 years old:												
Own log wage	1.043	.985	1.029	.981	.843	.791	.860	.814	.535	.496	.517	.485
Spouse log wage	-.557	-.563	-.565	-.559	-.345	-.348	-.321	-.318	-.395	-.387	-.353	-.343
Nonwage income (divided by 1,000)	-.006	-.006	-.006	-.006	-.005	-.006	-.004	-.004	-.004	-.003	-.002*	-.002^
Elasticities for age groups:												
Ages 25–34:												
Own log wage	.863	.716	.797	.677	.655	.565	.608	.540	.402	.340	.309	.283
Spouse log wage	-.378	-.326	-.407	-.348	-.237	-.211	-.258	-.221	-.204	-.184	-.221	-.186
Nonwage income (divided by 1,000)	-.003	-.004	-.003	-.004	-.004	-.004	-.004	-.004	.001^	.001^	.001^	.002^
Ages 35–44:												
Own log wage	.784	.763	.760	.706	.614	.603	.630	.589	.393	.400	.389	.367
Spouse log wage	-.352	-.339	-.369	-.381	-.285	-.246	-.268	-.254	-.277	-.219	-.238	-.208
Nonwage income (divided by 1,000)	-.009	-.009	-.009	-.009	-.009	-.008	-.007	-.008	-.005	-.004	-.004*	-.003*
Ages 45–54:												
Own log wage	1.084	1.066	1.056	1.030	.692	.686	.669	.653	.464	.472	.426	.418
Spouse log wage	-.339	-.333	-.347	-.350	-.190	-.186	-.214	-.217	-.171	-.153	-.169	-.165
Nonwage income (divided by 1,000)	-.008	-.008	-.008	-.008	-.004*	-.004*	-.004^	-.004^	-.008	-.007	-.008	-.007
Children controls	No	Yes	No	Yes	No	Yes	No	Yes	No	Yes	No	Yes
Own/spouse education[a]	No	No	Yes	Yes	No	No	Yes	Yes	No	No	Yes	Yes

Notes: All models include eight region dummies; a metropolitan area dummy; age and age squared; spouse age and age squared; three race and Hispanic origin dummies; three race and Hispanic origin dummies for spouse; and two year dummies. Elasticities are evaluated at the mean. All elasticities are significantly different from zero at the 1% level on two-tailed tests, except as noted otherwise.

[a] Includes spouse education only in the models estimated separately by education group.

* Denotes significance at 5%.

^ Denotes not significant.

than 1980. Thus, at least through the 2000 period, married women with young children appeared to behave very similarly to married women overall. Moreover, we obtained very similar findings when we restricted the sample to married mothers of children less than 3 years old.

6.5.2.3. Age Groups

In her Ely Lecture at the American Economic Association meetings, Goldin (2006) suggested that a number of substantial sharp changes in women's labor force behavior and outcomes occurred beginning with the cohort of women born in the 1940s. According to this view, unlike previous cohorts, members of these newer cohorts expected to be in the labor force for the long term, rather than to enter and exit depending on family responsibilities. This reasoning suggests that newer cohorts will have lower own wage and cross elasticities (in absolute value) and a greater commitment to work and careers. To examine these issues, we disaggregated our labor supply functions by age group, as shown in Table 6.2.

Table 6.2 indicates that own and cross wage elasticities declined in magnitude both between cohorts and within cohorts. First, reading horizontally for a given age group, one can assess between-cohort changes in labor supply behavior. Each age group is replaced 10 years later by one with much smaller (in magnitude) own and cross wage elasticities. The largest changes are for the 45–54-year-olds, where own wage elasticities fell from 1.03–1.08 in 1980 to .42–.47 in 2000. Interestingly, this is the age group where we have the cleanest "before" and "after" test of Goldin's (2006) conjecture about the 1940s being the key birth cohort: the birth years for the 1980 group span 1925–36 (a period completely before the 1940s), while the birth years for the 2000 sample span 1945–56; none of our other age groups completely precedes the key birth years.[15]

Second, reading diagonally in the southeast direction, one can follow the progress of individual birth cohorts. And in almost every case these show considerable within-cohort reductions in the magnitudes of own wage and cross wage elasticities. For example, among those born between 1945 and 1956, and therefore age 25–34 in 1979–81, own wage elasticities fall from .68–.86 in 1980 to .42–.47 in 2000; cross elasticities for this group fall in magnitude from -.35 to -.41 in 1980 to -.15 to -.17 in 2000. These reductions are actually comparable to the changes for the 25–34-year-old age group. The other cohorts also typically show declining magnitudes for own and cross wage elasticities.[16]

Our analysis of age groups does indeed show that members of newer cohorts have less responsive labor supply functions than earlier cohorts, as suggested by Goldin's (2006) reasoning. However, within cohorts, there have also been major reductions over time in the degree to which women's labor supply responds to their own and husbands' wages. This pattern suggests that the changing norms and expectations of labor force commitment affected adult women even after most had made their investments in schooling. These within-cohort changes and the similar changes that occurred even for lower education groups suggest that by 2000, women were becoming more committed to market work, even if this did not necessarily mean working in a high-level career.

6.5.2.4. *Other Subgroups*

We also estimated separate labor supply functions for black married women and single women (of all races), two groups with historically high labor force attachment for whom one might expect smaller changes in elasticities compared with white and married women, respectively. Married black women and single women had smaller elasticities than married white women and all married women, respectively, as expected. However, the elasticities for these groups fell by amounts similar to the declines for whites and married women, respectively, over the period. Specifically, own wage elasticities for single women ranged from .43 to .59 in 1980 (across specifications controlling or not controlling for education and children) but fell to the .15–.28 range by 2000. And figures for black women ranged from .38 to .53 in 1980, with a fall to the .08–.18 range by 2000. Own wage elasticities for married white women were similar to the full sample, not surprisingly: .72–.83 in 1980 and .36–.41 in 2000.

6.5.3. *Accounting for Changes in Women's Labor Supply: 1980–2000*

In this section, we consider the implications of the labor supply functions we have estimated for labor supply changes over the 1980s and 1990s. As we have seen, women's labor supply grew substantially faster in the 1980s than in the 1990s. To what extent can these changes be explained by exogenous factors such as wage offers and to what extent are the changes due to shifts in women's labor supply functions? Table 6.3 provides an accounting of the changes in women's labor supply by showing the contribution of changing levels of the explanatory variables, as well as the effect of shifts in the labor supply function (the "Total Unexplained Change") for each period (i.e., 1980–90 and 1990–2000). Of course, the answer one obtains potentially depends on the specification of the labor supply function and the weights one applies to the changes in the explanatory variables. Table 6.3 shows results for our most fully specified model, which includes own education, spouse's education, and children. We show results for this model since this specification gives the explanatory variables their best chance of explaining the observed changes in labor supply, although results were very similar for more parsimonious specifications. We show results using the 1980, 1990, and 2000 equations.

Table 6.3

Predicted Changes in Married Women's Unconditional Annual Work Hours, 1980–2000

	Predicted Changes in Labor Supply Using:					
	1980 Equation		1990 Equation		2000 Equation	
Variable	1980–90	1990–2000	1980–90	1990–2000	1980–90	1990–2000
Model 4 (includes own education, spouse's education, and children):						
Own log wage	86.51	145.43	85.15	143.15	56.71	95.34
Spouse log wage	6.99	-29.74	5.92	-25.19	5.26	-22.35
Nonwage income	-2.32	-3.43	-1.65	-2.45	-.76	-1.13
Education	15.50	9.55	17.90	11.12	33.51	28.21
Children	5.77	16.67	11.15	14.65	11.23	14.15
Age	-1.05	-19.56	.88	-18.67	4.70	-6.84
Race—Hispanic	.83	2.60	1.09	2.08	-.81	-.64
Spouse age	-.15	-4.40	-.74	-3.37	-3.54	-5.90
Spouse education	-3.36	-3.62	-1.50	-.23	-2.99	-4.15
Spouse race—Hispanic	2.97	2.80	.55	.60	.56	1.24
Region/MSA	-6.09	.20	-10.75	-1.44	-4.78	-.91
Total actual hours change	283.56	110.37	283.56	110.37	283.56	110.37
Total explained change	105.63	116.39	107.98	120.25	99.10	97.00
Total unexplained change	177.93	-6.02	175.59	-9.88	184.46	13.36

Notes: Based on model 4 in Table 6.1. Total actual hours change is the change in the predicted hours where, for each year, predicted hours are computed using that year's equation and that year's mean values for the explanatory variables.

Across the three years' equations shown in Table 6.3, measured factors explain 35%–38% of the growth in female labor supply over the 1980s, suggesting that the labor supply function shifted to the right over the 1980s. In contrast, using the 1980 and 1990 equations, measured factors are more than sufficient to account for the (smaller) increase in labor supply that occurred over the 1990s (explaining 106%–109%) and can account for a high proportion of the change (88%) using the 2000 function. Thus, in an accounting sense, one reason for the labor force growth slowdown between the 1980s and the 1990s is that the labor supply function did not shift to the right in the latter decade but rather remained relatively stable. In fact, when the same equation is used to evaluate the impact of the changes in the explanatory variables in the 1980s versus the 1990s, the larger unexplained increase in labor supply in the 1980s is sufficient or more than sufficient to fully account for the slowdown in the growth of annual hours of 173 hours between the two decades. We also obtained very similar decomposition results separately by education group as well as for mothers of children less than 6 years old.

Looking at the contribution of specific variables, increases in women's real wage offers were the single most important environmental change causing a rise in their labor supply in both decades. Within each year's equation, this factor actually had a larger positive effect in the 1990s than the 1980s, since women's real wages rose more in the latter decade. Thus, while rising real wages for women are an important part of the explanation for why women's labor supply grew in the 1980s and 1990s, they cannot explain why labor supply growth was slower in the 1990s than the 1980s. Overall, real own wage increases explain 20%–31% of the actual hours increase in the 1980s, and 87%–132%, in the 1990s. The estimated effect of this factor is largest in both models when the 1980 equation is used, reflecting the decrease in the responsiveness of married women to their own wages over the period. The 2000 function thus leaves less room for future wage increases to cause higher female labor supply than under previous labor supply functions. This suggests that demand increases will cause women's wages to rise to a greater extent than in the past.

We should point out that the effect of real wage increases may be overstated here, since they do not account for women's growing experience levels. In other words, wage offers to women of a given level of human capital probably rose more slowly than the increases assumed in Table 6.3. In our earlier work (Blau and Kahn 2006), we found that women's human capital levels (including actual experience and education) increased similarly relative to men's in both the 1980s and 1990s. Thus, given men's real wage increases in the 1980s and 1990s, the wage increases to women with given human capital levels would have led to decomposition results with a smaller contribution from own wage changes and a larger unexplained portion. But because of the similarity in women's relative human capital changes across the two decades, our conclusion about a larger rightward shift in the 1980s than the 1990s would remain unchanged.

Husbands' real wages on average fell slightly during the 1980s, providing a possible explanation for the rising labor supply of women during this period. However, consistent with Juhn and Murphy (1997), we find little effect of this factor, with declining husband's real wages explaining only 2% of the actual hours increase under all specifications. Rising male real wages during the 1990s do explain some of the reduction in the growth of female labor supply during this decade. The effect of husbands' wage increases in the 1990s lowered female labor supply by 22–30 hours. Thus, comparing the 1980s to the 1990s, changes in husbands' real wage growth between the two decades explained 28–37 hours of slower female labor supply growth in the 1990s than in the 1980s, or 16%–21% of the slowdown. Thus, women's labor supply grew more slowly during the 1990s than during the 1980s in part because husbands' real wages increased more in the 1990s than the 1980s.

Of the other explanatory variables, rising education levels accounted for hours increases of 16–34 in the 1980s and 10–28 in the 1990s, in each case a modest share of the actual increase in female labor supply (5%–12% in the 1980s and 9%–26% in the 1990s). And these hours effects were slightly larger in the 1980s than the 1990s. Thus changes in the growth in educational attainment, controlling for wages, accounted for a small portion (3%–4%) of the slowdown in women's labor supply growth. The decline in the number of children in each decade also raised women's labor supply modestly, with a slightly larger effect in the 1990s (14–17 hours) than the 1980s (6–11 hours).[17] Thus, in an accounting sense, smaller families can explain a small to modest portion of women's rising labor supply in the two decades (2%–4% in the 1980s and 13%–15% in the 1990s); however, differences across decades in changes in family size cannot explain the slowdown in women's labor supply growth since the contribution of changes in the number of children was more positive in the 1990s than the 1980s.

6.5.4. *Alternative Specifications and Estimation Methods*

In order to further investigate the robustness of the findings shown in Table 6.1, we implemented a variety of alternative specifications and methods of estimating married women's labor supply. Each of these alternatives leads to the same conclusion: married women's own wage elasticity fell dramatically between 1980 and 2000. With one exception (i.e., the aftertax results when husbands' earnings are included with asset income in an other family income measure), we continue to find that cross-elasticities fell in absolute value as well.

6.5.4.1. *Changing Selectivity of Married Couples*

As discussed earlier, the declining incidence of marriage may produce selection biases in our sample of married women. We account for this factor in several ways, as shown in Table 6.4. First, between 1980 and 2000, an increasing number of individuals lived together as couples but were not officially married, suggesting that the meaning of marriage may have changed over time. Thus, we reestimate our basic model on an expanded sample that includes likely cohabitors. Cohabitors were identified in a consistent fashion across years as pairs of unrelated adults (aged 15 or over) of the opposite sex living in the same household in which there were no other adults present using the Census Bureau's Partners of the Opposite Sex Sharing Living Quarters (POSSLQ) definition (as discussed in Casper and Cohen 2000). While imperfect, this procedure undoubtedly permits us to add to the sample many people who are in fact cohabiting. Table 6.4 shows that the results of this analysis are very similar to those using the traditional definition of marriage, suggesting that changes in the propensity to cohabit do not account for the falling labor supply elasticities of married women.

Second, we remove the least marriage-prone individuals for the years with higher overall marriage incidence, in the spirit of a similar adjustment for selection into employment used by Hunt (2002). We first estimate a marriage probit for each year using only own age, own education, race/ethnicity, and location as explanatory variables. Because marriage is the dependent variable, we of course did not include any spouse-related characteristics or presence of children variables, and we also did not include any wage data since wages may be endogenous with respect to marriage. We then adjusted the samples

Table 6.4

Selected Results for Women with Marriage Selection Corrections

	1979–81				1989–91				1999–2001			
	Model 1	Model 2	Model 3	Model 4	Model 1	Model 2	Model 3	Model 4	Model 1	Model 2	Model 3	Model 4
Instrumental variables estimation including likely cohabitors—elasticities:												
Own log wage	.856	.774	.811	.730	.557	.502	.524	.466	.401	.383	.363	.342
Spouse log wage	-.358	-.324	-.386	-.354	-.235	-.219	-.261	-.250	-.197	-.165	-.193	-.167
Nonwage income												
(divided by 1,000)	-.006	-.006	-.006	-.006	-.004	-.004	-.004	-.004	-.004	-.003	-.003	-.002
Removing some married women from earlier samples (specification 1)—elasticities:												
Own log wage	.885	.800	.856	.767	.651	.610	.644	.597	.413	.397	.371	.349
Spouse log wage	-.378	-.345	-.397	-.368	-.255	-.229	-.256	-.236	-.213	-.182	-.206	-.181
Nonwage income												
(divided by 1,000)	-.006	-.007	-.007	-.007	-.006	-.005	-.005	-.005	-.005	-.003	-.004	-.003
Removing some married women from elasticities:												
Own log wage	.826		.836		.594		.621		.352		.339	
Adding unmarried people to later samples[a]—elasticities:												
Own log wage	.835		.840		.578		.596		.347		.319	
Using all women in all periods[a]—elasticities:												
Own log wage	.800		.761		.578		.548		.318		.258	
Children controls	No	Yes	No	Yes	No	Yes	No	Yes	No	Yes	No	Yes
Own/spouse education	No	No	Yes	Yes	No	No	Yes	Yes	No	No	Yes	Yes

Notes: All models include eight regional dummies; a metropolitan area dummy; age and age squared; three race and Hispanic origin dummies; and where applicable, spousage and age squared; three race and Hispanic origin dummies for spouse; and two year dummies. All elasticities are computed at the respective means of the sample for which they are estimated, and all elasticities are significantly different from zero at the 1% level on two-tailed tests.

[a] Specification excludes spouses' characteristics.

for 1980 and 1990 by eliminating the least "marriage-prone" married women so that each year's sample of married women represents the same (2000) fraction of the full population, and reestimated the basic models.[18] As Table 6.4 indicates, the results for own wages, spouse's wages, and nonwage income are very similar to our results in Table 6.1.[19] In particular, the own wage elasticities evaluated at the mean of the sample included in the regressions fall from 0.77–0.89 in 1980, to 0.60–0.65 in 1990, to 0.35–0.41 in 2000.

Third, an alternative procedure is to add some nonmarried people (in order of marriage-proneness) to the later samples and estimate our basic labor supply models without controlling for spouse characteristics, children, or family nonwage income. In contrast to the earlier procedure of deleting some married people from the sample, this procedure adds observations and thus includes more of the population, although now we cannot investigate family effects. Table 6.4 reports three sets of results for this approach. The first provides results for the same specification (i.e., excluding family-related variables) for the sample that removes some married women from the earlier years' samples (denoted in the table as "specification 2" for this group). The second adds unmarried women to later years' samples (in order of their probability of being married) so that in each year the sample of women represents the same (1980) fraction of the full population. The third simply estimates the model for all women ages 25–54 (regardless of actual marital status), in effect allowing all decisions regarding marriage and children to be endogenous. Each specification yields dramatically declining own wage elasticities over time. For example, for the third specification (all women ages 25–54), at the mean of annual hours, the own wage elasticity fell from 0.76–0.80 in 1980, to 0.55–0.58 in 1990, to 0.26–0.32 in 2000. Overall, Table 6.4 shows that selection into marriage is not the cause of our estimates of falling labor supply elasticities.

6.5.4.2. Taxes

Marginal tax rates decreased dramatically over the 1980–2000 period, while the generosity of the Earned Income Tax Credit was greatly increased. Our basic wage and other income measures are defined gross of income taxes and thus may be biased by these changes. The net effect and size of these biases are uncertain. Thus, in this section, we examine the robustness of our findings by reestimating our models using after tax incomes and wages as the key explanatory variables.

In order to impute an after tax wage for each married woman, we assumed that husband's earnings were exogenous and included them in "other family income" for the purposes of computing a marginal tax rate for each woman, which is similar to the procedure in Eissa and Hoynes (2004). Thus, net other family income for women includes husband's wage and salary and self-employment earnings as well as asset income. Net other family income is calculated for each man under the assumption that his wife is not working at all. Given these values for other family income, women's wage rates are adjusted using the average tax rate faced by a worker shifting from zero hours to full-year, full-time work (i.e., 40 hours/ week for 52 weeks), again as in Eissa and Hoynes (2004). This procedure recognizes that a woman's marginal tax rate can be affected by her labor supply decisions and thus assigns a tax rate based on the assumption of full-time, full-year employment rather than the woman's actual work hours. This tax rate is exogenous to the woman's actual labor supply choice.

In computing after tax wages and other family income, we incorporated the effect of the federal income tax, social security taxes, and the Earned Income Tax Credit (EITC). The adjustments for the income tax assume that spouses are filing jointly and take the standard deduction plus personal exemptions for themselves and each of their own children 18 or younger. The adjustments for social security taxes, which include both Old-Age, Survivors and Disability Insurance (OASDI), and Hospital Insurance (HI), take into account the different tax rates that apply to wage income and self-employment income and also the maximum tax payable in each year. The adjustments for the EITC assume that all own children 18 or younger may be considered dependent children and that family investment income (used in an eligibility test in 1999–2001) consists of interest, dividends, and rent.

Selected results for before and after tax own wage and other family income are shown in Table 6.5. The before tax results for all married women are included because the specification differs from that in our basic results (see Table 6.1) in that, as just noted, husbands' earnings are now added to asset income to form what we call other family income. Before tax results for all married women closely track those for the basic results. Married women's own wage elasticity fell from .75 to .85 in 1980 to .34 to 39 in 2000. Their other family income elasticity fell in magnitude from -.18 to -.19 in 1980 to -.11 to -.14 in 2000, with most of the decrease occurring in the 1980s. Note that the other family income elasticities are smaller in magnitude than those estimated for

Table 6.5

Estimation Results for Net of Taxes Variables (Elasticities)

	1979–81				1989–91				1999–2001			
	Model 1	Model 2	Model 3	Model 4	Model 1	Model 2	Model 3	Model 4	Model 1	Model 2	Model 3	Model 4
Before taxes:												
Own log wage	.854	.778	.826	.747	.617	.578	.612	.568	.388	.380	.358	.344
Other family income[a]	-.190	-.176	-.187	-.176	-.145	-.132	-.136	-.126	-.138	-.119	-.125	-.110
Net-of-tax variables:												
Own log wage	.864	.807	.808	.760	.597	.560	.581	.541	.376	.369	.346	.333
Other family income[a]	-.106	-.088	-.127	-.107	-.162	-.143	-.157	-.140	-.140	-.118	-.129	-.111
Children controls	No	Yes	No	Yes	No	Yes	No	Yes	No	Yes	No	Yes
Own and spouse education	No	No	Yes	Yes	No	No	Yes	Yes	No	No	Yes	Yes

Notes: All models include eight regional dummies; a metropolitan area dummy; age and age squared; spouse age and age squared; three race and Hispanic origin dummies; three race and Hispanic origin dummies for spouse; and two year dummies. All elasticities are significantly different from zero at the 1% level, two-tailed tests.

[a] Includes husbands' income and asset income; divided by 1,000.

husbands' wages separately, and their magnitude declines less over the period. This makes sense since in these estimates husbands' earnings are combined with nonwage income; the elasticities obtained for the latter in Table 6.1 were considerably smaller in absolute value than for husbands' wages and decreased much less in magnitude over time.

The after tax results continue to show a dramatic decrease in own wage elasticities comparable in magnitude to the pretax results. They no longer show a decrease in responsiveness to other family income, but rather, taking the 1980–2000 period as a whole, the other family income elasticity remains roughly constant to slightly increasing in absolute value, depending on specification. This raises the possibility that the finding of a decreasing responsiveness to other family income (and by implication husband's wages) in the pretax models is an artifact of measuring the variable in before tax dollars. However, note that the trend for other family income is already considerably more muted than for husband's wages in our basic specification. Moreover, the treatment of taxes must necessarily be tentative because of the problems of observing true taxable income (e.g., deductions are unobservable) and the fact that tax rates are endogenous.

When education groups were examined separately (results available in Blau and Kahn 2005a), the tax-corrected results for the own wage elasticities are very similar to those presented in Table 6.2, showing sharp declines for all groups. For 2000, we continued to find negative and small (in absolute value) own wage elasticities for women with less than a high school degree even after accounting for income taxes, payroll taxes, and the Earned Income Tax Credit.[20]

6.5.4.3. Adjustments at the Extensive versus the Intensive Margin

The dependent variable in our basic estimations is unconditional hours, which are of course affected both by decisions to participate in the labor force (extensive margin) and to work more or fewer hours conditional on working (intensive margin). Recognizing that these two types of decisions may be differentially affected by our explanatory variables (Heckman 1993), we present in Table 6.6 the results of analyses separately estimating the determinants of positive hours and work hours conditional on working. In each case, we use predicted own and husband's wages as in Table 6.1, although, in the participation probits, we do not correct the standard errors, since we are primarily interested in the parameter estimates, which are consistent.

Table 6.6

Estimation Results for Adjustment along the Extensive and Intensive Margins

	1979–81				1989–91				1999–2001			
	Model 1	Model 2	Model 3	Model 4	Model 1	Model 2	Model 3	Model 4	Model 1	Model 2	Model 3	Model 4
Employment participation probit estimation:												
Own log wage	.610	.586	.568	.534	.438	.424	.433	.413	.297	.296	.279	.273
Spouse log wage	-.217	-.204	-.247	-.243	-.141	-.126	-.149	-.141	-.132	-.113	.124	-.109
Nonwage income												
(divided by 1,000)	-.002	-.002	-.005	-.005	-.003	-.003	-.003	-.003	-.004	-.004	.004	-.002*
Instrumental variables estimation of annual hours for those who worked:												
Own log wage	.279	.256	.274	.252	.235	.222	.229	.216	.140	.137	.126	.122
Spouse log wage	-.169	-.162	-.170	-.162	-.125	-.117	-.124	-.117	-.110	-.100	.109	-.100
Nonwage income												
(divided by 1,000)	-.001	-.001	-.001	-.001	-.001	-.001	-.001	-.001	-.001	-.001	.001	-.001
Instrumental variables estimation of annual hours for those who worked with selection correction:												
Own log wage	.279	.256	.274	.252	.333	.317	.334	.316	.123	.121	.106	.099
Spouse log wage	-.169	-.162	-.170	-.162	-.129	-.116	-.124	-.113	-.095	-.077	-.093	-.080
Nonwage income												
(divided by 1,000)	-.001	-.001	-.001	-.001	-.001	-.001	-.001	-.001	-.001^	-.001^	-.001^	-.001^
Children controls	No	Yes	No	Yes	No	Yes	No	Yes	No	Yes	No	Yes
Own and spouse education	No	No	Yes	Yes	No	No	Yes	Yes	No	No	Yes	Yes

Notes: Elasticities are computed at the mean. See Table 6.1 for additional details. All elasticities are significantly different from zero at the 1% level except those marked otherwise.
* Significant at 5%, on two-tailed tests.
^ Not significant, on two-tailed tests.

The probit results in Table 6.6 for the determinants of positive hours give the partial derivatives evaluated at the mean of the explanatory variables as well as the implied elasticities at the mean. Own wage participation elasticities fall sharply: from 0.53–0.61 in 1980, to 0.41–0.44 in 1990, and to only 0.27–0.30 by 2000. The effect of spouse wages on participation also falls in absolute value over the period, though less dramatically. The negative cross-elasticities decrease in magnitude from -.20 to -.24 in 1980 to -.11 to -.13 in 2000, with most of the decline occurring over the 1980s. These findings mirror the unconditional hours results.[21]

Conditional hours are analyzed in two ways. First, we simply use the same IV analysis as in Table 6.1 with the sample restricted to those with positive hours. Second, we explicitly recognize that there may be a selection bias problem in focusing on those with positive hours. Unfortunately, there are no good instruments for determining participation that do not theoretically affect hours given participation. Instead, we implement a procedure similar to that used in correcting for selection into marriage (see section 6.5.4.1). We begin by noting that the participation probability rises over time (Appendix Table 6.A2). To adjust for sample selection, we reduce the size of the 1990 and 2000 samples so that the same fraction of the population is observed in each year. To do this, we estimate participation equations based on the full set of exogenous variables in the IV labor supply models shown in Table 6.1. These include dummy variables for one's own wage decile, and spouse's wage decile; nonwage income; own and spouse age, education, and race; region; and year. We then drop from the sample those with the lowest predicted probabilities of participating in 1990 and 2000 to yield samples with the same relative likelihood of participation in each year. Note that this procedure imposes no a priori assumptions about the wage levels of nonparticipants versus participants.

Table 6.6 shows that both methods of analyzing conditional work hours yield very similar results for 1980 and 2000: the effect of own and spouse wages is similar across the methods, and they each decline sharply in magnitude between 1980 and 2000. At the mean conditional hours, the own wage elasticity ranges from .25 to .28 in 1980 and falls to a range of .10 to .14 by 2000. The estimation methods do give differing results for 1990, with the selectivity corrected own wage elasticity rising to .32–.33, and the elasticity without correcting for selectivity declining to the .22–.24 range. However, as just noted, by 2000, both methods yield the same basic result: own wage elasticities for conditional work hours were much smaller by 2000 than they were in 1980. And spouse wage elasticities fall continually in absolute value from 1980 to 2000 across both methods, as in the participation equations.

These results suggest that women's own wage and cross wage labor supply elasticities decreased in magnitude at both the extensive and intensive margin over this period. Of course, as in the previous literature on labor supply, we find that the participation own wage elasticities are much larger than the conditional hours own wage elasticities (Blundell and MaCurdy 1999). Moreover, our results indicate that the participation own wage elasticities fell by much more over the 1980–2000 period than the conditional elasticities, suggesting that the fall in women's overall own wage labor supply elasticity occurred mostly through a reduction of responsiveness at the extensive rather than the intensive margin.

6.5.4.4. Omitted Variable Bias: Using Grouped Data

As discussed earlier, using grouped data can eliminate asymptotic biases due to possible correlation of tastes for working with unmeasured productivity, without the exclusion restrictions needed for the IV approach. To implement the strategy of using group averages, we create own age/spouse age/own education/spouse education cells. We define three age groups - 25–34, 35–44, and 45–54 - and four education groups - less than high school, high school degree, some college, and college degree. Considering both own and spouse age and education, this breakdown potentially yields 144 cells: 3 own age groups × 3 spouse age groups × 4 own education groups × 4 spouse education groups.

Ordinary least squares (OLS) estimation of our basic labor supply models using individual data may produce biased estimates of the labor supply elasticity if, within age-education cells, married women with strong tastes for work are also more productive. Taking cell averages, we can eliminate this potential asymptotic bias. However, if there are cross-cell differences in the factors affecting tastes for work and in wage offers, then even using group averages may lead to biased estimates of the labor supply parameters. For example, college graduates may have higher wage offers and greater work orientedness than high school dropouts. This unmeasured factor can be accounted for by estimating the labor supply models using first differences of cell means. But it is also possible that wage offers for college graduates and their work orientedness rose relative to those of high school dropouts over the 1980–2000 period, suggesting that even first differences may yield biased estimates. We can account for these unobserved changes by estimating the models using first differences and including dummy variables for cell characteristics. These consist of main effects for dummy variables for categories referring to own age, spouse age, own education, and spouse education. The use of first differences and inclusion of the group effects allow for age and education cell fixed effects as well as a different trend for age groups and for education groups. Moreover, by including the change in the control variables, we adjust for changes in the race-regional composition of age-education cells.

Table 6.7

Results Using Grouped Data

	(1989–91) – (1979–81)		(1999–2001) – (1989–91)	
Elasticities:				
Own log wage	.445**	.898**	.195	.258
Spouse log wage	-.417*	-.652**	-.174	-.194
Nonwage income	.027	.027	-.039*	-.012
Own and spouse education and age cell dummies included?	No	Yes	No	Yes
Observations	129	129	129	129
R^2	.48	.59	.20	.34

Notes: Additional controls for all models include averages of eight regional dummies; a metropolitan area dummy; three race and Hispanic origin dummies; three spouse's race and Hispanic origin dummies; and two year dummies. All models are estimated in first differences. Elasticities are computed at the beginning period means.
* Denotes significance at 5%, two-tailed tests.
** Denotes significance at 1%, two-tailed tests.

The potential reduction in omitted variable bias produced by using grouped data is a substantial benefit to using this technique; however, it is obtained at the expense of constraining the labor supply parameters to be constant over a given 10-year period, an outcome we have reason to doubt based on our earlier estimates. Nonetheless, it is possible to estimate the grouped data first difference labor supply equation for the 1980–90 and 1990–2000 periods separately; in this way, we can determine whether the average effect of own and husband's wages on labor supply over the 1980s was larger than their effect in the 1990s.

Table 6.7 presents the results of two specifications for the grouped averages approach (i.e., with and without controlling for own and spouse age and education dummy variables). We included only cells with at least five observations in each year, although the results were not sensitive to other assumptions about cell inclusion. The regressions in Table 6.7 are weighted by the inverse of the sum of the cell sizes for the two years used to form the first difference.[22] The results are similar to our earlier findings for own wages and spouse wages; although the effects of nonwage income rise in absolute value, they still remain very small in magnitude.[23]

6.5.4.5. Further Specifications

We found results very similar to those reported in Table 6.1 for a number of additional specifications (see results reported in Blau and Kahn [2005a]). First, we used a traditional Heckman (1979) selectivity bias correction for predicted wages for those not working. In these models, we excluded education from the labor supply function but included it in the wage offer equations. Second, we used OLS on equations (1a) and (1b). Third, we estimated the model using Tobit instead of a linear hours model. And, finally, we disaggregated the nonwage income variable in equation (1b), as implied by bargaining models, although we obtained no evidence that the effect of own nonwage income differed from that of spouse's nonwage income.

6.6. Conclusions

This chapter has used March CPS data to investigate married women's labor supply behavior over the 1980–2000 period. Married women's labor supply rose dramatically in the 1980s, with a much smaller increase in the 1990s.We find that married women's real wages increased in both the 1980s and 1990s, and these caused comparable increases in labor supply in each decade, given women's positively sloped labor supply schedules. However, their labor supply function shifted sharply to the right in the 1980s, with little shift in the 1990s. In an accounting sense, this difference in the supply shift is the major reason for the more rapid growth of female labor supply in the 1980s than the 1990s. In addition, married men's real wages fell slightly in the 1980s but rose in the 1990s, a factor that contributed modestly to the slowdown in the growth of women's labor supply in the 1990s.

Moreover, during both decades, there was a dramatic reduction in married women's own wage labor supply elasticity. This is a significant new development. In addition, continuing a long-term trend, married women's labor supply became less responsive to their husbands' wages as well, particularly over the 1980s. Taking the 1980–2000 period as a whole, women's own wage elasticity was reduced by 50%–56%, while their cross wage elasticity fell by 38%–47% in absolute value. Thus, as predicted by Goldin (1990), women's own and cross wage labor supply elasticities were becoming more like men's, possibly reflecting increasing divorce rates and increasing career orientation of women.

The reduction in the magnitude of women's labor supply elasticities implies that government policies such as income taxes that affect marginal wage rates have a much smaller distortionary effect on labor supply than in the past. In addition, the potential of technological changes that raise the demand for female labor to bring women into the labor market is much smaller than previously; rather, these demand changes would instead raise women's relative wages to a greater degree than before.

Appendix

Data were obtained from the 1979–81, 1989–91, and 1999–2001 March supplements of the Current Population Survey. To ensure that each year was given equal weight, the March supplement person weights were divided by the sum of these weights over all observations in a given year. Husband and wife records were matched, with observations dropped if either spouse was a member of the armed forces, was not in the 25–54 age range, or had allocated annual weeks worked or allocated hours worked per week.

The number of children at each age was calculated for each married couple. Values for the highest grade completed by husbands and wives in the 1999–2001 sample were assigned using Jaeger's (1997) suggested correspondence. Annual hours worked were defined as the product of the number of weeks worked (WKSWORK) in the previous year and the number of hours usually worked (HRSWK) during those weeks; a respondent was considered to be in the workforce if HRSWK > 0.

All nominal earnings and income variables were converted into 2000 dollars using the National Income and Product Account price index for personal consumption expenditures. All top-coded values of total wage and salary earnings (WSAL - VAL) in 1979–81 were multiplied by 1.45. For our 1989–91 and 1999–2001 samples, wage and salary income was split into two variables by the CPS: wage and salary income on one's main job and wage and salary income on secondary jobs. The CPS top-coded value for main job earnings (ERN - VAL) was $99,999 for 1989–91 and $150,000 for 1999–2001. We multiplied these by 1.45. The top code on other wage and salary earnings (WS - VAL) was $99,999 in 1989–91 but was only $25,000 (in current dollars) during 1999–2001. For consistency, we forced a $25,000 top code for all years for secondary wage and salary earnings and multiplied these by 1.45 as well. The measure of wage and salary earnings used (WSINC) was equal to the modified value of WSAL - VAL in 1979–81 and the sum of the modified values of ERN - VAL and WS - VAL in 1989–91 and 1999–2001. Log of wages (lnw) was equal to the log of WSINC divided by the product of WKSWORK and HRSWK.

We also experimented with two other methods for adjusting top-coded earnings values. First, we followed Card and DiNardo's (2002) strategy of forcing the same top code ($99,999) for main job wage and salary earnings for data from 1989 onward, while keeping the $25,000 top code for secondary wage and salary earnings. Second, we followed Autor, Katz, and Kearney's (2005a) strategy of keeping our top-coded values the same as the CPS's and then multiplying by our correction factor (1.45) in each case. (Our correction factor was midway between the 1.4 value used by Card and DiNardo [2002] and Autor, Katz and Kearney [2005a] value of 1.5.) In both cases, the labor supply results were virtually unchanged.

Flags were generated for any observation that had an allocated value for any variable used in creating lnw or that had a wage value less than $2 or greater than $200 (in 2000 dollars). An imputed wage variable was created, using actual wages unless the individual was not employed or the calculated wage value was not valid, in which case predicted values were used from separate log wage regressions for each combination of gender, decade, and low/high work weeks (using a 20-week cut-off). The regressors used were own and spouse variables for age, age squared, three education categories, and three race/Hispanic categories, plus eight region categories and a metropolitan area indicator.

Table 6.A1

Means for Nonworkers and Those Working Less than 20 Weeks, Married Women Ages 25–54

	1980			1990			2000		
	(1) Nonworkers	(2) Less than 20 Weeks	(2) - (1) Difference	(1) Nonworkers	(2) Less than 20 Weeks	(2) - (1) Difference	(1) Nonworkers	(2) Less than 20 Weeks	(2) - (1) Difference
Less than grade 12	.253	.190	-.063	.212	.153	-.058	.168	.108	-.060
Grade 12	.476	.465	-.011	.443	.450	.007	.351	.339	-.012
Some college	.152	.181	.029	.178	.205	.027	.252	.294	.042
College graduate	.118	.164	.045	.168	.192	.025	.230	.260	.030
Spouse less than grade 12	.245	.205	-.040	.195	.155	-.040	.149	.109	-.040
Spouse grade 12	.360	.348	-.012	.352	.376	.024	.296	.303	.007
Spouse some college	.154	.189	.035	.168	.191	.023	.216	.267	.051
Spouse college graduate	.241	.259	.018	.285	.278	-.007	.339	.320	-.019
Number of children age less than 1	.070	.091	.021	.084	.091	.008	.075	.081	.006
Number of children age 1	.098	.094	-.004	.109	.115	.006	.097	.108	.011
Number of children age 2	.099	.083	-.016	.112	.089	-.022	.106	.091	-.014
Number of children ages 3–5	.315	.288	-.028	.355	.332	-.023	.327	.287	-.041
Number of children ages 6–11	.659	.687	.028	.626	.639	.013	.612	.674	.063
Number of children ages 12–17	.597	.553	-.043	.425	.427	.002	.433	.456	.024
Total children under 18	1.838	1.795	-.042	1.710	1.693	-.017	1.650	1.698	.048
Age	37.543	35.319	-2.224	37.410	35.702	-1.708	38.619	37.308	-1.311
Spouse age	40.029	37.816	-2.214	39.691	37.909	-1.782	40.746	39.539	-1.207

Table 6.A2

Selected Descriptive Statistics for the Full Sample

	1979–81		1989–91		1999–2001		Changes	
	Mean	*N*	Mean	*N*	Mean	*N*	1980–90	1990–2000
Women:								
Proportion married	.726	100,585	.666	99,557	.636	86,402	-.060	-.030
Total:								
Annual hours	1,081.3	100,585	1,330.3	99,557	1,451.7	86,402	249.1	121.3
Worked positive hours	.695	100,585	.775	99,557	.799	86,402	.081	.023
Annual hours conditional on working	1,556.9	69,986	1,716.1	77,263	1,817.9	68,688	159.2	101.8
Married:								
Annual hours	969.4	64,001	1,253.0	58,987	1,363.4	48,733	283.6	110.4
Worked positive hours	.667	64,001	.767	58,987	.780	48,733	.100	.013
Annual hours conditional on working	1,454.4	42,882	1,633.7	45,388	1,748.1	37,922	179.4	114.3
Nonmarried:								
Annual hours	1,397.1	26,888	1,519.2	32,458	1,615.3	30,754	122.1	96.1
Worked positive hours	.790	26,888	.814	32,458	.840	30,754	.024	.027
Annual hours conditional on working	1,768.3	21,246	1,867.3	26,382	1,922.7	25,674	98.9	55.4
Men:								
Proportion married	.742	92,365	.658	91,496	.625	80,193	-.084	-.033
Total:								
Annual hours	2,025.2	92,365	2,009.5	91,496	2,033.1	80,193	-15.7	23.6
Worked positive hours	.948	92,365	.938	91,496	.921	80,193	-.010	-.017
Annual hours conditional on working	2,136.4	87,856	2,143.0	86,249	2,208.1	74,295	6.6	65.1
Married:								
Annual hours	2,142.3	64,001	2,147.5	58,987	2,183.3	48,733	5.3	35.8
Worked positive hours	.969	64,001	.964	58,987	.955	48,733	-.005	-.009
Annual hours conditional on working	2,210.7	62,025	2,227.2	56,859	2,286.3	46,525	16.5	59.1
Nonmarried:								
Annual hours	1,729.0	21,597	1,758.0	28,461	1,799.4	28,229	29.0	41.4
Worked positive hours	.890	21,597	.888	28,461	.867	28,229	-.002	-.021
Annual hours conditional on working	1,941.6	19,337	1,979.7	25,529	2,075.8	24,782	38.1	96.1

Notes: Sample restricted to individuals ages 25–54. "Married" includes individuals who are married with spouse aged 25–54 present; "nonmarried" includes all individuals who are not married with a spouse present. "1980–90" refers to changes between the 1979–81 averages and the 1989–91 averages, and similarly for "1990–2000."

Table 6.A3

Mean Values of Selected Explanatory Variables, Estimation Sample of Married Women Ages 25–54

				Changes	
	1979–81	1989–91	1999–2001	1980–90	1990–2000
Own log imputed wage	2.192	2.308	2.504	.116	.196
Own log valid wage[a]	2.248	2.373	2.546	.124	.173
Spouse log imputed wage	2.834	2.814	2.900	-.020	.085
Spouse log valid wage[b]	2.829	2.815	2.896	-.013	.081
Nonwage income (divided by 1,000)	1.540	2.127	2.997	.587	.870
Less than grade 12	.185	.119	.084	-.066	-.035
Grade 12	.477	.433	.323	-.043	-.110
Some college	.171	.212	.288	.041	.076
College graduate	.168	.236	.305	.068	.069
Spouse less than grade 12	.210	.134	.092	-.076	-.042
Spouse grade 12	.362	.368	.314	.006	-.054
Spouse some college	.172	.201	.265	.029	.063
Spouse college graduate	.256	.296	.330	.041	.033
Number of children age less than 1	.058	.064	.055	.006	-.009
Number of children age 1	.065	.070	.063	.005	-.007
Number of children age 2	.068	.071	.067	.004	-.004
Number of children ages 3–5	.224	.236	.212	.012	-.024
Number of children ages 6–11	.554	.487	.482	-.067	-.005
Number of children ages 12–17	.577	.412	.430	-.165	.018
Total children under 18	1.545	1.341	1.310	-.204	-.031
Number of observations	64,001	58,987	48,733	—	—

Notes: Imputed wage equal to actual wage unless individual did not work, had a wage of less than $2 or more than $200 (in 2000 dollars), had allocated wage and salary income, or was self-employed, in which case predicted values are used from separate log wage regressions for each combination of gender, decade, and low/high weeks worked (using a 20-week cutoff). The regressors used were own and spouse variables for age, age squared, three education categories, and three race/Hispanic categories, plus eight region categories and a metropolitan area indicator.

[a] Sample sizes are 32,900, 36,666, and 28,807 in the three periods, respectively.

[b] Sample sizes are 43,146, 42,078, and 33,179 in the three periods, respectively.

7

Trends in the Well-Being of American Women: 1970–1995

7.1. Introduction

The major goal of this chapter is to chart the trends in the well-being of women in the United States over the last quarter of a century. This interval covers the period of the most significant shifts in women's wage outcomes since 1940 and is long enough to form reasonable conclusions regarding the extent and magnitude of changes in other indicators of well-being. The past 25 years are significant not only as a period in which women's labor market outcomes and family structure changed substantially, but also as a time of equally significant changes in the labor market as a whole. Chief among these has been the dramatic widening of wage inequality among workers. In a time of stagnating overall real wage increases for men, this has meant substantial declines in the real wages of less-skilled men. Moreover, substantial decreases in the relative employment of this group have also been documented. The sources, dimensions, and consequences of widening wage inequality, particularly as they affect male workers and family income distribution have been the focus of considerable research. Less attention has been directed at the implications of these trends for women's well-being, a major focus of this chapter.

This chapter is a revised version of Blau, F. D (1998). Trends in the Well-Being of American Women, 1970-1995, in: Journal of Economic Literature, 36(1): 112-165.

The author would like to thank Deborah Anderson, Marianne Ferber, Victor Fuchs, Joyce Jacobsen, Lawrence Kahn, Elizabeth Peters, Jane Waldfogel, Anne Winkler, and anonymous referees for helpful comments and suggestions. I am indebted to Deborah Anderson, Shub Depgupta, and Rana Sihwail for excellent research assistance.

Documentation of changes in women's well-being cannot proceed without the specification of a set of indicators by which well-being may be measured. A second major goal of this study is to propose a set of indicators for this purpose and demonstrate their usefulness for forming a more complete picture of changes in women's well-being than may be obtained elsewhere in the literature. While there is always likely to be some disagreement about the usefulness of including any particular indicator, I hope that the two basic principles which guided me in my selection will prove useful in future similar endeavors.

First, it is important that a broad range of indicators of well-being be employed, encompassing not only labor market outcomes like wages and occupations, but also time available for leisure, the level of family income, and the share of women who are single family heads, an important proxy for a family's economic resources. In this respect, this inquiry follows the example set by Fuchs (1986; 1988) and Smith and Ward (1989). In addition, work on bargaining models of the family and feminist economics[1] suggest that women's status within the family is also of interest. Thus, I have sought indicators with which to measure changes in this facet of well-being as well, including women's relative wages among married couples and data on the extent of domestic violence.

Second, in considering the trends, it is important to examine both changes in indicators of well-being for women relative to men, and changes in absolute levels for women over time, and to conduct these inquiries at a disaggregated as well as at an aggregate level. An interest in relative outcomes of women flows naturally from a concern that women are in some sense in a disadvantaged position in the labor market, in the family, and in the larger society. But such a perspective is not necessary to motivate this investigation. Even if gender differences in outcomes were entirely due to differences between men and women in preferences and qualifications, it is still of interest to know whether such factors have resulted in widening or narrowing differences in outcomes over time. In addition to permitting an appraisal of progress toward gender equality per se, women's relative progress is also of interest because data on males provide a useful benchmark against which to assess women's progress, in effect enabling us to estimate a "period effect." Thus, for example, we would assess a 10 percent decline in real wages for women differently depending on whether the real wages of comparable males fell by 20 percent or increased by 20 percent at the same time.

Absolute trends in indicators of well-being among women are also important. So, for example, it instructive to know not simply that the gender wage gap is declining, but also the magnitude of any real wages increases for women. Or, as another example, we may inquire as to whether women have been upgrading their occupations in some absolute sense or simply narrowing the gender difference in occupational distributions. The importance of a disaggregated analysis is suggested by the research on men which has pointed to growing disparities among them based on skill. This suggests the potential usefulness of a comparable investigation of how various groups of women are faring relative to others, both in terms of how quickly they are narrowing the gap with men, but also in terms of their standing on various indicators of well-being compared with other women. Because in most cases a great deal more is known about the trends for males and the trends in the relevant gender differences than about the absolute trends in indicators of well-being for women and the differences in these trends among various groups of women, I have sought in this review to place greater emphasis on the latter.

One contribution of this chapter is to supplement what can be learned from existing research by presenting new tabulations of a variety of indicators of women's well-being calculated primarily from Current Population Survey (CPS) data.[2] While the broad outline of many of the trends delineated here are generally known, it is useful to present data for the same years from a comparable source and across a wide range of outcomes. More important, data are presented here at a more disaggregated level than is generally the case so that significant differences in trends by education and age may be identified. Given constraints of space, however, I was not able to investigate these trends separately by race in comparable detail; this remains an important area for future research. I also present empirical results for indicators which have not been examined in the same way before, including information on trends in the wages of wives compared to their husbands from the CPS and in the time use of men and women from the Panel Study of Income Dynamics. Where possible, I compare my empirical results with the broader literature but I do not attempt to review this literature in its entirety, which would of necessity be a very different exercise. Similarly, I endeavor to summarize briefly and comment on what is known about the causes of these trends, but, here too, given the broad range of indicators which I review, it is not possible to fully consider this question in each case. Finally, it is important to note that when other work is considered, the primary focus is on the economics literature. Considerations of time and space preclude doing justice to the voluminous literature on these topics in other fields.

For virtually all age and education groups, I obtain substantial evidence of rising gender equality in labor market outcomes, notably labor force participation, wages, occupational distributions, and self-employment. I also find broad evidence of greater gender parity within married couple families as the housework time of husbands has increased relative to wives', and as the relative wages of wives have risen compared to their husbands'. However, parallel to the evidence of the declining labor market status of lower-skilled men, there has been a similar sharp decline for less educated women, especially high school dropouts, compared to other women. This decline has occurred across a wide variety of dimensions. For example, while overall female participation rates increased 23 percentage points over the 1970 to 1995 period, the participation rate of high school dropouts, already below that of their more educated peers in 1970, rose by only 4 percentage points. For those that were employed similar disparities are evident with respect to the progress of real wages, with average weekly wages of full-time workers rising by 31.2 percent in real terms for all women, but declining by 2.2 percent for female high school dropouts. Finally, while the headship rate of women with less than a high school education (12.1 percent) was fairly similar to that of all women (9.4 percent) in 1970, the incidence of single headship among high school dropouts increased 12.2 percentage points, compared to an increase of 6.5 percentage points among all women.

The deteriorating relative economic position of less educated women and their families is a major finding of this study, drawn both from existing studies and the original results presented here. One question that these results raise, and a question which has received remarkably little attention in the literature, is the possibility that such trends reflect shifts in the composition of the least educated category rather than changes in their opportunities or behavior. The share of the population with less than 12 years of education has fallen sharply over the period considered in this study, 1970-1995, declining by over 60 percent among both men and women. It is possible that as this group has dwindled in size it has become more negatively selected compared to more highly educated Americans. Were it possible to identify a similarly constituted group in each year, one might find smaller changes in outcomes, or, indeed, no changes at all. An additional compositional factor affecting the least educated is that the share who are foreign born has grown considerably more rapidly for them than for other education groups, and labor market outcomes of immigrants have been declining relative to natives, even compared to natives with the same measured characteristics (Borjas 1995). On the other hand, it could be argued that the college educated group which has fared especially well relative to high school dropouts, has increased its share markedly – by nearly two times among men and two and a half times among women – potentially making it a less positively selected group. This suggests that, to the extent that compositional factors are important, their impact is an empirical question.

Although these are undoubtedly complex factors which will take considerable effort to unravel completely, in their analysis of trends in wage inequality, Juhn, Murphy, and Pierce (1993) suggest a fairly simple method for gaining some insight into whether or not changes in the relative status of the less educated reflect true changes in outcomes and behavior versus solely compositional shifts. One can compare the magnitude of changes in outcomes for a cohort over time to changes experienced by successive cohorts of individuals of the same age. Because the former comparison could not have been affected by changes in the composition of the various education groups, similar findings for the "within cohort" and "across cohort" comparisons would suggest true changes in opportunities or behavior and not simply compositional effects. I apply this technique to a number of the indicators of welfare considered below. The findings strongly suggest that compositional shifts do not entirely account for the deteriorating economic position of less educated Americans.

In the sections that follow, a broad range of indicators of economic well-being are considered. I first focus on labor force participation and next turn to an examination of major labor market outcomes including wages and occupations, and trends in self-employment. I then consider indicators of women's standard of living, including family structure and income differences across families, as well as indicators of women's well-being within the family, including the relative wages of husbands and wives and housework hours of men and women, as well as trends in domestic violence. A more detailed rationale for the inclusion of each indicator and its relationship to women's economic well-being is presented below in conjunction with the empirical results. The focus is on individuals aged 25–64; and the following four age groups are distinguished: 25–34, 35–44, 45–54, and 55–64. Disaggregations by education are presented for the following four education groups: less than 12 years, 12 years, 13–15 years, and 16 or more years.[3] Throughout, the term "married" is used to refer to an individual who is married, spouse present. A "single head" of a family or subfamily is a person who is not married spouse present, i.e., was never married, or is separated, widowed, or divorced.

7.2. Labor Force Participation: Trends and Explanations

The labor force participation decision is viewed as the outcome of a utility maximizing decision by an individual, possibly in conjunction with his or her family, as to how much labor to supply to the market. Thus, the relationship between trends in participation and women's economic well-being is not obvious. One reason for examining participation trends is that they underlie the transformation in gender roles that has occurred and thus should be summarized, if only to provide the background for understanding changes in indicators more obviously linked to well-being. However, our consideration of labor force participation also rests on more direct links between female participation and women's well-being.

First, with the increase in the incidence of female-headed families and single person female households, admittedly not entirely exogenous developments, there exists a segment of the female population whose economic well-being is quite obviously heavily dependent on whether they participate in the labor force and their earnings levels, given participation. In addition, within married couples, the contribution of working wives has traditionally been important in averting poverty and has been found to play a role in determining the extent of inequality in family income (Cancian, Danziger, and Gottschalk 1993; Karoly and Burtless 1995). Thus, the finding that, for example, the growth in the labor force participation of female high school dropouts has lagged behind that of other groups is of concern in light of their rising incidence of single-headed families and the well documented declines in the relative earnings of the less educated men that they are likely to marry.

Second, family bargaining models suggest that, in married couple families, women's participation in the labor force and their level of earnings while employed is likely to affect the distribution of resources within marriage. These models assume that the preferences of husbands and wives may diverge and that outcomes for each spouse can be modeled using game theory. In the most widely applied of these models, the cooperative bargaining model of marriage, the utility received by each spouse in the Nash bargaining solution is positively related to the utility of each partner at the "threat point." Most commonly, threat point utility is taken to be the utility that each would receive if the marriage irretrievably broke down, i.e., in the event of divorce. The link to labor force participation is provided by assuming that, if a divorce occurs, each partner will maintain ownership of income received separately within marriage. Thus, a woman who works outside the home will have a higher utility at the threat point and hence a more favorable distribution within marriage. Studies reviewed by Lundberg and Pollak (1996) provide empirical support for this model in their finding that earned or unearned income received by the wife has a different effect on demand patterns than income received by the husband.[4]

Third, shifts in participation are also of importance because they influence the average levels of labor market experience of women, an important determinant of the gender pay gap (Mincer and Polachek 1974). The relationship between rising participation and women's average experience is not obvious a priori (Smith and Ward 1985; Goldin 1990). On the one hand, to the extent that rising participation reflects increased entry of women, female experience levels are likely to be diluted by new entrants. On the other hand, to the extent that participation increases reflect more continuous attachment over the life cycle, experience levels will be raised. While the net effect is an empirical question considered below, in either case, participation trends potentially affect gender differences in labor market outcomes.

7.2.1. Trends in Labor Force Participation: Gender Differences

An extensive literature documents the substantial increases in the labor force participation of women since World War II, including Mincer's (1962a) classic study and the influential papers in Smith (1980). Panel (A) of Table 7.1 illustrates these trends for our time period, while Panel (B) presents comparable tabulations for men. Data are for the standard measure of labor force participation based on survey week status; both the employed and unemployed are included in the labor force.

Table 7.1A

Labor Force Participation Rates of Women by Age and Education, 1970–95

	1970	1980	1990	1995
I. Total	0.490	0.596	0.689	0.715
II. By Age				
Age 25–34	0.456	0.660	0.737	0.745
Age 35–44	0.513	0.660	0.763	0.771
Age 45–54	0.544	0.598	0.706	0.752
Age 55–64	0.437	0.417	0.453	0.492
III. By Age and Education				
A. Education < 12 years	0.430	0.439	0.462	0.472
Age 25–34	0.403	0.490	0.505	0.505
Age 35–44	0.476	0.537	0.569	0.542
Age 45–54	0.479	0.476	0.507	0.538
Age 55–64	0.367	0.308	0.319	0.319
B. Education = 12 years	0.513	0.614	0.687	0.689
Age 25–34	0.455	0.642	0.721	0.722
Age 35–44	0.527	0.676	0.763	0.751
Age 45–54	0.578	0.625	0.716	0.731
Age 55–64	0.494	0.472	0.471	0.490
C. Education 13 to 15 years	0.509	0.665	0.759	0.773
Age 25–34	0.455	0.704	0.780	0.772
Age 35–44	0.527	0.700	0.803	0.824
Age 45–54	0.570	0.666	0.774	0.799
Age 55–64	0.506	0.491	0.555	0.586
D. Education 16 + years	0.608	0.736	0.811	0.828
Age 25–34	0.576	0.775	0.850	0.856
Age 35–44	0.576	0.749	0.824	0.835
Age 45–54	0.674	0.739	0.830	0.856
Age 55–64	0.641	0.545	0.595	0.636

Overall, female participation rose 23 percentage points between 1970 and 1995. While participation increased substantially for all but the oldest age group, the major development of these decades was the substantial rise in participation among younger women due partly to postponements and reductions in fertility and increases in the divorce rate, but also reflecting a substantial rise in labor force attachment among new mothers, especially among married women (e.g., Blau, Ferber, and Winkler 1998; Leibowitz and Klerman 1995). So, for example, published data indicate that the participation rate of married women with children under six rose from 18.6 percent in

1960 to 30.3 percent in 1970 and 63.5 percent in 1995. Participation growth of women slackened in the early 1990s, most notably in the two younger age groups. Given the high rates that their participation had attained by 1990, approximately three-quarters were in the labor force, such a slow-down is perhaps not surprising.

Table 7.1A (continued)

Labor Force Participation Rates of Women by Age and Education, 1970–95

	Change			
	1970–80	1980–90	1990–95	1970–95
I. Total	0.107	0.093	0.025	0.225
II. By Age				
Age 25–34	0.203	0.078	0.007	0.289
Age 35–44	0.147	0.103	0.008	0.258
Age 45–54	0.054	0.108	0.046	0.208
Age 55–64	–0.020	0.036	0.039	0.054
III. By Age and Education				
A. Education < 12 years	0.009	0.023	0.010	0.042
Age 25–34	0.087	0.014	0.000	0.101
Age 35–44	0.061	0.033	–0.027	0.066
Age 45–54	–0.003	0.030	0.031	0.059
Age 55–64	–0.059	0.011	0.001	–0.047
B. Education = 12 years	0.100	0.074	0.002	0.176
Age 25–34	0.187	0.079	0.000	0.267
Age 35–44	0.149	0.088	–0.012	0.224
Age 45–54	0.048	0.091	0.015	0.153
Age 55–64	–0.022	–0.001	0.020	–0.004
C. Education 13 to 15 years	0.156	0.094	0.014	0.264
Age 25–34	0.249	0.075	–0.007	0.317
Age 35–44	0.173	0.103	0.021	0.297
Age 45–54	0.095	0.108	0.025	0.229
Age 55–64	–0.015	0.065	0.031	0.080
D. Education 16 + years	0.127	0.076	0.016	0.219
Age 25–34	0.199	0.075	0.006	0.280
Age 35–44	0.172	0.076	0.011	0.259
Age 45–54	0.065	0.091	0.026	0.181
Age 55–64	–0.096	0.050	0.041	–0.005

Notes: Sample for each year includes all adult civilian women between ages 25 and 64. Labor force participation is measured during the survey week.
Source: Author's tabulations from the March Current Population Surveys.

As Goldin (1990) has shown, increases in female participation patterns have been fueled by rises in participation both across and within cohorts. This may be seen in Table 7.1 which shows, looking across the rows, that more recent cohorts have evinced greater labor force attachment than their predecessors, and, looking diagonally, that participation has also risen within specific cohorts as they age. An exception is that for the oldest age category, 55–64, where retirement begins to occur, there are some small cross-sectional increases due to cohort effects, but declining participation within cohorts (aging from 45–54 to 55–64). Male participation trends shown in Table 7.1B are in some respects the reverse of those for women. As emphasized in work by Juhn (1992), male participation has been declining, even in the prime working ages, though the changes have been considerably less than the shifts in female participation; overall, the male rate fell by 6 points. The net result of these participation trends is that the difference in participation rates between men and women declined substantially between 1970 and 1995 from 45 to 16 percentage points.

As discussed above, rising female labor force participation has ambiguous effects on the average experience levels of employed women depending on the relative importance of increases in entry and reductions in exits (i.e., increasing labor force attachment) in producing the trends. The central finding here too has been one of declining gender differences over this period (e.g., Goldin 1990; Smith and Ward 1985). However, this decrease did not occur immediately even though women's age-specific experience levels began to increase in the 1970s. This is because the especially large increases in participation of younger women which occurred over the decade resulted in a decrease in the average age of women workers (Goldin 1990). This is ironic in that it is precisely this growing labor force attachment of women during the childbearing years which was necessary to increase women's overall experience levels in the long run. In any case, by the 1980s, this process had played itself out and the "experience gap" between men and women began to fall. For example, Blau and Kahn (1997) find that, among full-time workers, the gender difference in full-time experience declined from 7.5 years in 1979 to 4.6 years in 1988; similar trends are reported in O'Neill and Polachek (1993). The gender difference in job tenure (i.e., length of time with an employer) was also reduced (Wellington 1993).

7.2.2. Trends in Labor Force Participation: Differences by Education within Gender Groups

The results presented in Table 7.1 also illustrate the well known strong positive association between educational attainment and labor force participation in each year. Of more significance for trends in well-being, however, are the sharp differences in participation trends by education for both men and women which resulted in a steepening association between education and participation among both groups, with an especially large increase in the participation gap between high school dropouts and others. The sharp declines in participation of less educated men have received considerable attention.

Table 7.1B

Participation Rates Of Men by Age and Education, 1970–95

	1970	1980	1990	1995
I. Total	0.935	0.898	0.888	0.874
II. By Age				
Age 25–34	0.965	0.950	0934	0.926
Age 35–44	0.971	0.953	0.942	0.914
Age 45–54	0.946	0.912	0.904	0.890
Age 55–64	0.834	0.726	0.671	0.661
III. By Age and Education				
A. Education < 12 years	0.893	0.794	0.751	0.720
Age 25–34	0.951	0.892	0.868	0.842
Age 35–44	0.947	0.885	0.818	0.756
Age 45–54	0.916	0.853	0.797	0.733
Age 55–64	0.793	0.621	0.537	0.508
B. Education = 12 years	0.963	0.922	0.899	0.869
Age 25–34	0.982	0.967	0.945	0.928
Age 35–44	0.982	0.965	0.939	0.910
Age 45–54	0.963	0.926	0.911	0.869
Age 55–64	0.888	0.773	0.693	0.650
C. Education 13 to 15 years	0.958	0.927	0.915	0.901
Age 25–34	0.958	0.946	0.942	0.939
Age 35–44	0.988	0.968	0.960	0.933
Age 45–54	0.975	0.929	0919	0.909
Age 55–64	0.875	0.794	0.694	0.704
D. Education 16 + years	0.961	0.955	0.945	0.938
Age 25–34	0.954	0.960	0.952	0.956
Age 35–44	0.988	0.985	0.983	0.970
Age 45–54	0.975	0.972	0.968	0.964
Age 55–64	0.900	0.850	0.797	0.777

Table 7.1B (continued)

Participation Rates Of Men by Age and Education, 1970–95

	Change			
	1970–80	1980–90	1990–95	1970–95
I. Total	–0.037	–0.010	–0.014	–0.061
II. By Age				
Age 25–34	–0.015	–0.015	–0.009	–0.040
Age 35–44	–0.018	–0.011	–0.028	–0.057
Age 45–54	–0.034	–0.007	–0.014	–0.055
Age 55–64	–0.108	–0.055	–0.010	–0.173
III. By Age and Education				
A. Education < 12 years	–0.099	–0.043	–0.032	–0.173
Age 25–34	–0.059	–0.025	–0.025	–0.109
Age 35–44	–0.062	–0.067	–0.061	–0.190
Age 45–54	–0.063	–0.057	–0.064	–0.183
Age 55–64	–0.172	–0.084	–0.030	–0.285
B. Education = 12 years	–0.042	–0.023	–0.030	–0.094
Age 25–34	–0.016	–0.022	–0.017	–0.055
Age 35–44	–0.016	–0.026	–0.029	–0.071
Age 45–54	–0.037	–0.015	–0.042	–0.095
Age 55–64	–0.115	–0.080	–0.043	–0.238
C. Education 13 to 15 years	–0.031	–0.012	–0.014	–0.057
Age 25–34	–0.012	–0.004	–0.003	–0.019
Age 35–44	–0.020	–0.008	–0.027	–0.056
Age 45–54	–0.045	–0.011	–0.010	–0.066
Age 55–64	–0.081	–0.101	0.010	–0.171
D. Education 16 + years	–0.006	–0.010	–0.006	–0.023
Age 25–34	0.006	–0.008	0.004	0.002
Age 35–44	–0.003	–0.001	–0.014	–0.018
Age 45–54	–0.003	–0.004	–0.005	–0.011
Age 55–64	–0.050	–0.053	–0.020	–0.123

Notes: Sample for each year includes all adult civilian men between ages 25 and 64. Labor force participation is measured during the survey week.
Source: Author's tabulations from the March Current Population Surveys.

But it has not been recognized that an analogous pattern of falling relative participation has occurred among women as participation increases of high school dropouts have lagged considerably behind those for other groups. Participation rates of the least educated women, already below those of their more highly educated counterparts in 1970, rose by only 4 percentage points over the 25 year period compared to increases of 19 to 26 points for the other education categories. By 1995, only 47 percent of women with less than a high school education were in the labor force compared to 83 percent of college graduates.

The role of compositional changes in explaining the trends in participation by education is investigated by comparing across and within cohort changes in participation for those with less than 12 years of schooling to the changes for high school and college graduates. Were compositional changes the full explanation for the weakening position of high school dropouts, we would expect to see considerable differences in across cohort changes in participation by education group but relatively little difference in within cohort changes. Table 7.2 which is derived from the data in Table 7.1 presents these comparisons. (Note that the oldest age group is dropped because only the across cohort changes would be available for them.) A positive sign indicates that the change for high school and college graduates is algebraically larger than for high school dropouts, i.e., more positive or less negative.

Table 7.2

Differences In Labor Force Participation Rates by Education, Across and Within Cohorts, 1970–90

	Across Cohort Change		Within Cohort Change	
	1970–80	1980–90	1970–80	1980–90
I. Women				
A. Difference: Ed = 12 minus Ed < 12				
Age 25–34	0.100	0.065	0.087	0.042
Age 35–44	0.088	0.055	0.098	0.071
Age 45–54	0.050	0.060	0.065	0.003
B. Difference: Ed = 16+ minus Ed < 12				
Age 25–34	0.112	0.060	0.039	–0.030
Age 35–44	0.111	0.043	0.162	0.112
Age 45–54	0.067	0.060	0.041	0.013
II. Men				
A. Difference: Ed = 12 minus Ed < 12				
Age 25–34	0.043	0.003	0.049	0.047
Age 35–44	0.045	0.041	0.038	0.034
Age 45–54	0.025	0.041	0.104	0.083
B. Difference: Ed = 16+ minus Ed < 12				
Age 25–34	0.064	0.017	0.096	0.098
Age 35–44	0.058	0.066	0.078	0.072
Age 45–54	0.060	0.053	0.170	0.141

Notes: Calculated from results presented in Table 7.1. Illustrating for the 1970-80 participation change of the 25-34 year age group, the "across" cohort change is the difference between the participation rate of the 25-34 year age group in 1970 and 1980; the "within" cohort change is the difference between the participation rate of the 25-34 year age group in 1970 and the 35-44 year age group in 1980.

Looking first at the results for women shown in panel I of the table, we see that, for the comparisons of high school dropouts to high school graduates, all the within and across cohort comparisons indicate a growing gap in participation between the two groups and all but one of the within cohort changes are quite similar in magnitude to the corresponding across cohort changes. The exception is that, by the 1980s, the size of the within cohort participation reduction as 45–54 year olds aged to 55–64 was similar for high school dropouts and high school graduates. Similarly, with one exception, the comparisons between high school dropouts and college graduates indicate a widening difference between the two groups over time both across and within cohorts. The exception is for the 25–34 year age group: within cohort increases in participation were smaller for college graduates than for high school dropouts over the 1980s. Similarly, over the 1970s, the within cohort advantage for college graduates was considerably smaller than their across cohort advantage. These results are likely due to the tendency of female college graduates to delay childbearing; thus, many of them are making first transitions into parenthood as they age from 25–34 to 35–44, at the same time that many women with a high school education or less are experiencing diminished child care responsibilities as their children get older and more self-sufficient. It may also be noted that the participation rate for college graduates in this age group was already extremely high by 1980 (77.5), thus limiting the scope for further increases and making their within cohort participation rate increase of 5 points particularly impressive. Finally, as was the case for the comparison with high school graduates, the participation rate drops off as the 45 to 54 year olds aged over the 1980s was similar for high school dropouts and college graduates.

Taken as a whole, these results strongly suggest that compositional factors are not the full explanation for the growing disparity in participation rates between high school dropouts and more highly educated women. The results for males shown in the lower portion of the table are, if anything, even stronger in this regard, indicating that the within cohort changes are consistently larger than the corresponding across cohort changes. Thus for males as well it appears that the declining relative participation of the least educated does not merely reflect compositional shifts.

Our discussion has focused on the labor force participation trends which show strikingly similar patterns for men and women of decreasing relative labor force participation among the less educated. Findings by Coleman and Pencavel (1993a; 1993b) strongly suggest that the patterns noted here also prevail along other dimensions of labor supply. They document remarkably similar trends of rising annual hours worked for well-educated male and female workers since 1940 and decreasing trends in annual hours among the less educated. The changes in magnitude were larger for women than for men. Further evidence of the deteriorating labor market position of less-skilled workers is presented by Farber (1995) who finds a decrease in the probability of being in long duration jobs for less educated men between 1973 and 1993, while women with at least a high school education were more likely to be in such jobs.

7.2.3. Explaining the Trends

In his pioneering study of the post-World War II increase in married women's labor force participation, Mincer (1962a) concluded that the rise was due to a dominance of the positive substitution effect generated by increases in wives' own wages over the negative income effect associated with increases in the real wages of their husbands. Extrapolating to our period of stagnating real wages for men, it would be tempting to suggest that married women's participation increased over the 1970s and 1980s at least in part to compensate for the disappointing wage growth of their husbands. This is the question posed in a study by Juhn and Murphy (1997) which convincingly demonstrates that, while such an interpretation appears plausible at the aggregate level, it does not match up well with the cross-sectional evidence. They find that the declines in male employment and earnings have been greatest for low wage men, but employment and earnings gains have been largest for wives of middle and high wage men.[5] Moreover, for married women, the positive relationship between employment and own wages has grown stronger over time while the negative relationship between employment and husband's earnings has grown weaker. Based on these findings, they conclude, as did Mincer (1962a), that own wage effects continue to dominate cross effects between husband and wife in accounting for changes in female employment.

These findings not only help to illuminate the aggregate participation trends, but also shed light on the widening differences in participation across education groups. As we shall see below, more highly educated women have experienced faster real wage growth than less educated women, and real wage declines have occurred for high school dropouts. Because women tend to marry men with similar levels of education, low wage couples tend to be comprised of men and women with low levels of education. Thus, the labor force participation rates of husbands and wives in these families has been declining relative to the participation rates of higher wage, more highly educated couples who experienced faster real wage growth for both partners. More generally, this suggests that worsening relative wage prospects for less educated women underlie their declining relative participation just as has been found to be the case in studies of male labor force participation (Juhn 1992; Pencavel 1997).

As discussed in detail below, another important development during the 1970–95 period was the especially large increase in the incidence of single-headed families among less educated women and blacks. Nonetheless, Table 7.3 which shows participation trends by education, headship, and race suggests that the differences in the overall participation trends across education groups were driven by the trends for married women. For all races combined, married women's participation rates rose by 8 percentage points among high school dropouts, but by 22 points among high school graduates, and by 29 points among women with some college. Differences in trends by education were much smaller for single heads and others. Moreover, the participation rates of high school dropouts were fairly similar across headship/marital status categories in 1995, with the highest rate being 49 percent for single heads. Thus, a slower growth in female headship would not have raised the participation rate of less educated women as a whole. Because the slow rise of participation rates among married women appears to be primarily responsible for the declining relative participation of less educated women, welfare is unlikely to have played a major role in explaining it. This conclusion is reinforced by Moffitt's (1992) finding based on an extensive review of the literature that higher AFDC guarantee levels have only a small negative effect on the labor supply of female family heads.

Table 7.3

Labor Force Participation Rates of Women by Headship, Education, and Race, 1970–95

	All			Whites			Blacks		
	1970	1995	Change 1970–95	1970	1995	Change 1970–95	1970	1995	Change 1970–95
I. Total	0.490	0.715	0.225	0.479	0.719	0.240	0.590	0.704	0.114
II. Education < 12 years									
Married, Spouse Present	0.393	0.469	0.076	0.380	0.466	0.086	0.500	0.531	0.031
Single Head	0.520	0.487	–0.033	0.531	0.514	–0.018	0.504	0.449	–0.055
Other	0.549	0.464	–0.085	0.544	0.478	–0.066	0.564	0.406	–0.158
III. Education = 12 years									
Married, Spouse Present	0.453	0.668	0.215	0.443	0.667	0.223	0.613	0.699	0.086
Single Head	0.762	0.722	–0.040	0.776	0.754	–0.022	0.714	0.653	–0.061
Other	0.795	0.742	–0.053	0.798	0.756	–0.041	0.767	0.686	–0.081
IV. Education > 12 years									
Married, Spouse Present	0.476	0.767	0.291	0.458	0.763	0.305	0.805	0.838	0.033
Single Head	0.785	0.851	0.066	0.784	0.863	0.079	0.791	0.826	0.035
Other	0.843	0.863	0.021	0.835	0.868	0.033	0.921	0.860	–0.061

Notes: Sample for each year includes all adult civilian women between ages 25 and 64. Labor force participation is measured during the survey week.
Source: Author's tabulations from the March Current Population Surveys.

Over the 1970-1995 period, there have been significant declines in the participation rates of blacks relative to whites. Among men this has taken the form of faster declines in participation among blacks. As may be seen in Table 7.3, among women this was due to considerably slower increases in participation among blacks than whites; by 1995, the historic participation advantage of black women had been eliminated. Table 7.3 also indicates that smaller participation increases for black women prevailed within all education and headship categories. Analyzing the growing overall race gap in employment rates among men, Juhn (1992) finds that declining wage opportunities for the low skilled combined with the lower education levels of black men explain a substantial part of the differences between blacks and whites. However, a significant component cannot be explained and is consistent with an inward shift in the supply curve of black males. A similar analysis of the slower growth of participation among black women and the role of behavior shifts versus labor market opportunities in producing it would be extremely valuable.

Rising educational attainment of women is also a factor in their increasing labor force participation via its impact on wages. The causation likely runs in the opposite direction as well: as women expect to participate in the labor force more continuously over the life cycle, they will be inclined to invest more in their human capital. While years of education have increased at only a slightly faster pace for women than men, women have been increasingly pursuing college, graduate and professional education and entering traditionally male fields of study (Blau, Ferber, and Winkler 1998; Jacobs 1995). While a human capital explanation for the educational shifts fits well in some respects, it should also be pointed out that, to the extent that women's expectations of encountering labor market discrimination have deterred their educational investments in the past,[6] expectations of reductions in discrimination would encourage them to invest more and to enter traditionally male fields.

Demographic factors have also contributed to the aggregate increases in labor supply for women. Decreases in fertility, declines in marriage rates, and increases in marital breakup move women into categories with higher participation rates (e.g., Goldin 1990). Moreover, there is some evidence that the higher probability of divorce has increased the participation rates of married women (Johnson and Skinner 1986). Of course to some extent these demographic trends may themselves be due to rising market opportunities for women (Becker 1991).

Of considerable importance in understanding the reasons for the intertemporal shifts in women's participation is the evidence that changes in measured variables, including wages and demographic factors can explain only a portion of the observed increase; frequently only a small portion. So, for example, focusing on the traditional economic variables, Juhn and Murphy (1997) find that increases in women's real wages can explain only 6–7 percent of the total increase in women's employment between 1969 and 1989. While changes in demographic factors likely explain some of the remainder, behavioral shifts even in the impact of demographic factors have played a part as well. Of particular significance, not just for the level of women's participation, but also for its growing consistency over the life cycle is that young children exert a smaller negative influence on wives' participation than formerly (Leibowitz and Klerman 1995).

Thus, a considerable portion of the change over time in female participation remains "unexplained" by variables conventionally used in our analyses. As we shall see, this appears to be the case in each of the broad areas examined. During a period of major shifts in gender roles, it is perhaps not surprising that a significant portion of the explanation for the changes in participation appear to be due to behavioral shifts of unknown or at least unquantified origin. Moreover, it can be informative to ascertain what particular aspects of behavior have changed. So, for example, the findings of a diminished negative effect on female participation of young children and higher husband's income, and of a growing positive effect of own wages, suggest that women's economic role within the family has changed and that their participation is increasingly determined by their own opportunities and less by the demographic and economic circumstances of their families.[7]

7.3. Labor Market Outcomes: Wages and Occupational Distributions

The inclusion of wages as an indicator of economic well-being requires little justification because they are of obvious fundamental importance as a major determinant of economic welfare for employed individuals, as well as of the potential gain to market employment for those not currently employed. Further they serve as a significant input into a myriad of decisions ranging from labor supply to marriage and fertility (Becker 1991), as well as a factor potentially influencing bargaining power and relative status within the family.

A major motive for considering sex differences in occupational distributions derives from their association with earnings. Considerable research suggests that predominantly female occupations pay less, even controlling for measured personal characteristics of workers and a variety of characteristics of occupations and industries.[8] Occupational differences between men and women may reflect differences in preferences or discrimination. It is not an easy matter to distinguish between these two empirically, and of course the outcome may reflect a combination of both. While most would allow that gender differences in preferences play some role, and there is considerable evidence to support that view (e.g., Gunderson 1989), the claim that discrimination is also important is more controversial. Some of the more convincing evidence of the importance of discrimination comes from descriptions of institutional barriers that have historically excluded women from particular pursuits or impeded their progress (e.g., Reskin and Hartmann 1986). In addition the finding that women are less likely to be promoted, all else equal, is also suggestive though it suffers from the standard problems of this type of exercise discussed at greater length below.[9] Moreover, to the extent that less on-the-job training occurs in female than in male jobs, the incentives for women to participate in the labor force continuously are increased when women enter traditionally male jobs. This is the case whether the changes are due to voluntary choice or declines in discrimination. It might also be argued that the tie to earnings is not the only reason for including occupations as an indicator of well-being. Occupational segregation itself may have deleterious effects on women's economic status by reinforcing exaggerated notions of gender differences in capabilities, preferences, and social and economic roles. Such views could adversely affect the labor market outcomes even of women who enter traditionally male pursuits. In addition to occupation, we also consider the growth in self-employment of women as at least potentially indicating an expansion in opportunities.

7.3.1. Issues in Measuring Wages

An important factor in interpreting our results for wages and other labor market outcomes is that they may be affected by changes over time in the self-selection of individuals into the labor force This is of particular concern in a study focusing on women because there have been considerable increases in their labor force participation rates over time, as well as differences in growth rates across education categories. Two types of selectivity are potentially at issue. The first relates to changes in the degree of self-selection by measured characteristics, as, for example, more highly educated women experience faster increases in participation. This type of selection is of lesser concern because all our results are disaggregated by important measured characteristics, i.e., education and age, thus in effect adjusting for such shifts. (Although it should be noted that age is a much poorer proxy for labor market experience for women than it is for men.) In addition, studies of the impact of changes in men's and women's measured characteristics, including actual labor market experience, on the gender gap over time are reviewed below.

Of considerably greater concern, however, are changes in the degree of selectivity of workers on the basis of their unmeasured characteristics; this important issue was brought to the fore in the highly influential work of Heckman (1980). The expected effect of this factor on the trends is uncertain. It is theoretically possible for labor force participants to be either a positively selected group of those with especially high wage offers, controlling for measured characteristics, or a negatively selected group of those with especially low values of nonmarket time, all else equal. In the former case, an increase in the relative size of the labor force group is likely to make it less positively selected. In the latter case, an expansion of the labor force could result in its becoming less negatively selected. A conventional approach to adjusting for selectivity bias in unmeasured characteristics is to employ a Heckman (1980) selectivity bias correction to obtain consistent estimates of the coefficients in the earnings equation. Using this approach, it would be possible to obtain estimated mean male and female wage offers after adjusting for selectivity bias. Such parametric models have, however, been criticized for their lack of robustness: "seemingly small misspecifications [including heteroskedasticity and nonnormality] may generate large biases in estimates" (Manski 1989: 356). For this reason, I do not employ such an approach here. If we take as the most plausible scenario that the female labor force has become less positively selected over time as it has grown, the degree of closing of the gender wage gap is understated in the results presented below, but, as our discussion above suggests, the possibility that women's relative wage growth is overstated cannot be completely ruled out. It may be noted, however, that where the Heckman correction has been used, it has uniformly been found that women narrowed the gender wage gap even after such an adjustment (Blau and Beller 1988 – discussed in Chapter 2; and Wellington 1993).

To study trends in wages, it is necessary to define an earnings measure for the CPS data which adjusts for time input. Weekly wages, defined for the calendar year preceding the survey, are used here; they are computed as annual earnings divided by annual weeks worked for full-time workers. This measure is employed because it is available in comparable form for each of the sample years; computation of a comparable hourly wage variable is complicated by the absence of data on usual weekly hours in the 1970 CPS. The issues involved are considered at greater length in the Data Appendix. A final point to note is that money wages, however measured, are an incomplete indicator of total compensation which would take into account not only nonwage benefits but also compensating differentials for job amenities. This is far from a trivial issue and particularly the latter is a concern given the likelihood of substantial differences in occupational preferences between men and women. Complex issues are also raised with respect to nonwage benefits because, in some instances, married women may be covered under their husbands' plans, thus reducing their demand for these benefits. Unfortunately, a full consideration of these issues would take us well beyond the scope of this chapter; at the same time the relevant data and prior research needed for such an investigation are considerably sparser than one would like. Thus the focus here is on the traditional wage.

Table 7.4

Female-Male Weekly Wage Ratios by Age and Education, 1969–94 (Full-Time Workers)

	Ratio				Percent Change			
	1969	1979	1989	1994	1969–79	1979–89	1989–94	1969–94
I. All workers	0.562	0.583	0.682	0.717	3.87	17.00	5.00	27.61
Age 25–34	0.598	0.665	0.785	0.827	11.20	18.06	5.37	38.33
Age 35–44	0.520	0.542	0.664	0.720	4.29	22.53	8.37	38.49
Age 45–54	0.541	0.535	0.620	0.651	−1.16	16.03	5.00	20.43
Age 55–64	0.600	0.554	0.582	0.615	−7.66	5.03	5.78	2.59
II. Education < 12 years	0.560	0.568	0.682	0.670	1.48	20.08	−1.79	19.67
Age 25–34	0.556	0.630	0.738	0.713	13.34	17.02	−3.32	28.22
Age 35–44	0.546	0.581	0.685	0.639	6.28	17.94	−6.74	16.89
Age 45–54	0.557	0.532	0.660	0.662	−4.48	24.00	0.36	18.87
Age 55–64	0.574	0.558	0.603	0.607	−2.84	8.09	0.77	5.82
III. Education = 12 years	0.553	0.577	0.662	0.710	4.22	14.79	7.24	28.30
Age 25–34	0.577	0.621	0.712	0.779	7.60	14.67	9.42	35.00
Age 35–44	0.526	0.539	0.657	0.700	2.53	21.95	6.42	33.06
Age 45–54	0.536	0.558	0.596	0.651	4.00	6.91	9.22	21.44
Age 55–64	0.563	0.567	0.606	0.633	0.83	6.83	4.44	12.51
IV. Education 13 to 15 years	0.568	0.608	0.680	0.715	7.06	11.89	5.11	25.91
Age 25–34	0.617	0.676	0.748	0.776	9.54	10.59	3.78	25.71
Age 35–44	0.538	0.565	0.665	0.711	4.93	17.68	6.93	32.05
Age 45–54	0.526	0.557	0.641	0.681	5.76	15.13	6.32	29.45
Age 55–64	0.569	0.534	0.612	0.663	−6.15	14.67	8.29	16.54
V. Education 16 + years	0.589	0.598	0.694	0.722	1.51	16.01	4.03	22.52
Age 25–34	0.660	0.715	0.796	0.831	8.36	11.34	4.34	25.89
Age 35–44	0.554	0.561	0.698	0.736	1.36	24.40	5.49	33.02
Age 45–54	0.540	0.526	0.645	0.685	−2.64	22.63	6.25	26.85
Age 55–64	0.542	0.570	0.617	0.647	5.17	8.34	4.80	19.40

Notes: The sample for each year includes full-time workers between ages 25 and 64. The weekly wage ratio is calculated as $WAGE_w/WAGE_m$, where $WAGE_w$ is the mean weekly wage of women and $WAGE_m$ is the mean weekly wage of men. See the Data Appendix for additional sample restrictions and wage definitions.

Source: Author's tabulations from the March Current Population Surveys.

7.3.2. *Trends in the Gender Wage Gap*

Gender wage ratios for all workers and for age and education categories separately are shown in Table 7.4. Overall, there has been a substantial reduction in the gender gap over the past 25 years as the gender ratio rose from 56.2 percent in 1969 to 71.7 percent in 1994. For the most part, gains were concentrated in the post-1979 period, as has been noted in a number of previous studies, although some progress is discernible among younger women in the earlier decade.[10] The largest increases were during the 1980s, but progress continued at a slower rate in the early 1990s. Women in all age and education groups substantially narrowed the gap with their male counterparts; increases were largest for women in the younger two age groups, 25–34 and 35–44, and smallest for those over 54. Relative gains were fairly similar in magnitude for high school graduates and women with some college. Increases were a bit lower among college graduates, but they started and ended the period with the highest gender ratios. While relative gains were actually a bit greater for high school dropouts over the 1980s, progress for them lagged over the early 1990s, and, by 1994, they had the lowest gender ratio.

7.3.3. Trends in Real Wages and Differences in Wage Gains Within Gender Groups

The declining gender gap has also meant that women as a group fared better than men in terms of real wage growth. Table 7.5 shows percentage changes in real weekly wages; adjusted using the 1990 Implicit Price Deflator. Overall, women's real wages increased by 31 percent between 1969 and 1994; rising at a similar average annual rate in the 1970s and 1980s, and at a somewhat slower pace in the early 1990s. In contrast, as has been widely noted, men's real wages stagnated, rising by only 3 percent over the 25 year period. If the Consumer Price Index had been employed to adjust for inflation, the real wage gains for women would have been smaller and men's real wages would have declined somewhat.[11]

Table 7.5 also shows that, as has been widely found by other researchers, more educated men fared better than less educated men in terms of real wage growth in the post-1980 period and cumulatively for the two decades (e.g., Juhn, Murphy, and Pierce 1993). Less well known is that a similar pattern prevailed among women. Real wage gains between 1969 and 1994 were 20.3 percent for female college graduates and 8 to 9 percent for women with high school degrees or some college, while real wages fell by 2.2 percent for high school dropouts. As was the case for men, declines in real wages among the least educated women were especially large for the younger two age groups, falling by 6.4 to 8.0 percent. For each educational group, however, the experience of women was more favorable than that of the corresponding male group. The real wages of male high school dropouts, for example, fell by 18.3 percent between 1969 and 1994, declining by 27.0 percent for the youngest men, while the real wages of male college graduates decreased by only 1.8 percent.

Table 7.5

Percentage Changes In Real Weekly Wages, by Sex, Age and Education, 1969–94
(Full-Time Workers)

	Women				Men			
	1969–79	1979–89	1989–94	1969–94	1969–79	1979–89	1989–94	1969–94
I. All workers	12.07	11.98	4.51	31.15	7.90	–4.29	–0.47	2.78
Age 25–34	13.30	6.78	–0.56	20.31	1.89	–9.56	–5.62	–13.03
Age 35–44	15.73	16.41	4.48	40.76	10.96	–4.99	–3.59	1.64
Age 45–54	10.72	15.83	7.65	38.06	12.01	–0.17	2.52	14.64
Age 55–64	8.12	7.12	7.43	24.42	17.08	1.99	1.56	21.28
II. Education < 12 years	7.18	–1.79	–7.11	–2.23	5.62	–18.21	–5.42	–18.30
Age 25–34	9.37	–7.33	–7.69	–6.44	–3.50	–20.81	–4.52	–27.03
Age 35–44	8.39	0.50	–15.57	–8.03	1.99	–14.79	–9.46	–21.32
Age 45–54	6.07	2.18	–2.95	5.19	11.05	–17.59	–3.30	–11.51
Age 55–64	7.42	–2.55	0.87	5.60	10.56	–9.84	0.11	–0.21
III. Education = 12 years	7.02	1.95	–0.71	8.33	2.69	–11.18	–7.42	–15.56
Age 25–34	7.73	–2.56	–1.16	3.76	0.12	–15.02	–9.67	–23.14
Age 35–44	7.76	5.29	–4.42	8.44	5.10	–13.66	–10.19	–18.50
Age 45–54	8.20	4.28	0.63	13.54	4.04	–2.46	–7.86	–6.50
Age 55–64	6.81	–0.01	3.04	10.05	5.92	–6.40	–1.33	–2.18
IV. Education 13 to 15 years	2.53	6.71	–0.34	9.05	–4.23	–4.63	–5.18	–13.39
Age 25–34	6.72	0.51	–3.77	3.22	–2.57	–9.11	–7.28	–17.89
Age 35–44	2.40	9.70	–0.31	11.99	–2.42	–6.78	–6.77	–15.19
Age 45–54	4.08	12.25	–1.91	14.59	–1.59	–2.50	–7.74	–11.48
Age 55–64	–0.29	8.94	1.01	9.72	6.25	–5.00	–6.72	–5.85
V. Education 16 + years	–2.00	16.26	5.55	20.26	–3.46	0.22	1.45	–1.84
Age 25–34	–0.18	15.52	–1.21	13.92	–7.88	3.75	–5.32	–9.51
Age 35–44	4.37	15.74	9.22	31.93	2.97	–6.97	3.53	–0.82
Age 45–54	–2.01	15.40	5.60	19.42	0.65	–5.89	–0.61	–5.86
Age 55–64	8.37	5.45	0.84	15.24	3.05	–2.66	–3.78	–3.49

Notes: The sample for each year includes full-time workers between ages 25 and 64. Wages are expressed in 1990 dollars, adjusted for inflation using the Implicit Price Deflator. See the Data Appendix for additional sample restrictions and wage definitions.
Source: Author's tabulations from the March Current Population Surveys.

Patterns of men's and women's real wage growth by education differed between the 1970s and the 1980s. These differences were related to movements in the return to a college education which fell in the 1970s, for both men and women, but has risen for both groups since then (Katz and Murphy 1992). Thus, the disparity in the experience of real wage growth among education categories was more pronounced in the 1980s and 1990s than for the period as a whole. Since 1979, the real wages of female college graduates have risen by 22.7 percent, while the real wages of female high school dropouts fell by 8.8 percent.

Finally, we may consider whether the declining relative wages of the least educated which are observed across cohorts represent a true change in outcomes or whether they can be entirely explained by compositional changes. In Table 7.6, I seek to shed light on this issue by comparing across and within cohort changes in real wages by education group. Again, the focus is on the comparison of the across and within cohort changes of high school dropouts to high school and college graduates shown in panels A and B. For women, we see that the within cohort changes generally exhibit the same basic pattern of changes for high school dropouts relative to the others as the across cohort changes. Moreover, the across and within cohort changes are quite similar in magnitude in the 1980s, the key period during which high school dropouts lost ground.

Table 7.6

Differences In Percentage Changes In Real Wages By Education Across and Within Cohorts, 1969–89

	Across Cohort Change		Within Cohort Change	
	1969–79	1979–89	1969–79	1979–89
I. Women				
A. Difference: Ed = 12 minus Ed < 12				
Age 25–34	–1.64	4.78	–2.53	4.26
Age 35–44	–0.63	4.79	1.12	3.83
Age 45–54	2.12	2.10	1.94	2.37
B. Difference: Ed = 16+ minus Ed < 12				
Age 25–34	–9.55	22.85	–0.25	27.40
Age 35–44	–4.02	15.24	–4.19	13.32
Age 45–54	–8.09	13.22	1.56	18.32
II. Men				
A. Difference: Ed = 12 minus Ed < 12				
Age 25–34	3.62	5.79	10.27	6.58
Age 35–44	3.12	1.13	–8.17	5.98
Age 45–54	–7.02	15.14	–3.85	5.81
B. Difference: Ed = 16+ minus Ed < 12				
Age 25–34	–4.38	24.56	24.86	39.09
Age 35–44	0.98	7.82	–1.54	10.56
Age 45–54	–10.41	11.70	–3.90	12.62

Notes: Illustrating for the 25–34 year age group in 1969–79, the "across" cohort change is the percentage change in the real wage of the 25–34 year age group between 1969 and 1979; the "within" cohort change is the percentage difference between the real wage of the 25–34 year age group in 1969 and the 35–44 year age group in 1979. See Table 7.5 and the Data Appendix for additional information.

Source: Author's tabulations from the March Current Population Surveys.

The same is true for males. As in the case of the participation trends, there is no evidence that the age specific trends identified for high school dropouts are merely due to shifts in the composition of this group.

7.3.4. Trends in Gender Differences in Occupations and Self-Employment

For many decades a high degree of segregation of men and women into different occupations appeared to be an unchanging feature of the labor market (Blau, Ferber, and Winkler 1998). A substantial break with this pattern occurred in the 1970s when occupational segregation began to decline noticeably (Beller 1985). This progress has continued into the 1980s (e.g., Jacobsen 1994; and Blau, Simpson, and Anderson 1997). Differences between women and men in occupations across a wide number of categories may be summarized by a segregation index which gives the percentage of women (or men) who would have to change jobs for the occupational distribution of the two groups to be the same. Estimates based on Census data for a comparable set of 470 detailed occupations indicate that the index fell by 11 to 12 percent in each decade, declining from 67.7 in 1970 to 59.3 in 1980 and 53 in 1990 (Blau, Simpson, and Anderson 1997).

Changes in the extent of segregation may be due to shifts in sex composition within occupations (i.e., integration of formerly male or female occupations) or shifts in occupation mix (i.e., growth in the size of integrated occupations or decreases in the size of male or female occupations). Changes in the sex composition of occupations were the predominant cause of the decrease in segregation in both the 1970s and 1980s, suggesting expanding opportunities for women played a significant role, although changing occupational mix was of more importance in the latter period (Blau, Simpson, and Anderson 1997). In terms of segregation per se, female college graduates made the fastest progress in reducing the segregation index over the decade and by 1990 the index was 46 among college graduates compared to 56–58 for less educated women (Jacobsen 2007).[12]

Another striking trend during our period is a substantial increase in the self-employment rate of women which rose over 60 percent from 4.1 percent in 1975 to 6.7 percent in 1990, compared to a 20 percent increase for men to 12.4.[13] Thus women have reduced the "self-employment gap" with men, increasing from less than one quarter to nearly one third of self-employed workers (Devine 1994a).

Similarly, a larger rise in female than in male self-employment prevailed within each of a large number of racial and ethnic groups included in a study (Fairlie and Meyer 1996). However, while the rise in female self-employment was fairly broad-based, here too the least skilled, as measured by quartile in the distribution of potential wage and salary earnings, have lagged (Devine 1994b).

An interesting question which has not yet been addressed is the relationship between the changes in the occupational distribution of women and their increased incidence of self-employment. As women have entered traditionally male pursuits, the opportunities for self-employment have likely increased. In evaluating the implications of the growth in self-employment for women's well-being, however, it should be noted that, for workers of both sexes, this expansion likely reflects, at least in part, the increase in independent contractors who comprise one component of the growing "nonstandard" workforce (that is, workers who do not have "regular" full-time jobs).[14] Nonetheless, a study by Lombard (2001) found that the rising earnings potential of women in self-employment compared to the wage and salary sector explains most of the upward trend in the self-employment of married women between 1970 and 1990. This suggests that the growing move of women into self-employment does represent an expansion in their opportunities.

7.3.5. *Explaining the Trends in Wages: The Overall Gender Gap*

As we have seen, the narrowing of the gender gap since 1980 has taken place in an environment of sharply rising wage inequality. Wage inequality has been increasing for women since at least 1979, and for men since 1970. The most widely accepted explanation for this trend links it to a rise in the returns to skill caused by an outward shift in the relative demand for highly-skilled workers (e.g., Katz and Murphy 1992; Juhn, Murphy, and Pierce 1993). This demand shift has in turn been related to such economy-wide forces as technological change and the impact of international trade. Institutional factors like the decline in unionism and the falling real value of the minimum wage may have also played a role. What is the relationship between these developments and trends in the gender wage gap?

An insightful paper by Juhn, Murphy, and Pierce (1991) suggests how these aggregate trends may influence the wage outcomes of particular demographic groups. Juhn, Murphy, and Pierce (1991) were concerned with explaining the slowing of convergence black and white wages among males over the late 1970s and the 1980s. (A similar slowing of race convergence occurred among women; see, e.g., Blau, Ferber, and Winkler 1998). Their approach not only links the outcomes of particular groups to the widening wage inequality which has been a dominant labor market trend of this period, but also introduces a new factor into the analysis of demographic wage differentials. Traditional analyses focus on what might be termed "group-specific" factors, i.e., the group's relative skills and the extent of labor market discrimination against them. However, outcomes for particular groups are also affected by "wage structure" in general. I would define wage structure to include overall skill prices and rents received for employment in favored sectors, although Juhn, Murphy, and Pierce (1991) emphasize the former. Because blacks are on average less skilled than whites, Juhn, Murphy, and Pierce show that they were especially adversely affected by trends in skill prices and that this helps to explain the slowing of convergence in the race gap.

The reasoning which Juhn, Murphy, and Pierce (1991) apply to understanding the trends in the race gap is applicable to understanding trends in gender wage differentials. Thus, while there have been a number of useful studies of the sources of the narrowing of the gender gap, including O'Neill and Polacheck (1993) and Wellington (1993), I focus on one by Blau and Kahn (1997) and discussed in Chapter 2, which incorporates these insights. As Blau and Kahn point out, analyzing women's progress in Juhn, Murphy, and Pierce's framework raises something of a paradox. As the prices of measured skills and rewards for employment in high-paying sectors have risen, women, who continue to have less experience, on average, and to be located in lower-paying occupations and industries, should have been increasingly disadvantaged. Yet the gender wage gap has declined substantially.

Blau and Kahn (1997) investigate this issue using data from the Michigan Panel Study of Income Dynamics.[15] They find that rising inequality and higher rewards to skills did indeed retard women's progress during the 1980s, "reclaiming" about one-third to two-fifths of women's potential gains in relative wages. The substantial decline in the male-female pay gap which nonetheless occurred is traced to "gender-specific" factors which were more than sufficient to counterbalance changes in both measured and unmeasured prices which worked against women. Specifically, improvements in women's relative qualifications and the "unexplained" portion of the pay gap declined substantially.

A decline in the unexplained gap is generally viewed as reflecting either an upgrading of women's unmeasured labor market skills or a decline in labor market discrimination against them. This ambiguity is due to the fact that empirical evidence for discrimination relies on the existence of a residual gender pay gap which cannot be explained by gender differences in measured qualifications. This accords well with the economic definition of labor market discrimination, i.e., pay differences between groups that are not explained by productivity differences, but may also reflect group differences in unmeasured qualifications. If men are more highly endowed with respect to these omitted variables then we would overestimate discrimination. Alternatively, if some of the factors controlled for (e.g., occupation, industry) themselves reflect the impact of discrimination, then discrimination will be underestimated. Blau and Kahn report that, controlling for human capital characteristics, including education and actual labor market experience, women earned 71.5 percent as much as men in 1979 and 80.5 percent in 1988. When the authors further control for major occupation and industry and for unionism, the ratio rose from 77.6 percent in 1979 to 88.2 percent in 1988.

Table 7.7

Impact of Changes In Characteristics on Changes in Men's and Women's Log Real Wages and The Gender Gap, 1979–88 (1983 Dollars)

	Men's Wages	Women's Wages	Gender Gap
I. All Workers			
Total Change	–0.104	0.048	–0.152
Due to: All Characteristics	–0.014	0.116	–0.124
Education Variables	0.040	0.049	–0.009
Experience Variables	–0.018	0.040	–0.053
Occupation Variables	0.002	0.048	–0.046
Collective Bargaining	–0.028	–0.011	–0.018
Industry Variables	–0.009	–0.011	0.001
II. Low Skill Group (0–20 in 1979)			
Total Change	–0.268	–0.159	–0.109
Due to: All Characteristics	–0.069	0.015	–0.083
Education Variables	0.030	0.019	0.011
Experience Variables	–0.006	0.005	–0.012
Occupation Variables	–0.009	0.032	–0.041
Collective Bargaining	–0.051	–0.029	–0.022
Industry Variables	–0.028	–0.016	–0.012

Table 7.7 (continued)

Impact of Changes In Characteristics on Changes in Men's and Women's Log Real Wages and The Gender Gap, 1979–88 (1983 Dollars)

	Men's Wages	Women's Wages	Gender Gap
III. Middle Skill Group (20–80 in 1979)			
Total Change	–0.144	–0.037	–0.107
Due to: All Characteristics	–0.067	0.003	–0.070
Education Variables	0.020	0.011	0.009
Experience Variables	–0.021	0.002	–0.024
Occupation Variables	–0.006	0.025	–0.031
Collective Bargaining	–0.046	–0.019	–0.027
Industry Variables	–0.011	–0.012	0.001
IV. High Skill Group (80–100 in 1979)			
Total Change	–0.038	0.080	–0.118
Due to: All Characteristics	–0.033	0.065	–0.098
Education Variables	0.008	0.026	–0.018
Experience Variables	–0.040	0.001	–0.040
Occupation Variables	–0.025	0.035	–0.060
Collective Bargaining	0.001	0.000	0.001
Industry Variables	0.023	0.004	0.019

Notes: These results are from Blau and Kahn (1997) and include some additional calculations. Data are from the Michigan Panel Study of Income Dynamics for 1980 and 1989. Wages are defined as annual average hourly earnings. Individuals are divided into skill groups based on their predicted wages using estimated coefficients from an overall male OLS regression estimated pooling 1979 and 1988 wage data which controls for education (years of schooling and dummy variables for college and advanced degrees), actual experience, actual experience squared, and year. In 1979, allocation to skill groups is determined by the own sex percentile ranking of the individual's predicted wage as follows: low-skill group (0–20); middle-skill group (20–80); high-skill group (80–100). Individuals are allocated to skill groups in 1989 based on the 1979 cut-offs for predicted wages. Thus the size of each skill group can change. For further details, see Blau and Kahn (1997).

The entries in the columns headed "men's wages" and "women's wages" show the contribution of changes in the means of the indicated category of variables to the 1979–88 change in the mean of real log wages for males and females respectively. This is calculated for all workers and separately by skill groups. The contribution of the indicated variables is:

$$(\overline{X}_1 - \overline{X}_0)\hat{\beta}_{1m}$$

where $\hat{\beta}_{1m}$ is a vector of coefficients from an OLS regression estimated for males overall or in the indicated skill group in 1988, and $\overline{X}_t$ is a vector of own means of the variables (i.e., for men or women) either overall or in the indicated skill group in year t (1 = 1988 and 0 = 1979). The results are based on the "full specification" reported in Blau and Kahn (1977) and include controls for education and experience (as described above), as well as dummy variables for major industry and occupation, and unionism. The difference in the entries for men and women is equal to the contribution of changes in the indicated characteristics to the change in the gender gap.

Source: Blau and Kahn (1997).

These results are shown in more detail in Table 7.7. Column (3) is drawn directly from the Blau-Kahn study and gives the contribution of changes in the characteristics of men and women workers to changes in the gender wage gap over the 1980s. However, these findings refer to relative changes and thus leave open the question of whether women's characteristics improved in some absolute sense. To shed light on this question, the first two columns of Table 7.7 provide new calculations based on the Blau-Kahn results. They give the contribution of changes in characteristics to each sex group's real wage changes over the period, both overall and separately by skill group. The weights are 1988 regression coefficients (including the constant term) from male wage equations estimated either for all workers or for workers in the indicated skill group. Differences in these changes for men and women separately equal the final column which gives the net result of the changes in characteristics on the change in the gender gap. (See the notes to Table 7.7 and Blau and Kahn (1997) for additional details.)

Results in column (3) indicate that improvements in women's relative experience[16] and broad occupational category were particularly important in narrowing the gender gap; changes in unionism also benefited women relative to men, but played a smaller a role, while shifts in industrial distribution had relatively little effect. Looking at columns (1) and (2), we see that women did upgrade their major occupations absolutely, that is they moved into higher paying categories, evaluated at the male returns, while changes in men's occupational distribution had no effect on men's real wage changes. Both men and women lost ground in terms of collective bargaining coverage, with larger declines for men than for women. Changes in industry distribution also lowered the real wage growth of both men and women, but by approximately the same amount for each.

The role of occupational upgrading in narrowing the gender gap raises the question of the reason for the decline in occupational segregation which occurred over the 1970s and 1980s. Here again, as in our consideration of the educational improvements of women, both the human capital and the discrimination models potentially provide viable explanations.[17] On the one hand, it may be that as women anticipated remaining in the labor force for longer periods it became profitable for them to invest in the higher amount of on-the-job training required in traditionally male occupations. On the other hand, women may have entered these areas in response to declining barriers to their participation. Unfortunately, there is no research explicitly examining this, but it is quite likely that both sets of factors played a role.

There is also some question as to how we should interpret the decline in the unexplained gender gap over this period; as noted above, it is unclear whether this is due to an upgrading of women's unmeasured labor market skills or a decline in labor market discrimination against them. Because women improved their relative level of measured characteristics, it is plausible that they also enhanced their relative level of unmeasured characteristics. For example, it is possible that with increasing labor force commitment, the quality of women's labor market experience may have also improved. A study by Royalty (1996), the first to explicitly examine the importance of predicted turnover probability in explaining the gender training difference, sheds some light on this possibility. Consistent with this expectation, she finds that predicted turnover probability does explain some of the gender training difference.[18] However, interestingly, a major portion remains unexplained even after this and other determinants of training are taken into account. This suggests that women's rising labor force commitment likely did reduce the gender training gap, though even if the gender difference in commitment had been eliminated some training difference would remain.

There is also evidence that the marketability of women's education improved. As noted above, gender differences in fields of study among college students decreased over the 1970s and 1980s. This development, which is not captured in the Blau and Kahn study and other similar work, likely contributed to the narrowing of the gender gap because gender differences in college major have been found to be strongly related to the gender wage gap among college graduates (Charles Brown and Mary Corcoran 1997). The male-female difference in SAT math scores has also been declining, falling from 46 points in 1977 to 35 points in 1996 (College Board 1996).[19]

On its face, the implication that discrimination against women declined seems less credible than that their unmeasured characteristics improved, because it is well known that the federal government scaled back its anti-discrimination enforcement effort during this period (Leonard 1989). However, there are a number of ways in which decreases in discrimination still could have played a role in reducing the pay gap in the 1980s. For example, it is possible that the female gains reflected delayed dividends to earlier anti-discrimination efforts which encouraged women to enhance their qualifications and enter traditionally male fields. Thus, decreases in discrimination may underlie some of the progress women made due to the enhancement of their measured qualifications relative to men's. And, to the extent that qualifications are not fully controlled for in the wage regression used to decompose the change in the gender wage gap, this may also help to explain the decline in the "unexplained" gap. Further, it may be that as women increased their commitment to the labor force and their other job skills, the rationale for statistical discrimination against them diminished. For example, controlling for measured characteristics, employers may discount women's wages due to their higher expected turnover rate. A reduction in the perceived turnover differential between men and women would result in a decrease in this discount and an increase in women's relative wages controlling for other factors (Aigner and Cain 1977). Moreover, in the presence of feedback effects, employers' revised views can generate further improvements in women's earnings by increasing returns to their investments in job qualifications and skills.[20] To the extent that some of these qualifications are unobserved in our analysis, the result will be a decrease in the unexplained gap. A final scenario might be that discrimination declined due to changes in social attitudes which make such discriminatory tastes increasingly unpalatable. Thus, an important role for decreases in discrimination in narrowing the gap may not be as implausible as it first appears.

Two more points may be noted about the finding that a decrease in the unexplained gap played a significant role in the narrowing of the gender gap. First, these findings do not, of course, imply that labor market discrimination has disappeared entirely. As reported above, ceteris paribus pay gaps between men and women, which are often taken as an estimate of discrimination, continue to exist, although their magnitude has been diminished. Second, the finding that a substantial portion of the closing of the gap is essentially "unexplained" parallels the findings in each of the major areas examined. This may be an indicator in this case of a decrease in discrimination. It is my own view that is the case at least to some extent. However, it may also be, in this area as in others, in part a reflection of the limitations of our models and the data sets at our disposal for estimating them.

7.3.6. Explaining the Trends in Wages: Differences by Skill Group

Blau and Kahn (1997) also investigate women's progress separately by skill group. Returning to Table 7.7, we see that the pay gap declined at about the same pace across all three skill groups defined in terms of experience and education. This is consistent with tabulations from the CPS presented above which showed similar gains for women across education groups prior to the early 1990s. However, the sources of the closing differed. Consistent with a greater negative effect of restructuring on male blue-collar and manufacturing jobs, the results in column (3) of Table 7.7 indicate that industry and union representation effects strongly favored women relative to men at the bottom and middle of the skill distribution; but worked to increase the gender gap slightly among high-skill workers. High-skill women nonetheless advanced at a similar pace as the other groups due to the larger improvement in their human capital characteristics and occupational distribution, although relative occupational gains were also substantial for low- and middle-skill women.

In terms of absolute progress, we see in Table 7.7 that women in each skill group also improved their occupational distribution absolutely over the period, while men's distribution declined slightly for low- and middle-skilled men and more substantially for high-skill men. With respect to industrial distribution and unionism, the experience of low- and middle-skilled men and women was less favorable than men and women in the high-skill group. Putting this somewhat differently, the decline of the gender wage gap among low- and middle-skilled workers was partly due to men losing ground at a faster pace than women. Taken together, changes in industry distribution and unionism worked to lower the real wages of low-skill men by about 8 percent and of low-skill women by about 5 percent. In the middle-skill group, these factors lowered real wages by 6 percent for men and 3 percent for women. In contrast, in the high-skill group, changes in industry and unionism (principally the former) worked to raise men's wages by 2 percent and left women's wages roughly unchanged.

7.4. Standard of Living: Differences Across and Within Families

In this section I review trends in a number of indicators of economic well-being related to the distribution of resources both between and within families. I first consider trends in marital status and family formation among women, chiefly focusing on single headship. I concentrate on headship because it is well documented that families headed by women are more likely to be poor or to have low incomes. There are also serious concerns about negative consequences for children of living in female-headed families, due in part to this economic deprivation (e.g., McLanahan and Booth 1989). Trends in well-being are influenced not only by trends in family structure but also by trends in family income both across family types and by differences in the trends within each type for particular education groups. Thus, I also explicitly consider these trends below.

In comparing income across family types we confront a conceptual issue raised by Fuchs (1988) which has generally not been addressed in the income distribution literature. Because full-time homemakers produce goods and services of value to their families, comparisons based only on money income are likely to overstate the difference in well-being between families in which the wife works outside the home and those in which she does not. In like manner, when labor force participation rates of married women are rising, the increase in the well-being of married couples compared to single-headed families is likely to be overstated when only money contributions to the economic well-being of the family are counted. However, Fuchs' (1988) careful adjustment for this problem did not alter his conclusion that the rise in the share of female-headed families adversely affected the economic well-being of women relative to men.

Another issue to be considered which Fuchs (1988) also brought to the fore is the sharing rule within the family. If the distribution of resources between husbands and wives within families is very unequal, we may overstate the advantage in well-being for women of being part of a higher income married couple family over a lower income single-headed family. While this is certainly a reasonable qualification, the differences in income between the two family types are so large that it seems justifiable to assume in general that women in married couple families do have more resources. Further, bargaining models (discussed above) suggest that higher relative wages of wives should increase their bargaining power within marriage. Thus, trends in wages of wives relative to those of husbands are reviewed as an indicator of bargaining power.[21] Relative wages of wives are found to have been increasing overall and within education groups. This implies that, if anything, women's share of resources within marriage should be increasing. Similarly, while domestic violence is a risk which married (or cohabiting) women may face to a greater extent than single women, the trends in domestic violence which are also considered below suggest that there was no increase in the incidence of such violence from the mid-1970s to the mid-1980s.

Finally, trends in the gender division of housework are considered. This is an important indicator of well-being for a number of reasons. First, as Fuchs (1986; 1988) has pointed out, access to leisure is important. Within families, women have traditionally had the major responsibility for housework, while men have had the major responsibility for market work. As market work has become more equally shared between men and women in the family, if the division of housework remains very unequal, the consequence is likely to be a reduction in leisure for women. An additional reason for concern over the division of housework is because women's greater responsibility for housework may adversely affect their labor market outcomes in at least two ways. First, it may cause women to constrict their hours of work, work schedules, and commuting time, and hence reduce their wages or occupational choice. Second, even controlling for hours of market work, it may result in their reducing their effective effort per hour compared to men who spend fewer off-job hours on homemaking tasks (Becker 1985). And, indeed, empirical evidence suggests that women who spend more time on housework do have lower wages, all else equal (e.g., Hersch and Stratton 1997). Of course, the causation could run in the opposite direction: women with lower wages face a lower opportunity cost of time spent in housework. However, Hersch and Stratton (1997) still find a significant negative effect of housework on wages when instrumental variables estimation is used.[22]

7.4.1. Trends in Marital Status and Family Formation

In this section I review trends in marital and family status for women. As noted above, "married" refers to women who are married spouse present. Single heads are women who head families or subfamilies and are not married spouse present; this excludes single person households. One problem with these definitions is that a significant and growing proportion of individuals who are officially defined as single heads are actually members of cohabiting couples. For example, in 1990, 7 percent of single mothers were cohabiting (McLanahan and Casper 1995). While this is certainly an important caution, it should also be noted that the extent of income pooling in cohabiting families is uncertain. Moreover, cohabitations tend to end very quickly either in marriage or a breakup (Bumpass and Sweet 1989).[23]

Table 7.8

Marital And Family Status of Women

	Marital Status			Single Head		Child/Children Present		
Year	Married, Spouse Present	Ever Married	Never Married	All	Never Married	All	Married, Spouse Present	Single Head
				All Women				
1970	0.777	0.161	0.062	0.094	0.008	0.545	0.484	0.061
1980	0.715	0.200	0.085	0.132	0.016	0.506	0.410	0.096
1990	0.666	0.211	0.123	0.148	0.032	0.462	0.356	0.106
1995	0.652	0.214	0.135	0.159	0.040	0.467	0.350	0.116
				Age 25–34				
1970	0.819	0.096	0.086	0.084	0.009	0.812	0.730	0.081
1980	0.687	0.159	0.154	0.141	0.029	0.686	0.551	0.135
1990	0.618	0.145	0.236	0.165	0.063	0.632	0.475	0.157
1995	0.589	0.144	0.266	0.183	0.081	0.620	0.446	0.174
				Education < 12 Years				
1970	0.736	0.218	0.046	0.121	0.009	0.474	0.397	0.077
1980	0.656	0.281	0.063	0.182	0.023	0.445	0.319	0.126
1990	0.596	0.287	0.117	0.217	0.056	0.404	0.258	0.146
1995	0.561	0.293	0.146	0.243	0.076	0.436	0.270	0.167
				Education = 12 Years				
1970	0.816	0.129	0.055	0.080	0.006	0.604	0.549	0.055
1980	0.754	0.180	0.065	0.125	0.015	0.534	0.441	0.092
1990	0.691	0.214	0.094	0.154	0.031	0.477	0.364	0.113
1995	0.669	0.219	0.113	0.166	0.043	0.459	0.337	0.122
				Education 13–15 Years				
1970	0.790	0.137	0.073	0.078	0.006	0.589	0.536	0.054
1980	0.711	0.193	0.095	0.127	0.015	0.551	0.449	0.102
1990	0.664	0.210	0.126	0.147	0.030	0.502	0.392	0.110
1995	0.647	0.233	0.121	0.172	0.037	0.501	0.368	0.133
				Education 16 + Years				
1970	0.754	0.103	0.144	0.060	0.009	0.523	0.489	0.034
1980	0.704	0.130	0.165	0.078	0.010	0.482	0.430	0.052
1990	0.671	0.144	0.185	0.082	0.016	0.441	0.387	0.054
1995	0.685	0.136	0.179	0.082	0.017	0.454	0.398	0.057

Notes: Sample for each year includes all adult civilian women between ages 25 and 64.
Source: Author's tabulations from the March Current Population Surveys.

Table 7.8 shows the trends in marital and family status for women and illustrates a number of well-known demographic shifts. Overall, the proportion of women who are married spouse present has declined, while the proportion of those who are single heads has increased. So, for example, the percentage of women who were married and living with their husbands fell from 78 to 65 percent between 1970 and 1995. At the same time, the incidence of single headship rose from 9 to 16 percent; and the proportion of women raising children on their own doubled from 6 to 12 percent. The fastest growth in female headship over this period occurred during the 1970s. A rise in headship occurred in all age groups with the exception of the oldest, and was particularly pronounced for younger women.

While these increases in single headship among women have received a great deal of attention, the pronounced differences across education groups in these trends have been less often noted. The contrast between high school dropouts and college graduates is particularly striking. In 1970, about three-quarters of both groups were married, less than either high school graduates or those with some college. But, by 1995, the proportion of women who were married had fallen to 56 percent among high school dropouts compared to 69 percent among college graduates. Of greater significance for economic well-being, this represented principally a postponement of marriage and family for more educated women but an increasing tendency toward single headship among less educated women. Although women with less than a high school education were more likely to be single heads than other groups in 1970, the differences were fairly moderate in absolute terms. For example, the proportion of single heads was 12 percent among high school dropouts compared to 6 percent among college graduates. By 1995, the incidence of headship had doubled to 24 percent among high school dropouts compared to a 33 percent increase to 8 percent among college graduates. As many as 38 percent of female high school dropouts with children were raising them on their own compared to only 13 percent of college graduates.

As has been widely noted in the literature, the rise in female headship has been particularly large among blacks. As Table 7.9 indicates, by 1995, 39 percent of black women were single heads and the race difference in the incidence of single female headship rose from 17 percentage points in 1970 to 26 points in 1995. A considerably higher incidence of single headship prevailed among blacks within all age and education groups. However, it is also true for both blacks and whites that, within each age category, high school dropouts had the highest rates of single headship. By 1995, among women aged 25–34 with less than 12 years of education, 65 percent of black women and 25 percent of white women were single family heads.

A final important aspect of the demographic shifts related to headship is the rise in the incidence of never married women among female heads. This is of concern because this group tends to be the least well-off economically. As may be seen in Table 7.8, never married single heads account for a rising proportion of women overall and within each education group. However, the share of never married heads has increased especially rapidly among blacks and among younger, less educated women in both race groups. By 1995, among younger women (aged 25–34) with less than 12 years of education, 44 percent of single white heads and 72 percent of single black heads were never married, up from 7 percent of whites and 19 percent of blacks in 1970.[24]

Table 7.9

Incidence Of Single Headship by Race, Age, and Education

	1970	1980	1990	1995	Change 1970–95
A. White Women	0.077	0.105	0.116	0.124	0.047
Age 25–34	0.063	0.106	0.121	0.140	0.078
Education < 12 years	0.091	0.199	0.223	0.253	0.162
Education = 12 years	0.060	0.115	0.145	0.178	0.118
Education > 12 years	0.042	0.067	0.075	0.097	0.056
Age 35–44	0.078	0.126	0.136	0.148	0.070
Education < 12 years	0.097	0.169	0.196	0.235	0.138
Education = 12 years	0.070	0.115	0.149	0.153	0.083
Education > 12 years	0.065	0.115	0.112	0.130	0.065
B. Black Women	0.244	0.347	0.381	0.388	0.144
Age 25–34	0.260	0.398	0.445	0.440	0.181
Education < 12 years	0.335	0.517	0.646	0.651	0.316
Education = 12 years	0.236	0.418	0.464	0.452	0.216
Education > 12 years	0.114	0.277	0.337	0.358	0.243
Age 35–44	0.274	0.396	0.413	0.416	0.142
Education < 12 years	0.319	0.456	0.484	0.536	0.217
Education = 12 years	0.227	0.369	0.432	0.421	0.194
Education > 12 years	0.184	0.348	0.351	0.375	0.192

Notes: Sample for each year includes all adult civilian women between ages 25 and 64.
Source: Author's tabulations from March Current Population Surveys.

Across and within cohort changes in headship are presented in Table 7.10. I focus on the two younger age groups (25–34 and 35–44) when across and (especially) within cohort changes in headship are still likely to occur. Comparisons of the across and within cohort rates are not as informative here as in the case of the other variables considered. Less educated women have children earlier and increasingly form single-headed families through out-of-wedlock births, thus reducing the scope for within cohort increases in headship over time. In contrast, more educated women are much more likely to form single-headed families through divorce or separation, and, especially in the case of college graduates, tend to have children considerably later. These factors tend to raise within cohort increases in headship of more educated women relative both to their own across cohort increases and to the within cohort increases of less educated women.

Table 7.10

Across and Within Cohort Changes in Single Headship of Women by Age and Education, 1970–90

	Across Cohort Change		Within Cohort Change	
	1970–80	1980–90	1970–80	1980–90
A. Education < 12 years				
Age 25–34	12.39	3.98	8.87	–0.73
Age 35–44	8.84	2.79	4.05	–1.62
B. Education = 12 years				
Age 25–34	7.48	3.95	6.50	3.31
Age 35–44	6.06	4.29	2.24	–2.63
C. Education 13 to 15 years				
Age 25–34	6.09	3.14	10.88	5.04
Age 35–44	8.39	0.25	2.76	–5.21
D. Education 16 + years				
Age 25–34	2.43	0.31	7.02	4.28
Age 35–44	4.31	–0.32	6.67	2.46
E. Difference: Ed = 12 minus Ed < 12 (B – A)				
Age 25–34	–4.91	–0.04	–2.37	4.04
Age 35–44	–2.78	1.49	–1.80	–1.01
F. Difference: Ed = 16+ minus Ed < 12 (D – A)				
Age 25–34	–9.96	–3.67	–1.84	5.00
Age 35–44	–4.52	–3.11	2.62	4.08

Notes: Illustrating for the 1970–80 change in single headship of the 25–34 year age group, the "across" cohort change is the difference between the single headship rate of the 25–34 year age group in 1970 and 1980; the "within" cohort change is the difference between the single headship rate of the 25–34 year age group in 1970 and the 35–44 year age group in 1980.

Taking these factors into account, the results in Table 7.10 are fairly supportive of the view that true changes in behavior and not just compositional shifts underlie at least some of the observed growth in headship of the least educated women. Focusing on the 1970s, when the largest across cohort increases in headship occurred for all groups, we find sizable within cohort increases in headship among high school dropouts, although in each case they are smaller than the corresponding across cohort increases. Moreover, with one exception, the within cohort increases of high school dropouts exceed those of high school and college graduates (panels E and F), although by considerably less than is the case for the across cohort differences. In contrast, in the 1980s, as the rate of increase in headship slowed and as more less educated women entered single headship through out-of-wedlock births, within cohort changes in headship of less educated women became smaller than their across cohort changes (in fact they are negative) and tended to be smaller than those of more highly educated women as well. Nonetheless, at least for the 1970s, these results suggest that the rise in headship of less educated women was due at least in part to behavioral changes.

7.4.2. Explaining the Trends in Family Formation

A variety of explanations have been offered for the movement of women away from marriage and toward female headship. One explanation links these developments to increasing labor market opportunities for women which increase their relative wages and thereby reduce the gains to marriage (Becker 1991). A second explanation focuses on the deteriorating labor market situation of less-skilled men and the resulting scarcity of "marriageable" males (Wilson 1987). A final explanation points to welfare availability as important in encouraging the formation of female headed families (Murray 1984; Becker 1991). Changes in social attitudes, including the greater social acceptance of divorce and the declining social stigma of unwed motherhood have also been cited as supplementary to the economic explanations (Blank 1995).

Some conclusions may be reached concerning the relative importance of each of these factors based on what has been learned regarding the fundamental causes of headship at a point in time as well as from a smaller number of studies that explicitly examine trends. On the basis of this research, welfare appears the least plausible explanation for a number of reasons. First, Moffitt's (1992) review of the literature suggests that welfare does not have strong incentive effects on demographic decisions. Second, the time pattern of changes in welfare benefits does not match the demographic trends. The real value of monthly support levels available from AFDC and food stamps combined have been falling steadily since the 1960s (Blank 1995). It is true, as we have seen, that labor market options of low-skilled men (and women) have also been declining, possibly making welfare relatively more attractive. However, to the extent this is the case, it is the labor market trends that are the causal factor. Finally, as Blank (1995) points out, international comparisons are very persuasive. While the U.S. provides much lower levels of government support for single mothers than other industrialized countries, it has one of the highest rates of single motherhood and the highest rate of teen pregnancy.

Greater empirical support has been obtained for the first two explanations: rising relative wages of women (e.g., Schultz 1994) and the declining economic prospects of low-skilled men (e.g., Darity and Meyers 1995).[25] Blank (1995) suggests that these two explanations may work together, with higher relative wages and labor market opportunities for women explaining the general rise in single parenthood across all income and skill groups, and declining labor market opportunities of low-skilled men explaining the higher increases among the low-skilled women they would generally marry. An additional factor that can be noted based on the labor market trends reviewed above is declining labor market opportunities for low-skill women. This has been true over the 1980s in both a relative sense, i.e., compared to other women, and an absolute sense, i.e., in terms of declining real wages. And the declines have been most pronounced for younger women. A substantial and growing proportion of single female heads, especially among low-skilled women, is comprised of unwed mothers, many of whom began their childbearing as teenagers. The declining market opportunities confronting this group imply that their opportunity cost of having children at an early age has been falling relative to others.[26]

While arguments structured in terms of the wage trends of men and women appear more promising than the welfare explanation, a review of the aggregate trends suggests that they too are unlikely to provide a full explanation. The largest growth in female headship during our period occurred over the 1970s, yet that was a time when real wage trends for those with a high school education or less were actually more favorable than the trends for college graduates among both men and women. This suggests that the 1970s trends were not driven by a declining desirability of male high school graduates or dropouts as husbands in economic terms, or by a falling opportunity cost of teen pregnancy. Moreover, research findings suggest that the decline in the supply of "marriageable" men is not the prime explanation for the sharp decrease in black marriage rates over the 1970s and 1980s. A particularly comprehensive study by Wood (1995) using SMSA level data for 1970 and 1980 finds that the decline in high earning young black men explains only 3 or 4 percent of the decline in black marriage rates during the 1970s. Moreover, Wood's review of previous research suggests that while the availability of marriageable men, defined in terms of employment or earnings, is often found to be statistically significant, its quantitative effect is small.

Rising relative wages of women also appear unlikely to be the principal cause of the trends, especially the large rise in headship in the 1970s. While there was some increase in the relative wages of women among younger workers in the 1970s, the largest increase even for this group as well as for other age groups occurred in the 1980s. Even the point estimate of this effect is in some doubt. An event history analysis of first marriages begun between 1967 and 1983 using data from the Panel Study of Income Dynamics by Hoffman and Duncan (1995) finds no evidence that higher wages of wives increase marital instability. Based on simulations using their estimated coefficients, they find that female wages, male incomes, and AFDC benefit levels did not play a large role in explaining the trends in divorce rates over this period.

A review of the trends presented above suggests that a closer correlation would be obtained between rising women's labor force participation per se and the decline in marriage than between the relative wages of women and the 1970s trends. This difference can occur both because absolute increases in women's wages can raise their participation even if their relative wages remain fairly constant – this appears to have occurred in the 1970s – and because, as we have seen, much of the increase in women's labor force participation cannot readily be explained by measured economic and demographic variables. As women and men become less specialized in homework and market work, the scope for gains to specialization is reduced. On the other hand, in reconciling an explanation based on participation with the aggregate trends, we now face an embarrassment of riches: the percentage point increases in female participation were similar in the 1970s and 1980s, but headship rose at a much faster pace in the 1970s.[27]

Thus, wage explanations framed in terms of changes either in levels of male wages or in women's wages relative to men's are unlikely to fully account for the particularly rapid increases in headship which occurred over the 1970s, though they might provide a more viable explanation for the post-1980 trends which have not yet been investigated. Considerably more work is needed to fully understand the importance of economic factors in explaining the trends. The role of increases in women's labor force participation, as distinct from trends in the wages of women relative to men, might be a fruitful area for future study. In addition, there is some evidence, particularly among blacks, that greater economic opportunity may reduce out-of-wedlock births to young women by raising its opportunity cost (Randall Olsen and Farkas 1990). This suggests that an investigation of the declining prospects of less-skilled women might also be a promising route to explore in explaining the post-1980 trends. Given the apparent inadequacies of each of the proposed economic explanations, a principal role in explaining the changes in family formation would at this point have to be assigned to changes in behavioral responses and shifts in social attitudes. While it is always difficult to know whether changes in behavior follow changes in attitudes or cause them, it is likely that, whatever the initial cause, changes in both areas reinforce each other through feedback effects.

7.4.3. Implications of Changes in Family Formation, Labor Force Participation, and Wage Trends for Income Differences Across Families

As we have seen, the rise in female headship has been heavily concentrated among less-educated women. At the same time, the labor force participation and wages of this group have also declined relative to other women. Thus, it is not surprising that the relative incomes of individuals in female-headed families have fallen. Equivalence incomes for individuals are based on family income after adjusting for the number of family members and economies of scale. In 1989, the mean equivalence income of individuals in married couple families was over double the income in female-headed families, up from 70 percent higher in 1969 (U.S. Department of Labor 1995, p.65). The consequences of being in a female-headed family are also more negative for less educated women, and are becoming increasingly so. Fifty-nine percent of individuals in families headed by a single woman with a high school education or less were in the bottom quintile compared to 30 percent when the head had more than a high school education. And, between 1969 and 1989, the equivalence income of individuals in families headed by single, less-educated women fell from 60 to 57 percent of individuals in families headed by women with more than a high school education (U.S. Department of Labor 1995).

There has also been a widening income gap between individuals in families headed by less educated couples compared to more highly educated couples. For example, in 1969, the average equivalence income of individuals in families headed by married couples who had a high school education or less, was 59 percent of that of individuals in families where both spouses had more than a high school education; by 1989 the ratio was 52 percent (U.S. Department of Labor 1995). This trend reflects a larger rise in labor force participation of wives of high earning husbands and also an increase in the correlation between the earnings of husbands and wives when both are employed (U.S. Department of Labor 1995; Karoly and Burtless 1995; Cancian, Danziger, and Gottschalk 1993). The consequences of these developments for income inequality across married couple families is unclear a priori. Increases in participation of wives lower wage dispersion across all persons (or families) because there are fewer families with zero earnings of the wife. On the other hand, the increasing tendency of participation to be concentrated among high income families and the increase in the correlation of husbands' and wives' earnings works to increase inequality (Karoly and Burtless 1995). Cancian, Danziger, and Gottschalk (1993) found that, on net, wives' earnings have continued to equalize family income among married couples. Karoly and Burtless (1995), however, using a different measure of inequality and a different decomposition technique, find that wives contributed to a rise in inequality of equivalence income of individuals since the late 1970s among married couples. One problem in reconciling these results is that, as Gottschalk and Smeeding (1997) point out, it is unclear how to allocate changes in correlations among income sources (e.g., between husbands' and wives' earnings) in such decompositions. They report that some of the differences between the Karoly and Burtless, and Cancian, Danziger, and Gottschalk results are due to differences in the treatment of changes associated with such correlations. In any case, it is clear, as we have seen, that the average equivalence income of individuals in families headed by less educated spouses has fallen relative to those in families headed by the more highly educated.

7.4.4. Trends in Intra-family Allocation: Wage Ratios of Husbands and Wives

We have seen that, overall, women's wages increased relative to men's, particularly over the 1980s. In this section, I examine how these trends have played out within the family. The focus is on the post-1979 period because preliminary results indicated little change in the wage ratio of wives to husbands in the 1970s. Because I do not include results from the 1970 CPS, it is possible to compute average hourly earnings. An advantage of this measure is that part-time workers may be included; part-time work is particularly prevalent among married women. In Table 7.11, data are presented for all women, and separately by education category of the wife; and for wives in the youngest age group. Wage ratios are calculated as the ratio of the mean wages of wives in the indicated group divided by the mean wages of husbands in that group. In addition, data are presented on the percentage of couples with a wage ratio of .9 or higher, i.e., with rough wage parity between the spouses (or, in some cases, superiority for the wife).

Looking first at the actual female-male wage ratios, it may be seen that, for the total group, there was considerable improvement in the 1980s and early 1990s. Overall, the wage ratio rose from 60.1 to 72.9 percent between 1979 and 1994. Also of interest is that the percentage of couples with a wage ratio of .9 or higher rose by 14 percentage points, from 23 to 37 percent. Potential market wages likely affect the behavior and bargaining power of women who are not currently employed, as well as that of labor force participants. Because, as we have seen, employment growth has been largest for wives of middle and high wage men who are likely themselves to be better educated, the figures in Table 7.11 may be affected by shifts in the composition of employed wives compared to their husbands. Thus, they may give a distorted impression of the extent of increases in the relative earnings of wives with given characteristics.

To get a rough indication of whether adjusting for changes in measured characteristics would affect our conclusions, I have calculated female-male wage ratios for all workers based on "fixed weight" averages; that is, based on mean earnings for each sex fixing the distribution of husbands and wives across education-age cells at their 1970 levels, but attributing current year wages to each cell.[28] These fixed weight averages thus adjust for any shifts in the composition of women relative to men across these measurable characteristics. The results suggest that some of female gains are due to improvements in working wives' characteristics relative to their husbands, because the pace of progress is somewhat reduced when the fixed weight measure is used. Nonetheless, bulk of the gains remain; the wage ratio based on fixed weight averages increased from 59.2 to 68.9 percent between 1979 and 1994. Of course, this approach only addresses the issue of gender differences in the selectivity of labor force participants in terms of their measured characteristics. Shifts in the distribution of unmeasured characteristics of wives relative to husbands could still have an impact on the observed progress (Heckman 1980).

Table 7.11

Female-Male Average Hourly Earnings Ratios Among Married Couples by Education, 1979–94

	1979	1989	1994	Change 1979–94
I. All Women				
Female/male wage ratio (actual)	0.601	0.684	0.729	21.3%
Female/male wage ratio (fixed weight average)	0.592	0.663	0.689	16.4%
Wage ratio .9 or higher	0.228	0.316	0.368	0.14
II. Education < 12 years				
All Women				
Female/male wage ratio	0.579	0.647	0.643	11.2%
Wage ratio .9 or higher	0.226	0.286	0.276	0.05
Age 25–34				
Female/male wage ratio	0.593	0.659	0.696	17.4%
Wage ratio .9 or higher	0.240	0.315	0.313	0.07
III. Education = 12 years				
All Women				
Female/male wage ratio	0.568	0.616	0.649	14.2%
Wage ratio .9 or higher	0.186	0.255	0.300	0.11
Age 25–34				
Female/male wage ratio	0.610	0.671	0.711	16.5%
Wage ratio .9 or higher	0.214	0.270	0.344	0.13
VI. Education > 12 years				
All Women				
Female/male wage ratio	0.646	0.742	0.772	19.5%
Wage ratio .9 or higher	0.286	0.380	0.419	0.13
Age 25–34				
Female/male wage ratio	0.718	0.799	0.830	15.5%
Wage ratio .9 or higher	0.330	0.424	0.440	0.11

Notes: The sample in each year includes husbands and wives (matched partners) both of whom are between ages 25 and 64 and worked for at least one week in the previous year. The additional sample restrictions detailed in the Data Appendix are applied to both partners except that respondents are not required to be full-time workers. Wages are defined as annual earnings divided by annual hours; ratios are calculated as the mean wages of wives divided by the mean wages of husbands. The ratio using "fixed weight averages" is calculated by fixing the distribution of husbands and wives across education-age cells at their 1970 levels, but attributing current year wages to each cell. Four age categories are employed: 25–34, 35–44, 45–54, and 55- 64; and three education categories: less than 12 years, 12 years, and greater than 12 years. The "proportion with a wage ratio of .9 or higher" is the mean of a dummy variable which takes a value of 1 if a couple's wage ratio is .9 or higher and 0 otherwise. Where averages are reported separately, couples are classified on the basis of the wife's education and age.

Source: Author's tabulations from the March Current Population Surveys.

The results for the gender ratios based on fixed weight averages indicate that most of the progress in narrowing the gender ratio among married couples occurred within age-education categories.

But this does not mean that the rate of progress was the same for each educational group. Table 7.11 indicates that the ratio of wages of wives to husbands increased in all education groups. However, in each year, the highest ratio was for wives with more than a high school education and, moreover, relative gains were larger for more highly educated wives. By 1994, the wage ratio for couples where the wife had more than 12 years of schooling was 77 percent, and rough wage parity existed for 42 percent of such couples. Among wives with less than 12 years of education, the wage ratio was 65 percent and rough wage parity prevailed for only 30 percent of couples. In each year, the wage ratio was higher for younger women (25–34) and they experienced similar wage gains across all education groups. Nonetheless, young wives with more than a high school education began and ended the period with the highest wage ratio.

7.4.5. Trends in Intra-family Allocation: Allocation of Housework

There are two potential sources of data on housework: time budget studies and self-reports based on recollections over some period of time. While the former are likely to be more accurate, the relevant surveys are generally not available on a regular basis and tend to have small samples. Given these data problems, there have been few efforts to examine trends in the allocation of housework between men and women. A notable exception is work by Fuchs (1986; 1988). Fuchs reports that, on average, women's total hours of work (housework plus market work) increased relative to men's between 1959 and 1979, and thus concludes that the increased employment of women outside the home had resulted in a relative decrease in leisure for them. One problem with these estimates, however, is that, given the limited data available, Fuchs relied on an imputation of housework time based on coefficients obtained from one time use study which he then merged with large, nationally representative data sets drawn from the Census and CPS for a number of time periods.[29]

Two other studies which use time budget data reach somewhat different conclusions from each other, but neither find that total work time of women increased relative to men's. Juster and Stafford (1991) report that women's total work time fell from 60.9 hours to 54.4 per week between 1965 and 1991 compared to a decrease from 63.1 to 57.8 for men, while a United Nations (1991) report found that women's total weekly work time remained roughly constant at about 56.5 hours between 1965 and 1986 while men's increased slightly from 58.3 to 59.4 hours. However, because these studies do not provide data separately by marital and employment status, it is not clear what role changes in the composition of the population play in producing these results nor is there any direct indication of the extent of reallocation of tasks between partners among married couples.

To investigate the extent of reallocation of housework between men and women, as well as trends in leisure, I provide some new tabulations on time allocation based on the Michigan Panel Study of Income Dynamics (PSID) in Table 7.12. There are some limitations to the data used here, most important, due to the phrasing of the housework questions, it is possible that time spent on child care or time spent outside of the home on housework, e.g., shopping, are not included, because respondents were not explicitly prompted about them.[30] Bearing this caution in mind, the opportunity to examine these trends for a large, nationally representative sample is nonetheless of interest. Tabulations are from the 1979 and 1989 PSID on reported average weekly housework and market work hours in 1978 and 1988. "Not employed" is defined as working less than 100 hours per year.

The results in Table 7.12 suggest a moderate but significant reallocation of time use between men and women. Overall, for women, average hours of market work increased and average hours of housework decreased, while hours of both market work and housework increased for men. The changes were larger for women. Their housework declined by 5.4 hours per week, on average. It fell a bit more for married than for single women and, surprisingly, more for nonemployed than for employed wives. Comparisons across a number of time use studies reported in Blau, Ferber, and Winkler (1998) indicate that women's housework time also appears to have declined for both employed and nonemployed wives between the 1960s and the 1970s, suggesting that the results in Table 7.12 for the 1980s represent the continuation of a longterm trend. The increase in wives' market work of 6.3 hours are, in part, the result of a shift of wives from nonemployed to employed status, but, even among employed wives, market work hours increased. Again, similar findings are reported by Blau, Ferber, and Winkler (1998) for the earlier period.

Table 7.12

Trends in Average Weekly Hours of Housework and Market Work by Marital Status and Education, Men and Women, 1978 and 1988

	1978			1988			Change 1978–88	
	Market Work	Housework	N	Market Work	Housework	N	Market Work	Housework
A. All individuals								
Women	20.1	26.7	2008	26.4	21.3	2320	6.34	–5.35
Single	27.2	17.2	412	32.1	13.4	507	4.96	–3.83
Married	18.3	29.1	1596	24.9	23.6	1813	6.58	–5.57
Wife not employed	0.3	37.1	607	0.3	33.0	415	–0.02	–4.01
Wife employed	29.3	24.3	989	32.2	20.8	1398	2.83	–3.52
Men	42.5	6.1	1812	43.3	7.4	2183	0.71	1.27
Single	38.3	8.2	216	41.2	7.0	370	2.99	–1.14
Married	43.1	5.8	1596	43.7	7.5	1813	0.54	1.63
Wife not employed	42.5	5.0	607	41.3	6.4	415	–1.19	1.40
Wife employed	43.5	6.4	989	44.4	7.8	1398	0.86	1.42
B. Married Couples by Education of Wife								
Education 12 years or less								
Wives	16.8	30.6	1088	23.1	24.9	941	6.36	–5.64
Wife not employed	0.2	37.5	462	0.1	33.3	248	–0.12	–4.26
Wife employed	29.0	25.4	626	31.4	21.9	693	2.39	–3.49
Husbands	42.0	5.7	1088	41.7	7.2	941	–0.30	1.58
Wife not employed	41.2	4.8	462	38.6	6.0	248	–2.63	1.13
Wife employed	42.6	6.3	626	42.8	7.7	693	0.22	1.42
Education 13 years or more								
Wives	21.5	26.1	508	26.7	22.1	872	5.22	–3.97
Wife not employed	0.4	35.5	145	0.4	32.7	167	0.07	–2.83
Wife employed	30.0	22.3	363	33.0	19.6	705	3.00	–2.69
Husbands	45.5	6.2	508	45.8	7.7	872	0.25	1.51
Wife not employed	46.7	5.4	145	45.4	7.0	167	–1.29	1.59
Wife employed	45.1	6.5	363	45.9	7.8	705	0.81	1.35

Notes:
Individuals and spouses are aged 25–64 in the indicated year and have valid data on both housework and market work hours. Married individuals are included only if their spouse also satisfies the inclusion criteria. Couples are allocated to education categories on the basis of the wife's education.

Source:
Based on author's tabulations from the Michigan Panel Study of Income Dynamics, 1979 and 1989.

In contrast to the changes for women, the increase in men's housework was entirely concentrated among married men: housework hours declined by 1.1 hours for single men but increased by 1.6 hours for married men. The increase in married men's housework in part represented a shift of their wives to the employed category where, even in the initial year, husbands' hours of housework were greater. But, primarily, it reflected a rise in hours of housework of equal magnitude, 1.4 hours, for husbands of both employed and nonemployed wives. Trends were similar among married couples where the wife had a high school education or less, and those where she had more than a high school education.

The increase in husbands' hours of housework was small and the allocation of hours of housework between husbands and wives remained quite unequal in 1988, even when the wife was employed. However, the significance of this change is magnified by the fact that housework hours decreased for wives. So, for example, in employed-wife families, the ratio of husbands' to wives' housework hours rose from 26 percent in 1978 to 38 percent in 1988.[31] Moreover, the fact that married men's housework hours increased when they decreased for all other demographic groups is also significant. This suggests the combined impact of demographic trends together with changes in household technology and in the availability of market substitutes was to reduce housework. Absent some reallocation between spouses, we would have expected married men's housework to have declined rather than to have increased. Finally, it may be noted that the comparison of results of time use studies for the 1960s and 1970s reported in Blau, Ferber, and Winkler (1998) finds no such trend toward increased housework by husbands for that period, either among those with employed wives or among those with nonemployed wives. This suggests that increased housework by husbands was an important new development of the 1980s.

Overall, these trends are consistent with a reallocation of housework between men and women due to the rising relative wage of women.[32] The timing of the change also matches well with the increase in married women's relative wages in the 1980s. Such a reallocation might occur in Becker's (1991) model of specialization within the family due to comparative advantage. As women's comparative advantage in this area declines, housework may be more evenly divided.[33] Alternatively, the increasing relative wages of women could signal an increase in their bargaining power (e.g., Lundberg and Pollak 1996), and the reallocation of housework between men and women could be viewed in that context. Our finding that housework hours increased for the husbands of both employed and nonemployed women seems more consistent with the bargaining explanation, with a shift in bargaining power between husbands and wives in response to changing market opportunities for women (regardless of their current employment status). However, calculations based on results in Table 7.11 indicate a faster growth in relative wages over the 1980s for wives with some college than for women with a high school education or less, yet the housework of more highly educated wives relative to their husbands fell no faster than for less educated women. This does not accord well with either theory.[34]

We may also consider the trends in relative leisure time of men and women implied by the results in Table 7.12, although an important qualification is that the measure of housework hours is likely incomplete. Overall, based on this measure, total work time (including both housework and market work) was a bit higher (2 hours) for men than for women in 1978. Total work time increased for both men and women, but a bit more for men (2 hours) than for women (1 hour). The trends were the same for married men and women: an increase of 2 hours in total work time for husbands and 1 hour for wives. The more favorable trend for women was due to the sizable decrease in the time spent on housework by both employed and nonemployed wives; this was sufficient to outweigh most of the positive impact on their total hours of the shift of wives to the employed category (employed wives work longer total hours than nonemployed wives in each year). Based on this data then it appears that, for this period, gender differences in trends in leisure time are small, and where differences exist they slightly favor women over men.[35]

7.4.6. *Trends in Intra-family Allocation: Domestic Violence*

Considerable public attention has focused on domestic violence, but economists efforts to model the determinants of the incidence of domestic violence are still comparatively recent. At the time the original version of this chapter was written, there had been very few studies of trends in domestic violence, let alone efforts to explain these trends. An endeavor of this type faces enormous measurement problems due to changes in the propensity to recognize and report such incidents, as well as changes in the particular questions asked over time in various surveys. However, as we shall see, it is possible to reach some reasonable conclusions about trends despite the data problems.

One potential source of data on domestic violence is the National Crime Victimization Survey (NCVS) which annually collects information about crimes from a nationally representative sample of U.S. households. This data set has a number of advantages for our purposes, but also some disadvantages. First, as a household survey, it includes information on crimes that are not reported to the police; this is important because many incidents of domestic violence are not reported. Second, it separately reports information on violent crimes committed against women by "intimates," although who precisely is included in that category has changed over time.[36] Finally, incidents reported in the survey must be considered "crimes" by the respondents. This is both an advantage and a disadvantage. On the one hand, it serves as an implicit control for the seriousness of the incident. On the other hand, while many people see domestic violence as wrong, they do not necessarily perceive it as criminal (Murray Straus and Richard Gelles 1988). Thus, data from the NCVS is likely to underreport the incidence of domestic violence, though perhaps to a lesser extent over time if people are increasingly inclined to see such acts as criminal. The inherent problems in using the NCVS to study trends are exacerbated by a redesign of the survey explicitly undertaken to produce more accurate reporting of violence by intimates and to increase the range of incident types that are reported.

Bearing the data issues in mind, it is nonetheless of interest to consider the magnitude of the problem based on this data source. In general, men in the U.S. are considerably more likely than women to be the victims of violence; during the 1980s and 1990s, the overall rate of violent crime victimization for men averaged 1.5–1.7 times higher than the female rate.[37] In contrast, as may be seen in Table 7.13, women are considerably more likely than men to be victims of violence by an intimate or relative, some 3.5 to 5.4 times more likely. The data in Table 7.13 show a jump in the incidence of violence by intimates for both men and women with the redesign of the survey, indicating considerable sensitivity of responses to how questions are phrased and whether or not additional cuing occurs. However, prior to the redesign of the survey, the incidence of violence by intimates and relatives is virtually constant for women at about 6.5 per thousand for the 1979–87 and 1987–91 periods, and fell somewhat for men from 1.8 to 1.2.[38] Given the many biases which would be expected to cause an upward trend in these figures over time, it seems reasonable to conclude that there was no increase in domestic violence between the early and the late 1980s.

Table 7.13

Average Annual Rate Of Single-Offender Violent Victimizations From The National Crime Victimization Survey, 1979–93

	Women			Men		
Victim-Offender Relationship	1979–87	1987–91	1992–93	1979–87	1987–91	1992–93
Intimates and Relatives	6.3	6.5	12.1	1.8	1.2	2.6
Intimate	na	5.4	9.3	na	0.5	1.4
Other Relative	na	1.1	2.8	na	0.7	1.2
Acquaintance/friend	7.0	7.6	12.9	12.1	13.0	17.2
Stranger	11.4	5.4	7.4	29.4	12.2	19.0

Notes: Rate per 1000 individuals, 12 years of age or over. Intimate includes spouse, ex-spouse, boy/girlfriend, and ex-boy/girlfriend. Data for 1979–87 include multiple offenders: na indicates not available. Results from the 1992–93 NCVS are based on a redesigned survey and thus may not be comparable to previous years.

Source: 1979–87: Harlow (1991); 1987–91: Bachman (1994); and 1992–93: Bachman and Saltzman (1995).

Another source of data on domestic violence is the 1975 and 1985 National Family Violence Surveys (NFVS) reported in Table 7.14. This nationally representative survey which includes married and cohabiting couples is portrayed to respondents as a survey of "family problems" rather than of crime. And respondents are explicitly questioned about the particular types of violent behavior which are itemized in the footnotes to the table. Two indexes are obtained, one for overall violence and the other for severe violence; the latter includes actions which are believed to have a high probability of causing injury. As may be seen by comparing the violence rates in Tables 7.13 and 7.14, the rates obtained from the NFVS, even for severe violence, are considerably higher than those obtained by the NCVS. For example, for 1992–93, after the redesign, the rate of violence against women by intimates from the NCVS is 9.3 per thousand compared to a rate of severe husband to wife violence of 30 per thousand from the NFVS for 1985. When all violence is considered, the NFVS rate of 113 for husbands to wives in 1985 is 12 times the NCVS rate and indicates that at least one incident of violent behavior of husbands to wives occurred among 11 percent of American couples in 1985, with serious incidents taking place among 3 percent. Are the rates from the NFVS, which are so much higher than the NCVS rates, credible? The answer seems to be yes. Straus and Gelles (1988) summarize findings from a large number of similar studies which obtain results of roughly the same magnitude. The difference between the NFVS and the NCVS appears to occur because the NFVS does not query respondents about "crimes," but rather "problems," and also because it asks them about specific types of violent behavior.

Table 7.14

Rate Of Victimization Based on Marital Violence Indexes, 1975 And 1985

	Husband to Wife		Wife to Husband	
Year	Overall Violence (1)	Severe Violence (2)	Overall Violence (1)	Severe Violence (2)
1975	121	38	116	46
1985	113	30	121	44
% Change	–6.6	–21.1	4.3	–4.3

Notes: Rate per 1000 wives (husbands): includes cohabiting couples.
(1) Includes: threw something; pushed, grabbed, or shoved; slapped; kicked, bit or hit with fist; hit or tried to hit with something; beat up; threatened with knife or gun; used gun or knife.
(2) Includes only: kicked, bit or hit with fist; hit or tried to hit with something; beat up; threatened with gun or knife; used gun or knife.
Source: Gelles and Straus (1986) based on the 1975 and 1985 National Family Violence Surveys.

Another surprising finding from the NFVS is that, when this methodology is employed, the violence rate of wives to husbands is similar to the rate of violence of husbands to wives. However, as Straus and Gelles and others have pointed out, the greater average size and strength of men and their greater aggressiveness means that the same act (e.g., a punch) is likely to inflict greater amounts of pain and injury when committed by a man. This reasoning is supported by the much lower rates of victimization of men by intimates reported in the NCVS where "crimes" are the focus. In addition, the data on homicide indicate that 28.3 percent of female homicide victims in 1992 were known to have been killed by an intimate compared to only 3.6 percent of males (Bachman and Saltzman 1995).[39] Moreover, Straus and Gelles argue that many of the assaults of women against their husbands are acts of retaliation or self-defense. Some evidence in support of this is that while these data suggest that women are violent as frequently within the family as men, they are very rarely found to be violent outside the family.

Nonetheless, the high rates of violence of wives against husbands reported in this data raise some concerns about the validly of the results for violence of husbands against wives. Specifically, if one dismisses much of the violence of women against men as insignificant because it is unlikely to cause injury, some unknown portion of the violence of husbands against wives should also likely be dismissed for the same reason. Putting this somewhat differently, though many reasonably feel that any domestic violence is wrong and should not occur, the statistics from the measure of violence employed by NFVS may give an inflated picture of the prevalence of violence that constitutes a serious problem in terms of harm or potential harm. On the other hand, as

Straus and Gelles point out, violence by women may be of substantive concern because it is dangerous to them. It may set the stage for a more serious immediate assault on them by their partners who, as previously noted, are generally bigger and stronger; or it may provide a precedent or rationale for violence on their partners' part at a later time.

Whatever the conclusion about the levels of violence reported in the two surveys, the data in Table 7.14 from the NFVS strongly support our conclusion from the NCVS that there is no evidence of an increase in the rate of domestic violence against women, in this case between the mid-1970s and mid-1980s. Indeed, there is even some evidence of a decrease, especially in the incidence of severe violence. If we again assume that, if anything, the tendency would be to increase reporting of such incidents, our confidence that a decrease has occurred would be strengthened further.

An interesting question that may be raised about these trends is whether economic variables played a role in causing the apparent decrease in the incidence of domestic violence. Specifically, it is possible that, as women's relative wages and employment rates have risen, they have become less likely to remain in an abusive situation. The increased establishment of shelters for battered women could also have contributed to the decrease. However, currently, there are no detailed studies of the causes of these trends and, indeed, as we have seen, there is some reason to feel less than completely confident that a decrease has even occurred. Perhaps the most reasonable conclusion is that there is no evidence that the inclusion of domestic violence would in any way change our finding, based on other indicators, that women's status within the family has, if anything, increased.

A last point to consider is what can be learned about the incidence of domestic violence among women by level of education and by race. For this purpose, the most recent NVCS figures are particularly useful because they provide the most accurate reporting of the relevant data for this survey. The findings are somewhat surprising. While high school dropouts and black women have higher overall violence victimization rates than others, rates of violence by intimates are similar for blacks and whites, and across education categories, with the exception of considerably lower rates among women college graduates. If it can be assumed that this pattern has been fairly stable,[40] here again, the bottom line is that the conclusions reached based on other indicators do not have to be revised by a consideration of domestic violence.

7.5. "Having It All": Combining Work and Family

Given traditional male and female roles, one potential source of gender differences in economic well-being is a difference in the ability to successfully combine work and family responsibilities so as to attain desired objectives in both areas. Men tend not to face the same dilemmas as women, or not to face them to the same extent, because desirability as a spouse and ability to contribute economically to one's family are positively correlated with labor market success for men. While shifting gender roles within the family may be increasing the prevalence of family responsibilities among men, as we have seen, considerable gender differences remain.

Differences in typical gender roles in the family are also indicated by research which widely finds a negative simple correlation between women's earnings and the presence of children. In general, it has also been found that children are negatively related to female earnings, all else equal, while marriage and children are positively related to male earnings.[41] The finding for women depends in part on what other variables are controlled for. A substantial part of the negative effect of children when education and potential experience (age) are held constant reflects the lower actual labor market experience of women with children, but some evidence of a negative effect has been obtained in a number of studies even when experience is controlled for (e.g., Jacobsen and Levin 1995; Waldfogel 1997). This may reflect that, in the past, the birth of a child often meant that a woman withdrew from the labor force entirely, thus breaking her tie to her employer and foregoing the returns to any firm-specific training she might have received, as well as any rewards for having made an especially good job match. Anticipation of this pattern could also deter both women and their employers from making large investments in firm-specific training to begin with.

This is by no means a new dilemma for women, but the terms of the choices perceived by the bulk of women have changed over time. The desire to "have it all," that is to successfully pursue a career and to have a family appears to have become an increasingly common goal among women, especially the college educated. While there is no way of knowing precisely how prevalent it is, work by Goldin (1997) shows how rarely women have been able to successfully combine career and family, even among a relatively recent cohort of college women.

Using National Longitudinal Survey data, Goldin looks at attainment of career and family by 1985–88 among white women who graduated from college between 1966 and 1979. These women ranged in age from 34 to 44 in 1988. Goldin uses a variety of definitions of career, but especially emphasizes results where career is defined as having hourly earnings in the selected years exceeding that of the 25th percentile of men with 16 or more years of schooling in the Current Population Survey (CPS) in the relevant year. When a three-year definition is employed, 1985, 1987, and 1988, only 26 percent of the women qualify as having careers. Using a two-year definition, 1987 and 1988, one third qualify, still a relatively low proportion. A still smaller proportion attain both career and family, where family is defined by the presence of children: only 13 percent using the three-year definition and 16 percent using the two-year definition. This reflects a considerably lower incidence of career among women with children. This is a relatively stringent definition of career, because a substantial proportion of men would not have attained a career by this definition either. However, when Goldin shifts to a lower cutoff – being in the labor force in each of three years and generally working full-time – the incidence of career and family among the women remains extremely low, only 22 percent. And, under all three definitions, approximately one half of the women with careers had not had a first birth.

Some qualifications may be noted concerning these findings. We do not know what fraction of the childless women were disappointed in not having children. However, Goldin (1997) does present evidence that a considerable fraction (half or more) had indicated that they desired children when surveyed in their early to mid twenties. Another qualification is that this cohort (aged 34–44 in 1988) has in general postponed marriage and childbearing. Thus, childlessness among them is likely to be overestimated, because some may still have children later, and their measured career attainments may appear especially low during the years surveyed because of the presence of young children among the women with families. Yet even these qualifications suggest that these women face the need to make decisions and tradeoffs seldom confronted by their male counterparts. This concern is reinforced by Waldfogel's (1997) finding that the wages of women with children lag increasingly behind those of women without children. On a more positive note, Waldfogel finds that access to family leave substantially mitigates the negative effect of children on women's wages. This suggests that the difficulties which women have faced in achieving career and family may be reduced as more firms adopt such policies.[42]

7.6. Conclusion

The goal of this chapter is to delineate the trends in the well-being of American women over the past quarter century. I argue for a broad range of indicators designed to capture changes in women's well-being in the family as well as in the labor market, and also for the importance of examining both women's progress relative to men and in some absolute sense compared to the initial levels of indicators for women. Moreover, given the trends of growing disparities across groups, the investigation must proceed at a disaggregated as well as at an aggregated level to be informative. I have undertaken this investigation both through direct analyses of data, primarily from the Current Population Surveys, and examination of existing research results.

Overall, I conclude that women have made substantial progress toward gender equality over the past 25 years across a number of dimensions. Gender differences in labor force participation have narrowed sharply and women now remain in the labor market more consistently over the life cycle. Differences between men and women in occupations, types of education, and rates of self-employment have been greatly diminished; and women have narrowed the gender wage gap substantially. Within the family, wages of wives rose relative to their husbands' and, perhaps as a consequence, there was a small but notable reallocation of housework between husbands and wives. And, while the data are not as reliable as one would like, there is no indication of any increase in domestic violence between the mid-1970s and mid-1980s which would tend to offset these gains. Relative gains also appear to have been widely distributed across education groups. These relative gains appear to be matched by progress for women overall in an absolute sense. Women's real wages increased substantially over the 1969–1994 period, while men's stagnated. Similarly, women upgraded their major occupations absolutely between 1979 and 1988, in that they moved into higher paying occupational categories, while, on net, men's occupational shifts left their real wages unchanged.

This does not mean that discrimination and other gender-related disabilities affecting women have disappeared. There still exists a considerable, although reduced, gender wage gap after controlling for measured characteristics, which is often taken as an estimate of discrimination. And the challenges of combining work and family appear to continue to pose serious obstacles and dilemmas for women but, at this point, do not seem to affect men in the same way or at least to the same extent. Moreover, trends in family structure and, in particular, the increase in families headed by single women, have adversely affected the economic well-being of women and their dependent children. But this development, unlike those cited above was heavily concentrated among women with little education (less than 12 years) and black women.

The faster rise in female-headed families was just one of a number of developments adversely affecting the relative economic well-being of less educated women. In a manner strikingly parallel to trends in the labor market for men, wage differentials by education widened among women in the 1980s and early 1990s, and female high school dropouts experienced real wage declines. While women at all skill levels upgraded their occupations, less-skilled and middle-skilled women lost union jobs, although at a slower pace than men, and their representation in higher paying industries declined, at about the same rate as men's. Less educated women have also increased their labor force participation less than other education groups, as have black women compared to white women. Finally, not only has female headship increased most rapidly among less educated women, the income of individuals in families headed by couples with lower educational attainment has fallen relative to that of more highly educated couples. Some simple analyses strongly suggest that compositional shifts do not entirely account for the deteriorating economic position of less educated Americans, but rather that real changes in behavior and opportunities underlie at least some part of them. My principal concern has been with the well-being of women. However, these findings for less educated women also serve to underscore the widening gap between more and less-skilled Americans of both sexes, as well as to emphasize its broad dimensions.

Much remains to be learned about the details of the trends outlined here, and even more about their fundamental causes. In each major area where we probed existing studies for explanations of the trends, whether in participation, relative wages, or single headship, a substantial portion of the explanation must at this point be allocated to behavioral shifts and changes in tastes. The sources of the growth in headship are particularly poorly understood. It may be that this is inescapable at a time of rapid change in gender roles and social attitudes toward women and family relationships. But perhaps we should take this as a challenge to develop and refine economic models which can account for a greater proportion of the changes. It is in any case clear that more serious empirical analyses of the reasons for these trends are needed if we are to understand these developments better. Such analyses also provide an excellent opportunity for testing the economic significance as well as the statistical significance of our models.

Appendix

The primary source of data for the empirical results presented here are the March Current Population Surveys (CPS) for 1970, 1980, 1990, and 1995. The CPS was used because it is a large, nationally representative sample which permits considerable disaggregation by subgroups. The CPS data for 1970, 1980, and 1990 were selected because the earnings measure which is based on the previous calendar year relates to years of comparable economic activity over broad ten year intervals; the 1995 CPS was the most recent year available at the time this research was conducted. While the Census of Population could have been used as an alternative data source for 1970–1990, providing still larger samples, the CPS provides a consistent data source throughout, including the most recent year.

There was a change in the coding of the CPS education variables affecting the 1995 CPS data. In earlier years, information is available on years of schooling completed, top-coded at 18. The 1995 codes, with years of education assigned in parentheses, are: less than 1st grade (1); 1st, 2nd, 3rd, or 4th grade (2.5); 5th or 6th grade (5.5); 7th or 8th grade (7.5); 9th grade (9); 10th grade (10); 11th grade or 12th grade no diploma (11); high school graduate (12); some college but no degree (13); associate degree (14); bachelor's degree (16); master's degree; professional school degree; and doctorate degree (18).

Wage results are generally for the weekly wages of full-time workers (i.e., those usually working 35 hours or more per week in the preceding year). While average hourly earnings (i.e., annual earnings divided by weeks worked multiplied by hours per week) would have been a preferable measure in some respects, weekly hours information in 1970 is available only for hours last week. This is in an error-ridden measure of the preferred variable, usual weekly hours, and, moreover, is only available for a selected group of workers, i.e., those employed last week. However, information on whether the individual usually worked part-time or full-time in the preceding year is available in each of the surveys, including 1970. I thus generally use the weekly earnings measure which can be computed on a comparable basis in each year and which applies to an identifiable group, full-time workers, rather than an arbitrary group, those employed in the previous week.[43]

Average weekly and hourly wage rates are calculated based on the previous calendar year and exclude individuals who were self-employed or for whom data on wage and salary income was either missing or imputed. Except when otherwise indicated, the sample was further restricted to full-time workers who worked at least one week in the preceding year and who participated in the labor force (i.e., were employed or unemployed) for at least 27 weeks. Following Katz and Murphy (1992), individuals with real weekly earnings of less than $67 or real hourly earnings of less than $1.68 in 1982 dollars (i.e., one half the value of the minimum wage, assuming a 40 hour week for the weekly earnings cutoff) were excluded; for individuals whose annual wage and salary income was top-coded by the CPS, annual income was imputed as 1.45 the top-coded value ($50,000 in 1970 and All tabulations employ the CPS sampling weights.

The CPS data are supplemented with information from the Michigan Panel Study of Income Dynamics (PSID) on average weekly hours of self-reported market work and housework. The PSID is a large, national sample which is available for a number of years making it attractive compared to smaller, and less frequently available time use studies. I employ data from the 1979 and 1989 PSID yielding information for the preceding years. I begin with 1979 because housework data were not consistently available before this. The 1989 PSID was the most recent publicly available when this work was commenced. These are two years of roughly comparable levels of economic activity. The poverty sample of the PSID was deleted in the tabulations presented.

8

Can Mentoring Help Female Assistant Professors? Interim Results from a Randomized Trial

Based on a paper with Janet M. Currie, Rachel T.A. Croson, and Donna K. Ginther

Since its inception in 1971, the American Economic Association (AEA) Committee on the Status of Women in the Economics Profession (CSWEP) has tracked the number of women at various ranks in the profession. CSWEP's statistics indicate a "leaky pipeline" from PhD programs into tenured academic jobs. The significant under-representation of women in economics at the tenured level prompted CSWEP to establish the CSWEP Mentoring Program (CeMENT) with the support of the National Science Foundation's (NSF) ADVANCE

This chapter is a revised version of Blau, F. D., Currie, J. M., Croson, R. T. A., Ginther, D.K. (2010). Can Mentoring Help Female Assistant Professors? Interim Results from a Randomized Trial, in: American Economic Review, 100: 348-352.

The authors are grateful to the many women who have volunteered their time to participate in this experiment. We are indebted to the National Science Foundation (SBE-0317755) and to the American Economic Association for their support and to Daniel Newlon, Alice Hogan, and John Siegfried, for supporting this program. David Munroe, Sarah Frazelle, Patricia Oslund, Joshua Goodman, Christine Pal, Johannes Schmeider, and Kerry Watson provided excellent research assistance. Gwyn Loftis and Pat Fisher provided invaluable help with implementing the workshops. Any errors are our own responsibility. Furthermore, the authors thank the following discussants: Henry Farber, Princeton University; Claudia Goldin, Harvard University; Mark Lopez, Pew Hispanic Center; Rhonda Sharpe, Bennett College for Women; Mary Daly, Federal Reserve Bank-San Francisco, Donna Ginther, University of Kansas; Debra Barbezat, Colby College; John Haltiwanger, University of Maryland; Nancy Jianakoplos, Colorado State University; Robert Pollak, Washington University in St. Louis; Olivia Mitchell, University of Pennsylvania.

program and the AEA. The program is aimed at assisting female junior faculty in preparing themselves for the tenure hurdle.

We are evaluating the success of the program using a randomized trial. Applicants were randomly assigned to be treatments (mentees who attended the workshop) or controls who did not participate. Our study will compare the academic performance (i.e., papers, grants) of these two groups. To our knowledge, this randomized trial of a mentoring program is unique in academia.[1]

There have now been three cohorts of program participants, in 2004, 2006, and 2008. A fourth cohort begins in January 2010, and another is planned for January 2012. This chapter thus presents an interim assessment. We find that CeMENT significantly increased publication rates and successful grant applications. While it is too early to tell what the eventual effect on tenure will be, the results suggest that this program may be a useful way to help women advance in the economics profession.

8.1. Background

Using data from the 1973–2001 Survey of Doctoral Recipients, Donna K. Ginther and Shulamit Kahn (2004) find gender differences in promotion to tenure in economics of 21 percentage points. A separate analysis of a sample of AEA members that controls for publications and citations finds a 14 percentage point gender gap in the probability of promotion to tenure. Moreover, they show that women are significantly less likely to be promoted in economics than in political science, statistics, life science, physical science, and engineering. John M. McDowell, Larry D. Singell and Mark Slater (2006) suggest that one possible cause of women's failure to advance in economics may be a lack of research networks. As one indicator of limited networks, they find that while coauthorship is common in economics, female economists are less likely to coauthor than their male colleagues, even after controlling for publication rates. Francine Blau, Marianne Ferber and Anne Winkler (2010) suggest a second possible cause, a lack of role models and informal relationships between young academics and those who are more senior.

8.2. The CeMENT Intervention

The national CeMENT workshops were designed to expose participants to role models (senior female economists), to transmit information about what it takes to get tenure, and to build peer networks of female junior faculty working in similar research areas. Each workshop lasted two days and was held in conjunction with the American Economic Association annual meetings. The workshops brought together junior and senior faculty mentors from various institutions, arranged into small groups (four or five participants and one or two mentors) based on research interests. The workshops were widely advertised and aimed at faculty in research departments.[2]

Each participant circulated a research paper or other related work (like a grant proposal) before the workshop. During the workshop, the small groups met to discuss and provide feedback on each participant's work (approximately one hour for each participant). In addition to the small group meetings, plenary sessions were held consisting of panels of the senior mentors. Topics included research and publishing, getting grants, professional exposure, teaching, the tenure process and work-life balance. At the end of each workshop an exit survey was distributed. On a scale of 1–7, where 1 is "not at all helpful" and 7 is "extremely helpful," the average rating of the workshop over all three years was 6.63. Anecdotal evidence based on discussions with former participants suggests that many women stayed in touch with other women whom they met through the program, and that these women became an important support network.

More than 80 people applied for each workshop. After elimination of incomplete or inappropriate applications, applicants were divided into groups by research area. Applicants were then randomly assigned to treatment or control status within each group. We selected more treatments than controls in an effort to maximize access to the program. For example, in a group of eight, we would select five to be treatments and three to be controls. Both controls and participants were told that we had received more applicants than we could accommodate, and that we had randomly selected participants from the pool of eligible applicants.

This interim evaluation focuses on information that has been systematically coded from vitae of participants and controls. These vitae were either obtained directly from the individual or downloaded from the Web. If no current vita was available (as of the follow-up date), we searched public databases for published articles and federal grants in order to update these outcomes. Most people who were missing recent vitas had left the tenure track.

8.3. Interim Results

We have data after one year for all three workshops; after three years for 2004 and 2006; and after five years for 2004. Table 8.1 shows a comparison of selected "pre-intervention" characteristics of treatments and controls based on information submitted as part of the initial applications for the workshops.

On average, applicants were about three years from their PhDs. Fewer than half were U.S. citizens. However, most applicants obtained the PhD in a U.S. school, and the majority were employed by U.S. institutions.[3]

Table 8.1

Pretreatment Means (Standard errors)

	Treatment	Control
Observations	126	91
Age	33.37	32.64
	(0.332)	(0.419)
US Citizen	0.429	0.505
Married/living with partner	0.640	0.600
Any children	0.240*	0.144
Years since PhD	3.05	2.90
	(0.159)	(0.191)
PhD at top ten	0.357	0.308
Intends to be in academia in 10 years	0.924*	0.978
Has mentor	0.659	0.567
Job at PhD granting institution	0.754	0.747
Job at top-ten department	0.135*	0.055
Any top-tier publications	0.111**	0.023
Total publications	2.94	2.67
	(0.311)	(0.466)
Total NSF grants	0.087	0.055
	(0.025)	(0.024)
Total NIH grants	0.079	0.077
	(0.037)	(0.032)
Total grants	0.476	0.626
	(0.075)	(0.191)

Notes: ** Differences significant at the 5 percent level.
* Differences significant at the 10 percent level.

A little over half were married or living with a partner, and about a fifth had children. Overall, treatments were significantly more likely to have children; this was driven by treatments in Cohort 2 (the 2006 workshop), who were also significantly older. 92.4 percent of the treatments and 97.8 percent of the controls planned to be in academia ten years from the time of their initial application. Most of the applicants were in academic jobs, and 75 percent were in PhD granting institutions.

Table 8.1 indicates that there are no significant differences in number of grants or total number of publications before the workshops. However, we do find that treatments were significantly more likely to hold a job at a top-ten department[4] and to have a publication in a top-tier journal.[5] The estimates by cohort show that these differences arose in Cohort 2, where, by unfortunate chance, all of the applicants from top-ten departments were selected for the treatment. Treatments in Cohort 2 had more publications and were significantly more likely to have a publication in a top-tier journal. We therefore present our results by cohort, as well as for the pooled cohorts.

Table 8.2 shows our main results. Each entry in the table is a coefficient from a separate regression of an outcome (indicated by the column heading) on a constant and an indicator for whether or not the woman was in the "treatment" group. The first four rows suggest that one year after the treatment, the program had had little impact, as one would expect given delays in grant writing and publications. The main exception is the second-cohort treatments, who were also more likely to have top-tier publications and more publications pretreatment.

The next three rows suggest that the intervention had a positive effect on publications in both Cohort 1 and Cohort 2 after three years. Since there was no pretreatment difference in publications in Cohort 1, this result is encouraging. The estimates suggest that by three years after the intervention, workshop participants were 20 percentage points more likely to have a top-tier publication and had two more publications than controls. There is also a positive effect on successful grants in the pooled cohorts.

Finally, the last row shows the results after five years for Cohort 1. We see positive and significant effects of the workshop on grants, top-tier publication and total publications. Those in the treatment group had 0.4 more NSF or NIH grants on average. They had 3 additional publications and were 25 percentage points more likely to have a top-tier publication. These results are especially persuasive in that there were no significant pretreatment differences in outcomes for this cohort.

Table 8.2

Regressions of Outcomes on Treatment
(Coefficients on treatment)

	Total NSF or NIH grants	Any top-tier publications	Total publications
1-year			
All cohorts	0.069	0.109**	0.583
	(0.084)	(0.039)	(0.652)
Cohort 1	0.179	0.067	1.099
	(0.166)	(0.074)	(0.834)
Cohort 2	0.117	0.194**	1.994*
	(0.112)	(0.067)	(1.024)
Cohort 3	−0.104	0.074	−1.378
	(0.141)	(0.060)	(1.473)
3-year			
Cohorts 1 and 2	0.227*	0.195**	1.850**
	(0.125)	(0.058)	(0.861)
Cohort 1	0.320	0.171*	2.039*
	(0.210)	(0.088)	(1.145)
Cohort 2	0.117	0.222**	1.628
	(0.112)	(0.070)	(1.312)
5-year			
Cohort 1	0.398*	0.252**	2.959**
	(0.241)	(0.103)	(1.472)

Notes: Estimated treatment effect from a regression of outcome on treatment and a dummy variable for each cohort (where applicable). Robust standard errors in parentheses. There are 79, 66, and 72 observations in cohorts 1, 2, and 3, respectively.
** Significant at the 5 percent level.
* Significant at the 10 percent level.

Given the evidence in Table 8.1, we have conducted a number of additional analyses to explore whether the estimated treatment effects in Table 8.2 are driven by preexisting differences between treatments and controls. Table 8.3 shows estimates similar to those in Table 8.2, except that the models included controls for having a pretreatment job at a top-ten department and for the number of pretreatment publications in top-tier journals. Adding these controls reduces the estimated effects somewhat, and there are no longer significant effects on grant activity, although all of the year 3 and year 5 estimates remain positive. We still find, however, that at year 5, treatments are 20 percentage points more likely to have a top-tier publication and have 2.7 more publications overall, compared to controls; at year 3, the comparable figures are 9 percentage points and 1.6 publications.

Table 8.3

Regressions of Outcomes on Treatment, Including Pretreatment Controls (Coefficients on treatment)

	Total NSF or NIH grants	Any top-tier publications	Total publications
1-year			
All cohorts	0.054	0.023	0.478
	(0.088)	(0.025)	(0.674)
Cohort 1	0.151	0.011	1.032
	(0.176)	(0.053)	(0.844)
Cohort 2	0.126	0.024*	1.898
	(0.116)	(0.013)	(1.205)
Cohort 3	−0.117	0.011	−1.480
	(0.143)	(0.050)	(1.500)
3-year			
Cohorts 1 and 2	0.179	0.090*	1.622*
	(0.136)	(0.046)	(0.890)
Cohort 1	0.256	0.112	1.843
	(0.221)	(0.078)	(1.124)
Cohort 2	0.126	0.058	1.414
	(0.116)	(0.037)	(1.484)
5-year			
Cohort 1	0.314	0.200**	2.677*
	(0.246)	(0.097)	(1.461)

Notes: Estimated treatment effect from a regression of outcome on treatment; total pretreatment top-tier publications; having a job at a top-ten school at pretreatment; and a dummy variable for each cohort (where applicable). Robust standard errors in parentheses.
** Significant at the 5 percent level.
* Significant at the 10 percent level.

Table 8.4 asks whether changes in outcomes between the pre-intervention and a later date are affected by the intervention. These models are equivalent to including person-specific fixed effects (since the difference in intervention status between time t and time 0 is always 1 or 0).

Table 8.4

Regressions of Change in Outcomes Between Pretreatment and Indicated Year on Treatment
(Coefficients on treatment)

	Total NSF or NIH grants	Any top-tier publications	Total publications
1-year			
All cohorts	0.039	0.016	0.308**
	(0.037)	(0.023)	(0.153)
Cohort 1	0.045	0.037	0.531*
	(0.078)	(0.048)	(0.275)
Cohort 2	0.072	—	0.361
	(0.075)	—	(0.275)
Cohort 3	—	0.007	0.000
	—	(0.048)	(0.238)
3-year			
Cohorts 1 and 2	0.134*	0.089*	0.795
	(0.075)	(0.042)	(0.481)
Cohort 1	0.186	0.141*	1.471**
	(0.122)	(0.073)	(0.670)
Cohort 2	0.072	0.028	-0.006
	(0.075)	(0.028)	(0.682)
5-year			
Cohort 1	0.265*	0.226**	2.387*
	(0.158)	(0.091)	(1.055)

Notes: Estimated treatment effect from a regression of the change in outcomes between pretreatment and the given year on treatment, and a dummy variable for each cohort (where applicable). Robust standard errors in parentheses. The missing estimates correspond to outcomes that do not change between pretreatment and the one-year follow up.
** Significant at the 5 percent level.
* Significant at the 10 percent level.

The year 1 results show that this specification effectively controls for the larger number of top-tier publications in Cohort 2 at baseline. At year 5, we continue to see significant gains in grants and publications for treatments: Treatments were 27 percentage points more likely to have an NSF or NIH grant, 23 percentage points more likely to have any top-tier publication, and they have 2.4 more publications overall. For Cohort 1, there are also significant (but smaller) effects on both outcomes at year 3, and effects that are smaller still in year 1. It is conceivable that the differences at year 3 and year 5 could reflect preexisting differences in trajectories between treatment and control members. However, the much smaller effects of the treatment on grants and top-tier publications after one year provides some evidence that the treatments were not simply on a better trajectory to start. Models excluding applicants with PhDs from top-ten departments, and models excluding applicants with first jobs at top-ten departments, produce similar results.

8.4. Conclusions

We find that CeMENT increased top-tier publications, the total number of publications, and the total number of successful federal grants in treated women relative to controls. The effects are monotonic with respect to time from the intervention and robust to several specification checks designed to control for possible preexisting differences between treatments and controls. These results are encouraging in that publications and grants are important predictors of tenure at most research institutions, and suggest that the intervention had a positive influence on academic productivity. Nonetheless, it is too early to say whether the intervention will have a significant effect on either the probability that women stay in academia, or the probability that they receive tenure.

V

Inequality by Race and Immigrant Status

Introduction

While much of my research has concentrated on gender inequality and gender issues, I have long been interested in inequality by race and ethnicity, as well as the economic status of immigrants. In this part, I consider some of my research on these dimensions of inequality, focusing on black-white differences in the case of race. Chapter 9, based on joint work with Andrea Beller, focuses on gender differences in trends in black-white earnings differentials and Chapter 10 discusses joint work with John Graham on race differences in wealth and asset composition. I then consider some issues related to immigrant status. Chapter 11 considers the extent and sources of immigrant-native differences in the receipt of transfer payments and Chapter 12 examines the impact of traditional gender roles in immigrant source countries on immigrant women's labor supply behavior in the United States.

Looking first at race, the discussions in Chapters 9 and 10 both focus on aspects of race differences that had gotten little attention at the time the research was undertaken. The issue that captured Beller and my attention is illustrated in Table V.I, based on published government data. After a marked trend towards convergence in the race earnings gap beginning in the 1960s for men and dating back to the 1950s for women, there was a notable slowdown in convergence for both sexes in the 1980s. The data in the table make clear that, unfortunately, there has been no renewed trend towards convergence since then. While the slowdown for men had gotten some attention at the time Beller and I undertook this work, the trends for women had not been analyzed. Even today, there has been relatively little work examining the reasons for gender differences in black-white wage gaps among women, particularly taking into account selection bias – for an important exception see, Neal (2004).

Table V.I

Black-White Ratios of Median Earnings by Gender for Full-Time, Year-Round Workers, 1955-2007

Year	Males	Females
1955	60.9	51.4
1960	66.1	67.8
1965	62.8	67.9
1970	69.0	82.2
1975	74.4	96.3
1980	70.7	94.6
1985	69.7	90.6
1990	70.1	88.6
1995	71.0	87.3
2000	73.0	84.1
2005	71.0	87.0
2007	71.7	84.6

Notes: Prior to 1970, data are for income rather than earnings. Data for 1980 onwards refer to workers 15 years of age and older; and for 1955-1975 to workers 14 years of age and older. Prior to 1970, blacks include blacks and other nonwhites. Beginning in 1990, data on whites are for white, non-Hispanics. After 2000, individuals were able to report more than one race. In this table, whites are defined as persons who selected this race group only; blacks are defined as persons who selected black alone or in combination with other races.

Sources: Blau, Ferber, and Winkler (2010). Original data sources: 1955-1965: U.S. Census Bureau, Current Population Reports, Consumer Income Series P-60, various issues; 1970 and beyond: U.S. Census Bureau, Historical Income Tables - People, Table P-38 "Full-Time, Year-Round Workers by Median Earnings and Sex" from, http://www.census.gov/hhes/www/income/histinc/incpertoc.html

Beller and I focused on trying to understand black-white earnings trends over the 1970s and 1980s, and, in particular, the role of educational and occupational shifts. In light of the much higher unemployment rates of blacks, we focused on annual earnings (rather than weekly wages) and specifically identified the impact of race differences in trends in part-time employment and annual weeks worked on the earnings differential. A challenge, as always, was sample selection, especially since labor force participation rates of blacks relative to whites had declined over the focal period. Thus, we were interested in examining the potential impact on the results of adjustment for selectivity bias in both measured and unmeasured characteristics. Adjusting for selectivity with respect to measured characteristics is straightforward. To adjust for selectivity in unmeasured characteristics, we expanded on a technique employed by Smith and Welch (1986). This involved simulating what the relative wage trends would have been had the participation rates of blacks and whites remained at their initial year (1971) level. Where participation has decreased, the dropouts are added back in. The details of the adjustment are described in the chapter. Essentially, we applied an "adjustment factor," i.e., the proportion of the wage of an otherwise similar participant which a nonparticipant would receive. In the empirical work, two adjustment factors were used: 0.8 and 0.6. This enabled us to estimate plausible bounds for the black-white ratio and see what the impact of these assumptions would be on the trends.

Overall, our findings indicated that, although black women fared better than men over the period in some respects, in other important respects their experience was similarly negative. Taking the period as a whole (1971-1988), black women gained in terms of both annual earnings and estimated wages relative to white women, while black men gained only in terms of wages. Moreover, black women made faster progress relative to white males than black males did relative to the same group. On the other hand, both black women and black men experienced stagnating or declining earnings and wages relative to whites of the same sex during the 1980s, with younger blacks faring particularly poorly. We noted that our results implied that the progressive entry of relatively higher earning younger blacks and the retirement of lower earning older blacks, a process which had in the past increased overall black wage ratios, would not be a source of wage gains for blacks in the 1990s (and by implication beyond). The continued stagnation of the relative earnings of blacks since the 1980s suggests that this was an accurate predication.

My work with John Graham on race differences in wealth and asset composition, discussed in Chapter 10, began with the observation that there was an extremely large difference in wealth between blacks and whites that dwarfed the race difference in income. In our sample of young families (the mean age of family heads was 30), black families held only 18 percent of the wealth of white families. In contrast, in these young families, black-white income ratios were 75 percent for married couples and 65 percent for single heads. Yet race wealth differences had up to that point received very little attention, with even fewer attempts to explain the difference (see Chapter 10). Unfortunately, these race wealth gaps have remained extremely large since the late 1970s when our data were collected.[1] For example, a recent study for the full age range of families found that black households held only 5 percent of the wealth of white households in 2009, down from 9 percent in 2005, prior to the recession of 2007 (Kochhar, Fry, and Taylor 2011).[2] The black-white wealth ratios reported by Kochhar, Fry, and Taylor for both years are lower than the ratio Graham and I obtained. This likely primarily reflects the difference in ages between the two samples, although there may also have been trends adverse to black wealth acquisition since the late 1970s.[3]

We focused on young families because, at the time of our writing, this was the group that had benefited the most from improvements in the labor market for black Americans shown in the table above. Thus, for this group, the effects of past discrimination and other disabilities which older blacks presumably suffered to a greater extent would be minimized. We felt that evidence of large unexplained racial differentials in wealth for this relatively advantaged group of younger blacks would be of particular concern, not only for the group itself, but also for future generations to the extent that wealth is used to finance children's education or given directly in the form of financial or physical assets. The persistence of a large race gap in wealth since the period we examined would seem to support our concern about these issues.

In accounting for racial differences in wealth, we employed a standard Oaxaca-Blinder decomposition, using either the black or white regression coefficients to evaluate the differences in the means of the explanatory variables. This turned out to raise an interesting problem that can arise in other contexts as well. The more dissimilar the underlying functions (in our case wealth functions of blacks and whites), the greater the likelihood of obtaining very different results depending on the weights employed. This is precisely what happened in our case. Differences in means explained 73.6% (96.6%) of the wealth differential for married couples (single heads) when the white coefficients were used, but only about 22.0% (for both groups) when the black coefficients were employed.[4] In contrast, racial differentials in income were not only smaller than wealth differentials (both absolutely and relatively), they were also more consistently explained by the characteristics of black and white families, regardless of which function was employed. Differences in means were found to explain 62 to 84 percent of the income gap among married couples, and 45 to 52 percent among families with single heads.

Given the sharply differing decomposition results for wealth based on the black and white functions, it is reasonable to inquire whether there are any grounds for emphasizing one set of results over the other. While the selection of weights is in some sense arbitrary, we argued that, from a policy perspective, the more relevant question was addressed when the black functions were employed: what would happen to black wealth if blacks were given the white means but retained their own functions? Our results indicated that even if society were successful in eliminating all the disadvantages of blacks in terms of their lower incomes and adverse locational and demographic characteristics, a large portion of the wealth gap - 78 percent - would remain. By this estimate, over three quarters of the observed racial differences in wealth was related to race per se, as reflected in the dissimilar black and white wealth functions.

The reader may or may not agree with our reasoning. For example, it might be argued that differences in coefficients between the two functions might converge as differential treatment of blacks and whites was reduced. Or, the coefficient differences could be ascribed to race differences in behavior, for example lower savings rates of blacks. However, at the time of our writing, past studies (cited in the chapter) appeared to rule out major differences in the propensity to save as an explanation. Based on this, we believed the coefficient differences more likely represented differences in rates of return, perhaps due to blacks facing barriers to acquiring certain assets such as businesses and housing which historically have paid among the highest real rates of return. We noted that there was a substantial literature on the effects of racial discrimination on home ownership. We also noted that higher unemployment and greater income uncertainty may increase the demand of blacks for liquid (relative to other types of) assets, and rates of return are often lower for liquid assets. We also speculated that racial differences in inheritance and other intergenerational transfers most likely play a part (particularly given the young age of our sample).

Turning now to immigrant status, with the increase in immigration to the United States and other advanced industrialized countries, considerable public attention and concern has focused on the impact of immigrants on destination countries. One area that has excited considerable controversy looks at the impact of immigrant flows on outcomes for natives. My research has not been concerned with this issue. However, if there are immigrant differences in outcomes or behavior, another way in which immigrants influence the destination country is by altering the composition of the population. This provides one motivation for research examining immigrant-native differences in outcomes, the issue which has been the focus of my research. Another motivation is that, for all of us with an interest in inequality, immigrant-native differences are one potential source of inequality within the polity, one that is potentially getting of greater importance as the size of the immigrant group increases. The discussion in Chapter 11 focuses on an aspect of immigrant-native differences that has been a perennial "hot button" issue – immigrant-native differences in transfer payments. Yet, for all the attention it received in the public discourse, at the time of my investigation of the issue, the 1980s, it had received very little systematic analysis. .

Julian Simon, a colleague at the University of Illinois where I was then on the faculty, first prompted my interest in researching the topic. He had earlier presented Congressional testimony, later published in Simon (1984), which sought to balance the costs and benefits of immigration at an aggregate level. I became interested in a more detailed analysis of the transfer system, focusing on identifying any immigrant-native differences that might exist, and understanding the extent to which they were due to immigrant-native differences in characteristics versus behavioral differences between the two groups.

This was a very interesting time to be studying immigration to the United States. Immigrant flows had previously peaked with the last great wave of immigration, from the late 1800s to the early 1920s. This wave excited considerable interest and concern at the time, both with respect to its large volume and the shift in composition of immigrants away from northern and western Europe and towards southern and eastern Europe. Writing at that time, economist and later U.S. Senator, Paul Douglas, confronted concerns that would be repeated in the next great wave of immigration. His 1919 article was entitled "Is the New Immigration More Unskilled than the Old?" (Douglas 1919). My own forebears were Eastern Europeans who had come in this wave, and I had done some earlier research examining how various nationality groups fared in the early twentieth century labor market more closely analyzing one of the data sources that Douglas had referenced – see Blau (1980).

Starting with some legislative changes in 1965, immigration to the United States began to pick up again and its origins shifted from Europe and North American to Asia and Latin America. Again, increases in the volume of immigration and shifts in its composition began to incite considerable interest and concern. With respect to transfer receipt, a priori, there was certainly reason to believe the "new" immigrants might be a transfer-prone group. They were less well educated relative to natives than their predecessors and increasingly comprised of racial and ethnic minorities that might face additional barriers in the labor market. But in this, as in other areas, it is my firm belief that one must actually go to the data to see what it tells you before reaching a final conclusion.

In this case, for the year my data referred to – 1975 – these concerns appear to have been overblown. I did find that the average level of transfers was considerably higher among families headed by immigrants, but this was almost entirely the result of the higher average age of family members among the immigrant group - a reflection of the large inflows of immigrants into the U.S. during the pre-1924 period. When age and other factors were held constant, immigrant families were found to be considerably less likely to rely on welfare than native families, and their receipts from social insurance programs were found to be only slightly higher.

This study was undertaken relatively early in the most recent wave of immigrants so its results may or may not hold currently. But the principle of going to the data most certainly does hold. Moreover, my conclusions are in some respects similar to more recent analyses. For example, Borjas and Hilton (1996), who focus on means-tested entitlement programs, find that the immigrant-native difference in the probability of receiving cash benefits (the type I studied) is small. However, they also find that the gap widens once noncash transfers are included. The inclusion of such programs where data are available is certainly valid and appropriate. When this is done, they find that 21 percent of immigrant households receive some type of assistance, as compared with only 14 percent of native households.

Chapter 12 considers the results of one of a recent set of papers with Lawrence Kahn that probe the influence of source country characteristics on the behavior of immigrants and their children in the United States. This work is potentially of interest not only because of the policy issues raised by immigrant behavior and outcomes but also because it is related to a broader literature examining the impact of culture or preferences and beliefs developed in a different time or place on current economic behavior (Fernández 2008). As I noted above, one of the major motivations for my work on immigration is a concern with how immigrants fare in the United States. But I also find the issue of the impact of culture on behavior extremely interesting because it sheds light on one set of factors that appear to influence individuals' preferences about labor supply, fertility, and education, to mention some of the areas we have examined. While individuals' preferences generally play an important role in economic models, preference formation itself tends to be a black box to economists. If culture, in the sense Fernandez defines it, does have a strong hold on people's behavior, it suggests that greater attention to preference formation would be fruitful. As early as the 1990s, I had been intrigued by evidence I found, in the course of a study on immigrant fertility, of a positive effect of source country fertility levels on immigrant fertility in the United States (Blau 1992); however I had not revisited the issue until Kahn and I decided to embark on the current set of projects.

In Chapter 12, our focus is on the impact of source country characteristics on the labor supply assimilation profiles of married adult immigrant women and men. While previous work by Antecol (2000) had indicated a positive association between source country labor supply and immigrant women's labor supply in the United States, our work raised the issue of the persistence of this effect – i.e., how did this source country characteristic affect the assimilation profile. This question is of interest both from a policy perspective and also for what it might suggest about the role and importance of source country culture on immigrant women's behavior. We examined this issue using the 1980–2000 U.S. censuses, augmented with an extensive set of source country characteristics. While our focus is on the impact of two indicators of the extent of traditional gender roles in the source country – female relative to male labor force participation and women's completed fertility – (particularly the former), we also control for a variety of other source country characteristics that may affect immigrants' labor supply behavior in the United States in order to more confidently parse out the effects of the gender role variables.

We find that immigrant women from countries with high-female labor supply persistently work more than those from low-female supply countries, that is that the gap in labor supply between women from high- and low-female supply countries is roughly constant with time in the United States. The persistence of this effect is consistent with the notion of an impact of culture, as is our finding that men's labor supply is unaffected by source country female participation, and other tests reported in the Chapter. It is important to point out, however, that while both groups of women work less than comparable natives on arrival, women from high-female-participation countries eventually close the gap with natives entirely, and women from low-female labor supply countries eliminate most of it.

In a recent paper (Blau and Kahn 2011), Kahn and I probe the mechanism behind the positive association between source country female supply and immigrant women's labor supply in the United States to get further insights on the role of culture on behavior. One possible mechanism would be that immigrant women from high-female labor supply source countries have more work experience prior to their arrival in the United States and that their higher labor supply in the United States is due to their the higher levels of job-related human capital that they accumulated before migration. On the other hand, it may be that higher female participation rates in the source country impart labor market-oriented values or additional skills beyond those directly tied to employment; this would be consistent with an effect of broader culture or social capital. Using a rich new data set, the New Immigrant Survey, which contains information on immigrant women's pre-migration employment, we are able to directly test the relative importance of each of these mechanisms. We find that most of the effect of source country female labor supply on immigrant women's labor supply in the United States remains when we further control for each woman's own work experience prior to migrating, and, further, that immigrant women's pre-migration labor supply also strongly positively affects their labor supply in the United States. Finally, we find a significantly negative interaction between pre-migration labor supply and source country female labor supply. These results suggest an important role for culture and norms in affecting immigrant women's labor supply, since the effect of source country female labor supply on immigrant women's work hours in the United States is still strong even controlling for the immigrant's own pre-migration labor supply. The negative interaction effects between pre-migration work experience and source country female labor supply on immigrant women's U.S. work hours and wages suggest that cultural capital can substitute for individual job-related human capital in affecting preparedness for work in the United States.

Another potential indicator of the potential importance of culture is if there is an effect of source country characteristics on the behavior of U.S.-born women descended from immigrants. This does indeed appear to be the case. For example, Antecol (2000) found a positive correlation between U.S. and source country participation for "second and higher generation" immigrants, defined by their answer to the Census question on ancestry. Similarly, the labor supply and fertility behavior of U.S.-born daughters of immigrants (the second generation) has been found to be positively associated with both female participation and fertility rates in their parents' country of origin (Fernández and Fogli 2009) and the U.S. female participation and fertility rates of immigrants from those origin countries (Blau, Kahn, Liu and Papps 2011).

9

Black-White Earnings over the 1970s and 1980s: Gender differences in Trends

Based on a paper with Andrea H. Beller

9.1. Introduction

Research on black/white earnings trends through the early 1970s (e.g., Freeman 1973; Smith 1979; Smith and Welch 1977) suggests that starting in the 1950s for women and in the 1960s for men, black earnings increased relative to those of whites of the same sex.[1] Both educational and occupational shifts appear to have contributed to these earnings increases, and some studies suggest that anti-discrimination legislation also played a significant role (e.g., Freeman 1973; Beller 1978; Brown 1984).[2] An additional finding of interest was that, particularly among males, gains tended to be larger for younger blacks. Under the assumption that younger blacks would retain a substantial portion of these gains as they

This chapter is a revised version of Blau, F. D., Beller, A. H. (1992). Black-White Earnings Over the 1970s and 1980s: Gender Differences in Trends, in: The Review of Economics and Statistics, 74(2): 276-286.

An earlier version of this paper was presented at the Population Association of America meetings, May 1990. The authors are thankful to Suzanne Bianchi, William Darity, Marianne Ferber, Daniel Hamermesh, Lawrence Kahn, Edward Montgomery, and the participants at the Northwestern University Labor Economics Workshop for helpful comments, and Jeffrey Hayes for providing the 1980 occupational recodes used in this paper. We are indebted to Mann Yoon, Denise Chachere, Lisa Reavlin, and Nichola Dyer for able research assistance. Research support from the Research Board of the University of Illinois is gratefully acknowledged.

aged, this was taken as an optimistic finding for the future economic progress of blacks.

Previous research has presented evidence of a slowdown in wage convergence for males during the 1980s which it is argued is associated with increasing returns to both measured and unmeasured skills (Juhn et al. 1989; O'Neill 1990). At the time this study was conducted, trends for black women had not yet been analyzed but we argued they were of importance for understanding the overall 1980s trends: to the extent that explanations for the 1980s slowdown that focus on skills are correct, we should expect to find similar patterns among females as among males.

In this chapter, we extend previous work by examining black-white earnings trends over the 1970s and 1980s focussing on gender differences and on the role of educational and occupational shifts in explaining the trends. Given the importance of age differences in earlier periods, the analysis is performed separately for three groups defined in terms of potential labor market experience. In light of race differences in unemployment rates, we focus on annual earnings (rather than weekly wages) and specifically identify the impact of race differences in trends in part-time employment and annual weeks worked on the earnings differential. While earnings are only one dimension of race differences in economic outcomes (Cotton 1989), we believe they are an important one worthy of detailed study. Since relative labor force participation rates of blacks have fluctuated over this period, we also examine the potential impact on the results of adjustment for selectivity bias in both measured and unmeasured characteristics (Butler and Heckman 1977; Darity 1980).

We use data from the 1972, 1982, and 1989 Annual Demographic Files of the Current Population Surveys (CPS). The 1972 and 1982 CPS data (with information on 1971 and 1981 earnings) were selected because they allow us to observe changes over a decade and because economic conditions were reasonably comparable, with both 1971 and 1981 following cyclical troughs in the preceding year (Moore and Zarnowitz 1986). The unemployment rate was higher in 1981 (7.6%) than in 1971 (5.9%) but that was generally the case in the late 1970s and the early 1980s compared to the earlier period.[3] Similarly, while black unemployment rates increased relative to white's between 1971 and 1981, and black relative labor force participation rates declined; this again reflects secular trends rather than cyclical factors.[4] The 1989 CPS (1988 earnings data) was selected as the most recent year available at the time the analysis was performed. Economic conditions differed considerably from 1981, but this reflects general differences between the poor performance of the economy in the early years of the decade and the economic expansion that followed. As the overall unemployment rate declined to 5.5% in 1988, the black-white unemployment rate gap decreased for both males and females, while the black-white labor force participation differential fell for males.[5]

9.2. Regression Model and Empirical Procedures

In order to analyze earnings trends, the following regressions are estimated separately for race-gender-experience groups in each year:

$$\ln Y = B_T' X + e_1 \quad (1)$$

$$\ln Y = B_D' X + B_O' OCC + e_2 \quad (2)$$

where ln Y is the natural log of annual earnings, X is a vector of variables measuring human capital, demographic and locational characteristics; OCC is a vector of dummy variables for major occupational category[6] and employment in the government sector; B_T, B_D and B_O are vectors of coefficients; and e_1 and e_2 are random error terms. The coefficient on an explanatory variable (x_j) in equation (2) (b_{dj}) measures the direct effect of x_j on log earnings, controlling for occupation, while the coefficient on x_j in equation (1) (b_{tj}) measures the total effect of x_j on earnings taking into account both its direct effect and its indirect effect via occupational attainment.

The variables in X include measures of education,[7] potential labor market experience and its square, the natural log of annual weeks worked, dummy variables for part-time work, veteran status (males only), and marital status, as well as number of children (women only),[8] and dummy variables for three regions and urban residence. OCC includes dummy variables for government employment and major occupational category. The occupational variables are specified somewhat differently for males and females because gender differences in employment distributions resulted in too few observations in some categories to form the same set of dummy variables for both sexes.[9]

Our sample consists of individuals aged 18 to 64 who worked at least one week during the previous year and whose wage and salary income was at least $100. We excluded individuals with any self-employment income, members of the military, those in farming occupations,[10] and, for the youngest experience group, those who were in school.[11] We also excluded all individuals for whom data on income from wages and salaries were missing and therefore imputed by the Census.[12]

The Oaxaca-Blinder decomposition (Blinder 1973; Oaxaca 1973a) is used to decompose black-white earnings differentials in each year into a component due to race differences in the means of the variables and a component that is unexplained (i.e., due to race differences in coefficients including the constant term). We consider both equations (1) and (2) to identify the role of occupational shifts in producing the observed earnings trends. The unexplained portion of the pay differential is commonly viewed as due to labor market discrimination or unmeasured skill differences or both.

As noted above, given shifting relative participation rates of blacks, sample selection bias is a concern in estimating black-white earnings trends. Selectivity with respect to either measured or unmeasured factors may occur. As an example of the former, suppose that the propensity of blacks with low educational attainment to participate in the wage and salary sector decreases relative to white's. Trends in wage ratios calculated on the basis of participants will then be biased upward. As an example of the latter, suppose that among those with the same measured characteristics, participation in the wage and salary sector becomes increasingly selective of those with higher wage offers among blacks in comparison to whites. Then the trend in black-white wage ratios will again be overestimated.

A conventional approach is to adjust for selectivity bias with respect to unmeasured characteristics by using a technique suggested by Heckman (1980) to obtain consistent estimates of the earnings equation. This approach has, however, come under increasing criticism for its lack of robustness: "[...] seemingly small misspecifications may generate large biases in estimates [...]" (Manski 1989: 356). In addition to being extremely costly given the large number of equations estimated here, we found in previous work (Blau and Beller 1988) that coefficients on the selectivity variable were very imprecisely estimated for blacks, making this approach not very informative for this group. Thus, we examine the sensitivity of our results to adjustments for selectivity in measured and unmeasured characteristics by expanding on a technique employed by Smith and Welch (1986).

To adjust for potential selectivity bias, we attempt to simulate what the relative wage trends would have been had the participation rates of blacks and whites remained at their initial year (1971) levels.[13] We refer to those included in the regression sample as "participants" and those excluded as "nonparticipants." Following Smith and Welch (1986), we begin with the following relationship for adjusted wages in year t (0 = 1971, 1 = 1981 or 1988).[14]

$$W_{A1} = W_{P1} \cdot w + W_{N1}(1-w) \tag{3}$$

where W_{A1} = the adjusted wage in year 1; W_{P1} = the observed wage of participants in year 1; W_{N1} = the wage attributed to "dropouts" (or "entrants") in year 1; and $w = p_1/p_0$ where p = the participation rate. The intuition behind equation (3) when the participation rate has declined is that "dropouts" are added back in, and W_A in, say, 1981 is computed as a weighted average of the wages of participants and nonparticipants (dropouts) with the weights being determined by the ratio of the 1981 to the 1971 participation rate. In the case in which participation has increased, W_A is the wage that would obtain in 1981 if the entrants were subtracted out.

To adjust for selectivity with respect to measured characteristics, we implement (3) using an estimated wage of nonparticipants to proxy W_N. That is, W_N is obtained by estimating equation (1) for participants and evaluating it at the observed means of nonparticipants. We adjust for possible participant-nonparticipant differences in unmeasured characteristics by assuming that a nonparticipant receives a lower wage than a participant with the same measured characteristics. We examine the impact of two arbitrarily selected "adjustment factors" (i.e., proportions of the wage of an otherwise similar participant which a nonparticipant receives), 0.8 and 0.6. (An adjustment factor of 1 assumes that nonparticipants receive the wage predicted by the earnings regression.)

While it is theoretically possible for nonparticipants to have either higher or lower wage offers than participants with the same measured characteristics,[15] we have focussed on the latter case since this would be the situation of most concern for an adverse effect on black-white trends.

9.3. Overview of Trends

Black-white unadjusted annual earnings ratios and estimated wage ratios for the 1971-88 period are shown in Table 9.1. Estimated wage ratios adjust for part-time employment and weeks worked over the year by evaluating equation (1) at the white (male) means for the part-time and log weeks variables.[16] The trends are shown for each race-gender group as a whole and for three experience groups defined by potential labor market experience equal to 0-9 years, 10-19 years, and 20+ years (figures for the group with 7-16 years of experience in 1988 are shown in parentheses).

Table 9.1

Trends in Black-White Annual Earnings and Estimated Wage Ratios, 1971-88[a]

	Annual Earnings			Estimated Wages[b]		
	1971	1981	1988	1971	1981	1988
Black males/White males						
All[c]	63.4	66.0	62.3	68.6	74.5	74.5
Experience 0-9	66.4	70.0	59.7	76.0	81.1	75.4
Experience 10-19	63.8	62.9	59.3	67.0	72.8	76.7
(Experience 7-16)			(60.0)			(76.7)
Experience 20 +	61.7	65.2	67.6	65.7	71.0	72.8
Black females/White females						
All[c]	82.2	92.4	92.6	81.2	89.7	88.2
Experience 0-9	93.4	86.3	79.4	91.5	91.5	87.6
Experience 10-19	102.1	104.4	102.9	85.8	97.0	91.5
(Experience 7-16)			(98.4)			(89.4)
Experience 20 +	70.1	88.7	94.5	72.5	86.1	87.3
Black females/White males						
All[c]	31.0	40.1	46.6	45.2	54.7	60.0
Experience 0-9	43.7	50.9	52.4	59.8	67.1	70.8
Experience 10-19	29.2	39.4	47.9	45.2	55.9	61.5
(Experience 7-16)			(50.3)			(63.9)
Experience 20 +	26.5	33.8	42.3	38.9	45.9	52.8
White females/White males						
All[c]	37.7	43.4	50.3	55.6	61.0	68.0
Experience 0-9	46.7	59.0	66.0	65.7	74.2	81.5
Experience 10-19	28.6	37.7	46.5	52.1	60.9	69.0
(Experience 7-16)			(51.1)			(73.3)
Experience 20 +	37.8	38.2	44.7	53.0	53.7	60.0

Notes: [a]Based on geometric means.
[b]Computed by evaluating regression equation (1) for each gender-race-experience group at the white (male) weighted means for the part-time and weeks worked variables and at own group means for the remaining variables.
[c]Computed as a weighted average of the means for each experience group.

Table 9.1 suggests that black women fared better than black men over the 1970s and 1980s in at least two respects. First, taking the 1971-88 period as a whole, they experienced increases in both annual earnings and estimated wages whereas black males gained only in terms of estimated wages. Gains in estimated wage ratios were, however, similar (8.6%) for the two groups. The less favorable trend in annual earnings for black males reflected declining relative time inputs of blacks in the 0-9 and 10-19 experience groups due to an increase in part-time work in the case of the former and both an increase in part-time work and a decrease in annual weeks in the case of the latter. In contrast, among women only the youngest group of blacks experienced decreases in relative time inputs, in this case because increases in annual weeks among blacks did not keep pace with increases among whites.

Second, during the 1971-88 period and especially in the 1980s, the gender gap narrowed substantially among whites, with the female-male wage ratio increasing by 22.3% (12.4 points). Thus, as the wages of black women increased relative to white women, the black female to white male wage ratio increased at an even faster pace, by 32.7% (14.8 points) in comparison to an increase of 8.6% (5.9 points) in the black male to white male ratio.

In a number of other respects, however, the experience of black men and women over the 1971-88 period was similar. First, for both groups, while earnings and wages relative to whites of the same sex rose during the 1970s, they stagnated or declined during the 1980s. Second, in contrast to the 1960s experience, younger blacks did not fare better than older blacks. Taking the period as a whole, the largest gains of any gender-experience group were for older (experience 20+) black women who increased their wage ratio from 72.5% in 1971 to 87.3% in 1988 and older black males were the only group of men to increase their relative annual earnings over the period. During the 1970s, wage gains for younger black males (0-9 experience group) were no greater than those for older males, and the relative wages of younger women were stable while those of older women increased substantially. Moreover, for both black men and women, wage ratios actually fell over the 1980s for the 0-9 experience group, with considerably larger declines in annual earnings ratios. Black women in the 10-19 experience group also saw a decrease in their wage ratio in the 1980s.

The consequence of these varying trends by age was a dramatic alteration in the relationship between estimated wage ratios and potential labor market experience. In 1971, for both men and women, the ratio was highest for labor market entrants and declined across experience groups from 76.0% (91.5%) for male (female) entrants to 65.7% (72.5%) for males (females) in the 20+ experience group. By 1988, estimated wage ratios were fairly similar across experience groups at 75% to 77% among males and 88% to 92% among females.

To track the experience of the 1960s (1970s) entry cohort over the 1970s (1980s), we may compare the wage ratios for the 0-9 experience group in 1971 (1981) to the ratios for the 10-19 (7-16) experience group in 1981 (1988). Among males, while the ratio for the 1960s and the 1970s entry cohorts did decline with age, they still exceeded the ratio for the 10-19 experience group ten (seven) years earlier. Thus, for males, as in the past, the higher wage ratios of entering cohorts relative to older blacks was a source of cross-sectional earnings growth for the 10-19 experience group throughout the 1970s and 1980s. For females, this was the case only in the 1970s as the 1960s black entry cohort not only retained but actually increased their relative wages as they aged. However, not only was the wage ratio of the 1970s entry cohort lower than that of the 10-19 experience group in 1981, it decreased further with age, causing the decline in the wage ratio of the 10-19 experience group between 1981 and 1988 noted above.

9.4. Adjustment for Selectivity Bias

The results of our illustrative adjustments for selectivity bias are shown in Table 9.2. The rows headed labor force give the estimated wage ratio for labor force participants as presented in Table 9.1. Under the rows headed adjustment factor, we present the results of the adjustments described above. The findings suggest that the 1970s trends for black males and females in the youngest experience group are most affected by the adjustment. Adjusting for the decrease in the relative probability of sample inclusion that occurred for blacks during that time[17] results in a stable to declining black-white wage ratio (rather than an increase) for males, and a declining (rather than a stable) ratio for females. While these results are illustrative rather than conclusive, they suggest that gains for younger blacks over the 1970s estimated on the basis of observed wages may be overstated.

There are also some indications of adverse effects for blacks in other experience groups in either the 1970s or the 1980s. However, in all but one case, the trends remain the same as those described above based on observed wages. The exception is that when an adjustment factor as low as 0.6 is employed (an extremely low value), all relative wage gains for black women in experience group 10-19 over the 1970s are eliminated. Finally, it is particularly noteworthy that the finding of large relative wage gains for older black women in the 1970s remains even after this adjustment for selectivity bias.

Table 9.2

Simulations of the Impact of Selectivity Bias on Black-White Trends in Estimated Wage Ratios[a]

	Males			Females		
	1971	1981	1988	1971	1981	1988
Experience 0-9						
Labor force	76.0	81.1	75.4	91.5	91.5	87.6
Adjustment factor						
1.0		77.2	74.5		88.1	86.2
0.8		73.6	73.4		83.1	84.4
0.6		69.1	72.0		77.1	82.1
Experience 10-19						
Labor force	67.0	72.8	76.7	85.8	97.0	91.5
Adjustment factor						
1.0		72.4	75.7		95.0	89.8
0.8		71.2	75.4		88.2	82.5
0.6		69.7	74.9		80.2	73.9
Experience 20+						
Labor force	65.7	71.0	72.8	72.5	86.1	87.3
Adjustment factor						
1.0		70.6	72.7		85.9	87.9
0.8		69.2	72.4		84.4	86.0
0.6		67.5	72.1		82.7	83.6

Notes: [a] Earnings are standardized for time input on the basis of the white means of those included in the wage regression sample.

9.5. Decomposition of the Earnings Trends

We now turn to an analysis of the observed trends in earnings ratios by experience group (Table 9.3). In each year, the white earnings functions are employed to evaluate the impact of race differences in the means of the variables on the log earnings differential ($\ln Y_W - \ln Y_B$). The remainder is considered "unexplained" and may reflect the impact of discrimination or race differences in unmeasured factors. Changes over the 1971-81 and 1981-88 periods are shown in the final four columns of Table 9.3. The final two rows for each experience group show the unadjusted and adjusted black-to-white earnings ratios.[18] Unless otherwise indicated, we focus on the total effects of the variables (given in the second column for each year) rather than the direct effects (given in the first column).

Table 9.3

Decomposition of the Log Earnings Differential (White Functions)

	1971		1981		1988		Change			
							1971-1981		1981-1988	
	Direct	Total	Direct	Total	Direct	Total	Direct	Total	Direct	Total
					Males					
EXPERIENCE 0-9										
Due to Means	0.306	0.284	0.233	0.192	0.324	0.282	-0.073	-0.091	0.091	0.090
Occupation	0.025	—	0.043	—	0.058	—	0.017	—	0.015	—
Education	0.113	0.114	0.030	0.030	0.057	0.068	-0.083	-0.084	0.027	0.037
Time	0.142	0.143	0.149	0.151	0.193	0.198	0.007	0.008	0.044	0.047
Unexplained	0.101	0.123	0.118	0.159	0.163	0.201	0.016	0.035	0.046	0.042
TOTAL	0.408	0.407	0.351	0.351	0.488	0.483	-0.056	-0.056	0.137	0.132
Unadj. Ratio	0.665	0.666	0.704	0.704	0.614	0.617	0.039	0.039	-0.090	-0.087
Adj. Ratio	0.904	0.884	0.889	0.853	0.849	0.818	-0.015	-0.030	-0.040	-0.035
EXPERIENCE 10-19										
Due to Means	0.251	0.209	0.260	0.227	0.373	0.331	0.009	0.018	0.113	0.104
Occupation	0.057	—	0.043	—	0.058	—	-0.014	—	0.015	—
Education	0.082	0.096	0.060	0.067	0.034	0.043	-0.022	-0.029	-0.026	-0.024
Time	0.061	0.061	0.135	0.137	0.223	0.228	0.075	0.075	0.087	0.091
Unexplained	0.203	0.243	0.192	0.221	0.136	0.174	-0.011	-0.022	-0.056	-0.047
TOTAL	0.454	0.452	0.453	0.448	0.509	0.505	-0.002	-0.004	0.057	0.057
Unadj. Ratio	0.635	0.636	0.636	0.639	0.601	0.604	0.001	0.003	-0.035	-0.035
					(0.612)	(0.615)				
Adj. Ratio	0.816	0.784	0.825	0.801	0.873	0.840	0.009	0.017	0.048	0.039
					(0.878)	(0.847)				
EXPERIENCE 20+										
Due to Means	0.315	0.246	0.265	0.211	0.275	0.205	-0.049	-0.035	0.010	-0.006
Occupation	0.104	—	0.082	—	0.098	—	-0.022	—	0.016	—
Education	0.079	0.112	0.078	0.102	0.068	0.094	-0.001	-0.010	-0.010	-0.008
Time	0.072	0.074	0.060	0.062	0.061	0.063	-0.012	-0.012	0.000	0.001
Unexplained	0.168	0.236	0.136	0.189	0.099	0.169	-0.031	-0.047	-0.038	0.019
TOTAL	0.482	0.482	0.402	0.400	0.374	0.374	-0.080	-0.083	-0.028	-0.026
Unadj. Ratio	0.617	0.617	0.669	0.670	0.688	0.688	0.052	0.053	0.019	0.017
Adj. Ratio	0.846	0.789	0.873	0.828	0.906	0.844	0.027	0.038	0.033	0.016

Table 9.3 (continued)

Decomposition of the Log Earnings Differential (White Functions)

	1971		1981		1988		Change 1971-1981		Change 1981-1988	
	Direct	Total	Direct	Total	Direct	Total	Direct	Total	Direct	Total
					Females					
EXPERIENCE 0-9										
Due to Means	0.066	0.040	0.081	0.058	0.179	0.159	0.014	0.018	0.099	0.101
Occupation	0.046	—	0.027	—	0.033	—	-0.019	—	0.006	—
Education	0.037	0.062	0.025	0.032	0.035	0.047	-0.012	-0.029	0.010	0.014
Time	-0.006	-0.008	0.021	0.020	0.098	0.100	0.028	0.029	0.077	0.079
Unexplained	0.011	0.039	0.038	0.057	0.048	0.070	0.027	0.019	0.011	0.013
TOTAL	0.077	0.079	0.118	0.115	0.228	0.229	0.041	0.036	0.109	0.114
Unadj. Ratio	0.926	0.924	0.888	0.891	0.796	0.795	-0.038	-0.033	-0.092	-0.096
Adj. Ratio	0.989	0.962	0.963	0.944	0.953	0.932	-0.026	-0.018	-0.010	-0.012
EXPERIENCE 10-19										
Due to Means	0.033	-0.105	-0.020	-0.056	-0.060	-0.095	- 0.053	0.049	-0.040	-0.038
Occupation	0.147	—	0.044	—	0.042	—	- 0.103	—	-0.002	—
Education	0.037	0.056	0.022	0.038	0.020	0.031	- 0.015	-0.018	-0.002	- 0.007
Time	-0.153	-0.160	-0.108	-0.116	-0.132	-0.139	0.045	0.044	-0.024	-0.022
Unexplained	-0.047	0.088	- 0.028	0.007	0.030	0.061	0.019	- 0.081	0.058	0.054
TOTAL	-0.014	-0.017	-0.048	-0.049	-0.031	-0.033	-0.034	-0.033	0.018	0.016
Unadj. Ratio	1.014	1.017	1.049	1.051	1.031	1.034	0.035	0.034	-0.018	-0.017
					(0.990)	(0.993)				
Adj. Ratio	1.048	0.915	1.029	0.993	0.971	0.941	-0.019	0.078	-0.058	-0.053
					(0.944)	(0.920)				
EXPERIENCE 20+										
Due to Means	0.375	0.141	0.093	-0.001	0.027	- 0.046	-0.282	-0.142	-0.066	-0.045
Occupation	0.279	—	0.120	—	0.090	—	- 0.159	—	-0.030	—
Education	0.049	0.085	0.031	0.056	0.029	0.048	- 0.018	-0.029	-0.002	-0.008
Time	0.027	0.031	-0.054	-0.056	-0.079	- 0.084	-0.080	-0.087	-0.025	-0.028
Unexplained	-0.021	0.216	0.000	0.097	0.025	0.095	0.022	-0.119	0.024	-0.002
TOTAL	0.354	0.357	0.093	0.096	0.052	0.049	-0.260	-0.261	-0.042	-0.048
Unadj. Ratio	0.702	0.700	0.911	0.908	0.950	0.953	0.209	0.208	0.039	0.044
Adj. Ratio	1.022	0.806	1.000	0.908	0.975	0.910	-0.022	0.102	-0.024	0.002

Notes:
In each year, the total differential (T), mean effect (M), and unexplained differential (U) are equal to

$$T = \sum_i b_{iw}x_{iw} - \sum_i b_{ib}x_{ib}$$

$$M = \sum_i b_{iw}(x_{iw} - x_{ib})$$

$$U = T - M = \sum_i x_{ib}(b_{iw} b_{ib})$$

where b_{ij} and x_{ij} are the regression coefficient and weighted mean of the ith variable for the jth race group (w = whites, b = blacks) and year subscripts are omitted to simplify notation. The unadjusted (R_X) and adjusted (R_A) ratios are equal to $R_X = e^{-T}$ and $R_A = e^{-U}$. Results for the 7-16 experience group in 1988 are shown in parentheses.

Looking first in greater detail at the role of annual time inputs, we see that among males, blacks' lesser annual time inputs produced a substantial earnings differential in favor of whites in each year in all experience groups. For the younger two, this differential increased, lowering the earnings ratio over the 1971-88 period by 16.6% for the 10-19 experience group,[19] with the effect roughly equally divided between the 1970s and the 1980s, and by 4.7% for the 0-9 experience group during the 1980s.

For women, the impact of race differences in time inputs tended to differ across experience groups, as did trends over the period. In 1971, time inputs contributed little to the differential in the youngest (0-9) experience group, lowered the differential in the 10-19 experience group, and raised the differential among the oldest (20+) experience group. Adverse trends in relative time inputs substantially slowed the earnings progress of blacks in the youngest (0-9) experience group, reducing the earnings ratio by 10.8% over the 1971-88 period. In contrast, relative time inputs increased substantially in the oldest (20+) experience group, explaining over one-third of their large earnings gains between 1971 and 1988.

In comparing the sources of earnings increases for men and women, especially for the 1970s when most of the gains occurred, the most striking finding is the larger role which occupational upgrading played for women than for men. In 1971, race differences in occupation lowered the relative earnings of blacks in all gender-experience groups, with larger effects for older blacks, particularly older black women. With the exception of men in the 0-9 experience group, shifts in occupational distributions by major occupational category worked to reduce black-white earnings differences over the 1970s.[20] For black men and younger black women the gains in earnings due to occupational upgrading were only moderate. But for older (experience 10+) black women the impact of occupational shifts was substantial. Between 1971 and 1988, changes in occupational distributions increased the earnings ratio by 10.5% for the 10-19 experience group (with virtually the entire effect occurring in the 1970s) and by 18.9% for the 20+ experience group (with 84.1% of the effect occurring in the 1970s). These gains were largely due to a reduction in private household employment of black women in these two experience groups.

In 1971, 27.1% (10.7%) of black women in the 20+ (10-19) experience group were private household workers in comparison to only

2.7% (1.5%) of whites. By 1981, black women in the 10-19 experience group were no more likely to be private household workers than whites. Race differences in the proportion employed in these jobs in the oldest (20+) experience group decreased substantially, to 11.1% of blacks versus 1.6% of whites in 1981 and to 7.2% of blacks versus 1.5% of whites in 1988. For the 10-19 experience group, this shift alone is sufficient to account for 87.4% of the contribution of occupation to the 1971-81 change in the race earnings differential (the period during which the equalization in private household employment occurred). For the 20+ experience group, it accounts for 69.8% of the 1971-88 earnings change attributable to occupation.

The decline in the concentration of black women in private household employment over the 1970s and 1980s was part of a long-term trend. In 1940, fully 60% of black women were private household workers falling to 36% in 1960 (Malveaux and Wallace 1987). Tabulations from our CPS data show a further decrease to 16.6% in 1971 and 3.5% in 1988. Our data further suggest that these observed cross-sectional changes represent a "vintage effect" where a younger cohort of blacks with a more similar occupational distribution to whites replaces an older cohort with a greater disparity. Tabulations of our CPS data indicate that in 1971, 4.2% of black women in the 0-9 experience group were private household workers, only slightly higher than the 1.4% figure for the 10-19 experience group in 1981. Similarly, in 1971, 17.6% of black women aged 54 or under with at least 10 years of potential experience were private household workers. This was not very much higher than the 11.1% of black women in the 20+ experience group who held such jobs in 1981. In 1981, 6.5% of black women aged 57 or under with at least 13 years of potential experience held private household jobs compared to 7.2% of the 20+ experience group in those positions seven years later.

The impact of occupational shifts on earnings differentials was considerably less for women in the 1980s, as this process played itself out. For men, adverse occupational shifts actually increased the earnings differential over the 1980s. This was due to a growing underrepresentation of blacks in managerial and professional jobs in conjunction with, for the 0-9 and 20+ experience groups, a rise in the returns to these jobs.

Examining next the role of educational attainment, we see that in 1971 blacks' lower educational attainment relative to whites increased the earnings differential in all gender-experience groups, but that rising relative educational attainment reduced the black-white differential for all groups over the 1970s. The largest effects were for young black males (0-9 experience) where a reduction in the black deficit in years of schooling from 1.28 in 1971 to 0.42 in 1981 increased the earnings ratio by 8.4%. Effects on other groups were considerably smaller. In contrast to the 1970s, educational shifts in the 1980s increased the earnings differential among younger (experience 0-9) workers of both genders. For males this was due to a small increase in the race disparity in educational attainment of 0.2 years coupled with an increase in the return to education beyond high school.[21] For females the education gap remained about the same (0.4 years), but the returns to years of schooling increased.

An interesting gender difference emerges in the nature of the impact of education on earnings. For men the direct and total effects of education on earnings changes are virtually identical, even where, as in the case of the 0-9 experience group in the 1970s, the impact of rising relative educational attainment is quite large. In contrast, among women, where education effects are substantial (in experience groups 0-9 and 20+ over the 1970s), over half of the total effect of education is due to its indirect effect on earnings via occupational upgrading of blacks.

Finally, we consider the impact of changes in the unexplained differential on the observed trends. These may reflect changes over time in the degree of labor market discrimination or in unmeasured characteristics. Since occupational differences may reflect the choices of employers as well as workers, we focus on the total rather than on the direct effects. As may be seen in Table 9.3, among both men and women in the 0-9 experience group, changes in the unexplained differential were unfavorable throughout the 1971-88 period resulting in falling adjusted ratios. Whereas in 1971 younger black men (women) were estimated to earn 88.4% (96.2%) of whites with the same measured characteristics, by 1988 this figure had fallen to 81.8% (93.2%). The adjusted ratio also fell for black women in the 10-19 experience group during the 1980s from virtual parity in 1981 (99.3%) to 94.1% in 1988.

In contrast, for other experience groups and years, declining unexplained differences worked to reduce the race differential. The largest impact occurred for older women during the 1970s where a reduction in unexplained differences increased the earnings ratio by 11.9% in the 20+ experience group and by 8.1% in the 10-19 experience group.

A comparison of the direct and total effects of the unexplained differential indicates that these large total effects were due to the occupational upgrading of women in these two experience groups described above. It may be noted that the fact that these unexplained differentials go in opposite directions for different experience groups suggests that they are more likely to reflect shifts in unmeasured characteristics (or in their returns) than in the extent of labor market discrimination.[22] Moreover, the similarity of our findings for males and females suggests that the same underlying factors were at work for both groups.

As in the case of the estimated wage ratios, we find a pronounced change in the relationship between the adjusted earnings ratio and potential labor market experience. While in 1971, for both men and women, the adjusted ratio was highest for labor market entrants, by 1988 ratios were fairly similar across experience groups ranging from 81% to 84% among males and from 91% to 93% among females. Also mirroring the results for the estimated wage ratios, we find that the higher ratios of entering cohorts relative to older blacks were a source of cross-sectional earnings growth for the 10-19 experience group for the 1971-88 period for males and for the 1971-81 period for females, but that the lower ratio of the entering cohort in 1981 was a source of a cross-sectional earnings decline for females in the 10-19 experience group in the 1980s.

9.6. Conclusion

In this chapter we analyze trends in black-white annual earnings differentials by gender over the 1970s and 1980s. We find that in at least two respects black women fared better than men over this period. First, a major obstacle to the earnings progress of black males, but not of black females, over this period was a decrease in their relative annual time inputs. As a result, while black women experienced increases in both annual earnings and estimated wages, black men gained only in terms of wages. Wage gains over the period were, however, similar (8.6%) for the two groups. Second, since the gender earnings gap among whites was narrowing during this time, as black women's wages rose relative to white women's, they also made substantial progress relative to white males. The black female to white male wage ratio increased by 32.7% (14.8 points) compared to a considerably smaller increase of 8.6% (5.9 points) in the black male to white male ratio.

In other important respects, however, the experience of black men and women over the period was similar. First, for both groups, while earnings and wages relative to whites of the same sex rose during the 1970s, they stagnated or declined during the 1980s. Second, in contrast to the 1960s, younger blacks did not fare better than older blacks. While in 1971, both unadjusted wage ratios and adjusted earnings ratios were highest within each gender group for labor market entrants, by 1988 these ratios were fairly similar across experience groups. Indeed, women in the 20+ experience group had the largest increases in relative earnings of any gender-experience group over the period. Their large gains were tied to a reduction in their concentration in private household employment, a development which also benefited women in the 10-19 experience group. Blacks of both sexes in the youngest experience group actually experienced declining wage ratios during the 1980s and our adjustment for selectivity bias suggests that the weakening of their relative wage position may have begun in the 1970s.

The evening out of adjusted and unadjusted ratios across experience groups may be viewed in part as a positive development in that it reflects considerable progress for older blacks. However, it is a disquieting development to the extent that it resulted not simply from earnings gains for older blacks but also from relative declines in earnings of younger blacks compared to whites with the same measured characteristics. The fact that trends in unexplained earnings differentials go in opposite directions for different experience groups - up for the youngest group and down for the others - suggests that they are more likely to reflect shifts in unmeasured characteristics (or in their returns) than in labor market discrimination. The similarity of our findings for males and females further implies that the same underlying factors were at work for both groups. Regardless of the source of these trends, they are of serious concern. They imply that the progressive entry of relatively higher earning younger blacks and the retirement of lower earning older blacks, a process which in the past increased overall black wage ratios, will not be a source of wage gains for blacks in the 1990s.

10

Black-White Differences in Wealth and Asset Composition

Based on a paper with John W. Graham

10.1. Introduction

The purpose of this chapter is to examine racial differences in the magnitude and composition of wealth and to identify the reasons for these differences. We present cross-sectional data which show that, on average, young black families hold only about 18 percent of the wealth of young white families and tend to hold this wealth in proportionately different forms. Blacks share a variety of characteristics that may lower their net worth relative to whites, most especially their lower income, but also such demographic factors as a higher incidence of central city residence and families with single heads. We find that the income difference is the largest single factor explaining racial differences in wealth, but that even after controlling for income and other demographic factors, as much as three quarters of the wealth gap remains. We speculate on the causes of these puzzling differences.

An investigation of wealth is important in formulating a more complete picture of racial differences in well-being. Most studies of

This chapter is a revised version of Blau, F. D., Graham, J. W. (1990). Black-White Differences in Wealth and Asset Composition, in: The Quarterly Journal of Economics, 105(2): 321-339. Oxford University Press.

The authors are grateful for the helpful comments of Lawrence Kahn, Joseph Altonji, Earl Grinols, Daniel Hamermesh, editor Lawrence Summers, and two anonymous referees of this Journal, and for the research assistance of Susan Schwochau, Bruce Lawrence, Keith Chauvin, Ed Sexton, Laura Mayer, and Denise Dorigo. Research support by the Research Board of the University of Illinois and by the Rutgers Research Council is gratefully acknowledged.

economic well-being focus solely on income, but if wealth differences are even greater, then these studies will underestimate racial inequality and policies that seek to narrow income differences will not be sufficient to close the wealth gap. Our sample of relatively young families (the mean age of the family heads is 30) focuses upon the group that has benefited the most from the improvements in the labor market for black Americans dating to the mid-1960s (Freeman 1980) and nets out the effects of past discrimination and other disabilities which older blacks presumably suffered to a greater extent. Evidence of large unexplained racial differentials in wealth for this relatively advantaged group of younger blacks is of particular concern not only for the group itself, but for future generations as well to the extent that wealth is used to finance children's education or given directly in the form of financial or physical assets.

Previous studies of racial differences in wealth, although relatively sparse, find black-white wealth ratios ranging from 0.08 to 0.19 (Terrell 1971; Smith 1975; Soltow 1972; Sobol 1979). In one of the few studies to investigate the causes of these differences, Terrell finds that racial differences in income are not sufficient to account for the observed wealth disparity; however, the effects of other variables are not controlled for. Studies of racial differences in asset composition are especially rare. Sobol finds that some assets such as net equity in a business are much more unequally distributed by race than other assets such as checking and savings accounts; however, the factors responsible for these differences in asset composition are not analyzed. This chapter builds on previous work by performing a much more comprehensive analysis of racial differences in both wealth and asset composition.

10.2. Data and Methodology

We combined separate data extracts from the 1976 National Longitudinal Survey (NLS) of young men and the 1978 NLS of young women to increase the overall sample size and to include more household types (i.e., married-couple families, families headed by single[1] males or females, and one-person households). In each survey the primary respondent was 24 to 34 years of age.[2] The sample was restricted to families (or individuals) in which the respondent (or spouse) was the family head and neither spouse was enrolled in school. Cases with missing data on any of the asset variables or other variables used in our regression analyses were excluded.[3]

Table 10.1 shows differences in wealth by race for married couples, single heads, and the full sample. Wealth is defined as the sum of the value of net liquid assets, net business assets, equity in house(s), and equity in car(s). All values are expressed in terms of 1976 dollars. The mean wealth of all black households is $4,177, or 17.6 percent of the white mean of $23,703. While blacks hold less of all assets than whites, they hold a higher proportion of their assets in the form of cars and houses, and a lower proportion in net liquid and net business assets.

Since households with single heads hold less wealth than married couples, the higher incidence of single heads among blacks (45.3 percent versus 23.4 percent) lowers their relative wealth. However, within each group, wealth differences remain quite large: the black-white wealth ratio is 0.23 for married couples and 0.135 for single heads. These wealth differences within each household type account for the major portion of the wealth differential in the full sample. If blacks (whites) had the same incidence of each household type as whites (blacks) but continued to differ in their mean levels of wealth, 95 (84) percent of the racial wealth differential would remain.[4] Thus, in the empirical work that follows, we focus upon explaining the racial differences in wealth within each of the two groups.

Why do families at roughly the same stage of their life-cycle hold different amounts of wealth? According to the standard model (Modigliani and Brumberg 1954), differences in wealth have three identifiable sources-differences in inherited wealth (or other intergenerational transfers), rates of return, and previous saving. Saving behavior, in turn, depends upon differences in lifetime (or permanent) income, age, and other sociodemographic factors related to tastes.

Even in our relatively young sample, it is likely that all three of these factors play a role in explaining individual wealth differences. First, while many of these families may not as yet have received substantial inheritances from their parents' estates, given current longevity and the typical age differences between generations, they are quite likely to have received gifts or "inter vivos" transfers in the form of, for example, money for college, a down payment on a house, or a share in a family-owned business. Second, given the importance of "liquidity constraints" (Tobin 1972), even young families are likely to have engaged in substantial amounts of past saving to accumulate wealth

Table 10.1

Wealth and Income by Race and Household Type[a]

	Married couples			Single heads			Total		
	Blacks	Whites	Ratio[b]	Blacks	Whites	Ratio[b]	Blacks	Whites	Ratio[b]
	($)	($)	(%)	($)	($)	(%)	($)	($)	(%)
Income	13,304	17,636	75.4	6,783	10,418	65.1	10,349	15,946	64.9
Wealth	6,210	27,039	23.0	1,725	12,795	13.5	4,177	23,703	17.6
Net liquid assets	-74	2,756	-2.7	246	3,604	6.8	71	2,955	2.4
Net business assets	569	7,874	7.2	281	4,793	5.9	438	7,152	6.1
Equity in house(s)	4,222	13,864	30.5	665	2,616	25.4	2,610	11,230	23.2
Equity in car(s)	1,492	2,544	58.6	533	1,782	29.9	1,057	2,366	44.7
Number of observations	485	2,204		402	674		887	2,878	

Notes: [a] Net liquid assets consist of checking and savings accounts; U. S. savings bonds; stocks and bonds and mutual funds; and personal loans to friends and relatives; less other debts. Other debts are defined as the value of all liabilities other than those against business, house, or cars. Net business assets equal the market value of farm, business, and real estate assets minus outstanding liabilities on such assets. Equity in house(s) equals the market value of owner-occupied housing minus the value of the unpaid mortgage. Equity in cars equals the market value of cars owned minus the value of outstanding loans on those cars.

[b] The black mean divided by the white mean.

as a cushion against unanticipated fluctuations in their income. Finally, differential information or access to certain asset markets and unequal capital gains especially on housing equity may cause rates of return to differ across families.

While the NLS data do not permit us to observe these factors directly, we can control for the income and demographic factors that may be related to them. To fully allow for behavioral differences by race, we estimate separate regressions for black and white families. Specifically, for each household type (married couples and single heads) we estimate

$$W_i = a + bY_i + cZ_i + e_i, \tag{1}$$

where W_i equals wealth of family i, Y_i is a vector of the family's permanent and transitory income, Z_i is a vector of sociodemographic characteristics, and ei is a normally distributed error term. To examine racial differences in asset composition, we also estimate

$$A_{ik} = a_k + b_kY_i + c_kZ_i + d_kW_i + e_{ik}, \tag{2}$$

where A_{ik} equals holdings of asset k by the ith family (k = net liquid assets, net business assets, equity in house(s), and equity in car(s)). The inclusion of total wealth (W_i) as a determinant of net asset composition is meant to capture market imperfections such as differential access to credit across families at different levels of wealth and their unequal ability to acquire certain assets with large minimum denomination restrictions.[5] Variable definitions and sample means are provided in Table 10.2.

Since current income may not be a very good proxy for the lifetime or permanent income upon which saving decisions are based, we estimate wealth and asset regressions with measures of permanent (PINC) and transitory (INCDIF) income estimated on the basis of family income regressions.[6] Both PINC and INCDIF are expected to have positive signs in the wealth regressions. However, since a given increment in INCDIF represents higher income only in the particular year, while an increment in PINC reflects higher income over a number of periods, we expect the coefficient on PINC to be larger than the coefficient on INCDIF. The inclusion of a measure of permanent income is particularly important for blacks in that, given their higher unemployment rates (14.0 percent for blacks versus 6.4 percent for whites in 1976), current income is likely to be a poorer indicator of their long-term income situation.[7]

Table 10.2

Means of Explanatory Variables by Race

	Married couples		Single heads	
	Blacks	Whites	Blacks	Whites
AGEHEAD = age of head	29.73 (3.64)	30.08 (3.73)	28.35 (3.20)	27.86 (2.97)
FEMHEAD = 1 if head is a single woman; and 0 otherwise	—	—	0.67 (0.47)	0.49 (0.50)
KIDS = number of children	2.06 (1.56)	1.59 (1.19)	1.43 (1.64)	0.44 (.90)
WKSWRK-W = weeks worked of wife	29.46 (22.08)	24.46 (22.53)	—	—
CENTCITY = 1 if resides in central city; and 0 otherwise	0.49 (0.50)	0.22 (0.42)	0.65 (0.48)	0.39 (0.49)
OTHSMSA = 1 if resides in SMSA outside central city; and 0 otherwise	0.16 (0.37)	0.44 (0.50)	0.18 (0.38)	0.38 (0.49)
SOUTH = 1 if resides in the South; and 0 otherwise	0.72 (0.45)	0.31 (0.46)	0.50 (0.50)	0.28 (0.45)
INCOME (1,000s) = actual income	13.30 (7.47)	17.64 (8.54)	6.78 (5.14)	10.42 (6.75)
PINC (1,000s) = estimated permanent income at AGEHEAD = 30	13.71 (4.13)	17.78 (3.50)	7.18 (1.78)	11.34 (2.75)
Number of observations	485	2,204	402	674

10.3. Empirical Results

Total wealth and individual asset regressions for married couples and single heads are given in Tables 10.3 and 10.4. As expected, the coefficients on PINC and INCDIF are consistently positive in the wealth regressions, with the coefficient on PINC greater than that on INCDIF. When PINC and INCDIF were replaced by current income (INCOME), the coefficient on INCOME was smaller than the corresponding coefficient on PINC, suggesting that PINC is indeed a better indicator of the long-term income position of the family. Furthermore, the dif-

Table 10.3

Regression Results for Total Wealth and Individual Assets, Married Couples (standard errors)

Explanatory variables	Blacks (*N* = 485)					Whites (*N* = 2,204)				
	Total wealth	Net liquid assets	Net business assets	Equity in house(s)	Equity in car(s)	Total wealth	Net liquid assets	Net business assets	Equity in house(s)	Equity in car(s)
PINC (1,000s)	1,156**	-13	-29	50	-8	3,229**	481	-1,021**	486**	54**
	(157)	(32)	(48)	(57)	(38)	(400)	(110)	(160)	(135)	(20)
INCDIF	353**	12	-51*	-7	45**	1,826**	235**	-331**	38	58**
(1,000s)	(71)	(14)	(21)	(25)	(16)	(149)	(42)	(60)	(51)	(8)
WEALTH	795**	79**	198**	631**	92**	2,497**	98**	679**	210**	13**
(1,000s)	(117)	(9)	(13)	(16)	(11)	(321)	(6)	(84)	(71)	(1)
AGEHEAD	—	16	-55	43	-4	—	103	-1,169**	1,028**	38*
		(23)	(36)	(42)	(29)		(88)	(128)	(109)	(16)
KIDS	683*	109	-68	368**	191**	2,803*	-298	-300	817*	-219**
	(314)	(60)	(92)	(108)	(73)	(1,159)	(315)	(457)	(388)	(58)
WKSWRKW	-9	-3	-44	90	-43	-164**	-352*	196	156	0.04
(10s)	(22)	(41)	,(63)	(74)	(SO)	(54)	(146)	(211)	(179)	(2.67)
CENTCITY	-5,322**	206	13	2	191	8,364**	1,080	1,085	2,007	158
	(1,093)	(214)	(325)	(386)	(260)	(3,163)	(860)	(1,246)	1,058)	(158)
OTHSMSA	-3,855*	288	-687	2	397	8,606**	817	948	83	214
	(1,587)	(305)	(464)	(551)	(371)	(2,813)	(765)	(1,109)	(942)	(140)
SOUTH	1,262	512*	360	98	54	4,698	213	2,987**	3,241**	41
	(1,110)	(212)	(323)	(383)	(258)	(2,486)	(675)	(978)	(831)	(124)
CONSTANT	-32,079**	-214	1,484	-2,758	1,488	-98,833**	-10,157**	41,251**	-31,652**	559
	(4,543)	(911)	(1,388)	(1,648)	(1,110)	(12,174)	(3,352)	(4,860)	(4,127)	(616)
R^2	0.220	0.220	0.343	0.818	0.203	0.120	0.178	0.758	0.377	0.128

Notes: * Coefficient is significant at the 5 percent level on two-tailed test.
** Coefficient is significant at the 1 percent level on two-tailed test.

Table 10.4

Regression Results for Total Wealth and Individual Asset, Single Heads (standard errors)

Explanatory variables	Blacks (N = 402) Total wealth	Net liquid assets	Net business assets	Equity in house(s)	Equity in car(s)	Whites (N = 674) Total wealth	Net liquid assets	Net business assets	Equity in house(s)	Equity in car(s)
PINC	672*	-353*	243*	-21	-21	2,408**	548	-772	136	87
(1,000s)	(312)	(142)	(99)	(125)	(125)	(901)	(420)	(428)	(167)	(150)
INCDIF	319**	14	-6	-48	-48	2,264**	751**	-843**	-14	106*
(1,000s)	(73)	(34)	(24)	(30)	(30)	(251)	(123)	(126)	(49)	(44)
WEALTH	—	610**	126**	205**	205**	—	429**	465**	76**	30**
(1,000s)		(23)	(16)	(20)	(20)		(18)	(18)	(7)	(6)
AGEHEAD	83	-48	29	19	19	1,409*	-137	-251	390**	-2
	(116)	(53)	(36)	(46)	(46)	(547)	(255)	(260)	(101)	(91)
KIDS	28	-54	1	67	67	269	-346	-709	1,326**	-270
	(284)	(129)	(89)	(113)	(113)	(2,127)	(985)	(1,004)	(392)	(353)
FEMHEAD	-979	-662	292	765	765	-883	5,664**	-5,561**	426	-530
	(1,004)	(456)	(316)	(401)	(401)	(4,259)	(1,973)	(2,010)	(785)	(708)
CENTCITY	542	112	247	-207	-207	-10,100*	2,366	-407	-1,190	-769
	(1,063)	(483)	(334)	(424)	(424)	(4,496)	(2,090)	(2,130)	(831)	(750)
OTHSMSA	-792	348	-348	-638	-638	-4,749	2,507	-1,585	81	-1,003
	(1,409)	(640)	(443)	(562)	(562)	(4,294)	(1,991)	(2,029)	(792)	(714)
SOUTH	779	-1,194**	834**	327	327	1,229	1,818	-705	-694	-419
	(972)	(442)	(306)	(388)	(388)	(3,439)	(1,593)	(1,623)	(634)	(571)
CONSTANT	-5,448	4,091*	-3,234*	-710	-710	-48,098**	-9,266	18,561*	10,935**	1,641
	(4,302)	(1,957)	(1,355)	(1,720)	(1,720)	(17,964)	(8,366)	(8,524)	(3,327)	(3,000)
R^2	0.072	0.663	0.176	0.220	0.220	0.136	0.551	0.507	0.220	0.070

Notes: * Coefficient is significant at the 5 percent level on two-tailed test.
** Coefficient is significant at the 1 percent level on two-tailed test.

ference in the coefficients on PINC and INCOME is relatively larger for blacks than whites, as would be expected given blacks' higher transitory income.[8] The regression results indicate that for both races and household types, wealth tends to be positively related to AGEHEAD and KIDS, all else equal. Among married couples, WKSWRKW, CENTCITY, OTHSMSA, and SOUTH are negatively related to wealth, although the effects are not always significant. Among households with single heads, FEMHEAD is negatively related to wealth, although not significantly, and, of the location variables, only one, CENTCITY, is significant in the white regressions with a negative sign.

Black households have lower permanent income, are more likely to live in the central city (but less likely to live in the suburbs), have a higher proportion of families headed by women only, and, among married couples, have wives who work a greater number of weeks on average (see Table 10.2) – all characteristics associated with lower wealth. At the same time, the magnitude of the impact of these explanatory variables is often quite different in the black and white regressions (see Tables 10.3 and 10.4). Most notable are the considerably smaller coefficients on PINC and AGEHEAD for blacks than for whites – 64.5 (72) percent lower for PINC and 68.2 (94.1) percent lower for AGEHEAD among married couples (single heads).[9]

In accounting for racial differences in wealth, we employ a standard means-coefficients analysis (e.g., see Blinder [1973]) using either the black or white regression coefficients to evaluate the difference in the means of the explanatory variables. In general, the more dissimilar the two wealth functions, the greater the likelihood of obtaining very different results depending on the weights employed. This is precisely the situation revealed in the decomposition shown in Table 10.5. Differences in means explain 73.6 (96.6) percent of the wealth differential for married couples (single heads) when the white coefficients are used, but only about 22 percent when the black ones are employed.[10] In contrast, racial differentials in income are not only smaller than wealth differentials (both absolutely and relatively), they are also more consistently explained by the characteristics of black and white families. Differences in means are found to explain 62 to 84 percent of the income gap among married couples, and 45 to 52 percent among families with single heads.

Given the sharply differing decomposition results for wealth based on the black and white functions, it is reasonable to inquire whether there are any grounds for emphasizing one set of results over the oth-

Table 10.5

Decomposition of Recial Differences in Wealth and Income

	Wealth[a]				Income[b]			
	Black functions		White functions		Black functions		White functions	
	($)	(%)[c]	($)	(%)[c]	($)	(%)[c]	($)	(%)[c]
I. Married couples								
(1) Evaluated at black means	6,210	23.0	11,704	43.1	13,304	75.4	14,950	84.8
(2) Evaluated at white means	10,755	39.8	27,039	100.0	16,937	96.0	17,636	100.0
(3) Unadjusted differential	20,829	77.0	20,829	77.0	4,332	24.6	4,332	24.6
(4) Explained (2)-(1)	4,545	16.8	15,335	56.7	3,633	20.6	2,686	15.2
(% of unadjusted)		(21.8)		(73.6)		(83.9)		(62.0)
Explained by income	4,707	17.4	13,150	48.6	—	—	—	—
(% of unadjusted)		(22.6)		(63.1)				
(5) Unexplained (3)-(4)	16,284	60.2	5,494	20.3	699	4.0	1,646	9.3
(% of unadjusted)		(78.2)		(26.4)		(16.1)		(38.0)
II. Single heads								
(1) Evaluated at black means	1,725	13.5	2,096	16.4	6,783	65.1	8,531	81.9
(2) Evaluated at white means	4,153	32.5	12,795	100.0	8,414	80.8	10,418	100.0
(3) Unadjusted differential	11,070	86.5	11,070	86.5	3,636	34.9	3,636	34.9
(4) Explained (2)-(1)	2,428	19.0	10,699	83.6	1,631	15.7	1,877	18.1
(% of unadjusted)		(21.9)		(96.6)		(44.9)		(51.9)
Explained by income	2,796	21.9	10,024	78.3	—	—	—	—
(% of unadjusted)		(25.3)		(90.6)				
(5) Unexplained (3)-(4)	8,642	67.5	371	2.9	2,004	19.2	1,748	16.8
(% of unadjusted)		(78.1)		(3.4)		(55.1)		(48.1)

Notes: [a]Based on wealth regressions reported in Tables 10.3 and 10.4.
[b]Based on family income regressions availabe from the authors upon request.
[c]As a percentage of the white mean wealth.

er. While the selection of weights is in some sense arbitrary, we would argue that, from a policy perspective, the more relevant question appears to be the one addressed when the black functions are employed: what would happen to black wealth if blacks were given the white means but retained their own functions? Our results indicate that even if society were successful in eliminating all the disadvantages of blacks in terms of their lower incomes and adverse locational and demographic characteristics, a large portion of the wealth gap - 78 percent - would remain. By this estimate, over three quarters of the observed racial differences in wealth appears to be related to race per se, as reflected in the dissimilar black and white wealth functions.

Why are the black and white wealth functions so different? Possible reasons for ceteris paribus racial differences are suggested by the basic determinants of wealth discussed above. First, black families will have less wealth than white families if they engage in proportionately less saving. If blacks expect faster future income growth than whites, they may have saved less out of past income, thus lowering the ratio of current wealth to income. However, studies by Lazear (1979) and Smith and Welch (1986) find no racial differences in wage growth for males in our particular cohort.[11] More generally, Friedman (1957), Alexis (1971), and Hamermesh (1982) find that the saving rate of blacks exceeds that of white, while Galenson (1972) finds that black and white saving rates are identical. Thus, past studies appear to rule out major differences in the propensity to save as an explanation.[12]

A second potential source of wealth differences is differences in rates of return, both within and across asset categories. If blacks face barriers to acquiring certain assets such as businesses and housing which historically have paid among the highest real rates of return, they are likely to earn a lower overall return on their portfolios than do whites. In the case of business assets, blacks may face customer discrimination, difficulty in securing loans, or poor information about investment opportunities due to prior discrimination in education. While it is difficult to assess the importance of such factors for business assets, there is a substantial literature on the effects of racial discrimination on home ownership. Previous studies (e.g., Kain and Quigley [1972]; Jackman and Jackman [1980]) find clear evidence of racial differences in home ownership rates and housing values favoring whites after controlling for income and demographic differences, although these differences are much less pronounced among recent movers (Roistacher and Goodman 1976), or controlling also for differences in total wealth (Birnbaum and Westin 1974). Further, Kain and Quigley (1975) find that homes in black neighborhoods have much lower rates of appreciation than those in white neighborhoods.

The labor market situation of blacks may also produce racial differences in asset composition and hence in rates of returns. Higher unemployment and greater income uncertainty may increase the demand of blacks for liquid (relative to other types of) assets. Since rates of return are often lower for liquid assets than for other types, blacks may earn a lower overall return on their portfolio, particularly if they lack information about or access to higher yielding liquid assets, such as stocks and bonds.

While race differences in rates of return are a plausible source of unexplained race differences in wealth, simulations suggest that such differences are unlikely to explain more than a very small income coefficient difference at plausible levels of rates of return for each group.[13] While we take race differences in location (and their impact on housing equity) as given in reaching this conclusion, location does not appear to be a very important determinant of the wealth differential (see below).

This leaves differences in inheritance and other intergenerational transfers as the most likely explanation. While there is little direct information on intergenerational transfers by race, Smith (1975), examining estate records for deceased persons in 1967 in Washington, D.C., finds that mean black net worth for males was less than one sixth of white male net worth. Intergenerational transfers are likely to be an important source of unexplained racial differences in our wealth regressions because, given the labor market progress of younger blacks during the 1960s and 1970s, a black's family of origin is likely to have had lower income and wealth than that of a white with similar levels of our control variables. Intergenerational transfers may also affect wealth through their effect on asset composition and hence rates of return. Blacks may find it more difficult to purchase a home without a gift or low interest loan from their parents for the down payment. Similarly, blacks may be less likely to have inherited property or a family business or farm, or to have the opportunity to join an on-going family enterprise.[14]

Given the overall effect of racial differences in characteristics on the wealth gap, it is also of interest to ascertain the impact of various sets of variables taken separately. Income is by far the most important factor, although its magnitude differs considerably depending upon which coefficients are used: Income differences account for approximately one quarter of the wealth differential based on the black functions and from 63.1 percent (married couples) to 90.6 percent (single heads) when the white functions are used. In results not shown, controlling for income and other factors, racial differences in wife's work status, incidence of female-headed families, and other demographic factors had relatively little impact on the wealth differential. Among married couples, residence had relatively little effect on the wealth gap because the negative effect of the greater tendency of blacks to live in central cities was approximately offset by the greater tendency of whites to live in the suburbs which also reduces wealth relative to nonSMSA residence. The continued greater tendency of blacks to be located in the South was estimated to explain 9.4 percent of the wealth difference among married couples when the white function was used, but to lower the differential slightly when the black function was employed.[15] Among single heads, blacks' concentration in the central cities was found to adversely affect their wealth only when the white function was used, in which case it accounted for 15.7 percent of the wealth differential.

A decomposition of race differences by individual asset is shown in Table 10.6. Again, the results are sensitive to the weighting scheme employed. Using the white functions, we find that racial differences in the means of the explanatory variables (including wealth) are more than sufficient to account for the observed differential in net liquid assets and that the unexplained differential is thus negative. This remains the case among single heads, but not among married couples, when the black functions are employed. Thus, while black families with single heads unambiguously hold a higher proportion[16] of their wealth in the form of liquid assets than their white counterparts hold, among married couples this is only true at the lower levels of income and wealth represented by the black means.

Thus, we find some support for the hypothesis that blacks' higher unemployment rates (and transitory income) result in their holding a higher proportion of their wealth in liquid form, particularly at lower levels of income and wealth. This is consistent with the holding of a minimum cash reserve against the contingency of unemployment which, among married couples, increases less than in proportion to wealth with increasing affluence. It may also reflect a smaller utili-

Table 10.6

Decomposition of Racial Differences in Asset Composition[a]

	Net liquid assets		Net business assets		Equity in house(s)		Equity in car(s)	
	$	%[b]	$	%[b]	$	%[b]	$	%[b]
I. Married couples Unadjusted differential	2,830	100.0	7,305	100.0	9,642	100.0	1,052	100.0
A. Explained differential (black functions)	2,003	70.8	3,692	50.5	13,095	135.8	2,039	193.8
Unexplained differential (white means)	827	29.2	3,614	49.5	-3,453	-35.8	-988	-93.9
B. Explained differential (white functions)	3,754	132.7	8,350	114.3	8,160	84.6	565	53.7
Unexplained differential (black means)	-924	--32.7	-1,045	-14.3	1,482	15.4	487	46.3
II. Single heads								
Unadjusted differential	3,358	100.0	4,513	100.0	1,951	100.0	1,249	100.0
A. Explained differential (black functions)	5,790	172.4	2,016	44.7	1,936	99.2	1,329	106.4
Unexplained differential (white means)	-2,432	-72.4	2,497	55.3	15	0.7	-80	-6.4
B. Explained differential (white functions)	5,859	174.5	3,732	82.7	322	16.5	1,156	92.6
Unexplained differential (black means)	-2,502	-74.5	780	17.3	1,628	83.4	93	7.4

Notes: [a]Based on asset regressions reported in Tables 10.3 and 10.4.
[b]As a percentage of total differential.

zation of more sophisticated forms of holding liquid assets (such as stocks and bonds) among married blacks relative to whites due, say, to poorer information about these options.

In the case of equity in house(s) (and, among married couples, car equity), we find that, at lower levels of income and wealth, blacks hold a smaller proportion of wealth in this form (these forms). However, if black married couples were given the higher levels of income and wealth represented by the white means, they would "overinvest" in housing (and cars) relative to whites, while the home and car equity of black single heads would be about the same as their white counterparts. Thus, our evidence is not consistently supportive of the notion that housing discrimination lowers the proportion of wealth held by blacks in the form of housing.[17] While we control for residence in drawing this conclusion, racial differences in residence explain none of the racial differences in house equity when the black functions are employed.

At the white means, blacks are found to have a considerably smaller amount of net business assets than do whites. This is the case at the black means as well among single heads, although not among married couples.[18] Barriers to the accumulation of business wealth among blacks, particularly at the higher levels of income and wealth represented by the white means, may in part explain the tendency of black married couples to hold a higher proportion of their wealth in the form of home equity (and cars) at the white means.

10.4. Conclusion

In this chapter we have examined black-white differences in wealth and asset composition among younger families. We have found large racial differences that cannot be explained by differences in income and other demographic, and locational characteristics. Our findings suggest that even if policies designed to reduce racial differences in income and other differences in characteristics were completely successful, as much as three quarters of the gap in wealth would remain. This large unexplained differential (due to differences in coefficients between black and white wealth functions) appears not to be primarily the result of racial differences in saving behavior or rates of return, although, particularly the latter, may play a role. Thus, we conclude that racial differences in inheritance and other intergenerational transfers most likely play an important part. Some support was also found for the possibility of barriers to the accumulation of business and housing wealth among blacks, although our evidence on this is somewhat mixed. Our findings suggest that additional policies which might help to lower the racial gap in wealth include increases in estate and gift taxes, the promotion of small businesses among blacks, and the removal of obstacles to their home ownership.

11

The Use of Transfer Payments by Immigrants

The large influx in the 1970s and early 1980s of refugees from Southeast Asia, Cuba, and Haiti, and of illegal immigrants from Mexico, Latin America, and elsewhere have focused public attention on the consequences of these population movements for the U.S. economy. When considering the advisability of admitting immigrants to the United States, policy-makers necessarily weigh their use of the income-transfer system as a major consideration. But although this issue is one that excited much public interest, relatively little research had been done on the topic before the current study.[1]

Some of the current concern over the economic impact of immigrants may stem from the belief that recent arrivals differ in important respects from earlier immigrants. Nevertheless, given the protracted nature of the "Americanization" process – the process by which immigrants adapt to their new surroundings – and the importance of age-related factors in determining transfer payments, it is helpful to assess the experiences of the entire immigrant population, including earlier arrivals, in forming judgments about the likely impact of newcomers. This is the strategy pursued in this chapter, and the conclusion considers the specific implications of the findings for recent immigrants.

This chapter is a revised version of Blau, F. D. (1984). The Use of Transfer Payments by Immigrants, in: Industrial and Labor Relations Review, 37(2): 222-239.

The author is grateful for the comments and suggestions of Julian Simon, Glen Cain, Barry Chiswick, Sheldon Danziger, Marianne Ferber, Jean Grossman, Daniel Hamermesh, Marjorie Honig, Lawrence Kahn, Robert Plotnick, and Cordelia Reimers. The author is also indebted to Julian Simon for making the SIE data available, to Jeremy Atack and Mark Browning for preparing the data tapes, and to Judi Catlett, Denise Dimon, Susan Schwochau, and Andy Jaske for research assistance.

Table 11.1

Receipt of Transfer Payments by Immigrant and Native Families, 1975

	Male Heads		Female Heads	
Payment Type	Natives	Immigrant	Native	Immigrant
Welfare (W)	$ 73.29	$ 93.18	$ 416.41	$ 295.24
Social Insurance (S)	$ 979.09	$ 1,505.09	$ 1,095.05	$ 1,411.84
Total (W + S)	$ 1,052.38	$ 1,598.27	$ 1,511.46	$ 1,707.08
Participation in Welfare [P(W > 0)]	.046	.055	.211	.147
Participation in Social Insurance [P(S > 0)]	.365	.456	.449	.575
Welfare, Given Participation [W|(W > 0)]	$ 1,585.49	$ 1,683.93	$ 1,974.18	$ 2,002.66
Social Insurance, Given Participation [S|(S > 0)]	$ 2,679.95	$ 3,301.38	$ 2,437.20	$ 2,453.93
N	7,787	6,317	2,539	2,298

Notes: †Welfare payments include income received by the family from public assistance, welfare (including Aid to Families with Dependent Children), or supplemental security income. Social insurance payments include income received by the family from social security, railroad retirement, veterans' payments, unemployment compensation or workers' compensation. Observations are weighted by sampling weights reported in the SIE.

Source: Unpublished data from the Survey of Income and Education, 1976, U.S. Department of Commerce, Bureau of the Census. For a description of these data, see, for example, U.S. Bureau of the Census, Money Income and Poverty Status in 1975 of Families and Persons in the United States by Divisions and States, Current Population Report, Series P-60, Nos. 110 - 113 (Washington, D.C.: GPO, 1977).

Throughout, this chapter distinguishes between welfare payments (such as public assistance, Aid to Families with Dependent Children, and supplemental security income) and social insurance payments (such as social security, railroad retirement, veteran's payments, unemployment compensation, and workers' compensation). This distinction is desirable because the two types of programs differ in eligibility requirements and in the criteria for determining payment levels and thus should be analyzed separately. Moreover, families who receive social insurance payments have generally made some, and often substantial, previous contributions to the program (or their employers have done so). Such contributions are generally not the case for welfare payments, since these are financed out of general revenues. Such a difference may be significant from a policy perspective.

Table 11.2

Mean Values of Variables[a]

Variables	Male Heads		Female Heads	
	Natives	Immigrants	Natives	Immigrants
Personal Characteristics				
BLACK	.09	.04	.19	.06
OTHER	.01	.10	.01	.06
HISP	.02	.23	.02	.18
PER18T64	.99	.90	.21	.26
PERGE65	.09	.21	.03	.03
KIDSLT18	.91	.80	—[c]	—[c]
KIDSLT5	—[c]	—[c]	.12	.07
KIDS5T17	—[c]	—[c]	.49	.31
HDAGE	44.47	51.16	48.73	57.84
HD18T44	.52	.42	.46	.29
HD45T59	.27	.22	.18	.17
HD60T64	.07	.07	.07	.06
HD65T67	.04	.05	.05	.05
HD68PLUS	.10	.25	.24	.42
HDEDUC	12.07	10.73	11.55	9.70
OTHERY	840.53	1,114.61	865.39	887.04
HOUSEQ	15,170.49	15,833.62	8,259.61	9,060.46
MAR	.82	.81	—[c]	—[c]
SPEDUC	9.91	8.59	—[c]	—[c]
VET	.47	.18	—[c]	—[c]
Location				
METRO	.66	.86	.69	.88
SOUTH	.33	.17	.33	.15
WEST	.18	.28	.18	.27
CENTRAL	.28	.17	.27	.16
NORTHEAST	.21	.38	.22	.42
ENGPOOR	.002	.15	.004	.15
Foreign Birth				
(FOR) (1970-74)	—[c]	.15	—[c]	.10
(FOR) (1965-69)	—[c]	.14	—[c]	.11
(FOR) (1960-64)	—[c]	.10	—[c]	.09
(FOR) (1950-59)	—[c]	.19	—[c]	.16
(FOR) (1920-49)	—[c]	.35	—[c]	.40
(FOR) (BEFR20)	—[c]	.07	—[c]	.15
Predicted LNWAGE	1.52	1.44	.95	.97
N	7,787	6,317	2,539	2,298

Notes: [a] See Table 11.3 for variable definitions. Observations are weighted by sampling weights reported in the SIE.
[b] Predicted on the basis of wage regressions with a selectivity-bias correction.
[c] Not applicable.

Table 11.3

Variable Definition

Variable	Definition
BLACK	Equals 1 if the head is black and 0 if otherwise.
OTHER	Equals 1 if the head is other nonwhite and 0 if otherwise.
HISP	Equals 1 if the head is of Hispanic origin and 0 if otherwise.
PER18T64	Number of family members, excluding head, aged 18 to 64.
PERGE65	Number of family members, excluding head, aged 65 or older.
KIDSLT18	Number of children under 18 years of age.
KIDSLT5	Number of children under 5 years of age.
KIDS5T17	Number of children between 5 and 17 years of age.
HDAGE	Age of family head.
HD18T44	Equals 1 if the head is aged 18 to 44 and 0 if otherwise.
HD45T59	Equals 1 if the head is aged 45 to 59 and 0 if otherwise.
HD60T64	Equals 1 if the head is aged 60 to 64 and 0 if otherwise.
HD65T67	Equals 1 if the head is aged 65 to 67 and 0 if otherwise.
HD68PLUS	Equals 1 if the head is aged 68 or older and 0 if otherwise.
HDEDUC	Highest grade completed by family head.
OTHERY	Amount of the family's nonlabor, nontransfer income.
HOUSEQ	Market value of the family's house minus the value of the mortgage outstanding.
MAR	Equals 1 if the head is married with spouse present and 0 if otherwise.
SPEDUC	Equals highest grade completed by spouse, if married, and 0 if otherwise.
VET	Equals 1 if the male head is a veteran and 0 if otherwise.
METRO	Equals 1 if metropolitan area and 0 if otherwise.
SOUTH	Equals 1 if South and 0 if otherwise.
WEST	Equals 1 if West and 0 if otherwise.
CENTRAL	Equals 1 if North Central and 0 if otherwise.
NORTHEAST	Equals 1 if Northeast and 0 if otherwise.
ENGPOOR	Equals 1 if the head does not speak or does not understand English well, and 0 if otherwise.
(FOR) (1970-74)	Equals 1 if the head is foreign born and entered the U.S. between 1970 and 1974, and 0 if otherwise.
(FOR) (1965-69)	Equals 1 if the head is foreign born and entered the U.S. between 1965 and 1969, and 0 if otherwise.
(FOR) (1960-64)	Equals 1 if the head is foreign born and entered the U.S. between 1960 and 1964, and 0 if otherwise.
(FOR) (1950-59)	Equals 1 if the head is foreign born and entered the U.S. between 1950 and 1959, and 0 if otherwise.
(FOR) (1920-49)	Equals 1 if the head is foreign born and entered the U.S. between 1920 and 1949, and 0 if otherwise.
(FOR) (BEFR20)	Equals 1 if the head is foreign born and entered the U.S. before 1920, and 0 if otherwise.
LNWAGE	Equals the natural log of the hourly wage.

Immigrant-native differences in receipts from major transfer programs during 1975 are shown in Table 11.1. At a superficial level, these figures lend some support to fears that immigrants constitute a burden on the transfer payment system. On average, the transfers received by families headed by a male immigrant[2] were 52 percent ($546) higher than the receipts of families headed by native-born males. This differential reflects both male-headed immigrant families' greater likelihood of participating in each type of program (welfare and social insurance) and their higher average payment levels conditional on participation. On average, female-headed immigrant families received lower welfare payments, but higher social insurance payments, resulting in total payments that were 13 percent ($196) higher than those to their native-born counterparts – primarily a result of their higher probability of participating in social insurance programs.

The purpose of this study is to develop a fuller understanding of the reasons for these immigrant-native differences in the receipt of transfer payments. It is hoped that the investigation may be useful in formulating immigration policy. If policymakers wish to minimize the size of outlays for transfers, for example, such information may be relevant to the selection of criteria for admitting immigrants or for determining the level of immigration permitted. On the other hand, a deeper investigation of the causes of these observed differentials may suggest that immigrants do not, in fact, burden the transfer payment system any more than do the native born and that a reduction of transfer payments to immigrants need not be a major policy concern.

To elucidate these issues, this study first seeks to determine whether immigrant families place greater or lesser demands on the transfer system than native families with similar characteristics, that is, whether immigrant families are more or less apt to receive transfer payments than native families. The chapter also investigates the role of differences in characteristics across immigrant and native families in producing a higher use of the transfer system on the part of the former group. Of particular interest in this comparison is the role played by age and age-related variables.

The age distribution of the native population is determined primarily by domestic birth and death rates,[3] but in the case of immigrants, the major factor is the historical pattern of immigration. Such inflows peaked during the late nineteenth and early twentieth centuries. In 1921 and again in 1924, restrictive federal legislation sharply curtailed the entry of immigrants. As a result, the age distribution of immigrant and native-born heads differs in important respects. Table 11.2 shows (for HD68PLUS) that a considerably higher proportion of immigrant than of native-born heads were elderly (over 68), many having arrived during the less restrictive period.[4] In the case of male heads of households, 25 percent of the immigrants were over 68 in 1976, whereas only 10 percent of the native-born were those ages in that year. In the case of female heads, these figures were 42 and 24 percent, respectively.

On the other hand, a considerably smaller proportion of immigrant than of native-born heads belonged to the post-World War II "baby boom" cohort, since immigration rates for that cohort showed no upswing comparable to birth rates. Among the male (female) heads, 27 (29) percent of the native-born, but only 17 (13) percent of immigrants, were 18 to 30 in 1976 (subgroup of HD18T64, Table 11.2).[5] Thus, the average age of immigrant male heads exceeded that of native-born male heads by 6.7 years, while the average age of immigrant female heads exceeded that of native-born female heads by 9.1 years. Male-headed immigrant families also included considerably more older family members than male-headed native families: on average, there is one additional family member 65 years of age or over for every five immigrant families, and less than one such older individual for every ten native families (PERGE65 in Table 11.2).

Although immigrants have other characteristics that could raise their reliance on transfers (such as a lower educational attainment, or a higher representation among minority groups), the role of age-related factors has particular relevance for public policy. To the extent that the differences in the receipt of transfer payments shown in Table 11.1 are the result of age and age-related factors, a fairly good case may be made for the view that the higher level of transfer payments among immigrants does not represent a cause for concern. First, as with any investment in human capital, immigration is more profitable the earlier in the life cycle it takes place (the longer the remaining working life in which the returns may be collected). Thus, the vast majority of older immigrants have spent most of their working lives, including their most productive years, in the United States.[6]

Second, to the extent that the collection of transfer payments by older individuals may be conceptualized as an intergenerational transfer, older immigrants' own working-age children make positive contributions to the system, in the form of income and social security taxes.[7] Third, in the decision of which and how many immigrants to admit, higher costs many years in the future in the form of transfer payments to older individuals would have relatively little weight in a present-value calculation, at most discount rates (Simon 1981). Finally, the age distribution of immigrants can be manipulated by public policy in a beneficial manner, for example, to even out population imbalances in age composition resulting from past fluctuations in domestic birth rates.[8]

11.1. Conceptual Framework

This study examines the impact on transfer payments of foreign birth and two important characteristics of immigrants – their length of residence in the United States and their ability to speak and understand English – while controlling for the other factors that influence transfers. Since virtually all transfer programs have work disincentives associated with them, the labor-leisure trade-off is at the heart of the transfer decision. Potential recipients may be viewed as comparing the value of work with the benefits of participation in the transfer program. Thus, an individual's potential market earnings are expected to be negatively related to transfer receipts.[9]

Foreign birth, length of residence, and English ability are therefore expected to influence the transfer utilization of immigrants both directly, holding constant the effect of economic success on transfers, and indirectly through their impact on potential market earnings. From a policy point of view, we are also interested in the total or full effect of the foreign-born variables on transfers, which is the sum of the direct and indirect effects. The total effect is a measure of the ultimate impact of the foreign-born variables on transfers for immigrants and native families of similar other characteristics.

The indirect effects of these variables - foreign birth, length of residence, and English ability - on transfers depend, first, on their effects on potential wages, and, second, on the effect these potential wages in turn have on transfers. Although recent immigrants may initially be at a disadvantage in the labor market because of their lack of knowledge of customs or of job opportunities, for example, their earnings are expected to increase over time as they accumulate experience of their new country and as they seek out the best opportunities to deploy their skills and abilities. All else equal, the earnings of male immigrants have been found to be positively related to the length of their residence in the United States and eventually, to catch up to and even to surpass those of their native-born counterparts (Chiswick 1978; Blau 1980).[10] The last finding has been taken as an indication that immigration, particularly economically motivated immigration' is selective of the more able or more highly motivated individuals (Chiswick (1978). On the other hand, an inability to speak and understand English well is expected to have a negative effect on earnings.

Thus, to the extent that higher wages are associated with lower participation in transfer programs, the indirect effect of foreign birth and of length of residence on the receipt of transfer payments (through the wage) is likely to be negative. Nevertheless, poor English ability, other things equal, is expected to increase reliance on transfer programs through its negative effect on wages.

Controlling for the wage, the direct effect of length of residence and English ability on transfers is unclear, a priori. On the one hand, the increased labor market information accumulated over time should reduce the incidence and duration of unemployment, all else equal (Chiswick 1982). Reduced unemployment, in turn, is expected to reduce the receipt of transfer payments after the immigrant has spent some time in the country. On the other hand, over time, immigrants may accumulate more information about transfer programs, serving to increase their receipt of transfer payments, all else equal. Further, their eligibility for and, in some cases, benefit levels in social insurance programs are expected to increase as they accumulate employment experience in covered sectors.

Poor English ability may be hypothesized to increase the incidence or duration of unemployment through its influence on access to labor market information, resulting in a positive effect on the use of transfer payments. Nonetheless, the expected negative impact of poor English ability on information about transfers and possibly employment in a covered sector can also be expected, instead, to lower transfer payment use, other things equal. The foregoing discussion suggests that the total (direct plus indirect) effects of these variables are ambiguous a priori, since the signs of the direct effects are unknown.

The direct effects on transfer receipts of foreign birth, length of residence in the United States, and English ability are estimated from structural transfer equations that control for potential labor market wages or economic need (Tables 11.4 and 11.5). The total effects of these variables, shown in Tables 11.6 and 11.7 (see pages 438 and 439), are inferred from reduced-form equations that include all the exogenous variables in the wage and the structural transfer equations, but they omit potential market wages as an explanatory variable.[11]

As noted earlier, in analyzing the use of transfers, it is helpful to distinguish between welfare (W) and social insurance (S) programs. Specific welfare programs are targeted to particular groups (such as the disabled and elderly or broken families), but the basic requirement for eligibility is economic need as determined on the basis of current sources of income and assets. Guarantee levels (that is, benefit levels at zero work hours) are designed to bring actual family income up to a stated level of need.

Social insurance programs, on the other hand, are targeted to individuals who have had a "firm attachment to the labor force" (Lampman 1976: 165). Eligibility is determined by employment of a specified duration in a covered sector. The determination of guarantee levels is guided primarily by the replacement-ratio principle, whereby a specified portion of the income lost (through disability, unemployment, or retirement, for example) is replaced by the program. The level of the individual's nonwage income or assets is typically not taken into account in determining payments under social insurance programs. Other indicators of need, however, such as number of dependents, do play a role in determining benefit levels in some social insurance programs.

Because of these differences between the two types of programs (W and S), the programs are analyzed separately in the empirical work that follows. As we have seen in Table 11.1, differences between any two groups in the average level of transfer receipts may arise from group differences in the probability of participating in a transfer program $[P(T > 0)]$ or in the level of payments received, given participation $[T|(T > 0)]$, or a combination of both. As part of the effort here to explore a variety of potential sources of the observed differences between immigrants and natives, these two issues are also analyzed separately.

The control variables included in the structural transfer equations may be seen in Tables 11.4 and 11.5. As noted earlier, all else equal, potential market wages are expected to affect negatively $P(T > 0)$ and $T|(T > 0)$. We must qualify this prediction somewhat, however, in the case of social insurance programs, in which benefits are determined on the basis of the replacement principle, namely, they are a positive function of earnings. It is important that the wage measure used in the empirical analysis reflect potential market wages, since actual earnings are influenced by labor-supply behavior, which is in turn determined by the transfer-participation decision.

Potential market wages are predicted on the basis of wage equations that include the traditional human capital variables and other control variables.[12] Since potential rather than actual labor market experience is used, the number of children is included in the wage equations for female heads of households to control for potential labor-force interruptions. Education and experience are omitted from the structural transfer equations, under the assumption that they influence transfers only indirectly through their effects on wages.

The income and asset variables ($OTHERY$ and $HOUSEQ$) are proxies for the demand for leisure as well as for eligibility and benefit levels under welfare programs. To ensure exogeneity to the transfer decision, income from other transfer programs is excluded from $OTHERY$. The race and ethnic variables ($BLACK$, $OTHER$, and $HISP$) may reflect the impact of labor market discrimination, after wages and other factors are controlled. If, for example, individuals from these groups expect slower future wage growth as a result of their labor market experience (that is, if they earn lower rewards to their current labor-force participation) or encounter more difficulty locating a job (that is, if they experience a higher unemployment rate

Table 11.4

Structural Results for Male Heads

	Participation Probability (Probit)[b]		Level of Receipts Among Participants (OLS)[c]	
Variables[a]	Welfare	Social Insurance	Welfare	Social Insurance
Personal Characteristics				
BLACK	547***	-.021	193.32	1.45
	(.075)	(.060)	(158.80)	(121.42)
OTHER	.267***	-.169***	181.49	-201.56*
	(.084)	(.058)	(192.30)	(115.69)
HISP	.269***	-.137***	453.11**	149.79
	(.075)	(.053)	(178.24)	(106.33)
PER18T64	.277***	.186***	105.64*	115.49***
	(.028)	(.020)	(63.94)	(35.96)
PERGE65	.583***	.994***	133.64	1083.20***
	(.063)	(.057)	(130.06)	(66.11)
KIDSLT18	.135***	-.037***	88.67**	66.01**
	(.016)	(.011)	(36.49)	(26.12)
HD45T59	.179***	-.021	260.45*	336.31***
	(.059)	(.035)	(142.74)	(79.50)
HD60T64	.154	.348***	306.39	749.60***
	(.095)	(.050)	(237.47)	(103.31)
HD65T67	.430***	1.278***	96.25	1756.20***
	(.104)	(.070)	(245.77)	(104.87)
HD68PLUS	.305***	1.719***	116.69	1925.50***
	(.091)	(.070)	(210.42)	(95.66)
OTHERY	$-.509 \times 10^{-4}$***	$-.102 \times 10^{-4}$**	-.002	.021***
	$(.163 \times 10^{-4})$	$(.423 \times 10^{-5})$	(.041)	(.007)
HOUSEQ	$-.151 \times 10^{-4}$***	$-.405 \times 10^{-5}$***	-.008*	-.002*
	$(.161 \times 10^{-5})$	$(.747 \times 10^{-6})$	(.004)	(.001)
MAR	-.085	.452***	233.34	345.64**
	(.098)	(.074)	(221.21)	(115.58)
SPEDUC	035***	-.035***	-23.77	-.220
	(.008)	(.005)	(19.47)	(8.92)
VET	-.001	.403***	-100.50	114.42**
	(.050)	(.030)	(127.60)	(54.88)

that that of the general population), they may be more likely to use transfers than comparable white non-Hispanics.[13] There may also be racial and ethnic differences in the demand for leisure, all else equal, resulting from noneconomic factors.

The other personal-characteristic variables are proxies for the demand for leisure, family responsibilities, and the potential earnings of other family members, as well as eligibility and benefit levels under a variety of transfer programs. Given the number of factors represented by these variables, it is not possible to predict all their signs a priori. Nevertheless, all else equal, a positive association between the ages of the family head and the other adult family members and the collection of transfers is expected, because of both an increased demand for lei-

Table 11.4 (continued)
Structural Results for Male Heads

	Participation Probability (Probit)[b]		Level of Receipts Among Participants (OLS)[c]	
Variables[a]	Welfare	Social Insurance	Welfare	Social Insurance
Location				
METRO	-.015	.062**	310.30***	124.12**
	(.046)	(.029)	(110.17)	(51.03)
SOUTH	-.068	-.279***	-574.14***	-152.90**
	(.063)	(.040)	(151.71)	(75.35)
WEST	.016	-.158***	-241.81*	-119.02*
	(.056)	(.034)	(141.28)	(63.25)
CENTRAL	-.183***	-.166***	-444.86***	-41.12
	(.062)	(.036)	(160.82)	(64.16)
ENGPOOR	.143*	-.106	-243.65	-191.90*
	(.085)	(.068)	(189.70)	(114.26)
Foreign Birth				
(FOR) (1970-74)	-.435***	-.333***	-120.27	-177.90
	(.104)	(.066)	(250.74)	(165.33)
(FOR) (1965-69)	-.307***	-.062	-103.34	-98.55
	(.104)	(.063)	(247.43)	(143.86)
(FOR) (1960-64)	-.202*	.055	-75.46	-54.68
	(.112)	(.068)	(267.54)	(153.54)
(FOR) (1950-59)	-.219**	.101**	-332.94	-80.87
	(.089)	(.046)	(225.39)	(100.76)
(FOR) (1920-49)	-.217***	.216***	-462.10***	99.68
	(.068)	(.042)	(167.02)	(64.74)
(FOR) (BEFR20)	-.317***	.114	-257.76	-29.55
	(.104)	(.131)	(238.28)	(96.53)
Predicted LNWAGE	-.492***	-.629***	3.01	200.21**
	(.083)	(.068)	(179.18)	(86.21)
Constant	1.027***	.139	1325.80***	835.44***
	(.123)	(.095)	(278.24)	(137.29)
-2 × Log-Likelihood Ratio	878.373	5,915.775		
Adjusted R^2			.062	.290
N	14,104	14,104	652	5,896

Notes: [a]See Table 11.3 for variable definitions.
[b]Asymptotic standard errors in parentheses.
[c]Standard errors in parentheses.
*Significant at the .10 level in a two-tailed test.
**Significant at the .05 level in a two-tailed test.
***Significant at the .01 level in a two-tailed test.

sure and an increased eligibility for welfare (such as supplemental security) and for social insurance (such as social security retirement and disability) programs.

The locational variables employed in this analysis are intended to control for area differences in the eligibility requirements and benefit formulas of transfer programs, as well as in stringency with which the program criteria and formulas are administered at the local level. The inclusion of these variables also adjusts for locational differences in economic conditions and the cost of living.

Table 11.5

Structural Results for Female Heads

	Participation Probability (Probit)[b]		Level of Receipts Among Participants (OLS)[c]	
Variables[a]	Welfare	Social Insurance	Welfare	Social Insurance
Personal Characteristics				
BLACK	.689***	-.188**	232.41**	-481.56***
	(.079)	(.082)	(113.23)	(121.80)
OTHER	.312**	-. 252*	324.35	66.45
	(.134)	(.131)	(213.18)	(196.62)
HISP	.459***	-.380***	355.31**	-595.53***
	(.106)	(.114)	(164.81)	(156.22)
PER18T64	.093**	.315***	84.17	529.23***
	(.044)	(.042)	(68.79)	(46.43)
PERGE65	.531***	1.145***	202.03	1473.30***
	(.138)	(.175)	(223.31)	(113.47)
KIDSLT5	.796***	-.166**	450.81***	83.91
	(.072)	(.077)	(88.21)	(165.82)
KIDS5T17	.367***	.108	520.54***	417.67***
	(.028)	(.026)	(35.07)	(45.34)
HD45T59	.235***	.370***	81.26	435.07***
	(.081)	(.067)	(136.10)	(122.23)
HD60T64	.373***	1.032***	-.493	708.08***
	(.113)	(.089)	(206.70)	(137.85)
HD65T67	.303**	2.022***	299.37	761.84***
	(.131)	(.121)	(238.25)	(136.27)
HD68PLUS	.072	2.340***	-82.75	1104.50***
	(. 100)	(.094)	(176.83)	(119.61)
OTHERY	$-.197 \times 10^{-3}$***	$-.958 \times 10^{-5}$	-.201***	.012
	$(.279 \times 10^{-4})$	$(.887 \times 10^{-5})$	(.049)	(.009)
HOUSEQ	$-.196 \times 10^{-4}$***	$-.251 \times 10^{-5}$	.001	.003*
	$(.250 \times 10^{-5})$	$(.160 \times 10^{-5})$	(.005)	(.002)

11.2. The Data

This study uses from the 1976 Survey of Income and Education (SIE) conducted by the U.S. Bureau of the Census for the Department of Health, Education, and Welfare. The immigrant sample comprises all families in which the male or female head is foreign-born, is 18 years of age or over, and had arrived in the United States during or before 1974. Since the income data in the SIE refer to calendar year 1975, those arriving after 1974 were excluded from the analysis, either because they did not receive income and transfer payments in the United States during 1975 or because their income and transfer data did not represent a full year. To minimize data-processing costs, the author constructed a random subsample of native families from

Table 11.5 (continued)

Structural Results for Female Heads

Variables[a]	Participation Probability (Probit)[b]		Level of Receipts Among Participants (OLS)[c]	
	Welfare	Social Insurance	Welfare	Social Insurance
SOUTH	-.271***	-.187***	857.82***	-141.59*
	(.078)	(.071)	(128.31)	(83.96)
WEST	-.028	-.088	451.68***	-6.53
	(.068)	(.064)	(114.71)	(71.08)
CENTRAL	-.078	-.092	401.71***	-35.49
	(.071)	(.069)	(117.54)	(68.74)
ENGPOOR	.011	.078	178.17	-160.30
	(.110)	(.128)	(181.50)	(119.80)
Foreign Birth				
(FOR) (1970-74)	-.515***	-.286**	-95.21	-327.49
	(.144)	(.135)	(227.90)	(251.95)
(FOR) (1965-69)	-.404***	-.317**	40.62	-22.35
	(.140)	(.136)	(220.19)	(262.74)
(FOR) (1960-64)	-.370**	.016	393.69	-229.86
	(.149)	(.122)	(246.88)	(192.24)
(FOR) (1950-59)	-.088	.022	-211.03	-403.99***
	(.105)	(.090)	(176.15)	(135.95)
(FOR) (1920-49)	-.128	.168**	-34.27	-22.39
	(.078)	(.072)	(148.02)	(66.34)
(FOR) (BEFR20)	.050	.317**	292.31	-278.45***
	(.106)	(.139)	(194.62)	(84.84)
Predicted Lnwage	-.905***	-.370***	148.92	423.20***
	(.094)	(.096)	(165.91)	(82.30)
Constant	-.372***	-.567***	1475.60***	1043.80***
	(.127)	(.126)	(217.31)	(146.13)
-2 × Log-Likelihood Ratio	1,095.448	3,074.325		
Adjusted R^2			.390	.179
N	4,837	4,837	818	2,549

Notes: [a]See Table 11.3 for variable definitions.
[b]Asymptotic standard errors in parentheses.
[c]Standard errors in parentheses.
*Significant at the .10 level in a two-tailed test.
**Significant at the .05 level in a two-tailed test.
***Significant at the .01 level in a two-tailed test.

the SIE in which the male or female head was native born and 18 years of age or over (native men married to immigrant women were not included in the native sample). Individuals born in Puerto Rico and other U.S. territories were excluded from the sample.[14]

There is a potential bias. No information is available on the legal or illegal status of the immigrants in the SIE sample. It seems likely, however, that illegal immigrants are underrepresented, since no special efforts were made to include them. The receipt of government transfers by illegal immigrants may be less common than that by legal immigrants, other things equal, since the former may be ineligible if their illegal status is discovered (U.S. House of Representatives 1978). On the other hand, many of the characteristics of illegal aliens, such as their low levels of education, are likely to increase their use of transfers. Thus, the probable underrepresentation of illegals in the SIE is an important qualification to the results reported below.

One problem in estimating these equations is that a potential-wage variable based on an OLS regression for labor-force participants is subject to a possible censoring bias, if the probability of being employed is correlated with the wage offer. This bias may be important in the sample employed here, since wages were not observed for 29 percent of the male heads and 51 percent of the female heads. The possible censoring bias in estimating wages can be eliminated using a technique developed by Heckman.[15]

It should also be noted that a possible censoring bias may exist in the case of the transfer-receipt regression as well, since it is estimated for a censored sample of transfer program participants. No correction for this bias problem is made in this case however, since the explanatory variables included in the transfer-probability and transfer-receipt equations are identical.[16] Censoring bias is essentially an omitted-variable problem, and to the extent that proxies are included for the major determinants of the level of transfer payments, it may not be important in this case. Further, even if censoring bias exists, there is no reason to suppose that immigrants and natives are differentially so affected as to bias findings for group differences in transfer receipts in one direction or another.

11.3. Control Variables

Tables 11.4 and 11.5 present estimates of the probability of participating in welfare and social insurance programs [$P(T > 0)$] and of the level of receipts from each type of program, given participation [$T|(T > 0)$]. Let us first briefly consider some of the findings for the control variables that are particularly relevant in comparing immigrants with natives and then proceed to a detailed examination of the impact of foreign birth on the receipt of transfers.

Potential wages are found to have a significantly negative effect on the probability of participating in both welfare and social insurance programs (despite the ambiguity of their expected effect in the latter case). Specifically, computations based on the estimated coefficients indicate that among male- (female-) headed families, a 10 percent increase in potential wages is associated with a 5.5 (8.9) percent reduction in the probability of participating in welfare programs and a 5.8 (2.7) percent reduction in the probability of participating in social insurance programs.[17] Among participants in social insurance programs, the estimated potential-wage coefficient is significantly positively related to the level of receipts for both male and female heads, probably reflecting the influence of the replacement-ratio principle. Among male- and female-headed families that participate in welfare programs, the coefficient on the predicted *LNWAGE* is not significant. This may indicate little labor-supply response to potential wages among welfare recipients or may in part be a result of the truncated nature of the recipient sample.

Among both male- and female-headed families, other things equal, members of minority groups are more likely to participate in welfare programs and less likely to participate in social insurance programs, although the coefficient on BLACK is not statistically significant for male heads in the case of social insurance programs. Among participants in transfer programs, there is some tendency for members of minority groups to receive higher welfare payments, ceteris paribus. In the regression for social insurance payments, other nonwhite males and black and Hispanic females receive significantly lower payments than comparable whites.

The lower usage of social insurance programs by minorities may reflect such factors as the depletion of unemployment benefits or employment in an uncovered sector. Domestic work, for example, had only recently been brought into the social security system when this study was conducted and was generally not covered by unemployment insurance or workers' compensation. This lower usage of social insurance transfers, all else equal, works to increase minorities' reliance on welfare programs.

In light of the differences in age composition between immigrant and native households, it is particularly interesting to note that among the other personal-characteristic variables, there is a sizable effect of the age variables on the probability of participating in both types of transfer programs. Having a male head aged 68 or over, for example, substantially raises the probability of a family receiving welfare payments (by 1.8 percentage points) over that of a family headed by a male aged 18 to 44, all else equal. For female-headed families, this probability increases by 1.3 percentage points. Similarly, a family's probability of participating in social insurance programs is estimated to be 68.1

(92.3) percentage points higher when the head is 68 or over, ceteris paribus, than when the family is headed by a male (female) aged 18 to 44. Among social insurance recipients, families headed by a male (female) aged 68 or over receive \$1,926 (\$1,105) more than families headed by a male (female) aged 18 to 44, other things equal.

All these effects are large relative to the means of the dependent variables given in Table 11.1. All else equal, the presence of additional family members over 65 (excluding the head) also has a strong positive effect on the collection of transfers, raising the probability of participation in welfare and social insurance programs, and raising the payments received by participants in social insurance programs.

Veterans have a significantly higher probability of receiving social insurance benefits than other groups. Such benefits include the veterans' payments for which only they are eligible. They also receive higher social insurance payments, all else equal, suggesting that veterans' programs either are more generous than other social insurance programs or have a larger work disincentive effect, or both. Immigrant male heads are considerably less likely to be veterans than native male heads (see Table 11.2).

11.4. Direct and Indirect Effects of Foreign Birth

We now turn to a consideration of the impact of English ability, foreign birth, and time spent in the Unites States on immigrants' use of transfer programs. The estimated direct effects of these variables holding wages constant, may be found in Tables 11.4 and 11.5 (the reference category for the foreign-born-year-of-entry interactions is the native-born group). Poor English ability of the male head significantly raises the probability of a family's being on welfare, all else equal, possibly through its hypothesized positive impact on the unemployment of the head. On the other hand, families headed by a male who does not speak or understand English well have an insignificantly lower probability of collecting social insurance transfers, ceteris paribus, possibly because of the head's difficulty in obtaining employment in the covered sector. These effects are insignificant and small relative to their standard errors for females.

Furthermore, among both male- and female-headed families, the head's poor English ability is negatively associated with the level of receipts from both types of transfer programs, although the coefficients on *ENGPOOR* are generally not significant. This is consistent with the hypothesis that those with poor English ability are poorly informed about transfer programs, which in turn results in a lower level of receipts. In the case of social insurance programs, this finding may also reflect a shorter duration of covered employment among this group. On net, the direct effect of poor English ability on total transfers (W + S), all else equal, is to lower total transfers by $179 in the case of male heads and by $40 in the case of female heads.[18]

Let us now turn to the direct impact of the family head's foreign birth and length of time in the United States on the family's receipt of transfers. All else equal, including potential wages, all male immigrant cohorts are significantly less likely to participate in welfare programs than male-headed native families. There is a similar tendency among female-headed families, although the effects are not always significant, and one cohort, the before-1920 group, is insignificantly more likely to participate. All cohorts of male and female heads receive lower welfare payments than natives, although these effects are almost never significant.

Within the immigrant group, there does not appear to be a consistent pattern linking length of time in the new country to the probability of receiving welfare or to the level of welfare receipts for either male or female heads. The length of U.S. residence appears to have a stronger direct effect on the collection of social insurance transfers. Among both male- and female-headed families, immigrants initially are significantly less likely than natives to participate in social insurance programs. Their relative participation probability increases over time until they are significantly more likely to participate- after they have resided here more than 16 (men) or 26 (women) years. These findings suggest increased participation in social insurance programs by immigrants over time, ceteris paribus, as they gain access to and accumulate experience in covered sectors. The coefficients for the foreign-born-year dummy variables in the social insurance payments regression are negative, but generally not significant. Evaluated at the mean of the length-of-U.S. residence dummy variables for immigrants, the direct effect of foreign-birth on total transfers (W + S), other things equal, is to increase slightly the transfers of male heads by $34 and to lower substantially the transfers of female heads by $102.[19]

Table 11.6

Total Effects of Foreign Birth, Length of U.S. Residence, and English Ability on Wages and the Receipt of Transfer Payments, for Male and Female Heads[a]

	0–5 Years	6–10 Years	11–15 Years	16–20 Years	21–30 Years
1. Effect of own source country characteristics					
Fertility rate	-2.205	-29.804	-34.341	-18.649	-39.733
	(14.805)	(19.318)	(20.199)	(21.450)	(22.884)
Activity rate ratio	243.009*	370.203*	549.509*	249.191	-53.800
	(98.040)	(117.711)	(128.320)	(129.407)	(156.859)
2. Effect of spouse's source country characteristics					
Fertility rate	-8.931	-37.064*	20.602	-28.569	40.606*†
	(15.487)	(16.861)	(16.066)	(17.759)	(18.389)
Activity rate ratio	188.021	65.948	330.028*	-32.009	213.050
	(104.406)	(124.158)	(114.166)	(120.646)	(132.778)
3. Sum of effects of own and spouse source country characteristics					
Fertility rate	-21.136	-66.869*	-13.739	-47.218	0.873
	(19.920)	(23.675)	(25.470)	(26.889)	(25.711)
Activity rate ratio	431.030*	436.150*	879.538*†	217.182	159.250
	(122.542)	(150.591)	(167.485)	(179.909)	(189.006)

Notes: [a]Based on wage and reduced-form transfer regressions available from the author upon request.

[b]See Table 11.3 for variable definitions.

[c]Based on the estimated OLS regression coefficients: see note *f*.

[d]Computed as $\beta_k f(\beta'\overline{X})$, where β_k is the estimated probit coefficient on an exogenous variable, X_k, and $f(\beta'\overline{X})$, is the value of the normal density function evaluated at the weighted sample means of the exogenous variables. See note *f*.

[e]Computed as $T_{\overline{X}}\frac{\partial PT}{\partial X_k} + PT_{\overline{X}}\frac{\partial T}{\partial X_k}$,

where $T_{\overline{X}}$ and $PT_{\overline{X}}$ are the level of welfare or social insurance receipts (given participation) and the probability of participating, respectively, evaluted at the weighted sample means of the exogenous variables; and the computation of

$\frac{\partial PT}{\partial X_k}$ and $\frac{\partial T}{\partial X_k}$,

is described in notes d and c, respectively. The "total" column is obtained by summing the entries under "welfare" and "social insurance": see note f.

[f] The foreign-born-education interaction term is evaluated at the weighted sample mean level of HDEDUC.

English ability, foreign birth, and length of U.S. residence also influence the receipt of transfers indirectly through their impact on wages. Table 11.6 shows that for male heads, as expected, poor English ability is significantly negatively related to wages, decreasing wages by 8.9 percent, all else equal.[20] Among female heads, this variable is not significant, however. Among both males and females, wages tend to increase with the length of residence in the United States. All else equal, including English ability, immigrant male (female) heads who arrived between 1970 and 1974 receive wages 5.9 (1.8) percent lower than those of the native born, but the wages of male (female) heads in the 1965 - 69 cohort exceed those of comparable native-born workers by 7.6 (2.5) percent. Evaluated at the mean of the length-of-U.S.-residence variables for immigrants, the predicted wages of immigrant male heads are 10.6 percent higher than those of comparable natives, and the wages of female heads are 20 percent higher (Table 11.7, row 7).[21] This finding supports the view that immigrants are self-selected because of their ability or motivation or both.

Table 11.7

Decomposition of the Immigrant-Native Wage and Transfer Differential[a]

Characteristic	Men's Wages[b]	Men's Expected Transfer Receipts			Men's Wages[b]	Women's Expected Transfer Receipts		
		Welfare[c]	Social Insurance[c]	Total[d]		Welfare[c]	Social Insurance[c]	Total[d]
	(1)	(2)	(3)	(4)	(5)	(6)	(7)	(8)
(1) Race or Ethnic Group	-.031	10.07	-27.56	-17.49	-.010	11.24	-61.55	-50.31
(2) Age-Related Factors[e]	-.081	9.88	717.64	727.52	-.077	-46.65	454.93	408.28
(3) Education	-.075	8.97	81.70	90.67	-.130	123.31	-15.63	107.68
(4) Other Personal Characteristics	-.021	3.09	-90.71	-87.62	—	-3.75	-1.24	-4.99
(5) Location	.045	6.95	52.80	59.75	.045	42.28	50.03	92.31
(6) Poor English Ability	-.013	.52	-19.36	-18.84	.013	1.38	-22.85	-21.47
(7) Foreign Birth[f]	.101	-21.66	17.53	-4.13	.182	-141.54	27.84	-113.70
(8) Total Predicted Differential[g]	-.076	3.89	733.25	737.14	.023	-84.21	446.65	362.43

Notes: [a]Based on wage and reduced-form transfer regressions available from the author upon request. All means are weighted by the sampling weights reported in the SIE.

[b]Computed as: $W_{N(I)} - W_N$, where W is the predicted value of wages; the subscript $N(I)$ indicates that the value was obtained using immigrant means for the indicated variables and native means for the remaining explanatory variables; and the subscript N indicates the value was obtained using native means for all explanatory variables.

[c]Computed as: $T_{N(I)} \cdot PT_{N(I)} - T_N \cdot PT_N$, where T is the predicted value of transfer receipts, given participation; PT is the predicted value of the transfer-participation probability; and $N(I)$ and N are as defined above. Note that in the case of receipts, the means of the explanatory variables are computed for the relevant subgroup, namely, welfare or social insurance program participants.

[d]Computed as the sum of columns 2 and 3, or columns 6 and 7, for males or females, respectively.

[e]Includes potential experience and experience squared, and PER18T64, PERGE65, KIDSLT18 (males), KIDSLT5 and KIDSST17 (females), HD45T59, HD60T64, HD65T67, and HD68PLUS, where relevant.

[f]Includes a foreign-birth-education interaction term and (FOR) (1970-74), (FOR) (1965-69), (FOR) (1960-64), (FOR) (1950-59), (FOR) (1920-49), and (FOR) (BEFR20).

[g]Because of the nonlinearity of the probit function, the total predicted differential does not necessarily equal the sum of rows 1 through 7.

These findings imply that the indirect effect of poor English ability on the probability of participating in both types of transfer programs is positive for males, whereas the indirect effect of foreign birth on transfer program participation is negative for both males and females. On the other hand, it may be recalled that the wage coefficient in the regression for the receipt of social insurance payments, given participation, was significantly positive. We find that the indirect effect of poor English ability on total transfer payments (W + S) through lesser labor market success is to raise the transfers of male-headed families by $45.[22] Evaluated at the mean of the length-of-U.S.-residence variables for immigrants, the indirect effect of foreign birth on total transfer payments through greater labor market success is to lower the transfers of male-headed families by $38 and those of female-headed families by $12.

11.5. Total Effects of Foreign Birth

The total effects of these explanatory variables on the utilization of transfers shown in Table 11.6 take into account both direct and indirect effects. As noted earlier, they are estimated on the basis of reduced-form transfer equations. For both male and female heads, we find that those who do not speak or understand English well are more likely than those who do to receive welfare payments, but less likely to participate in social insurance programs. Those with poor English ability receive a lower level of both types of payments, given that they participate in a transfer program. On net, those who do not speak and understand English well have higher expected payments from welfare programs but lower expected payments from social insurance programs, resulting in total expected payments that are $134 lower among male heads and $185 lower among female heads than those whose command of English is superior.

With respect to foreign birth, after controlling for English ability and other factors, immigrant families are estimated to be less dependent on welfare and to receive lower levels of welfare payments than native families, regardless of the sex or length of U.S. residence of their head. All else equal, the expected welfare receipts of immigrant families range from $27 to $36 less for male-headed families and from $57 to $157 less for female-headed families, depending on the length of residence of the head.

On the other hand, although participation in social insurance is initially less for immigrant than native families, immigrant cohorts arriving more than 16 years ago in the case of male heads and more than 26 years ago in the case of female heads begin to have a higher incidence of participation at those times, all else equal. The increased participation of immigrants in social insurance programs over time (a positive total effect) indicates that their increasing eligibility for social insurance programs (a positive direct effect) outweighs their rising relative wages (a negative indirect effect). The social insurance receipts of immigrant families, given participation, are about the same as or less than native families, all else equal, for female-headed families. This is also the case among males, if the head arrived after 1949. Among the families headed by longer-term male immigrants, however, receipts are higher than for native families, ceteris paribus.

All else equal, the expected social insurance receipts of male- and female-headed immigrant families are less than those of native families initially, but they eventually surpass them. Among both male- and female-headed families, total expected transfer receipts are initially lower than those of comparable native families, but they exceed them among cohorts having arrived more than 26 years ago – a time pattern that primarily reflects the time path of social insurance payments.

We may obtain an overall foreign-born effect by evaluating the foreign-born length-of-U.S.-residence interactions at their mean levels for immigrants (Table 11.7, row 7). Overall, immigrant families rely on welfare payments to a lesser extent than do native families with similar characteristics (columns 2 and 6). Among male-headed families, the expected welfare payment among immigrants is thus estimated to be 59 percent ($22) lower than the predicted level for the native born with mean native-born characteristics ($37); and among female-headed families, the payment for immigrants is 57 percent ($142) lower than that predicted for the native born ($248). On the other hand, the expected social insurance payment of an immigrant family is estimated to be 2 percent higher than the predicted value for a typical male-headed ($969) or female-headed ($1,123) native family (columns 3 and 7). On net, all else equal, the total expected transfer payment of a male-headed immigrant family is about the same as the predicted level for a male-headed native family with mean native characteristics and actually 8 percent ($114) lower among female-headed families.

11.6. Immigrant-Native Differences in Characteristics

Since differences in immigrant and native responses to the same set of variables do not appear to account for the observed differences in transfer receipts between the two groups reported in Table 11.1, the transfer differential must be the result of immigrant-native differences in the levels of the explanatory variables. The role of such group differences in characteristics is evaluated in Table 11.7. The table seeks to answer the following questions: What would the predicted immigrant-native differential be if immigrants had their own particular levels of a given characteristic (such as race or ethnic group) but had the native means for all the other variables? Or, what would the immigrant-native differential be if the two groups differed only with respect to the indicated characteristic?[23] This is considered the contribution of that characteristic to the predicted differential. These findings were outlined earlier when the relevant characteristic was foreign birth. We now consider the contribution of other variables.

Table 11.7 suggests that, as expected, age and age-related variables play a major role in explaining the observed differences between immigrants and natives. Among males, age-related factors are more than sufficient to account for the predicted immigrant-native differential in expected welfare receipts; they explain 98 percent of the predicted differential in expected social insurance receipts and 99 percent of the predicted differential in total expected transfer receipts. Among female-headed families, age-related factors account for 55 percent of the lower levels of welfare received by immigrants. (The opposing effect of age-related factors on the welfare receipts of male and female heads probably reflects the greater relative importance of Supplemental Security Insurance among the former and Aid to Families with Dependent Children among the latter.) Age-related factors are sufficient to explain all of the predicted higher use of social insurance and total transfers (W + S) by female-headed immigrant families.

Immigrants' lower levels of education and greater concentration in metropolitan areas and in the Northeast tend to raise their expected receipts from transfer programs.[24] The higher representation of minority groups among immigrants increases their expected welfare payments but lowers their expected social insurance payments, resulting in lower amounts of total expected transfer receipts. On net, the other personal characteristics of immigrants serve to lower their total transfer receipts, with a major factor among male heads being the lower proportion of veterans among immigrants (which lowers their utilization of social insurance transfers). The higher representation of individuals who have poor English ability among immigrants reduces their total transfer receipts, on balance. This reduction reflects their lower probability of participating in social insurance programs, as well as their lower receipts, given participation, from both types of programs.

11.7. Conclusion

Policy-makers often express concern over the possibility that immigrants constitute a burden on the U.S. transfer payment system. This study shows that total transfer payments to an immigrant family are indeed higher on average than to a native family - in 1975, 52 percent higher among families with male heads and 13 percent higher among families with female heads. A closer examination of these differences casts considerable doubt on the validity of the above concern, however.

We have found that immigrant families are, in fact, considerably less likely to rely on welfare than native families with similar characteristics. (Indeed, the unadjusted welfare receipts of immigrant families headed by a woman are also lower than those of native families.) As a result, expected receipts from welfare programs in 1975 were significantly lower for immigrants than for the native born: 59 percent lower among comparable families with male heads and 57 percent lower among comparable female-headed families. In addition, the expected social insurance payments of an immigrant family in 1975 were found to be only slightly (2 percent) higher than those of a comparable native family.

Overall, we estimate that total expected transfer payments to male-headed immigrant families in 1975 were about the same as total payments to their native counterparts, and total payments to female-headed immigrant families were actually 8 percent lower. Thus, we conclude that behavioral differences in the response of immigrant and native families to the same variables do not account for the observed higher receipts of transfer payments by immigrant families. That is, families headed by immigrants appear to be no more apt to receive transfers than otherwise comparable native families. This implies that the observed differences between the two groups are the result of group differences in characteristics, or of ways in which immigrant and native families differ from each other.

We have found that immigrant-native differences in age-related variables are sufficient to account for virtually all of the higher use of transfers by immigrant families. Since the age distribution of immigrants is determined by historical trends in immigration (particularly the adoption of restrictive immigration laws in 1921 and 1924) rather than by domestic birth and death rates, immigrants tend to be older, on average, than natives. Their age, therefore, tends to increase their use of transfers, all else equal. Nonetheless, since the vast majority of older immigrants have spent most of their working lives in the United States and have working-age children who contribute taxes to finance social programs, their higher reliance on transfers for reasons of their age does not appear to burden the transfer payment system unduly.

The policy implications of these findings must be drawn in full awareness of the fact that the findings are in part dependent on the past composition of the immigrant group studied. If, in the future, we were to see, for example, a widening of the immigrant-native disparity in educational attainment or an increase in the proportion of refugees among immigrants,[25] the relative use of transfers by immigrants might begin to pose a social problem. For the most part, however, the findings of this study provide grounds for cautious optimism.

One issue often raised about more recent immigrant cohorts is, for example, the high representation of minority individuals among them. But, as we have seen, the higher representation of minority groups among immigrants in the past has actually worked to lower their total transfer receipts, on net, by increasing their expected welfare payments but lowering their expected social insurance payments. Similarly, the higher representation among immigrants of individuals who have poor English ability has also reduced their total transfer receipts, on balance, because of their lower probability of participating in social insurance programs, as well as their lower receipts, given participation, in both types of programs.

On the hand, policy-makers may wish to distinguish between contributory social insurance programs and noncontributory welfare programs. If that is the case, the higher representation of minority individuals and those with poor English ability among immigrants might be cause for concern. Moreover, the findings here must be further qualified by the fact that the sample drawn from the Survey of Income and Education most likely underrepresents illegal immigrants.

12

Gender, Source Country Characteristics, and Labor Market Assimilation among Immigrants

Based on a paper with Lawrence M. Kahn and Kerry L. Papps

12.1. Introduction

A steady flow of new immigration has resulted in an increase in the foreign-born share of the U.S. population from 4.8% in 1970 to 11.1% in 2000. Perhaps more dramatically, the percentage of the foreign-born population that came from Europe or Canada fell from 70.4% to 18.4% between 1970 and 2000, with a corresponding increase in the Asian and Latin American share from 28.3% in 1970 to 52.4% in 1980 and 78.2%

This chapter is a revised version of Blau, F. D., Kahn, L. M., Papps, K. L. (2011). Gender, Source Country characteristics, and Labor Market Assimilation among Immigrants, in: Review of Economics and Statistics, 93(1): 43-58. © 2011 The MIT Press.

The authors are indebted to Alberto Abadie, Martha Bailey, Charlie Brown, John DiNardo, Andrew Oswald, Mark Rosenzweig, Jeff Smith, and Dean Yang and two anonymous referees. We are indebted as well to participants at the Society of Labor Economists meetings in Chicago, May 2007; the Wang Yanan Institute for Studies in Economics 2007 International Symposium on Contemporary Labor Economics, Xiamen University, Xiamen, China, December 2007; the Herman Colloquium, University of Michigan, March 2008; the Centre for European Economic Research (ZEW) Workshop on Gender and the Labour Market, Mannheim, Germany, March 2008; the Sixth Annual Migration Meeting, IZA, Bonn, Germany, May 2009; and the Cornell University Labor Economics Workshop for helpful comments and suggestions. We also thank Fidan Kurtulus and Albert Yung-Hsu Liu for excellent research assistance, and the Russell Sage Foundation for financial support. Portions of the research for this paper were completed while Blau and Kahn were visiting fellows in the Economics Department of Princeton University, supported by the Industrial Relations Section.

in 2000.[1] An additional feature of the immigrant population that is less frequently noted is that immigrants typically come from countries with a more traditional division of labor by gender than the United States. Moreover, during the 1980–2000 period, the gender gap in labor supply in the United States narrowed much more than in immigrant source countries. If immigrant women's labor supply behavior mirrors that in their home countries, rising shares of the U.S. population composed of immigrants from countries with more traditional gender roles will cause the U.S. female labor force participation rate to be lower than otherwise. On the other hand, if immigrant women's labor supply eventually assimilates to U.S. levels, this effect would be lessened.

While some evidence suggests that source country female participation does influence immigrant women's labor supply behavior in the United States (Antecol 2000), little is known about its effect on the assimilation process. The assimilation profile can shed light on what will happen in the long run as these women are exposed to labor market conditions and social norms in the United States. For example, suppose women from a more traditional source country have on average a 20% shortfall in hours relative to comparable immigrant women from less traditional countries. This could reflect a substantial and persistent 20% shortfall throughout their time in the United States or, say, a 40% shortfall during the early stages of their time in the United States, which falls to 0 with longer residence. The two scenarios have different implications for convergence of the group to comparable natives and may affect the labor supply behavior of the second generation of immigrants as well.

In this chapter, we study the impact of traditional gender roles in immigrant source countries on the assimilation of married immigrant women and men into the U.S. labor market. This chapter contributes to a broader literature examining the impact of culture or preferences and beliefs developed in a different time or place on current economic behavior (Fernández 2008), and, in particular, the impact of source country characteristics on immigrant women's behavior in the United States. We build on Antecol (2000), who found, using the 1990 Census, that source country female labor force participation rates were positively correlated with U.S. labor force participation of immigrant women, even controlling for human capital characteristics. In addition, Blau's (1992) study of the effect of source country fertility rates on immigrant women's fertility also suggests an impact of gender roles in source countries on the behavior of immigrant women in the United States. Also of interest is Antecol's finding of a positive, though weaker, correlation between U.S. and source country participation for "second- and higher-generation" immigrants, defined by their answer to the census question on ancestry. Similarly, the labor supply and fertility behavior of U.S.-born daughters of immigrants (the second generation) has been found to be positively associated with both female participation and fertility rates in their parents' country of origin (Fernández and Fogli 2009) and the participation and fertility patterns of immigrants from those origin countries (Blau, Kahn, Liu et al. 2008).

To examine the impact of source country characteristics on immigrant women's assimilation into the U.S. labor market, we use the 1980–2000 U.S. censuses, which we augment with an extensive set of source country characteristics, as described in the Appendix. These include two indicators of the extent of traditional gender roles in the source country: female relative to male labor force participation and women's completed fertility. In addition, in contrast to most earlier work,[2] we control for a variety of other source country characteristics that may affect immigrants' labor supply behavior in the United States, thus increasing the likelihood that our models estimate the true effect of source country female labor supply and fertility rather than the impact of omitted factors that are correlated with these variables. Moreover, results for the impact of these control variables on the assimilation profile are of considerable interest in themselves in shedding light on the economics of immigration generally. Our design allows us to characterize the impact of these source country characteristics on the entire labor supply assimilation profile, an analysis that previous research on immigrant assimilation has not performed. We measure source country characteristics at the time each immigrant came to the United States, although our results are robust to alternative specifications. This is appropriate, since we would like a measure of the tastes or economic incentives one left behind in deciding to migrate and changes in the strength of their effect over time in the United States. We focus on married immigrants for whom gender roles are expected to have a greater effect and in order to explicitly consider the division of labor in the family among immigrants compared to natives.

Higher female labor force participation rates in the United States than in many immigrant source countries may ultimately be due to tastes and beliefs about women's appropriate roles in society, although they may also be due to different economic incentives (e.g., higher female relative wages) in the United States than in the countries of origin. If differences in labor supply behavior between immigrant women from high and low participation source countries tend to persist over time in the United States, cultural factors may indeed be important. If, however, the labor supply of women from both groups tends to converge as both assimilate to the U.S. native levels, one might conclude that the hold of home country beliefs on women's appropriate roles is relatively weak in the face of U.S. work incentives and possibly a U.S. market work-oriented culture. By investigating the impact of source country relative female labor supply on the labor supply assimilation profiles of immigrant women, we provide an explicit test of the persistence of these effects and hence of the potential role and strength of source country culture on immigrant behavior in the United States. Because immigrants are likely to differ from natives in significant unmeasured ways, comparing labor supply assimilation paths of immigrants from more and less traditional source countries is a useful way to study the impact of cultural factors. The great variety of immigrant source countries from which immigrants to the United States originate, spanning such diverse cultures as those in Scandinavia, Latin America, Asia, and the Middle East, provides considerable variation in the source country gender division of labor. Our research design uses this variation to study the issue of assimilation.

In addition to its focus on the assimilation process, our research design provides evidence on the impact of source country culture in a number of other ways. First, we examine the effect of female relative labor supply in the source country on immigrant male labor supply behavior. An effect of traditional source country patterns that is unique to or stronger for women than men suggests that the effect for women reflects source country gender roles rather than other unmeasured factors that may be expected to have a similar effect for both men and women. Second, we investigate the impact of source country relative female participation of immigrant men on the labor supply behavior of their native-born wives. A positive correlation between immigrant husbands' source country female participation and the labor supply of native-born wives may be due to immigrant men selecting marital partners with similar preferences or directly affecting the labor supply behavior of their wives, for example, by being more or less helpful with family chores or supporting, or opposing their labor force entry or career commitment. In either case, an effect of husband's source characteristics on these wives is suggestive of an effect of source country culture on U.S. behavior.[3] Finally, unlike previous work on immigrants, we distinguish between the effects of a woman's own source country from that of her husband's country of origin in the cases where the couple migrated from different countries. This sheds light on the relative importance of wives' and husbands' source country characteristics in influencing wives' labor supply when both spouses are foreign born.

A study of the impact of source country characteristics on immigrant women's labor supply assimilation raises the question of the shape of that profile and how (or if) it may differ between women from more and less traditional source countries. The standard expectation might be that the assimilation profile would be upward sloping for both husbands and wives, where the immigrant would start at a disadvantage relative to otherwise similar individuals due to the disruptions of immigration that could lead to difficulty in finding a job or to temporarily working positive but less-than-desired hours. The impact of these disruptions is expected to decrease over time, and immigrant labor supply is expected to approach that of natives. A period of disruption may be even more likely for married women than married men to the extent women are "tied movers" (Mincer 1978). In addition, some visas obtained by husbands (generally the primary earner) may not permit their spouse to work.[4]

An alternative possibility is raised by the family migration model proposed by Baker and Benjamin (1997) that predicts women will initially take dead-end jobs to finance their husbands' human capital investments and eventually drop out of the labor market or reduce their labor supply as their husbands' labor market outcomes improve. Rather than convergence toward native labor supply levels, this model predicts a negatively sloped labor supply profile for immigrant women relative to natives, a finding that has been observed for Canada (Baker and Benjamin 1997) but not for the United States (Blau et al. 2003). A recent study by Cobb-Clark and Crossley (2004), using Australian data, focuses on immigrant families who migrated together and examines the behavior of the secondary worker (the spouse of the family member who applied for admission to the country) in such families. When the secondary worker in the family is a woman, she works more on arrival than immigrant women in mixed (immigrant-native) families, supporting the family migration model; but when the secondary worker is male, he works less than in mixed families, a finding inconsistent with the model.[5]

The logic of the family migration model, as well as the findings by Cobb-Clark and Crossley (2004), suggest that gender roles within the family are potentially important in determining its applicability. One might expect the family migration model to hold more strongly for families coming from countries with a more traditional division of labor by gender. If so, couples migrating from such countries may be expected to exhibit more specialization by gender, implying that immigrant women's assimilation profiles will have a higher intercept and more negative (or perhaps less positive) slope the more traditional the source country is. While a complete test of the family migration model is outside the scope of this study, we may contribute to the literature on this topic by providing evidence on this hypothesis.

12.2. Data and Descriptive Patterns

Our basic data sources are the 1980, 1990, and 2000 U.S. Census of Population public use microsamples. In addition, we assembled a time-series, cross-sectional database on source country characteristics, which we merged into the census microdata for immigrants based on their country of origin and the date they arrived in the United States. Because of changes in the list of countries across censuses, it was necessary in some cases to aggregate countries and compute appropriately weighted country characteristics. We also performed some imputations for missing data. (See the Appendix for further details.) Note that the measure of source country female labor supply we employ is women's labor force participation relative to men's (female LFP/male LFP). This relative measure is appropriate in that it captures the gender division of labor explicitly. A further advantage is that it implicitly adjusts for problems in measuring the labor force, particularly at different levels of economic development, at least to the extent that such problems affect men's and women's measured participation rates similarly.

We focus on individuals aged 18 to 65 who are married to someone aged 18 to 65 and restrict the immigrant sample (respondents and spouses) to those who migrated as adults - age 18 or over.[6] This is desirable because our empirical approach relies on within-immigrant arrival cohort changes to estimate assimilation effects. If child immigrants are included, some immigrants who recently arrived in the United States as children will be excluded from the sample of those aged 18 to 65 in an initial census but will have attained age 18, and therefore eligibility for sample inclusion in subsequent censuses. Thus, the composition of the immigrant sample would change with time in the United States, as those arriving as children comprise a higher share of those with a longer duration of residence (Friedberg 1993). This is likely to bias the results because those migrating to the United States as children may be less affected by home country characteristics and more similar to native-born Americans when they reach adulthood than those migrating as adults. This also implies that adult immigrants, the large majority of immigrants, are the more appropriate sample on which to study the assimilation process in any case. We use all immigrants for whom we can match source country characteristics, and, for tractability, we take a 4% sample of natives, whom we appropriately weight in all analyses. Overall, we were able to match over 99% of immigrants who had valid, nonallocated values for country of birth and year entering the United States to source countries for which we were able to obtain the source country variables.

Table 12.1 contains descriptive information on labor market outcomes and personal characteristics in our sample of married individuals for (adult) immigrants and natives in the 1980 and 2000 Censuses, although we additionally use the 1990 Census in the regression analyses. Table 12.1 indicates that in both years, immigrant women have lower labor supply (measured by either the probability of positive hours or average annual work hours, including those with 0 hours) and more children than U.S. women, even though they are about the same age. Moreover, while both immigrant and native women increased their labor supply between 1980 and 2000, the native-immigrant gap grew considerably: in 1980, natives worked 66 hours (8%) more than immigrants; by 2000, the gap was 319 hours (32%). In contrast to women, immigrant men worked only 8% fewer hours than native men in 1980, a gap that increased only slightly (to 11%) by 2000. Thus, the gender gap in labor supply fell much more for natives than for immigrants. Table 12.1 also shows a widening educational gap between immigrants and natives, and an increase in the relative share of minorities among immigrants.

Table 12.1

Mean Values of Selected Variables for Immigrants and U.S. Natives, 1980 and 2000 (Married Individuals)

	1980		2000	
Variables	Immigrants	U.S. Born	Immigrants	U.S. Born
A. Women				
Annual work hours	822.51	887.13	983.06	1301.98
Participated in labor market	0.542	0.608	0.578	0.758
Number of children under 18	1.401	1.157	1.220	1.043
Speaks English well	0.697	0.996	0.652	0.995
Age	40.814	39.231	40.942	41.574
High school dropout	0.395	0.221	0.249	0.061
Exactly high school diploma	0.286	0.470	0.247	0.312
Some college	0.148	0.177	0.184	0.340
College graduate	0.171	0.133	0.320	0.287
White, non-Hispanic	0.418	0.891	0.229	0.867
Black, non-Hispanic	0.037	0.066	0.051	0.065
Other, non-Hispanic	0.268	0.40	0.404	0.022
Hispanic	0.277	0.032	0.316	0.046
Sample size	69,431	76,940	111,283	71,198
B. Men				
Annual work hours	1823.52	1969.47	1855.07	2052.51
Participated in labor market	0.905	0.922	0.889	0.912
Speaks English well	0.731	0.996	0.704	0.996
Age	43.617	41.755	43.521	43.658
High school dropout	0.383	0.248	0.238	0.081
Exactly high school diploma	0.191	0.366	0.211	0.300
Some college	0.130	0.174	0.159	0.306
College graduate	0.296	0.212	0.392	0.314
White, non-Hispanic	0.407	0.891	0.240	0.867
Black, non-Hispanic	0.050	0.067	0.061	0.069
Other non-Hispanic	0.236	0.011	0.372	0.020
Hispanic	0.307	0.031	0.327	0.044
Sample size	60,259	86,112	104,866	77,615

Notes: Immigrant samples include only those from countries with observations in each census year and only adult immigrants.

The finding of a growing immigrant-native labor supply gap among women in the United States raises the question of whether there are similar trends when female labor supply in immigrant source countries is compared to that in the United States. To the extent that source country labor supply patterns mirror the growing native-immigrant gap in labor supply, we may also ask whether this is associated with a shift in the composition of countries from which immigrants originate versus different time trends within sending countries and the United States. These questions are addressed in Table 12.2, based on our sample of 106

Table 12.2

Mean Values of Selected Source Country Characteristics, 1980 and 2000 (Married Woman)

Variables	1980			2000		
	Source Countries		United States	Source Countries		United States
	1980 Weights (1)	2000 Weights (2)	1980 Weights (3)	1980 Weights (4)	2000 Weights (5)	2000 Weights (6)
Total fertility rate	4.473	5.301	2.817	3.055	3.663	1.957
GDP per capita (1995 US$)	4,768.3	3,012.4	16,807.3	7,919.3	4,705.6	25,786.9
Female LFP/male LFP	0.445	0.464	0.513	0.572	0.566	0.716
Percentage refugees	0.061	0.057	0.000	0.105	0.117	0.000
Primary school enrollment rate	98.73	94.00	100.05	102.55	100.59	100.40
Secondary school enrollment rate	41.57	34.68	89.42	70.12	58.78	94.92
English-speaking country	0.157	0.091	1.000	0.157	0.091	1.000
English official language (non–English speaking)	0.105	0.169	0.000	0.105	0.169	0.000
Miles from country	3,834.5	4,247.7	0.0	3,834.5	4,247.7	0.0

Notes: Source country characteristics are measured as of each immigrant's arrival period and averaged across immigrants. Country weights are fixed by giving each immigrant a weight for her source country corresponding to the frequency of immigrants from that source country in the indicated year (1980 or 2000). U.S. characteristics are weighted by the number of immigrants in each arrival period cell in the indicated year. Census sampling weights are taken into account. Immigrant samples include only those from countries with observations in each census year and only adults.

countries, which shows the mean characteristics of source countries of immigrant women for 1980 and 2000, with source country characteristics measured at the time immigrants migrated to the United States. (We omit a corresponding table for men, since the source countries of immigrant men and women tend to be quite similar.) The table also shows the corresponding means for the United States, similarly weighted by the number of immigrants in each arrival period cell. For immigrants, two sets of weights are employed: contemporary-year weights (1980 in 1980 and 2000 in 2000) and fixed-year weights that hold the mix of source countries constant at the indicated year (1980 or 2000).

Looking first at the results for contemporary-year weights (columns 1 and 5 for immigrants; columns 3 and 6 for the natives), Table 12.2 indicates that in each year, the average immigrant woman came from a country that, at the time of her arrival in the United States, had lower relative female labor force participation and higher fertility than the United States had at the same time. Moreover, although average home country relative female labor supply at the time of arrival increased over the period, the corresponding U.S. value increased by considerably more, resulting in a growing gap between U.S. and source country relative female labor force participation - mirroring what we found for immigrant-native differences in the United States. Similarly, source country fertility at time of arrival is higher than U.S. fertility in each year and fell, but by less than the corresponding U.S. fertility decline. We note, however, that for recent immigrants (those who arrived in the past five years), source country fertility decreased substantially relative to U.S. fertility and was only 44% above the U.S. level for recent immigrants in 2000, compared to 2.3 times the U.S. level in 1980 (results not shown).[7] Thus, although origin countries have higher fertility than the United States, the gap is closing at the margin. Table 12.2 also indicates that had the distribution of origin countries stayed the same, source country fertility would have been reduced considerably (compare column 2 with 1 and column 5 with 4). However, the relative female participation rate - the key variable for our study - remains roughly constant when source country mix is fixed.

There were some trends in the control variables as well. The gap between U.S. and source country GDP per capita increased both absolutely and relatively; this trend was fueled by shifts in source country mix. Immigrants were less likely to have come from English-speaking countries in 2000 than in 1980, and average distance between the United States and the source country increased. (Since these variables are fixed over time, these shifts were entirely due to the shifting composition of source countries.) On the other hand, primary and secondary enrollment gaps between the United States and immigrant source countries have narrowed. However, the convergence would have been greater had the source country mix remained constant and, moreover, the secondary enrollment gap remains quite large.

12.3. Empirical Procedures

Our analysis of the impact of source country characteristics on the labor supply assimilation of immigrants compares immigrants to natives with the same observable characteristics. Thus, assimilation here refers to the degree to which immigrants' labor supply patterns converge to those of otherwise comparable natives. We estimate equations of the following form on our pooled census microdata separately for men and women:

$$(1) \qquad H_{it} = B'X_{it} + \sum_{c} a_c A^0_{cit} + \sum_{y} b_y T^0_{yit} + \sum_{y,j} d_{yj} T^0_{yit} Z^0_{jit} + \sum_{c} e_c A^s_{cit} + \sum_{y} f_y T^S_{yit} + \sum_{y,j} d_{yj} T^S_{yit} Z^S_{jit} + k_{90} C90_{it} + k_{00} C00_{it} + u_{it},$$

where for individual i in immigrant arrival cohort c, immigrant years since migration category y, and census year $t(t = 1980, 1990, \text{or } 2000)$, H is annual hours worked in the previous year (usual weekly hours times weeks worked, including those with 0 hours), X is a vector of controls, A^0_{cit} and A^S_{cit} are a series of own and spouse (o and s superscripts) immigrant cohort-of-arrival dummy variables, T^0_{yit} and T^s_{yit} are a series of dummy variables referring to own and spouse years since migration (YSM), Z^0_{jit} and Z^s_{jit} are a series of own and spouse source country characteristics indexed by j, $C90_{it}$ and $C00_{it}$ are year dummies for 1990 and 2000, and uit is an error term.[8] The dummy variables for immigrant arrival cohort and years since migration category (A^0_{cit}, A^s_{cit}, T^0_{yit}, and T^s_{yit}) and the immigrant source country characteristics (Z^0_{jit} and Z^s_{jit}) are all set to 0 for native-born respondents or spouses. We cluster the standard errors at the respondent's year of arrival–source country level, treating the United States as a source country for natives. We cluster in this way because this is the level of variation of our group-level explanatory variables; however, results were robust to alternative assumptions, including clustering at the source country and source country–census year level. After creating sampling weights to reflect the random sample of natives and taking into account census sampling weights for 1990 and 2000, we adjust each year's weights so that the total weight of each year's observations is the same.

We define the cohort of arrival and years-since-migration variables for immigrants and their spouses as follows. Since the immigrant arrival period is defined in interval form in the 1980 and 1990 Censuses, we define sets of cohort of arrival and years-since-migration dummy variables that are consistent across the three censuses. We specify the years-since-migration variables as dummies rather than forming a continuous variable (say, by evaluating the intervals at their midpoints) in order to capture all the available information in the most flexible form. The full set of years-since-migration dummies is included: 0–5, 6–10, 11–15, 16–20, and 21–30 years in the United States (these are the T^0_{yit} and T^s_{yit} dummies). The sum of the years-since-migration dummy variables for the respondent (the T^0_{yit}) would be identical to a respondent immigrant dummy variable, and the sum of the spouse years-since-migration dummies (the T^s_{yit}) would be identical to a spouse immigrant dummy variable; therefore, respondent and spouse immigration indicators are not separately included in equation (1). Using the full set of years-since-migration dummies requires us to omit one of the possible arrival cohort dummy variable categories; we have omitted the 1950–1959 cohort for both the respondent and spouse. Thus, the cohort of arrival dummies are 1995–2000, 1991–1994, 1985–1990, 1980–1984, 1975–1979, 1970–1974, 1965–1969, and 1960–1964 (these are the A^0_{cit} and A^s_{cit} dummies). Pooling the sample across three census years and assuming common period effects for immigrants and natives together allow us to separately identify immigrant cohort and assimilation effects (Borjas 1985).

The interval form of the arrival period in the 1980 and 1990 Censuses also affects our restriction of the sample to adult immigrant respondents and spouses. For each arrival interval, we include only immigrants whom we can definitely conclude were at least 18 years old on arrival in the United States.[9] For comparability, similar procedures are followed for the 2000 Census data. This requires us to exclude individuals in the open-ended arrival category in the earlier censuses (pre-1950), since we cannot ascertain whether they migrated as children or adults. The resulting maximum years since migration is thus thirty for 1980, and, for comparability, a maximum of thirty years since migration is also set for 1990 and 2000. This explains why the above years-since-migration dummies exhaust the sample of adult immigrants.

The source country characteristics Z^0_{jit} and Z^S_{jit} are measured at the time the individual migrated to the United States and are set equal to 0 for natives. Thus, they are in effect interactions between an immigrant dummy variable and the source country characteristics. Because the years-since-migration dummies (T^0_{yit} and T^S_{yit}) add up to 1 for each immigrant respondent or immigrant spouse, for each country characteristic, the sum of its interactions with the years-since-migration variables equals the country characteristic itself. Therefore, we do not include main country characteristics effects (Z^0_{jit} and Z^S_{jit}). The specification in equation (1) allows the source country variables to affect both the level of labor supply and the impact of time in the United States on labor supply.

Source country variables were selected to serve as indicators of the degree to which the home country has a traditional division of labor by gender and the extent of labor market preparedness of men and women and to address possible issues of selective migration. They include the female labor force participation rate/male labor force participation rate; the total fertility rate (an estimate of completed female fertility); GDP per capita in 2000 U.S. dollars; the proportion of immigrants arriving in the period who were refugees; the female (female regression) or male (male regression) enrollment rates in primary school and secondary school; a dummy variable for whether the country is English speaking; a dummy variable for countries that are not English speaking but in which English is an official language;[10] and the distance between the source country and the United States.

Female relative labor supply and fertility rates in the source country are indicators of traditional gender roles in the source country. Moreover, these variables, as well as GDP per capita, education, and use of English, are all likely to be related to preparedness for work in the U.S. labor market. In addition, migration likely involves a disruption of work patterns due to housing and job search in the United States. Refugees and those who have come a long distance may suffer the largest disruption, possibly steepening their work assimilation profiles. Alternatively, because of the fixed costs of migration, those who come from a greater distance are likely to have higher labor market returns to migration than those coming shorter distances, all else equal (Chiswick 1978), and this potential selectivity could also be reflected in work assimilation patterns. For example, migrants moving from a longer distance may be more likely to have jobs lined up in the United States (contributing to their higher rate of return to migration), thus raising their work hours at entry and flattening their assimilation profiles (i.e., the opposite predictions from the disruption mechanism). Thus, the impact of distance on assimilation profiles is theoretically ambiguous.

The combination of the cohort and years-since-migration dummies allows us to completely characterize immigrant labor supply over time in the United States relative to that of natives, controlling for the X variables and year effects. The X variables include the following for respondent and spouse: age, age squared, three education dummies (high school diploma, some college, and college degree, with less than high school as the omitted category), interactions between an immigrant dummy and the three education dummies, and three race/Hispanic origin dummy variables (black non-Hispanic, other non-Hispanic, and Hispanic, with white non-Hispanic the omitted category). X also includes eight census region dummies and dummy variables for each of California, Texas, New York, Florida, Illinois, and New Jersey, the states with the largest immigrant populations. Of special note in our controls is the inclusion of immigrant-education and spouse immigrant-education interaction terms.[11] These variables allow the impact of education on labor supply to be affected by whether the education was obtained in the United States and further allow an immigrant's (or immigrant spouse's) level of education to affect the assimilation process. In addition, because we have included source country school enrollment levels, these interactions in effect transform the immigrant and spouse immigrant education impacts into effects relative to source country schooling. Implicitly, then, these variables control for self-selection of immigrants by education, as well as for the substantive effect of education. Immigrants who are higher up in the educational distribution of their country of origin may differ in their unmeasured characteristics from those with an equal level of education who place lower in their home country's educational distribution. To the extent this type of selection is controlled for by our specification, we expect to obtain estimates of the effects of other explanatory variables that are less biased by selectivity. We also note that equation (1) is a reduced-form specification. We seek to estimate the total effects of the source country variables on the immigrant assimilation process in the United States. We exclude variables such as number of children and wages, which may be considered endogenous to the assimilation process.[12]

We initially estimate equation (1) for all married women and all married men in order to characterize the overall effects of source country characteristics on the married immigrant population's labor supply assimilation profiles. These estimates pool a number of immigrant family types – immigrants married to immigrants from the same and different countries, as well as immigrants married to natives – with our reference group of natives married to natives. In addition to estimating our models on these subsamples, we implement a number of robustness checks and alternative specifications on the basic sample of married women. These include breaking up the annual labor supply into the intensive (hours given employment) and extensive (incidence of employment) margins, measuring source country characteristics as of age 17 (a perhaps formative age), measuring them as of the current period (perhaps reflecting changing norms in one's source country), adding country dummy variables (in order to eliminate any possible correlation between omitted country-specific factors and the key country characteristics examined), and using all adults – married and nonmarried (in order to address the possibly changing selection into marriage).

12.4. Results

12.4.1. Source Country Characteristics and Assimilation Profiles for Labor Supply: All Married Couples

The basic findings from estimating equation (1) are summarized in Table 12.3 and Figure 12.1 for women and Table 12.4 and Figure 12.2 for men. We focus on the sum of the own and spouse effects of the source country characteristics. The sum corresponds to an experiment in which we compare a married couple who migrated together from one source country to an otherwise similar couple who migrated together from a different source country. This is a reasonable way to summarize the results in that data from the 1980 Census suggest that a couple migrating together from the same source county is the modal family type for immigrant couples. In 1980, we have information on individuals' age at first marriage and the number of times they have been married. (Unfortunately, there is no comparable information in the 1990 and 2000 Censuses.) Among immigrant women who were in their first marriage (91.0% of immigrant women), 73.8% were married to immigrants. Of these women, between 62.9% and 78.4% were married before arriving in the United States to a spouse who arrived at the same time. (This range occurs because the arrival year is coded in intervals.)[13] For both estimates, 89% of the women identified as married at arrival were from the same source country as their husband. A further reason for summarizing our results by summing the coefficients for respondents and spouses is precisely because a high proportion of immigrant couples do come from the same source country; pooling all census years, 90.3% of immigrant women married to immigrant men came from the same source country as their husband. This results in considerable collinearity between respondent and spouse source country characteristics among immigrant couples; for example, the correlation between wives' and husbands' source country female relative activity rate is 0.942,[14] making precise estimates of their individual effects problematic in the specification that pools all family types. Below, we investigate this issue by looking at various family types separately (e.g., immigrants migrating from different source countries or immigrants married to natives).

Looking first at the results for relative female labor supply in the female regressions, we see that the source country relative activity rate has a positive, significant effect on annual hours in each YSM category. Thus, source country female labor supply is strongly positively associated with immigrant women's labor supply behavior in the United States. Table 12.3 indicates that this effect is roughly stable across YSM categories; the effect of the activity rate ratio on labor supply at 6–10 through 21–30 years since migration is not significantly different from its effect at arrival (0–5 years), although the point estimate rises somewhat through the 16–20 year category before dropping back in the 21–30 year group. Thus, the factors mentioned earlier that might potentially cause the gap between women from high and low activity rate source countries to intensify or decay over time in the United States appear to roughly cancel out.

These effects and the relationship of immigrant women's labor supply to the native-born reference group are illustrated in Figure 12.1. The figure shows simulated assimilation profiles for adult immigrant women married to adult immigrant men who came to the United States from the same country and at the same time, assuming the couple migrates from a country with a high female relative activity rate, at the 75th percentile of our sample, or a low female activity rate, at the 25th percentile. This calculation uses individual immigrants, not individual source countries, as the unit of analysis, thereby giving countries sending larger numbers of immigrants more weight in computing

Figure 12.1

Simulated Profiles, Annual Work Hours, Married Adult Immigrant Woman, By Source Country Relative Female Activity Rate

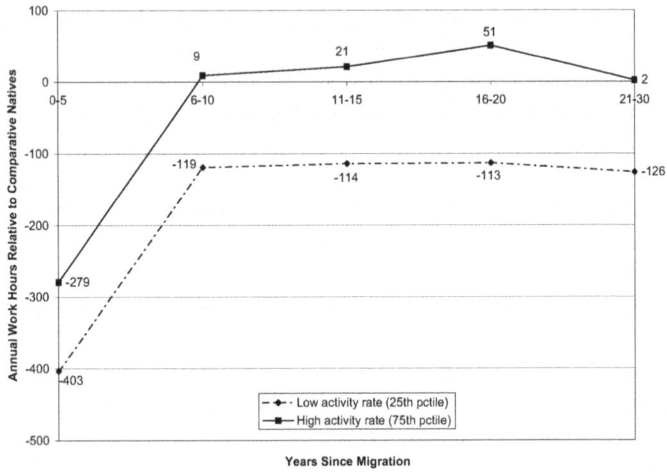

Notes: Profiles assume the same cohort arrival values, years since migration, and source country characteristics for women and spouses.

Figure 12.2

Simulated Assimilation Profiles, Annual Work Hours, Married Adult Immigrant Men, by Female Relative Activity Rate

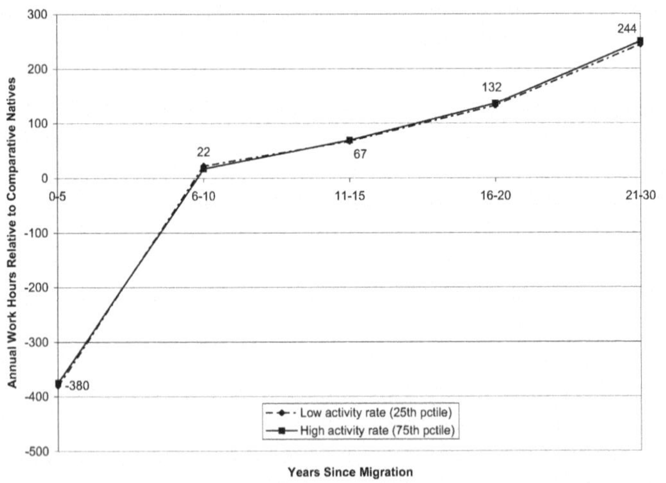

Notes: Profiles assume the same cohort arrival values, years since migration, and source country characteristics for men and spouses.

the percentiles. The 75th percentile figure is 0.636 and corresponds roughly to the Austrian value for the relative female activity rate for 1996, while the 25th percentile is 0.368 and roughly the level for Pakistan in 1994.[15] In order to construct the profiles, we assume the sample averages for the cohort arrival dummies and the source country characteristics apart from the female relative activity rate.

Table 12.3

Sum of Own and Spouse Effects on Annual Work Hours For Models, Including Source Country Interactions, Married Women, Selected Variables

Variable	0–5 Years	6–10 Years	11–15 Years	16–20 Years	21–30 Years
Fertility rate	-25.304	-55.094*	-59.015**†	-43.161**	37.180**
	(19.829)	(22.741)	(17.460)	(14.039)	(13.336)
GDP per capita	-0.023**	-0.037**††	-0.050**††	-0.037**†	-0.026**
	(0.003)	(0.004)	(0.004)	(0.004)	(0.004)
Activity rate ratio	464.656**	476.427**	506.396**	614.289**	476.716**
	(101.708)	(122.639)	(96.208)	(90.313)	(76.358)
Refugee proportion	-122.953	-95.503	-60.999	-58.982	-162.381**
	(81.161)	(100.055)	(74.057)	(52.989)	(55.254)
Primary enrollment rate	1.215	1.474	3.572**	3.850**	3.253**
	(1.426)	(1.257)	(1.134)	(0.999)	(0.822)
Secondary enrollment rate	1.064	1.523	1.095	-0.010	-0.953†
	(1.314)	(1.479)	(1.126)	(0.954)	(0.858)
English-speaking country	145.288**	104.985*	78.503	68.430	114.505**
	(46.724)	(51.190)	(47.035)	(44.064)	(31.250)
English-official country	244.429**	233.019**	234.421**	156.219**	85.371††
	(79.532)	(66.247)	(59.633)	(57.896)	(62.062)
Miles from home country	-0.029**	-0.013†	-0.017	-0.009†	0.007††
	(0.008)	(0.010)	(0.010)	(0.008)	(0.006)
Immigrant × high school	-137.091*	-133.062*	-125.533*	-86.181	-98.029
	(54.434)	(58.426)	(58.041)	(59.656)	(53.946)
Immigrant × some college	-259.760**	-181.136*†	-180.449**†	-92.290††	-104.491††
	(63.288)	(70.264)	(64.322)	(73.111)	(58.749)
Immigrant × college	-338.209**	-111.660††	-139.472††	-94.509††	-24.270††
	(77.202)	(86.335)	(80.039)	(74.487)	(70.008)
Observations			490,939		
R^2			0.09		

Notes: Immigrants are restricted to adult immigrants only. All models also include own and spouse variables for age, age squared, five-years-since-migration dummies, eight arrival cohort dummies, three education dummies, and three race/Hispanic origin dummies, as well as eight region, six state, and two year dummies. Standard errors are clustered at the country-year level. * and ** denote significance levels of 5% and 1%, respectively; † and †† denote significance levels of the difference between the indicated coefficient and the corresponding effect at 0–5 years since migration, 5% and 1%, respectively.

As may be seen in the figure, there is a substantial and persistent gap between the annual hours of women from high- and low-activity-rate countries: an unweighted average of 136 hours across YSM categories, corresponding to 14% of immigrant women's mean hours of 939. Both groups of women work less than comparable natives on arrival: 279 hours less for women coming from a high-female-activity-rate country and 403 hours less for those migrating from a low-female-activity-rate country. These are sizable deficits of 26% and 37% relative to the sample average work hours (including natives) of 1,093. Work hours for women from both types of countries assimilate dramatically over time relative to comparable natives. Women from high-female-labor-supply countries work roughly the same number of hours as natives after 6 to 10 years and work at or above the native levels thereafter. Women in families migrating from low-female-labor-supply countries continue to work less than natives throughout their residence in the United States, but by the 21 to 30-year mark, they have reduced their deficit to 126 hours (12%). These upward-sloping assimilation profiles for women from both high- and low-female-labor-supply source countries are not consistent with the family migration model.

Table 12.4

Sum of Own and Spouse Effects on Annual Work Hours For Models, Including Source Country Interactions, Married Men, Selected Variables

Variable	0-5 Years	6-10 Years	11-15 Years	16-20 Years	21-30 Years
Fertility rate	-41.517**	-65.100**	-32.310**	-56.701**	-40.331**
	(14.985)	(16.670)	(11.412)	(16.230)	(15.364)
GDP per capita	0.017**	-0.002††	-0.001††	-0.006††	-0.002††
	(0.004)	(0.003)	(0.003)	(0.004)	(0.005)
Activity rate ratio	28.845	-39.190	10.258	10.513	59.368
	(112.415)	(105.507)	(74.384)	(93.415)	(74.686)
Refugee proportion	-430.768**	-309.112**	-273.005**	-175.966	-215.118*
	(119.940)	(93.214)	(92.224)	(133.265)	(108.341)
Primary enrollment rate	1.931	0.240	0.458	1.336	1.069
	(1.226)	(0.972)	(0.877)	(0.934)	(0.818)
Secondary enrollment rate	-2.834	-0.585	0.062	-2.322*	-2.319*
	(1.556)	(1.202)	(1.007)	(1.104)	(0.948)
English-speaking country	120.359*	52.887	16.392	62.106	2.552
	(56.527)	(35.624)	(31.894)	(36.785)	(32.357)
English-official country	370.358**	118.107**††	18.505††	-18.639††	-72.810††
	(58.918)	(39.509)	(38.464)	(55.201)	(63.633)
Miles from home country	-0.035**	-0.008†	0.006††	0.014††	0.004††
	(0.011)	(0.008)	(0.009)	(0.011)	(0.009)
Immigrant × high school	-219.416**	-111.804*††	-112.898**††	-119.238**††	-105.256**††
	(48.801)	(45.033)	(40.328)	(39.203)	(37.376)
Immigrant × some college	-345.472**	-176.690**††	-157.331*††	-116.512††	-92.634††
	(74.931)	(64.969)	(65.385)	(68.128)	(63.260)
Immigrant × college	-376.920**	-188.083*††	-165.535††	-66.687††	12.613††
	(95.688)	(88.581)	(87.732)	(85.581)	(83.109)
Observations			490,939		
R^2			0.15		

Notes: Immigrants are restricted to adult immigrants only. All models also include own and spouse variables for age, age squared, five-years-since-migration dummies, eight arrival cohort dummies, three education dummies, and three race/Hispanic origin dummies, as well as eight region, six state, and two year dummies. Standard errors are clustered at the country-year level. * and ** denote significance levels of 5% and 1%, respectively; † and †† denote significance levels of the difference between the indicated coefficient and the corresponding effect at 0–5 years since migration, 5% and 1%, respectively.

The assimilation results for married adult immigrant women can be compared to those for married men, as shown in Table 12.4 and Figure 12.2. The activity rate ratio interactions are not significant, and, in the figure, the profiles for men born in high- and low-female-labor-supply countries are virtually identical. Thus, source country female labor supply clearly has a much more important effect on immigrant women's than immigrant men's labor supply. The gender difference in findings is suggestive of an impact of culture and norms of the source country rather than unmeasured factors associated with labor supply that might be expected to affect men and women similarly.

A further indicator of a traditional source country division of labor is its fertility rate. Tables 12.3 and 12.4 indicate that for each YSM category, work hours are negatively related to source country fertility for both men and women. These differences are significant for men in each case and for women in four of the five cases (all but the 0–5 years since migration category). Evaluating these effects at the 25th (2.49 children, or roughly Chile's 1996 value) and 75th percentiles (5.63 children, or roughly Iran's 1990 level) of the source country fertility rates yields an impact of between 79 and 185 hours for women (8–20% of the immigrant mean) and 101 and 204 hours for men (5–11% of the immigrant mean). There is no evidence that the effect of source country fertility differs with time in the United States for men; for women, the effect of fertility is significantly more negative at 11 to 15 years since migration than at arrival. Thus, as in the case of the activity rate, we find substantial and persistent differences in the labor supply behavior of women from high- and low-fertility-source countries; however, in this case, we find similar evidence for men as well.

In addition to the effect of traditional gender roles (i.e., relative female activity rates and fertility), Tables 12.3 and 12.4 show some interesting effects of other source country characteristics on immigrants' labor supply assimilation profiles. First, coming from a country where English is an official language has large, statistically significant positive effects on both women's and men's labor supply on arrival: 244 hours for women (26% of the immigrant mean) and 370 hours for men (39% of the immigrant mean). For both men and women, this difference falls dramatically with years since migration. For men, the interactions with YSM are no longer significant after 10 years in the United States; for women the interactions remain significant until the YSM category of 21 to 30 years. The impact of coming from an English-speaking country also shows a pattern of positive effects on men's and women's labor supply that decline with time in the United States, although coefficients are smaller and less often significant.

Second, for both men and women, coming from a greater distance significantly reduces work hours at arrival. For example, increasing the distance by 5,000 miles (roughly the difference between Canada's distance and Japan's distance to the United States) reduces women's work hours at arrival by 145 and men's by 175. However, for both men and women, the interactions of distance with YSM category are no longer significant after 0 to 5 years and are smaller in absolute value than the effect at arrival. Thus, coming from a long distance appears to produce an initial disruption for both men and women that is made up after a relatively short time in the United States. Since distance does not affect long-run work hours for either men or women, it does not appear to be an indicator of positive or negative selection with regard to work behavior. It is also worth noting that refugee proportion has a negative effect on labor supply that is substantial and significant for men. The effect for males falls in magnitude from -431 at arrival to -215 after 21 to 30 years, consistent with a disruptive effect of leaving as a refugee (as argued earlier); however, this difference (between the effect at arrival and at 21 to 30 years) is not statistically significant.

Third, the assimilation profiles differ in interesting ways by level of schooling. For both men and women, the immigrant-native gap in work hours at arrival (immigrant hours minus native hours, all else equal) is much more negative for immigrants with at least a high school diploma than it is for high school dropouts, and these differences are large and highly significant. Moreover, the gap increases in magnitude with level of education and is largest for college graduates. For each education category, these effects relative to high school dropouts diminish in magnitude with time in the United States, indicating steeper assimilation profiles relative to natives for the more highly educated.[16] It is possible that the labor market is more specialized for those with higher levels of schooling and that it therefore takes a longer period of job search or a need for additional training for these workers to locate an acceptable job. Additionally, the more specialized labor markets for those with higher levels of schooling may require additional visas not needed in more menial jobs, again potentially explaining the lower relative work hours at arrival and steeper slopes for the more highly educated.[17]

Table 12.5

Selected Results for Annual Work Hours For Models, Including Source Country Interactions, Married Women, by Family Type

Family Type/Sample	0–5 Years	6–10 Years	11–15 Years	16–20 Years	21–30 Years
1. Immigrants married to immigrants (sum of own and spouse coefficients)[a]					
Fertility rate	-29.824	-63.493**	-63.244**	-40.921**	-35.776**
	-20.304	-22.149	-17.279	-12.621	-12.067
Activity rate ratio	414.490**	454.375**	451.660**	605.092**	378.508**
	-106.636	-122.912	-108.563	-91.752	-80.362
2. Immigrants married to immigrants arriving at same time from same country (own source country effects)[b]					
Fertility rate	-26.774	-59.675*	-63.401**	-40.632**	-29.615*
	-22.776	-24.707	-15.751	-13.586	-12.71
Activity rate ratio	464.493**	472.357**	452.270**	642.027**	338.758**
	-110.365	-134.52	-104.152	-98.706	-92.494
3. Immigrants married to natives (own source country effects)[b]					
Fertility rate	0.239	16.02	-8.102	1.543	-0.017
	-16.193	-15.291	-15.796	-13.968	-14.923
Activity rate ratio	320.692**	385.207**	254.157*	309.000**	413.756**
	-111.245	-91.506	-104.89	-95.723	-102.359
4. Natives married to immigrants (effects of husband's source country on wife's hours)[c]					
Fertility rate	13.905	16.464	19.536	-15.695	-21.789
	-8.729	-12.59	-14.041	-16.118	-16.236
Activity rate ratio	198.726*	94.137	196.085*	225.961*	244.614*
	-87.872	-83.423	-91.111	-107.144	-101.864

Notes: Immigrants are restricted to adult immigrants only. Each set of results comes from a sample of the indicated group augmented by the sample of natives married to natives. All models also include own and spouse variables for age, age squared, three education dummies, and three race/Hispanic origin dummies, as well as eight region, six state, and two year dummies. Standard errors are clustered at the country-year level.

* and ** denote significance levels of 5% and 1%, respectively; † and †† denote significance levels of the difference between the indicated coefficient and the corresponding effect at 0–5 years since migration, 5% and 1%, respectively.

[a] Includes own and spouse years since migration and arrival cohort dummies.

[b] Includes wife's years since migration and arrival cohort dummies.

[c] Includes husband's years since migration and arrival cohort dummies.

12.4.2. Source Country Characteristics and Assimilation Profiles for Labor Supply: Separately by Family Type

The findings in Table 12.3 and Figure 12.1 suggest a permanent, roughly constant gap in work hours in favor of women coming from countries with high female labor force participation relative to low participation for the overall sample of immigrant women. In Tables 12.5 and 12.6, we probe the results further by examining them for a number of different family types separately. In each case, the estimated regressions include the indicated subsample of immigrant women and the base group of native women married to native men. The first two panels show findings for immigrant women married to immigrant men and immigrant women married to immigrant men arriving at the same time from the same country. In panel 1, we continue to sum own and spouse source country effects, while in panel 2, there is only one set of source country characteristics by construction. In either case, the results are almost identical to those in Table 12.3 for both activity rate and fertility.

And Figure 12.3 shows very similar assimilation profiles among immigrant women married to immigrant men coming from the same country and at the same time by source country female relative activity rate to those in Figure 12.1, which was estimated for all married immigrant women. This close correspondence is perhaps not surprising, given the substantial share of immigrant women married to immigrant men arriving at the same time from the same source country noted above.[18] The results in panel 2 are of interest in that they allow a sharper test of the family migration model in that it might be argued that this model applies most strongly to couples arriving from the same country at the same time. However, the results continue to be inconsistent with the family migration model.

Table 12.6

Selected Results for Annual Work Hours For Models, Including Source Country Interactions and Immigrant Women Married to Immigrant Men From A Different Source Country

	0–5 Years	6–10 Years	11–15 Years	16–20 Years	21–30 Years
1. Effect of own source country characteristics					
Fertility rate	-2.205	-29.804	-34.341	-18.649	-39.733
	(14.805)	(19.318)	(20.199)	(21.450)	(22.884)
Activity rate ratio	243.009*	370.203*	549.509*	249.191	-53.800
	(98.040)	(117.711)	(128.320)	(129.407)	(156.859)
2. Effect of spouse's source country characteristics					
Fertility rate	-8.931	-37.064*	20.602	-28.569	40.606*†
	(15.487)	(16.861)	(16.066)	(17.759)	(18.389)
Activity rate ratio	188.021	65.948	330.028*	-32.009	213.050
	(104.406)	(124.158)	(114.166)	(120.646)	(132.778)
3. Sum of effects of own and spouse source country characteristics					
Fertility rate	-21.136	-66.869*	-13.739	-47.218	0.873
	(19.920)	(23.675)	(25.470)	(26.889)	(25.711)
Activity rate ratio	431.030*	436.150*	879.538*†	217.182	159.250
	(122.542)	(150.591)	(167.485)	(179.909)	(189.006)

Notes: Immigrants are restricted to adult immigrants only. Sample includes natives married to natives and immigrants married to immigrants from a different source country. All models also include own and spouse variables for age, age squared, years-since-migration dummies, arrival cohort dummies, three education dummies, and three race/Hispanic origin dummies, as well as eight region, six state, and two year dummies. Standard errors are clustered at the country-year level. * and ** denote significance levels of 5% and 1%, respectively; † and †† denote significance levels of the difference between the indicated coefficient and the corresponding effect at 0–5 years since migration, 5% and 1%, respectively.

Figure 12.3

Assimilation Profiles, Annual Work Hours, Adult Immigrant Women Married to Immigrant Men Who Arrived From the Same Country and the Same Time, by Source Country Relative Female Activity Rate

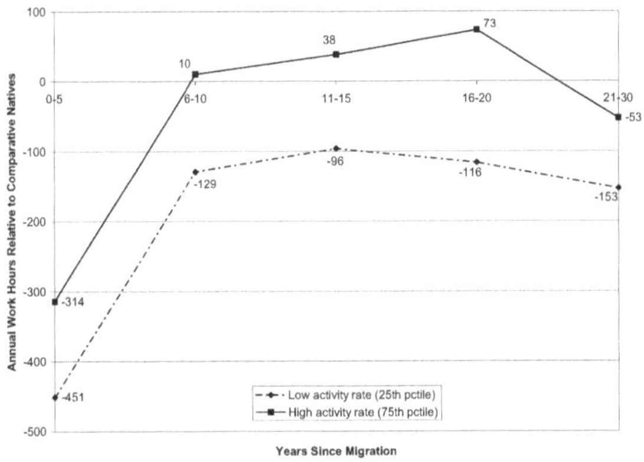

Notes: Profiles assume the same cohort arrival values, years since migration, and source country characteristics for women and spouses.

The fact that the impact of source country female relative activity on wife's labor supply was found to be smaller for native women married to immigrant men (panel 4) than for immigrant women married to native men (panel 3) suggests that the impact of a women's own source country characteristics on her behavior is greater than the impact of her husband's. We probe this question further in Table 12.6, where we contrast the effects of a woman's own source country characteristics and those of her spouse in the case where the members of the couple have migrated from different countries. There are about 20,000 such cases in our pooled census data. A caution we note here in disentangling these effects is that even among this sample, there is a high correlation (0.429) between wives' and husbands' female relative activity rate, a correlation that in itself is suggestive of a cultural effect. The results indicate that the effect of women's own country female relative activity ratio is more positive through the first twenty years in the United States than the effect of female labor supply in the spouses' source country; it is also more often significant. The effect of the respondent's own source country fertility is generally more negative than that of fertility in the spouse's source country, although these effects are generally not significant in either case. Overall, women are more responsive to their own source country's culture, but that of their husband also generally affects their labor supply in the expected direction. Again, these results are consistent with the findings in Table 12.5, which show a larger effect of source country female relative activity ratio for immigrant women married to native men than for native women married to immigrant men.

12.4.3. Alternative Specifications

We attempted a number of alternative specifications of equation (1). Each of these led to qualitatively similar results to those shown in Tables 12.3 and 12.4 and Figures 12.1 and 12.2. First, we included a full set of country dummy variables, in effect transforming the country characteristics effects into within-country effects. The effects on married immigrant women of the female relative activity rate remained highly significant and positive for each category of years since migration. The coefficients rose from 467 hours at 0 to 5 years, to 899 hours at 16 to 20 years, before falling back to 828 hours at 21 to 30 years since migration.[19] The rise in this case was statistically significant, indicating that within countries, an increase in the activity rate raises both the level and the slope of the profile. (Recall from Table 12.3 that the slope was increased through 16 to 20 years but not significantly so.) The effect of the relative female activity rate controlling for country dummies is actually larger in magnitude than the results in Table 12.3. This comparison implies that controlling for the other country characteristics, the female relative activity rate is negatively correlated with unmeasured country-specific factors raising immigrant women's labor supply. The significantly positive impact controlling for country dummies gives us more confidence that our basic results reflect the impact of source country female labor supply rather than unmeasured country-specific factors. In contrast to the results for the female activity rate, the impact of fertility on women's labor supply in the country fixed-effects specification was positive but statistically insignificant. And the impact of female activity rate for men's labor supply was positive, much smaller in magnitude than for women, and statistically insignificant for each years-since-migration category except for 16 to 20 years.[20]

Second, we estimated equation (1) with two alternative dependent variables: (1) a dummy variable indicating that one had positive work hours (a linear probability analysis) and (2) work hours given employment. In these models, the female relative activity rate had significantly positive effects for each years-since-migration category on both employment incidence and hours given employment for married immigrant women. These effects were relatively stable with time in the United States, ranging from .205 to .285 for employment and 162 to 248 for hours given employment. A 75–25 difference in female relative activity rate raises employment incidence by 5.5 to 7.6 percentage points (about 9.6% to 13.3% of the immigrant mean of .573) and hours given employment by 43 to 66 hours (or about 2.6% to 4.0% of the immigrant mean of 1,640 hours given employment). Thus, effects on employment were larger relative to the mean than effects on hours given employment, but source country characteristics have noticeable effects on both margins for women.[21] Effects of fertility were negative for both dependent variables and significant four of five times for hours given employment and three of five times for the incidence of employment. A 75–25 difference in fertility lowered employment by 4.4% to 15.3% and hours given employment by 1.8% to 8.2% of the respective immigrant averages.[22] As before, the effect of fertility was similar for men to what it was for women, and the effect of female activity rate was small and insignificant.

Third, our basic results were very similar when we measured source characteristics at age 17, in the current census year (1980 for the 1980 Census, 1990 for the 1990 Census, and 2000 for the 2000 Census), or at the same year for the full sample (two models: one using 1980 values and one using 1990 values). Thus, our findings are robust to a number of alternative assumptions about the timing of when one's source country might affect one's values and tastes. Fourth, because one might be concerned that selection into marriage may have changed between 1980 and 2000 (as discussed by Blau and Kahn 2007, see Chapter 6), we estimated our models using all adults and controlling only for one's own source country characteristics. In effect, these models allow marriage to be endogenous. We obtained very similar results to those reported in Tables 12.3 and 12.4 and Figures 12.1 and 12.2. Finally, results were also broadly similar when we performed separate pairwise analyses for 1980–1990 and 1990–2000, rather than pooling all three years as we do in our main specifications.

12.5. Conclusions

In this chapter, we have examined the assimilation of married immigrant women into the U.S. labor market. We found that controlling for personal characteristics, women from high-female-labor-supply countries work more than those from low-female-labor-supply source countries and that this gap is substantial and roughly constant with length of residence in the United States. The work hours of women from both types of source countries do, however, assimilate dramatically over time relative to comparable natives. Women from high-female-labor supply countries (at the 75th percentile of the distribution) work roughly the same number of hours as natives after 6 to 10 years in the United States. While women migrating from low-female-labor-supply countries (at the 25th percentile of the distribution) continue to lag behind natives, they greatly reduce their initial work hours deficit.

Our findings suggest that growing up in a country with less traditional gender roles facilitates the labor market assimilation of women, perhaps by giving them higher (unmeasured) human capital levels or by affecting their views about women's appropriate roles and hence their work orientation. A number of our findings are consistent with the latter possibility or an impact of culture on economic behavior. First, we find that the relationship between source country female participation and immigrant women's labor supply is persistent over time in the United States, consistent with a relatively strong hold of source country culture. This inference is reinforced by our finding that men's labor supply levels and profile slopes are unaffected by source country female labor supply, suggesting that the female findings reflect notions of gender roles rather than the overall work orientation or human capital of all immigrants from a particular type of source country. Second, when we disaggregate by family type, we find that the labor supply of the native-born wives of immigrant husbands is positively related to female participation in the husband's country of origin. This could be due to a direct effect of husbands on the behavior of wives or selection of spouses who share similar values, but either way again suggests an impact of culture. A final result of interest is that unlike previous work on immigrants, we distinguish between the effects on labor supply of an immigrant woman's own source country from that of her husband's, finding that the women's own source country has a larger impact on her behavior.

Findings for another indicator of traditional gender roles, source country fertility rates, are broadly similar for women, with substantial and persistent negative effects of source country fertility on the labor supply of female immigrants for the full sample of immigrant wives. However, we also find a similar result for immigrant men, suggesting that source fertility may be an inverse proxy for general preparedness for work in the United States.

The nature of gender roles in the source countries of immigrants to the United States is changing in potentially offsetting ways. On the one hand, fertility rates are falling dramatically in immigrant source countries relative to the United States, potentially raising immigrant women's labor supply here. On the other hand, while female labor force participation relative to men's grew around the world between 1980 and 2000, it grew even faster in the United States than in immigrant source countries. These trends could potentially widen the relative gap in labor supply between native and immigrant women. More recently, however, female participation rates in the United States have leveled off, suggesting that source country rates may begin to catch up to the U.S. rate. Thus, the future assimilation of immigrant women into the U.S. labor market will depend on the strength of these opposing forces.

Appendix A: Individual Variables

Data were obtained from the 1980, 1990, and 2000 5% extracts of the U.S. Census. Those people born in the United States or a U.S. territory or possession, or born abroad to an American parent are classified as natives; others are classified as immigrants. All immigrants in the extracts are included, along with all natives who were married to immigrants. A 4% random sample was taken of the remaining observations, with the 1990 and 2000 Census person weights multiplied by 25; comparable weights were created for the 1980 Census, for which no census weights are provided. (Hence, we have a 1/500 sample of natives.) To ensure that each year was given equal weight, the adjusted weights were then divided by the sum of these weights over all observations in a given year.

For the married sample, husband and wife records were matched, with observations dropped if either spouse was not in the 18–65 age range, had 0 weight, had allocated annual weeks worked, allocated hours worked per week, allocated birthplace or year of immigration, or had missing source country information. For the total sample, observations were dropped if a person was not in the 18–65 age range, had 0 weight, had allocated annual weeks worked, allocated hours worked per week, allocated birthplace or year of immigration, or had missing source country information.

Since we focus on adult immigrants, the preceding samples were further restricted by excluding immigrants who arrived in the United States before age 18. Data on arrival period in the 1980 and 1990 Censuses is in interval form. For each interval, we include only immigrants for whom we can definitely conclude that they were at least 18 years old on arrival in the United States. That is, if the immigrant arrived between A0 and A1, we take only individuals for whom, where BY is birth year as calculated from the individual's reported age. For comparability, similar procedures were followed for the 2000 Census data. This also required us to exclude individuals in the open-ended arrival category for 1980 and 1990 (pre-1950), since we cannot ascertain whether such individuals migrated as children or adults. The resulting maximum years since migration are thus 30 for 1980, and, for comparability, a maximum of 30 years since migration is also set for 1990 and 2000. We define sets of cohort of arrival and years-since-migration variables dummies that are consistent across the three censuses. The cohort of arrival dummies include all but one possible arrival cohort: 1995–2000, 1991–1994, 1985–1990, 1980–1984, 1975–1979, 1970–1974, 1965–1969, and 1960–1964 (1950–1959 is the omitted category). The full set of years-since-migration dummies is included: 0–5, 6–10, 11–15, 16–20, and 21–30 years in the United States.

Values for the highest grade completed by husbands and wives in the 1990 and 2000 samples were assigned using Jaeger's (1997) suggested correspondence. Annual hours worked were defined as the product of the number of weeks worked in the previous year and the number of hours usually worked during those weeks; a respondent was considered to be in the workforce if annual hours were greater than 0.

Appendix B: Source Country Variables

The source country characteristics were collected at five-year intervals for the period 1950 to 2000. To form a consistent list of source countries, we combine some countries that were not available in some Census years (e.g., subsets of countries in Africa, the Pacific Islands, and the West Indies) and countries that split or combined between 1980 and 2000 (e.g., the former USSR countries, East and West Germany, former Czechoslovakia, and former Yugoslavia). Some countries were combined because data on source country characteristics were available only in a combined form. The data set contains 106 source countries. The characteristics for each composite group are the average values over constituent countries weighted by each country's population age 18 to 65 from the 2000 Census 1% extract. Due to missing values of source country variables in some years, we have, in some cases, interpolated for intervening years, used earliest (most recent) values for preceding (subsequent) years, and imputed source country characteristics from neighboring countries. Source country characteristics were matched to arrival cohorts as follows: 1950–1959: 1955; 1960–1964: 1960; 1965–1969: 1965; 1970–1974: 1970; 1975–1979: 1975; 1980–1984: 1980; 1985–1990: 1985; 1991–1994: 1990; and 1995–2000: 1995.

Table 12.A1

Source Country Characteristics: Definitions and Sources

Variable	Description
Fertility	Total fertility rate: Number of children who would be born per woman, assuming no female mortality at child-bearing ages and the age-specific fertility rates of a specified country and reference period. The data are available between 1955 and 2000 at five-year intervals. Source: United Nations Statistics Division (2006a).
GDP per capita	GDP per capita (1995 US$): GDP is an aggregate measure of production equal to the sum of the gross values added of all resident institutional units engaged in production. The total population of a country may comprise either all usual residents of the country (de jure population) or all persons present in the country (de facto population) at the time of the census. The data are available annually between 1960 and 2000. Source: United Nations Statistics Division (2006b, 2006c), with supplemental data from U.S. Arms and Control Disarmament Agency (various years and U.S. Department of State (various issues).
Female/male Activity rate	Female LFP / male LFP: Economically active population ("usually active" or "currently active" (currently active is also known as "the labor force") comprises all persons who furnish the supply of labor for the production of economic goods and services (employed and unemployed, including those seeking work for the first time), as defined by the System of National Accounts (SNA). The rates are calculated for individuals age 15 and up. The data are available between 1950 and 2000 at 10-year intervals and in 1995. Source: United Nations Statistics Division (2006d, 2006e).
Refugee proportion	Refugees as a proportion of total immigrants. The data are available between 1950 and 2000 at five-year intervals. Sources: U.S. Immigration and Naturalization Service (various years) and U.S. Department of Justice (various years).
Primary school enrollment rate	Female or male primary school enrollment rate: Gross enrollment ratio is the ratio of total enrollment, regardless of age, to the population of the age group that officially corresponds to that level of education in question. The World Bank data are available in 1970, 1975, 1980, 1985, and 1990–1998; Barro-Lee data are available between 1960 and 1985 at five-year intervals. Source: World Bank (2002a), with supplemental data from Barro and Lee (1994).
Secondary school enrollment rate	Female or male secondary school enrollment rate: Gross enrollment ratio is the ratio of total enrollment, regardless of age, to the population of the age group that officially corresponds to that level of education in question. The World Bank data are available in 1970, 1975, 1980, 1985, and 1990-1998; Barro-Lee data are available between 1960 and 1985 at five year intervals. Source: World Bank (2002b), with supplemental data from Barro and Lee (1994).
English-speaking country	English-speaking country. Source: Bleakley and Chin (2004); their data were from the World Almanac and Book of Facts (1999).
English official language	English is an official language of the country (for non-English-speaking countries). Source: Bleakley and Chin (2004); their data were from the World Almanac and Book of Facts (1999).
Distance to United States	Distance to the United States (miles): computed as the distance between the capital of the foreign country and the closest of three U.S. gateways: New York, Los Angeles, or Miami. See http://www.indo.com/distance/ and http://www.cia.gov/cia/publications/factbook.

VI

Concluding Thoughts

The chapters in this book cover a number of areas related to inequality and indeed it was in large part my interest in inequality that drew me to the economics profession. The issues that particularly concerned me initially were poverty and the disadvantaged status of African Americans. As a child, the pictures of African-American children my age braving hostile crowds in integrating previously segregated schools in the American South made a deep impression on me, as did other aspects of the black civil rights movement that were captured in the news. In graduate school, I began working on issues related to immigrants. This issue also had deep roots for me in that my first paper in this area concerned immigrant outcomes in early twentieth century America, the period during which my immigrant forebears came to the United States in the last great wave of immigration. My interest in gender issues came a bit later during my graduate program. When I first started in the economics profession, women were a rarity - women received only 7 percent of PhDs in economics in the early 1970. Work on gender was sparse and considered a risky undertaking, especially for a woman. The evolution of my interest in the study of gender issues and my decision to make it a focus of my research is related to my own personal journey into the economics profession.

When I entered graduate school at Harvard in 1966 having just turned 20, there were only 4 women out of a class of 63 students. In some respects I was prepared for the experience. I was always very career-oriented, even though at the time most social pressures were for women to think primarily in terms of marriage and family, so I knew (or should have known) I was taking a nontraditional path. I also had previous experience in a predominantly (though not so overwhelmingly) male environment, since women comprised only 15 out of some 90-100 students in my freshman class at Cornell's ILR School where I was an undergraduate. But I found that I was unprepared for the subjective feeling of being a member of such an extremely small minority; this included the faculty - there were virtually no female economics faculty members at Harvard at that time.[1] Until I was well into graduate school I had never even set eyes on a woman PhD economist. Moreover, although the modern women's movement in the United States is often dated from 1963 when Betty Friedan published The Feminine Mystique, I for one was almost completely ignorant of these ideas. And I doubt that I was unusual in this respect. Thus, I had no tools to analyze the problems caused by what we would now identify as an absence of role models and a feeling of being on the outs of the "old boy" network. I was left with a vague sense of unease and a feeling that I did not fit in, exacerbated occasionally by overt discrimination. More seriously, as a minority, you can doubt your own ability to succeed since you see no or few examples of others who have been successful. These problems are intensified by and add to the already difficult situation of being a graduate student or an Assistant Professor in a demanding environment.

My growing awareness of the women's movement was a great help to me in gaining perspective on some of these issues. In addition, through my interest in gender issues, as well as my activities in working to establish CSWEP (the American Economics Association Committee on the Status of Women in the Economics Profession) and my role as a committee member, I came in contact with others with similar interests and concerns, many of them women economists. I am very grateful to those role models, including Barbara Bergmann, Caroline Shaw Bell, Marianne Ferber, Barbara Reagan, and Myra Strober who showed that women could "walk the walk and talk the talk." In addition, Heidi Hartman (also a graduate student at the time) and I encouraged each other about the legitimacy and importance of working on gender and urged each other to keep at it.

My growing interest in women's issues also turned out to be of enormous importance to me intellectually. I initially read widely on the topic, including not only the relatively little that had been written at the time in economics, but also in other fields like sociology and history. I found this exposure to a new set of issues that I viewed of great social importance, combined with the relative dearth of previous work by economists, extremely stimulating. This became the area of my dissertation research and much of my subsequent work.

As I have already noted, however, the decision to work in this area was not without its potential costs. At the time, research on women was generally not seen as central. For a member of a "marginal group" to work on a subject that is viewed as "marginal" is risky. In addition, a woman working in this area, especially one known to have feminist leanings or concerns over equity issues, was suspected of lacking objectivity. The latter point, the role of values in social science research is an interesting and important one. But it has always seemed to me a bit illogical to assume that, for example in the case of gender, women would be more likely to be ideologues whereas men would tend to be more neutral, or that an individual, regardless of sex, who favors social change would necessarily be less objective in his or her research than one who upholds the status quo. Either might be tempted to try to fit the facts to their views. I personally have always endeavored, on the one hand, to benefit from the insights which my concern over gender inequities may give me into what would be interesting problems to study as well as possible explanations for observed outcomes, while, on the other hand, to be as objective as possible in reporting my results, even if those results do not accord with what I would have at some level liked to find. Indeed, one quickly learns that a source of great excitement as well as of great frustration to the empirical economist is that the data may fail to confirm our a priori expectations.

In the long run it was certainly the right decision for me to stick with my interests. I have been able to work on topics that I find engaging and important. While not all of these have related to gender issues, many have. I have also been lucky in that circumstances have become more favorable to research in this area. I cannot claim great foresight in this outcome or even great courage in holding the course. I think what I intuitively realized is that you have to work on what you are interested in, without being unduly concerned with the current status within the profession of your topic or approach. It is only in this way that you will do your best work. That is, it is the topics that most engage and interest us that will stimulate our best ideas and insights and enable us to perform at the highest levels of our abilities. And, in the long run, doing one's best work, regardless of the topic, is what will most contribute to success. So, I do think there is a lesson here – to be a successful researcher, you have to follow your interests.

What forces have increased research on gender by economists and brought it into the mainstream? I would argue that one set of factors is that current events thrust gender-related issues to the fore and economists responded. The outcome has been not only a better understanding of the nature and causes of gender differences, but also an enrichment of the discipline itself.

A critical external factor that helped to focus economists' attention on gender was the large increase in married women's labor force participation after World War II. This is because, one reason for the historical neglect of gender issues by the economics discipline is that, traditionally, economists focused on market transactions and, traditionally, most married women were primarily engaged in nonmarket activities. Thus, as women have come to comprise a larger share of the paid labor force and as market work has loomed larger in the typical woman's life, interest in the determinants of gender differences in behavior and labor market outcomes has grown. In this respect it is not surprising that some of the earliest important contributions of economists to research on gender were prompted in part by their desire to understand the causes of the growth in the labor force participation of married women. This enterprise led economists like Gary Becker (1965) and Jacob Mincer (1962b) to extend the traditional theory of labor supply to consider household production.[2] This development in turn contributed to economists' growing interest in analyzing nonmarket work; the division of labor in the family and household decision making; and demographic outcomes such as marriage, divorce and fertility.[3] The growth of interest and research in these areas was an important development in and of itself, and also one which further increased economists' attention to gender-related issues.

As in the case of the analysis of women's roles in the family, the catalyst for the development of analyses of gender differences in pay and occupations was provided to some extent by external events. Some moderate degree of interest in the pay issue was generated in England by the World War I experience when there was some substitution of women into traditionally male civilian jobs, although not nearly to the degree that would later occur during World War II. Questions of the appropriate pay for women under these circumstances arose and stimulated early economic analyses of the gender pay differential. These included the work of Fawcett (1918) and Edgeworth (1922), both of whom assigned a prominent causal role to occupational segregation, thus providing the antecedents for Bergmann's (1974) important overcrowding model. As female participation in the labor force continued to increase, it was logical that economists would begin to more closely examine the extent and sources of gender differentials in labor market outcomes. An important further impetus to such investigations occurred in the 1960s, this time in the United States, with the development of the women's liberation movement and the passage of anti-discrimination legislation. Early important work by Mincer and Polachek (1974) developing the human capital analysis of the gender wage gap and empirically testing it dates to around this time as do a number of analyses of labor market discrimination against women. It was in this context that the widely used Oaxaca-Blinder decomposition was developed (Blinder 1973, Oaxaca 1973a).

Some additional factors have contributed to the growth in research on gender issues and its acceptance into the mainstream. The entry of increasing numbers of women into the economics profession itself has resulted in more research in this area as women have chosen gender-related topics at greater rates than their male colleagues. Also, the very high caliber of the work done in this area, by both women and men, as well as its objectivity and even-handedness, have undoubtedly contributed to its acceptance within the profession. I am especially gratified that the IZA award, in part for my work on gender, further marks the full entry of research in this area into the mainstream.

While considerable progress has been made along a number of dimensions, it is my view that the study of inequality remains an extremely important area and one that must address an evolving and challenging set of problems. With respect to gender, wage differences between men and women, though generally decreasing in most advanced economies, remain substantial (Blau and Kahn 2008). And, while discrimination appears to have declined, it has not in my opinion been eliminated. A major challenge here is that as gender discrimination has become less socially acceptable, it has become less overt and more subtle. Indeed, there is growing evidence from social psychologists that suggests discriminatory attitudes and stereotyping may even be unconscious (e.g., Fiske 1998, Valian 1998, and Bertrand, Chugh, and Mullainathan 2005). Thus, although discrimination appears to be declining, the residual discrimination that remains may be getting more difficult to identify and counter. Moreover, work-family issues remain a challenge – this is in some respects the cutting-edge problem facing women in the labor market today. I would argue that policies in this area should keep two goals in mind if they are to contribute to gender equity. First, while such policies are currently of particular interest and concern to women, it is important that they be formulated in a gender-neutral fashion that encourages greater sharing of family responsibilities between women and men. In the long run it is precisely this type of sharing that will be particularly beneficial in reducing gender gaps in labor market outcomes. And, second, it is important that policies designed to assist workers, particularly women, with their family responsibilities not end up creating a "mommy track" whereby women are channeled into separate and unequal work arrangements that concentrate them in jobs with limited advancement opportunities. In my view, this means that we should emphasize policies that allow women (and men) workers to successfully combine work and family relative to policies that encourage parents, especially mothers, to take long leaves and work part-time for extended periods.

Along other dimensions of inequality, income and wage inequality remain extremely high by historical standards in the United States and many other countries. Moreover, the major recession that occurred in the United States and elsewhere in the late 2000s, with the weak labor markets that followed, may well have long term effects magnifying differences across individuals and groups well into the future (e.g., Kahn 2010). Concerns about racial inequality also remain pressing. Little progress in narrowing black-white wage gaps has taken place in the United States since the 1970s. At the same time, partly due to immigration, the minority share of the population has increased in the United States and elsewhere. Understanding the sources of inequality across the various racial and ethnic groups that now constitute the minority population, both native- and foreign-born, has become correspondingly more challenging as it has increased in importance.

I owe a great debt to the many colleagues, collaborators, and students who have enriched my professional life and contributed directly and indirectly to the recognition I have received from IZA. These include my colleagues and students at the University of Illinois, Urbana-Champaign, where I spent the first half of my academic career, and Cornell University where I have been since 1994. Space does not permit individual recognition of all those I would like thank, but let me mention a few of those to whom I am especially indebted.

As a young assistant professor at Harvard, Richard Freeman (who won the IZA Prize three years ago) was on my thesis committee. I was not then in residence at Harvard and may have had only one extended conversation with him, but it will probably not surprise those who know Richard, that that conversation really turned things around for me. More broadly, like so many other labor economists, I owe Richard a great debt - through his own work and his leadership role at the National Bureau of Economic Research - for his contribution to elevating the status and importance of empirical work in labor economics, and improving the tools we use to analyze data and reach conclusions.

I want to sincerely thank all my research collaborators. I always feel that collaborating raises the possibility that the whole can be greater than the sum of the parts. And that has definitely been my experience. I would like to especially thank my coauthors who generously gave their permission to include our joint work in this volume, including, Andrea H. Beller, Rachel T. A. Croson, Janet M. Currie, Donna Ginther, John W. Graham, Lawrence M. Kahn, and Kerry Papps. I would also like to express my deep gratitude to Marianne Ferber and Anne Winkler who have toiled with me on our textbook - "The Economics of Women, Men, and Work" - currently in its 6th edition. It has been hard work but deeply rewarding; I hope it has contributed to advancing the economics of gender in the curriculum, as well as serving as a broad reference for all those interested in this area.

Finally, I am sure none of my collaborators will begrudge my especially singling out my husband, Lawrence Kahn. I think there is something in our joint work that brings out the best in both of us and we both feel that we have done some of our best work together. But my debt to Larry does not stop there - he has been a friend, advisor, technical consultant, and partner in every aspect of my life, including the household. I am deeply grateful for the family that Larry and I have built with our now grown children, Daniel Blau Kahn and Lisa Blau Kahn, that has supported and sustained me through all my professional endeavors.

Notes

Part II

Introduction

1 See Blau, Ferber and Winkler (2010), Chapter 7 for a review.
2 Other scholars have contributed valuable insights into the sources of the trends in the gender pay gap in the United States over this period. For a review see Blau, Ferber and Winker (2010: 250-4) (and references therein).

Chapter 1

1 See, for example, such economy-wide studies as Sanborn (1964); Fuchs (1971); Oaxaca (1973b); and Sawhill (1973). For studies of within occupation pay differences employing aggregate establishment data, see McNulty (1967) and Buckley (1971).
2 See, for example, Bergmann (1974); Fuchs (1971); Sawhill (1973); and Blau and Jusenius (1976).
3 See Blau (1977, Chapter 3) for further discussion of the literature, in addition to Doeringer and Piore (1971). Note that an extensive later literature utilizing firm-worker matched data provides considerable support for the assumption of a wage hierarchy of firms, or "firm effects." See, for example, Abowd, Kramarz and Margolis (1999).
4 For discussions of the importance of this factor, see Rees and Schultz (1970: 36-44).
5 See Hammermesh (1971: 161-2); Raimon and Stoikov (1969); and Rees and Schultz (1970: 181-4). The union variable employed by Rees and Schultz for white-collar workers was "union in the establishment." This is roughly the same as our "plant-only" variable, since white-collar workers were unionized in only a few of the establishments in their sample.
6 An interaction variable reflecting the joint effect of manufacturing and size was not found to be significant and thus is not reported in the second set of regressions.

Chapter 2

1 Unfortunately, these inferences about the gender gap in experience are made without directly examining data on the average work experience of male workers. It is likely that the average experience of the male work force declined as the younger baby boom cohort entered the labor market and as retirement rates of older men increased. In addition, male work experience was likely to have declined due to increased educational attainment (and hence later school-leaving ages).

2 Our selection of the 1972 CPS (1971 earnings data) was determined by the fact that this is the first year with occupational data comparable to data for later years (Beller 1985). We selected the 1982 CPS (1981 earnings data) because it allows us to observe changes over a decade and because economic conditions were reasonably comparable in 1971 and 1981.

3 Such individuals are excluded because in 1976 the Census changed its method of imputing or allocating income to individuals with missing data, breaking the comparability of income series data (Lillard, Smith, and Welch 1986).

4 Results for the arithmetic means of earnings are quite similar to those reported above for the median.

5 When blacks and whites are combined, our data show a small rise of 2 percent (1.2 percentage points) in the female-male ratio of median earnings for year-round, full-time workers, in contrast to the stability reported in the published statistics (see above). This small discrepancy occurs because the particular age range and sample we study differ somewhat from those employed in calculating the published statistics

6 For a study that emphasizes the importance of changes in this type of selectivity for the average gender differential, see Smith and Ward (1984).

7 Specifically, $\lambda_i = f(C'Z_i)/F(C'Z_i)$, where C is a vector of coefficients estimated from a probit equation predicting inclusion in the wage regression, Z is a vector of variables in the probit, and $f(-)$ and $F(-)$ are, respectively, the standard normal density and cumulative distribution functions. We included in Z the explanatory variables in X measuring the individual's education, experience, demographic characteristics, veteran status, and location, as well as the individual's non-labor income, a dummy variable for whether the individual is 62 years of age or over (the age at which early Social Security benefits become available), and the number of other family members between the ages of 18 and 64 and 65 or over. Transfer payments are included in non-labor income because, although there may be a degree of endogeneity, the availability of transfers is an important determinant of labor supply and hence sample inclusion.

8 The sign or magnitude of b will be affected by changes in participation rates if they are, in fact, accompanied by changes in the covariance between the unmeasured factors in the sample-inclusion and wage equations - a question that can be answered only by empirical study.

9 The definition of MALOCC and INTOCC employed here is designed to capture the intuitive notion that "male" ("female") jobs are not only *disproportionately* male (female) compared to their 1970 share of the labor force of about 60 (40) percent, but also that each is *predominantly* male or female as well. Except as noted below, the results (in OLS regressions) were quite similar when other plausible definitions of these variables were used - specifically, MALOCC, 70 percent or more male, and INTOCC, 51-69 percent male; and MALOCC, 80 percent or more male, and INTOCC, 41-79 percent male.

10 Similar findings for men are reported by Reimers (1983).

11 This finding accords with the results of other studies (see Smith 1980).

12 The intuitive expectation is borne out, however, with respect to measured characteristics. Relative to the female population, women included in the sample were less highly educated and more likely to be married and to have children in

1981 than in 1971. The ratios of sample to population means are available from the authors on request.

13 The same result is found when we evaluate the male functions at the female means.

14 When the male functions are evaluated at the female means, the results by experience level are quite similar except that white female cohorts do not improve their earnings ratios as they age.

15 This finding does not hold for blacks when INTOCC is defined as 51-69 percent male.

16 Of course, if occupational representation reflects employer hiring decisions, then controlling for occupation may lead to us to underestimate the full extent of discrimination against women.

17 Given the relatively small size of the union sector in the United States, such effects are not likely to be large empirically, and indeed Farber (2005) does not find much evidence of them.

18 Datta Gupta, Oaxaca, and Smith (2006) suggested performing Juhn/Murphy/Pierce decompositions on pooled male and female wage samples. We chose not to do this because the coefficients for male equations are more likely to reflect true returns to human capital and rents than unmeasured human capital. However, in supplementary models, we pooled men and women for each year and obtained results that were very similar to those presented below.

19 After the 1997 survey, the PSID began surveying respondents every other year rather than annually. Thus, there are no PSID data for 2000.

20 The unemployment rate was 5.8% in 1979, 5.3%in 1989, and 4.5% in 1998 (BLS web site: www.bls.gov, accessed June 9, 2003).

21 In view of the possibility that the returns to education changed differently for different experience groups (Card and Lemieux 2001), we also implemented the JMP decomposition interacting the three education variables with full-time experience and its square; the results were unchanged.

22 The negative occupational price effect contrasts with our earlier work and is likely due to our ability to more finely define occupation in the larger samples we now use. Our earlier study employed only the PSID random sample, whereas the current study uses both the PSID's random sample and its poverty over sample populations (employing appropriate sampling weights).

23 The All X's effect in the full specification was significantly more negative in the 1980s than the 1990s.

24 Using re-weighting techniques introduced by DiNardo, Fortin, and Lemieux (1996), we reestimated our models holding constant first the age composition and second the human capital composition of the male and female samples over time. These analyses, which correct for cohort size (partial equilibrium) effects as well as sample composition effects with respect to the residual as suggested by Lemieux's (2006) work, yielded results very similar to those reported here. In addition, in our longer paper (Blau and Kahn 2004), we performed JMP decompositions on March CPS data for the same years used in Table 2.9 and obtained similar results.

25 Applying these assumptions to individuals who had observed wage offers misclassifies 9–15% of men and14–21% of women in the low-education, low-experience group and 17–22% of men and 11–20% of women in the high-education, high-experience group. Thus, while the imputation clearly makes some errors, they appear to have a low incidence. Results were not sensitive twosome alternative education and experience cutoffs for inclusion in these imputed wage samples.

26 For the regression-based approach to evaluating raw and human-capital gender wage gaps that we employ, which is based on separate human-capital wage regressions for men and women, we need some additional assumptions about unobserved wage offers. Specifically, for individuals without observed wage offers, we need to assume that those with less than a high school degree and less than eight years' full-time experience had below-median wage offers conditional on their human capital levels; by the same token, we must assume that those with college degrees and at least eight years' full-time experience had above-median

wage offers conditional on their human capital. A similar point is made by Neal (2004). These assumptions are discussed further below.

27 Those who were self-employed or agricultural workers as of the time wages were observed (1979, 1989, or 1998) are excluded from both the numerator and the denominator in these percentages. For further details on the process of obtaining past wages, see Blau and Kahn (2004).

28 Note that, unlike OLS regressions, quantile regressions do not necessarily pass through the median of the dependent variable and the means of the independent variables. Thus, the predicted value of the male and female medians and the resulting gender gap is not necessarily equal to the actual male and female medians or the gender gap calculated from them. For the imputed wages, we assigned a log wage of 1 for those below median and 4 for those above median. Our analyses of the gender pay gap here focus on medians rather than means, since we do not know the actual earnings levels of these presumed below - and above median wage individuals.

29 For men, predicted median log wages of full-time, employed workers (group a) were .10 to .14 log points higher than those added to the full-time employed to form our most inclusive group (d); for women, they were .22 to .29 log points higher.

30 The estimated wage offers for women not included in group (a) were 25.2% lower than those in group (a) in 1979, but 33.2% lower in 1989 - again indicating that the full-time employed had become more positively selected relative to those not included.

31 See also Blau (1998, see Chapter 7) and references therein.

32 After we wrote the first draft of this paper, we became aware of a paper that uses a structural approach to investigate the impact of selectivity bias on the observed gender pay gap over the 1975–2001 period (Mulligan and Rubinstein 2005). The authors found that selection accounts for all of the apparent improvement in women's relative wages since 1975, although they did not study the sub periods separately as we do. In contrast, as noted in the text, we find that selection is only part of the explanation for the 1979–98 period. And using a selection correction similar to ours, Olivetti and Petrongolo (2006) found that selection explains about 60% of the cross-country (negative) correlation between the gender pay gap and the gender employment gap.

33 As noted, in order to reach conclusions about changes in the gender pay gap when those with imputed wages are included (as in group d in Table 2.10), we must assume that their wage offers are above median or below median, conditional on their human capital levels. This assumption is more likely to be valid for the group with low education and low experience than for the high-education, high-experience group. When we performed analyses like those in Table 2.10 adding only the former group, the results were virtually identical: selection is estimated to have accounted for 25% of the slowdown in the convergence in the unexplained pay gap. Moreover, as may be seen in Table 2.10, when we make no imputations and include only those for whom we observe a wage offer at some time in the past four years (group c in Table 2.10), we obtain results very similar to those for group d: selection accounts for 27% of the slowdown in the closing of the unexplained gender pay gap. Thus, our conclusions about selection do not appear to be sensitive to adding those with imputed wage offers

34 These conclusions were not affected by taking account of childcare, which was not analyzed in the regressions. Specifically, Aguiar and Hurst (2006:47) found that the gap in average childcare hours between working women and all men was 2.0 hours in 1975, 2.1 hours in 1985, 1.7 hours in 1993, and 2.6 hours in 2003 (the authors did not present data that would allow us to infer the pattern of changes in housework hours between working women and men).

35 Women's work attitudes and ambition are examples of other unmeasured factors that potentially influence wages and could have changed at a different rate over the two decades. In this regard, it is interesting that Fortin (2006) found evidence that gender differences in these factors were much smaller in 2000 than in1986,

although her data do not allow us to determine whether this convergence happened at a faster pace in the 1980s than in the 1990s.

36 That is, the unexplained gap is calculated as $(B_M - B_F)X_F$, where B_M and B_F are vectors of coefficients from male and female quantile regression equations and X_F is a vector of female characteristics.

37 The simulated female wage distribution created using the sample of 100 women and the 99 female quantile regressions was very similar to the actual female wage distribution, suggesting that the 100 randomly chosen women were representative of the working female population. Note that Albrecht, Björklund and Vroman (2003) also employed a similar strategy in their implementation of the Machado and Mata (2005) procedure.

38 Autor, Katz, and Krueger (1998), for example, noted that the groups having the most rapid increase in computer usage in the 1980s and early 1990s (the highly educated, whites, white-collar workers, and women) also had the largest wage increases.

39 Friedberg provided data on computer use only for 1984, 1989, 1993, and 1997. The estimates in the text use linear interpolation to obtain computer use in 1998 and assume zero incidence of computer use in the workplace in 1979. The latter is consistent with Autor, Katz, and Krueger's (1998) observation that the IBM PC was introduced in 1981 and the Apple II in 1977. If we instead use linear interpolation to estimate 1979 computer use, we estimate that rising computer use increased women's share of hours by 0.027 log points (Weinberg low estimate) to 0.044 log points (Weinberg high estimate) over the 1980s; and 0.018 log points (Weinberg low estimate) to 0.030 log points (Weinberg high estimate) over the 1990s.

Part III

Introduction

1 See the edited volume, by Freeman and Katz (1995), including our contribution (Blau and Kahn 1995).

2 The source of this tabulation of the OECD data is Blau and Kahn (2008). The included countries are Australia, West Germany, Japan, New Zealand, United Kingdom, Finland, Netherlands, and Sweden; the specific years of data included vary somewhat by country due to availability. In some cases the data are available as weekly or monthly earnings of full-time workers, and in others as annual earnings of full-time, year-round workers; both sets of countries are combined here.

3 The role of selection in explaining the international differences in the gender pay gap is examined further in Olivetti and Petrongolo (2008).

4 High European unemployment in the 1990s led to some efforts to increase labor market flexibility in some European countries. However, the United States still stands at an extreme in terms of labor market flexibility, see Kahn (2012) for a recent review of international differences.

Chapter 3

1 Of course, under different wage-setting institutions, U.S. women might have different incentives to acquire labor market skills.

2 For descriptions of these data, see Blanchflower and Freeman (1992) for ISSP; Rosenfeld and Kalleberg (1990) for CSCC; Blackburn and Bloom (1994) for IDS; Erickson and Ichino (1995) for BI; Blau and Kahn (1994b) for PSID; and Edin and Holmlund (1995) for HUS.

3 Unfortunately there are some differences across countries in the exact definitions of the income variables. While in most cases the income data are measured before taxes, for Austria, Germany, and Switzerland income is measured after taxes. Similarly, while in other cases income from earnings is available, in the case of Sweden (1980), the income measure includes income from all sources. While these differences are of some concern, it is reassuring that the international rankings of the gender ratios that we computed based on our microdata are consistent with published sources and other studies (see below). In addition, our results for Sweden are quite similar when we use the 1984 HUS data, which do enable us to identify earnings. The impact of the tax system on the labor force behaviour, and hence on the earnings of men and women, is itself a question of some interest. Unfortunately it is not one that we are in a position to investigate.

4 There is information on weeks worked for Australia and for a subset of the 1982 Norwegian data. Analyses correcting for weeks worked yielded very similar results to those reported here, with slightly lower adjusted gender differentials. Lack of information on hours worked for those with multiple jobs forced us to limit the 1980 Swedish sample to those with one job only.

5 The Australian earnings data were originally reported as a continuous variable. However, to maintain comparability with the other countries, we recoded the Australian earnings into the ISSP's intervals for Australia. When the analysis was performed for Australia using the original continuous variable, the results were virtually identical to those reported here. The BI data were also continuous but did not match up with the ISSP categories for Italy. We therefore used the continuous earnings variable for Italy.

6 The country rankings here are similar to those based on published data (when available) or other studies. Note, however, that the ratios for the Scandinavian countries and Australia are below those reported in OECD publications. This discrepancy appears to be due to the OECD data being restricted to manufacturing workers for Sweden and Norway and to non-supervisory employees for Australia. The magnitudes of the gender ratios that we obtain are consistent with other studies that use microdata for these countries.

7 That is, we assign each woman in country j a percentile ranking in country j's male wage distribution. The female mean of these percentiles by country is presented in Figure 3.2.

8 Bernhardt, Morris, and Handcock (1995) use a similar methodology to examine the distribution of women's wages relative to the male distribution over time in the United States.

9 Child care is another important area of public policy that affects women, but one that is more difficult to summarize across our large set of countries. In addition, non-governmental initiatives may be important. Below we summarize the extent of voluntary provision of parental leave by private employers in the United States during the period covered by our data.

10 Switzerland incorporated the principle of equal pay for work of equal value into its constitution in 1981 (Simona 1985), but there is no indication that it has been implemented as yet.

11 In 1993 the United States passed the Family and Medical Leave Act, mandating that employers provide up to 12 weeks of unpaid leave to parents for the birth or adoption of a child.

12 A more detailed examination of these institutional differences is provided in Blau and Kahn (1996a, see Chapter 5).

13 The high incidence of part-time work for Scandinavian women may be due in part to the generous family leave policies in these countries. In addition to policies guaranteeing paid parental leave in both Sweden and Norway, Sweden has since

1979 allowed working parents of small children the right to have a six-hour day on demand (Haavio-Mannila and Kauppinen 1992).

14 Our conclusion regarding labor force commitment might be altered if U.S. women were more likely than women in other countries to work part-year, if not part-time. However, an examination of the countries in our sample for which we have "weeks worked" information does not yield a consistent pattern regarding this issue. For example, U.S. employed women worked an average of 45 weeks per year (1984, PSID), while Swedish women worked an average of 41 weeks (1984, HUS), and those in Australia (1986, IDS) and Norway (1982, CSCC) were employed 46 and 49 weeks, respectively.

15 This conclusion regarding the U.S. position largely holds true when the segregation index is calculated using published data from the ILO (Blau and Ferber 1992: 309). Note that our findings for Switzerland must be interpreted with caution, given the small size of our sample. A segregation index computed on the basis of ILO data does not indicate a lower level of segregation for Switzerland than for the United States.

16 This is not to say, however, that they are completely uncontaminated by discrimination. This is discussed further below.

17 Countries may differ in their definitions of "part-time". We adopt the 35-hour cut-off which is employed by the OECD in its tabulations of part-time employment (OECD 1989a). Hours information was not available for self-employed workers in Italy. Earlier results suggested that the gender ratio for Italy was overstated when the self-employed were excluded. Thus, hours were imputed for this group based on hours regression equations estimated for wage and salary workers including the full-set of explanatory variables.

18 For countries with more than one year of data, the log earnings variable was obtained by including dummy variables for year in equation (4) and transforming each observation into its 1989 (or end-year) equivalent in calculating YFULL in equation (5).

19 For Hungary, Australia, and Italy, industry and/or occupation differ from those for the rest of the countries. In addition, for the latter two countries and for the Sweden (1984), union membership status is not available. For the purposes of comparing the United States and these countries, we estimated U.S. equations that conformed to the same specification as each country.

20 It would have been possible, however, to construct a proxy for number of children: number of non-spouse others in the household.

21 Reasons for the low estimated pay gaps among single workers include the likelihood that they are disproportionately young (the pay gap is lower for young workers – see Mincer and Polachek 1974), and that single males are less productive than married males (see Korenman and Neumark 1991).

22 For each country, this is the mean of the percentile ranking of each woman's residual from the male regression (e_{if}) in the distribution of male wage residuals (e_{im}).

23 Although Swiss women have a higher mean percentile ranking than U.S. women, the gap effect is positive. Such inconsistencies can arise because in essence a different set of weights are employed in calculating the mean percentile rankings and the gap effects. Specifically, as noted above, based on her residual from the male wage equation, each Swiss woman is given a percentile ranking in the Swiss male distribution of wage residuals. She is then allocated a wage residual based on these percentile rankings and the U.S. male distribution of wage residuals. The mean of these imputed residuals (multiplied by -1; i.e. $\Delta\theta_j\sigma_k$) may be larger than the actual mean wage residual of U.S. women (multiplied by -1; i.e. $\Delta\theta_k\sigma_k$) even if the mean of the percentile rankings of each woman's residual from the male regression is higher in Switzerland than in the United States.

24 These calculations include, for Norway, a weighted average of the two observations for that country where the weights are determined by sample sizes. The United States and Sweden (1984) are not included because the earnings measure employed – average hourly earnings – differs from that available for the other countries.

25 Marital status is not available for Italy.
26 Illustrating for married workers, the mean residuals for married males (m) and married females (f) are:

$$e_m = Y_m - X_m B \text{ and } e_f = Y_f - X_f B,$$

where Y_m, and Y_f are the mean earnings of married males and married females, X_m and X_f are the vectors of means of the explanatory variables for married males and married females, and B is a vector of estimated coefficients from the overall male earnings regression. Thus, the gender difference in residuals is:

$$(e_m - e_f) = (Y_m - Y_f) - (X_m - X_f)B.$$

27 A primary exception is the comparable worth approach pursued in Australia, which might be expected to produce a larger immediate impact on wages.
28 Another source of differences in the gender ratios for these two countries in Table 3.7 and Figure 3.1 is the time periods: 1980 for Sweden and 1985-89 for the United States in Figure 3.1 compared with 1984 for both countries in Table 3.7.
29 In these analyses, the two observations on Norway were averaged using sample size as weights. The United States and Sweden 1984 were excluded since the wage variable in these analyses was defined as the log of actual hourly earnings, unlike the rest of the sample.
30 The degree of centralization for the other countries in our sample was: West Germany 6·943; United Kingdom 12·632; Switzerland 10·904; Sweden 2·736; Norway 2·536; Australia 10·766; and Italy 14·325.

Chapter 4

1 This is an unweighted average of the raw gender pay gaps by country presented in Table 4.2. Below, we explain in detail how the estimated pay gaps were obtained.
2 The countries were Australia, Austria, Britain, Hungary, Italy, Norway, Sweden, Switzerland, and West Germany.
3 This framework has been subsequently adopted by other researchers, who have also found evidence of the impact of wage-setting institutions on the gender gap in pay; see Kidd and Shannon (1996) and Edin and Richardson (2002).
4 Russia's law prohibited discrimination against pregnant women.
5 Switzerland incorporated the principle of equal pay for work of equal value into its constitution in 1981 (Simona 1985), but there is no indication that it has been implemented as yet. And, in 1991, Ontario required virtually all employers to practice the principles of comparable worth, but other Canadian provinces have not passed such legislation (Gunderson and Robb 1991).
6 This reasoning applies whether women's gains come through reductions in discrimination or through improvements in women's relative human capital levels.
7 Data were also available for Spain in 1993, but these were not included here because the estimated gender gap, .061, was not credible in comparison with other sources. Data on Australia for 1985 were also excluded due to data problems noted in Blau and Kahn (1995).
8 Countries may differ in their definitions of part-time. Until 1997, the OECD used each country's own definition in reporting on the fraction of workers employed part-time. For our data period (1985–94), this was 35 hours in most cases, leading us to use the 35 hours definition here. Starting in 1997, in recognition of some recent trends in the definition of full-time work, the OECD began using a common 30-hour cutoff in its statistics (see, e.g., OECD 1999). Because of changing norms with respect to what is considered full-time work, we tested the robustness of our results by using a 30-hour cutoff and obtained findings very similar to those reported below.

Notes

9 That is, for each male (female) worke r i, we have (suppressing the country and year subscripts): $\ln EARN40_i = \ln EARN_i - b_1 PART_i - b_2 HRPART_i - b_3(HRFULL_i - 40)$.

10 We used this methodology in our earlier work (Blau and Kahn 1992; 1995; 1996b, see Chapter 3) and obtained estimated gender pay gaps that were similar in country rankings to those reported in published data based on average hourly earnings.

11 As noted above, data on industry and unionism are not consistently available across our sample of countries.

12 We have also estimated our models with the raw 50-10 male wage gap as the indicator of wage compression, with results very similar to those reported below.

13 The increasing availability of matched firm-worker data should facilitate future efforts to assess international differences in the magnitude of these firm effects (Abowd and Kramarz 1999).

14 Since data on industry were not consistently available across countries in the ISSP, we used published sources to obtain this information for each country and year, e.g., International Labor Organization, various years.

15 In earlier international work (Blau and Kahn 1996a, see Chapter 5), we did not find evidence of a consistent relationship between female net supply and male wage inequality. Similarly, Juhn and Kim (1999) found little evidence that female supply affected male wage inequality within the United States; see also Blau and Kahn (1997).

16 The control for year also provides an adjustment to the price variability terms, which are computed using a given year's U.S. male sample. Year dummies in effect control for differences over time in the composition of the U.S. male sample of workers in the ISSP.

17 The quadratic term is included in light of our earlier discussion of the impact of short versus long parental leave entitlements.

18 In some cases, these variables were not available for the full set of country-year observations, in which case we omitted the observation from these particular analyses. Results for the basic model specified in eq. (8) were very similar for these subsamples.

19 It is possible to keep East and West Germany separate even after unification in the ISSP data. We follow this procedure due to sizable differences between the two in the dependent and many of the explanatory variables. The country rankings here tend to be similar to those based on published data or other studies, when available (Blau and Kahn 1995). The gap for Australia is larger than that reported in OECD publications. This discrepancy appears to be due to the OECD data restriction to nonsupervisory employees; the gender gap we obtain from the ISSP data is consistent with studies that use other microdata for Australia (Gregory and Daly 1991; Blau and Kahn 1995). The extremely small gender gap we estimate for Italy may be in part a result of its large unreported sector (Erickson and Ichino 1995). Since the wages of many secondary workers are "off the books," respondents may be reluctant to report this income.

20 In the regression sample of 100 country-year data points, the correlation between TOTALGAP and GAPUSCHARS is .8680.

21 Overall, our two measures of labor market prices are modestly positively correlated. Across the regression sample, SD yus and SD MALERES have a correlation coefficient of .2376, while 50:10yus and 50-10MALERES have a correlation coefficient of .3170.

22 The results were very similar when we omitted the year dummy variables.

23 Results were similar when we used the unexplained gender gap (the mean female residual from the country's male wage equation) as the dependent variable. See Blau and Kahn 2001.

24 We focus on the Western country average as the comparison under the assumption that it would be made up of the most comparable countries. However, the results are similar when we consider the full range of countries included in the regression analysis.

25 With the United States omitted, the average values of the male inequality and gender gap variables over the remaining 21 countries are: TOTALGAP (.303);

GAPUSCHARS (.265); SD yus (.264); SD MALERES (.445); 50:10yus (.367); and 50:10MALERES (.508). These may be compared to the figures for the United States in Table 4.2.

26 The countries were Australia, Canada, Germany, Ireland, Netherlands, New Zealand, Poland, Sweden, Switzerland, the United Kingdom, and the United States. Since Switzerland's scores were broken down into French and German regions, we averaged them, although they were very similar to each other. The literacy variable is available only at one point in time, 1994–96.

27 When we used country averages, we obtained results similar to those in Table 4.3, further underscoring the conclusion that our time-series, cross-section results are driven primarily by between-country effects.

28 Seventy-five percent or more of the variation in the male inequality variables and 95% of the variation in net supply are associated with between-country variation.

29 The countries were Austria, Australia, Britain, Canada, West Germany, Ireland, Italy, Japan, the Netherlands, New Zealand, Norway, Sweden, Switzerland, and the United States.

30 The sample in Table 4.7 includes one less observation than that in Table 4.6 because we lack data on minimum wages in Switzerland.

31 See Neumark and Wascher (1999) and Nickell and Layard (1999) for further discussion of minimum wage systems.

32 This difference in the impact of the policy variables depending on whether we control for net supply and segregation is not due to the smaller sample (66 observations) for which segregation data are available. When we reestimated the second specification shown in Table 4.8 on this subsample, the policy variables remained jointly and individually insignificant.

33 While we have used the degree of collective bargaining coverage, it is also possible that the degree of coordination of collective bargaining can have an independent effect on wage inequality and thus on the gender pay gap. We investigated the impact of coordination using Nickell's (1997) six-point scale, which improves upon Calmfors and Driffill's (1988) original centralization measure by taking into account pattern bargaining and coordination. Unfortunately, in the sample of 14 countries for which we had data, collective bargaining coverage and coordination were too closely correlated to reliably disentangle their separate effects; the two variables had a correlation coefficient of .67. Collective bargaining coverage and Calmfors and Driffill's (1988) original centralization measure were correlated at 0.71 with country rankings for collective bargaining coverage (OECD 1997: 73).

34 The countries were Australia, Canada, Germany, Italy, Japan, Sweden, Switzerland, the United Kingdom, and the United States.

35 Specifically, over the 1985–88 period, the ratio of the female to the male labor force participation rate was 58.6% in West Germany, 73.3% in the United States, and 94.5% in Sweden (Blau and Ferber 1992). The experience gap accounted for only about .03 log points of the 1984 difference in the Swedish-U.S. gender gaps of .21 log points (Blau and Kahn 1996b, see Chapter 3).

Chapter 5

1 An example of the importance of labor market inequality is provided by the U.S. experience in the 1980s when rising wage inequality was sufficient to counteract the effects of economic expansion in reducing poverty (Cutler and Katz 1991; Blank 1993).

2 Employers have voiced both these complaints about Sweden's "solidarity" wage policy, and that country's generous student stipends and subsidized loans for higher education may be viewed in part as a means of offsetting the distortions caused by wage compression (Edin and Holmlund 1995; see also Edin and Topel 1994).

Notes

3 The impact of administered wages on employment is a controversial issue. For research on both sides, see Neumark and Wascher (1992), Card, Kramarz, and Lemieux (1994), Edin and Topel (1994), Abowd, Kramarz, and Lemieux et al. (1995), Card and Krueger (1995), and Katz, Loveman, and Blanchflower (1995).

4 This difference between the United States and other countries is due to the greater compression at the bottom of the wage distribution in these other countries, which disproportionately benefits employed women (Blau and Kahn 1996b).

5 For evidence of rising inequality in several countries, see Gottschalk and Joyce (1991), Bound and Johnson (1992), Davis (1992), Katz and Murphy (1992), Juhn, Murphy, and Pierce (1993), OECD (1993), Edin and Holmlund (1995), Erickson and Ichino (1995), and Katz et al. (1995).

6 In Blau and Kahn (1992; 1995; 1996b), we consider the consequences of differences in wage inequality across countries for international differences in the gender gap.

7 Among the countries in our sample for which the OECD also had data (i.e., Austria, Germany, Italy, Norway, Sweden, and the United Kingdom), the 50-10 gap averaged 0.59 log points higher in the United States, whereas the 90-50 gap averaged 0.25 log points higher. (Australia was also included in the OECD data, but only for nonsupervisory workers.) In our hours-corrected microdata for these countries, the 50-10 gap averaged 0.61 log points higher in the United States, whereas the 90-50 gap averaged 0.032 log points higher. The higher U.S. level of relative inequality at the top in the OECD data appears to reflect differences for the United States between the Current Population Survey data, which the OECD used, and the International Social Survey Programme (ISSP) data, which we employ in this chapter. In this regard, it is interesting to note that our ISSP results closely correspond to those we obtain with Michigan Panel Study of Income Dynamics data (see below). In any case, the same qualitative pattern of considerably larger differences between the United States and other countries at the bottom of the distribution than at the top emerges regardless of the data source.

8 The claim about poverty holds if we are comparing countries with similar average real wage levels, as is the case here. For example, in 1988, hourly compensation in manufacturing in the OECD countries other than the United States averaged 98 percent of the U.S. level, when one adjusts for exchange rates (U.S. Department of Commerce 1992: 841).

9 This assumes barriers to the mobility of capital, labor, or goods across national boundaries so that skill prices are not equalized.

10 Freeman (1980) uses such a decomposition to assess the role of unionism on U.S. wage inequality. See also Juhn et al. (1993), who employ a similar approach to measuring the impact of industry on wage inequality.

11 Much of this higher U.S. union-nonunion wage differential is due to a higher ceteris paribus U.S. union-nonunion wage gap rather than to differences in the personal characteristics of union and nonunion workers (Blanchflower and Freeman 1992). Thus a strong causal role for the industrial relations system is suggested.

12 This will be the case if union "threat" effects dominate any negative "crowding" effects in the nonunion sector caused by the adverse employment effects of unionism. Kahn and Curme (1987) found for the United States that, other things equal, nonunion wage dispersion was lower in highly unionized than in less unionized industries.

13 This discussion of recent trends is based on OECD (1989b), Katz (1993), Edin and Topel (1994), and Edin and Holmlund (1995).

14 See Kennedy (1980), Tomandl and Fuerboeck (1986), Treu (1990), and "Minimum Pay in 18 Countries" (1992). A sizable proportion of Italian workers are self-employed or work in an underground or informal sector in which government-mandated benefits are not paid. The self-employed are not included in our analysis because of our interest in the wage determination process for wage and salary workers. Further, it is likely that since informal-sector employment is illegal, it is underreported by the respondents in our survey-based data. Thus we may understate wage inequality in Italy.

15 Blanchflower and Freeman (1992) describe the ISSP data; Rosenfeld and Kalleberg (1990) the CSCC data; Blackburn and Bloom (1994) the IDS data; and Erickson and Ichino (1995) the Bank of Italy data. The ISSP had information on Italy, but it did not collect data on the respondents' industrial sector. We therefore used the Bank of Italy data instead. Further, preliminary results indicated that the Australian data in the ISSP were inconsistent with other sources, leading us to use the more consistent IDS data.

16 For a description of the PSID, see Blau and Kahn (1997), and for information on the HUS, see Edin and Holmlund (1995).

17 For Australia and Norway in 1982, weeks worked information is available. We thus are able to compute hourly earnings for these two countries in addition to the 1984 Sweden-United States comparison. However, we treat these countries like the others in order to maintain comparability. As we note below, the difference between the United States and these countries in the distribution of hourly wages is quite similar to that for our hours-corrected earnings variable (described below), increasing our confidence in the data correction method.

18 The Australian earnings data were originally reported as a continuous variable, and the 1989 Norwegian data were also available in continuous form. However, to maintain comparability with the other countries, we recoded the Australian earnings into the ISSP's intervals for Australia and used the interval 1989 Norwegian data. Wage distributions for Australia and Norway in 1989 using the original continuous variables were virtually identical to those reported here. These findings for the cases in which we are able to construct a continuous earnings variable give us some confidence in the cases in which we are forced to use interval data. The Bank of Italy data were also continuous but did not match up with the ISSP categories for Italy. We therefore used the continuous earnings variable for Italy.

19 Marital status was not available for Italy; union status was not available for Australia or Italy; and, as indicated in Table 5.A2, available occupation and industry classifications differ for some countries. For the purpose of comparing the United States to these countries, we estimated U.S. equations that conformed to the same specification as each country. In analyses of the U.S. PSID and the Swedish HUS data shown below, actual labor market experience is used; union status is not available in the HUS.

20 The impact of unmeasured productivity is discussed below.

21 An alternative procedure is to first adjust earnings for hours by regressing In EARN on the hours variables and year dummies only and use the resulting coefficients to create hours-adjusted earnings, which are then regressed on X. When we implemented this alternative, we obtained very similar wage distributions, X coefficients, and wage residuals as those obtained using eq. (2).

22 For the U.S. PSID sample, we excluded anyone earning less than \$1.00 per hour or more than \$250 per hour in 1983 dollars. The U.S. minimum wage was \$3.35 per hour at the time. For Sweden, we excluded anyone earning less than 7 kroner per hour, or about one-seventh the average measured wage. This exclusion restriction was made since \$1.00 was about one-seventh the U.S. average. Since the U.S. wage distribution is more dispersed than the Swedish, any error caused by these exclusion restrictions will lead us to understate the Swedish-U.S. difference in wage dispersion.

23 As noted above, it is possible for us to compute distributions of hourly wages among full-time workers for Australia and Norway (1982). When we compare them to the distribution of hourly wages among full-time workers for the United States using the PSID, the differences in wage distributions between the United States and these countries are quite similar to those obtained using the hours-corrected data.

24 Country j's estimated values of θ are also used in computing $Y(1)_{ij}$, but they are standardized across countries and therefore do not directly contribute to international differences in the distribution of wages. However, to the extent that θ is more strongly correlated with X for one country than another, the difference

between the distribution of $YFULL_u$ and $Y(1)_j$ will also reflect the effects of this difference in correlation.

25 In the Swedish data, information on actual experience since age 16 is collected, whereas in the PSID, the variable refers to years of experience since age 18. To make the two variables comparable, we added two times the U.S. white male employment/population ratio for ages 16-17 to the PSID experience figure. These data were collected from the U.S. Bureau of Labor Statistics (1985).

26 For the full specification, the analysis proceeds in one step, as described above, in which we estimate eq. (2) to obtain all the coefficients necessary for the adjustment of earnings and for the decomposition at the same time. For the human capital specification, estimation proceeds in two steps. We first obtain YFULL using eqq. (2) and (3). That is, we adjust earnings for hours input using an equation with all the explanatory variables included. This procedure was followed in order to obtain an hours-correction factor with the least possible contamination by omitted variable bias. We then estimate the coefficients in the modified X vector (i.e., including human capital variables only) using YFULL as the dependent variable. Thus the basic dependent variable in comparisons of the human capital and full specifications is the same.

27 These figures differ slightly from those presented above because Sweden (1984) is now included in the non-U.S. average.

28 To some degree union status, while treated here as a measured characteristic in panel B of Tables 5.2 and 5.3, could be considered part of the wage-setting institutions. The effects of collective bargaining are discussed below.

29 Italy, Australia, and Sweden (1984) were excluded for lack of data, and Sweden (1980) could not be included because of the small sample of nonunion workers (59) in the data set. With a unionization rate of 85.7 percent, Sweden may be considered essentially a unionized country in any case.

30 That is, we employ the overall regressions for the full specification to obtain the estimated coefficients but then examine the distributions of YFULL, Y(1), and Y(2) separately for union and nonunion workers. Ideally one would like to estimate separate union and nonunion equations to allow the coefficients to vary across sectors, but small sample sizes precluded this approach.

31 Equation (7) was run using weighted least squares, with the weights being EMP/sample size, where EMP is average male employment in the country for the years in question and sample size is the size of the microdata sample for the given country. In effect, we weight by the worldwide likelihood that each worker is a member of the sample. Employment information was taken from International Labor Organization (1991). The results were similar when unweighted regressions were used. Marital status was excluded in order to include Italy in the analysis.

32 The intervals are closed at the bottom and open at the top, except for the 67-100 group, which is closed at each end.

33 In the demand indexes, the actual entries have the form $\ln(1 + \Delta D_k)$ and are approximate percentage effects. The occupation-industry categories include six industries crossed with three occupation groups. The industries are (1) agriculture; (2) mining, manufacturing, and construction; (3) transportation, communication, and public utilities; (4) trade; (5) finance, insurance, real estate, and services; and (6) government. The occupations are (1) managers and professionals; (2) clerical and sales workers; and (3) craft workers, operatives, laborers, and service workers. For the purposes of constructing the demand and supply indexes, the self-employed are included in all countries. For the 1984 Sweden-United States comparison, part-time workers are included (in addition to full-time workers and the self-employed) in measures of labor input.

34 This is also the case in nine out of a possible 11 pairwise (United States versus country j) comparisons for both the hours and earnings measures.

35 The degrees of centralization for the other countries in our sample were West Germany 6.943, Britain 12.632, Switzerland 10.904, Sweden 2.736, Norway 2.536, Australia 10.766, and Italy 14.325.

36 In these analyses, the two observations on Norway were averaged using sample size as weights. Sweden (1984) was excluded since, in contrast to the rest of the sample, the wage variable was defined as the log of actual hourly earnings.
37 For the price effects, the United States was included and given zero for the dependent variable. Also, note that the results were unchanged when female labor input was measured as the share of all earnings accounted for by women.
38 The United States was included and given zeroes for relative wages and relative female labor supply. Up to a constant, DECENT is already defined relative to the United States.
39 That is, we divided the full population of men aged 18-65 into three skill groups (i.e., high, medium, and low) on the basis of the U.S. cutoffs for employed workers described above. Countries for which we lacked data on nonparticipants in the labor force were omitted.
40 Consideration of labor supply effects strengthens our confidence in these results. Specifically, the lower relative wages of low-skilled workers in the United States should reduce their labor supply and hence their employment/population ratios compared to workers elsewhere. (Some support for such an expectation is provided by Juhn's [1992] finding that the labor supply of low-skilled males in the United States fell during the 1980s, primarily because of their declining real wages.) Thus the fact that we generally find *higher* relative employment among the low-skilled in the United States is some evidence for the existence of demand effects.
41 The 11.3 percent figure comes from the adjustment of the United States' actual 852/1,000 employment/population ratio to Germany's 756/1,000 level. We delete the bottom 96/852 (.113) from the U.S. distribution to make its simulated employment/population ratio .756.
42 Details of this test are available on request.
43 While Bjorklund and Freeman (1994) find roughly equal government relative employment between skilled and unskilled workers in Sweden in 1991, their 1981 findings show a larger representation of skilled workers, a pattern similar to our microdata, which come from 1980 and 1984.

Part IV

Introduction

1 The labor force is increased by entries and decreased by exits. When the number of entrants exceeds the number of exiters, the size of the labor force is increased. Thus, both increases in flows of entrants (which potentially dilute average experience levels) and decreases in flows of exits (which potentially increase average experience levels) contribute to the growth of the female labor force, making the relationship of rising female participation rates to average experience levels of a group ambiguous. As we have seen in Part II, the evidence suggests that, at least since 1980, women's average experience levels have been increasing and the gender gap in experience has been decreasing. For the pre-1980 period, see Goldin (1990) and Smith and Ward (1985).
2 This literature is summarized in Chapter 7; see also, Gregory (2009).
3 As we were completing work on a revision of our paper, we became aware of a recently completed working paper by Bradley Heim, eventually published as Heim (2007), which covered some of the same ground and found similar results for the trends in the elasticities.

4 Another factor that modestly contributed to the slowdown was that married men's real wages fell slightly in the 1980s but rose in the 1990s.

5 Macunovich (2010) reports a modest increase in the magnitude of both elasticities between 1999-2001 and 2007-2009, but they remained considerably below their earlier levels.

6 A number of these indexes are referenced in Guiso, Monte, Sapienza et al. (2008) who report the fascinating result that, looking across countries, girls' math scores – whether measured at the means or based on performance at the highest levels – are positively related to indicators of country-level gender equity (as measured by the various indicators).

7 This earlier program had subsequently been evaluated but, unlike our evaluation, did not use random assignment; see Bartlett and Ziegert (2000).

8 CSWEP also ran "regional" workshops associated with the meetings of regional economics associations. These workshops, organized by KimMarie McGoldrick, were aimed at faculty in teaching institutions and were not evaluated using random assignment as were the national workshops.

Chapter 6

1 Data in this paragraph are from published government sources summarized in Blau, Ferber, and Winkler (2006).

2 Similarly, Jacobsen (1998) summarizes existing work as showing a median male labor supply elasticity of -0.09 and a female elasticity of 0.77; and Filer, Hamermesh, and Rees (1996) characterize the middle-level estimates of labor supply elasticities as equaling 0.0 for men and 0.80 for women.

3 In the process of completing a revision of the August 2004 version of the original article we became aware of a recently completed working paper on this topic, Heim (2007), which finds, as we do, declining own wage and income elasticities of labor supply for married women over a roughly similar period (1979–2003 in his case). Although his paper also uses CPS data, there are a number of differences in our approaches, further suggesting that this finding is quite robust. Our study considers a wider range of robustness and specification checks than Heim's and also examines the sources of the slowdown in the increase in married women's labor supply in the 1990s compared to the 1980s.

4 A family bargaining approach also suggests disaggregating nonlabor income A according to ownership, and we estimate some models with this specification as well.

5 We include two year dummy variables in each regression. Since the CPS samples the same household in two 4-month periods that are separated by 8 months, there will be many cases in which the same household appears in two different March CPS files. We used these observations to increase sample size. However, our results were virtually identical when we restricted the number of times an individual could appear in the sample to once only.

6 Labor supply results for married women ages 25–54 with no restrictions on their spouse's age were virtually identical to the labor supply results for those married to men ages 25–54.

7 Work hours and wages refer to the previous year, so we are in effect studying the years 1978–80, 1988–90, and 1998–2000. Each of these periods is centered near a business cycle peak, although there were mild downturns in 1980 and 1990 but continued expansion in 2000 (see, e.g., the Bureau of Labor Statistics unemployment statistics, at http://www.bls.gov, accessed March 15, 2006). If anything, this difference should have raised women's hours in the last period, but in fact we see a slowdown in the growth of their hours which is perhaps understated due to this factor. To some degree, our control for year mitigates these differences in economic conditions, at least within each of the periods.

8 While Juhn (1992) found declining participation rates for unskilled men during the 1980s, evidently these were not large enough to cause the aggregate male participation rate to decline.

9 We use Jaeger's (1997) algorithm for assigning education levels to respondents in the 1999-2001 CPS files, in light of the change in the CPS education coding scheme.

10 As noted above, Juhn and Murphy (1997) find an increase in married women's own wage employment elasticities for the 1968–70 to 1988–90 period as a whole. However, inspection of results reported in their Table 6.6 (Juhn and Murphy 1997, 92) indicates that, consistent with our results, they find a roughly stable coefficient on own wages for the 1978–80 to 1988–90 period. And, as we point out in the text, with rising female hours, this would imply a declining elasticity for this period.

11 Note that we have not corrected the standard errors in the final stage median regressions for the fact that they use estimated regressors (i.e., predicted wages), since we are primarily interested in the magnitude of the labor supply parameters rather than significance tests.

12 Note that the estimated negative effect of number of children less than one is smaller in absolute value than for number of children age 1. Recall that the dependent variable is annual hours, so some of the labor supply observed for mothers of children under age 1 may be prior to the birth (or adoption) of the child.

13 An alternative hypothesis potentially consistent with the decline in the own wage effect on labor supply during the 1990s is that welfare reform and expansions in the earned income tax credit (EITC) in the 1990s induced the labor force entry of low wage women, thus flattening the observed relationship between wages and labor supply. However, this reasoning applies most strongly to single mothers, for whom the welfare system's changes were most salient. Thus, changes in the welfare system are unlikely to explain our results. Moreover, while expansions of the EITC in the 1990s raised single mothers' labor supply, they lowered married mothers' labor supply, due to the marriage penalty built into its rules (Eissa and Hoynes 2004). Since this effect is more likely to be observed among low wage women, expansions of the EITC are likely to have steepened the relationship between labor supply and wages for married women, unlike the results we have found. Moreover, as shown below, the labor supply elasticity fell within education groups, suggesting that whatever the effects of the EITC or welfare reform, something more than these policy changes was responsible for the declining estimated labor supply elasticities we document. And estimates presented below that take into account the effect of the EITC (as well as other taxes) continue to show declining labor supply elasticities.

14 In addition, we investigated the possibility that the 2000 results for the less educated were influenced by the fact that this group has a relatively large share of immigrants (Borjas 2003). Specifically, we reestimated our models for 2000 using only natives. The results for this sample using either before tax or after tax wages on models with all education groups pooled or treated separately were similar to those based on the full sample of all residents. Unfortunately, the CPS for 1979–81 and 1989–91 did not collect nativity data, but the similarity of the 2000 results for natives and for the full sample is reassuring.

15 The 35–44-year-olds in 1980 come the closest; however, even their birth years spanned 1935–46. These birth year intervals reflect our pooling of 3 years of CPS data for each period.

16 The only exception is the cohort that was 25–34 in 1990. For this group, the cross wage elasticity stays roughly constant between 1990 and 2000, although the own wage elasticity falls sharply.

17 The effect of changes in the number and ages of children was larger in the 1990s than the 1980s despite Table 6.A3's data that show a larger fall in the total number of children in the 1980s than the 1990s. The two observations can be reconciled by noting that in the age groups where children have their most negative effect on labor supply (i.e., the preschool ages), the number of children rose in the 1980s and

fell in the 1990s. While the number of school age children fell sharply in the 1980s, our estimates imply that these declines did not have a large impact on labor supply. This analysis illustrates the value of disaggregating the number of children by their ages.

18 To illustrate this process, recall from Table 6.A2 that in 2000, 63.6% of women were married, while in 1980, 72.6% were married. From the 1980 sample of married women, our procedure would eliminate the lowest 12.4% (i.e., [(0.726–0.636)/(0.726)]) of individuals with respect to their estimated probability of being married. The actual percentages are very slightly different from those in this example, because in the regression samples, we have excluded married women whose spouses have allocated income variables, while in Table 6.A2, we include the full set of married women. We perform a similar adjustment for 1990.

19 Note that the coefficients for the 2000 regressions differ very slightly from those in Table 6.1 even though the sample is the same in both tables. The reason for this is that in calculating wage deciles (i.e., the instruments in the IV analysis) for the Table 6.1 analyses the married sample is used. However, for all analyses in Table 6.4 (with the exception of the specification that includes cohabitors), the full sample (married and unmarried) is used. This is done so as to treat current marital status as endogenously as possible.

20 Eissa and Hoynes (2004) estimate an own after tax wage participation elasticity for married women with less than 12 years of schooling of 0.267 using data from 1985–97. The after tax hours elasticities that we estimate for this group fall from .64 to .65 in 1990 to -.14 to -.17 in 2000. Our small and negative estimated elasticities for 2000 are not necessarily inconsistent with Eissa and Hoynes' findings, given that 2000 (1999–2001) is outside their sample period and our 2000 elasticities represent a sharp drop from 1990.

21 We obtained results similar to the participation probits when we estimated models of the determinants of the probability that a woman worked full-time, full-year, an alternative participation measure used by Welch (1997).

22 This weight is based on the assumptions of constant variance in annual hours for individuals and independence of the sample 10 years apart. In this case, we have

$$Var(\Delta H_{jk}) = VarH_{jkt} + VarH_{jkt+1} = [(1/N_{jkt})+(1/N_{jkt+1})]\sigma^2,$$

where for cell jk N_{jkt} is the cell size for year t and σ is the individual residual standard deviation of work hours. The cell sizes (N_{jkt}) are themselves based on weighted counts of the individuals in the cells, where the individuals are given their adjusted CPS sampling weight, where as discussed earlier, we scale the raw CPS weights to have the same sum for each year.

23 Devereux (2004) uses 1980 and 1990 Census data to estimate grouped data labor supply models, although in his case the dependent variable is the log of hours conditional on supplying labor. Nonetheless, our results for the 1980–90 spouse wage elasticity are similar to his. However, his findings for the own conditional labor supply elasticity range from 0.7 to 1.2 without controlling for group indicators, and 0.002 to 0.4 controlling for group indicators.

Chapter 7

1 See Lundberg and Pollak (1996) for a review of the literature on family bargaining models and the contributions in Ferber and Nelson (1993) for examples of issues raised by feminist economics.

2 See the Data Appendix for details of the data analysis.

3 The specification of education in the 1995 CPS differs significantly from previous years. These differences and how they were dealt with are described in the Data Appendix.

4 A common finding of such studies is that children appear to do better when their mothers control a larger fraction of family resources. Additional support for this view is provided by a substantial literature in sociology which finds that employed wives have a greater say in household decision making than nonemployed wives (England and Farkas 1986).

5 The rising correlation of wife's and husband's earnings has also been noted by others, e.g., Cancian, Danziger, and Gottschalk (1993); and Karoly and Burtless (1995). We return to this issue below when we consider income trends across families.

6 Blau and Ferber (1991) find that while female college seniors expected equal starting salaries with men in the same field, they expected much lower salaries later in their career, even under the assumption of equal labor force attachment. It should also be noted that a reduction in discrimination in educational institutions themselves may have also played a role; Title IX which bans such discrimination was passed in 1972.

7 Goldin (1990: 136-8) provides an excellent example of how evidence of shifts in supply responsiveness may be interpreted to suggest insights into the underlying factors that caused them.

8 See, e.g., Sorensen (1990). A recent study by Macpherson and Hirsch (1995) using a 1973–93 panel of data from the CPS, however, finds that the negative wage effect of percent female in the occupation is substantially reduced when longitudinal wage change models are estimated to control for unobserved fixed effects.

9 For citations of such studies, see, Blau, Ferber, and Winkler (1998).

10 This also accords with published data summarized in Blau, Ferber, and Winkler (1998).

11 Note that estimated changes in real wages will vary depending on the wage measure used, the data set employed, and the starting and ending years selected. However, the findings reported here are broadly consistent with those reported in the literature.

12 Some caution must be observed in such comparisons because the 3-digit occupational categories employed by the Census for blue-collar, manufacturing occupations distinguish an especially large number of occupations thus making it easier to detect segregation than for (relatively) more aggregated white-collar jobs.

13 The self-employment rate is the percentage of nonagricultural workers who are self-employed.

14 For more information on these trends, see, e.g., Blau, Ferber, and Winkler (1998).

15 In a companion paper, Blau and Kahn (1996b, see Chapter 3) present evidence that wage structure is very important in explaining international differences in the gender pay gap.

16 Similar results are reported by O'Neill and Polachek (1993) and Wellington (1993).

17 England (1982) provides the strongest critique of the human capital explanation for occupational segregation. Some particularly interesting recent evidence implicitly supporting the human capital model is Macpherson and Hirsch's (1995) finding of a substantial effect of skills in explaining the lower pay in predominantly female jobs. Theirs are among the higher estimates; for a review see Sorensen (1990).

18 Considerable empirical evidence indicates that women have traditionally received less on-the-job training than men; see Barron, Black, and Loewenstein (1993) and the references therein.

19 SAT scores were recentered by the College Board in 1996; scores for the earlier year have been converted to the recentered scale by the College Board.

20 Lundberg and Startz (1983) develop an interesting model of statistical discrimination based on women's productivity being less accurately predicted than men's that includes feedback effects. See also, Blau, Ferber, and Winkler (1998).

21 This is preferable to looking at earnings, because earnings are influenced by labor supply decisions which could well change after a divorce.

Notes

22 The Hersch and Stratton study finds these conclusions to be quite robust to alternative specifications of the instrument set. They do not, however, find consistent evidence of a significant negative effect of housework on men's wages.

23 For example, 40 percent of cohabitations do not continue (as cohabitations) beyond one year, and two-thirds do not continue beyond two years.

24 Based on tabulations from the CPS.

25 In the black community, relatively high homicide and incarceration rates are also believed to contribute to a scarcity of marriageable males.

26 Recent work suggests that the negative effects of teen childbearing may have been overstated in earlier studies due to overestimates of the alternative prospects for these young women (Geronimus and Korenman 1992). At present there exists a considerable range of estimates of the magnitude of this adverse effect (Hoffman, Foster, and Furstenberg 1993).

27 The percentage increase in participation did decline a bit, however, from 21.8 percent over the 1970s to 15.6 percent over the 1980s.

28 Four age categories: 25–34, 35–44, 45–54, and 55–64; and three education categories: less than 12 years, 12 years, and greater than 12 years are employed.

29 For a critique of the Fuchs' approach, see Manchester and Stapleton (1991).

30 This and other data issues are evaluated in detail by Hersch and Stratton (1997); they conclude that, despite these data problems, the PSID yields a useful measure of household production.

31 Using data from the 1975 Time Use Study based on time diaries and the 1987 National Survey of Families and Households based on direct questions about specific tasks, Shelton (1992) also finds an increase in employed men's housework time as a percentage of employed women's over the 1975 to 1987 period, due in part to a decline in women's time. Similarly, Juster and Stafford (1991) report a decrease in women's housework time and an increase in men's between 1965 and 1981; however, because as noted above, they do not report results separately by employment or marital status, trends in these factors could account for some of the observed changes.

32 See Hersch and Stratton (1994) for evidence on the responsiveness of husband's and wife's housework time to relative wages.

33 This conclusion would require some modifications of the simple comparative advantage model presented in Becker (1991). For example, there might be a number of household activities, with the degree of comparative advantage of each spouse differing across activities. Then, as the wife's relative wage increases, some activities might be transferred from wife to husband.

34 Specifically, the ratio of husband's to wife's housework time increased by 57 percent among less educated wives (39 percent for nonemployed wives and 42 percent for employed wives); the ratio increased by 47 percent among more highly educated wives (41 percent for nonemployed wives and 37 percent for employed wives).

35 Based on diary reports of time specifically spent on leisure activities, Shelton (1992) finds little difference between women and men in total leisure time in 1975 or 1981.

36 An intimate is currently defined as a spouse, ex-spouse, boy/girlfriend, or ex-boy/girlfriend. In earlier data, figures for intimates are included in the same category as "other relatives."

37 Calculated from U.S. Department of Justice (1994); and Bachman and Saltzman (1995).

38 Another discontinuity in the table is the sizable fall in the rate of violence by strangers for both men and women between 1979–87 and 1987- 91. This likely reflects the inclusion of multiple-offender victimizations in the 1979–87 data, but not in the later period.

39 The relationship of the offender to the victim was not identified in 30.9 percent of the cases with female victims and 41.3 percent of the cases with male victims.

40 Tabulations for previous years in Harlow (1991) and Bachman (1994) suggest similar patterns.

41 See for example, Korenman and Neumark (1991), Waldfogel (1997), and Fuchs (1988). A number of serious econometric issues are raised in seeking to measure the effect of children on women's wages due to unmeasured heterogeneity among individuals and endogeneity of the decision to have children. For an especially thorough treatment of these issues, see Korenman and Neumark (1992 and 1994). While Korenman and Neumark's earlier findings were ambiguous, their more recent and preferred results do indicate a negative effect of children on wages for white women.

42 The Family and Medical Leave Act of 1993 requires all employers over a minimum size to offer 12 weeks of unpaid job-protected leave.

43 The weekly wage measure has been used quite extensively in recent studies of trends in wages, wage inequality, and race wage differentials; see, for example, Katz and Murphy (1992), and Juhn, Murphy, and Pierce (1991 and 1993).

Chapter 8

1 An earlier, one-shot CSWEP mentoring effort was offered in 1998 and subsequently evaluated but did not use random assignment. See Bartlett and Ziegert (2000).

2 CSWEP also ran "regional" workshops associated with the meetings of regional economics associations. These workshops, organized by KimMarie McGoldrick, were aimed at faculty in teaching institutions and were not evaluated using random assignment.

3 In order to be included in the pool eligible for random assignment, the applicant needed to have a North American PhD or be employed at a North American research institution.

4 We defined department rank using Kalaitzidakis, Mamuneas, and Stengos (2003) because it included non-North American schools. The top-ten departments were Harvard University, University of Chicago, Massachusetts Institute of Technology, Northwestern University, University of Pennsylvania, Yale University, Princeton University, Stanford University, University of California at Berkeley, and New York University.

5 We defined the top-tier journals as the American Economic Review, the Journal of Political Economy, the Quarterly Journal of Economics, and Econometrica.

Part V

Introduction

1 Our data were from the 1976 National Longitudinal Survey (NLS) of young men and the 1978 NLS of young women.

2 Kochhar, Fry, and Taylor report similar large wealth differences between whites and Hispanics that also increased over the recession.

3 However, data reported in Kochhar, Fry and Taylor (2011) for selected years in the 1984-2009 period suggest this was not the case - the wealth ratio was fairly constant (with some year-to-year fluctuations) between 1984 and 2005, before declining in 2009.

4 Interestingly, later work by Altonji and Doraszelski (2005) reports the same discrepancy in results depending on whether the black or white functions are employed.

Chapter 9

1 Smith and Welch (1986) have also emphasized long-term gains for black males over the 1940-1980 period. Montgomery and Wascher (1987) have examined race differentials within the manufacturing and service industries during the 1970s.

2 Others, e.g., Smith and Welch (1986) argue that anti-discrimination legislation played a minor role.

3 The unemployment rate was 2.3 points higher in 1979 (the most recent cyclical peak prior to 1981) than in 1969 (the most recent cyclical peak prior to 1971).

4 Between 1971 and 1981, the difference in unemployment rates between black and white males (females) increased by 5.0 (4.2) points, compared to an increase of 4.1 (3.8) points between 1969 and 1979. Similarly, the race difference in participation rates for males increased by 3.2 points (1971-81) compared to 4.0 points (1969-79), while the black female advantage in participation rates declined by 5.0 points (1971-81) compared to 5.4 points (1969-79).

5 Between 1981 and 1988, the race difference in unemployment rates decreased by 2.2 points (males) and 1.7 points (females). The race difference in participation rates decreased by 2.2 points for males and remained unchanged for females.

6 Since CPS occupational codes were changed from 1970 to 1980 Census categories by 1989, the 1989 detailed categories were recoded to major occupational categories on the basis of U.S. Department of Commerce (1983).

7 That is, years of school completed and splines for education less than 8 years (experience group 20+ only) and more than 12 years.

8 This is included to capture the impact of time out of the labor force for childbearing and child-rearing (Hill 1979).

9 The categories are: professional or managerial, clerical or sales, and, for males, craft worker, operative, and laborer; and, for females, blue-collar worker and private household worker. The reference category is service worker.

10 The proportion of individuals meeting other sample selection criteria who were in farm occupations was small: 1.3%, 1.4% and 1.3% of white males in 1971, 1981 and 1988; 3.1%, 3.2% and 1.9% of black males; 0.6%, 0.5% and 0.5% of white females; and 1.6%, 0.9% and 0.3% of black females.

11 Those reporting school as their major activity during the survey week or as the reason for part-year work were excluded.

12 In 1976 (and again in 1989) the Census changed its method of imputing income to individuals with missing data, breaking the comparability of income series data (Lillard, Smith, and Welch 1986).

13 A common reference year is used to facilitate comparisons across all three years.

14 While our approach is similar to Smith and Welch (1986), they apply the adjustment to within cohort comparisons and focus solely on one variable, education, in making the adjustment.

15 Both Reimers (1983) and Blau and Beller (1988) find evidence that, among males, participants are a negatively selected group.

16 We adopt this procedure rather than simply calculating a wage because in the 1972 CPS hours information is available only for the week preceding the survey. In light of this data limitation, adjustment for part-time versus full-time employment in a regression context was believed to be the preferable approach.

17 The probability of sample inclusion is related to participation rates but is also affected by other factors such as school enrollment, employment at some time during the year, self-employment, and participation in the military.

18 The predicted differentials are computed using weighted means (based on sampling weights provided by the CPS). Thus, the predicted unadjusted earnings ratios shown in Table 9.3 may differ slightly from the actual unadjusted earnings ratios shown in Table 9.1.

19 For ease of exposition we refer to these as percentage effects although they are only approximately so.

20 The finding for younger black males was actually due to rising occupational premia for professional, managerial, and craft jobs where blacks were underrepresented rather than to an increase in occupational differences between blacks and whites.

21 O'Neill (1990) presents evidence of a decrease in the race-education gap among 20-34 year olds between 1980 and 1988 using CPS data. Given her broader (14 year) age range and her exclusion of 18 and 19 year olds, her 20-34 year old group most likely represents a combination of our experience groups 0-9 and 10-19. We also found a decrease in the education gap for the latter group.

22 In this respect our findings are consistent with the conclusions reached by Juhn et al. (1989) and O'Neill (1990).

Chapter 10

1 We use the term single to refer to all respondents who are not married with a spouse present.

2 To keep the sample relatively homogeneous with respect to age, we required that the respondent's spouse be age 18 to 40 (if wives of male respondents) or 21 to 40 (if husbands of female respondents).

3 The proportion of cases remaining after exclusion for missing data was quite similar for whites and blacks. Most exclusions were due to missing data on assets or income. Cases with negative values of total wealth or of particular assets are included in the analysis.

4 These calculations are intended to provide only a rough indication of the impact of family status on the racial wealth differential. If marriage is selective of the more economically advantaged, increasing the proportion of married couples among blacks may not lower the racial wealth differential by as much as our calculations suggest. Wealth levels may also be behaviorally related to marital status. On the one hand, the lower asset levels of black married couples may raise their probability of marital dissolution. On the other hand, to the extent that black couples anticipate a higher probability of marital breakup, they may have a lower incentive to accumulate assets.

5 Brainard and Tobin (1968) have shown that there are important cross equation restrictions that apply to the system of four equations in (2), specifically the coefficients ak, bk, and ck must each sum to zero across the four equations and the four coefficients on wealth (dk) must sum to one. These restrictions are met by OLS estimation of (2). While these restrictions imply that it is necessary to estimate only three of the four regressions to obtain the four sets of coefficients, for the reader's convenience we present the results of OLS estimation of each equation.

6 The explanatory variables in the income regressions include age and age squared of head (and spouse), education and health of head (and spouse), as well as KIDS, CENTCITY, OTHSMSA, SOUTH, and FEMHEAD (single heads). Permanent income was set equal to predicted income evaluated at AGEHEAD equal to 30. (The wife's age was set equal to what her age would be when her husband was 30.) This provides a consistent measure of permanent income that can be compared across families which may be at somewhat different stages of the life-cycle. Transitory income (IN CD IF) is defined as the difference between observed income and predicted income evaluated at the actual age of the head (and wife).

7 Since transitory income is disproportionately saved, we would expect the coefficient on current income in a savings regression to be greater for blacks than whites (Friedman 1957). However, this does not necessarily imply that the coefficient on current income in a wealth regression would also be greater for blacks. This is because, while a higher proportion of a given increment in transitory income is saved, it is available for a smaller number of periods than an equal increment in permanent income. In the long run, for a given family, the impact of years of positive transitory income and positive saving on wealth will

be offset by years of negative transitories and hence dissaving. To the extent that our measures of permanent and transitory income are less adequate for blacks than whites, our finding of smaller coefficients on permanent income in the black wealth regressions (see below) may be partially due to this factor. This is unlikely, however, in that the use of our estimate of permanent income rather than actual income increases the income coefficients of blacks to a considerably greater extent than whites (see notes 8 and 10).

8 Results are available upon request. Among married couples (single heads), the coefficient on PINC is 120 (98) percent higher than the INCOME coefficient for blacks, compared with 45 (2) percent higher for whites.

9 These differences are significant at the 1 percent level in the case of married couples and at the 2 percent level in the case of single heads.

10 When the INCOME specification is employed, a smaller proportion of the wealth differential is explained: 59.4 (89.4) percent for married couples (single heads) using the white coefficients and 19.4 (11.3) percent using the black coefficients. When a PINC squared term is included in the permanent income specification to allow for possible nonlinearities in the relationship between income and wealth, the results are quite similar to those reported in the text.

11 Using longitudinal data from the NLS, Lazear finds no significant race difference in wage growth over the 1966-1969 period. Similarly, using Census data, Smith and Welch find that for the cohort with a median labor market entry of 1963 (1968), the black-white wage ratio was 70.1 (75.1) percent in 1970 and 71.2 (73.5) percent in 1980. Published data from the Current Population Survey suggest that black and white women in this cohort also experienced similar wage growth. The ratio of black to white median income of full-time, year-round workers was 93.4 percent among those aged 20-24 in 1970 and 95.6 percent among those aged 30-34 in 1980.

12 To the extent that these results relate to current rather than to permanent income, the larger coefficient on income for blacks is expected (see note 7) and consistent with similar saving rates out of permanent income for blacks and whites. If black saving rates out of permanent income are actually lower than those of whites, that could explain some of the observed racial differences in income coefficients in our wealth regressions.

13 Suppose that saving is identically s percent of permanent income $\overline{Y}$ in each year; that is,

$$S_1 = S_2 = \ldots = S_t = s\overline{Y}.$$

Wealth at time t can be written as

$$W_t = W_0\,(1 + r)^t + s\overline{Y}\sum_{i=1}^{t}\,(1 + r)^{t-1} = W_0(1 + r)^t + s\overline{Y}\left[\frac{(1 + r)^t - 1}{r}\right],$$

where W_0 is initial wealth and r is the rate of return. If s is the same for white and black families, then the income coefficient differs only because of racial differences in r (for a given date t). Assume that s is 0.1 and $t = 10$. If blacks earn $r = 0.03$ on their portfolio, then their income coefficient would be 1.146, which is quite close to the coefficient on PINC for black married couples reported in Table 10.3 of 1.156. However, even if whites earned $r = 0.09$ – three times the black rate of return – their income coefficient would be only 1.519. Thus, for reasonable parameter values, it would appear that interest rate differences could not account for more than a small differential in the income coefficient.

14 Note that the value of access to a family business most likely exceeds the market value of the business itself. The individual is likely to have received informal training in the conduct of the business as well as many useful contacts.

15 The concentration of blacks in our sample in the South (see Table 10.2) is higher than figures obtained from census data which indicate that in 1980, about 56 percent of married and 48 percent of single (nonmarried) black men and women aged 25 to 39 lived in the South. This difference most likely results from the

oversampling of households in predominantly black enumeration districts which was employed to increase the number of blacks in the sample. Adjustment for this factor would, however, have only a modest effect on the decomposition results reported above.

16 Note that since the regressions control for total wealth, a dollar differential in favor of blacks implies that they hold a higher proportion of their wealth in this form.

17 Birnbaum and Weston (1974) find similar results for the probability of home ownership, controlling for wealth. At the black means, whites were more likely to own homes than blacks; however, at the white means, blacks were more likely to be home owners. It might be argued that barriers to home ownership among blacks lower their wealth levels so that, controlling for wealth, the black disadvantage is not apparent. When similar calculations are performed based on regressions in which wealth is not included as an explanatory variable, it is found that house equity is indeed lower, evaluated at both the white and black means. The unexplained differential ranged from 27.3 (black means) to 70.7 percent (white means) of the total differential among married couples and from 84.9 (black means) to 91.7 (white means) among single heads. However, among married couples, blacks would hold a higher proportion of their wealth in the form of housing, regardless of whether the functions are evaluated at the black or at the white means. The findings for the proportion of wealth held in house equity for single heads remain the same as those reported in the text.

18 In this case, it is found that when wealth is omitted as an explanatory variable, blacks would hold a smaller proportion of their wealth in the form of business assets when the functions are evaluated at either the white or the black means.

Chapter 11

1 For an attempt to balance the costs and benefits of immigration at an aggregate level, see Simon (1981). The U.S. House of Representatives, Special Committee on Population (1978: 32): "Immigrants undoubtedly have an effect on the cost of providing a whole range of public services [...]. Few of these effects, however, have received more than cursory attention by immigration researchers or by the administrators of these public services."

2 In the interests of clarity, I reluctantly follow the traditional practice of designating the husband in a family with a husband and wife as the "head."

3 Outmigration is a relatively minor factor in the case of the United States.

4 Among immigrant heads who were 68 or older, 28 percent of the men and 34 percent of the women arrived before 1920. An additional 62 percent of the men and 58 percent of the women arrived between 1920 and 1949; unfortunately, no more detailed breakdown on the latter group is available from the SIE.

5 These figures were computed from the SIE data, but are not shown in Table 11.2.

6 See note 4. Among immigrant heads who were 65 or over, 88 percent of the men and 91 percent of the women arrived before 1950.

7 Using 1970 census data, Chiswick (1977) has found that, other things equal, the native-born sons of immigrants have higher earnings than the native-born sons of native-born parents. For a similar finding for sons and daughters using data from the early 1900s, see Blau (1980).

8 This possibility is mentioned by Wachter (1980) although he does not necessarily advocate this policy for the 1980s.

9 See, for example, Hamermesh (1978).

10 The results from contemporary data for female immigrants show a less consistent time pattern; see Long (1980).

11 Alternatively, one may estimate the total effects by solving for them using the structural-transfer and wage equations. The reduced-form equations were used because they necessitate fewer restrictive assumptions. Similar results were

obtained when the alternative was employed. Reduced-form results are available from the author upon request.

12 The wage equations included controls for potential labor market experience and potential experience squared. HDEDUC and a foreign-born-education interaction term. BLACK, OTHER, HISP, KIDSLT5 and KIDS5TI7 (women). MAR and VET (men), location (METRO through CENTER), ENGPOORand foreign birth (FOR 1970-74 through FOR BEFR20). Results are available from the author upon request.

13 In 1975. the unemployment rate of men (women) 20 years of age and over was 12.4 (12.1) percent among blacks, 9.7 (11.6) among those of Hispanic origin, but only 6.2 (7.5) percent among whites. See U.S. Department of Labor (1976: 223).

14 Puerto Ricans are excluded from the analysis because they have some characteristics of the native born (such as free access to the mainland and coverage under federal programs in their place of origin) and some characteristics of immigrants (such as language and cultural differences). The results of preliminary analyses for male heads in which Puerto Ricans were included as immigrants were essentially the same as the results obtained when they were excluded.

15 For each individual i, λ_i is included as an additional explanatory variable in a wage regression; and λ_i is computed as

$$-\frac{f(B'X_i)}{F(B'X_i)},$$

where $f(-)$ and $F(-)$ are, respectively, the standard normal density and cumulative distribution functions; B is a vector of probit coefficients from an equation estimating the probability of being employed at the time of the survey; and X includes all the exogenous explanatory variables present in the wage and transfer equations. See Heckman (1980).

16 Although it would be technically possible to include an estimate of λ based on the transfer-probability equation in the transfer-receipt equation (due to the nonlinear estimation technique), the collinearity between λ and the other explanatory variables would be too severe to draw any meaningful conclusions.

17 In general, the partial derivative of the transfer probability with respect to an exogenous variable (X_k) is computed as: $B_{kT}f(B_T'\bar{X})$, where B_{kT} is the estimated probit coefficient on X_k; B_T is the estimated vector of probit coefficients; and $f(-)$ is the density function for a standard normal random variable. To find the percentage change in the participation probability for a 10 percent increase in waged, we multiply this partial derivative by ln 1.1 and divide by the weighted mean of the dependent variable.

18 These effects are computed as in Table 11.6.

19 These effects are computed as in Table 11.7.

20 Since the dependent variable in the wage equation is $\ln \omega$, the percentage effect of an independent variable on wages is equal to $e^b - 1$, where b is the effect of the variable as given in Table 11.6. Our findings for the impact by length-of-U.S.-residence variables for female heads (discussed below) differ from those of Long (1980) but are similar to those of Blau (1980) for the early 1900s. The estimated coefficients on λ (see note 20) indicate that employed individuals have unobservable characteristics that are positively related to wages.

21 See note 25: in this case, the figure in the text is based on Table 11.7.

22 The indirect effects are computed as the difference between the total effects given below and the direct effects given above. Computed in this way, the indirect effect of poor English ability is found to lower the total transfers of female heads. This effect is the result of an insignificant positive association between wages and poor English ability for this group.

23 Since the decomposition of expected transfer payments is based in part on probit coefficients, the answer to these questions differs depending on whether immigrants are given their own means for the characteristic and the native means for all the other variables (as reported in Table 11.7) or natives are given their own means for the characteristic and the immigrant means for all the other variables.

In fact, these differences were small and did not affect the results. It should be noted that the predicted immigrant-native differentials do not equal the actual differentials because of the nonlinearity of the probit function and the use of weighted means in the decomposition.

24 Among immigrants, an additional year of schooling lowers total expected transfer receipts by $41 among male heads and $44 among female heads.

25 To the extent that refugee immigrants are less motivated by economic considerations than other groups, they may be economically less successful and thus utilize more transfers.

Chapter 12

1 These figures on the presence and source region of the foreign born were taken from http://www.census.gov/population/www/documentation/twps0029/tab02.html and http://www.census.gov/population/www/socdemo/foreign/STP-159-2000tl.html.

2 Blau (1992) is an exception.

3 This is similar to Fernández, Fogli, and Olivetti's (2004) finding of a positive effect on wife's labor supply of a husband coming from a family in which his mother worked, a result that they interpret as evidence of an impact of culture.

4 We do not have data on visa type, which may be correlated with country-of-origin characteristics. However, in one of our specifications, we control for source country fixed effects, which may absorb some of the effects of visa requirements, thus making the interpretation of the measured country characteristics stronger than otherwise.

5 The data did not allow us to compare immigrant labor supply to that of natives or to follow the immigrants over a long time period, thus preventing analysis of long-term changes in immigrant labor supply.

6 The spouse restriction means that natives or adult immigrants who are married to child immigrants are excluded from the sample.

7 When we used recent arrival weights (the U.S. values for five years before each census), U.S. fertility fell between 1980 and 1990 and then rose back to its 1980 level by 2000.

8 We also interact own and spouse education with the YSM dummies.

9 That is, if the immigrant arrived between A_0 and A_1, we take only individuals for whom $(A_0 - BY) \geq 18$, where BY is birth year as calculated from the individual's reported age. An alternative would have been to evaluate the arrival intervals at their midpoints and calculate age of arrival accordingly. We follow the former procedure due to its greater accuracy in excluding child immigrants (see Bleakley and Chin 2004).

10 The English-speaking and English official variables are from Bleakley and Chin (2004).

11 Recall that since the own and spouse cohort YSM dummies add up to an own and a spouse immigrant dummy, respectively, we do not include main effects for immigrant and spouse immigrant.

12 Results are broadly similar in models including these variables; see Blau, Kahn, and Papps (2011).

13 The lower figure uses the start point of each arrival interval; the higher figure uses the end point.

14 This high correlation also partly reflects a substantial correlation (0.429) between wives' and husbands' female relative activity rate even among immigrants married to immigrants from different source countries.

15 For these and other examples in the text of the countries corresponding to the percentiles, we sometimes refer to interpolated data.

16 Differences relative to 0–5 years since migration are significant in all cases for men and for those with a college education (some college and graduates) for women. To

calibrate the education effects in Tables 12.3 and 12.4 relative to natives, we may, as in Figures 12.1 and 12.2, evaluate the immigrant-native difference in work hours for high school dropouts for immigrant women married to immigrant men who came to the United States from the same country and at the same time, assuming the sample averages for the cohort arrival dummies and the source country characteristics. These differences for women (men) are: 0–5: -146 (-136); 6–10: 57 (137); 11–15: 72 (180); 16–20: 48 (210); 21–30: .3 (297).

17 It is possible that the need for specialized visas for highly technical work or for study at U.S. universities is correlated with some of the country characteristics we have included in our regressions. However, as noted above, our basic conclusions hold even when we include country fixed effects.

18 For the full sample (pooling all census years), 77% of married immigrant women are married to immigrant men, 70% are married to immigrant men from the same country, and 53% are married to immigrant men who migrated from the same country at the same time.

19 Like the results in Table 12.3, these represent the sum of the own and spouse country characteristics effects.

20 The effects of relative female activity rate for men ranged from 33 to 333 hours. These were more positive than the results in Table 12.4, which did not control for country dummies, again suggesting that controlling for the other source country characteristics, female relative activity rate is negatively correlated with unmeasured country-specific factors increasing immigrant men's labor supply (as was the case for women as well).

21 The similarity of the effects of the female relative activity rate on both employment incidence and hours given employment gives us some confidence in this variable as an indicator of the gender division of labor in the source country, despite our lack of information on the hours actually worked by source country.

22 The effect of fertility on hours given employment was significantly more negative for 21 to 30 years than at arrival, although, again, the magnitude of these effects relative to the mean was small.

Concluding Thoughts

1 "Prior to 1966 there were no women in the economics faculty at Harvard. In 1966 [Anne P.] Carter became the first [female] assistant professor of the Harvard Economics Department but, while she was permitted to offer seminars on topics of her choice and to advise students, she was never given any teaching assignments" (Akhabbar 2001, p.2). I later had the great pleasure to get to know Anne Carter but I did not know her at that time.

2 An early pioneer in analyzing household production was Margaret Reid (1934), but it was the work of Gary Becker and Jacob Mincer in the 1960s that was particularly influential in bringing these issues into the mainstream.

3 Much of the foundation was laid by Becker (see Becker 1991, orig. published 1981). In addition, important early work by Manser and Brown (1980) and Horney and McElroy (1981) introduced household bargaining models.

References

1. Introduction by the Editors

Akerlof, G.A., Kranton, R.E. (2000). Economics and Identity, in: Quarterly Journal of Economics, 115: 715-53.
Bertrand, M. (2011). New Perspectives on Gender, in: Ashenfelter, O., Card, D. (Eds.), Handbook of Labor Economics, Vol. 4, Elsevier: 1543-90.
Blau, F. D. (1977). Equal Pay in the Office, Lexington, MA: Lexington Books.
Blau, F. D. (1984). The Use of Transfer Payments by Immigrants, in: Industrial and Labor Relations Review, 37(2): 222-39. [Chapter 11 in this volume]
Blau, F. D., Beller, A.H. (1988). Trends in Earnings Differentials by Gender: 1971-1981, in: Industrial and Labor Relations Review, 41(4): 513-29.
Blau, F. D., Ehrenberg, R. G. (1997). Gender and Family Issues in the Workplace, New York: Russell Sage Foundation.
Blau, F. D., Ferber, M. A. (1986). The Economics of Women, Men, and Work, Englewood Cliffs, NJ: Prentice-Hall.
Blau, F. D., Kahn, L. M. (1996). Wage Structure and Gender Earnings Differentials: An International Comparison, in: Economica, 63(250): S29-S62. [Chapter 3 in this volume]
Blau, F. D., Kahn, L. M. (2000). Gender Differences in Pay, in: Journal of Economic Perspectives, 14(4): 75-99.
Blau, F. D., Kahn, L. M. (2002). At Home and Abroad – U.S. Labor Market Performance in International Perspective, New York: Russell Sage Foundation.
Blau, F. D., Kahn, L. M. (2006). The U.S. Gender Pay Gap in the 1990s: Slowing Convergence, in: Industrial and Labor Relations Review, 60(1): 45-66.
Blau, F. D., Currie, J. M., Croson, R. T. A. et al. (2010). Can Mentoring Help Female Assistant Professors? Interim Results from a Randomized Trial, in: American Economic Review, 100: 348-52. [Chapter 8 in this volume]
Croson, R., Gneezy, U. (2009). Gender Differences in Preferences, in: Journal of Economic Literature, 47(2): 1-27.
Dohmen, T.J. , Falk, A., Huffman, D. et al. (2011). Individual Risk Attitudes: Measurement, Determinants and Behavioral Consequences, in: Journal of the European Economic Association, 9(3), 522-50.
European Commission (2010). Strategy for Equality Between Women and Men, SEC(2010) 1079, Brussels.
Fernandez, R., Fogli, A., Olivetti, C. (2004), Mothers and Sons: Preference Development and Female Labor Force Dynamics, in: Quarterly Journal of Economics, 119(4): 1249-99.
Gneezy, U., Niederle, M., Rustichini, A. (2003). Performance in Competitive Environments: Gender Differences, in: Quarterly Journal of Economics, 118: 1049-74.
Goldin, C. (2006). The Quiet Revolution that Transformed Women's Employment, Education, and Family, in: American Economic Review, 96(2): 1-21.

Goldin, C., Katz, L. F. (2002). The Power of the Pill: Oral Contraceptives and Women's Career and Marriage Decisions, in: Journal of Political Economy, 110(4): 730-70.
Krause, A., Rinne, U., Zimmermann, K.F. (2010). Anonymisierte Bewerbungsverfahren, IZA Research Report No. 27.
Kuiper, E. (2001). The Most Valuable of All Capital, A Gender Reading of Economic Texts, Amsterdam: Thela Thesis.
Lalive, R., Stutzer, A. (2010). Approval of Equal Rights and Gender Differences in Well-being, in: Journal of Population Economics, 23(3): 933-62.
Lee, J., Lee, S. (2011). Does it Matter who Responded to the Survey? Trends in the US Gender Earnings Gap Revisited, IZA Discussion Paper No 5512, IZA, Bonn.
Pande, R. , Ford, D. (2011). Gender Quotas and Female Leadership: A Review, Background Paper for the World Development Report on Gender, April 2011.
OECD (2010). PISA 2009 Results: What Students Know and Can Do - Student Performance in Reading, Mathematics and Science, Vol. 1.
Stanley, T. D., Jarrell, S. B. (1998). Gender Wage Discrimination Bias? A Meta-Regression Analysis, in: Journal of Human Resources, 33(4): 947-73.
Stanley, T. D., Jarrell, S.B. (2004). Declining Bias and Gender Wage Discrimination? A Meta-Regression Analysis, in: Journal of Human Resources, 39(3): 828-38.
Stevenson, B., Wolfers, J. (2009). The Paradox of Declining Female Happiness, in: American Economic Journal: Economic Policy, 1(2): 190-225.

2. Bibliography Sections II-VI

Abowd, J. M., Kramarz, F., Margolis, D. N. (1999). High Wage Workers and High Wage Firms, in: Econometrica, 67: 251-333.
Abowd, J., Kramarz, F. (1999). Econometric Analyses of Linked Employer-Employee Data, in: Labour Economics, 6: 53–74.
Abowd, J., Kramarz, F., Lemieux, T. et al. (1995). Minimum Wages and Youth Unemployment in France and the US, paper presented at the NBER Summer Institute, Cambridge, MA.
Acemoglu, D. (2003). Cross-Country Inequality Trends, in: Economic Journal, 113: F121–F149.
Aguiar, M., Hurst, E. (2006). Measuring Trends in Leisure: The Allocation of Time over Five Decades, NBER Working Paper No. 12082.
Akhabbar, A. (2001). Anne P. Carter: A Biographical Presentation, in: Dimand, R. W., Dimand, M. A., Forget, E. L. (Eds.), A Biographical Dictionary of Women Economists, Cheltenham, UK and Northampton, MA: Edward Elgar Publishing, available at http://mpra.ub.uni-muenchen.de/30209/.
Aigner, D. J., Cain, G. G. (1977). Statistical Theories of Discrimination in Labor Markets, in: Industrial and Labor Relations Review, 30(2): 175–87.
Albrecht, J., Björklund, A., Vroman, S. (2003). Is There a Glass Ceiling in Sweden?, in: Journal of Labor Economics, 21(1): 145–77.
Alexis, M. (1971). Some Negro-White Differences in Consumption, in: Joyce, G., Govoni, N. A. P. (Eds.), The Black Consumer, New York: Random House: 257-74.
Altonji, J. G., Doraszelski, U. (2005). The Role of Permanent Income and Demographics in Black/White Differences in Wealth, in: Journal of Human Resources, 40(1): 1-30.
Angrist, J. D. (1991). Grouped-Data Estimation and Testing in Simple Labor-Supply Models, in: Journal of Econometrics, 47: 243–66.
Angrist, J. D., Evans, W. N. (1998). Children and Their Parents' Labor Supply: Evidence from Exogenous Variation in Family Size, in: American Economic Review, 88: 450–77.
Anker, R. (1998). Gender and Jobs: Sex Segregation of Occupations in the World, Geneva: International Labour Organization.
Antecol, H. (2000). An Examination of Cross-Country Differences in the Gender Gap in Labor Force Participation Rates, in: Labour Economics, 7(4): 409–26.

References

Arrow, K. (1973). The Theory of Discrimination, in: Ashenfelter, O., Rees, A. (Eds.), Discrimination in Labor Markets, Princeton, NJ: Princeton University Press.

Ashenfelter, O., Heckman, J. J. (1974). The Estimation of Income and Substitution Effects in a Model of Family Labor Supply, in: Econometrica, 42: 73–85.

Ashenfelter, O., Johnson, G. E. (1972). Unionism, Relative Wages, and Labor Quality in U.S. Manufacturing Industries, in: International Economic Review, 13: 488-509.

Autor, D. H., Katz, L. F., Kearney, M. S. (2005a). Trends in U.S. Wage Inequality: Re-assessing the Revisionists, NBER Working Paper No. 11627.

Autor, D. H., Katz, L. F., Kearney, M. S. (2005b). Rising Wage Inequality: The Role of Composition and Prices, NBER Working Paper No. 11628.

Autor, D. H., Katz, L. F., Krueger, A. B. (1998). Computing Inequality: Have Computers Changed the Labor Market?, in: Quarterly Journal of Economics, 113(4): 1169–213.

Autor, D. H., Levy, F., Murnane, R. J. (2003). The Skill Content of Recent Technological Change: An Empirical Exploration, in: Quarterly Journal of Economics, 118(4): 1279–333.

Bachman, R. (1994). Violence Against Women. A National Crime Victimization Survey Report, U.S. Department of Justice.

Bachman, R., Saltzman, L. E. (1995). Violence Against Women: Estimates from the Redesigned Survey, Washington, DC: U.S. Department of Justice.

Baker, D., Boushey, H. (2004). Plunging Employment: Blame Mom?, Washington, DC: Center for Economic and Policy Research.

Baker, M., Benjamin, D. (1997). The Role of the Family in Immigrants' Labor-Market Activity: An Evaluation of Alternative Explanations, in: American Economic Review, 87(4): 705–27.

Barro, R. J., Lee, J.-W. (1994). Sources of Economic Growth, in: Carnegie-Rochester Conference Series on Public Policy, 40: 1–46.

Barron, J. M., Black, D. A., Loewenstein, M. A. (1993). Gender Differences in Training, Capital, and Wages, in: Journal of Human Resources, 28(2): 342–64.

Barth, E., Zweimüller, J. (1992). Labour Market Institutions and the Industry Wage Distribution: Evidence from Austria, Norway, and the U.S, in: Empirica – Austrian Economic Papers , 19(2): 181–201.

Bartlett, R., Ziegert, A. (2000). Creating Career Opportunities for Female Economists: CCOFFE, National Science Foundation Final Project Report 1997–1999, Economics Program, Division of Social, Behavioral, and Economic Research and Information Dissemination Activities and Women and Girls, Division of Human Resource Development, HRD-9710136.

Bayard, K., Hellerstein, J., Neumark, D. et al. (1999). New Evidence on Sex Segregation and Sex Difference in Wages from Matched Employee-Employer Data, NBER Working Paper No. 7003.

Bayard, K., Hellerstein, J., Neumark, D. et al. (2003). New Evidence on Sex Segregation and Sex Differences in Wages from Matched Employee-Employer Data, in: Journal of Labor Economics, 21(4): 887–922.

Becker, G. S. (1957). The Economics of Discrimination. Chicago, IL: University of Chicago Press.

Becker, G.S. (1964). A Theory of the Allocation of Time, in: Economic Journal, 75: 493-517.

Becker, G. S. (1971). The Economics of Discrimination, 2nd ed., Chicago, IL: University of Chicago Press.

Becker, G. S. (1985). Human Capital, Effort, and the Sexual Division of Labor, in: Journal of Labor Economics, 3(1): S33–S58.

Becker, G. S. (1991). A Treatise on the Family, enlarged ed., Cambridge, MA: Harvard University Press.

Beller, A. H. (1978). The Economics of Enforcement of an Antidiscrimination Law: Title VII of the Civil Rights Act of 1964, in: Journal of Law and Economics, 21: 359-80.

Beller, A. H. (1982a). The Impact of Equal Opportunity Policy on Sex Differentials in Earnings and Occupations, in: American Economic Review, 72(2): 171-5.

Beller, A. H. (1982b). Occupational Segregation by Sex: Determinants and Changes, in: Journal of Human Resources, 17(3): 371-92.

Beller, A. H. (1985). Changes in the Sex Composition of U.S. Occupations, 1960-81, in: Journal of Human Resources, 20(2): 235-50.

Bergmann, B. R. (1974). Occupational Segregation, Wages and Profits When Employers Discriminate by Race or Sex, in: Eastern Economic Journal, 1(2): 103-10.

Berman, E., Bound, J., Griliches, Z. (1994). Changes in the Demand for Skilled Labor within U.S. Manufacturing Industries: Evidence from the Annual Survey of Manufactures, in: Quarterly Journal of Economics, 109(2): 367–97.

Bernhardt, A., Morris, M., Handcock, M. (1995). Women's Gains or Men's Losses? A Closer Look at the Shrinking Gender Gap in Earnings, in: American Journal of Sociology, 101(2): 302-328.

Bertola, G., Blau, F. D., Kahn, L. M. (2007). Labor Market Institutions and Demographic Employment Patterns, in: Journal of Population Economics, 20(4): 833-867.

Bertrand, M., Chugh, D., Mullainathan, S. (2005). Implicit Discrimination, in: American Economic Review, 95(2): 94-8.

Bianchi, S. M., Rytina, N. (1986). The Decline of Occupational Sex Segregation during the 1970s: Census and CPS Comparisons, in: Demography, 23: 79-86.

Birnbaum, H., Weston, R. (1974). Home Ownership and the Wealth Position of Black and White Americans, in: Review of Income and Wealth, 20:103-18.

Bjorklund, A., Freeman, R. B. (1994). Generating Equality and Eliminating Poverty, the Swedish Way, NBER Working Paper No. 4945.

Blackburn, M. L., Bloom, D. E. (1994). Changes in the Structure of Family Income Inequality in the U.S. and Other Industrialized Nations during the 1980s, NBER Working Paper No. 4754.

Blanchard, O., Wolfers, J. (2000). The Role of Shocks and Institutions in the Rise of European Unemployment: The Aggregate Evidence, in: Economic Journal, 110: C1–C33.

Blanchflower, D., Freeman, R. (1992). Unionism in the US and Other Advanced OECD Countries, in: Industrial Relations, 31: 56-79.

Blank, R. (1993). Why Were Poverty Rates So High in the 1980s?, in: Papadimitriou, D. B., Wolff, E. N. (Eds.), Poverty and Prosperity in the USA in the Late Twentieth Century, London: Macmillan.

Blank, R. (1995). Teen Pregnancy: Government Programs Are not the Cause, in: Feminist Economics, 1(2): 47–58.

Blank, R. M. (2000). Distinguished Lecture on Economics in Government - Fighting Poverty: Lessons from Recent U.S. History, in: Journal of Economic Perspectives, 14(2): 3–19.

Blau, F. D. (1977). Equal Pay in the Office. Lexington, MA: Lexington Books, D.C. Heath.

Blau, F. D. (1980). Immigration and Labor Earnings in Early Twentieth Century America, in: Simon, J. L., DaVanzo, J. (Eds.), Research in Population Economics 2: 21-41.

Blau, F. D. (1984). Occupational Segregation and Labor Market Discrimination, in: Reskin, B. F. (Ed.), Sex Segregation in the Workplace: Trends, Explanations, Remedies, Washington, DC: National Academy Press: 117-43.

Blau, F. D. (1986). The Economics of Women, Men and Work, Englewood Cliffs, NJ: Prentice-Hall.

Blau, F. D. (1992). The Fertility of Immigrant Women: Evidence from High-Fertility Source Countries, in: Borjas, G. J., Freeman, R. B. (Eds.), Immigration and the Work Force: Economic Consequences for the United States and Source Areas, Chicago, IL: University of Chicago Press: 93–133.

Blau, F. D. (1998). Trends in the Well-Being of American Women, 1970–1995, in: Journal of Economic Literature, 36(1): 112–65. [Chapter 7 in this volume]

Blau, F. D., Beller, A. H. (1988). Trends in Earnings Differentials by Gender 1971-1981, in: Industrial and Labor Relations Review, 41(4): 513-29.

Blau, F. D., Brummund, P., Liu, A. Y.-H. (forthcoming). Occupational Segregation by Gender 1970-2009: Adjusting for the Impact of Changes in the Occupational Coding System, in Demography.

Blau, F. D., Ehrenberg, R. G. (Eds.) (1997). Gender and Family Issues in the Workplace, New York: Russell Sage Foundation.

References

Blau, F. D., Ferber, M. A. (1987). Women's Progress in the Labor Market: Should We Rest on Our Laurels? Proceedings of the Thirty-Ninth Annual Meetings, Madison, WI: Industrial Relations Research Association: 70-6.

Blau, F. D., Ferber, M. A. (1991). Career Plans and Expectations of Young Women and Men, in: Journal of Human Resources, 26(4): 581–607.

Blau, F. D., Ferber, M. A. (1992). The Economics of Women, Men and Work, 2nd ed., Englewood Cliffs, NJ: Prentice-Hall.

Blau, F. D., Ferber, M. A., Winkler, A. E. (1998). The Economics of Women, Men and Work, 3rd ed., Englewood Cliffs, NJ: Prentice-Hall.

Blau, F. D., Ferber, M. A., Winkler, A. E. (2002). The Economics of Women, Men, and Work, 4th ed., Englewood Cliffs, NJ: Prentice Hall.

Blau, F. D., Ferber, M. A., Winkler, A. E. (2006). The Economics of Women, Men and Work, 5th ed., Englewood Cliffs, NJ: Prentice Hall.

Blau, F. D., Ferber, M., Winkler, A. E. (2010). The Economics of Women, Men and Work, 6th ed., Upper Saddle River, NJ: Prentice-Hall.

Blau, F. D., Hendricks, W. E. (1979). Occupational Segregation by Sex: Trends and Prospects, in: Journal of Human Resources, 14(2): 197–210.

Blau, F. D., Jusenius, C. L. (1976). Economists' Approaches to Sex Segregation in the Labor Market: An Appraisal, in: Signs, 1: 181-200.

Blau, F. D., Kahn, L. M. (1992). The Gender Earnings Gap: Learning from International Comparisons, in: American Economic Review, 82: 533–8.

Blau, F. D., Kahn, L. M. (1994a). International Differences in Male Wage Inequality: Institutions versus Market Forces, NBER Working Paper No. 4678.

Blau, F. D., Kahn, L. M. (1994b). Rising Wage Inequality and the US Gender Gap, in: American Economic Review, 84: 23-8.

Blau, F. D., Kahn, L. M. (1995). The Gender Earnings Gap: Some International Evidence, in Freeman, R., Katz, L. (Eds.), Differences and Changes in Wage Structures, Chicago, IL: University of Chicago Press (for NBER): 105–43.

Blau, F. D., Kahn, L. M. (1996a). International Differences in Male Wage Inequality: Institutions versus Market Forces, in: Journal of Political Economy, 104: 791–837. [Chapter 5 in this volume]

Blau, F. D., Kahn, L. M. (1996b). Wage Structure and Gender Earnings Differentials: An International Comparison, in: Economica, 63(250, suppl.): S29–62. [Chapter 3 in this volume]

Blau, F. D., Kahn, L. M. (1997). Swimming Upstream: Trends in the Gender Wage Differential in the 1980s, in: Journal of Labor Economics, 15(1): 1–42.

Blau, F. D., Kahn, L. M. (1999). Institutions and Laws in the Labor Market, in: Ashenfelter, O., Card, D. (Eds.), Handbook of Labor Economics, Vol. 3a, Amsterdam: North-Holland: 1399–461.

Blau, F. D., Kahn, L. M. (2000a). Gender and Youth Employment Outcomes: A Comparison of the US and West Germany: 1984–91, in: Blanchflower, D. G., Freeman, R. B. (Eds.), Youth Employment and Joblessness in Advanced Countries, Chicago, IL: University of Chicago Press: 107–67.

Blau, F. D., Kahn, L. M. (2000b). Gender Differences in Pay, in: Journal of Economic Perspectives, 4: 75-99.

Blau, F. D., Kahn, L. M. (2001). Understanding International Differences in the Gender Pay Gap, NBER Working Paper No. 8200.

Blau, F. D., Kahn, L. M. (2004). The U.S. Gender Pay Gap in the 1990s: Slowing Convergence, NBER Working Paper No. 10853.

Blau, F. D., Kahn, L. M. (2005a). Changes in the Labor Supply of Married Women: 1980–2000, NBER Working Paper No. 11230.

Blau, F. D., Kahn, L. M. (2005b). Do Cognitive Test Scores Explain Higher US Wage Inequality?, in: Review of Economics and Statistics, 87(1): 184-193.

Blau, F. D., Kahn, L. M. (2006). The US Gender Pay Gap in the 1990s: Slowing Convergence, in: Industrial and Labor Relations Review, 60: 45–66.

Blau, F. D., Kahn, L. M. (2007). Changes in the Labor Supply Behavior of Married Women: 1980–2000, in: Journal of Labor Economics, 25(3): 393–438. [Chapter 6 in this volume]

Blau, F. D., Kahn, L. M. (2008). Women's Work and Wages, in: Durlauf, S., Blume, L. (Eds.), The New Palgrave Dictionary of Economics, Vol. 8, New York: Palgrave Macmillan: 762-772.

Blau, F. D., Kahn, L. M., Liu, A. Y.-H. et al. (2008). The Transmission of Women's Fertility, Human Capital, and Work Orientation across Immigrant Generations, NBER Working Paper No. 14388.

Blau, F. D., Kahn, L. M., Moriarty, J. et al. (2003). The Role of the Family in Immigrants' Labor-Market Activity: An Evaluation of Alternative Explanations: Comment, in: American Economic Review, 93(1): 429–47.

Blau, F. D., Kahn, L. M., Papps, K. L. (2011). Gender, Source Country Characteristics and Labor Market Assimilation among Immigrants: 1980–2000, in: Review of Economics and Statistics, 93(1): 43-58. [Chapter 12 in this volume]

Blau, F. D., Simpson, P., Anderson, D. (1997). Continuing Progress? Trends in Occupational Segregation Over the 1970s and 1980s, Cornell University.

Bleakley, H., Chin, A. (2004). Language Skills and Earnings: Evidence from Childhood Immigrants, in: Review of Economics and Statistics, 86(2): 481–96.

Blinder, A. S. (1973). Wage Discrimination: Reduced Form and Structural Estimates, in: Journal of Human Resources, 8(4): 436-55.

Blundell, R., Duncan, A., Meghir, C. (1998). Estimating Labor Supply Responses Using Tax Reforms, in: Econometrica, 66: 827–61.

Blundell, R., MaCurdy, T. (1999). Labor Supply: A Review of Alternative Approaches, in: Ashenfelter, O., Card, D. (Eds.), Handbook of Labor Economics, Vol. 3a, Amsterdam: Elsevier: 1559-695.

Blyth, C. A. (1979). The Interaction between Collective Bargaining and Government Policies in Selected Member Countries, in: Collective Bargaining and Government Policies, Paris: OECD: 59-94.

Blyth, C. A. (1987). The Interaction between Collective Bargaining and Government Policies in Selected Member Countries, in: Collective Bargaining and Government Policies, Paris: OECD.

Boeri, T. (2000). Social Europe: Dramatic Visions and Real Complexity, Discussion Paper No. 2371, London: Centre for Economic Policy Research.

Borghans, L., Weel, B., Weinberg, B. A. (2005). People: Social Capital and the Labor-Market Outcomes of Underrepresented Groups, IZA Discussion Paper No. 1494, Bonn, Germany.

Borjas, G. J. (1985). Assimilation, Changes in Cohort Quality, and the Earnings of Immigrants, in: Journal of Labor Economics, 3(4): 463–89.

Borjas, G. J. (1995). Assimilation and Changes in Cohort Quality Revisited: What Happened to Immigrant Earnings in the 1980s?, in: Journal of Labor Economics, 13(2): 201–45.

Borjas, G. J. (2003). The Labor Demand Curve is Downward Sloping: Reexamining the Impact of Immigration on the Labor Market, in: Quarterly Journal of Economics, 118: 1335–74.

Borjas, G. J., Hilton, L. (1996). Immigration and the Welfare State: Immigrant Participation in Means-Tested Entitlement Programs, in: Quarterly Journal of Economics, 111(2): 575-604.

Bound, J., Johnson, G. (1992). Changes in the Structure of Wages in the 1980's: An Evaluation of Alternative Explanations, in: American Economic Review, 82: 371–92.

Brainard, W., Tobin, J. (1968). Pitfalls in Financial Model Building, in: American Economic Review, 58: 99-122.

Brainerd, E. (2000). Women in Transition: Changes in Gender Wage Differentials in Eastern Europe and the Former Soviet Union, in: Industrial and Labor Relations Review, 54: 138–62.

Brown, C. (1984). Black-White Earnings Ratios Since the Civil Rights Act of 1964: The Importance of Labor Market Dropouts, in: Quarterly Journal of Economics, 99: 31-44.

Brown, C., Corcoran, M. (1997). Sex-Based Differences in School Content and the Male/Female Wage Gap, in: Journal of Labor Economics, 15(3): 431–65.

Bruno, M., Sachs, J. D.(1985). The Economics of Worldwide Stagflation, Oxford: Basil Blackwell.

References

Buckley, J. E. (1971). Pay Differences Between Men and Women in the Same Job, in: Monthly Labor Review, 94: 36-9.

Bumpass, L. L., Sweet, J. A. (1989). National Estimates of Cohabitation, in: Demography, 26(4): 615–25.

Butler, R., Heckman, J. J. (1977). The Government's Impact on the Labor Market Status of Black Americans: A Critical Review, in: Hausman, L. J. et al. (Eds.), Equal Rights and Industrial Relations, Madison, WI: Industrial Relations Research Association: 235-81.

Calmfors, L., Driffill, J. (1988). Centralization of Wage Bargaining, in: Economic Policy, 6: 14-61.

Cameron, D. R. (1984). Social Democracy, Corporatism, Labour Quiescence and the Representation of Economic Interest in Advanced Capitalist Society, in: Goldthorpe, J. H. (Ed.), Order and Conflict in Contemporary Capitalism, Oxford: Clarendon Press: 143-78.

Cancian, M., Danziger, S., Gottschalk, P. (1993). Working Wives and Family Income Inequality Among Married Couples, in: Danziger,S., Gottschalk, P. (Eds.), Uneven Tides: Rising Inequality in America, New York: Russell Sage Foundation: 195–221.

Caplow, T. (1954). The Sociology of Work (Minnesota Archive Editions), Minneapolis MN: University of Minnesota Press.

Card, D. E., Kramarz, F., Lemieux, T. (1994). Changes in the Relative Structure of Wages and Employment: A Comparison of the United States, Canada, and France, Manuscript, Princeton, NJ: Princeton University Press.

Card, D. E., Krueger, A. B. (1995). Myth and Measurement: The New Economics of the Minimum Wage, Princeton, NJ: Princeton University Press.

Card, D., DiNardo, J. E. (2002). Skill-Biased Technological Change and Rising Wage Inequality: Some Problems and Puzzles, in: Journal of Labor Economics, 20: 733–83.

Card, D., Krueger, A. B. (1995). Myth and Measurement: The New Economics of the Minimum Wage, Princeton, NJ: Princeton University Press.

Card, D., Lemieux, T. (2001). Can Relative Supply Explain the Rising Return to College for Younger Men? A Cohort-Based Analysis, in: Quarterly Journal of Economics, 116(2): 705–46.

Carrington, W. J., Troske, K. R. (1995). Gender Segregation in Small Firms, Journal of Human Resources, 30(3): 503-33.

Carrington, W. J., Troske, K. R. (1998). Sex Segregation in U.S. Manufacturing, in: Industrial and Labor Relations Review, 51(3): 445-64.

Carrington, W. J., McCue, K., Pierce, B. (2000). Using Establishment Size to Measure the Impact of Title VII and Affirmative Action, in: Journal of Human Resources, 35: 503–23.

Casper, L. M., Cohen, P. N. (2000). How Does POSSLQ Measure up? Historical Estimates of Cohabitation, in: Demography, 37: 237–45.

Chamberlain, G. (1991). Quantile Regression, Censoring, and the Structure of Wages, Harvard Institute of Economic Research Working Paper No. 1558.

Chiswick, B. R. (1977). Sons of Immigrants: Are They at an Earnings Disadvantage?, in: American Economic Review, 67(1): 376-80.

Chiswick, B. R. (1978). The Effect of Americanization on the Earnings of Foreign-Born Men, in: Journal of Political Economy, 86(5): 897–921.

Chiswick, B. R. (1982). The Employment of Immigrants in the United States, Washington, D.C.: American Enterprise Institute.

Cobb-Clark, D., Crossley, T. F. (2004). Revisiting the Family Investment Hypothesis, in: Labour Economics, 11(3): 373–93.

Coleman, M. T., Pencavel, J. (1993a). Changes in Work Hours of Male Employees, 1940–1988, in: Industrial and Labor Relations Review, 46(2): 262–83.

Coleman, M. T., Pencavel, J. (1993b). Trends in Market Work Behavior of Women Since 1940, in: Industrial and Labor Relations Review, 46(4): 653–76.

College Board (1996). College Board Reports Continuing Upward Trend in Average Scores on SAT 1, Press Release, Aug. 22, 1996.

Cotton, J. (1989). Opening the Gap, in: Social Science Quarterly, 70: 803-19.

Cutler, D. M., Katz, L. F. (1991). Macroeconomic Performance and the Disadvantaged, Brookings Papers Economic Activity, 2: 1-61.

Darity Jr., W. A. (1980). Illusions of Black Economic Progress, in: The Review of Black Political Economy, 11: 153-68.

Darity Jr., W. A., , Myers Jr., S. L. (1995). Family Structure and the Marginalization of Black Men: Policy Implications, in: Tucker, M. B., Mitchell-Dernan, C. (Eds.), The Decline in Marriage Among African Americans, New York: Russell Sage Foundation: 263–308.

Datta Gupta, N., Oaxaca, R. L., Smith, N. (2006). Swimming Upstream, Floating Downstream: Comparing Women's Relative Wage Progress in the United States and Denmark, in: Industrial and Labor Relations Review, 59(2): 243–66.

Davies, R. J. (1983). Incomes and anti-inflation policy, in: Bain, G. S. (Ed.), Industrial Relations in Britain, Oxford: Basil Blackwell: 419-55.

Davis, S. J. (1992). Cross-Country Patterns of Change in Relative Wages, NBER Working Paper No. 4085.

Davis, S. J., Haltiwanger, J. (1991). Wage Dispersion between and within U.S. Manufacturing Plants, 1963-86, Brookings Papers Economic Activity: Microeconomics: 115-80.

Deaton, D. R., Beaumont, P. B. (1980). The Determinants of Bargaining Structure: Some Large Scale Survey Evidence for Britain, in: British Journal of Industrial Relations, 18: 202-16.

Devereux, P. J. (2004). Changes in Relative Wages and Family Labor Supply, in: Journal of Human Resources, 39: 696–722.

Devine, T. J. (1994a). Characteristics of Self-Employed Women in the United States, in: Monthly Labor Review, 117(3): 20–34.

Devine, T. J. (1994b). Changes in Wage-and-Salary Returns to Skill and the Recent Rise in Female Self-Employment, in: American Economic Review, 84(2): 108–13.

DiNardo, J., Fortin, N. M., Lemieux, T. (1996). Labor Market Institutions and the Distribution of Wages, 1973–1992: A Semiparametric Approach, in: Econometrica, 64(5): 1001–44.

Doeringer, P. B., Piore, M. J. (1971). Internal Labor Markets and Manpower Analysis, Lexington, MA: D.C. Heath.

Dolado, J., Kramarz, F., Machin, S. et al. (1996). The Economic Impact of Minimum Wages in Europe, Economic Policy, 23: 319–72.

Douglas, P. H. (1919). Is the New Immigration More Unskilled than the Old?, in: Publications of the American Statistical Association, 16(126): 393-403.

Duncan, O. D., Duncan, B. (1955). A Methodological Analysis of Segregation Indexes, in: American Sociological Review, 20: 210-7.

Echeverri-Carroll, E., Ayala, S. G. (2006). High Technology Agglomeration and Gender Inequalities, paper presented at the American Economic Association Meetings, Boston, MA.

Edgeworth, F. Y. (1922). Equal Pay to Men and Women for Equal Work, in: Economic Journal, 32: 431-57.

Edin, P.-A., Holmlund, B. (1995). The Swedish Wage Structure: The Rise and Fall of Solidarity Wage Policy?, in: Freeman, R. B., Katz, L. F. (Eds.), Differences and Changes in Wage Structures, Chicago, IL: University of Chicago Press (for NBER).

Edin, P.-A., Richardson, K. (2002). Swimming with the Tide: Solidarity Wage Policy and the Gender Earnings Gap, in: Scandinavian Journal of Economics, 104: 49–67.

Edin, P.-A., Topel, R. H. (1994). Wage Policy and Restructuring: The Swedish Labor Market since 1960, in: Freeman, R. B., Topel, R., Swedenborg, B. (Eds.), The Welfare State in Transition: Reforming the Swedish Model, Cambridge, MA: NBER: 155-202.

Edin, P.-A., Zetterberg, J. (1992). Interindustry Wage Differentials: Evidence from Sweden and a Comparison with the United States, in: American Economic Review, 82: 1341–9.

Ehrenberg, R. G. (1989). Commentary, in: Michael, R. T., Hartmann, H. I., O'Farrell, B. (Eds.), Pay Equity: Empirical Inquiries, Washington, DC: National Academy Press: 243-6.

Eirr (1992). Minimum Pay in 18 Countries, in: European Industrial Relations Review, 255, 14-21.

References

Eissa, N., Hoynes, H. W. (2004). Taxes and the Labor Market Participation of Married Couples: The Earned Income Tax Credit, in: Journal of Public Economics, 88: 1931–58.

England, P. (1982). The Failure of the Human Capital Theory to Explain Occupational Sex Segregation, in: Journal of Human Resources, 17(3): 358–70.

England, P., Farkas, G. (1986). Households, Employment, and Gender: A Social, Economic, and Demographic View, Hawthorne, NY: Aldine de Gruyter.

Erickson, C. L., Ichino, A. C. (1995). Wage Differentials in Italy: Market Forces, Institutions, and Inflation, in: Freman, R. B., Katz, L. F. (Eds.), Differences and Changes in Wage Structures, Chicago, IL: University of Chicago Press (for NBER): 265-305.

European Industrial Relations Review (1992). "Italy", No. 223: 9-10.

Fairlie, R. W., Meyer, B. D. (1996). Ethnic and Racial Self-Employment Differences and Possible Explanations, in: Journal of Human Resources, 31(4): 757–93.

Farber, H. S. (1995). Are Lifetime Jobs Disappearing? Job Duration in the United States: 1973–1993, NBER Working Paper No. 5014.

Farber, H. S. (2005). Nonunion Wage Rates and the Threat of Unionization, in: Industrial and Labor Relations Review, 58(3): 335–52.

Fawcett, M. G. (1918). Equal Pay for Equal Work, in: Economic Journal, 28: 1-6.

Ferber, M A., Nelson, J. A. (Eds.) (1993). Beyond Economic Man, Chicago, IL: University of Chicago Press.

Fernández, R. (2008). Culture and Economics, in: Durlauf, S. N., Blume, L. E. (Eds.), The New Palgrave Dictionary of Economics, 2nd ed., New York: Palgrave Macmillan: 333–40.

Fernández, R., Fogli, A. (2009). Culture: An Empirical Investigation of Beliefs, Work, and Fertility, in: American Economic Journal: Macroeconomics, 1(1): 146–77.

Fernández, R., Fogli, A., Olivetti, C. (2004). Mothers and Sons: Preference Formation and Female Labor Force Dynamics, in: Quarterly Journal of Economics, 119(4): 1249–99.

Filer, R. K., Hamermesh, D. S., Rees, A. E. (1996). The Economics of Work and Pay, 6th ed., New York: Harper-Collins.

Fiske, Susan T. (1998). Stereotyping, Prejudice, and Discrimination, in: Gilbert, D. T., Fiske, S. T., Lindzey, G. (Eds.), The Handbook of Social Psychology, 4th ed., New York: Oxford University Press USA, Volume 2: 357-411.

Flanagan, R. J., Kahn, L. M., Smith, R. S. et al. (1989). Economics of the Employment Relationship. Glenview, III.: Scott, Foresman.

Fortin, N. M. (2006). Greed, Altruism, and the Gender Wage Gap, University of British Columbia, http://www.econ.ubc.ca/nfortin/Fortinat8.pdf.

Fortin, N. M., Lemieux, T. (1998). Rank Regressions, Wage Distributions, and the Gender Gap, in: Journal of Human Resources, 33: 610–43.

Fortin, N. M., Lemieux, T. (2000). Are Women's Gains Men's Losses? A Distributional Test, in: American Economic Review, 90: 456–60.

Freeman, R. B. (1973). Changes in the Labor Market for Black Americans, 1948-1972, in: Brookings Papers on Economic Activity, 1: 67-131.

Freeman, R. B. (1980). Black Economic Progress Post-1964: Who Gained and Why?, in: Rosen, S. (Ed.), Studies in Labor Markets, Chicago, IL: University of Chicago Press: 247–94.

Freeman, R. B. (1980). Unionism and the Dispersion of Wages, in: Industrial and Labor Relations Review, 34: 3-23.

Freeman, R. B. (1982). Union Wage Practices and Wage Dispersion within Establishments, in: Industrial and Labor Relations Review, 36: 3-21.

Freeman, R. B. (1988). Labour Markets, in: Economic Policy, 3: 63–80.

Freeman, R. B., Katz, L. F. (Eds.) (1995). Differences and Changes in Wages in Wage Structures, Chicago, IL: University of Chicago Press.

Freeman, R. B., Medoff, J. L. (1984). What Do Unions Do?, New York, NY: Basic Books.

Friedberg, L. (2003). The Impact of Technological Change on Older Workers: Evidence from Data on Computer Use, in: Industrial and Labor Relations Review, 56(3): 511–29.

Friedberg, R. M. (1993). Immigration and the Labor Market, Cambridge, MA: MIT (doctoral dissertation).

Friedman, M. (1957). A Theory of the Consumption Function, Princeton, NJ: Princeton University Press.

Fuchs, V. R. (1968). The Service Economy, New York: National Bureau of Economic Research.
Fuchs, V. R. (1971). Differences in Hourly Earnings Between Men and Women, in: Monthly Labor Review, 94: 9-15.
Fuchs, V. R. (1986). His and Hers: Gender Differences in Work and Income, 1959–1979, in: Journal of Labor Economics, 4(3, pt. 2): S245–72.
Fuchs, V. R. (1988). Women's Quest for Economic Equality, Cambridge, MA: Harvard University Press.
Galenson, M. (1982). Do Blacks Save More?, in: American Economic Review, 42: 211-16.
Geronimus, A. T., Korenman, S. (1992). The Socioeconomic Consequences of Teen Childbearing Reconsidered, in: Quarterly Journal of Economics, 107(4): 1187–214.
Ginther, D. K., Kahn, S. (2004). Women in Economics: Moving Up or Falling off the Academic Career Ladder?, in: Journal of Economic Perspectives, 18(3): 193–214.
Goldin, C. D. (1990). Understanding the Gender Gap: An Economic History of American Women, New York: Oxford University Press.
Goldin, C. D. (1997). Career and Family: College Women Look to the Past, in: Blau, F. D., Ehrenberg, R. G. (Eds.), Gender and Family Issues in the Workplace, New York: Russell Sage Foundation: 20–58.
Goldin, C. D. (2006). The Quiet Revolution That Transformed Women's Employment, Education, and Family, Ely Lecture delivered January 6, 2006, at the American Economic Association meetings, Boston; also NBER Working Paper No. 11953.
Gornick, J. C., Meyers, M. K., Ross, K. E. (1997). Supporting the Employment of Mothers: Policy Variation across Fourteen Welfare States, in: Journal of European Social Policy, 7: 45–70.
Gottschalk, P., Joyce, M. (1991). Changes in Earnings Inequality: An International Perspective, Manuscript, Boston: Boston Coll.
Gottschalk, P., Smeeding, T. M. (1997). Cross-National Comparisons of Earnings and Income Inequality, in: Journal of Economic Literature, 35(2): 633–87.
Gould IV, W. B. (1993). Agenda for Reform: The Future of Employment Relationships and the Law. Cambridge, MA: MIT Press.
Gregory, M. B. (2009). Gender and Economic Inequality, in: Salverda, W., Nolan, B., Smeeding, T. M. (Eds.), Oxford Handbook on Economic Inequality, Oxford: Oxford University Press: 284-312.
Gregory, R. G., Daly, A. E. (1991). Can Economic Theory Explain Why Australian Women Are So Well Paid Relative to Their U.S. Counterparts?, in: Willborn, S. L. (Ed.), Women's Wages: Stability and Changes in Six Industrialized Countries, Greenwich, CT: JAI Press: 284-312 .
Gronau, R. (1974). Wage Comparisons-a Selectivity Bias, in: Journal of Political Economy, 82(6): 1119-43.
Groshen, E. L. (1991). The Structure of the Female/ Male Wage Differential: Is It Who You Are, What You Do, or Where You Work?, in: Journal of Human Resources, 26(3): 457–72.
Gross, E. (1968). Plus ça Change ... ? The Sexual Structure of Occupations Over Time, in: Social Problems, 16: 198-208.
Guiso, L., Monte, F., Sapienza, P. et al. (2008). Education Forum: Culture, Gender, and Math, in: Science, 320: 1164-1165.
Gunderson, M. (1989). Male-Female Wage Differentials and Policy Responses, in: Journal of Economic Literature, 27(1): 46–72.
Gunderson, M., Robb, R. (1991). Equal Pay for Work of Equal Value: Canada's Experience, in: Sockell, D., Lewin, D., Lipsky, D. (Eds.), Advances in Industrial and Labor Relations, Vol. 5, Greenwich, CT: JAI Press: 151–68.
Haavio-Mannila, E., Kauppinen, K. (1992). Women's Lives and Women's Work in the Nordic Countries, in: Kahne, H., Giele, J. (Eds.), Women's Lives and Women's Work in Modernizing and Industrial Countries, Boulder, CO: Westview Press: 224-47.
Hamermesh, D. S. (1971). White-Collar Unions, Blue-Collar Unions, and Wages in Manufacturing, in: Industrial and Labor Relations Review, 24: 159-70.
Hamermesh, D. S. (1978). Entitlement Effects, Unemployment Insurance and Employment Decisions, in: Economic Inquiry, 86(5): 89-121.

References

Hamermesh, D. S. (1982). Social Insurance and Consumption, in: American Economic Review, 72: 101-13.

Hamermesh, D. S. (1993). Labor Demand, Princeton, NJ: Princeton University Press.

Hamermesh, D. S. (2000). The Craft of Labormetrics, in: Industrial and Labor Relations Review, 53: 363–80.

Handbook of Labor Statistics (1980). Bulletin 2070: 118.

Harlow, C. W. (1991). Female Victims of Violent Crime, Washington, DC: U.S. Department of Justice.

Heckman, J. J. (1979). Sample Selection Bias as a Specification Error, in: Econometrica, 47(1): 153–62.

Heckman, J. J. (1980). Sample Selection Bias as a Specification Error, in Smith, J. P. (Ed.), Female Labor Supply: Theory and Estimation, Princeton, NJ: Princeton University Press: 206–48.

Heckman, J. J. (1993). What Has Been Learned About Labor Supply in the Past Twenty Years?, in: American Economic Review, 83: 116–21.

Heim, B. T. (2007). The Incredible Shrinking Elasticities: Married Female Labor Supply, 1978–2002, in: Journal of Human Resources, 42(4): 881-918..

Hendricks, W. E., Kahn, L. M. (1982). The Determinants of Bargaining Structure in U.S. Manufacturing Industries, in: Industrial and Labor Relations Review, 35: 181-95.

Hersch, J., Stratton, L. S. (1994). Housework, Wages, and the Division of Housework Time for Employed Spouses, in: American Economic Review, 84(2): 120–5.

Hersch, J., Stratton, L. S. (1997). Housework, Fixed Effects, and Wages of Married Workers, in: Journal of Human Resources, 32(2): 285–307.

Hill, M. S. (1979). The Wage Effects of Marital Status and Children, in: Journal of Human Resources, 14(4): 579-94.

Hoffman, S. D., Duncan, G. J. (1995). The Effects of Incomes, Wages, and AFDC Benefits on Marital Disruption, in: Journal of Human Resources, 30(1): 19–41.

Hoffman, S. D., Foster, E. M., Furstenberg Jr., F. F. (1993). Reevaluating the Costs of Teenage Childbearing, in: Demography, 30(1): 1–13.

Horney, M. J., McElroy, M. B. (1981). Nash-Bargained Household Decisions: Toward a Generalization of the Theory of Demand, in: International Economic Review, 22(2): 333–49.

Hunt, J. (2002). The Transition in East Germany: When is a Ten Point Fall in the Gender Wage Gap Bad News?, in: Journal of Labor Economics, 20: 148–69.

Hyland, S. L. (1990). Helping Employees With Family Care, in: Monthly Labor Review, 113: 22-6.

International Labour Organization (ILO) (various issues). Yearbook of Labour Statistics, Geneva: ILO.

International Labour Organization (ILO) (1988). Work and Family: The Child Care Challenge, Conditions of Work Digest, 7(2), Geneva: ILO.

International Labour Organization (ILO) (1994). Maternity and Work, Conditions of Work Digest, 13, Geneva: ILO.

Jackman, M. R., Jackman, R. W. (1980). Racial Inequalities in Home Ownership, in: Social Forces, 58: 1221-34.

Jacobs, J. A. (1995). Gender and Academic Specialties: Trends Among Recipients of College Degrees in the 1980s, in: Sociology of Education, 68(2): 81–98.

Jacobsen, J. P. (1994). Trends in Workforce Sex Segregation, 1960–1990, in: Social Science Quarterly, 75(1): 204–11.

Jacobsen, J. P. (1998). The Economics of Gender, 2nd ed, Malden, MA: Blackwell.

Jacobsen, J. P. (2007). The Economics of Gender, 3rd ed., Malden, MA: Blackwell.

Jacobsen, J. P., Levin, L. M. (1995). Effects of Intermittent Labor Force Attachment on Women's Earnings, in: Monthly Labor Review, 118(9): 14–9.

Jaeger, D. A. (1997). Reconciling the Old and New Census Bureau Education Questions: Recommendations for Researchers, in: Journal of Business and Economic Statistics, 15(3): 300–9.

Johnson, G. E., Solon, G. (1986). Estimates of the Direct Effects of Comparable Worth Policy, in: American Economic Review, 76: 1117-25.

Johnson, W. R., Skinner, J. (1986). Labor Supply and Marital Separation, in: American Economic Review, 76(3): 455–69.

Juhn, C. (1992). Decline of Male Labor Market Participation: The Role of Declining Market Opportunities, in: Quarterly Journal of Economics, 107(1): 79–121.

Juhn, C., Kim, D. Il (1999). The Effects of Rising Female Labor Supply on MaleWages, in: Journal of Labor Economics, 17: 23–48.

Juhn, C., Murphy, K. M. (1997). Wage Inequality and Family Labor Supply, in: Journal of Labor Economics, 15 (1, pt. 1): 72–97.

Juhn, C., Murphy, K. M., Pierce, B. (1989). Accounting for the Slowdown in Black-White Wage Convergence, Chicago, IL: University of Chicago.

Juhn, C., Murphy, K. M., Pierce, B. (1991). Accounting for the Slowdown in Black-White Wage Convergence, in: Kosters, M. H. (Ed.), Workers and Their Wages: Changing Patterns in the United States, Washington, DC: AEI Press: 107–43.

Juhn, C., Murphy, K. M., Pierce, B. (1993). Wage Inequality and the Rise in Returns to Skill, in: Journal of Political Economy, 101(3): 410–42.

Juster, F. T., Stafford, F. P. (1991). The Allocation of Time: Empirical Findings, Behavioral Models, and Problems of Measurement, in: Journal of Economic Literature, 29(2): 471–522.

Kahn, L. B., (2010). The Long-Term Labor Market Consequences of Graduating from College in a Bad Economy, in: Labour Economics, 17(2): 303-16.

Kahn, L. M. (1998). Collective Bargaining and the Interindustry Wage Structure: International Evidence, in: Economica, 65: 507–34.

Kahn, L. M. (2000). Wage Inequality, Collective Bargaining and Relative Employment from 1985 to 1994: Evidence from Fifteen OECD Countries, in: Review of Economics and Statistics, 82(4): 564–79.

Kahn, L. M. (2012). Labor Market Policy: A Comparative View on the Costs and Benefits of Labor Market Flexibility, in: Journal of Policy Analysis and Management, 31(1): 94-110.

Kahn, L. M., Curme, M. (1987). Unions and Nonunion Wage Dispersion, in: Review of Economics and Statistics, 69: 600-7.

Kain, J. F., Quigley, J. M. (1972). Housing Market Discrimination, Home Ownership, and Savings Behavior, in: American Economic Review, 72: 263-77.

Kain, J. F., Quigley, J. M. (1975). Housing Markets and Racial Discrimination: A Microeconomic Analysis, New York: National Bureau of Economic Research, Columbia University Press.

Kalaitzidakis, P., Mamuneas, T. P., Stengos, T. (2003). Rankings of Academic Journals and Institutions in Economics, in: Journal of the European Economic Association, 1(6): 1346–66.

Karoly, L. A., Burtless, G. (1995). Demographic Change, Rising Earnings Inequality, and the Distribution of Personal Well-Being, 1959–1989, in: Demography, 32(3): 379–405.

Kassalow, E. M. (1967). White-Collar Unionism in the United States, in: Sturmthal, A. (Ed.), White Collar Trade Unions: Contemporary Developments in Industrial Societies, Urbana, IL: University of Illinois Press.

Katz, H. C. (1993). The Decentralization of Collective Bargaining: A Literature Review and Comparative Analysis, in: Industrial and Labor Relations Review, 47: 3–22.

Katz, L. F., Loveman, G. W., Blanchflower, D. (1995). A Comparison of Changes in the Structure of Wages in Four OECD Countries, in: Freeman, R., Katz, L. (Eds.), Differences and Changes in Wage Structures, Chicago, IL: University of Chicago Press (for NBER): 25–65.

Katz, L. F., Murphy, K. M. (1992). Changes in Relative Wages, 1963–87: Supply and Demand Factors, in: Quarterly Journal of Economics, 107(1): 35–78.

Kennedy, T. (1980). European Labor Relations: Text and Cases, Lexington, MA: Heath.

Kidd, M. P., Shannon, M. (1996). The Gender Wage Gap: A Comparison of Australia and Canada, in: Industrial and Labor Relations Review, 49: 729–46.

Killingsworth, M. (1990). The Economics of Comparable Worth, Kalamazoo, MI: Upjohn Institute for Employment Research.

Killingsworth, M. R. (1983). Labor Supply, New York: Cambridge University Press.

Killingsworth, M. R. (1990). The Economics of Comparable Worth, Kalamazoo, MI: Upjohn Institute for Employment Research.
Kitagawa, E. M. (1955). Components of a Difference Between Two Rates, in: The Journal of the American Statistical Association, 50: 1168-93.
Kmenta, J. (1971). Elements of Econometrics, New York, NY: Macmillan.
Kochhar, R., Fry, R., Taylor, P. (2011). Wealth Gaps Rise to Record Highs Between Whites, Blacks and Hispanics, Report Pew Research Center, available at http://pewsocialtrends.org.
Koenker, R., Bassett Jr., G. (1978). Regression Quantiles, in: Econometrica, 46(1): 33–50.
Korenman, S., Neumark, D. (1991). Does Marriage Really Make Men More Productive?, in: Journal of Human Resources, 26(2): 282–307.
Korenman, S., Neumark, D. (1992). Marriage, Motherhood, and Wages, in: Journal of Human Resources, 27(2): 233–55.
Korenman, S., Neumark, D. (1994). Sources of Bias in Women's Wage Equations, in: Journal of Human Resources, 29(2): 379–405.
Kosters, M. H. (Ed.) (1991). Workers and Their Wages, Washington, DC: AEI Press.
Krueger, A. B., Summers, L. H. (1988). Efficiency Wages and the Interindustry Wage Structure, in: Econometrica, 56: 259-93.
LaLonde, R. J., Topel, R. H. (1992). The Assimilation of Immigrants in the U.S. Labor Market, in: Borjas, G. F., Freeman, R. B. (Eds.), Immigration and the Work Force: Economic Consequences for the United States and Source Areas, Chicago, IL: University of Chicago Press (for NBER): 67-92.
Lampman, R. J. (1976). Employment versus Income Maintenance, in: Ginzberg, E. (Ed.), Jobs For Americans, Englewood Cliffs, NJ: Prentice-Hall.
Layard, R., Nickell, S., Jackman, R. (1991). Unemployment, Oxford: Oxford University Press.
Lazear, E. (1979). The Narrowing of Black-White Wage Differentials is Illusory, in: American Economic Review, 69: 553-64.
Lazear, E. P. (1995). Personnel Economics (The 1993 Wicksell Lectures), Cambridge, MA: The MIT Press.
Leibowitz, A., Klerman, J. A. (1995). Explaining Changes in Married Mothers' Employment Over Time, in: Demography, 32(3): 365–78.
Leion, A. (1985). Sweden, in: Roberts, B. C. (Ed.), Industrial Relations in Europe: The Imperatives of Change, London: Croom Helm.
Lemieux, T. (2006). Increasing Residual Wage Inequality: Composition Effects, Noisy Data, or Rising Demand for Skill?, in: American Economic Review, 96(3): 461–98.
Leonard, J. S. (1989). Women and Affirmative Action, in: J. Econ. Perspectives, 3(1): 61–75.
Lester, R. A. (1954). Hiring Practices and Labor Competition, Princeton, NJ: Industrial Relations Section, Princeton University.
Lewis, H. G. (1963). Unionism and Relative Wages in the United States: An Empirical Inquiry. Chicago, IL: University of Chicago Press.
Lillard, L. A., Smith, J. P., Welch, F. (1986). What Do We Really Know About Wages? The Importance of Nonreporting and Census Imputation, in: Journal of Political Economy, 94: 489-506.
Lofstrom, A., Gustafsson, S. (1991). Policy Changes and Women's Wages in Sweden, in: Willborn, S. L. (Ed.), Women's Wages: Stability and Changes in Six Industrialized Countries, Greenwich, CT: JAI Press: 313-30.
Lombard, K. V. (2001). Female Self-Employment and the Demand for Flexible, Non-Standard Work Schedules, in: Economic Inquiry, 39 (2): 214-237.
Long, J. E. (1980). The Effect of Americanization on Earnings: Some Evidence for Women, in: Journal of Political Economy, 88(3): 620-9.
Lundberg, S. J., Startz, R. (1983). Private Discrimination and Social Intervention in Competitive Labor Markets, in: American Economic Review, 73(3): 340–7.
Lundberg, S., Pollak, R. A. (1994). Noncooperative Bargaining Models of Marriage, in: American Economic Review, 84: 132–7.
Lundberg, S., Pollak, R. A. (1996). Bargaining and Distribution in Marriage, in: Journal of Economic Perspectives, 10(4): 139–58.
Machado, J. A. F., Mata, J. (2005). Counterfactual Decomposition of Changes in Wage Distributions Using Quantile Regression, in: Journal of Applied Econometrics, 20(4): 445–65.

Machin, S., Manning, A. (1994). The Effects of Minimum Wages on Wage Dispersion and Employment: Evidence from the U.K. Wage Councils, in: Industrial and Labor Relations Review, 47: 319–29.

Macpherson, D. A., Hirsch, B. T. (1995). Wages and Gender Composition: Why Do Women's Jobs Pay Less?, in: Journal of Labor Economics, 13(3): 426–71.

Macunovich, D. J. (2010). Reversals in the Patterns of Women's Labor Supply in the United States, 1977–2009, in: Monthly Labor Review, 133: 16-36.

Malveaux, J., Wallace, P. (1987). Minority Women in the Workplace, in: Koziara, K. S. et al. (Eds.), Working Women: Past, Present, Future, Washington, DC: Bureau of National Affairs: 265-98.

Manchester, J. M., Stapleton, D. C. (1991). On Measuring the Progress of Women's Quest for Economic Equality, in: Journal of Human Resources, 26(3): 562–80.

Manser, M., Brown, M. (1980). Marriage and Household Decision-Making: A Bargaining Analysis, in: International Economic Review, 21: 31–44.

Manski, C. F. (1989). Anatomy of the Selection Problem, in: Journal of Human Resources, 24(3): 343-60.

McDowell, J. M., Singell Jr., L. D., Slater, M. (2006). Two to Tango? Gender Differences in the Decisions to Publish and Coauthor, in: Economic Inquiry, 44(1): 153–68.

McElroy, M. B., Horney, M. J. (1981). Nash-Bargained Household Decisions: Toward a Generalization of the Theory of Demand, in: International Economic Review, 22: 333–49.

Mclanahan, S., Booth, K. (1989). Mother-Only Families: Problems, Prospects, and Politics, in: Journal of Marriage and the Family, 51(3): 557–80.

McNulty, D. J. (1967). Differences in Pay Between Men and Women Workers, in: Monthly Labor Review, 90: 40-3.

Meyer, B. D., Rosenbaum, D. T. (2001). Welfare, the Earned Income Tax Credit, and the Labor Supply of Single Mothers, in: Quarterly Journal of Economics, 116(3): 1063–114.

Mincer, J. (1962a). Labor Force Participation of Married Women: A Study of Labor Supply, in: Lewis, H. G. (Ed.), Aspects of Labor Economics, Princeton, NJ: Princeton University Press: 63–105.

Mincer, J. (1962b). On-the-Job Training: Costs, Returns and Some Implications, in: Journal of Political Economy, 70(5, pt. 2): 50–79.

Mincer, J. (1978). Family Migration Decisions, in: Journal of Political Economy, 86(1): 749–73.

Mincer, J., Polachek, S. (1974). Family Investments in Human Capital: Earnings of Women, in: Journal of Political Economy, 82(2, pt. 2): S76–S108.

Minimum Pay in 18 Countries (1992). European Industrial Relations Review, 225: 14-21.

Minimum Pay Setting: Germany (1992). European Industrial Relations Review, 226: 14-6.

Modigliani, F., Brumberg, R. (1954). Utility Analysis and the Consumption Function: An Interpretation of Cross-Section Data, in: Kurihara, K. K. (Ed.), Post-Keynesian Economics, New Brunswick, NJ: Rutgers University Press.

Moffitt, R. (1992). Incentive Effects of the U.S Welfare System: A Review, in: Journal of Economic Literature, 30(1): 1–61.

Montgomery, E., Wascher, W. (1987). Cross-Industry Differences in Race and Gender Wage Differentials, in: Industrial Relations, 26: 284-90.

Moore, G. H., Zarnowitz, V. (1986). The Development and Role of the National Bureau of Economic Research's Business Cycle Chronologies, in: Gordon, R. J. (Ed.), The American Business Cycle, Chicago, IL: University of Chicago Press: 735-79.

Mroz, T. A. (1987). The Sensitivity of an Empirical Model of Married Women's Hours of Work to Economic and Statistical Assumptions, in: Econometrica, 55: 765–99.

Mulligan, C. B., Rubinstein, Y. (2005). Selection, Investment, and Women's Relative Wages Since 1975, NBER Working Paper No. 11159.

Murphy, K. M., Topel, R. H. (1985). Estimation and Inference in Two-Step Econometric Models, in: Journal of Business and Economic Statistics, 3: 370–9.

Murray, C. (1984). Losing Ground: American Social Policy 1950–1980, New York: Basic Books.

Neal, D. A. (2004). The Measured Black-White Wage Gap among Women Is Too Small, in: Journal of Political Economy, 112(1): S1–S28.

References

Neal, D. A., Johnson, W. R. (1996). The Role of Pre-Market Factors in Black-White Wage Differences, in: Journal of Political Economy, 104(5): 869–95.

Neumark, D., Wascher, W. (1992). Employment Effects of Minimum and Subminimum Wages: Panel Data on State Minimum Wage Laws, in: Industrial and Labor Relations Review, 46: 55-81.

Neumark, D., Wascher, W. (1999). A Cross-National Analysis of the Effects of Minimum Wages on Youth Employment, NBER Working Paper No. 7299.

New Industrial Relations Talks Continue (1990). European Industrial Relations Review, 192: 7.

Nickell, S. (1997). Unemployment and Labor Market Rigidities: Europe versus North America, in: Journal of Economic Perspectives, 11: 55–74.

Nickell, S., Layard, R. (1999). Labor Market Institutions and Economic Performance, in: Ashenfelter, O., Card, D. (Eds.), Handbook of Labor Economics, Vol. 3c, Amsterdam: North-Holland: 3029–84.

O'Neill, J. (1985). The Trend in the Male-Female Wage Gap in the United States, in: Journal of Labor Economics, 3(1): S91-S115.

O'Neill, J. (1990). The Role of Human Capital in Earnings Differences Between Black and White Men, in: The Journal of Economic Perspectives, 4: 25-46.

O'Neill, J. (2003). The Gender Gap in Wages, circa 2000, in: American Economic Review, 93(2): 309–14.

O'Neill, J., Polachek, S. (1993). Why the Gender Gap in Wages Narrowed in the 1980s, in: Journal of Labor Economics, 11(1, pt. 1): 205–28.

Oaxaca, R. (1973a). Male-Female Wage Differences in Urban Labor Markets, in: International Economic Review, 14(3): 693–709.

Oaxaca, R. (1973b). Sex Discrimination in Wages, in: Ashenfelter, O., Rees, A. (Eds.), Discrimination in Labor Markets, Princeton, NJ: Princeton University Press.

Offices of Representatives John D. Dingell and Carolyn B. Maloney (2002). A New Look through the Glass Ceiling: Where Are the Women?, Report.

Olivetti, C., Petrongolo, B. (2006). Unequal Pay or Unequal Employment? A Cross-Country Analysis of Gender Gaps, IZA Discussion Paper No. 1941, Bonn, Germany.

Olsen, R. J., Farkas, G. (1990). The Effect of Economic Opportunity and Family Background on Adolescent Cohabitation and Childbearing Among Low-Income Blacks, in: Journal of Labor Economics, 8(3): 341–62.

Organisation for Economic Cooperation and Development (OECD) (1988). Employment Outlook, September 1988, Paris: OECD.

Organisation for Economic Cooperation and Development (OECD) (1989a). Employment Outlook, July 1989, Paris: OECD.

Organisation for Economic Cooperation and Development (OECD) (1989b). OECD Economic Surveys: Norway 1988/1989, Paris: OECD.

Organisation for Economic Cooperation and Development (OECD) (1993). Employment Outlook: July 1993, Paris: OECD.

Organisation of Economic Cooperation and Development (OECD) (1994). Employment Outlook: July 1994, Paris: OECD.

Organisation of Economic Cooperation and Development (OECD) (1997). Employment Outlook: July 1997, Paris: OECD.

Organisation of Economic Cooperation and Development (OECD) (1998). Human Capital Investment: An International Comparison, Paris: OECD.

Organisation of Economic Cooperation and Development (OECD) (1999). Employment Outlook: July 1999, Paris: OECD.

Organisation for Economic Cooperation and Development (OECD) (various issues). Labour Force Statistics, Paris: OECD.

Pencavel, J. (1997). Changes in Male Work Behavior and Wages, Stanford University.

Pencavel, J. (1998). The Market Work Behavior and Wages of Women, in: Journal of Human Resources, 33: 771–804.

Polachek, S. W. (1979). Occupational Segregation Among Women: Theory, Evidence, and a Prognosis, in: Lloyd, C. B. et al. (Eds.), Women in the Labor Market, New York: Columbia University Press: 137-57.

Raimon, R. L., Stoikov, V. (1969). The Effect of Blue-Collar Unionism on White-Collar Earnings, in: Industrial and Labor Relations Review, 22: 358-74.
Rees, A., Schultz, G. P. (1970). Workers and Wages in an Urban Labor Market, Chicago, IL: University of Chicago Press.
Reid, M. G. (1934). Economics of Household Production, New York: Wiley.
Reimers, C. W. (1983). Labor Market Discrimination Against Hispanic and Black Men, in: Review of Economics and Statistics, 65(4): 570-9.
Reskin, B. F., Hartmann, H. I. (Eds.) (1986). Women's Work, Men's Work: Sex Segregation on the Job, Washington, DC: National Academy Press.
Reskin, B. F., Roos, P. A. (1987). Status Hierarchies and Sex Segregation, in: Bose, C. E., Spitze, G. (Eds.), Ingredients for Women's Employment Policy, New York, NY: SUNY Press: 3-21.
Reskin, B., Padavic, I. (1986). Women's Work, Men's Work, Washington, DC: National Academy of Sciences.
Rezler, J. (1973). The Industrial Relations System in Hungary after the Economic Reform, in: Annaire de L'URSS et des Pays Socialistes Europiens, 1972-73, Paris: Libraire ISTRA (for Centre National de la Recherche Scientifique).
Roistacher, E. A., Goodman Jr., J. L. (1976). Race and Homeownership: Is Discrimination Disappearing?, in: Economic Inquiry, 14: 59-70.
Rosenfeld, R. A., Kalleberg, A. L. (1990). A Cross-National Comparison of the Gender Gap in Income, in: American Journal of Sociology, 96: 69-106.
Rosenzweig, M. R., Wolpin, K. I. (1980). Life-Cycle Labor Supply and Fertility: Causal Inference from Household Models, in: Journal of Political Economy, 88: 328–48.
Rowthorn, R. E. (1992). Centralisation, Employment, and Wage Dispersion, in: Economic Journal, 102: 506–23.
Royalty, A. B. (1996). The Effects of Job Turnover on the Training of Men and Women, in: Industrial and Labor Relations Review, 49(3): 506–21.
Ruhm, C. J., Teague, J. L. (1997). Parental Leave Policies in Europe and North America, in: Blau, F. D., Ehrenberg, R. G. (Eds.), Gender and Family Issues in the Workplace, New York: Russell Sage: 133–56.
Ruhm, C. J. (1998). The Economic Consequences of Parental Leave Mandates: Lessons from Europe, in: Quarterly Journal of Economics, 113: 285–317.
Sanborn, H. (1964). Pay Differences Between Men and Women, in: Industrial and Labor Relations Review, 17: 532-50.
Sawhill, I. V. (1973). The Economics of Discrimination Against Women: Some New Findings, in: Journal of Human Resources, 8: 383-95.
Schmitter, P. C. (1981). Interest Intermediation and Regime Governability in Contemporary Western Europe and North America, in: Berger, S. D. (Ed.), Organizing Interests in Western Europe: Pluralism, Corporatism, and the Transformation of Politics, Cambridge: Cambridge University Press: 287-327.
Schultz, T. P. (1994). Eroding the Economic Foundations of Marriage and Fertility in the United States, paper presented at the conference on "Changes in Family Patterns in Western Countries," Bologna, Italy, Oct. 6–8.
Segal, M. (1964). The Relationship Between Union Wage Impact and Market Structure, in: Quarterly Journal of Economics, 78: 96-114.
Sen, A. (1999). Development as Freedom, Oxford: Oxford University Press.
Shelton, B. A. (1992). Women, Men, and Time: Gender Differences in Paid Work, Housework and Leisure, New York: Greenwood Press.
Simon, J. L. (1981). What Immigrants Take From, and Give to, the Public Coffers, in: Select Commission on Immigration and Refugee Policy, United States Immigration Policy and the National Interest, Appendix D to the Staff Report of the Commission, Papers on Legal Immigration to the United States, Washington, D.C.: GPO: 223-62.
Simon, J. L. (1984). Immigrants, Taxes, and Welfare in the United States, in: Population and Development Review, 10(1): 55-69.
Simona, I. (1985). Switzerland, in: Farley, J. (Ed.), Women Workers in Fifteen Countries, Ithaca, NY: ILR Press: 147-53.
Smith, J. D. (1975). White Wealth and Black People: The Distribution of Wealth in Washington, D.C. in 1967, in: Smith, J. D. (Ed.), The Personal Distribution of Income and Wealth, New York: Columbia University Press.

Smith, J. P. (1979). The Convergence to Racial Equality in Women's Wages, in: Lloyd, C. et al. (Eds.), Women in the Labor Market, New York: Columbia University Press: 173-215.
Smith, J. P. (Ed.) (1980). Female Labor Supply: Theory and Estimation, Princeton, NJ: Princeton University Press.
Smith, J. P., Ward, M. P. (1984). Women's Wages and Work in the Twentieth Century, Santa Monica, CA: Rand Corporation.
Smith, J. P., Ward, M. P. (1985). Time-Series Growth in the Female Labor Force, in: Journal of Labor Economics, 3(1, suppl.): S59–90.
Smith, J. P., Ward, M. P. (1989). Women in the Labor Market and in the Family, in: Journal of Economic Perspectives, 3(1): 9–23.
Smith, J. P., Welch, F. (1977). Black-White Earnings and Employment: 1960-1970, in: American Economic Review, 67: 323-38.
Smith, J. P., Welch, F. R. (1986). Closing the Gap: Forty Years of Economic Progress for Blacks, Santa Monica, CA: Rand Corporation, R-3330-DOL.
Sobol, M. G. (1979). Factors Influencing Private Capital Accumulation on the "Eve of Retirement", in: Review of Economics and Statistics, 61: 585-93.
Soltow, L. (1972). A Century of Personal Wealth Accumulation, in: Vatter, H. G., Palm, T. (Eds.), The Economics of Black America, New York: Harcourt Brace Jovanovich.
Sorensen, E. (1990). The Crowding Hypothesis and Comparable Worth Issue, in: Journal of Human Resources, 25(1): 55–89.
Straus, M. A., Gelles, R. J. (1986). Societal Change and Change in Family Violence from 1975 to 1985 as Revealed by Two National Surveys, in: Journal of Marriage and the Family, 48(3): 465–79.
Straus, M. A., Gelles, R. J. (1988). How Violent Are American Families? Estimates from the National Family Violence Resurvey and Other Studies, in: Hotaling, G. T. et al. (Eds.), Family Abuse and Its Consequences: New Directions in Research, Newbury Park, CA: Sage: 14–36.
Suen, W. (1997). Decomposing Wage Residuals: Unmeasured Skill or Statistical Artifact?, in: Journal of Labor Economics, 15, pt. 1: 555–66.
Summers, L., Gruber, J., Vergara, R. (1993). Taxation and the Structure of Labor Markets: The Case of Corporatism, in: Quarterly Journal of Economics, 108: 385–411.
Terrell, H. S. (1971). Wealth Accumulation of Black and White Families: The Empirical Evidence, in: Journal of Finance, 26: 363-77.
Teulings, C., Hartog, J. (1998). Corporatism or Competition? Labour Contracts, Institutions and Wage Structures in International Comparison, Cambridge: Cambridge University Press.
Thorsrud, E. (1985). Norway, in: Roberts. B. C. (Ed.), Industrial Relations in Europe: The Imperatives of Change, London: Croom Helm.
Tobin, J. (1972). Wealth, Liquidity, and the Propensity to Consume, in: Strumpel, B., Morgan, J. N., Zahn, E. (Eds.), Human Behavior in Economic Affairs (Essays in Honor of George S. Katona), Amsterdam: Elsevier.
Tomandl, T., Fuerboeck, K. (1986). Social Partnership: The Austrian System of Industrial Relations and Social Insurance, Ithaca, NY: ILR Press.
Topel, R. H. (1994a). Regional Labor Markets and the Determinants of Wage Inequality, in: American Economic Review, 74: 17–22.
Topel, R. H. (1994b). Wage Inequality and Regional Labor Market Performance in the US, in: Tachibanaki, T. (Ed.), Labour Market and Economic Performance: Europe, Japan and the USA, London: Palgrave Macmillan: 93-127.
Treu, T. (1985). Italy, in: Bull. Comparative Labour Relations, 19: 227-50.
U.S. Arms and Control Disarmament Agency (various issues). World Military Expenditures and Arms Transfers.
U.S. Bureau of Labor Statistics (1985). Handbook of Labor Statistics, 1985, Washington: Government Printing Office.
U.S. Department of Commerce (1992). Statistical Abstract of the United States 1992, Washington: Government Printing Office.
U.S. Department of Commerce, Bureau of the Census (1973). U.S. Census of the Population, 1970, Detailed Characteristics. Final Report PC(1)-D1, U.S. Summary, Washington, DC: U.S. Government Printing Office.

U.S. Department of Commerce, Bureau of the Census (1983). 1970 Census Major Occupation Groups in Terms of 1980 Census Occupational Categories.
U.S. Department Of Justice (1994). Criminal victimization in the United States: 1973–92 Trends, Washington, DC: U.S. Department of Justice.
U.S. Department of Justice (various issues). Annual Report of the Immigration and Naturalization Service, Washington, DC: U.S. Government Printing Office.
U.S. Department of Labor (1976). Employment and Training Report of the President, Washington, D.C.: GPO.
U.S. Department of Labor (1984). Foreign Labor Trends: Norway 1983, Washington: Government Printing Office.
U.S. Department of Labor (1992). Foreign Labor Trends: Hungary 1991-2, Washington: Government Printing Office.
U.S. Department of Labor, Bureau of Labor Statistics (1970). Occupational Outlook Handbook, 1970-71, Washington, DC: Government Printing Office.
U.S. Department of Labor, Bureau of Labor Statistics (1987). Usual Weekly Earnings of Wage and Salary Workers: Second Quarter 1987, News, USDL 87-327.
U.S. Department of Labor, Bureau of Labor Statistics (1995). Report on the American workforce, Washington, DC: U.S. GPO.
U.S. Department of State (various issues). World Military Expenditures and Arms Transfers.
U.S. General Accounting Office (GAO) (2001). Women in Management: Analysis of Selected Data from the Current Population Survey, Report to Congressional Requesters, Washington, DC.
U.S. House of Representatives (1978). Legal and Illegal Immigration to the United States, US #962-17.
U.S. Immigration and Naturalization Service (various issues). Statistical Yearbook of the Immigration and Naturalization Service, Washington, DC: U.S. Government Printing Office.
United Nations (1991). The World's Women 1970–1990: Trends and Statistics, New York: United Nations.
United Nations Statistics Division (2006a). Fertility Rate (13700): Total Fertility Rate, New York: U.N. Population Division, Quinquennial Estimates and Projections, http://unstats.un.org/unsd/cdb/cdb_series_xrxx.asp?series_code¼13700.
United Nations Statistics Division (2006b). GDP (22918): Gross Domestic Product at Market Prices, Constant US$, World Bank Estimates, http://unstats.un.org/unsd/cdb/cdb_series_xrxx.asp?series_code=29918.
United Nations Statistics Division (2006c). Population (13660): Population Total, UN Population Division, Annual Estimates and Projections [code 13660], http://unstats.un.org/unsd/cdb/cdb_series_xrxx.asp?series_code¼13660.
United Nations Statistics Division (2006d). Economic Activity Rate (4270): Economic Activity Rate by Sex, Thirteen Age Groups, 1950–2010, ILO Estimates and Projections, http://unstats.un.org/unsd/cdb/cdb_series_xrxx.asp?series_code=4270.
United Nations Statistics Division (2006e). Economically Activity Population (4230): Economically Active Population by Sex, Thirteen Age Groups, 1950–2010, ILO Estimates and Projections, http://unstats.un.org/unsd/cdb/cdb_series_xrxx.asp?series_code=4230.
U.S. Bureau of Labor Statistics (various issues). Handbook of Labor Statistics, Washington, DC: U.S. Government Printing Office.
Valian, V. (1998), Why So Slow? The Advancement of Women, Cambridge, MA: The MIT Press.
Wachter, M. L. (1980). The Labor Market and Illegal Immigration: The Outlook for the 1980s, in: Industrial and Labor Relations Review, 33(3): 342-54.
Waldfogel, J. (1997). Working Mothers Then and Now: A Cross-cohort Analysis of the Effects of Maternity Leave on Women's Pay, in: Blau, F. D., Ehrenberg, R. G. (Eds.), Gender and Family Issues in the Workplace, New York: Russell Sage Foundation: 92–126.
Waldfogel, J. (1998). The Family Gap for Young Women in the United States and Britain: Can Maternity Leave Make a Difference?, in: Journal of Labor Economics, 16(3): 505–45.

References

Weinberg, B. A. (2000). Computer Use and the Demand for Female Workers, in: Industrial and Labor Relations Review, 53(2): 290–308.

Weiss, L. W. (1966). Concentration and Labor Earnings, in: American Economic Review, 56: 96-117.

Welch, F. (1997). Wages and Participation, in: Journal of Labor Economics, 15, pt. 2: S77–S103.

Welch, F. (2000). Growth in Women's Relative Wages and in Inequality among Men: One Phenomenon or Two?, in: American Economic Review, 90(2): 444–9.

Wellington, A. J. (1993). Changes in the Male/Female Wage Gap, 1976–85, in: Journal of Human Resources, 28(2): 383–411.

Wilson, W. J. (1987). The Truly Disadvantaged, Chicago, IL: University of Chicago Press.

Wood, R. G. (1995). Marriage Rates and Marriageable Men: A Test of the Wilson Hypothesis, in: Journal of Human Resources, 30(1): 163–93.

World Almanac and Book of Facts (1999), New York: World Almanac Books.

World Bank (2002a). World Development Indicators, Series SE.PRM.ENRR.FE, CD-ROM.

World Bank (2002b). World Development Indicators, Series SE.SEC.ENRR.FE, CD-ROM.

Wrong, G. (1987). Switzerland, in: Bulletin of Comparative Labour Relations, 16: 183-201.

Index

A

B

C

D

E

Index

F

G

H

I

Index

J

K

L

M

R

S

T

Y

About the Author...

Francine D. Blau is Frances Perkins Professor of Industrial and Labor Relations and Professor of Economics at Cornell University, and a Research Associate of the National Bureau of Economic Research. She received her Ph.D. in Economics from Harvard University and her B.S. from Cornell University. She has served as President of the Society of Labor Economists, the Labor and Employment Association, and the Midwest Economics Association, as Vice President of the American Economic Association, and as Chair of the American Economic Association Committee on the Status of Women in the Economics Profession. She is a fellow of the Society of Labor Economists, the American Academy of Political and Social Science, and the Labor and Employment Relations Association. Furthermore she acts on the Editorial Boards of the Journal of Labor Economics, the ILR Review, the Journal of Labor Research, the Annals, and Research in Labor Economics, and as an Associate Editor of Labour Economics. Formerly she was an Editor of the Journal of Labor Economics, on the Board of Editors of the American Economic Review, on the Advisory Board of the Journal of Economic Perspectives, and an Associate Editor of the Journal of Economic Perspectives. Francine Blau has written extensively on gender issues, wage inequality and international comparisons of labor market outcomes and is among the most renowned experts in these fields. She is the author of Equal Pay in the Office, At Home and Abroad: U.S. Labor Market Performance in International Perspective (with Lawrence Kahn) - recipient of the Richard A. Lester Prize, and The Economics of Women, Men, and Work (with Marianne Ferber and Anne Winkler) - currently in its 6th edition. In 2001 she was honored with the Carolyn Shaw Bell Award from the American Economic Association Committee on the Status of Women in the Economics Profession for furthering the status of women in the economics profession. Francine Blau joined IZA as a Research Fellow in April 2004. In 2010 she was awarded the IZA Prize in Labor Economics.

...and the Editors

Anne C. Gielen is a Senior Research Associate at IZA and an Assistant Professor at the Erasmus University Rotterdam. She received her Ph.D. from CentER Graduate School, Tilburg University in 2008. Previously, she studied Economics at Tilburg University, where she has received her Master's degree. Her research interests include labor and health economics. In her work, she has studied labor market transitions, and how they relate to improvements in the quality of the worker-job match as well as to improvements in the quality of worker's lives. Most recently, she started working on how work, and various dimensions of work, affects individual's health.

Klaus F. Zimmermann has been Full Professor of Economics at the University of Bonn and Director of the Institute for the Study of Labor (IZA Bonn) since 1998. From 2000 until 2011 he was President of the German Institute for Economic Research (DIW Berlin). Zimmermann is Honorary Professor of Economics at the Free University of Berlin (since 2001) and Honorary Professor at the Renmin University of China (since 2006), and was Chairman of the Society of the German Economic Research Institutes (ARGE)from 2005 until 2011. He is Editor-in-Chief of the Journal of Population Economics and a member of the German Academy of Sciences Leopoldina and the Academia Europaea. Zimmermann regularly advises the World Bank, the European Commission, and various national governments. His main research interests are in migration, labor economics, and population economics.

The manufacturer's authorised representative in the EU for product safety is Oxford University Press España S.A. of El Parque Empresarial San Fernando de Henares, Avenida de Castilla, 2 - 28830 Madrid (www.oup.es/en or product.safety@oup.com). OUP España S.A. also acts as importer into Spain of products made by the manufacturer.
Printed and bound by CPI Group (UK) Ltd, Croydon, CR0 4YY
14/09/2026
02216293-0006